Rome's Religious History

This book explores the way in which three ancient historians, writing in Latin, embedded the gods into their accounts of the past. Although previous scholarship has generally portrayed these writers as somewhat dismissive of traditional Roman religion, it is argued here that Livy, Tacitus and Ammianus saw themselves as being very close to the centre of those traditions. The gods are presented as a potent historical force, and a close reading of the historians' texts easily bears out this conclusion. Their treatment of the gods is not limited to portraying the role and power of the divine in the unfolding of the past: equally prominent is the negotiation with the reader concerning what constituted a 'proper' religious system. Priests and other religious experts function as an index of the decline (or restoration) of Rome and each writer formulates a sophisticated position on the practical and social aspects of Roman religion.

JASON P. DAVIES is a Research Fellow at the Department of Education and Professional Development, University College London.

Rome's Religious History: Livy, Tacitus and Ammianus on their Gods

JASON P. DAVIES

CAMBRIDGE UNIVERSITY PRESS

PUBLISHED BY THE PRESS SYNDICATE OF THE UNIVERSITY OF CAMBRIDGE
The Pitt Building, Trumpington Street, Cambridge, United Kingdom

CAMBRIDGE UNIVERSITY PRESS
The Edinburgh Building, Cambridge CB2 2RU, UK
40 West 20th Street, New York, NY 10011–4211, USA
477 Williamstown Road, Port Melbourne, VIC 3207, Australia
Ruiz de Alarcón 13, 28014 Madrid, Spain
Dock House, The Waterfront, Cape Town 8001, South Africa

http://www.cambridge.org

© Jason P. Davies 2004

First published 2004

Printed in the United Kingdom at the University Press, Cambridge

Typeface Times 10/12 pt.   *System* LATEX 2$_\varepsilon$ [TB]

A catalogue record for this book is available from the British Library

ISBN 0 521 83482 1 hardback

Contents

Acknowledgements   *page* vii
Note on the texts   ix

1 Introduction   1
  1.1 Religion and its reception   1
  1.2 Historiography   12
  1.3 Religion and historiography   17

2 Livy and the invention of Roman religion   21
  2.1 The reception of Livy   21
  2.2 Actuality of phenomena   27
  2.3 Interpretation   61
  2.4 Choice   78

3 Gods and men in Livy   86
  3.1 Introduction   86
  3.2 Explanation   86
  3.3 The agency of the gods   96
  3.4 Interpretation and power   123
  3.5 Conclusions   138

4 Tacitus and the restoration of Rome   143
  4.1 Religious categories   144
  4.2 Tacitus: a man of distinctions   153
  4.3 Conclusions   221

5 Ammianus and a final settlement   226
  5.1 Introduction   226
  5.2 A religion for Rome   236
  5.3 The fundamentals of Ammianus' Roman religion   265
  5.4 Ammianus and the Roman tradition   282

v

6   Conclusions   286

Bibliography   292
Index locorum   319
Subject index   333

Acknowledgements

Sole authorship is a marvellous fiction if this monograph is anything to go by and these Acknowledgements will exhaust the synonyms for 'generosity'. Countless blunders and errors of a lesser order have been pointed out to me at every stage, as well as insights too numerous to list, from the days when this was a doctoral thesis, through to its present form. Professor John North's unstinting support, whether as supervisor or friend, through the last decade or so made the task considerably easier than it might otherwise have been. C. Robert Phillips III, an unofficial supervisor if ever there was one, shamed me repeatedly with his attentive reading of the many drafts. I must also thank Christina Kraus for her endless efforts to improve on almost every version. Emma Dench and Denis Feeney made the generous transition from examiners to supportive advisers, and Gavin Kelly read the proofs and offered humbling suggestions on the entire work, not just the requested Ammianus chapter: like all the others, his pertinent observations made a considerable difference. The insightful Press readers also found considerable room for improvement, for which I am grateful.

A substantial debt of gratitude is owed also to Rhiannon Ash, Rebecca Flemming, Alan Griffiths, David Levene, John Marincola, Gary Miles, Stephen Oakley, Susan Palmer-Jones, Christopher Pelling, Russell Shone, Charles Stewart and all the staff at the Library of the Institute of Classical Studies in London. Innumerable others made often vital contributions.

Much of the rewriting was undertaken during a fellowship at the Wellcome Trust Centre for the History of Medicine at UCL, in tandem with a wider medically orientated religious project: Professors Vivian Nutton and Hal Cook provided an enviable working environment, as did Alan 'punctuation' Shiel, Debra Scallan and Gwyn Griffiths. Dominic Wujastyk, also of the Centre, initiated a poor student into LATEX, which made the production of the final version much more efficient. The manuscript was finally completed during a Research Fellowship in the Department of Education and Professional Development at UCL as part of the interdisciplinary project on Evidence funded by the Leverhulme Trust and the ERSC.

The research underpinning the book could not have been possible without BBEdit, from Bare Bones Software, whose technical support staff, both past and present, enabled me to keep track of the hundreds of different references required to discuss the religious material and produce the various manuscripts: special (but far from exclusive) thanks go to Christian Smith in this regard. Another program, Nisus Writer, was indispensable for much of the writing, not least by virtue of the expert assistance of Yusuke 'Kino' Kinoshita. The final burden, of publication, was shared generously by the various officers of Cambridge University Press to whom I also owe thanks.

In the face of such assistance, the only part of the work for which I can claim sole responsibility is the errors. Last and never least, my wife Wendy and elder son Ryan showed their patience with the long-term loan of husband or father to this project, and baby Jack's smiles also made the task a lighter one.

Finally, I must thank my mother, F. Hilary Ecclestone.

Note on the texts

Since the editions offered no consistency, spelling has been standardised (i.e. 'u' for 'v' and 'V' for 'U'). Lower case for the first letter of a sentence has also been applied throughout, notwithstanding the editions used.

For Livy the following texts have been used:

1–10 Oxford Classical Texts:
   1–5 Ogilvie (1974)
   6–10 Walters & Conway (1919)
21–45 Teubner:
   21–22 Dorey (1971)
   23–25 Dorey (1976)
   26–27 Walsh (1982)
   29–30 Walsh (1986)
   31–40 Briscoe (1991: 2 vols.)
   41–45 Briscoe (1986)

For Tacitus:
Teubner (both edited by Heubner):
   Annals (1983)
   Histories (1978)

For Ammianus:
Teubner (Seyfarth: 2 vols., 1978)

1
Introduction

1.1 Religion and its reception

This book is an exploration of the form(ul)ation of knowledge in a given context – a process which might well be called education. More specifically, it is about the presentation of religious knowledge in an ancient historiographical context, though, like its subjects, it is occasionally given to 'digressions' which either enhance or detract from the text, depending on the reader's expectations and criteria for relevance. Like its subjects, it *can* be plundered for individual items of information but will only make proper sense when taken as a whole, where each item is defined to a large extent by its context.

It assumes that the historians in question were highly intelligent and deliberate men who went a long way towards achieving a fundamental cohesion in their works. It also works on the premise that they built up an image of religious systems as a whole, not by describing a system *ex nihilo* for outsiders. They represented their model of religion to their world by offering refinements of the understanding that they assumed would be brought to their text by their readers. They presumed to know roughly what this understanding was, though their frequent and deliberate refinements indicate that they also acknowledged that the details would be more or less negotiable and could be debated. What they did *not* cater for was a fundamentally different matrix of understanding, such as the modern reader brings to bear when reassembling the worlds they created. Without a compatible matrix of knowledge as a context, any statement as an intentional communication is doomed.

Any 'religious' statement in these historians has two contexts: firstly the (now-incomplete) text itself within which it is situated and, secondly, the cognitive context of the reader. The first of these has, in each case, been the centre of interest as a means of deciphering what Livy, Tacitus and Ammianus 'thought'. The rather mixed results are, it is suggested, the inevitable product of relative inattention to the latter rather more nebulous cultural context, a concern which is given more weight here than has generally been the case. But before this can be done, some effort must be made to distinguish the interpretative strategies that we habitually bring to the material in question. This discussion therefore aims not only to decipher the meanings of the many religious moments in the historiographical texts but also, after exploring the ways in which we have tended to understand them, to reconstruct the cultural knowledge that informed the text in antiquity: the extra-textual context of the accounts is in fact the most decisive factor in shaping our understanding. Though we shall be attentive to similarities in these authors, it will not be at the expense of a sensitivity to the distinctive contexts in which they wrote – one during the death throes of the Republic and the establishment of empire, another after imperial rule had become the norm and the last in a world where Christianity had effectively eclipsed 'pagan' state cult. Historiographical uses of religious categories, whether the 'wrath of the gods', 'fate' or '*fortuna*', are often treated as if their audience, utterly ignorant of any religious and cultural ideas of their own, were expecting the baldest and most simplistic theological statements, deployed primarily to address broad questions of belief or scepticism about religion. Here, in contrast, it is argued that these terms and other similar categories were important and subtle parts of ancient reasoning.

Such an argument is not overdue: our tools for studying historiography have become increasingly, even exponentially, refined in recent years, and we detect subtlety in almost every part of a narrative – except where the religious is concerned. Here a simple formula of 'belief' or 'scepticism' (unbelieving) is almost universally applied. Yet these men were writing for a society that was not, for the most part, concerned *whether* the gods existed but rather with how they would impact on the human world, how they should be understood to act and, more importantly, the effects and means of placation – and the consequences of failing to do so. Read from this perspective, these three historians have a great deal to offer to both their expected (contemporary) audience and the present one, whose assumptions are about as alien to their own as is imaginable.[1]

Even among the three we will find important differences, most notably (but not exclusively) between Ammianus and his predecessors. Livy might just have become aware of the very beginnings of a new cult, if the traditional dating is correct, before he died; Tacitus certainly knew of the Christians but, I suspect, would never have anticipated the religious change

---

[1] I use the term 'audience' with caution. For my purposes, 'audience' presumes 'readership': I make no claims to distinguish them. We know less than we often assume about public recitals of texts and their readers: see Kraus (1994a) 2–4, esp. n.9 for the little we know about recitations of Livy's work. Pelling (2000) is a useful discussion of the ways that ancient authors (though Greek in this case) worked with their audiences.

as we know it from 'pagan' to 'Christian'. These two could work without moving outside the framework that we refer to as 'paganism': Ammianus, on the other hand, was writing in a society where large-scale violence could break out on the basis of the difference. His relatively understated (yet determined) drive to paganism drew, by definition, on the traditions of the past, and a strong tendency to continuity underpins his (re)formulation of religious matters. All three, it is argued, offered strong correctives to what they perceived as current and pressing issues pertaining to religion: but the relevance of these discussions is lost if we do not consider the social, political and epistemic climates in which they wrote.

Given this attention to interpretative context, I might best begin by declaring my intended extra-textual context: those who are committed to doubting whether religion could ever be 'taken seriously' in ancient Rome are about to embark on a lengthy and persistent example of special pleading; those who are readily sympathetic to ancient religion will find it unnecessarily pedantic and overstated, if ultimately in harmony with their interests. Any who are willing to entertain the suggestion that religion was a fundamental, even immovable, part of ancient thinking but find themselves repeatedly unable to find in practice that this is the case will hopefully benefit from the accounts that follow.

The argument depends on the assertion that there can never have been a single unchangeable entity that we can call 'Roman religion', easily recognisable in any context.[2] It will become obvious that the literary and political context exercised a powerful effect on the way that religion was formulated and presented: different ages posed different questions and a similar issue might be addressed in a very different way as the time and context varied.

The prevalent model of ancient religion is now that of 'civic paganism', which grew out of an attempt to move away from discussions that measured paganism against largely Christian expectations of 'communion with the divine' that dominated scholarship of the early twentieth century.[3] In its

---

[2] A banal version of the hypothesis of 'brain-balkanisation' put forward by Veyne (1988): his work represents a watershed in the study of both historiographical and religious (in his case, mythical) material in Greek historians. Many of his arguments can be applied to Roman historians, though his hypothesis of 'brain-balkanisation' has often (paradoxically, and certainly wrongly) been used to 'demonstrate' 'irrationality' in ancient authors. It was not Veyne's intention to 'prove' irrationality once and for all: rather the opposite. Veyne's arguments rely on the observation that moderns are just as 'balkanised' as ancients and that this is an inevitable, even useful, function of cognition: the latter point is often elided.

[3] The results of applying 'civic paganism' to the material can be seen in Beard North and Price (1998) each of whom has written extensively to criticise the older models and develop the 'civic model'. Rives (1995a) usefully takes the analysis to its logical conclusion by treating Carthage over the centuries; Rogers (1990) looks at Ephesos from a similar angle. For an application to the Greek *polis*, see Zaidman and Pantel (1996).

maturity, it has begun to encounter criticism of its own. It has, for instance, been asserted that we should not allow an approach that stresses civic identity to obscure the plethora of possible religious identities available to a Roman with his or her familial, professional, local and political ties; but this is hardly a fundamental criticism – none of these is mutually exclusive. We should think in terms of expanding the civic focus of recent approaches, considering them limited and ripe for expansion rather than flawed.[4] Civic paganism endeavoured (perfectly legitimately) to shift the goalposts to a more suitable location, chiefly that of the negotiation of identity rather than an attempt to commune with the divine. However, we shall find that in discussing the historians under scrutiny, the older models and approaches still generally hold sway, even in recent publications: we must therefore outline the older approaches in order to appreciate how these texts have been formally understood. My strong suspicion is that they are still instinctively read in this way for the most part.

The 'old' model asserted the decline and subsequent poverty, even vacuity, of Roman religion in any *historical* period:[5] any 'genuine' religion was deferred backwards (conveniently) into the past (just) before any useful documentation was begun.[6] All subsequent religious phenomena were therefore spinning hopelessly further and further away from their origin, the only place where they had any meaning.[7] Later religious 'revivals' (such as the so-called 'Augustan restoration') were therefore portrayed as doomed from the start,[8] even if there was some grudging admiration for the sheer effort of the upper classes of Rome. In Phillips' formulation we recounted to ourselves their 'mindless cult acts for the elites and superstitious mumblings for the lower orders'.[9]

This interpretation inevitably shaped our understanding of the various texts on which they were based, in a logical circle. As one text was taken to

---

[4] For criticism, see Woolf (1997) and Bendlin (1997) and (2000) who move away from the focus on civic cult and into other, 'private' or 'local' arenas.

[5] Wissowa (1912) is the fullest exposition of this approach, though not everyone saw decline: see e.g. Geffcken (1978; originally 1920) 9–14 on the vitality of paganism in late antiquity.

[6] Many of these criticisms are of little relevance to another school of thought founded by, and largely represented by, Dumézil, for which see Bélier (1991); Dumézil (1969) and (1970).

[7] A trend probably introduced into Rome by Varro and gratefully preserved by Augustine (*City of God* 4.31 = Varro fr. 13 (56) and 18 (59) Cardauns). Feeney (1991) 47–48 notes it for earlier (Greek) thought. On the inadequacies of the idea of decline see (amongst others) North (1976); Scheid (1987a); most recently Beard North and Price (1998) I 10–11. The alternative to a chronological displacement of 'real' religion is the tradition of 'simple rustic piety' disposed of by North (1995). There is also the assumption that 'private' religion was somehow more authentic than 'state' religion, but the evidence (see e.g. Bakker (1994); Dorcey (1992)) still requires nuanced analysis and is not so different from that for religion at a civic level.

[8] See e.g. Warde Fowler's analysis, dating from 1911 (428–429).

[9] Phillips (1986) 2703.

be sceptical (because we 'knew' there was entrenched scepticism within the élite), so the next could be more easily read this way: not surprisingly, applying a different set of criteria, more sympathetic to religion, produced a more favourable reading.[10] The 'old school' derived its methodology almost exclusively from Christianising tendencies, and the model was not even *ancient* Christianity: 'religion' was, we would now say, unproblematised and unreconstructed. We, for all our recent efforts, persist in assuming that religion functions as a set of propositions to which someone agrees (or not), an idea which is probably irrelevant even to the early Christian Church.[11] The greatest handicap to any sympathetic understanding of Roman religion was this insistence that it should behave according to Christian principles: 'belief' was seen as the cornerstone of religion, and 'belief' could hardly be accorded to these rites by men as evidently *sensible* as our three 'great historians'. The opposite pole from this unacceptable 'belief' was 'scepticism' – the 'rational' objection to such superstitious 'mumbojumbo'.[12] Romans, like Christians, had a choice: they could believe – or they could reject the 'canons' of their religion. There was no acceptable (or recognised) position between these two.[13] Thus most formulations, searching in vain for some intense personal experience in ancient religion, located 'true spirituality' in mystery cults and derided state cult, with its complex rituals of divination and propitiation as utterly 'arid'.[14]

'Belief' is, however, deeply problematic: it may be that this paradoxical concept is one peculiar to the Christianised West.[15] Moreover, to reject religion as an interpretative system that gives events meaning, quite apart from being fashionable, is, in the present age, *easy*. There are rival cosmological claims to which one can pledge allegiance and from which one

---

[10] For detailed examples see North (1990a) 58–60, on Cato *On Agriculture* 7.4 and Beard (1986) on Cicero.

[11] Phillips (1986); also e.g. Feeney (1998) esp. 14, 22–25; Price (1984) 247; Smith (1979) 77. See also Bendlin (2000).

[12] Elliott (1983) 209 refers thus to magic.

[13] Though we might read of Tacitus' 'profound religiosity' that acknowledged no gods, (better described as a state of confusion than a position): some examples of these arguments are given in chapter 4.

[14] Toynbee's description, dismantled by North (1976) 9–10. On mystery cults, Cumont (1911) and, more recently, Burkert (1987), strongly criticised by North (1992) 183. Particular studies on these cults include Mylonas (1961); Gordon (1980); Cole (1984); Sfameni Gasparro (1985). For a (Jungian) psychological study of ritual see Shorter (1996).

[15] A major topic: Needham (1972) is the fullest discussion but see also Pouillon (1982). For a discussion more centred on classical sources, see Price (1984) 10–11 and especially Phillips (1986) 2697–2710; for some of the consequences of these arguments, Beard North and Price (1998) I 42–43. Smith (1979) is a very different and highly sympathetic book (in contrast to many more recent works) which asserts the value and universality of belief and faith; his conclusions may not however be easily applied to ancient cultures. But they are a useful corrective to anachronism; see esp. chs. 5 ('*Credo*') and 6 ('Believe').

can derive worlds of meaning. The favourite is that of science which has established its own orthodoxy. But this was not the case in the ancient world: in the absence of any comprehensive alternative formulation,[16] the rejection of religion was altogether more difficult to accomplish psychologically and would actually have represented an extreme position, more like abandoning 'science' (the dominant interpretative paradigm in the present day) than 'religion' (now thoroughly marginalised in the West). It can only claim to have existed in philosophical circles, and even then the majority of philosophers acquiesced in, or even encouraged, traditional cult.[17] 'Ancient religious scepticism', as a widespread and normative social phenomenon, is an illusion whose chief function is to preserve a specious similarity between the ancient past and the present.[18]

Perhaps this is an overstated position; it is certainly the kind of generalisation that scholars normally do well to avoid. But given a choice between one insecurely founded assumption and another, we will perhaps benefit more from beginning with an overly generous acceptance of the overwhelmingly positive evidence. What occasional evidence there is for scepticism is steadily decreasing; almost every area of ancient religion is being reinterpreted along more subtle lines. The process of our reassessment has been under way for three decades[19] on various fronts,[20] and for the most part has been based on internal evidence[21] but has also drawn on wider comparative initiatives.[22] Indeed a survey of comparative work provides a rude awakening: the formulations of anthropologists on religion bear little resemblance to the traditional formulations of classicists.[23] Uncritical comparisons would be inappropriate here since the dialectic continues in that field, but a brief survey of some of the major issues and players will place this predominantly localised discussion in a broader context.

---

[16] Phillips (1986) 2697–2710.
[17] Attridge (1978) 63.
[18] See North (1983) 216–218 for the same sentiment.
[19] Feeney (1998) 3 dates the beginning of the process to Jocelyn (1966). Others (e.g. Liebeschuetz (1979) Acknowledgements and *passim*) often refer to North (1968).
[20] Greek material has received distinct treatment for the most part; the work of Vernant, Détienne and Calame has been particularly influential as is visible in (e.g.) Zaidman and Pantel (1996). For the differences (often prejudices) between the treatments of Greek and Roman religious affairs, see Beard (1993) and Feeney (1998) 6–11, 22–31, 47–64, 77–78.
[21] To the list of authors mentioned thus far, we might add Phillips (1992) and Feeney (1998) on poetry; Feeney (1991) on epic; Harrison (2000) on Herodotus. But recent studies dedicated to particular authors are relatively rare.
[22] E.g. Price (1984); Beard has also drawn on works such as Douglas (1966). Feeney (1998) and Beard North and Price (1998) draw on a number of comparative efforts.
[23] For instance, Détienne's studies of Dionysos (Détienne (1979) and (1989)) heavily influenced by French anthropology, are virtually ignored at times (they are certainly absent from bibliographies where one would expect to find them). The irony is that one (Détienne (1979)) opens with detailed response to classicists who had criticised his anthropological work on empirical grounds. See Bourque (2000) for some perspective on anthropological methods.

It may well be that the very idea of religion as a category is in itself misinformed and simply a further legacy of Christianity. Not all cultures even recognise it as a distinct phenomenon.[24] Nor, if we do construct such a category, do religions necessarily obey our expectations, largely formed as these are from Christianity. Many aspects of anthropological discussions are directly relevant to ancient religions: consider for instance Eliade's observations that many religions look back to a sacred past, forever recreated in ritual,[25] which go a long way to answering complaints about a 'lack of spirituality'. Smith coined the term 'locative' to indicate a society that places a higher value on its present integrity and well-being than on eschatology:[26] he distinguished a profoundly different constellation of values and *desiderata* in such a society. The act of identifying (and thereby validating) a different value-system frees it to some extent from direct comparison with 'open' or 'soteriological' (as he calls them) systems such as Christianity: in other words, predominantly locative societies simply have different agendas. Another strategy, which avoids the thorny issue of truth values, is to treat any knowledge system as a social transaction: thus Kapferer, writing on sorcery, asserts that 'the logic of science and sorcery as systems of abstract explanation. . . is of far less significance than the fact they are both social practices.'[27] The same could be said for religious knowledge in antiquity, and the social value placed on religious knowledge of all kinds will emerge as a severely under-deployed aspect of the religious aspects of our narratives. Moreover this will apply both to the agents in the narratives and also to the historians themselves.

Many of these frames of reference have been eagerly adopted in recent years:[28] one result of this reformulation is that the theme of *interpretation* has become central to religion. Furthermore, there is an increasing awareness of the specific workings of genre in religious dialectic: it has become a legitimate concern not just *what* is said, but *who* spoke, and in which idiom, a process probably 'begun' in Rome by Varro when he followed the Greek habit in schematising the threefold idiom of 'mythical, physical and civil', relevant to poets, philosophers and political society.[29] If we assume

---

[24] Feeney (1998) 12–13.

[25] Eliade (1957).

[26] Smith (1970).

[27] Kapferer (1997) 14.

[28] It is not always social anthropology that is drawn upon: other accounts are centred on biology, most famously (for classicists) Burkert on Greek religion (Burkert (1985) and especially Burkert (1997)). On some of these issues see Phillips (1998).

[29] Frr. 7–10, in Augustine *City of God* 6.5. For discussions of idiomatic religion, see (e.g.) Feeney (1991); Beard (1986). More generally Lamberton's (1986) discussion of philosophical exegesis of Homer is excellent; most of their interest is abstract and what we can reasonably call 'religious'. One wonders what Varro would have made of Mithraism with its astrological significations (Beck (1988)).

the existence of religious 'knowledges'[30] the various sources on religion go from 'deviating from' or 'representing' some unified central position to being a constellation of varied positions; Roman religious meaning becomes the whole of that constellation with all its readjustments, dichotomies, contradictions[31] and ultimate unity. The whole transformation of the field is reflected in the delicate change of title between Warde Fowler's *The Religious Experience of the Roman People* and Beard North and Price's *Religions of Rome*; the plural reflects an appreciation of diversity, and 'experience' has moved to the background.

This new approach is not without its difficulties: in some ways we might look back enviously on the days when things were almost literally black and white – belief or scepticism – because to explore rather than simply classify does not make for easy analysis. Consider Feeney's example of the (modern) Shintoist cult of Amaterasu: her temple is regularly demolished and rebuilt a few yards away. A senior priest, on being asked why this ritual was performed replied, 'I'm not really sure... there are many theories... but we are not sure which of them are true.'[32] Analysed along lines of 'belief' or 'scepticism' it is not hard to see how this instance would be taken: it would almost certainly 'prove' that some section of the movement was consciously and deliberately engaged in a huge deception. What indeed should we make of Feeney's closure with his assent to Dr Johnson's 'Why, Sir, we know very little about the Romans'?[33] Does this invalidate all his arguments? The background to any informed position may well be not a central canon to be reproduced exactly but a melting pot of possibilities, out of which individual voices arise. We should beware of overly privileging any of these voices: a 'true' orthodoxy, or even a normative position, is not to be found in a single account, even that of an expert.[34] What we have is an ongoing process of self-creation which *precludes* the existence of a central canon by its very nature: no sooner has a position been formulated than it becomes open to challenge, reassessment and refinement. Though we should expect certain features to command a general consensus, details will vary. Our criteria are no longer centred on the search for some 'original' 'authentic' Roman

---

[30] I borrow the term from Worsley (1997) whose use is broader than in this study, but nonetheless relevant.

[31] Liminality has become a key interpretative issue, often providing useful analysis of situations formerly thought of as confused or confusing; see e.g. Beard (1980) and (1995). It seems ironic that prodigies have not received a similar treatment until recently: Rosenberger (1998) has a section on this.

[32] Feeney (1998) 128, citing *The New York Times* of 7.10.93.

[33] Feeney (1998) 143, citing Chapman *Boswell's Life of Johnson* (Oxford, 1970) 464.

[34] Compare the difficulties encountered (even in antiquity) of defining 'good' and 'bad' magic (Phillips (1991b)).

religion, but the urge to understand the dynamic creation of identity and systems of meaning by and within a society.

Thus Ovid, for instance, is no longer 'confused' about religion: rather his *Fasti* make a statement about religious behaviour and organisation;[35] Cicero is no longer simply 'sceptical' but engaged in a complex inter-cultural negotiation.[36] Roman religion is a woven pattern of positions in a particular relationship to the gods and all the other religious positions represented within Roman society: to select which ones are to be excluded in favour of others is to miss the point.[37] This kind of approach is the one that is now generally taken in connection with religious phenomena of all types, and it has proved most fruitful.

But there are still gaps: whatever the progress in widening our understanding of religious motifs in (e.g.) poetry, certain debates that we might expect in Roman religious dialogue are simply *absent*. If identity can be shown to be a concern in actuality,[38] we should not be surprised that we can detect it as an organising principle in texts and rituals. By the same logic, we would expect to find commentary on another fundamental issue for Roman religion as it was practised, namely its ability to deliver *practical* results.[39] Yet such questions hardly loom large in our new understanding of Roman religion. We know that they performed rites in order to obtain the active support of the gods: we can also reasonably assume that when results matched their expectation from ritual, this would reinforce the expectation that the next ritual would have the same result. But there must also have been failures and setbacks, and reasons to consider, discuss and debate the details of both success and failure. We have not identified much material of this type in our sources: and I suspect that this is due to some extent to a lack of ease with paganism. We have for so long been concerned with the very modern question of whether 'they believed' in religion that we have often failed to detect more nuanced debate in our sources.

The issue of identity, while unquestionably pertinent and meaningful, also offers a way to sidestep the implication that ancient Romans did more

---

[35] For Phillips (1992) Ovid is defying the Augustan reformulation of the calendar. See also Scheid (1992); Feeney (1992) and (1998) 123–133; Parker (1993). On the *Fasti* more generally, see Newlands (1992a and b) and (a more pro-Augustan reading) Herbert-Brown (1994).

[36] Beard (1986); cf. Schofield (1986) 63 ('A Chinese box like this does not have, and can never have had, a single meaning').

[37] As is one that demands static meanings for (e.g.) festivals: for reinterpretation of a festival over time, see Beard (1987).

[38] E.g. Claudius' organisation of the *haruspices* was motivated partly by the hope of preserving what was, and what was not, proper Roman practice (Tacitus *Annals* 11.15; see further Briquel (1995)).

[39] So North (1976) 1: 'For the Romans of any generation, the real validation of their religion lay in the fact that it had worked ... for the Romans of the last generation of the Republic, it was a fact that their ancestors had won more battles and eaten better dinners than anybody else.'

than 'believe' in their religion, they also *used* it: they expected the cosmos to operate in a certain, largely predictable way, and when they performed rite, they were not just deliberately constructing their identity, they were also negotiating with the future course of events.

The intrinsic practicality of religion and the range of different rituals for different purposes should mean that they had a sophisticated set of expectations and remedies for all kinds of situations. Yet, while we have noted the importance of rite in Roman religion, we have not focussed on their discussion of this 'technology' in practice. This becomes a glaring omission when we consider the comparative material. Horton, studying a wide range of African religions, suggests a perspective from which

> [R]eligion is seen as growing, persisting and declining under the influence of two completely independent strivings: on the one hand, the striving to achieve an adequate level of explanation, prediction and control of the world; and on the other, the striving to achieve certain communion relationships not permitted in the purely human context.[40]

Horton's position has not been received with universal favour; his collected articles bear witness to the ongoing debate.[41] But his argument, though criticised, still carries weight[42] and bears a striking resemblance to certain aspects of Roman religion, with its emphasis on interpreting the cosmic *status quo* and acting to exert control by obtaining or maintaining the *pax deum*.

Faced with the kinds of 'contradictions' familiar to the student of Roman religion, Horton uses modern science as an analogy: by demonstrating that science functions routinely and comprehensibly with different and apparently contradictory 'levels', he demonstrates that *any* knowledge system (including religion) will do the same. We either understand the structure, or are so accustomed to this, that we see no contradictions. Taking Horton's

---

[40] Note how easily applicable his position is to antiquity: see e.g. Woolf's formulation (with no reference to Horton): 'All religions are primarily means of making sense of the world of mankind, of each individual's place in it, devices that offer a consistent account of the origins and workings of the cosmos and some explanations of and remedies for common misfortunes' (Woolf (1997) 74).

[41] There have been many responses, many of which Horton addresses in his collected articles (1993). See especially Penner (1971–2) and (1989); Tambiah (1990), esp. 90–92, 131–132; rejected by (e.g.) Kapferer (1997) 25, 225. In a classical context Lloyd (1996) argues against any universalist position (see esp. 137–139); for a (virtually univeralist) critique of anti-relativism see Penner (1989) 72–79. For a (not unfairly) more sympathetic overview of Horton's work see Segal (1993). Horton emphatically distances himself from Frazer but claims a heritage from Tylor via Durkheim.

[42] Many criticisms depend on stressing the aspect of communion, which critics claim Horton has ignored (e.g. Tambiah (1990), amongst other objections), which Horton does in fact appreciate, as the quote indicates. A common criticism is that his observations are too obvious (Boyer (1993b) 16) which does no harm to their use here.

lead, we can approach Roman religion with the expectation that it will have overlapping levels of explanation. It may be less 'contradictory' to speak of mortal efforts and the gods' actions in the same sentence after all, or, at least, no more so than when we speak of atomic bonds and superglue, or magnetism and gravity: if I drop an iron nail onto a magnet, why does it fall?

Horton's main claims made about science (and its implicit relativisation) are not our concern here: the analogy of science is simply a more useful one than an implicit, largely Christianised, model that stresses the aspect of 'religion as communion' rather than 'religion as technology'. Important aspects of the relationship of ancient Romans (and, implicitly, other similar cultures) with religion are more easily understood if we draw on our own relationship with science as an analogous system of knowledge and our predominant way of understanding and relating to the cosmos. I do not wish to press the analogy very far: there are many obvious differences, particularly in the results and details of operation. But we are accustomed to operating on different levels of thought that might appear inconsistent to an outsider lacking familiarity with our ways of understanding. The greater our knowledge of science, the more refinements of different 'levels' appear. The movement between 'levels of explanation' is largely effortless and unconscious. For the most part, we operate at an 'everyday' level, relating to objects as solids, for instance, rather than a confluence of atomic forces, waves and particles. But when a different level is called for, we will, as Horton argues, 'shift levels'. Anyone who has shown children the 'magic' of aligning iron filings with a nearby magnet, watched grit melt an icy road, seen bleach remove a stain or used a vacuum thermos has negotiated not with the 'immediately apparent', 'everyday' level but with 'higher' levels of operation and explanation. It is not inconsistent to expect water to retain its heat for hours in one vessel but not another, or to note the change in water's freezing point in the presence of salts: but these cannot be explained without recourse to a different level of explanation.

In the normal course of events we deal with perhaps a handful of different levels of explanation; a nuclear physicist or molecular chemist will deal with many more, and even theirs could be arranged in a hierarchy. Furthermore, the overall system is not particularly harmed by disagreements, inexplicables or limits: it is flexible enough to include competing theories. Despite the perception of constant testing and updating, science also freely moves between different models: Einsteinian physics may be the accepted theoretical model but Newtonian physics is perfectly usable for the vast majority of practical work. Quantum theory and relativity are simply not relevant until one requires a certain level of explanation, which is well beyond the needs of a great number of situations. Such is the nature of *our* system of explanations. The hypothesis offered here is that *their* systems also displayed this kind of complexity which scholars dubbed 'confusion' or 'inconsistency': alternatively, it became invisible because what was sought was a simple answer to the simple question 'Did they believe in their religion?'

Redefining religion as a dynamic system of knowledge and interpretation drastically changes the questions we bring to it: we hardly need reminding that where knowledge accumulates, power is not far away. The act of interpretation becomes a social and political transaction, fraught with considerations that simple facts never had to contend with. This will emerge as a central factor in all three historians; mastery of the complex understandings that informed religion is appropriated and dispensed sparingly to their textual agents. More frequently than mastery we encounter the *failure* to master religious lore: this serves chiefly to indicate the manifold and various possibilities for error – one hallmark of a nuanced set of knowledge. In each text, we meet a representative range of interpreters, from bungling amateurs to reasonably successful practitioners and – all too rarely – a true expert whose mastery encompasses many aspects of religious understanding. Presiding over them all is the omniscient historian. The representation is not exhaustive by any means but indicative of the kinds of errors that were likely to be found. In a similar way, no expert is shown to be proficient in all fields of religious learning. In fact, they are not permitted to do so, since religious acumen must never be located too securely in any one individual, even the historian, who tends towards cataloguing error without tastelessly foregrounding his own seasoned knowledge.

Even with this goldmine of interpretations, the explicit formulations that we have are only the tip of an intellectual iceberg: as Thomas (1993) 200 points out:

> [W]hat is stored in public representations is not necessarily identical with the conceptual system that is actually represented in the heads of ritual participants, especially when such a conceptual system has very complex cognitive relationships to other cognitive systems. In fact even the public information often presupposes hidden cognitive structures which only adequate theory can bring to light.

What we seek to explore here is the nature of the complex cognitive relationship between historiography and religion: we must also decide what sort of creature historiography was.

1.2 Historiography

Genre will affect the type of material and its presentation profoundly. A historiographical god in action will not necessarily resemble a poetic divinity, because genres are not simply static types of literature, but strategies in representation, as Conte has argued.[43] This means that we must consider how we are to read historiography with deliberate care: not only is it markedly different from its modern counterpart, but it will represent a different type of understanding from our own.

For instance, Feeney (1991) 260–1 notes a comment on historiography from Servius on the *Aeneid* 1.235: 'History is something that is related according to nature, whether it happened or not' (*historia est quicquid secundum naturam dicitur, siue factum siue non factum*) and continues: '"natural" is best understood as opposed to "mythic, unnatural and fabulous"... the "likely" is what is left over when you have disqualified the "fabulous" and is therefore a considerably more comprehensive category than we would allow under such a label'.

Servius' *secundum naturam ... siue factum siue non factum* will provide more than one key to our understanding of religious material in these historians; it alludes to an ethos that permeates the accounts, a genre-specific strategy *preference*, and we will find our authors scrupulously acknowledging a preferred *manner* of reporting. However, as we shall see, even the familiar terms such as 'likely' and 'unnatural', themselves the offspring of much broader expectations, will not necessarily correspond to categories of experience that we recognise without effort: and 'truth-value' in our sense will have little to do with this process. Ancient categories of understanding cannot be simplistically mapped onto our own, and the linguistic overlaps in terms such as 'nature' can tempt the reader to assume (mistakenly) that their *natura* is our nature and that their expectations of what can physically occur correspond with our own: thus liberal doses of 'scare-quotes' and untranslated Latin terms such as *fortuna* will be scattered throughout this monograph. These categories do not exist in isolation but are defined to a large extent not just by what they include but by other categories: we would not, for instance, see a distinction between nature and chance, but they did, as we shall see.

With the sort of formulation provided by Feeney and others, it becomes possible to explore authorial identity more fully, perhaps as fully as poetic *personae* have been treated.[44] What would a generous combination of approaches such as that of Détienne (1967) do for (some might say 'to') historiography? There are differences of course; but how far does Livy intend

---

[43] 'Every genre is a model of reality which mediates the empirical world ... The genre, a paradigm of the things to represent, makes reality recognisable and meaningful by translating it into something it is not' (Conte (1994a) 112 (writing specifically, but not exclusively, about poetry)).

[44] Poets have had more sustained treatment than historians, for the most part. Compare the acknowledged complexity of authorial *personae* in Latin poetry: I note virtually at random Harries (1989); Newlands (1992a and b); Phillips (1992) and Myers (1994) on Ovid; Lowrie (1997) on Horace.

to elide the gap with his 'mock invocation' of the gods *ut poetis* (*Pr.* 13)? While poets are generally thought to 'enrapture' their audience, historians usually (merely) provide 'entertainment'. The difference made to our reception by our choice of terms to describe an (arguably very similar) aspect is worth exploring and in the last ten years a number of scholars have given us far more sophisticated ancient historians.[45] This is part of a wider tendency to see deliberate sophistication where once we saw poor execution of an assumed historiographical norm. Whereas previous analyses were prone to treating ancient historians as flawed, and often demonstrating a weak mastery of their genre, there has been a growing tendency to treat them on their own terms. They have, not surprisingly, tended to fare rather better.

Where the attempt is made, there are interesting results: Moles (1993) shows intricate and sophisticated complexity in Livy's preface, for instance; Jaeger (1997) shows how our 'confusion' is often Livy's subtlety. The collaboration of Kraus and Woodman (1997), for all its brevity, shows the rigorous application (and contains many benefits) of a less anachronistic approach for a range of Latin[46] historians. Woodman's various other publications, especially his *Rhetoric in Classical Historiography*, have contributed to the habit of reading historians as fundamentally rhetorical. This has made it possible to examine organisational themes, issues of identity and exemplification in more detail than was previously admitted. Indeed we might question whether it is possible *not* to:

> The notion that sequences of real events possess the formal attributes of the stories we tell about imaginary events could only have its origin in wishes, daydreams, reveries. Does the world really present itself to perception in the form of well-made stories, with central subjects, proper beginnings, middles and ends, and a coherence that permits us to see 'the end' in

---

[45] Henderson (1987) on Tacitus, simplified to some extent in the version in Henderson (1998a), is perhaps the most immediately striking. Woodman's work is essential to such readings, but see Fowler's comment on his being 'bludgeoned back into line after some suspicious signs of imminent desertion to the good guys in recent years' (in *G* and *R* 40 (1993 227); Kraus' work (e.g. Kraus (1994b) and (1997)) also discusses the role of the Livian *persona* in a way that leaves an empirical approach looking redundant; Jaeger (1997) is equally sophisticated, and sympathetic, in her discussions. See now also Feldherr (1998) esp. 51–63 on Livy who reaches some similar conclusions to those presented here from a different angle; his discussion of religious material has much to commend it.

[46] Given the complexities of authorial identity, I follow their lead in preferring the epithet 'Latin' to 'Roman'; the issue of cultural identity is discussed for each author. 'Latin' has the advantage that it does not deliberately broach issues of culture, which become especially pertinent in connection with Ammianus, a Greek writing in Latin. Though it inevitably has allusions, these are less fixed than those associated with 'Roman'. Here we are concerned only with these specific historians of Rome writing in Latin.

every beginning? . . . and does the world, even the social world, ever really come to us as already narrativised, already 'speaking itself' from beyond the horizon of our capacity to make scientific sense of it? Or is the fiction of such a world, capable of speaking itself and of displaying itself as a form of story, necessary for the establishment of that moral authority without which the notion of a specifically social reality would be unthinkable? . . . could we ever narrativise without moralising?[47]

Woodman and Kraus come to similar conclusions for ancient historians, and state their preference for an analysis whereby it can be 'taken for granted that since these ancient texts are as much literary as historical, a literary approach, in which one reads for structure, style and theme, can offer new insights'.[48] Like them, we are interested in the interpretation that shapes the 'record of facts'.

In accordance with such cross-disciplinary arguments, interest in Latin historians has shifted its focus and desire, to the gain of the historians:

The catalogue of [Livy's] deficiencies is familiar: ignorance of geography and warfare, confusion on legal and constitutional matters, willingness to sacrifice accuracy to clarity etc. His greatness as a historian evidently does not lie in searching critical investigation of the past. It lies rather in his own imaginative reconstruction of the past and his representation, or rather evocation, of it to the reader . . . Livy's main engagement is not so much with the records of the Roman past as with the mind of his reader.[49]

Tacitus has similarly received attention on his own terms, and the results are equally striking.[50] For 'lonely'[51] Ammianus, perhaps doomed forever to isolation, and certainly not subjected to any fundamental reappraisal in recent years, a similar paradigmatic and epideictic approach is adopted.[52] Thus historians have moved from being 'themselves' (Livy) and gained

---

[47] White (1987) 25. Cf. the formulation of van Seters (1997) '[A] national history expresses what a nation is and what principles it stands for' (2). Such conclusions run counter to the implicit assumptions usually made of history. Veyne (1984) is a useful deconstruction of what history is usually thought to be. For a similar awareness of 'value-laden' perspective, even in scientific discourse, see Midgley (1992) 37.

[48] Kraus and Woodman (1997) 6.

[49] Solodow (1979) 258–259.

[50] I refer principally to Sinclair (1991a and b) and (1995) and Plass (1988) in addition to the detailed and various studies of Woodman.

[51] As Momigliano (1974) dubbed him.

[52] Kelly's 2002 DPhil makes a good start on this process but is, as yet, unpublished.

identities ('Livy').[53] The fact that a historian's material was 'factual' did not prevent him from moulding an account that resonated powerfully with contemporary concerns.[54]

Thus this study takes each historian as he comes, and presumes deliberate re-casting and selection from (rather than helpless subjugation to) their sources.[55] They represented a Roman world to their audience, and included within it material that we can call 'religious': cult action, various traditional signs such as prodigies and the operation of religious institutions. None of these is neutral: they all form part of a wider strategy which must be elucidated in each individual case. However they also made numerous religious diagnoses and interpretations as well as commenting on those that they represented: *fatum*, *fortuna* and *fors* have all been linked to 'religion', either as interpretative categories that bear witness to the gods (*fatum* and *fortuna*, depending on the argument) or as denials of the gods' action (*fors* and *fortuna*, in some cases). What 'religion' was to a Roman of the time is of course a somewhat elusive phenomenon but these categories all pertain to the interpretative spectrum that sought to explain or represent the workings of the gods. In short, anything that involved the gods, whether implicitly or explicitly, is fair game for this study. Other issues of both composition and reception are also explored here, though I shamelessly sidestep the deeper issues of reception brought to our attention by the suitably ill-defined postmodernist phenomenon, not because it brings a hopeless relativism (a common charge) but because it generates more possible meanings than can be dealt with, or even registered. True, many readers would potentially generate unpredictable responses. In fact, all our authors document the variety of interpretation that religious phenomena could stimulate – it would be entirely wrong to seek more than a vague consensus on what anything 'meant', even then. But the wider spectrum of plausible responses is left largely untouched. Thus the unregulatable reception is assumed to have a centre of

---

[53] For example: Kraus' work (e.g. Kraus (1994b) and (1997)); Jaeger (1997); Feldherr (1998) esp. 51–63. Further details are given in the specific chapters.

[54] I have only identified occasional and arbitrary points here: items with a direct bearing on individual authors or passages are included in the relevant chapters. See also Luce (1989); Rich (1996); for studies dealing with *ueritas* as the absence of bias see Woodman (1988); Wheeldon (1989); Blänsdorf (1992); Percival (1992); Marincola (1997) ch. 3.4 ('Impartiality') 158–174; on *inuentio* generally, Woodman (1988) 87–89, Marincola (1997) 160–162; on Livy, Oakley (1997) 4–12; on truth and fiction more generally in antiquity, Gill and Wiseman (1993). Most of these studies deal with our earlier two historians, though the point is no less valid for Ammianus who, as we shall see, is concerned with present conduct and issues.

[55] Oakley (1997) 13–100 establishes this for Livy; it is assumed in recent studies of Tacitus and asserted here for Ammianus (as lonely as ever with his omission from Kraus and Woodman (1997)). On the annalistic tradition and the different positions taken by scholars on evidence for early periods, Oakley (1997) 21–109: on the *annales maximi*, Frier (1979), Bucher (1987). For the argument that the term *annales* can refer specifically to a history of Rome see Verbrugghe (1989).

gravity, an 'intended audience', in antiquity. In this way it is possible to treat a text as a historical moment in the life of a particular society. The results of this strategy, adopted to make discussion more manageable, should not be mistaken for orthodoxy.

1.3 Religion and historiography

Religious issues of one sort or another pervaded ancient historiography. They were there from the start (in Classical terms) with Herodotus.[56] It should therefore come as no surprise that Livy and his successors included so much religious material. But this vague similarity should not disguise the fact that each formulates his own distinct position even if they all use comparable material. The arguments presented here do not depend on any demands made by the genre. They focus on reconstructing the sophistication of the religious strategies of each author on its own merits. In this way can we draw preliminary conclusions about the religious habits of these Latin historians.

Hitherto, accounts of religion in these authors, especially Livy[57] and Tacitus, have focussed on the issue of 'belief'. Opinions have been divided, as we shall see, since all three authors seem resistant to providing unambiguous evidence. Here, virtually the opposite sort of answer is sought: how *complex* can Roman religion be in a historian? How *nuanced* was religion as a system of interpretation? Discussion of 'belief' or 'scepticism' implies polarisation (what would the middle of such a spectrum be called?) and tends to be rather two-dimensional. 'Constellation' would be a better metaphor to describe the interpretative possibilities assumed in this discussion: some categories will have an immediate bearing on related features (such as prodigies and *fors*) while others will be relatively distinct (e.g. prodigies and the standing of the *augures* in a text). What emerges is that there was no single feature to which a Roman reader could give or deny assent, unless it is the actual existence of the gods, a reality which not even Epicureanism, the point farthest from state cult that we know of, chose to deny.

This discussion is thoroughly deductive: it reconstructs the largely implicit modes of understanding by close intratextual comparison and for the most part avoids intertextual reference, since importing contextless material is more likely to mislead us than clarify matters. Only by focussing on the

---

[56] Trompf (2000) discusses the theme of divine retribution in a variety of (principally Greek) authors in antiquity. On Herodotus in particular, Harrison (1997) and (2000).

[57] Levene (1993) sees far more sophistication on Livy than his predecessors. However he tends to represent two opposing poles (scepticism and belief): thus our strategies are rather different.

individual text at hand is it possible to speak of the dynamics of that particular text. That is not to say that these texts functioned in a vacuum: all four are clearly expecting their readers to note plentiful allusions. However, all too often, the argument that Tacitus (for instance) thinks little of the gods has meant that Ammianus' text is expected to show a similar tendency. As a result, any discussion that wishes to demonstrate his religious credentials begins with the handicap of this assumption. However, those arguments that establish Tacitus' 'disbelief' or (more often) untraditional and somewhat distant dealings with the gods often turn out to be based, to some extent, on the assumption that his predecessor Livy is a sceptic, and that Tacitus is aligning himself with *that* 'tradition'. Livy's supposed 'rationalism' is based in part on the prevailing reading of his contemporaries – and so on. In religious terms, these texts have rarely been examined closely without the argument being prejudiced by precedent. In this discussion, each is read as far as possible in isolation before any comparisons are made.

The discussion, especially that concerning Livy, establishes different aspects of the argument in stages. Initially, the basic categories of religion are established in the texts: if it could not be shown that prodigies, for instance, had meaning in these historical accounts, then it would be pointless attempting to clarify the cultural understandings that were supposed to inform them. Thus, after first contextualising Livy as a writer, we engage with previous interpretations of Livy's material and establish that where he has at times been thought to be sceptical about prodigies as a category, it is more useful to see an expert discriminating between genuine and mistaken diagnoses, a man who was almost mockingly familiar with the various pitfalls of deciding whether the gods had indicated their displeasure – or just that something unusual had occurred.

The official and procedural classification of an event as a prodigy also turns out to be more complicated than has often been assumed. This leads, necessarily, to a set of discussions on *oratio obliqua*, since much of Livy's material is presented in this way: once again, matters are deliberately complicated rather than simplified in order to show that the historian encodes his material in a surprising range of ways. In fact, very few of the religious moments are *not* nuanced in their deployment. Even apparently 'routine' moments, such as temple dedications, cast an interpretative shadow on the subsequent text, and serve to explain and elucidate the progress of events. After thus fixing some of the religious categories, the role of different experts within the text is explored, and it becomes possible to consider issues other than the acceptance or rejection of prodigies, such as the variety of religious customs and the deployment of a distinctively Roman *cultus deorum* in a meaningful sequential narrative.

At this point, a further element is introduced: 'causal over-determination' (also known as 'double motivation') whereby an author provides explanations of events simultaneously on both the human and the divine level. Two things emerge: firstly, that the over-determination is in fact multiple, not just double; and more pertinently, that such 'levels' of explanation are typical of explanatory systems, just as Horton argued. Rather than representing contradiction, superfluity or confusion, they are evidence of a sophisticated system of interpretation and classification. This distinction of levels creates a basis for exploring *fors*, *fortuna* and *fatum*, further categories for events that are even more contextually bound than those examined previously. Practically *anything* could be designated within these classifications, depending on the overall strategy of their context. Nor was this designation necessarily fixed or distinct: as we shall see, the same event might well be linked to *fortuna* in one context and *fatum* in another, without any inconsistency. Finally, for Livy, the politics is put back into religion as the implications of religion as interpretation are realised in the historian's text: like all knowledge systems, it attracted amateurs and experts, and was articulated within social protocols, checks and balances.

Much of this discussion is present only implicitly in the subsequent accounts: most of the basis for understanding the religious habits of Tacitus and Ammianus can be achieved by reference to the elucidation of these factors in connection with Livy. What is explored in chapters 4 and 5 is the particular orientation of religion in the changed climates of the imperial historian Tacitus, and Ammianus, writing when state paganism's time was finally up – though he may not have realised it. Tacitus wrote an account steeped in religious and political expertise, where errors of understanding – like so many other errors – attracted profound scorn. Yet this should not be mistaken for cynicism, least of all about religion. Despite the fragmentary nature of his depiction of the years 14 to 70, a religious framework for the extreme political disruptions of the first century can be discerned. Tacitus, far from being a sceptic, articulated a process spanning decades within a sophisticated religious structure.

Ammianus, writing in the fourth century under Christian emperors, appears rather different at first. Despite the profound transformation of the Roman world, his historical account shares a great number of its concerns with his predecessors: the refinement of an appropriate set of rites for Rome; the castigation of the various errors made in religion (not least the patronage of Christianisation by a long series of emperors); and the patterning of the narrative according to the will of the gods. The similarities in his method are not matched by his interpretative system however: for Ammianus, negotiation with the gods is not exercised primarily through ritual but rather by the justice of one's conduct. This is at once reminiscent of Herodotus and deliberate strategy that (re)appropriated central religious concerns from the contemporary discourse of Christianity. Ammianus' is a remarkable synthesis of historiographical *topoi*, traditional Roman concerns and practices with the foremost interpretative strategies of his day, in the last extant historiographical attempt to articulate a pagan religion for Rome.

2

Livy and the invention of Roman religion

2.1 The reception of Livy

2.1.1 Religious material in Livy

Our reception of Livy has tended to be determined by our requirements. As a source of historical information, he has been considered disappointing when judged by modern standards and methods. Though there are undoubtedly problems recovering historical facts from our author,[1] recent, more 'literary' studies have brought more favourable results that show Roman identity to have been a key factor in shaping the *Ab Vrbe Condita (AVC)*.[2] The following discussion belongs firmly in this latter category.

Livy is of course familiar to students of religion: without him our knowledge of Republican religion would be infinitely poorer.[3] The historian is generally treated as a store of material that can be taken, by and large, as it comes: little discussion of Livy's specifically religious methodology is thought to be necessary.[4] But there is also a tradition of scholarship examining Livy's 'belief' as an object of study in itself. For this school, religion has been a puzzling and contradictory phenomenon, and no clear consensus has been reached: the most recent – and probably the fullest – attempt to examine the material is the work of Levene in his *Religion in Livy* which therefore merits some attention. Levene makes central to his argument the issue that had previously confounded most attempts to understand the presentation of the religious material – namely that the author appears to contradict himself at various points on religious matters: Levene endeavours to retain this tension rather than favour one side to the detriment of the other.

---

[1] Cornell (1995) makes a case for the broad authenticity of much of the material; see also Walsh (1961), (1974) and (1982). For other angles and the understanding of historiographical material as 'myth', see Bremmer and Horsfall (1987), Wiseman (1995) and Fox (1996), amongst others.
[2] E.g. Jaeger (1997), Miles (1995), Feldherr (1998) and Kraus (1997).
[3] As a glance at the general list of prodigies in MacBain (1982) 83–105 or Cohee's (1994) list of repeated rites will easily demonstrate; Liebeschuetz (1979) grew out of undergraduate courses on Livy according to the Preface.
[4] For instance Orlin (1997) does not mention Livy's methodology, least of all when faced with uneven reporting of religious features, though he relies heavily on Livy's narrative. North (1979) is unusual in discussing the text so fully, if only with regard to specific passages.

Essentially his argument is that Livy is deliberately forging an account within which there are two possible readings at any moment: one ('believing') incorporates the religious material as integral to the record and explanation of past events, while the other ('sceptical') includes it only as 'traditional ornamentation' to be discarded by the educated élite. The reader must decide whether to believe the 'religious' account or not.[5]

Levene's indispensable contribution is his demonstration that, at almost any given moment, religious factors are eminently *relevant* in Livy's historical narrative: Roman success is consistently linked with Romans' piety and good relations with the gods. Impiety on the other hand leads to (temporary) setbacks, inevitably followed (in Rome's case) by religious and military recovery (in that order). This also applies to other agents in the narrative: Hannibal, for instance, attributes his successes and final downfall to the intervention of the gods.[6] Livy's method is not just explicit mention of the mood of the gods at any given moment but also, more commonly, the significant juxtaposition of religious material to other events, often those on the battlefield: Roman piety consistently leads to success and impiety to failure. It is perfectly understandable that in a culture which by and large accepted that the gods played a very active role in the world of men, such juxtaposition should be sufficient to leave the reader in no doubt as to the sort of intervention that was to follow. Levene shows that Livy 'is unlikely to be inventing such material outright, but ... he is prepared to expand it, shorten it, change the order of events within it, alter its position within its year, and even occasionally place it in the wrong year altogether':[7] in other words the organisation of his narrative *is* an interpretation that demonstrates the power of the gods.

However the suggestion that Livy is also simultaneously offering an account that 'denies' religious causation is more problematic. The 'believing' account is perfectly coherent as it stands, and Livy does not actually offer a full parallel and secular version as an alternative; rather, even if we were to accept Levene's analysis of the moments of apparent scepticism, it could only be said that Livy casts occasional doubt on his one coherent account. The use of *oratio obliqua* and deferred authority, combined with the explicit

---

[5] Liebeschuetz (1967) 45 suggests a comparable position, though (to simplify it somewhat) it seems that he prefers that the educated and rational Roman readership would not be so foolish as to believe the 'religious' version, which was for the unenlightened masses: 'I shall argue that thoroughgoing rationalism and earnest advocacy of religion are closely associated'. It is not always clear what he means by 'rationalism' since this term is usually synonymous with 'scepticism about religion' *per se*. For the most part, he (unusually) seems to mean 'discriminating' rather than 'absolutely sceptical'.

[6] 30.30.4 (speaking of himself, '*Hannibalem, cui tot de Romanis ducibus uictoriam di dedissent*'); 30.30.30 (he succeeded '*quoad ipsi inuidere di*'). The most recent of the many general discussions of Hannibal is Lancel (1998).

[7] Levene (1993) 242.

questioning of specific religious notices, it is alleged, are to be understood by the reader as representative of a more general scepticism. Ignoring the 'discredited' material is supposed to leave behind a fully formed 'rational' account for a discerning reader to choose.

There is a great number of possible nuances in Livy's handling of prodigies and it seems simplistic to assimilate these comments to an overarching, implicit and absolute denial of the whole category of prodigies, as Levene (1993) 17–18 does in connection with these reports. Despite his endeavour to give credit to Livy for his understanding of, and acquiescence in, contemporary ideology and beliefs, Levene is still reliant on the two opposite poles of belief/scepticism. Nothing, however, could be more anachronistic than the assumption that ancient Romans chose, as we do, between a predominantly materialistic and self-declared 'scientific' cosmology and a religiosity that is taken to be rationally indefensible (if liberally permissible) for those feeble-minded enough to require it. That perhaps is somewhat polemically put, but this assumption does represent the framework for analysing ancient religion until very recently.

In fact the introduction of the rather extreme 'sceptical' argument has only been possible because of its supposedly self-evident claim to consideration. This is due partly to an uneasy alliance between modern 'rationalism' and ancient anti-religious polemic, for which the most obvious Roman spokesperson is Lucretius. There seems no reasonable argument that would render Livy an Epicurean but we have to consider the possibility that some of his readership was: thus, Levene's ingenious suggestion that the historian writes two parallel accounts for different sensibilities. Indeed, the historian seems occasionally to acknowledge the existence of a thought system that rejected tradition but his narrative weighs strongly against sympathy for such a school. When a *pullarius* wrongly reports positive omens before battle, this comes to the attention of the consul's son, 'born before the school of thought that rejects the gods' (*iuuenis ante doctrinam deos spernentem natus*, 10.40.10). He duly informs his father Papirius, who is not daunted: he merely declares that the man had attracted the prognosticated *ira deum* to himself. Placing the man in the front line, he is soon proved right when a chance javelin, thrown before battle had even commenced, caught the *pullarius* and killed him. While Papirius noted that the gods had duly punished the man, a nearby raven apparently confirmed his diagnosis by cawing (10.40.13-14).

However, passing acknowledgement of a school of thought is not tantamount to tailoring an account for its adherents. In fact, such views are deliberately marginalised. Firstly, Livy simply notes that some, extremely ill-defined, people did not adhere to traditional interpretations. He does not dignify them with a title. Secondly, the logic of the first narrative in particular tends strongly towards a judgement so negative as to be rebuttal of such a position: one rather hopes that the *pullarius* who ignored the poor signs and reported good ones *was* an Epicurean, since he might have met his death with greater equanimity.[8] The episode as a whole is a striking vindication of the consul's judgement that the gods would avenge themselves on whoever misreported ill omens.

If we cannot convincingly detect that Livy was catering for a contemporary sceptical audience, then we are left only with *our* preference for scepticism. Only within a modern agenda does the assertion, for instance, that prodigy reports may have been flawed (the 'may' often gets lost or discarded) sound like a tacit admission that all reports were fake or meaningless. There is a number of reasons to object to this methodology: one of the problems is that all the religious material thereby becomes polarised – it is categorised as either absolutely sceptical or absolutely credulous. To ask the question in these terms deprives Livy of any opportunity to express reservations (rather than scorn), explicitly weigh up evidence or introduce subtle distinctions. In addition it is gravely misleading to assume that *all* these varying techniques should necessarily be taken to indicate the same methodological position of scepticism. If we adopt a more positive assumption, such as one that included the divine and supernatural as an absolutely fundamental and unshakeable feature of contemporary cosmology, our authors would gain substantial freedom, even license, to criticise aspects of that cosmology without running the risk of undermining it completely. If we were, for the sake of argument, to assume that prodigies were an undeniable reality for Livy's Roman audience, then our response to his comments and contextualisation would be vastly different from those hitherto suggested.

In fact, we shall see that an examination of these instances does not seem to require that they even be taken as part of one monolithic strategy: it will be argued, from a close reading of the text, that it is misleading to deploy 'scepticism' as a methodological position *at all*. Thus, the following argument will often engage with Levene's 'sceptical' argument, though we should remember that this is only part of his discussion: his synthesis of previous arguments makes him a useful reference point. If we are to understand the religious position of Livy's work, we must seek a different

---

[8] The task of observing the sacred chickens seems an unusual task for an Epicurean, whether he chose it or was appointed, so if we feel inclined to speculate about this incident, we should remain within the boundaries of traditional religious reasoning. His rather desperate move was perhaps based on foolish optimism or fear that the bringer of bad news would be blamed. Alternatively, since the incident came to light because there was an altercation between the various *pullarii*, it is possible that an ambiguous or unusual response was given a positive interpretation by a careless or inexperienced interpreter.

methodology, and one which belongs within a better general understanding of the historian's purpose as a whole.

2.1.2 Livy in general

Livy, like all historians, is competing for an audience, for credibility, for conviction;[9] his Rome must prevail over that of his competitors. His choice of strategy is totalising: the whole of Roman history. This gives him a particular perspective, and a particular impact on his reader:

> Annalistic history, even more than history generally, is not only an account of individual events, but of events that are formally similar or even identical … The yearly pattern – which is the Republican constitution in its continuing operation – is meant by Livy to be seen as subsuming the vicissitudes of men and events to itself. A decision to write annalistic history is more than a matter of style or tradition; it is the choice of an interpretation of history as well.[10]

Phillips highlights one of the key tensions in our reading of historiography: *any* organisation of data is necessarily interpretative. Miles (1995) also argues strongly for an interpretation of Livy whereby 'historical facts' are integrated into a strategy that owes more to identity than 'facticity': he encourages us to see Livy not as a misplaced modern empiricist but as an élite practitioner of politics, in its broadest sense – Livy the historian is another in a series of founders and refounders of Rome's history. Rather than accumulating the past, Livy negotiates with it to produce a new Rome, an identity born of negotiated memory.

This elaboration and this revision are a fundamental part of Livy's narrative, but we might single out one specific aspect which will have particular relevance for us, namely the historiographical use of *exempla*: his prologue famously offers that in history, 'for yourself and your state (*tibi tuaeque rei publicae*), you can choose what to imitate, and from that what you should avoid, what is loathsome in its beginning and loathsome in its end'.[11] Nor

---

[9] On which see especially Marincola (1997) ch. 2.

[10] Phillips (1974) 273. Cf. the formulation of Hickson (1993) 145 in connection with prayer formulae: 'Together they reminded Livy's contemporary audience that the Roman state, with its political and religious machinery, had been and continued to be a stable and enduring entity'.

[11] Kraus (1997) 53–54 comments, '*tibi tuaeque rei publicae* is a striking phrase, which suggests that Livy is thinking about his potential reader not simply as an individual, but as a citizen. By looking carefully at the monument (i.e. by reading Livy's history attentively), by understanding its representations (distinguishing good and bad), and then by implementing that understanding, *you* make history work. In turn, if you get it right, this imitation and avoidance will provide a cure for the current evils of your state.' See further Kraus (1994b) 13–15. On the prologue generally, Moles (1993).

are *exempla* limited to explicitly flagged examples: Livy shows his own characters negotiating with (unflagged) *exempla*, implying that any or all of the narrative can be usefully imitated, avoided or otherwise noted.[12]

The link between individual and *res publica* is a complex one in Livy's account. In many ways, the unfolding of Roman history is the story of individuals, whether glorious, average or ignominious. But the *res publica* amounts to more than any individual in Livy; that, above all else, is its central characteristic. The succession of years – all variations on a theme with their magistracies, triumphs, disasters, prodigies and other perennials – becomes impersonal, rising above individual issues and personalities, to the point of being an almost timeless and eternal process. Yet it is this mighty entity that has 'tottered' and must be restored with the use of history. Livy's epideictic and remedial programme influences the level at which he must explicitly design and represent his Republic; he suggests that his readers need reminding of better ways and better times. He will bring to the forefront *exempla*, both good and bad, to be followed or avoided[13] and he proceeds on the basis that his readers will read his account accordingly.

2.1.3 Religion and *exempla*

This exemplificatory agenda has been accepted as part of Livy's presentation of Romans as generals and statesmen. Yet it has not been applied to religious conduct as thoroughly as it has been discerned in political and military behaviour: this has meant that a great deal of religious comment has been misunderstood. The deliberate and exemplificatory level of explicitness influences both Livy's choice of religious phenomena and his mode of presenting them. Obviously the availability of material is relevant in a broad sense but this cannot be considered to be overly important. It seems almost certain that the Bacchist affair of 186 is subject to detailed expansion,[14] whatever Livy's sources were, while other opportunities for elaboration (for instance in the prodigy lists)[15] are not exploited: in fact the vast majority of religious entries are brief to the point of obfuscation. Livy, in evoking and recreating Rome in its beginnings, heyday and decline, is not intending to be exhaustive: he selects from, or builds on, the available material

---

[12] Chaplin (2000) 2. See also 29–31 for the centrality of *exempla* in Livy's history. The expectation that the ancient reader is concerned, in reading literature, with the 'care of the self', that is, the education and negotiation of the reader with posited norms and preferences, is argued by Foucault (1978–1986).

[13] For exemplarity in Livy's work see Chaplin (2000); Miles (1995), 249f.; Kraus (1997) 53–56.

[14] North (1979).

[15] For the historical sources of the prodigy lists see North (1986) 255, commenting on MacBain (1982) and Rawson (1971).

according to his overall objectives of 'creating' Rome (and with it, Roman religion in its various aspects). Many comments that have been understood as general statements of fact (usually on whether prodigies really occurred) are, on closer analysis, more usefully taken as highly specific assessments, included to *advise* the reader on religious practices and demonstrate the historian's expertise in discriminating between genuine and mistaken prodigy reports. Thus Livy's religious material is governed by his overall agenda; it is intended not so much to 'establish the facts', but to reaffirm what he presents as traditional religious practice through his portrayal of behaviour and its consequences. In fact, rather than being disposable or ornamental, the religious material is embedded deeply within the account, and presented with sophistication, as was appropriate for such a major aspect of Roman cultural life.

This assertion is the Ariadne's thread through the diverse material of the following chapters. We will be left, not with an account framed in a dialectic of belief or scepticism, but rather with a nuanced series of preferences centred on identity, 'practicality' and propriety. The hallowed practices of ancient Rome are integrated into a history that cannot be divorced from the current state of Rome. Indeed, it is argued that the *Ab Vrbe Condita* has little value as a nostalgic record: it is written with the present in mind. At the forefront of the account is the recommended 'norm', privileged by its repetition and brought into sharp relief by error, which is nonetheless subdued in its frequency in order that its shadow should not intrude on the showpiece of Rome at peace (or not so far from it) with its gods. With Livy as her guide, a tottering Rome could relearn her 'true' identity from her past: and was central to Livy's Rome. With the *Ab Vrbe Condita* in mind, Rome *could* begin to leave her recent errors behind and provide material for a future historian or another guardian of the 'real' Rome.

2.2 Actuality of phenomena

Before any attempt is made to analyse the significance that Livy (or his agents) ascribe to 'supernatural' events, there is the issue of whether he accepts that they occur(red) in actuality. We therefore begin with Livy's documentation and presentation of prodigial or supernatural phenomena. The argument distinguishes a series of different aspects, all or any of which might be relevant to any given example. These various aspects are deliberately treated separately, despite the modern tendency to conflate them; the argument presented here seeks rather to demonstrate that they are in fact distinct issues, each with a different bearing on the evidence.

2.2.1 Prodigy reports

Most of the discussion in Livy, and most of the material, centres on prodigies. This is not surprising: prodigies appear at (fairly) regular intervals in the text; most importantly, they usually appear as part of the year's report, and therefore have a role in the structure of Livy's history. However, they are *also* most problematic, for a number of reasons. Prodigies are the items most likely to offend modern taste. There are two aspects to this: while we might accept the factual possibility of some of the events (e.g. the numerous mentions of lightning strikes on a significant landmark, or an attack by a wolf one night on a guard at Capua at 27.37.4), others seem downright incredible to a *modern* perspective (such as statues sweating blood among the Sabines, 22.36.7).[16] But there is another aspect to which modern readers are even less sympathetic, which is the *interpretation* placed on these events (whether we think they happened or not). Prodigies were said to indicate the wrath of the gods: in Livy's text the response is to expiate them, thus obtaining afresh the good will of the gods, and the success of impending Roman endeavours. Though nowadays we generally afford the Romans the professional courtesy of not ridiculing their beliefs in print, I confess to harbouring the suspicion that little credence is given amongst modern scholars to their interpretative system and their use of sacrifice as means of communications with the gods. The problem is that this has unconsciously been compounded with certain types of evidence to incline us to see scepticism in the ancient sources where there is none. For our purposes, the world occurs as an interpretation from the ground up, and to note that we construct it differently (i.e. to note that their world does not make sense to us) testifies to the need for elucidation of the assumptions that shaped events into a meaningful sequence. Dismissal of their cognitive world is not a discovery or an insight.

However it *is* true that there *are* aspects of the presentation of prodigies that lead us to doubt whether Livy acquiesced in this sort of interpretation: not only can we be told that, 'time and again, when [Livy] reports stories of the supernatural, he qualifies them with words like *dicitur*, *fama est*, *traditur* or *nuntiatum est*, thus including the stories, but avoiding vouching for them himself',[17] but also there are moments where Livy has seemed to

---

[16] It is worth stressing that I refer here to judgements made, explicitly or implicitly, by modern writers. I am not arguing a position that supports this judgement; some occasional attempts have been made to rationalise the accounts, such as those made by Krauss (1930), but establishing prodigies' plausibility for a modern audience is not my concern here, though I do note that far fewer need any explanation than is often assumed.

[17] Levene (1993) 19, citing also Bornecque (1933) 61–62; Kajanto (1957) 32–34 and Walsh (1961) 47–48.

be dismissing specific prodigies outright. The combination of these factors has been a potent force in the formulation of interpretations of Livy that have him 'sceptical', 'rational' (for which we can effectively read 'sceptical') or 'distanced' (my rather clumsy term for Levene's twofold approach). Yet it has also been impossible to ignore the fact that prodigies as an indicator of the gods' wrath *do* seem to function in the text to explain the course of events. Thus we are left with something of a dilemma: there are reasons to think that Livy prefers not to accept the traditional Roman position on prodigies, and equally good textual reasons to think the opposite. Discussions have hitherto marginalised one type of evidence to favour its opposite; or, most recently, in the case of Levene, acknowledged the apparent dilemma and celebrated it as irreducible. Any attempt to prefer one side of the argument about prodigies must therefore address the whole range of issues and produce explanation(s) of this type of presentation that bring them into an integrated discussion, rather than privileging a pre-selected position.

2.2.1.1 *Definitions*

The items we are investigating at this point are usually called *prodigia*. As for definitions, modern discussions usually focus on the classification: we follow their lead in some ways in classifying prodigies as some kind of violation of nature. Festus, on the other hand (and writing later), defined prodigies by their *function*: they foretold future events.[18] The casual use of the term by ancient historians, including Livy, implies that prodigies did not need defining for their audience. But any definition of prodigies that seeks to oppose it to another term (in this case 'nature') must insist that 'nature' is taken in a Roman sense, whatever that was: any apparent semantic and linguistic similarities with the present are likely to play us false. Nonetheless, it seems that prodigies were at least sometimes defined as 'unnatural' events by the Romans.[19] To demonstrate the need for caution, we might also throw another criterion into the melting pot of definition: all too often what is termed prodigious is a complex of factors that 'should' not belong together. Lightning, for instance, is not apparently prodigious unless it hits

---

[18] Because of the similarity of the words *prodico* and *prodigium* (relying of course on the understanding of what prodigies 'were' as events: *prodigia – quod prodicunt futura, permutatione g litterae; nam quae nunc c appellatur, ab antiquis g vocabatur.* (254L). *Prodicunt* is an interesting term to use, implying that the outcomes are in some way shaped by the prodigies.

[19] Tacitus opposes the categorisation of events as prodigies when they were actually 'natural' events, as we shall see, and the Elder Pliny seems to offer support for this when he explicitly moves back to discussing *natura*, after digressing into the story of one who apparently came back to life: *idque ita euenit. post sepulturam quoque uisorum exempla sunt, nisi quod naturae opera, non prodigia, consectamur* (*NH* 7.178).

a significant building.[20] Nor are oxen troublesome, not unless they speak or find themselves in inappropriate places. It is not enough to speak of liminality as Rosenberger (1998) 103–126 does, however useful the concept is: the prodigy notices we have would seem to be very specific violations of particular norms. Thus the gloss at 27.37.6 *incertus mas an femina esset natus erat* underlines the troubling (liminal) status of a hermaphrodite; though many examples could be furnished of wolves within the city limits,[21] we cannot say simply that these are examples of a wild/civilised liminary violation, even if we adduce misplaced swarms of bees and the like. Though these *can* be thus classified, we do not know what other factors help to discriminate between the reported incidents and others which were not of interest: we have deformed mules from Reate scattered throughout the text, but no similar oxen; likewise we have no speaking mules. Some other criteria were surely applied in making initial assessments, far more specific than wild/civilised, urban/rural, cultivated/uncultivated and any others we might care to speculate on: what we can say for certain is that they are mostly irrecoverable.

2.2.1.2 The status of prodigy notices in Livy: reported speech

Prodigies, then, clearly have some role to play within the *AVC*: they are not only structurally embedded within the annalistic account, they are also part of the explanatory structure (Levene (1993)). Given this structural and explanatory importance, it is somewhat surprising to find that the prodigy notices themselves are so problematic. We should not underestimate the importance of this aspect: it is the mainstay of all arguments that render Livy sceptical or profoundly questioning about religion.[22] The issue must therefore be addressed in some detail. We begin with the alleged 'distancing' of *oratio obliqua*: but before any headway can be made, a number of distinctions must be made: *oratio obliqua* ('reported speech') is technically the name given to a linguistic phenomenon, and is contrasted with *oratio recta* ('direct speech'). More specifically, in Latin and Greek, it is associated with particular grammatical constructions such as the accusative (or nominative, in Greek) and infinitive.[23] Outside the linguistic context, it is also associated with the *topos* in literature whereby an author assigns authority and origin

---

[20] We never hear of a simple case of lightning in Livy; we always hear of the building, monument or construction involved.

[21] Livy typically goes to the trouble of noting their entry and/or exit points (or the point to which they penetrated: see 3.29.9, 21.46.2, 33.26.9 and 41.9.6).

[22] Levene (1993) 19; Bornecque (1933), 61–2; Kajanto (1957) 32–4; Walsh (1961) 47–8.

[23] In Latin, there *are* other methods of indicating *oratio obliqua* (such as 'virtual *oratio obliqua*'; Woodcock (1959) §240, 285). These are beyond our scope here.

of a statement to an outside agency, which might range from no one in particular to a specific agency, such as Valerius Antias. There are additionally particular words associated with *oratio obliqua*, such as *dicitur*, *fertur* and *ferunt*.[24]

However, much of our material is not, despite our normal terminology, literally reported *speech*: 'true' reported speech is the enactment of a speech in the text, and many of our examples are reported *events*. In fact, it is argued here that to place the vast majority of prodigies into an undistinguished mass labelled 'reported speech' is a mistake: there are a number of justifications for this, beginning with the fact that they are not introduced by the normal terminology of *oratio obliqua*.

Though Levene includes forms of the verb *nuntiare* along with *dicitur* and the like, there are several reasons to distinguish *nuntio* from this grouping. Firstly, *nuntio* is not used interchangeably with *traditur*, *proditur*, *dicitur*, *ferunt* and so on. Outside the prodigial context, it always constitutes an utterance, an event of speech *within* the time frame of the text, rather than outside it. This is clearly reflected in another key distinction, that the customary terms associated with *oratio obliqua* are typically, even universally and distinctively, in the present tense. *Nuntio*, on the other hand, is always in the past tense in connection with prodigies: that is, it represents an event, a factual utterance, in the time-frame of the narrative. On the other hand, where Livy explicitly names his sources, he still uses the present tense – *dicitur*, *traditur*, etc. – even if the source is contemporaneous with events in the text.[25] Furthermore, when we do encounter a present tense verb with *oratio obliqua*, what we are often dealing with is in fact better described as reported *narration* rather than speech, for instance when a head 'is said' to have been found on the Capitol (*caput humanum integra facie aperientibus fundamenta templi dicitur apparuisse*, 1.55.6). In contrast we normally read that a prodigy *was* announced (*nuntiatum* or a similar word). There are, as it turns out, good grounds for differentiating what has generally been included in one general category of *oratio obliqua*.

For the sake of clarity I propose to use a set of terms in order to distinguish different types of material previously grouped without distinction under the heading of *oratio obliqua* or reported speech. The phrase 'reported words' will, for our purposes, be limited to a literal usage – the representation, usually with the accusative and infinitive construction, in the text of a speaker uttering words ('the messenger said that Hannibal had

---

[24] This list could easily be expanded to include other words or phrases (e.g. *fama est*). The terms explored here are those that occur in conjunction with religious material.

[25] E.g. *artem adhibitam ferunt a patriciis, cuius eos Icilii tum quoque insimulabant* (4.56.3).

said. . . ') using *dixit* or a similar term in the past tense, and this category will not concern us here. 'Reported narration', on the other hand, indicates here that *events* are formulated with a word such as *dicitur* in the *present* tense, and also typically given in the accusative and infinitive ('it is said that the senate voted to. . . '). Finally, and somewhat liminally, we shall distinguish 'reported announcements', the act within the text of reporting events elsewhere, almost universally by the use of *nuntio*; these, as we shall see, while often appearing in the accusative and infinitive, also appear in *oratio recta* in the past tense and are characteristically succinct ('it was reported [to the senate] that a mule had been born. . . ') The rationale for these distinctions, which may not initially be obvious, will soon become evident as a practical concern; it should be emphasised that there are also good linguistic and methodological reasons for them.[26]

It will be argued that in reported *announcements*, there is no deferral of authority, nor any 'distancing': there is the representation of a report, which should, unless we are told otherwise, be assumed to be trustworthy or at least neutral. When a report is obtained in the text, it is an utterance, and constitutes an event. A messenger arrived and said that lightning had struck a temple, for instance, or that Hannibal was on the move: though this would be (grammatically speaking) in *oratio obliqua*, it would be misleading to emphasise this in determining the status of the content of the message. The messenger could, of course, be lying or mistaken. But it is not in question that a message was delivered to (e.g.) the Roman senate.[27] Verification of the *contents* of the message is a different matter, an issue for the constituent members of the textual audience, and indeed this process can at times be observed, as we shall see. This is essentially a fairly simple idea, and examples of straightforward accurate messages are plentiful. The most sceptical approach to 'reported announcement' can only doubt the veracity of the contents of the message within the narrative, but not (if we are to be at all reasonable) that the messenger(s) arrived and gave a report.

With this in mind, we can in fact modify Levene's comment to say that the majority of prodigy notices are presented as reported *announcements*, which has a very different impact and implication.[28] Rather than

---

[26] We shall necessarily be dealing with lists and Latin terms: where appropriate, the pertinent moments are translated and fuller passages footnoted in Latin.

[27] We do have an example of an untrustworthy messenger, and much is made of this, with explanations for his conduct (24.31.14-15), and another of one who was not trusted (but did his job anyway: 1.54.6-7). But Livy is hardly at pains to undermine the many messages that are delivered, often invisibly, within his text. His agents virtually always act on such information without any problems.

[28] Some religious material (but only one prodigy report, at 3.29.9) is presented as reported narration: these will be addressed in due course.

introducing prodigial material with *nuntio* because he wishes to emphasise its status as unverified, Livy is constituting the reports as events in themselves, with a textual impact on events. For a citizen of Rome it was not just significant in theory that mules were being born with the wrong number of legs, it was significant *now* that the gods were far from pleased with Rome. Given that the vast majority of prodigy notices in Livy are framed as reports (the alternative being that they are straightforward events in the text), we must next ask ourselves why there is much emphasis on this mode of inclusion. It seems that rather than being employed to reduce the factual status of the prodigies, *nuntio*'s chief role is to make the city of Rome the *locus* of these announcements, placing the reader at the centre of the action.

To demonstrate this, some kind of breakdown of the reports as a whole would seem useful: however, there is no straightforward way to *count* the prodigy notices since they vary in length, geographical origin and placement in the year. Sometimes two distinct prodigies occur in the same place at the same time, and at others it is not clear whether two items listed are prodigial in themselves, or only as a coincidence. Furthermore, Livy at times mentions 'other prodigies' which he did not see fit to list or specifically says that his list is selective (e.g. [*prodigia*] *in quis* 21.62.2 or *inter alia prodigia* ...at 3.10.6). Thus it is not possible to produce a list statistically showing (for example) that reports from outside Rome are more likely to be preceded by *nuntio*. However, the examination of a number of examples and citation of the remaining notices that show similar characteristics should, rightly, convey the impression that this is the general tendency, and that the exceptions do not violate the general principle.

Oratio obliqua 1: reported announcements   Firstly, announcements are clearly treated as factual events in time and/or the series of events: just how precisely the event of the announcement is located varies. Often Livy only places reports vaguely at some point in a year, but occasionally there is very specific information, as at 36.37.1 when one consul has left and another is still to set off, or at 40.2.1 when Livy refers to the timing of a specific report – after prodigies and expiation in Rome, *simul procuratum est quod tripedem mulum Reate natum nuntiatum erat...* (40.2.4). The timing is quite possibly *inuentio* of course; the point here is that they are *constructed* to have occurred at a specific time.[29]

The second consideration is far more compelling for our argument: there is the distinction made at times between prodigies that were seen (*uisa*

---

[29] For Livy's deliberate chronological (dis)placement of prodigial material and expiation see Levene (1993) 242.

in tandem with *oratio recta*) and announced (*nuntiata*, followed by *oratio obliqua*). This is consistently used to distinguish between events in Rome and abroad (by which I mean outside the City). For instance at 40.19.1-2, we have *prodigia multa foeda et Romae eo anno uisa et nuntiata peregre*. But even this is used with discrimination. Consider 40.19.2-3: we move from indicative *pluuit* in Rome to announcement from *within* Rome by the priests (presumably because they were the only ones to see the prodigy), before the sense of *nuntiauere* is carried over to cover the report of the delegates from Lanuvium.[30] Finally we shift back to indicative *oratio recta* for the plague in, around and outside Rome. No formal announcement is made here, because for the reader, relocated to ancient Rome, the prodigy itself is an event rather than the report. Therefore it is logical that when prodigies are encountered on campaign, they are not *nuntiata*, they simply 'happen' (e.g. 21.46.2). We even have a combination of the two stages of viewing and reporting when it is *reported* that at Hadria, an altar *had been seen* in the sky with men clothed in white standing round it; *Hadriae aram in caelo speciesque hominum circum eam cum candida ueste uisas esse* (24.10.11).[31]

One further example reinforces the hypothesis: at 34.45.6-7 we are told that 'some prodigies were also seen that year at Rome and others were reported' (*prodigia quoque alia uisa eo anno Romae sunt, alia nuntiata*). Though the summary lacks an explicit contrast between Rome and abroad, it is transparent in the list that follows: *in foro et comitio et Capitolio sanguinis guttae uisae sunt; et terra aliquotiens pluuit et caput Volcani arsit. nuntiatum est Nare amni lac fluxisse...* The list continues in the accusative and infinitive as the locations are given. As if that were not enough the same list includes a postscript to the remedies prescribed by the *pontifices*: *et sacrificium nouemdiale factum est, quod Hadriani nuntiauerant in agro suo lapidibus pluuisse* (34.45.8), where instead of the customary anonymous passive report we have agents and an active mood.

This is not the only mention of delegates sent specifically to Rome to make a formal announcement to the senate: at 32.1.10, it is *Formiani legati* who relate that the shrine of Jupiter has been struck by lightning and they are followed by *Ostienses...et Veliterni* who announce similar events in their localities. Presumably the choice to personalise the announcement (we are accustomed to reading a simple passive) is a matter of *uariatio*, as is

---

[30] *in area Vulcani et Concordiae sanguine pluuit; et pontifices hastas motas nuntiauere, et Lanuuini simulacrum Iunonis Sospitae lacrimasse. pestilentia in agris forisque et conciliabulis et in urbe.*
[31] Cf. *prodigiis nuntiatis...Lanuui fax in caelo uisa erat* at 45.16.5 and events at Falerii at 22.1.11; also at Mantua at 24.10.7.

the decision to use the term *legati* rather than the simple term for a citizen of the relevant town. Nonetheless these examples indicate that we are not dealing with rumours or material of a dubious nature for the townsfolk but rather matters that were taken seriously enough to equip messengers.[32] The distinction between a prodigy and a report is underlined at 34.55.4, where the senate is so preoccupied with earthquakes that an edict was issued to the effect that on a day when business had *already* been suspended, further reports were not to be made.[33]

While it is normal to find prodigies listed in syntactical *oratio obliqua*, it is also not uncommon for them to be listed in the indicative after *nuntio* for variation: at 43.13.3 we have an example not only of foreign reports being listed in this way, but even of the insertion of *nuntio* for events within Rome: 'at Anagnia two prodigies were reported that year… at Reate it rained stones … in Rome two temple attendants reported … '[34]

The variation seems perfectly reasonable: the standard introduction of *nuntio* draws the events in Anagnia into accusative and infinitive, but Livy shifts to the more vivid indicative for the subsequent events. Finally, when shifting to Rome, he notes the specific authors of the announcement and thus it is entirely appropriate to re-introduce *nuntio* since the prodigies occurred away from the public gaze in the privacy of the shrines.[35] Then there is the moment when there is an announcement of a hermaphrodite born at Frusino and another is discussed as a precedent in *oratio recta*.[36] We also find the occasional list that lacks any mention of *announcements* of events from Rome and beyond: *oratio recta* is the order of the day throughout, even abroad.[37]

---

[32] See 27.37.3 for the delegation of the *Minturnenses*. Where legates of some kind are mentioned they are always in the plural; this evidence is almost certainly impossible to prove historically, but at least we can say that Livy certainly sees nothing strange in the mission requiring more than one.

[33] *Contra* Liebeschuetz (1979) 193.

[34] *Anagnia duo prodigia eo anno sunt nuntiata, facem in caelo conspectam et bouem feminam locutam; <eam> publice ali. Menturnis quoque per eos dies caeli ardentis species affulserat. Reate imbri lapidauit. Cumis in arce Apollo triduum ac tris noctes lacrimauit. in urbe Romana duo aeditui nuntiarunt, alter in aede Fortunae anguem iubatum a conpluribus uisum esse, alter in aede Primigeniae Fortunae, quae in Colle est, duo diuersa prodigia, palmam in area enatam et sanguine interdiu pluuisse* (43.13.3-6).

[35] For indicatives following *nuntio*, see also 33.26.6-9, 21.46.2-5 (which shows more *uariatio*), 24.44.7 and 28.11.2 (especially *Lanuui fax in caelo uisa erat*, since the others are lightning strikes and a shower of stones, typically listed in *oratio recta*, on which see below).

[36] *at liberatas religione mentes turbauit rursus nuntiatum Frusinone natum esse infantem quadrimo parem nec magnitudine tam mirandum quam quod is quoque, ut Sinuessae biennio ante, incertus mas an femina esset natus erat* (27.37.5-6).

[37] *priusquam consules praetoresque in prouincias proficiscerentur, prodigia procurari placuit, quod aedes Volcani Summanique Romae et quod Fregenis murus et porta de caelo tacta erant, et Frusinone inter noctem lux orta, et Aefulae agnus biceps cum quinque pedibus natus, et Formiis duo*

The proof of this particular pudding would seem to be the interchange-ability of the *same prodigy* between accusative and infinitive after *nuntio*, and the pluperfect indicative, which occurs at 21.62.5 and 8. We initially hear that... *et Caere sortes extenuatas*, but that, as part of the expiation, *lec-tisternium Caere, ubi sortes attenuatae erant, imperatum*. Where prodigies are listed in the indicative they are nearly always listed as pluperfect; in other words they are events preceding the announcement (e.g. 45.16.5-6). It might be argued that a report in a provincial town does not indicate a factual event in reality (that is, we are not obliged to accept it into our histories as an event and nor was Livy), and certainly there would be some resistance to *our* accepting (e.g.) that an ox spoke the words '*Roma, caue tibi*' (35.21.5) without some speculative rationalising. But that is not the same as arguing that the announcement of a prodigy is not a *textual* event: in other words, Livy is not disputing its actuality, *we* are, and we are not concerned with the latter aspect here.

Of such pluperfect indicatives there are many examples and, as we might expect, they are often in Rome (e.g. 32.29.02), though they *can* easily be abroad, even some distance from Rome (e.g. 43.13.4, 45.16.05). However the inverse is also true: a number of prodigies in the City itself are heralded by *nuntio*, as we have already seen. We should, for completeness' sake, verify that our conclusions are not affected by the *lack* of *nuntio* in a prodigy list before examining the dynamics of prodigies in the City itself.

Prodigies outside Rome without nuntio There are relatively few prodigy notices from outside Rome that are not framed as announcements. We do have a list almost entirely devoid of *nuntio*, but this is one that clearly ex-hibits *uariatio*: we begin with urban indicatives (lightning), then several witnesses reported prodigies within Rome; moving abroad, it 'was agreed' that various prodigies had happened.

> *prodigia quoque priusquam ab urbe consules proficisceren-tur procurari placuit. in Albano monte tacta de caelo erant signum Iouis arborque templo propinqua, et Ostiae lacus, et Capuae murus Fortunaeque aedis, et Sinuessae murus por-taque. haec de caelo tacta: cruentam etiam fluxisse aquam Albanam quidam auctores erant, et Romae intus in cella aedis Fortis Fortunae de capite signum quod in corona erat in manum sponte sua prolapsum. et Priuerni satis constabat*

lupi oppidum ingressi obuios aliquot laniauerant, Romae non in urbem solum sed in Capitolium penetrauerat lupus (32.29.1-2).

bouem locutum uolturiumque frequenti foro in tabernam deuo-
lasse, et Sinuessae natum ambiguo inter marem ac feminam
sexu infantem, quos androgynos uolgus, ut pleraque, faciliore
ad duplicanda uerba Graeco sermone appellat, et lacte plu-
uisse et cum elephanti capite puerum natum (27.11.1-6).

We shall establish in due course that *quidam auctores* and *satis constabat* allude, not to profound concern about 'facts', but rather to the procedures of verification. This example also introduces us to the exception of what appears to be a particular category, or categories: that of lightning strikes and showers of stones. Lightning does appear after *nuntio* as a reported announcement but for the most part these particular prodigies are placed in *oratio recta*, even disruptively to the tone of the list, which most frequently reverts to reported announcement immediately following the notice of lightning.[38] The fact that lightning nonetheless appears in reported announcements[39] means that we cannot speak of a fixed pattern amounting to more than a preference which probably has at least some of its roots in the internal dynamics of individual lists. What we can say with some confidence is that lightning introduced without *nuntio* is almost without exception at the head of a list. That this seems deliberate can be supported by noting that at 27.11.2-5, Livy separates two prodigies, both from Sinuessa, to group them with similar types: the locality is mentioned in the opening catalogue of lightning strikes as well as the malformed children later in the list. However, while it does seem to be the case that these prodigies are

---

[38] So at 35.9.3f (showers of stones at Aricia and Lanuvium and on the Aventine); 27.11.2f (lightning at the statue of Jupiter on the Alban Mount and a tree near his temple, a grove at Ostia, the city wall and temple of Fortune at Capua and the wall and one of the gates at Sinuessa – which has a hermaphrodite further down the list as a reported announcement, implying the thematic differentiation of lightning); lightning is included in the list at 32.9.1-5 but the prodigies are a mixture of reported announcements and *oratio recta*; at 40.45.1-4 a storm causes much disruption in Rome (which is how the list opens) before there are lightning strikes, both within and outside Rome in *oratio recta*; the list then proceeds with reported announcements of other prodigies outside Rome; at 27.37.1-2, we hear of a shower of stones that *Veiis de caelo lapidauerat* but this is followed by *sub unius prodigii, ut fit, mentionem alia quoque nuntiata*, which illustrates nicely Livy's tendency to elide the announcement of these prodigies in particular; at 35.9.3-4 a flood in Rome introduces the list; it is followed by lightning strikes around the city and then showers of stones at Aricia, Lanuvium and on the Aventine in *oratio recta* before the narrative shifts to reported announcements abroad. Finally, we learn at 37.3.2 that there was a lightning strike at Puteoli in *oratio recta*, preceded by a notice of lightning at the temple of Juno Lucina, but otherwise at the head of a list of reported announcements. A shower of stone occurs at 39.22.3 without announcement, though there is a gloss *ignesque caelestes multifariam orti adussisse complurium leui adflatu uestimenta maxime dicebantur*, where *dicebantur*, in the past tense, should not be bracketed with *dicitur*: the relatively short list exhibits a range of variety in introducing the prodigies.
[39] 27.11.2-5f., 35.21.4, 26.23.5 (at Anagnia and Fregellae, and immediately following a strike in Rome, in *oratio recta*), 24.10.10 (a collection, including strikes at Rome), 28.11.2 (also in *oratio recta*), and 29.14.3.

sometimes highlighted, whether by being placed at the beginning of a list, or, more rarely, at the end,[40] or even both (28.11.1-4), we have no criteria for deciding whether they are thus emphasised (by their dramatic positioning at the beginning or end of a list as events), deprioritised (since some lists seem to begin with the most striking prodigies, and others to end that way) or otherwise contextualised by this. The process is hardly uniform and speculation on its significance would most likely, at this stage, be a breeding place for anachronism rather than insight. It is tempting to suggest that lightning strikes at significant places are treated as important, but such a bland conclusion does not noticeably further our understanding. What we can say is that if we discount lightning and showers of stones, it is distinctly uncommon for a prodigy outside Rome to be simply narrated as an event without *nuntio*. It remains to drive home some of these points by examining the prodigies as announcements and events in Rome itself.

Prodigies in Rome Quite a number of prodigies are presented simply as events in Rome, and Livy has a number of methods of distinguishing Roman prodigies from those outside the City: he might switch from reported announcement to factual reporting; more than once, as we have seen, he differentiates between prodigies that were *uisa* rather than *nuntiata*. Where he does so, the distinction is *always* between events in Rome and reports from abroad. For the most part, prodigies in Rome are simply listed as events.[41] In many cases, they would have been so visible or widespread that any effort to report them would have been superfluous.[42] However, it was possible to use some kind of formal procedure for notification even within Rome, as we see from the fact that Livy occasionally notes the announcement of prodigies within Rome by isolated witnesses: the use of *nuntio* in these

---

[40] At 24.10.10 the list is divided into two sections, bridged by *iam alia uolgata miracula erant*: the lightning appears at the end of the first half; the lightning at Formiae at 35.21.4 is followed by an ox belonging to Cn. Domitius issuing the unambiguous warning '*Roma, caue tibi*', *quod maxime terrebat*, which *closes* the list.

[41] Prodigies as events in Rome: at 3.10.6 the list is succinct and suppression of *nuntio* might well be attributed to the pace of the narrative; 32.29.2 sees lightning at the head of a list that lacks *nuntio*; at 34.45.6 prodigies are *uisa* in Rome and *nuntiata* from elsewhere; at 40.59.6 we hear of *prodigia, quae euenerant*; there is an extended account of one prodigy at 41.15.1; while most of the list is *nuntiata* at 40.45.3, the opening events, in Rome, are not; at 40.19.2, the first prodigies of the list in Rome are given in the indicative, then reported by *pontifices* (these collectively *uisa*) before we move on to those that are *nuntiata peregrine*; 37.3.2 sees lightning at Rome, then elsewhere, then reported announcements of other prodigies; a plague is treated as a prodigy at 41.21.5f.; the *stuprum* of a Vestal is considered a prodigy at 22.57.2-4; and at 40.2.1-3 a storm is considered prodigial and introduces further announcements from elsewhere.

[42] E.g. drops of blood in different locations in Rome (34.45.6); or the disruption of the Latin festival at 40.45.2.

circumstances seems perfectly logical.[43] The other exceptions indicate that while Livy prefers to include Roman prodigies as events,[44] he is not overly anxious pedantically to fix the distinction,[45] but is content to establish it as a general norm. At least some of the examples are distinctly said to have been seen by specific witnesses and virtually all of the others are organised into reported announcements when Livy is editing the lists. Such a distinction would be meaningless if the function of *nuntio* was to indicate that prodigies were factually dubious.

Announcements as textual events It emerges then, that reports of prodigies are more use to Livy as 'indexical'[46] events than as a forum for establishing categories of events. Obviously the overall point of focalisation shifts repeatedly and is often somewhat diffused, but when we are dealing with prodigies, there is often a strong sense that we are sitting either in the senate or at the gates of the *curia*, listening to reports; or perhaps watching the consul as he is delayed in setting out by the need for expiation. This serves (at least) two functions: it allows Livy to employ announcements as events in themselves but, more importantly, it permits him to locate announcement (or more diffused reporting) within a series of procedures, of which reporting was only the beginning.

Collecting reports of and expiating prodigies was not apparently a hit and miss affair: there was in fact a degree of caution applied to reports. We know that some were not recognised, for various reasons. It might be because of a

---

[43] As at 40.19.2 (*pontifices*) and 43.13.4 (*duo aeditui*, each with their own prodigy). Both examples include *nuntio*. At 43.16.6, T. Marcius Figulus *nuntiabat* a prodigy, but it was not expiated because it was on private soil.

[44] He reliably lists prodigies even *around* Rome as reported announcements (4.21; those at 28.11.4 and 41.9.5 occurred *in agro Romano*); the almost daily signs at 2.42.10 are both within and around Rome, and Livy gives these as events; this is also true of the plague at 5.14.3.

[45] He groups a Roman prodigy with another that is a reported announcement (as at 24.10.7, where rains of blood occurred at Rome and at Cales); at 21.62.1, the Roman prodigies are reported announcements but, as we shall see below, there is emphasis on the reporting procedure in this example; a particularly frightening portent occurs at 35.21.5 as an announcement at the end of a list dependent on *nuntio* (but it is quite likely that few or only one witness heard the ox speak); the virtual *oratio obliqua* alludes to a report at 39.46.5 but is best explained as *uariatio* since the item appears as a postscript to a list of already expiated prodigies; at 24.10.6 lightning is grouped from within and outside Rome after *nuntio* and shortly afterwards, at 24.10.11-12, a swarm of bees is *uisum*, still dependent on the *nuntio* that opened the list some lines previously. There is one other example, where we read that *lupos uisos in Capitolio ferunt a canibus fugatos; ob id prodigium lustratum Capitolium esse. haec eo anno gesta* (30.30.4). While we shall return to *ferunt* shortly, it is worth noting that it is *not* equivalent to *nuntio* here: Livy is speaking of the historical record's transmission, not the textual event of an announcement. He is rather summarising events for completeness at the end of the year.

[46] I.e. one of their functions is to designate the arena where the narrative is taking place – Rome in this case.

paucity of witnesses, or even a lack of expertise to assess and a response, as occurs at 5.15.1-2.[47] Livy mentions *quidam auctores* at 27.11.3 and a simple *quidam* at 24.10.6.[48] Not just numbers but status clearly entered into this equation: when M. Valerius reported a trickle of blood from his hearth at 45.16.5, the prodigy, presumably accepted on his authority, was the chief reason for consulting the Sibylline Books.[49] Livy explicitly tells us that the plebeian Caedicius was ignored at 5.32.6-7 when he reported a voice warning of the impending arrival of the Gauls: this was because of his plebeian status along with the novelty of the Gauls. It seems that if an aristocrat had heard the warning, it might have been taken more seriously. Propitiation was later made not just to acknowledge the voice's intervention, but also for the failure to act on it any earlier.[50] There is one particularly striking example: when Cn. Cornelius Scipio had made a sacrifice, he was brought news that the liver had vanished at 41.15.3. The news was so surprising (or unwelcome) that he had the contents of the cauldron poured out to reveal, or rather *not* reveal, a liver. One of the earliest examples of verification occurs at 1.31.1 with the first shower of stones. After this, it was, it seems, more plausible because of a precedent; it is referred to as the *uetus prodigium* at 7.28.7 and thereafter accepted without question.[51] There is also the speaking ox at 3.10.6, a phenomenon that was not accepted the previous year:[52] perhaps more or 'better' witnesses came forward this time.

The *technical* term for acknowledging that a prodigy had indeed occurred would seem to be *credo*. Though Livy is not famed for his use of technical language, especially of foreign terminology, he is extremely consistent in this: *credo* occurs almost as regularly as *nuntio*, though mention

---

[47] *prodigia interim multa nuntiari, quorum pleraque et quia singuli auctores erant parum credita spretaque, et quia, hostibus Etruscis, per quos ea procurarent haruspices non erant.* Even then, one sign was not ignored: the passage continues *in unum omnium curae uersae sunt quod lacus in Albano nemore, sine ullis caelestibus aquis causaue qua alia quae rem miraculo eximeret, in altitudinem insolitam creuit.*

[48] *Quidam* might best be translated 'a number of (disparate) people'.

[49] 32.1.12 mentions two presumably trustworthy witnesses: Q. Minucius, the propraetor in Bruttium, wrote to say that a foal had been born with five feet, and three chickens with three feet each and P. Sulpicius, the proconsul in Macedonia, that, amongst other things, laurel leaves had shot forth on the stern of a warship. Similarly the testimony of priests and shrine attendants at 43.13.3-6 seems to have weighed sufficiently to be convincing.

[50] They dedicated a temple to *Aius Locutius* (5.50.5).

[51] That is, in Livy's version of events: any subsequent caution about the prodigy is suppressed.

[52] This brief mention of the interpretative process is a mixed blessing: on the one hand it seems to allude to assessment before accepting prodigy reports. However it also presents problems for the question of the transmission of prodigy reports. We might expect *rejected* prodigies to disappear from the reports, especially so far back. The likeliest scenario is that Livy has compressed some discussion in his sources which explained why the second occurrence should count while the previous one does not. What seems most unlikely is that there was a complete change of attitudes so quickly on the significance of speaking oxen.

of it, like every stage of the process, can be suppressed.[53] Furthermore, there seems to be another technical term for a distinct process, though the evidence is less plentiful: *suscipio* is apparently used to indicate not only that a prodigy is valid as a prodigy, but also that the senate is deciding to undertake expiation.[54] It occurs once in this sense (in the negative), when *duo non suscepta prodigia sunt*: a prodigy reported by T. Marcius Figulus is declined on the grounds that it is a private matter (43.13.6)[55] and another is rejected at the same time on the grounds that it is foreign. The word is also used when Livy laments the relative failure of prodigy notices in recent times: he speaks of *prodigia . . . quae illi prudentissimi uiri publice suscipienda censuerint* (43.13.2). Equally, it may be that *sperno* has formal usage of rejecting a religious procedure or obligation, including prodigies.[56]

2.2.1.3 Hallucinations and prodigy types

Despite the fact that prodigies are a repeated and often formulaic part of Livy's narration, he exercises caution in his assessments. There are other signs of expertise and discrimination in understanding these phenomena. Livy mentions a number of prodigies which, as we assume and as he implies (or states), were hallucinatory, whether auditory or visual: at 24.44.7-8 people imagined they saw warships at Tarracina, heard the clash of arms in a temple at Compsa and that the river at Amiternum ran with blood. These are specifically said to be *ludibria oculorum auriumque*. The theme of hallucination also occurs at 3.5.14 when the sky 'seemed to be all on fire', and other portents were either actually seen, or people in their fright imagined that they saw them (*caelum uisum est ardere plurimo igni; portentaque alia aut obuersata oculis aut uanas exterritis ostentauere species*). The temptation has been to see dismissal, since Livy is at pains to record that these things were hallucinations and therefore did not happen: *ludibria* is then taken to apply widely to the contents of the list.

Yet once again the effort to draw a generalising inference from a passing comment proves unsustainable: we cannot, for instance, translate *alia*

---

[53] It is found at 3.10.6; 5.15.1; 21.62.1; 24.44.8; 29.14.2; 30.2.10 and 39.56.6. We might be better off translating it as 'accept' rather than 'believe'. (See for instance what effect this would have on Feeney's (1998) examples at 45). Cf. also Smith (1979) on the very similar meaning of *credo* for the early Christians (ch. 5), esp. 118.

[54] Cf. §*OLD* 7a and 8a.

[55] See MacBain (1982) 29f.: he is surely right that many considerations that we would not call religious are present here. He suggests that Livy is impressed with the punctilious *religio* although he treats it as an isolated example.

[56] It is used four times about the rejection of the nocturnal voice designated *Aius Locutius* (5.15.1, 5.32.7, 5.32.7 and 5.51.7) and also of *expiationem spretam* (9.1.5) and at 21.63.7 of *spretorum. . . uotorum*. We also have the variant formula *cui fides non fuerat* at 3.10.6.

ludibria oculorum auriumque as 'other visual and auditory hallucinations' (i.e. implying that the phenomena immediately previous are also *ludibria*) because the full listing at 24.44.8-9 includes lightning striking the temple of Jupiter, an eminently physical event, and verifiable at the time from the damage that one would expect. Even if there were no physical evidence of lightning, why should such a common occurrence be ontologically questioned? Despite the strong temptation to see scepticism in this assertion, we would be better advised to observe simply that Livy has noted a subcategory of prodigies. It seems that a hallucination was a perfectly acceptable prodigy; 'everybody' knows that the appearance of two suns is impossible in reality, but what was noteworthy was that widespread delusion was in itself a prodigial event. Enough people saw it happen for the senate to take the mass hallucination as a sign of the *ira deum*.

To summarise our progress thus far: Livy shows discrimination in presenting prodigies as witnessed generally in Rome, witnessed specifically in Rome, and reported as happening, usually elsewhere; he establishes this as a norm, though there are specific exceptions, mostly for reasons of *uariatio*, the pace of the text and the attraction of prodigies into different presentation types. The balance of probability should rest on the affirmative side, since communities, often some distance from Rome, were not likely to send embassies without what would seem to them good reason. But these accounts were not necessarily accepted automatically by the senate: the means existed to verify prodigies, presumably with a 'sliding scale' of scrutiny for those they thought more or less likely. It is quite possible that the messengers from abroad were the witnesses themselves (though this neatly logical idea is a speculation without textual support). Though we might reasonably argue that a message is of a different order of 'truth' from simple narration, we cannot say that this is Livy's concern: his interest is in reflecting the procedures involved. As we shall see, they had slipped in recent times and he is anxious to refresh them in the minds of his readers. This will become more evident after Livy's preoccupation with procedure has also made sense of other problematic areas.

2.2.1.4 The 'deluge' effect

There are a number of moments in the text where Livy alludes to other aspects of the social realities of reporting prodigies. Though they tend to be strung together in modern discussions as if near-identical, they are not: the comment at 27.37.2, after expiation of a prodigy announced from Veii that *sub unius prodigii, ut fit, mentionem alia quoque nuntiata*, should simply be taken to mean that several prodigies were reported (almost?) simultaneously since the majority of the opening entries are multiples.[57] The other passages are relatively similar in tone: at 21.62.1, we have many prodigies happening or, at least, being accepted because, once people's minds are excited to religious fears, many are announced and accepted rashly.[58] Similarly, at 24.10.6 many prodigies were announced: they grew in proportion to simple-minded and superstitious people accepting them (*prodigia eo anno multa nuntiata sunt, quae quo magis credebant simplices ac religiosi homines, eo plura nuntiabantur*).

None of these comments is sufficiently strong to warrant the conclusion that Livy is dismissing prodigies *per se*. Rather they represent a number of distinct criticisms which can be examined separately. At 21.62.1, Livy is presumably responding to the anticipated objection of the reader that the list is excessively long; if we ignore for now the first *aut* clause that proposes that the number of prodigies genuinely *was* unusually high, the two distinct points of criticism are the assertions that it is common to find that, when people are stirred up and already concerned about the mood of the gods (*motis . . . in religionem animis*), prodigies are reported more frequently and then accepted (*credita*) without sufficient thought (*temere*). The latter point is not difficult to deal with; at all times Livy is concerned to see that proper procedures are followed conscientiously: thus the insinuation that there was not a proper rigour in ascertaining the veracity of the prodigies has no bearing on any postulated scepticism. Rather, the allegation of haste implies that there were legitimate practices for the reception and scrutiny of prodigies that may not have been followed; the result is a longer list than he would expect, even in difficult circumstances. Nor is the suggestion that at times of stress people were more likely to report prodigies indicative of any generalised scepticism. The comments about the effect of fear on the number of reports, or the 'deluge' effect of one report anticipating many at 24.10.6 (*prodigia eo anno multa nuntiata sunt, quae quo magis credebant simplices ac religiosi homines, eo plura nuntiabantur*) should be considered with care. Essentially we have an instance of what is now called 'moral panic', where the perceived likelihood of an event far outstrips (genuine) factual occurrence.[59] Such are the 'worldly wise' comments made occasionally by Livy about reports of prodigies: 'people always report, and then uncritically accept as true, prodigies when someone else has done it first/when

---

[57] *Minturnis aedem Iouis et lucum Maricae, item Atellae murum et portam de caelo tactam; Minturnenses, terribilius quod esset, adiciebant sanguinis riuum in porta fluxisse. . .* (a relatively long list follows).

[58] *Romae aut circa urbem multa ea hieme prodigia facta aut, quod euenire solet motis semel in religionem animis, multa nuntiata et temere credita sunt.*

[59] On this see more generally La Fontaine (1998) 20.

everyone is already over-excited'. It is therefore an acknowledged feature of prodigy reporting that people are more observant, or more meticulous about the troublesome process of reporting, when tension is high for one reason or another: in these circumstances it is also to be expected that non-prodigial trivia would be reported, or that attention-seekers would appear with inflated tales.

In the event of unexpected numbers of reports, we might reasonably assume, just as Livy does, either that there were many (genuine) prodigies (thus reinforcing the fact that the gods were displeased) or that the process of verifying prodigies had been applied less stringently than should have been the case (i.e. *some* of the 'trivia' was accepted when it should have been ignored). Thus we have Livy's position at 21.62.1 without any doubt cast on the ontological category of prodigies, though perhaps we have had a glimpse into the 'ordinariness' of documenting the extraordinary. In the light of this the more elaborate notice at 24.10.6 seems to be more a learned and witty variation on a well-known theme than an uncomplicated statement of scepticism.

2.2.1.5 *Fine distinctions and the neglect of the gods*

There remains only one moment where we can say with some certainty that Livy finds an individual prodigy problematic. Apart from the gloss on the prodigy itself, the context is significant. The entry in question occurs at 27.23.2: provisionally we can translate it 'at Cumae – to such an extent does debased religion see the gods even in trivial things – rodents were said to have nibbled at the gold in the temple of Jupiter' (*Cumis – adeo minimis etiam rebus praua religio inserit deos – mures in aede Iovis aurum rosisse*).[60] Levene, taking a largely traditional line, comments that 'the "*etiam*" qualifying "*minimis rebus*" suggests that those who see the divine in larger events, also, are similarly affected by "*praua religio*". In short the passage is clearly implying that any connection between prodigies and the gods is quite spurious' (17). However, as he himself points out (25), 'the single clearest statement of divine causation in Livy comes at 27.23.4, with the deaths of the consuls Marcus Claudius Marcellus and T. Quinctius Crispinus, which he foreshadows with their inability to expiate the same set

---

[60] It may be that the notice immediately following is also scorned (*Casini examen apium ingens in foro consedisse*), joined asyndetically as it is to the notice. *Minimae res* cannot just refer to the size of the animals involved though: bees are part of a valid list at 21.46.2 and 24.10.11, and mice at 40.59.8. It is striking that Plutarch *Marcellus* 28.3 not only includes what seems to be the same portent as valid, but links it specifically to the approaching death of Marcellus. The difference between the two accounts is a useful index of how the same material can be handled in a different genre. Fate is also invoked in Plutarch's account with his quoting Pindar on the inevitability of *to pepromenon* (fr. 232 Snell).

of prodigies': Livy informs us that despite repeated attempts, the *pax deum* was not obtained. He adds as a gloss that the disaster prognosticated for the state was, in the event, diverted to the consuls (*in capita consulum re publica incolumi exitiabilis prodigiorum euentus uertit.*) Livy's 'sceptical' comment therefore merits some attention.

A number of objections can be made to Levene's suggestions: to begin with, there seems no reason to agree that the first passage implies the folly of those who see the divine in 'larger' things. It seems much more likely that Livy is saying the opposite of this: in 'major' (or whatever we would oppose to *minimus*) affairs the hand of the gods appears, but that their names should not be invoked in connection with trivia. Furthermore, it was a divine disapproval that proved very real for the consuls in question, according to Livy. It is from this, and other instances, that Levene adopts his 'twin approach' to Livy's religious material; but here, as elsewhere, it is not that there are two parallel versions, one requiring, and the other ignoring, divine action within the narrative. In fact it is clear from the context that to treat this episode as evidence of a widespread and fundamental scepticism about prodigies is unsustainable. The passage in its entirety contains at least seven prodigies (one mentions several lightning strikes) of which only this one is problematic (27.23.1-4).

In such a sustained list it seems churlish to pick one passing comment as indicative of an overarching scepticism: the query looks far more like an isolated example, the exception that proves the rule. It is surely more logical to accept the reading that Livy's criticism here is a specific one and relevant only to one prodigy. By implication the remaining portents are judged to be perfectly acceptable indicators of the displeasure of the gods; this would be the more likely meaning even if Livy had not explicitly offered the diagnosis that it is the consuls who suffered the effects of the *ira deum*, rather than, as one would have initially expected, the *res publica*.[61] Livy, far from undermining the entire narrative, is exhibiting his skill in discerning genuine prodigies from mistaken ones. As an expert addressing the knowledgeable, he is only required to give us extra material sufficient to explain what 'we' (as a Roman audience) would not have known, such as that repeated efforts (*per dies*) at expiation had failed. His analysis assumes the

---

[61] Such would seem to be the implication of *uertit*. Levene, unless I am mistaken in imputing such a strong position to him, seems to consider *praua* to be a gloss on *religio*, that is, he takes Livy to mean that all *religio* is necessarily *praua*. However we should probably understand *praua religio* as referring to one (degenerate) type of religious practice – the acceptance of a particular 'prodigy' – rather than all religion. The phrase occurs twice elsewhere in the extant Livy: it is used of Tullus just before he is annihilated by Jupiter for his botched secret rites (1.31.8); and it is used of the Bacchists by the consul before the people (39.16.6).

'knowledge' that prodigies indicate disaster for the *res publica*; and so Livy informs us that the *uitium* affected the consuls instead, thus demonstrating his ability to interpret the religious situation comprehensively. The issues of absolute credulity and scepticism are simply not present; far more pressing are issues of explanation, expertise and interpretation within the traditional framework.

An examination of the way that the tale unfolds makes the hypothesis that scepticism is involved seem even more remote; it also gives an opportunity to note the process of deciding how much explanation is needed for a Roman audience. Marcellus runs into further difficulties when he fails to dedicate the hastily constructed temples vowed to *Honos* and *Virtus* before going to war (27.25.9); his relationship with the gods is thus severely problematised. Shortly before the sortie that will lead to his death and his colleague's fatal wounding, the sacrificial signs are poor and the *haruspex* concerned (27.26.13-14). The other consul, Crispinus, dies from his wounds at 27.33.6 and the episode is closed with Livy's comment that, despite the Roman setbacks and vulnerability, the gods took pity on Rome, and 'condemned' the hastiness of the consuls (27.33.11).[62]

Far from forming a part of a 'parallel' account that can be discarded without affecting the historical record, the religious material is an integral part of a unified narrative here: in addition, this is a useful example of a situation in which the historian gives a relatively detailed exegesis for the simple reason that what occurred was not quite what was expected. But he never questions that the gods intervened in affairs, just as the prodigies portended.

Virtually every aspect of this argument is formative in one particular moment in Livy's text: his lament at the decline of the practice of reporting prodigies, at 43.13.1-2:

> I am not unaware that, because of the same [religious] neglect
> that has people generally think that the gods do not give warnings of the future, prodigies are nowadays neither announced
> publicly nor recorded in the annals. Nonetheless, while I write
> of these days of old, somehow my own spirit becomes old-
> fashioned, as it were, and keeps me from considering unworthy
> of inclusion in *my* annals the things which those exceptionally
> knowledgeable men judged worthy of acting on.[63]

---

[62] *ceterum deos immortales miseritos nominis Romani pepercisse innoxiis exercitibus, temeritatem consulum ipsorum capitibus damnasse*: a neat interpretative move that dovetails the poor signs with the human errors.

[63] With acknowledgements to Christina Kraus for discussion regarding translation.

Non sum nescius ab eadem neglegentia qua[64] nihil deos por-
tendere uulgo nunc credant, neque nuntiari admodum ulla
prodigia in publicum neque in annales referri. ceterum et mihi
uetustas res scribenti nescio quo pacto antiquus fit animus et
quaedam religio tenet, quae illi prudentissimi uiri publice sus-
cipienda censuerint, ea pro indignis habere, quae in meos an-
nales referam.

Obviously Livy, ever mindful of the ease with which errors could be
made in the complex art of categorising and validating prodigies, wishes to
demonstrate his mastery of the long list of signs that follows.[65] But this passage is somewhat more complex and presents the modern reader with not a
few difficulties.[66] A close survey suggest Livy is doing more than cautiously
validating an unusually long list. Firstly, there are problems with taking the
statement at face value in its precise setting within the text. It is not as if
Livy's own supply of prodigies began to run short: although this notice is
placed towards the end of the extant text, the *Periochae* and Obsequens,
both heavily dependent on Livy's record, indicate that prodigies continued to be reported and expiated long after this date, albeit in diminishing
numbers.[67] Since the historical record seems reasonably complete until we
approach his time of composition, it seems that Livy is talking about the
present rather than the period in which the comment is set. Secondly, he
alleges that people no longer generally believe that portents herald future
events, something that would seem to be denied a century later by the account given by Tacitus, which includes not just prodigies (admittedly in
comparatively reduced numbers), but also omens: consider the detailed deductions reported by the consular historian at the death of Augustus, not
long after the completion of Livy's work, at *Annals* 1.31. Even in Livy's
present, ascribing significance to prodigies was apparently far from obsolete. Thirdly, despite the historian's apparent hesitation in accepting prodigies, there is no other indication in the text that Livy is uncertain about
prodigies as a category, rather the opposite. This leads to the final problem:

---

[64] *Quia*, Madvig's emendation of *qua* has been widely adopted: see Levene (1993) 22 n.114. He
adopts this and then goes on to say in his footnote that 'it is striking that Livy does not go on to
counter those who have neglected prodigies by suggesting that they are genuine signs from the
gods'. But if we restore *qua* then he *has* implied his severe disapproval of the failure to accept
prodigies as divinely instigated.

[65] As is his custom: most of the discriminatory comments we have examined have prefaced long lists
of prodigies.

[66] Levene (1993) 23 has a useful survey of what people have made of it over the years.

[67] On the sources of the *Periochae*, see Begbie (1967); on continuing prodigies (i.e. from 169),
MacBain (1982)'s table of prodigies continues to list Livy, Obsequens and the *Periochae* until 17,
and other authors regularly until the end of the Republic. However there is a marked decrease in
frequency during the last century of the Republic.

there is an abrupt change in tone when moving from the first sentence to the second. *Neglegentia* is a strong and confident condemnation of the attitude under discussion, but in the latter sentence Livy seems to adopt a much more uncertain stance.

All these considerations – timing, the question of credence, Livy's erratic hesitancy – can be dealt with. Levene (1993) 116 finds that 'the decline during the Third Macedonian War (which is the context for this comment) is only the symptom of a larger decline' which helps to explain the location of this complaint within the chronological narrative: Livy is highlighting the beginning of a process that has reached its sorry depths in the present. But this still leaves the questions of the apparently mistaken idea that prodigies (and presumably omens) are not taken to indicate the future, and of Livy's rather strange hesitation.

Linderski sees a subtle agenda at work in this passage, namely a muted criticism of the Augustan practice of interpreting supernatural events in favour of a charismatic leader when a more traditional interpretation would have diagnosed disfavour. To give one example: according to Cassius Dio, the overflowing of the Tiber (which occurred just after Octavian adopted the name Augustus) was interpreted to indicate the greatness of the emperor's rule. However such floods, if treated as religious matters, had traditionally been interpreted as prodigial, that is, heralding disaster.[68] Linderski, commenting on Dio, continues: 'no republican *haruspex*, *pontiff*, *quindecimuir* or *augur* would subscribe to this interpretation. Did Livy? When he complained that prodigies are not reported, not recorded, not heeded, he did not think of the era of Cicero but of his own time, the time of the Augustan restoration.'[69] Linderski's position might be considered to be broadly supported by Miles' (1995) analysis of 4.20.5-11 (41f.), where Augustus' assertion that A. Cornelius Cossus was consul, rather than (just) a military tribune, is treated in such a way to 'allow the author to challenge his social and political superiors with a degree of safety' (53).[70] Miles discusses the difficulties of authority in the historical tradition and comments that:

> [B]y exposing the weakness of his narrative on important matters of fact, by himself submitting, conspicuously, to the

---

[68] A religious issue at 30.38.10 (*aquarum insolita magnitudo in religionem uersa*) and 35.9.3 (part of a list of prodigies) but not at 24.9.6, 35.21.6 or 38.28.4. See also 7.3.2.

[69] Linderski (1993) 64. He cites the overflowing of the Tiber, interpreted to indicate the greatness of the emperor's rule (Cassius Dio 53.20.1), after his adoption of the new title of Augustus: cf. Suetonius *Caesar* 32, 77; Plutarch *Caesar* 47. Rosenberger (1998) 245 examines the same question, arguing that the prodigy/expiation divinatory structure was held in place principally by the republican system of government and thus lost its meaning with the appearance of monarchy.

[70] This is a bare summary of Miles' salient conclusions; see his excellent discussion of the various permutations of the episode at 40–47. See also Badian (1993) and on the emperor as guarantor of the *pax deum*, Gordon (1990b).

> limitations of the evidence, Livy deprives Augustus of the power to impose his authority on history more effectively than if Livy had attempted to present himself as an authority – an act that would tacitly have conceded that factual certainty was attainable... [T]he combination of his argument against factual certainty and his own exemplification of its consequences is not unique to this immediate situation. (47)

In other words, Livy is deliberately underplaying his hand, and losing a battle, in order to redefine the rules about authority, thereby winning the historical war; he reduces all authorities to a relativity that deprives Augustus of the certainty that the *princeps* hoped to establish. The warning that ideology is often present in Livy's comments, disguised as strategic tact, should alert us to the fact that our passage may not speak plainly. Linderski's suggestion that Livy is complaining about the new, 'optimistic' style of interpretation can be explored in more detail along these lines, as Livy's presentation of the situation owes a lot to the kind of subterfuge detected by Miles: it does not seem that the 'new', favourable, interpretations included a blatant refusal to believe that the gods indicated future events, rather that daring interpretation could somehow avert or transform the prognosticated outcome. However, either Livy is not, as Linderski suggests, referring to this new habit of interpretation or, as seems more likely, he is *equating* the process of reinterpretation with a cynicism whereby the proponents of the new interpretation, by denying the traditional interpretations and asserting new and favourable ones instead, are *as good as* saying that the gods give no warnings. In other words, despite the apparent understatement, the issue is presented by Livy in polemic fashion: either one adopts the traditional, pessimistic, interpretations of prodigies and portents or one is simply neglecting the gods; playing with interpretations is simply nonsense – there is no middle ground.

This hypothesis is attractive for a number of circumstantial reasons. Firstly, Livy elsewhere indicates his displeasure at the sort of 'clever' interpretation that was practised in connection with vows, which is usually linked to the late Republic:[71] we might compare this sort of legalistic

---

[71] See e.g. 22.58.8 where a Roman, held hostage by the Carthaginians, attempts to cheat his vow to return to Hannibal's camp by leaving his party shortly after departure and returning as if he had forgotten something; Livy describes him as 'unroman' (*minime Romani ingenii homo*) and the senate is none too impressed when he attempts to remain in Rome while the others return – he is arrested and sent back to Hannibal's camp (22.61.4): see also the alternative version on the same theme, where the punishment of all the errant hostages is delayed until the census. Liebeschuetz (1979) 25–26 discusses this kind of legalistic interpretation, and its exploitation in the late Republic. Livy preserves the integrity of signs and their reporting in the story of the errant *pullarius* (10.40.4-5; 10.40.11-13): one could not simply alter signs by declaration that they were auspicious when they were not.

trickery with the 'new' interpretations of prodigies referred to by Linder-ski. Alternatively or quite possibly in tandem with this, the sense that the accusation is somewhat off-target is a superb strategy for avoiding offence. To mention that 'people in general' thought that adverse prodigies could be interpreted *favourably* would be an ill-concealed criticism indeed: the charge is too specific for offence to be avoided. But by knocking down a straw man Livy creates an opportunity to reassert traditional interpretations, thus he can offend no one and correct anyone. This is surely his intention: it is certainly in keeping with the presentation of religious material through-out his account. Additionally, if Livy *is* criticising imperial policy, to direct the accusation of *neglegentia* at 'everyone' (i.e. no one in particular) is in keeping with his method of deflecting criticism by an assumed modesty and apparent hesitancy that pervades his work.[72] Livy is marvellously vague and wrong: and he simultaneously issues a spectacular criticism and correction. He could not be explicit as he is with regard to Cossus because he wishes to introduce the idea of neglect, a far more serious charge than the allegation that there is a problem with the sources on a particular point (even with the implication that Augustus is falsifying the tradition); the accusation must be deflected further off target to be palatable – thus the virtually anonymous *uulgo*. Livy has managed to criticise imperial religious policy without leav-ing any scope for counter-accusation against him.[73]

The latter part of the passage, in assimilating a 'cured' Livy to the Ro-mans of the past, is reminiscent of his 'mission statement' in the Prologue, where morality (*mores*) was said to have declined. It is tasteful and polite to suggest that the 'process of decline' had affected the historian as much as his contemporaries: even with the new-found *Pax Augusta*, the question of the decline of traditional Roman *uirtus* still troubled the subjects of the newly emerging monarch.[74] Roman *uirtus* was to be (re)discovered in *ex-empla*, and the study of history allowed one to rediscover lost virtue as *Praef.* 10–11 clearly states.

In the light of this, the implication of the passage discussing the inclusion of prodigies is that Livy himself is also taking part in this process of learning from *exempla*. It may be that *nec uitia nostra nec remedia pati possumus*,

---

[72] Miles (1995) 48f. has a good discussion on what is known about the historian's background; his birthplace, Patavium, was on the 'margins of Roman political life... [Livy] appears... to have been... open to criticism that he was incompetent to write history' (49). Kraus (1997) 72 speaks of a habitual 'kind of arrogant deference'. Moles (1993) 159 speaks of Livy's 'ambiguous, disin-genuous, but formally striking, modesty'. See also Marincola (1997) 141 and 153.

[73] Whatever his status *was* with the Augustan régime. On Livy's supposedly 'personal' relationship with Augustus see Badian (1993) and Woodman (1988) 136–40.

[74] Moles (1993) argues that the preface was written after Actium; Woodman (1988) 128–134 prefers an earlier date.

but Livy is apparently confessing to making the attempt to cure himself, and is reporting on the patient's progress at 43.13.1-2. The success of the treatment invites others, perhaps not even aware of their malady, to join him. The uncertainty of the second sentence is disingenuous: the clumsy, misinformed and slightly bewildered apology is a political wolf in sheep's clothing, as Linderski has suggested.

Embedded within these contexts, Livy's presentation of prodigies has become more three-dimensional: prodigy reports are part of a complex of social and political negotiations, with which, for the most part, he assumes the reader is more or less conversant. This kind of complexity can also be found in Livy's presentations of a great number of other religious moments.

2.2.1.6 Oratio obliqua II: reported narration

Since we have separated reported announcements from reported speech, we should now attend to those moments in the text when Livy uses terms, and syntax, associated with *oratio obliqua*: we have labelled these 'reported words' and 'reported narration'. We shall be dealing exclusively with the latter.[75]

This discussion will be less exhaustive than the preceding analyses of prodigy reports: *oratio obliqua* is a broad topic that has a bearing on most authors in antiquity, and it is not possible to reach any firm conclusions without casting our net wider than Livy, which would be inappropriate for this study. Nonetheless, there is enough material for us to note unusual cases and to make suggestions about Livy's use of *oratio obliqua*. But the attempt must necessarily, and in fact *should*, be made to reconsider firmly held convictions about *oratio obliqua*: it may be that our customary assumptions are at odds with the material. Nonetheless, any working conclusions that are devised here must remain highly provisional. On the other hand, there is specific religious material which must be accounted for if this account is to deal comprehensively not just with the material in the *AVC*, but also the authorial construction of religion. We cannot use his evidence while its status is considered questionable.

Traditionally, *oratio obliqua* is taken to mean simply 'distancing' by an author. This is entirely consistent with an understanding of historiography as an accurate, factual record of the past. We have often tended to think of the 'ordinary narrative' as immediate, to be read unproblematically and without interpretative filters: thus it is taken to be 'true' (for Livy at least), that deviations from this type of presentation, such as those introduced by

---

[75] Though the dynamics of reported words do have a bearing on our discussion: see Laird (1999) for a revision of our customary readings.

dicitur, can only be deviations from 'the truth'. We have accordingly concluded that reported speech *necessarily* indicates doubt or scepticism, since
any change of register implies departure from historical truth. This assumption has been held to be true for *all* ancient writers, especially (but not exclusively) historiographical ones and the supposed universal applicability has
been a major factor in leaving the assumption unquestioned since a fully
convincing discussion would have to deal with at least the 'major' authors –
an enormous undertaking.

Nonetheless, the topic has been addressed from time to time: Westlake
(1977) suggested that Thucydides is, at times, *vouching* for reported narrative and Harrison (2000) criticises the assumption that reported speech
in Herodotus necessarily implies doubt;[76] Cook (2001) does the same for
Plutarch's lives.[77] Both these discussions are hedged with caution, but if
we took a leaf out of Feeney's book, our historiographical accounts would
be transformed: 'the fiction of the *Aeneid* must be asserted with so much
power that it will itself become a tradition... [Said] by whom? By none
other than the poet, the author of the new tradition which is evolving as we
read' (Feeney (1991) 186–7). Feeney, it will be objected, is dealing with
poetry: the same rules will not apply to a 'factual' account. However contentious *that* assertion might be, it seems most prudent to work with Livy's
own text before drawing any conclusions.

Even without acknowledging the more sophisticated readings of historiographical material, the inference of 'distancing' brings often insurmount-
able problems. The first of these is the sheer inconsistency in the narrative
that results from seeing *oratio obliqua* as indicative of factual problems.
Miles (1995), after examining a series of passages that include reported
narrative, speaks of 'the apparent hopelessness of finding a consistent rationale for the disposition of direct and indirect discourse in the narrative' (29)
and offers that 'if we look for some objective basis in historical evidence or
in the nature of the sources to explain the narrator's choice of emphasis, we
can find none ... Livy discourages the reader from seeking actively to evaluate his narrative objectively, in terms of historical reliability' (31). Livy
repeatedly introduces an element in reported narration, only to rely on its
historicity in the factual narrative. To add to Miles' examples, we can adduce specifically religious ones: at 1.45.3-6, an enormous ox is sacrificed to
Rome's benefit by a cunning Roman. The episode opens as a report: *bos in
Sabinis nata cuidam patri familiae dicitur miranda magnitudine ac specie.*

---

[76] '[I]t is worth noting that, while he may indeed distance himself from his reports, he equally considers it possible that *ta legomena* might be clear accurate and reliable' (Harrison (2000) 23–27).
[77] '*[L]egetai* or *legousi* serves to... mark reliance on a source... any hint of scepticism is absent'.

The story went that whoever sacrificed this ox would gain empire for his city: the Sabine owner was tricked by a Roman, who sacrificed the animal to Diana while the owner was washing himself, as instructed, in preparation for the sacrifice. Moreover, the size of the creature is affirmed when Livy notes that the horns were displayed as a *miraculum* (*fixa per multas aetates cornua in uestibulo templi Dianae monumentum ei fuere miraculo*, 1.45.4-5) and adds directly that it was treated as a prodigy 'which is what it was' (*habita, ut erat, res prodigii loco est*). To affirm that the animal was in fact (*ut erat*) prodigious if we are unsure of its existence would seem a little odd: even if we associate *dicitur* exclusively with the animal's dimensions, his comment in *oratio recta* that its horns hung for many years in public surely contradicts any factual concerns we might have had about the creature's existence or magnitude.

Miles offers a variety of alternative approaches to such accounts; reported narration is not scattered at random in the account. Rather, he detects precision in the usage of reported narration at several moments, most cogently in the episode of the murder of Servius Tullius by his daughter Servia, where 'Livy's implicit incredulity, his reluctance to report Tullia's violation of her father on his own authority... constitute a moral judgment... [T]o say that it is difficult to believe that anyone could act as Tullia did is to offer a measure of how extremely unacceptable her behaviour is' (64). For Miles then, distance persists but is not limited to issues of fact. The episode in question makes far better sense when approached from this angle, but we cannot apply his conclusions wholesale: it makes no sense, for instance, in the case of our *miranda bos*. To detect broader patterns, we must take a closer look at Livy's use of reported narration and analyse the use of some of the specific terms, which are all too rarely differentiated. The following discussion is far from exhaustive in its scope (though it is usually exhaustive on the particular terms under discussion), since the varieties of terminology and construction are innumerable. Our purpose is strictly limited to acquiring permission to treat the religious material as integral to the text. Some leeway can be gained by examining a few particular terms associated with *oratio obliqua*.

Terminology   There is a notable pattern when Livy cites his sources, such as Valerius Antias: in the middle extant books (but therefore early in the full *AVC*), Antias is frequently said to *tradere* his material.[78] Then, somewhat

---

[78] 25.39.14; 26.49.5 (*deditumque Romanis Antias Valerius, Magonem alii scriptores tradunt*); 30.29.7; 32.6.5; 33.30.8 and, much later, 41.27.2 and 45.40.1).

abruptly (in fact, in mid-book), he is cited most often with *scribit*.[79] Livy's *uariatio* should not surprise us, but what is noteworthy is that only *once* is a verb of speaking used (*ait*, 30.19.11).[80] We see a similar set of terms with other authors, e.g. Piso.[81] Livy shows a tendency to prefer specific terms in conjunction with named sources: *tradit*, *scribit* and *auctor est* are the principal terms used here, though there are others, *prodit* among them. This raises the possibility that when terms such as *traditur* are used without a 'speaker', Livy is particularly aligning himself with the historiographical tradition, a suggestion that can be supported tentatively by a representative survey of the evidence.

Traditur   *Traditur* is used thirty-five times in the extant *AVC*, but not all of these are linked to *oratio obliqua*.[82] These would seem to be part of Livy's representation of himself as an assiduous student of the past, dependent on, yet master of, the records, an interpretation which accommodates the material in question better than the aspect of historical veracity. At 1.31, after a shower of stones, the Romans hold a *nouemdiale*, either because of a voice from the Alban Mount, or after a haruspical warning: both are recorded (*nam id quoque traditur*). At 2.8.8, when Horatius is dedicating the temple of Jupiter Capitolinus and his rivals attempt to deflect him with news of his son's death, Livy is unsure of the precise reasons for the consul's steadfastness: *nec traditur certum nec interpretatio est facilis*. Numerous other examples of a similar nature are found throughout the text.[83] At 22.7.4,

---

[79] 33.36.13; 34.15.9; 35.2.8; 36.19.12 (*scribenti*) and later 36.38.6; 37.60.6 (*scripsit*); 42.11.1 before an uneven transition to the phrase *auctor est* (followed by the accusative and infinitive): 36.36.5; 37.48.1; 38.23.8; 38.50.5; 39.22.10; 39.56.7 and 45.43.8.

[80] We also have 3.5.12 (*ceciderintue exacto adfirmare numero; audet tamen Antias*); 4.23.1 (*Valerius Antias et Q. Tubero M. Manlium et Q. Sulpicium consules in eum annum edunt*); 30.3.6 (*Valerius prodit, in castra Romana ad conloquium uenisse*); 33.30.10 (*adicit Antias Valerius*); 39.43.1 (*Valerius Antias...peragit*); 40.29.8 (*[libros] adicit Antias Valerius Pythagoricos fuisse*) and 38.55.8 (*apud Antiatem inueni*).

[81] 1.55.9 (*scribit*); 2.32.3 (*ea frequentior fama est quam cuius Piso auctor est*); 2.58.2 (*auctor est*); 9.44.3 (*suggerit*); 10.9.12 (*auctor Piso effecit*) and 25.39.16 (*scribit*).

[82] My count is twenty-nine: 1.13.7; 1.16.5; 1.31.4; 1.48.7; 1.55.3; 2.8.8; 2.18.4; 3.70.14; 4.9.2; 4.12.7; 4.37.1; 4.60.1; 5.21.16; 5.33.2; 6.18.16; 6.38.12; 8.26.6; 9.28.6; 9.29.10; 10.11.10; 10.42.6; 22.7.3; 29.14.12; 38.24.11; 39.21.9; 44.14.1 (twice); 45.1.6 and 45.28.10. *Tradunt* is used almost exclusively of the historical tradition (forty-five out of fifty occasions: *Praef.* 6; 1.1.6; 1.31.8; 2.14.3; 2.40.10; 4.21.10; 4.29.6; 5.27.12; 5.31.3; 7.28.9; 8.30.7; 9.36.2; 9.44.7; 10.9.10; 10.17.12; 10.41.5; 21.28.5; 21.47.6; 22.31.8; 22.40.4; 24.17.6; 25.11.20; 25.16.3; 25.17.4; 25.17.6; 25.36.13; 26.6.8; 26.16.1; 26.49.6; 27.33.7; 29.21.2; 30.43.12; 32.6.8; 34.22.2; 37.34.6; 38.55.2; 38.55.10; 38.56.8; 39.49.2; 40.40.11; 42.7.9; 42.11.2; 44.13.12; 44.15.3 and 45.40.2: in a physical sense ('conveying') at 21.51.6; 21.59.10; 22.53.13; 23.34.4 and 27.43.5, as is *traduntur* (nine times in an historical sense (*Praef.* 6; 2.14.3; 5.27.12; 7.28.9; 8.30.7; 24.17.6; 34.22.2; 40.40.11 and 42.7.9); three times in a physical sense (at 21.51.6; 21.59.10 and 27.43.5)).

[83] See e.g. 2.18.4-5: at 4.37.1, Livy thinks a *peregrina res* worth reporting (*digna memoria traditur*). The scrutinising process continues at 8.26.6, when Livy offers that he is quite aware of another

we find once again that Livy is working explicitly with the tradition and preferring one account over others.[84] Finally, there are examples where the tradition is said to be silent on specific details: *nihil traditur, quae causa numero aucto infirmiores eos fecerit* (39.21.9); *ab regulo Gallorum – Balanus ipsius traditur nomen; gentis ex qua fuerit, non traditur* (44.14.1).

None of these examples can be adduced to argue that *oratio obliqua*, as a general feature, 'allows the historian to introduce material without vouching for it': the process is far more nuanced. They are not exhaustive but, paired with the observations of the language used in connection with named historians, they are sufficient to demonstrate that *traditur* is at the very least capable of specifically referring to Livy's sources, and probably the annalistic ones.[85] As such, other, simpler, examples of the term without further clarification (as at 4.9.2) would surely carry at least a strong implication that it was the written tradition that 'spoke'. In addition, we should note that *traditur* is veridically *neutral*: at times he will disagree, at others he will assent. He does not avoid vouching for the material in question, but does signify its status as part of the tradition, and by its inclusion indicates his preference that it should remain part of that tradition.

The extent to which this tradition is invoked, and thereby intrudes upon the ordinary narrative, is persistent in its occurrence yet restricted in its scope. In the vast majority of cases, the reported content is limited to one detail, perhaps two, within episodes that otherwise proceed without interruption. For instance, when a captive woman ingeniously arranges for the murder of her rapist-captor (a Roman centurion) Livy concludes the episode with the notice that *ut traditur* she retained the *sanctitas* and *grauitas* of the act for life (38.24.11).

This subdued invocation of the tradition thus has the effect of establishing Livy as its master, free to survey the variant threads that are woven together to produce his measured and unified account, and authoritatively its superior: though he derives his own authority from the records that vouch for his *ueritas*, they are not allowed to displace him. This plausibly accounts for the overall degree of the historical record: Livy is, above all, *discerning*;

---

tradition but he has chosen to follow 'the authorities whom I consider most worth trusting' *(haud ignarus opinionis alterius, qua haec proditio ab Samnitibus facta traditur, cum auctoribus hoc dedi, quibus dignius credi est)*; and when he relates the story of the Potitii (who died out within a year after surrendering the cult of Hercules), with the admonition that his reader should take note of this particular lesson of history: *traditur inde, dictu mirabile et quod dimouendis statu suo sacris religionem facere posset* (9.29.10). We need not worry that the story is *mirabilis* and 'therefore unreliable', since it is included as a moral lesson: its historicity is explicitly secondary.

[84] *multiplex caedes utrimque facta traditur ab aliis; ego praeterquam quod nihil auctum ex uano uelim, quo nimis inclinant ferme scribentium animi, Fabium aequalem temporibus huiusce belli, potissimum auctorem habui.*

[85] A refinement suggested by Stephen Oakley.

dismissing this, confirming that and content to include the other in the absence of anything better. If so, we are on very difficult ground for assessing distancing, since the content of a report, while it might be distanced in some way, might equally be affirmed by *ut traditur* or the like.[86]

Dicitur　It might well be argued that the conclusions reached thus far amount to a minor footnote – a gloss on the normal assumptions: but this is because most of the material discussed so far is that most intimately bound up with the 'factual' account, which is of course *one* of Livy's concerns. But hopefully it is clearer that any scepticism or criticism that we bring to the text is our importation: if Livy evokes the historian's task of sifting, weighing and choosing (or not) his path through the variant traditions, it is far from clear that he wishes to do away with those paths he has not trodden. With *dicitur*, however, we may be dealing with a different type of material.

The material introduced with *dicitur*, while not entirely homogeneous, does seem to fall into thematically distinguishable groups. Most notably, it is almost uniformly a matter of *details*, even more so than was found with *traditur*. There are the two moments where a consul weeps, apparently at the extremes to which Fortune can take man. Both are framed by *dicitur*.[87] Or there is the moment where a consul is acquitted for military failure, not least, *dicitur*, because of his resemblance to his father.[88] While under siege, the Romans 'are said' to have thrown bread out of the city to convince the Gauls that their attempts to break the city are doomed.[89] In fact a great proportion of moments reported by *dicitur* are linked to instances of unusual or noteworthy behaviour, and Livy, as we know, is *interested* in behaviour.

Livy alters the register, or tone, of many incidents by introducing them with *dicitur*, to bring them to our attention: we have extremes of behaviour (the suggestion of murdering a consul, 2.32.2) to the role model of the escaped hostage Cloelia; on returning to the Etruscan camp, she was given the chance to choose half the hostages for freedom. 'It is said' that she

---

[86] The traditional interpretation at least had the virtue of simplicity, even if it did mask rather than solve problems. Many of the potential examples fall into a Catch-22 of analysis: if they are unlikely, does their inclusion under the aegis of *traditur* mean that it is being affirmed (included and attested despite their apparent unlikelihood) or undermined (obviously too unlikely to believe)? No amount of internal reference is going to move us beyond speculation on this point.

[87] The imminent fall of Syracuse at 25.24.11-2 (*Marcellus...inlacrimasse dicitur partim gaudio tantae perpetratae rei, partim uetusta gloria urbis* (i.e. at the prospect of its ruin)) and and the downfall of Perseus at 45.4.3 (*Paulus Aemilius...ipse inlacrimasse dicitur sorti humanae*).

[88] *profuisse ei Cincinnati patris memoria dicitur, uenerabilis uiri* (4.41.12).

[89] *dicitur auertendae eius opinionis causa multis locis panis de Capitolio iactatus esse in hostium stationes* (5.48.4). They are unsuccessful.

chose the youngest, a choice called appropriate to her 'virginity' according to Livy, and also approved by the other hostages who felt that these were the most vulnerable (2.13.10-11). Of course we *can* attempt to apply the old rules of interpretation to these situations: there is no way of disproving that Livy doubted Cloelia's choice. But this is far from being the only plausible reading. 'Noteworthy' behaviour, a visibly common thread with *dicitur* statements, seems as good an interpretation as any other.[90]

Other 'types' of record also emerge from systematic analysis of the material: statements dealing with the beginnings of traditional habits – good or bad – also seem to attract the change of register provided by *dicitur*. After the betrayal of the plot to restore Tarquin to the throne, and Brutus' execution of his sons, the slave informant 'is said' to have been the first to receive his freedom by the *uindicta*, (2.5.10); Livius Andronicus 'is said' at 7.2.7 to have been the first to have a separate singer to accompany him while he acted (the beginning of the degeneration of theatre from innocence to decadence). There are other examples:[91] in other words, we seem to be encountering items of special interest – fascination perhaps – that had a bearing on the present.[92]

What has to an extent hampered our efforts to classify and appreciate many of these moments of reported speech is simply that we lack suitable classifications for them: they have therefore tended to drift into the closest fit, a framework that is driven theoretically by factual historicity. But they could also be said to bring varying and variant degrees of depth to the narrative; they personalise, or demonstrate the dignity, the potential disgrace, the curiosities, the singular moments of being Roman. In fact, we might go so far as to say that these (and many other moments) are better described as *lore* than history. 'Lore' is defined, somewhat inadequately, as 'the body of traditional facts or beliefs relating to some subject' by the *Oxford Shorter Dictionary*. What is inadequate in this definition is that it fails to address or describe the elevated register of lore, the supposed dignity that such 'information', if it can be reduced to such a class, conveys to (most) readers. Such a reaction would no doubt be taken to approximate to gullibility in an

---

[90] Cf. the documentation of the reactions of two of Rome's major enemies: *ipse etiam interdum Hannibal de fuga in Galliam dicitur agitasse* (22.43.4); Philip of Macedon *admiratus esse dicitur et uniuersam speciem castrorum et discripta suis quaeque partibus cum tendentium ordine tum itinerum interuallis* (31.34.8).

[91] At 9.40.16 we have the origin of festival customs; at 9.46.15, the institution of the annual parade of the knights by Fabius Maximus is also preceded by *dicitur*.

[92] *Ferunt* has been omitted so far. It would seem to belong somewhere between the more distinct types of information enshrined by the families of *traditur* and *dicitur* reports: it is linked to the historical tradition (e.g. at 1.5.1, 3.29.9, 4.56.3 and 3.24.10) but also to behavioural patterns and similar types (e.g. 6.8.3, 7.6.3 and 29.1.11).

audience as educated as I might expect here, but that does not mean that we should assume the same response in Livy's audience.

So (to return at last to my 'proper' subject matter) when we read, for instance, that 'it is said' (*dicitur*) that the two consuls shared the same terrible dream at 8.6.9, or of the voice that 'is said' to have warned the pillaging Latins away from the temple of Mater Matuta at Satricum (6.33.5), or perhaps the chasm that 'reportedly' opened in the Forum (7.6.2), we should not be so quick to dismiss or distance these from Livy's record: these moments are formative in Roman history, moments of mystery and awe. The dream and the chasm in the Forum in particular are stories of enormous interest, since they mark the prelude of Decius' *deuotio*[93] and Curtius' similarly unselfish self-sacrifice for Rome when he throws himself on horseback into the chasm, thus fulfilling the prediction of the *uates* that it would only be closed when the 'greatest strength of Rome' (*quo plurimum populus Romanus posset*, 7.6.3) was sacrificed. What we see here is a change of register (it is tempting to speak of 'hushed tones'). The irruption of the immense power of the gods into fragile human lives is not something to which Livy 'raised a sceptical eyebrow but included just in case'. These are powerful, evocative and often formative moments in Roman history.

Livy weaves together the narrative of men with a depth of understanding of their characters, of life, of the real motivations and causes of human behaviour. Their detailed historicity is relatively irrelevant in this, given the ancient practice of *inuentio*. While the material associated with *traditur* seems to have a tendency to be linked with Livy's visible and self-conscious – even flaunted – reflection on the tradition, *dicitur* in particular generally heralds exemplary, insightful and momentous events.

2.2.2 Unambiguous reticence

The final aspect of Livy's supposedly 'distancing' presentation of supernatural phenomena is the use of words such as *uideri* and *uelut*. Essentially, it has been generally assumed that any indication of dissonance between the historian and his religious diagnoses indicates an unbreachable gap and therefore scepticism. It is quite true that Livy frequently talks about how things 'appeared', and in such cases, as with *oratio obliqua*, the modern temptation is to assume an opposition between appearances and 'reality'. When Valerius attacks the Aequi, we are told that the consul deduced that

---

[93] 10.28.12-29; for the younger Decius see 10.28.12-29.7; also Cicero *On the Ends of Good and Evils* 2.61; *Tusculan Disputations* 1.89; Dio 10 in Zonaras 8.5. Analyses of Livy 8.9-11.1 are given by Versnel (1976) and (1981b). On *deuotio* in Livy see also Feldherr (1998) 82-111. On the rite more generally, Versnel (1976).

the gods were acting on behalf of the enemy: he was prevented by a violent storm, with hail and thunder (*cum grandine ac tonitribus caelo deiecta*). On his withdrawal, the sky cleared, 'as if' a god was defending them (*ut uelut numine aliquo defensa castra oppugnare iterum religio fuerit*, 2.62.1-2).

The modern temptation is to single out *uelut* and assert that it implies doubt, and doubt ('of course') constitutes scepticism. But it is more profitable to assume the categories of understanding established in connection with prodigies: was the storm to be attributed to the gods or not? Valerius would seem to answer positively, which leaves us wondering why there is *any* indication of 'distance' (*uelut*). Is Livy undermining Valerius' deduction or is there more to this? The answer, as with prodigies, is related not to phenomenology, but to conduct and interpretation: in the unnecessary statement that the storm and hail were 'from the heavens' (*caelo*), Livy is not informing his readers of the origins of storms and the provenance of hail; he is evoking the sense of the grandeur of the storm that seemed to the consul to be more than an ordinary phenomenon. *Velut* therefore represents the act of assessing the visible evidence.[94] In his style of reporting, Livy would seem to be *commending* the consul for his circumspection by representing the deductive process.

This use of *uelut* is mirrored in a context where it seems unlikely that outright scepticism is a factor: in the rare notices of the announcement of an augural diagnosis, the formulaic presentation often includes some aspect of 'distance'. At 8.23.14, when asked to provide an opinion, they announced that the Dictator's election seemed to be flawed (*uitiosum uideri...pronuntiauerunt*).[95]

The augurs' use of *uideri* does not indicate their fundamental doubt about their conclusions: it reflects their careful expertise. Evidence is sought and marshalled in accordance with interpretative principles, and deductions made from 'what is evident' (a preferable translation to 'what seems', which is often unconsciously compounded by modern readers with an unwritten 'deceptively'). Nor is this process random and unsystematic in the sense that Livy's agents receive all unusual phenomena in some undifferentiated way: there is a highly complex process of assessment of the relative weight of phenomena that are 'known' to indicate a particular explanation. It would have been sufficient for the Roman reader to be presented with the relevant

---

[94] Cf. the very similar conclusion on Herodotean material by Gould (1994) 94, who cites what he calls 'the built-in "uncertainty principle" which is a necessary part of any phenomenological religion'. See also Gould (1985). In both cases, he refuses to endorse the diagnosis of 'scepticism'.

[95] A highly formulaic construction: see also 8.15.6 (*religio inde iniecta de dictatore et, cum augures uitio creatum uideri dixissent, dictator magisterque equitum se magistratu abdicarunt*) and 23.31.13 (*uocati augures uitio creatum uideri pronuntiauerunt*). Cf. *OLD uideri* §24.

material from which to form, what were for him, obvious deductions. To draw an explicit conclusion is nothing less than crass, and probably insulting to the educated reader. Livy can inform his reader of his interpretation of events *purely* by his presentation of evidence if he so chooses. He might, on the other hand, present more explicit evidence, especially if he is touching on controversy, as he does when he reports the flooding that prevented the *ludi scaenici*, of which the historian disapproves, from going ahead *uelut auersis iam dis aspernantibusque* (7.3.2). *Velut* preserves the necessary distance between evidence and deduction. It does not make the religious notices superfluous, or indicate that we should ignore them.[96]

Apart from the endemic use of prodigies or failed sacrifices to indicate approaching danger, we might pick out one example where the explicit is skilfully *avoided*: the fragmentation of authority has a variety of subtle purposes, none of which involves genuine 'doubt'. When the Bastarnae begin their approach to Rome at the instigation of Philip of Macedon, they are struck down by a storm on Mount Donuca while attacking the Thracians who had withdrawn there: the storm is compared to the one that afflicted the Gauls when they attacked Delphi. Driven back by hail, crashes of thunder and lightning flashes all around them, they attributed their retreat to the gods rather than the pursuing Thracians, and ultimately returned to their camp 'like men escaping from a shipwreck' (*tamquam ex naufragio*, 40.58.3-7).

The deferred attribution of the disaster to the gods (*ipsi deos auctores... aiebant*) might be considered ambiguous and as giving an example of superstition on the part of the tribesmen, with suitable 'distancing' by the historian, except that the last mention of the Romans in the narrative was the dedication and inscription of thanks on the new temple of the *Lares Permarini* (40.52.2-6), vowed eleven years previously for the sea victory over Antiochus. The narrative structure makes the vivid comparison of the situation to a shipwreck rather significant. Livy has not explicitly stated that the new divine residents of Rome are looking after their own, but he has left little room for doubt: the Bastarnae, explicitly compared to the Gauls sacking Delphi, are opposed by the gods (presumably because of their anti-Roman intentions, since there was no revered shrine on Mt Donuca). The leaders are convinced that the gods are at work, and the mention of a shipwreck is not only dramatically satisfying but, in view of the sequence of events, extremely telling. Given the frequent failure of foreigners to understand

---

[96] One further example will underline the point: when Appius offers a temple to Bellona, Livy speaks of the situation being 'as if' the goddess were taking a hand (*uelut instigante dea*, 10.19.17-18). The rapidly ensuing success of the Roman force is not to be taken lightly in a narrative that relies for its coherence on the significant juxtaposition of piety and success.

religious matters properly,[97] the tribesmen's diagnosis of divine agency indicates not doubt, but greater certainty: even the primitive and unsophisticated tribesmen could see the divine in these events. Livy revels in the divine support without it being reduced to a gross and bald statement. Such 'unambiguous reticence' is frequent in the text of Livy, though it is rare to find an example with such specific features. We should not be thinking in terms of Livy's failure to draw explicit conclusions but rather understanding how the presentation of events leads unmistakably to an acknowledgement of the gods' aid in a climate that disliked strongly the sort of simple 'factual' statement that scholars have sought in vain.[98]

All this is not to say that Livy does not explicitly acknowledge the gods: but he is concerned to remain within appropriate interpretative habits that we are only beginning to outline here – his language reflects the process of deduction.

Rather than representing a monolithic scepticism, the four issues discussed here (discrimination between genuine and false prodigies, his evocative reporting of reports, *oratio obliqua* and 'unambiguous reticence') emerge as completely distinct aspects of Livy's reporting: what was treated as an impassable gulf between the historian and his religious material is often far more complex and the complexity reflects a number of different considerations, 'religious' as well as 'historiographical'. Livy is not simultaneously undermining religious phenomena on a number of fronts, as has so often been thought: he is sifting and sorting, distinguishing between the genuine and the erroneous, constantly aware of the need for and processes of validation. There is a 'distance' but it is one that Livy appropriately notes but does not over-reify; the vast majority of religious phenomena are *validated* rather than undermined. A whole array of checks and balances is evident in Livy's narrative, both as a display of skill and as allusion to proper procedure.

2.3 Interpretation

Thus far it has become evident that there is a premium on correctly understanding whether the gods have 'really' intervened. Where Livy is critical in connection with prodigies, he is criticising *particular* assessments: mice nibbling gold should not have been taken as a prodigy; people panic at times of stress and mistakenly report phenomena that might well not have been

---

[97] See e.g. 2.44.12; 10.11.2.
[98] Cf. 10.36.11-12, where Livy again includes both evidence and diagnosis: the ease of the victory confirms the help of the gods.

prodigies. This is perfectly consistent with his exemplary purpose: just as a consul might be criticised for rashness, so too can people be censured for their religious mistakes. We should, however, also note the *rarity* of such criticisms. Livy is not intending to insult his educated readers with a tedious list of minor quibbles but rather to work with them: there are considerations in the way he writes beyond some tedious and pedantic desire to sift belatedly through prodigy notices. His is one of many interpretative voices in the text and the position he makes for himself has a direct bearing on how we should understand his presentation of the polyphony that is Roman religious interpretation. It is a selection of those voices that are now examined: opinions are being weighed as well as counted in the *Ab Vrbe Condita*.

2.3.1 The historian as interpreter

If Livy is to write an exemplary history, he must first establish his right to do so: his non-senatorial origins – and therefore weak credentials – have already been mentioned. Throughout the narrative he takes care both to espouse modesty and hesitancy, and also to establish the authority that he needs to make explicit criticism. This difficult combination demands that he select his criticisms with a sense of measure: it would be out of keeping with his strategic display of insecurity to *flaunt* his ability to discern correctly the hand of the gods in events. Incessant intervention to question prodigy reports would be crude and in all likelihood spoil the desired effect – to indicate to the audience that Livy is perfectly capable and knowledgeable in religious matters. Thus his criticisms are much reduced in frequency and the level of authorial intervention is governed by this factor, probably more than any other. In his selection and presentation of material, Livy is as much constructing his own position as designing the Republic, and expert knowledge coupled with polite restraint are his trademarks.

Indeed we might go further: it is not so much that Livy is opposing his own assessment to that of the *maiores* as that he is following their lead in exercising his judgement. Thus he partakes of the proper Roman activity of distinguishing genuine from false prodigies: but he does not press the point. Even his distinctions between 'objective' prodigies (i.e. those that physically happened) and hallucinatory ones bears the hallmark of the expert at work, classifying the material with ease and skill. Anyone can spot a prodigy, but it is the mark of an expert that not only are such patterns detected, they are noted merely in passing.

Tastefully presented in this way, Livy's subdued omniscience translates directly into power. The question is therefore, to what end does he deploy it? For the most part the differential in authority is invisible as Livy merges his perspective with that of the venerable *res publica* for which he has such respect; the leading men soberly practise their art in the clear and uninterrupted gaze of the historian who keeps himself approvingly in the background. Thus there is often a sense of consensus – at times, we might even forget the existence of the historian but for the occasional reminders that his history is self-consciously a construction. But this seamless coherency between *auctor* and *actor* is only applied to certain processes and then with differing levels of assent. There are moments where Livy exercises his right to discriminate between proper and improper conduct and we have a whole range of levels of his consensus or disagreement with the agent(s). This arrogation of absolute authority should not go unstressed: an epideictic historian requires nothing less in his task of restoring a tottering Rome. Livy's specific gambit of underplaying his hand, given his lowly origins and low political status, should not deceive us; there is no surrender to the authority of the tradition or his sources and he will readily criticise where he feels it is necessary.

None of this should surprise us: just because an aristocrat has been made a consul, there is no reason to think that he will make a good, or exemplary, magistrate and general. Livy is very happy to criticise individuals who, he considers, have not performed well enough.[99] What is less well explored is the extent of his selectivity in validating different officials. This is most notable between those concerned with what we might, with caution,[100] call 'political' and 'religious' spheres of action. There is a temptation, based on modern parallels, to assume that priests had a monopoly on religious matters. In fact, it is more complicated than that: there are different centres of gravity with respect to religious interpretation in Livy's Roman society, different voices granted different weight and jurisdiction; of these it is the priests to which we turn first.

2.3.2 The authority of the priests

In considering the role of the priests, we should perhaps first note what is *not* present in Livy's narrative. The potential for conflict between historian and priest is extremely limited in a modern context since each is specialised to the extent that they would appropriate the authority to speak of each other's

---

[99] Frequently implicitly: see Chaplin (2000) for the often erroneous or incomplete negotiation of *exempla* by the textual agents and audiences.

[100] Central to this argument, and to a great deal of current and recent work on Roman religion, is the tenet that religious and political activity should not, and cannot, be divorced. It was the acting magistrate, for instance, who recited the prayer formula dictated by the priest: nonetheless the fact remains that certain men were *functioning* as priests, and others as annual magistrates, and their authority was distinct and peculiar to the position they held. See especially the introduction to Beard and North (1990); North (1986) 257–258 on Scheid (1985a); for the status of priests Scheid (1978); Szemler (1986); on priesthood and families North (1990b).

specialised areas only very rarely, if at all. But in a society where religious interpretations were at a premium, and positively sought, the potential for rivalry between the two is enormous. This would be true even if the historian restricted himself to 'human' matters but, as we have seen, Livy is keen to have his say on religious matters also. In the context of the *possible* disagreements the failure of rivalry to appear, and the almost seamless continuity between historian and priest, are hardly accidental. This should not be glossed over too quickly. A close analysis shows that this is deliberate, and consistent: Livy is careful to give the priests their proper place in his interpretative Rome.

The deliberations of the various priestly colleges are either, as with *haruspices*, inserted into the narrative at the relevant moment,[101] or more often included after implicit or explicit reference by the senate. The colleges of the *decemuiri sacris faciundis* and *pontifices*,[102] and the *ordo* of the *haruspices*[103] functioned rather like 'committees' of the senate which would call upon them for their expert opinion. Thus we can see immediately that the collegiate priests are *removed* from the most direct interpretative venture, of discerning whether the gods were involved or not.[104] Their roles are specialist, namely the interpretation of signs. Validation of signs was, as we shall see, the responsibility of the senate. In Livy's text, either we are simply given priestly remedies or we are told that they were consulted.[105] In both scenarios the decision as to whether Rome was genuinely faced with the *ira deum* has already been taken. In the case of the *decemuiri* we are expressly told that summoning them required some persuasion that the situation was extreme: Fabius 'managed' to get a decree passed that

---

[101] I.e. when warnings are given, often before battle.

[102] For a study of the meaning of the word *pontifex* see Fugier (1963), 161–172; Hallett (1970). Dowden (2000) 55 cheerfully dismisses the debate and plumps for 'bridge-makers' as the derivation.

[103] MacBain (1982) 49 suggests that the *haruspices* began to function as a distinct organised body in 278 BC while Rawson (1978) prefers to place this as late as the Augustan period. For our purposes it is clear that *haruspices* were summoned from Etruria by the senate, that is, in a consultative role, early on in Livy's account. This is specifically assumed in their second appearance, at 5.15.1, while at 1.31.4 they are mentioned briefly as issuing advice. The latest (published) opinion prefers an imperial date (Beard North and Price (1998) I 101). For the different extiscipal rites see Schilling (1979b) 83–90; North (1990a) 55.

[104] The only clarification between the human and divine realms explicitly assigned to any priests is the declaration of the *pontifices* that expense is not an issue with regard to the Great Games for Jupiter at 39.5.9, and that is a technical matter, as befits the college. The other priesthoods, the *flamines*, the *Salii* and the Vestals, are concerned with the performance of rituals and do not appear in connection with interpretation.

[105] It seems most likely that this was the normal procedure and that notice of it was suppressed for reasons of *uariatio* rather than the *collegia* having any *right* to be consulted; certainly the language of 'reporting back', which is the normal style, strongly implies their consultative role. For the difference between *decreta* and *responsa* see Cohee (1994) 18–27, who also has a useful table indicating the variety of Livy's expressions. We know of only one historical occasion when the advice of the priests was not heeded (Frontinus *de Aqua* 7).

the Sibylline books be consulted.[106] As Livy would have it, the senate was happy to avail itself simultaneously of their various talents if it felt so inclined.[107] Thus both initiation of priestly discussion and the final decision on remedies resides with the senate in Livy's account. Whatever the undoubted expertise of the various priests, it is not they but the senate which makes final decisions regarding action and consultation. Thus any overlap between the various priestly groups is a senatorial issue; it is the *patres* who decide which *collegium* to consult. Nor do the priests comment on whether a particular item is, or is not, a prodigy: they assume that the correct diagnosis has been made of whether the gods are involved or not. Thus their roles are strictly delimited: they are experts in their own domains.[108]

Livy's treatment of priesthood is distinct from his treatment of (for instance) magistracy. There are indications that he considers Roman priesthoods to be ennobling in themselves, at least in one well-known example: on being appointed unwillingly to the flaminate of Jupiter (27.8.4), C. Valerius Flaccus reforms his disreputable ways to such an extent that he could successfully plead for the restoration of the ancient, and virtually forgotten, right of the *flamen dialis* to attend the senate. Nor is this the only sign of respect for the venerable priesthoods.

There is a curious pattern in the naming of priests, or priestesses in the case of Vestals.[109] The *decemuiri, haruspices, augures* and *pontifices* (with the notable exception of the *Pontifex Maximus*, who is consistently named in a ritual context)[110] are consistently referred to in the anonymous plural when they are practising their duties, with the singular exception of the

---

[106] *peruicit ut...decemuiri libros Sibyllinos adire iuberentur* (22.9.8-9). Cf. the statement of Dionysius to similar effect (4.62.5).

[107] There appears to be a whole complex of expertise on offer at 27.37 (though it should be stressed how unusual the density of religious action was): the *pontifices* deal with prodigies; *haruspices* are called in to deal with a precocious hermaphrodite; the *pontifices* resume their activities with a ceremony including a hymn by Livius Andronicus; during rehearsals a lightning strike requires interpretation by the *haruspices* once again; finally the *decemuiri* appear without formal introduction to prescribe a further ceremony.

[108] Their *precise* domains are not always entirely clear: in some respects they do seem to overlap. Each has its own peculiar *modus operandi*, as noted in each section but it is not immediately clear to us why any one in particular, especially of the *haruspices* and the *pontifices*, should be consulted at any given moment. MacBain (1982) discusses (somewhat inconclusively) the evidence for specialisation of the *haruspices* in his Appendix D: Patterns of Haruspical Activity (118–126).

[109] For discussion of the ritual and symbolic role of Vestals see Beard (1980) and (1995); Beard North and Price (1998) I 51–54; for their relationship with the *Pontifex Maximus*, Beard North and Price (1998) I 57–59.

[110] He is also right in cases of conflict: at 37.51.1f. between P. Licinius, the *Pontifex Maximus*, and the *flamen quirinalis*, Q. Fabius Pictor, due to take up his praetorship. Livy notes that there had been a similar dispute many years previously between L. Metellus and Postumius Albinus. Metellus was *Pontifex Maximus* at the time, and Albinus the newly elected consul. In both cases the *Pontifex* carried the day (Bleicken (1957b)). Compare the provisions made for the *flamen dialis* at 31.50.7f.

old man of Veii who was captured at 5.15.4 after being heard to predict
that Roman victory would only follow the draining of the Albine Lake.
His circumstances rather preclude his collective anonymity, but Livy, or his
sources, has still refrained from giving him a name.[111] They are however,
with the exception of the *haruspices* (who were not an official *collegium*),
named at their inauguration or death.[112] This observation can be extended
in the case of the other priesthoods in a consistent pattern, whereby a fall
from grace involves the naming of a Vestal or a minor *flamen* in connection
with their failure. Of the Vestals, we know of Opimia and Floronia (found
guilty of impropriety at 22.57.2); Postumia was acquitted at 4.44.11 but
told to improve on her manners even though her morals were considered
above reproach.[113] However there is also the ritual error committed by an
anonymous Vestal at 28.11.6 which was attributed to human error,[114] and
the anonymity does not seem to be random.[115] The Vestal, who apparently
continued in her duties, was not 'named and shamed': presumably ritual error, however undesirable, was not taken to be such a threat as moral failure
in a priestess. This principle applies equally to the *flamines*: the only minor
flamen named in the text is Floronia's partner in disgrace, L. Cantilius, at
22.57.3. However the underlying tone is of reverence for the Vestals: they

---

[111] For the historical issues concerning the identity of *haruspices* see Rawson (1978). North (1990a)
notes that anonymity of *haruspices* was a Roman habit, and comments that 'we scarcely know
the names of any *haruspices*' (67). This may be largely due to Livy's habit of only naming collegiate priests (usually at inauguration and/or death), which of course did not include *haruspices*.
Szemler (1972) collects the evidence that we have for the names of priests.

[112] Though the listing is frequent, it is far from full. See Szemler (1972); Palmer (1997) Appendix 1
(107–115).

[113] Minucia, condemned at 8.15.7, combines elements of both stories: Opimia and Floronia are
guilty; Postumia is accused because of her dress and behaviour but acquitted; Minucia is suspected for similar reasons and these lead to her conviction after investigation. For the punishment
of Vestals see also Plutarch *Numa* 10; *Roman Questions* 96: Dionysius of Halicarnassus 2.67.4,
Cornell (1981).

[114] Presumably the discovery of an identifiable act of human negligence in the case of our anonymous Vestal (28.11.6) was considered sufficient explanation, and the inquiry ceased at that point,
although we are told that *quamquam nihil portendentibus dis, ceterum hostiis maioribus procurari et supplicationem ad Vestae haberi placuit*. This does not seem to have been the case in the
beginning of book 41, where there is a lacuna of about eight chapters (Luce (1977) 121). *Periochae* 41.1 records that *ignis in aede Vestae extinctus est*: this was apparently taken as a prodigy.
See also Obsequens 8: *incendio circa forum cum plurima essent deusta, aedes Veneris sine ullo
uestigio cremata. Vestae penetralis ignis extinctus. uirgo iussu M. Aemilii pontificis maximi flagro
caesa negauit ulterius interiturum. supplicationibus habitis in Hispania et Histria bella prospere
administrata.* Levene (1993) 104 suggests that 'possibly the mere mention of the prodigy by the
Periochae suggests its importance to Livy's narrative'.

[115] It could plausibly be argued of course that Livy found omissions in the record and that his account
merely reflects this. However, given the consistency in connection with other priesthoods, it does
not seem unreasonable to maximise the argument. If it does reflect the way that records were
kept, then the argument that it was inappropriate to name a Vestal who had not committed moral
errors would simply apply more generally.

are praised at 5.40.7, along with the nameless *flamen quirinalis*, for their selfless care for the *sacra* of the *res publica*. Like the anonymous Vestal, they are not named while their care for their duties is being performed. By keeping them anonymous, Livy places the minor *flamines*, Vestals and collegiate priests beyond criticism. Only when they descend from propriety do they become individuals again.[116] The anonymity of the priests in action merges them with the 'eternal' image of Rome; even more than other (annual) processes, they form part of the very substance of the city over time, impersonal ever-present servants of the ephemeral. The perspective portrayed is centred on the senate: just as they did not hear individual priests debating interpretations, nor do we. Thus also is their integrity placed beyond reproach: we cannot take issue with particular points of discussion, we must accept or reject their diagnosis as it comes, which stands in sharp contrast to the frequent debates in the senate.

The three priesthoods which appear the most frequently are the *haruspices* and the *duumuiri sacris faciundis* (later the *decemuiri* (6.37.12 and 6.42.20): hereafter, simply *decemuiri* although in the earlier period they did only number two) and the *pontifices*.[117] Though they have different jurisdictions, their presentation shares certain common features. The *decemuiri*, as Livy himself informs us, were normally consulted only when ordinary expiation was not considered to be sufficient.[118]

The task of the *decemuiri* is to consult the Sibylline Books of Fate[119] and prescribe suitable expiation.[120] Notices of their appearance, as we also

---

[116] The major *flamines* are often named in a political context, e.g. on their being appointed to a magistracy, but they are not named in a ritual context except in the case of C. Claudius, the *flamen* of Jupiter, who resigned his office in a most exemplary manner at 26.23.8 after committing a ritual error.

[117] For details of these priestly groups see Dumézil (1970) 594–610. Beard North and Price (1998) I 18–30 is a good overview with full references to older bibliography. Particular (recent) studies: MacBain (1982) 43–59 on the *haruspices*; Linderski (1986) on *augures*; Vanggaard (1988) on *flamines*. The *decemuiri* became the *quindecemuiri* under Sulla according to Servius (*Aen.* 6.73) and are first attested in one of Caelius' letters to Cicero (*Letters to His Friends* 8.4.1) dating from 51 BC. See also Scheid (1998b) on the records and practices of the *decemuiri*; North (1998) on the *pontifices*; Giovanni (1998) on the *augures* and Beard (1998) on religious archival process in general.

[118] *[Quintus Fabius Maximus] peruicit ut, quod non ferme decernitur nisi cum taetra prodigia nuntiata sunt, decemuiri libros Sibyllinos adire iuberentur* (22.9.8).

[119] The story of the old woman who sold the three remaining books to Tarquin after burning six of the original nine is not found in Livy's extant text, though it is possible that he alluded to it in his full work: it is recorded by Aulus Gellius 1.19; Lactantius *Inst.* 1.6.10-13; Servius *Aen.* 6.72; Dionysius of Halicarnassus 4.62; Zonaras 7.11.1; Tzetzes, *On Lycophron* 1279. See further Gagé (1955) 24–38, 196–204, 432–61, 542–55, 677–82; Parke (1988) 190–215. Phlegon of Tralles claims to record part of such an oracle (*FGrH* 257 F36 X).

[120] 'The responses of the Sibylline books recorded in Livy consist almost entirely of ritual prescriptions' (North (1990a) 54).

found with Livy's delivery of prodigy lists, are varied[121] but the procedure alluded to is consistent. They are summoned in their official role by the senate,[122] they report back, and the senate follows their advice – at least they do in Livy's account. As has been said, we do not hear of the deliberations of the *decemuiri*; we simply hear of their instructions in a consistently terse manner and varying degrees of factual detail (such as specific instructions for different prodigies). With one exception, it should be emphasised that Livy treats the solutions provided by the Sacred Books as beyond reproach. The procedures of this Roman priesthood thus underpin the ongoing greatness of the city.

Only once does Livy cast any doubt on the prescriptions of the *decemuiri*. At 22.57.2-7, the historian implies an error in judgement when certain prodigies are responded to. After the burial alive in the forum of two Greeks and two Gauls, he moves on with a unique link: 'After appeasing the gods *as they thought*'...[123] A number of items alert the reader, by now accustomed to a sense of release at the intervention of the *decemuiri*, to the fact that this is an unusual situation; the mention of *sacrificia aliquot extraordinaria* suggests some surprise on the part of the author; furthermore, the sacrifice is described as *minime Romano sacro*,[124] but most damning is the effect of the aside *ut rebantur* which can only imply that in fact the gods are far from *placati*.[125] In addition, before Pictor can return from Delphi, Pacuvius brings Capua over to Hannibal (23.2-4); this especially underlines

---

[121] E.g. *pestilentia ciuitatem adorta coegit senatum imperare decemuiris ut libros Sibyllinos inspicerent* (7.27.1); or *ob cetera prodigia libros adire decemuiri iussi* (21.62.6); *cum decemuiri libros inspexissent* (22.1.16); *eorum prodigiorum causa libros Sibyllinos ex senatus consulto decemuiri cum adissent, renuntiauerunt* (36.37.4); etc.

[122] Orlin's analysis and conclusions (1997 86) that 'consultation of the Sibylline books [only] followed the announcement of prodigies' is too simplistic, as his own discussion shows; he is too rigid in requiring the Roman state to need prodigy reports as a 'pretext'. For a discussion of the evidence for these procedures in Cicero and Dionysius of Halicarnassus, see Scheid (1998b) 13–17; for the accidental destruction of the books and a 'surprisingly calm' collection of new or alternative oracles, see most recently Scheid (1998b) 23.

[123] *placatis satis, ut rebantur, deis...*

[124] With respect either to the shedding of blood or to the sacrifice as a whole: Fabre (1940) argues that it is the shedding of blood – *imbutum* – that qualifies *minime Romano sacro* but Levene (1993) 50 n.38 suggests that 'the words "*iam ante*" imply that the current sacrifice is a further example of the "*minime Romano sacrum*" of earlier days'. *Imbutum* could be metaphorical ('inaugurated') in which case it is the choice of victim that is being criticised. It might just as well be, as I would prefer, that the sacrifice of a pair of Gauls and Celts had been performed before, but that it was done without directly shedding blood (thus reading a contrast between *iam ante...hostiis* and *minime...imbutum*). MacBain (1982), in suggesting an Etruscan origin for the rite, points out (62) that the inhumation of the Vestal *uti mos est* stands in contrast to the *sacrificia aliquot extraordinaria*. It is tempting to see Livy's retrojection of the ban on human sacrifice of 97 BC but 'the context makes it clear that this was sacrifice by magicians not state priests' (Beard North and Price (1998) I 81 n. 30). See also North (1979) 99 n.5; Beard North and Price (1998) I 80–82. For other speculations, see Bémont (1960); Porte (1984).

[125] Cf. 27.38.1 *dis rite placatis...*

the Romans' ill-fortune, for Livy precedes that narrative with the comment at 22.61.10 that the loyalty of the allies, previously unshaken, now began to waver as they despaired of Rome's empire. Clearly the religious procedures have proven insufficient.

It is not until the return of Pictor from Delphi at 23.11.1 that Roman fortunes begin to change; the oracle, in uncharacteristically unambiguous mood, promises victory if certain conditions are met, which they duly are. The entire atmosphere of the narrative begins to change: though the Roman failures and losses are detailed with the arrival of Mago back in Carthage with evidence of substantial booty, in the middle of the celebrations, Hanno wisely speaks up to warn Carthage that at best they have a good opportunity to make peace; he is, of course, unwisely ignored. The other aspects of the narrative also leave us with the sense that the *decemuiri*'s prescriptions have not been sufficient to rectify the situation, whereas those detailed by the oracle at Delphi have.

It is worth taking the opportunity to speculate about Livy's reasoning. His shaping of the narrative itself to imply divine disapproval presumably follows his diagnosis that the *decemuiri* had not propitiated the gods. But what prompted this conclusion? It might be that the answers received from Delphi were inconsistent with those of the priests. At a previous consultation, Delphi concurred with the Old Man of Veii.[126] It seems, however, more likely that Livy found his answer in the untraditional rite. Whatever the reason for Livy's complaint that the rite was not Roman, that seems to be the point at which he decides that the rite was not appropriate – nor successful – and shapes the rest of his account to fit this conclusion. For our purposes, what is interesting is that in this presentation Livy has noted the error with the least possible damage done to Roman republican religion; a mistake is acknowledged by the historian[127] but the correct response is obtained by the embassy to Delphi. The priests are not condemned for their error, for this is a very particular quibble: it is not an *exemplum* to be followed or avoided – there is no scope for doing so. In this one institutional error, Rome slips but catches itself. The failure of one department does not mean that the *res publica* fails. As with our misdiagnosed prodigy, we can consider this error to be the exception that proves the rule and that, for Livy, the institutions of Roman as a whole are equal to the task before them.

Livy's notice of the error notwithstanding, he retains a deferential attitude towards the priests: whereas at 27.23.2 he was confident in his ability to identify a genuine prodigy in competition with anyone else, here he

---

[126] *sortem oraculi adferentes congruentem responso captiui uatis* (5.16.8).
[127] We might consider his style of reporting muted: he does not use more emotive words such as *superstitio* in recording the rite.

deduces the error. The sacrifice may well have been a glaring anomaly in the tradition by the time of the late Republic, *requiring* comment from one who is claiming to be familiar with the workings of Roman religion. The effect on his appropriation of authority is significant, however: he has indicated that the customary smooth assimilation with the priests is subject to his consent. Thus we should infer his full agreement in other instances; their other remedies are presented as successful. Placing priests beyond the scope of unprompted criticism sets a boundary to the reader's response. *Exempla* will be constructed with the prescriptions of the priests as a given. The foolhardy ignore the warnings that the diviners offer; the wise embrace them and work with the situation as they are advised. What neither can do in Livy's text is to dispute details and offer alternatives.

It is not just the *decemuiri* who are generally trusted. The *haruspices*, too, receive a comparable treatment in that there is no outright contest between the historian, the man of hindsight, and the interpreter, the man of foresight. Though they were not incorporated into the *res publica* in a formal sense at this point, they figure frequently in Livy's narrative as if they were a recognised part of the Roman religious system. Their exact role is not easily specified in Livy's narrative:[128] they are often called on to interpret prodigies but also to interpret the omens evident in entrails at sacrifices. In contrast to the reliably pessimistic deductions of the *decemuiri* they 'introduced to the Romans the concept that a prodigy... may portend something favourable – a prediction never met with in Sibylline oracles'.[129] Most of their comments are not, however, positive: at 8.6.12 they confirm, typically in the anonymous plural, the suspicions of the two consuls who have had a night-time vision. Later on (8.9.1) a *haruspex* indicates that Decius' sacrifice is ill-omened. Here, as elsewhere, Livy's *haruspices* share the impersonal and unquestioned authority of his *decemuiri*; their response appears without any refinement beyond the needs of the narrative.[130]

The successes of the *haruspices* are many.[131] The way in which Livy reports their announcements is minimal, restrained and precise. Despite

---

[128] North (1990a) 51 distinguishes between *haruspices* as (Etruscan) interpreters of prodigies and (apparently Roman) *haruspices* who practised extispicy (the examination of entrails).

[129] MacBain (1982) 126 calls this 'their most substantial contribution': the *decemuiri* seem to have always drawn a pessimistic conclusion about signs and portents (Bloch (1963) 49f.).

[130] Our one haruspical response, as preserved by Cicero in the *De Haruspicum Responsis*, is multi-layered and complex, unlike the responses included by Livy, who usually limits his report to one (straightforward and practical) response. Livy suppresses causes and details of ritual responses though we can detect the presence of them both in the record: causes are mentioned in passing at 2.42.10 and 40.59.6, and rituals are simplified to formulaic notation such as *quibus diis uideretur* (e.g. 32.6.13).

[131] The prediction of Seppius Loesius' rule over Capua (26.6.14); the warning delivered to Fabius of a trap set by Hannibal (27.16.15); their concern for Marcellus at 27.26.13-4; and their promise of victory in the impending war with Philip of Macedon (31.5.7). For further positive prediction see also 36.1.3, 42.20.4, 42.30.9 etc.

his brevity, Livy's specificity unmistakably indicates their competence; at 23.36.10, for instance, Fabius Maximus is warned that he will expiate a string of prodigies *haud facile*. Thus their expertise is simultaneously precise and limited; there is a possibility that Fabius can ignore at his peril or explore with effort. In fact he quietly persists until we hear at 23.39.5 that he has succeeded *tandem* in obtaining favourable signs.

As with the *decemuiri*, if we look for criticism, we search in vain for more than one example, and even that is not a failure of the priests, although their skills are not sufficient to prevent the death of a consul.

In book 25, the consul Tiberius Gracchus, on campaign against Hannibal's forces in Lucania, was warned by the *haruspices* after three vitiated sacrifices that he should be on his guard against ambushes and plots.[132] Livy, however, adds his own conclusion that *nulla tamen prouidentia fatum imminens moueri potuit*. In the variants given for the story of Gracchus' death, plots are, as predicted, a consistent feature, whether he was killed after the plot of Flavus, while washing, or trying to make expiation. What Livy feels is necessary to add to the priests' diagnosis is the *inevitability* of Gracchus' death. Though we know from Fabius' successful ritual after a haruspical warning at 27.16.15 that there *was* scope for avoiding prognosticated events, this did not apparently apply to all instances. No fault is attached to the *haruspices* here:[133] no one explicitly criticises them; it seems that they have done their job. Had his death not been fated, perhaps Gracchus' expiation would have gone as planned; indeed, Livy's confident ascription of the cause to fate clears them of blame – to expect an interpreter to alter fate would be idiocy.

The *decemuiri* and the *haruspices* represent the priests most intimately concerned with interpretation but there are also moments in Livy's text when another college of priests becomes active, namely the *pontifices*. Like the *decemuiri* and the *haruspices*, these priests might be consulted with regard to the expiation of prodigies[134] but for the most part, as is said at their creation (1.20.5-6), they were concerned with regulatory issues. In one respect the anonymity of the other priesthoods is abandoned; the *Pontifex Maximus* reliably appears by name. Although these three colleges appear to overlap in that they might each or all be asked to comment on prodigial

---

[132] *ad imperatorem id pertinere prodigium praemonuissent et ab occultis cauendum hominibus consultisque* (25.16.4).

[133] This applies also to the variant at 25.17.3, whereby the *haruspices* indicate a suitable place for Gracchus to expiate the omens, where he is killed by Numidians: *sunt qui haruspicum monitu quingentos passus a castris progressum, uti loco puro ea quae ante dicta prodigia sunt procuraret, ab insidentibus forte locum duabus turmis Numidarum circumuentum scribant*. Again there seems a fine line between failure and limitation; the *haruspices* warned him that he ought to expiate, and found a place that was suitable (whatever we decide to make of *loco puro*).

[134] E.g. 41.16.6. See also MacBain's (1982) Appendix A 82–106.

affairs there is never any hint of rivalry between them.[135] As with the other important priests their authority is never questioned: the *pontifices* are grave and competent men in their execution of their professional duties.[136]

The last group of men required to provide expertise are the *augures* who appear in their traditional role of overseeing the taking of the auspices, which included the right to veto elections on religious grounds. The *augures* are the only group of Roman priests to receive criticism from characters in the text: though elections are cancelled on their advice without comment at 4.7.3, 8.15.6 and 23.31.13, there is the suggestion that their veto is politically motivated at 8.23.16: the accusation, certainly one familiar to Livy's peers,[137] is thoroughly discredited by the context and the speakers. At 8.23.14-17 it is rowdy tribunes who attribute patrician envy to the priests. Their speech betrays them as disrespectful and almost certainly mistaken. Their claim is that the augurs were politically motivated since they could not have known that the nomination of the Dictator (which happened in Samnium) was flawed since there was no one present to observe any irregularity, least of all the augurs, 'sitting quietly in Rome' at the time. But we know from elsewhere that specific questions could be put to the gods by augury: Numa asked specific questions in deciding on ritual procedures at 1.20.7. The dignified silence of the *augures* in response to these criticisms in Livy's narrative allows the speakers to condemn themselves: any contradiction of the opponents' discreditable interpretations would be superfluous.

We might add that the critics of the *augures* tend not to keep good company; a similar accusation is made at 22.34.3 by Q. Baebius Herennius, another tribune and a relative of Terentius Varro (opponent of the hero Fabius Maximus and the plebeian consul who was destined to lead Rome with memorable incompetence into the disaster at Cannae). He is outrageous in his criticism, attacking not only the *augures* but also the senate. The pairing of the priests in conjunction with the august senate does much to suggest that such accusers are not to be heeded; to underline the point, Baebius' success on behalf of his relative is a disaster for Rome. The *augures* gave

---

[135] It has been alleged that the episode at 27.37, where the *decemuiri, pontifices* and *haruspices* all feature at various times, indicates religious rivalry or contradictory purposes, but this is rightly dismissed by Champeaux (1996). We might add to her arguments that the *haruspices*, at least, are specifically summoned to play their part (*ex Etruria acciti*): they do not (textually) take the initiative. Boyce (1937) stresses the incorporation of rites both for and following this series of ceremonies. Compare 42.20.2, where both the *haruspices* and the *decemuiri* are consulted; the former probably because of the appearance of lightning, a typical haruspical province according to MacBain (1982) 119.

[136] E.g. at 24.44.9, 37.3.2.

[137] See Liebeschuetz (1979) 15–17, 20–21, 24–5, and *contra* Beard and Crawford (1985) 27–30. North's (1990a) formulation (65–71) is more useful on political motivation in religious matters.

a warning when they were the ones to declare the election of the *dictator* L. Veturius Philo invalid (23.31.13): this effectively blocked the elections in which Baebius was so sure that Varro would have succeeded. It does not seem beyond the pale to presume that Livy's readers would have seen a connection between this religious scruple and the subsequent disaster of Varro's election. This example would seem to confirm the reading that Livy expects his readers to know only too well that accusations of corruption against *augures*, official priests of Rome, are better taken as a judgement on the accuser rather than the accused. In their professional anonymity and the manner of their presentation,[138] the authority of the *augures* is placed beyond dispute.

Livy's presentation of priests is carefully weighed: while he scrutinises their record, he assumes – unless he cannot ignore an error – that they are competent in their duties. He does not attempt to advise the priests of the *collegia* through examples: he treats functioning priests of all types with respect, declining to use them – or even make them available – as *exempla*. For this, he is far more interested in the senate.

2.3.3 The senate

If all the roads that messengers trod with news of religious issues led to Rome, then they did not, for Livy, end at the City gates: they went on to the senate. Whatever the historical realities, it was the Livian senate to whom reports pertaining to religion were directed in his text.[139] For Livy, the senate seems to have ultimate jurisdiction over religious interpretation. It is not surprising that consuls acted on their instructions (often on the priests' advice) to perform rituals and that the consuls would report back on their progress.[140] The priests, who were of course mostly constituent members of the senate, intervened only on the express orders of the senate[141] though

---

[138] I.e., as with the other priests, not enough for the audience to quibble the workings of the decision. There clearly was a great store of augural lore, some of which must have been relatively common knowledge: the fullest discussion is Linderski (1986).

[139] So Beard (1990) 17–48, especially 31. North (1990a) 53 is less certain: 'our texts themselves sometimes seem confused over who had the final authority'. Beard is also criticised by Brennan *et al.* (1990). Most recently, Orlin (1997) 88–90 stresses that 'the Senate reserved discretionary power over exactly when to consult the Books'. None of these particularly explores the Livian *persona* although Livy is usually the principal source.

[140] E.g. 28.11.5 (*prodigia consules hostiis maioribus procurare iussi et supplicationem unum diem habere – ea ex senatus consulto facta*).

[141] The non-senatorial *haruspices* are normally 'called in' (*uocati*, e.g. 32.1.14; *acciti* 27.37.6); the *decemuiri* are directly instructed at 40.19.4-5 (*patres decreuerunt, ut...decemuiri libros adirent*) as is the *Pontifex Maximus* at 40.37.2 (*C. Seruilius pontifex maximus piacula irae deum conquirere iussus, decemuiri libros inspicere*). At 34.55.1-4, the senate wait some considerable time before instructing the *decemuiri* to consult the Sibylline Books during a period of frequent earthquakes.

Livy is hardly at pains to emphasise this fact, probably out of respect for the priestly colleges and a typical process of compression and *uariatio*.[142] Its supreme authority in religious matters is generally assumed rather than asserted by the historian.[143] It therefore seems to have been the senate who were the specific audience for prodigy announcements.[144] Livy never tells us that the opinions of those members who were priests were given more weight (though it seems highly likely that this would have occurred in reality): the senate acts as a responsible body in its own right. It is therefore to the deliberations of the senate that we must turn if we are to explore the boundaries of the divine and human (or 'natural') realms.

Livy's depiction of the senate, like his depiction of the priests, bears the hallmarks of his exemplary programme. Some of the material has already been introduced in the discussion concerning Livy's attitude to prodigies, where he was seen to be criticising procedure and public credulity, but it would be a mistake to overemphasise this disparity between historian and textual agents. For the most part, the senate is not questioned. When Livy does note error, we should not ignore the implication that the senate is perfectly correct most of the time: his carefully orchestrated account of procedures reflects ideal practice, and the annalistic account designs a role for the senate. How far Livy's account reflects historical practice of the Middle and Early Republic is not particularly our concern here: our enquiry relates to what he makes of the material that he had.

The first interpreters of any reported prodigy must have been those making the report itself. As already discussed, the lines of communication for prodigies were not fixed but some initial assessment of whether unusual climatic or animal phenomena should be reported to Rome would be required: obviously precedent and a culturally specific sense of the supernatural would have been applied. Livy is not atypical in being superior in his dismissals of mistaken reports[145] so ridicule might well have been a disincentive for those tempted to make a report.[146] No doubt there were those who would have tried their hand at predicting the expiatory procedures as

---

[142] The *haruspices* offer advice at 42.30.9 without the appearance of any formal request, as do the *pontifices* at 27.37.4 and (distinctly) at 27.37.7 before the *decemuiri* offer diagnosis with no textual intervention at 27.37.11.

[143] Apart from their other regular areas of jurisdiction, the old man of Veii was taken specifically to the senate 5.15.8 and it was the senate who discussed the verses of Marcius (25.12.11) before asking the *decemuiri* to attend to the prophecies and expiation.

[144] Rarely explicit but attested at 42.20.2 (*ea res prodigii loco habita ad senatum relata est*).

[145] Tacitus is far more caustic, as we shall see.

[146] The politeness that MacBain (1982) 30 shrewdly ascribes to the senate in the case of Figulus (43.13.6) would not have been extended to the plebs as M. Caedicius discovered when his prodigy report at 5.32.7 was spurned partly because of his status (as well the obscurity of the Gauls, about whom his mysterious voice had warned).

well; it is hard not to imagine self-appointed experts, given that prodigy reports were in the public domain and were obviously a matter of great interest. But none of this is reported in Livy's narrative beyond the vaguest indication of the panic that arose so often in connection with purported prodigies. Clearly the opinions of the rabble made as much difference as do modern conversations about the tactics in the latest England World Cup disaster. These amateurish efforts are largely suppressed in our text; the *patres* had no need of such prompts or advice and to give them credence, or present their deliberations as something to be taken seriously, would mar the splendid sight of the august senate at work. These are the experts, who do not panic, but simply take appropriate action after making their decisions on the various reports. It is *their* criteria that we are interested in.

Like Livy, the *patres* evidently felt quite capable of rejecting prodigies on various grounds at different times. These are sometimes what *we* might call 'jurisdictional' (for example) rather than 'religious'; at 43.13.6, two prodigies are rejected on the grounds of their irrelevance to the Roman senate – one of the two was considered to be private, the other foreign.[147] These examples do not help us understand why a phenomenon would or would not be classified as prodigial, though they do alert us to a wider range of issues. We must look elsewhere for 'religious criteria' but any examination of this question must remain exploratory and highly circumspect.[148] The various distinguishing features that we do have are extremely problematic: though we can always speculate, it is difficult, for instance, to see exactly why Livy should dismiss the prodigial status of mice nibbling gold in Cumae when we find that mice nibbling a golden crown at Antium (30.2.10) or crows building a nest in a temple (24.10.6) seem to pass whatever tests are being applied. We should not even rule out the possibility that Livy may be discriminating with a sense of proportion; there may be other questionable prodigies in his lists that he refrains from highlighting. We cannot do more than begin to experiment with the criteria that seem to be repeatedly or explicitly deployed.

---

[147] MacBain (1982) 29f.

[148] It is difficult to avoid seeming facetious when illustrating how homogeneous the prodigy lists are: examples do rather underline the difference between those days and these. But we might note in passing the absence of interest in unexpected colours (green cows? blue pigs?). It is not unthinkable that a society might choose to focus on unusual features such as these: compare the elusive 'white heather' in Scotland, or, from another angle, the four-leafed clover. The absence of other plausible documented phenomena that might sit well in the lists, such as humans with six fingers, might go some way to illustrating that if the lists are bizarre for modern tastes, they do nonetheless seem to know limits which we can only grope towards. Of course a Roman might well have responded to a six-fingered child with total disinterest, saying that it was just unusual but certainly not prodigial.

Once a report had been factually verified, the next question would seem to have been whether the gods were involved or not. When the flame of Vesta went out, it would seem that there was an announcement specifying the cause: human error.[149] That would seem to be enough explanation: more subtle criteria would not have been invoked. In cases where the issue of prodigiality was answered affirmatively, we can also detect recurring criteria in the patterns of our brief reports. The majority of prodigies tend to be characterised by their unpredictability and unusual nature. Sometimes there are even additional local peculiarities: Reate is known for its malformed mules, for example. Particular phenomena also repeat themselves and the reader of Livy becomes accustomed to rains of stones, blood and flesh, not to mention androgynes.[150] It stands to reason – and this is on the whole supported by the evidence – that patterns of reporting and acceptance would emerge whereby certain repeated events would be accepted as prodigial without much ado. Verification would still, presumably, be required, but the phenomenon would not arouse such astonishment if it had happened before; the level of proof might well have been less stringent.[151]

There are also examples where it is not the phenomenon itself but its particular orientation that would seem to be the critical criterion. This might be the specificity of the target, as seems to be the case with the storm at 40.2.1-3 which was considered a prodigy (*uersa in prodigium*) after it knocked down statues and damaged temples; similarly, lightning strikes on particular temples are taken to be indicative of that deity's displeasure.[152] In addition to the 'violation of the natural order',[153] prodigies might be located in the human realm. An interesting phrase occurs occasionally in the prodigy lists whereby an event or cluster of events is said to be taken as *loco prodigii*. These appear, from the few examples furnished by Livy, to be events that might not appear at first sight to be prodigial, but in fact it turns out (with the help of experts) that they are: thus when the column erected by

---

[149] 28.11.6.

[150] One interesting feature of these is that they all appear between the years 209 and 92 BC: for a full list from all sources, see MacBain's (1982) Appendix E (The Androgyne Expiations) 127–135. By the Imperial period, they were seen as entertaining rather than frightening: Pliny *NH* 7.34 offers that *olim androgynos uocatos et in prodigiis habitos nunc uero in deliciis*.

[151] One thinks of lightning striking temples or rains of stones which move from detailed verification at 1.31.1 to the acknowledgement of familiarity (it is called the *uetus prodigium* at 7.28.7) amongst many possible examples.

[152] Thus the *pontifices* do not allow Marcellus to dedicate a joint temple to Honos and Virtus (27.25.8) because they would not know to which deity propitiation would be made in the case of a lightning strike.

[153] So the formulation of Rosenberger (1998) 103–126, 242–243. He notes that prodigies are usually a disruption of a constructed cultural or social boundary: 'Endlich sind alle Prodigien in der einen oder anderen Form als die Überschreitung einer Grenze zu verstehen' (243: examples follow). Expiation is therefore the restoration of that order.

Marcus Aemilius, colleague of Servius Fulvius, is struck by lightning, we are notified that this was accepted *loco prodigii* (42.20.1), possibly because it portended the victory of the Punic War, and was therefore considered to be important and symbolic. Equally it might have been because of the total (*tota ad imum*) destruction, which would have been unexpected. A similar decision also occurs, after consideration, when a cluster of men of all ranks die at the same time (*postremo prodigii loco ea clades haberi coepta est*, 40.37.1): the poisonings perpetrated by a vast number of matrons at 8.18.11 are also considered to be due to divine influence (*prodigii ea res loco habita*). There is also the story of the oversized heifer that is sacrificed by cunning after the prediction that whoever should sacrifice it to Diana would earn for his country the destiny of empire. Not only does Livy testify to the existence of the creature, asserting that its horns were still visible much later at the temple of Diana, but also affirms that it could correctly be taken to be a prodigy (*habita, ut erat, res prodigii loco est*), as we saw earlier. The evidence given for its being portentous is that it was *miranda magnitudine ac specie*; presumably this means that it went *well* beyond the bounds of natural size and appearance (1.45.4). There is surely a similar process going on with the floodings of the Tiber, prodigial at 30.38.10 (*inter quae etiam aquarum insolita magnitudo in religionem uersa*)[154] and 35.9.3 (part of a list of prodigies) but not at 24.9.6, 35.21.6 or 38.28.4. Pestilence could also be either treated as a religious issue, or not.[155] The common factor in these examples is scale.[156]

The little we have to work with implies that there are different types of prodigies, not in any strictly formalised sense, but rather whereby the senate became accustomed to using precedents and forming the habit of recognising particular prodigies. From certain criteria, presumably after

---

[154] The phrase *loco prodigii* and the verb *uertere* appear to be formalised terminology like *credere*: cf. 40.2.3 *in prodigium uersa ea tempestas*; 40.59.8 *oleas quoque praegustasse mures in prodigium uersum est*. Cf. also Tacitus *Histories* 1.86.

[155] Not designated prodigial, e.g. 2.34.5, 3.32.2; interpreted as religious by Rome's allies at 3.6.5 (probably wrongly; see 3.7.1): Livy follows the notice of their entreaties to the gods at 3.8.1 with *seu pace deum impetrata seu grauiore tempore anni iam circumacto*. Natural causes are cited at 5.31.5. At 4.9.3, Livy informs us that pestilence is one of a series of calamities that are 'ascribed to the wrath of the gods as the last evil which a *res publica* can suffer'. At 7.3.3-4 the practice of driving in a nail to expiate plague is revived and at 7.27.1 the *decemuiri* are consulted. 40.19.3 sees a plague included with portents as reason for once again consulting the *decemuiri* and at 41.21.10 a plague goes on so long that consultation of the same priests is made (*cum pestilentiae finis non fieret, senatus decreuit, uti decemuiri libros Sibyllinos adirent*).

[156] *Contra* Orlin (1997) 88: 'the severity of the plague, however, appears *not* to have been a factor in consulting the Sibylline Books' (original emphasis) on the grounds that the timing of the introduction of the *decemuiri* varies in each example. But the lack of automaticity would surely suggest that there was some assessment of the situation and severity (or at least persistence) seems a very strong candidate for the decision to designate the plague prodigial.

discussion, they deduced the hand of the gods in events. Thus, a process that has so frequently been placed in the domain of the 'irrational' emerges as an ordered and complex phenomenon. For the Romans there was decipherable meaning in such disruptions of 'natural' expectation. However cautious *we* must remain about reconstructing specific lines of enquiry, it is clear that the senate was employing a set of criteria that made sense to them, and apparently with some care for procedure. Understanding the constituent elements of the gods' intervention and distinguishing them from natural phenomena was part and parcel of an élite Roman lifestyle.

There is a variety of religious voices in Livy's text: his own, the admittedly muted voice of the people as a whole, the senate and the priests. With the notable exception of the last group Livy assesses these voices and presents them accordingly: the people, a key part of the transmission of prodigy reports, were predictable in so often over-reacting. The senate, however is required and expected to understand with greater discrimination whether the gods are active or not in a particular event: he will censure them for error, but ultimately relies on them to do their job. But there were clearly a great number of verdicts to be heard in Livy's Republican Rome, some dissonant, others inclining to a unity. Livy's strategy is to dissipate or ignore the rival voices, and in so doing he firmly plants the senate at the centre of these debates, and affirms their success.

2.4 Choice

2.4.1 Introductory comments

Thus far material has been presented to illustrate that, for Livy, the key task of religious governance would have been to distinguish between those actions that were due to the intervention of the gods and those that were not: then for the senate to take appropriate action, sometimes on the advice of the priests. We have also seen that the Romans did not feel compelled to take responsibility for *all* acts that could be ascribed to the influence of the divine; they had to be relevant to the *res publica*. The gods' disfavour or favour with a Manlius was the affair of a Manlius.[157] This example, however, merely

---

[157] MacBain (1982) 30 is surely right to detect 'political' motives in this episode and I am not intending to prove that senatorial thinking was not subject to all kinds of deviation from the ideal in these interpretations: Livy chastises them for what he suggests is haste and a failure to apply proper procedures at 21.62.1, as we have seen, so he is clearly aware of the difficulties inherent in retaining high standards. Perhaps a virtually obsolete regulation was invoked in the knowledge that a technicality was being exploited: but consider a modern analogy, such as insisting on a fire regulation that had been ignored for years, and would continue to be ignored after its temporary resurrection. None of this has any bearing on a belief in fire regulations.

points the way; *praua religio* is more than simply a failure to address properly the question 'are the gods involved?' It also prompts the questions 'which gods?' and 'how does one address them?'

The consul of 186 BC makes some striking distinctions in his speech about the Bacchic cult: he distinguishes ancestral gods from those who, having 'captured' (*captas*) men's minds with their depraved and foreign rites, drive them to all sorts of crimes and acts of lust (39.15.2). He concludes that nothing is so deceptive as *praua religio* (39.16.6).

Here we encounter *praua religio* not as mistaken attribution to the gods, but in association with foreign rites and foreign gods, who are most potent in degrading their worshippers. This is evidently different from the error of the Cumaeans who *inser[unt] ...deos minimis rebus* (27.23.2). Here, the Romans are dealing with a different error, an *alternative*. In suppressing a cult of (purportedly) foreign origin,[158] Rome was policing a different boundary from that between mistaken or accurate assessment of divine activity. Roman religion was not merely a question of discriminating between genuine communications from the gods and natural occurrences, or foreign and domestic jurisdiction (the question '*whose* prodigy?'): there is also specialisation within the realm of events influenced by the gods.

The Bacchist affair is a useful one for us, since it highlights a number of key points. Firstly, we might note the difference made between one set of gods and another (*hos...illos*): in addition, it seems that *praua religio* can be a form of religious practice distinct from the traditional Roman as well as a tendency to see the intervention of the gods when it is not there. Finally there is mention of *superstitio*, which deserves further exploration. These themes will be taken up in sequence.[159]

2.4.2 Aspects of selection

At only two other points in Livy's extant text do we hear of foreign gods: at 4.30.9-11, for instance, when the City is filled with people performing foreign rites, care is taken that henceforth only Roman gods are worshipped, and in Roman ways (*ne qui nisi Romani di neu quo alio more quam patrio colerentur*). This distinction between gods is remarkable.[160] Livy's normal operating principle is that the gods are equally available to all: we encounter

---

[158] The cult had undergone some organisational changes since its introduction by a Greek *ignobilis...sacrificulus ac uates* (39.8.3): see North (1979) 88–89.

[159] The argument presented here is broadly similar to that of Liebeschuetz (1967) 49, though we differ on points of detail.

[160] It is only extantly found in Livy here and in connection with the Bacchist cult, though rites and the nature of the gods are closely aligned at 25.1.6 (*tanta religio, et ea magna ex parte externa, ciuitatem incessit ut aut homines aut dei repente alii uiderentur facti*).

interpretatio Romana at 38.41.4 (*praeter Apollonis Zerynthium quem uocant incolae templum*) and the *templum Dianae, quam Tauropolon uocant*
(44.44.4). Livy can speak of the exceptional *sanctitas* of (non-Roman)
Delos at 44.29.1 (*sanctitas templi insulaeque inuiolatos praestabat omnes*);
and Delphi is also mentioned with the greatest of respect – when Rome
seeks the advice of the Pythia, her authority is fully validated in the text.[161]
When, on the other hand, Q. Fulvius Flaccus goes to Bruttium and strips
the temple of Juno Lacinia of its roof at 42.3.1f., Livy calls it a *sacrilegium*
(42.3.3) and there is the rhetorical protest in the senate that the censor acted
'as if the immortal gods were not the same everywhere' (*tamquam non
iidem ubique di immortales sint*).[162] The designation of a god as foreign
or non-Roman has no bearing on its existence or power: the consul does not
doubt the power of Bacchus to 'drive people to crime and lust' (39.15.3), nor
does the senate take the risk of destroying all the shrines, which would have
incurred the wrath of the god(s).[163] Presumably, if pressed, Livy would indicate his knowledge of other gods whose worship and gifts were considered
unsuitable for some reason.[164] But the majority of the gods are considered at
least potentially appropriate for the *res publica*, and even those with somewhat unsavoury characteristics could be represented in the most Roman
way. Thus foreign gods are generally introduced to Rome in Livy's text –
through appropriate channels – without any apparent difficulty.[165] Where

---

[161] Brutus' fateful visit to Delphi begins at 1.56.9; at 5.16.9 the prediction of the old man of Veii,
already supported by his inspiration, the *libri fatales* and the *Etrusca disciplina* (5.15.10-11) is
supported by the oracle; Q. Fabius Pictor brings home instructions that are a turning point at
23.11.1; at 29.10.6 victory is promised by Delphi; etc.

[162] 42.3.9. If further proof is required that Livy implies divine retribution, we might refer to Levene (1993) 108–109, who says 'all of this foreshadows the theme of Roman ill-treatment of
allies... [and] the prodigy lists... cast the shadow of divine retribution for such actions over the
book'. Flaccus' death, recorded at 42.28.12, has a nexus of reports on his insanity and Livy notes
the popular opinion that this was due to the goddess' wrath.

[163] For the (un)likelihood of the cult's historical continuance, see North (1979) 90–91, though witness the (historical) care taken not to offend the god: the cult is virtually suppressed, though the
Romans are careful not to attempt to remove the god's shrines completely. On this episode see
the *Senatus Consultum de Bacchanalibus* (*ILS* 18); Frank (1927); Tierney (1947); North (1979)
90–92; Pailler (1986) and (1988); most recently Gruen (1990) 35–78; Beard North and Price
(1998) 91–96.

[164] Virgil's *Allecto* is not a particularly desirable deity (*Aeneid* 7.324-7). But compare Cicero's comments on the Furies in *On The Nature of the Gods* 3.46: *deae sunt, speculatrices credo et uindices
facinorum et sceleris*. Even 'bad' gods have their reasons and their place.

[165] Aesculapius is said to be required by the *decemuiri* at 10.47.7 and the god is said to have been
already obtained from Epidauros at 29.11.1. Cybele, of course, is often cited as a most unroman
god, that is until she *was* a Roman god, at which point, for Livy at least, she has impeccable credentials in contrast with other historians, e.g. Dionysius of Halicarnassus 2.19.4. Livy reports her
Games most matter-of-factly at 36.36.4, but he is aware of the unorthodox behaviour of the priesthood: at 38.18.9 he mentions their *fanaticum carmen*. There is a discussion of the introduction

Livy differentiates people in religious terms, it is predominantly with respect not to deities but to rites.

2.4.3 Foreign rites

The protection of Rome from foreign rites is far more prominent as a religious priority than the exclusion of foreign gods. Numa foresaw the need to remind the people of proper Roman rites when he set up the college of *pontifices* to preserve *patrios ritus*, ancestral (if we can thus label them so early) against foreign rites (1.20.6). The virtual synonymity of the introduction of foreign, and the neglect of traditional, rites is reinforced in the polarities used by the consul in the Bacchanalian affair: what is more, he stresses the role of the priests in preserving (constructing) appropriate rites for the Roman populace, naming the pontifical and augural colleges individually, as well as stressing the role of the senate, who are included in the description of 'masters of all human and divine lore' (*prudentissimi uiri omnis diuini humanique iuris*, 39.16.9).

Such statements are typically ascribed to a preference for 'tradition' in a sense that is more sentimental than anything, but that is essentially the only possible explanation if one assumes the vanity of religious practice. If we are to posit a profoundly embedded religiosity instead, it becomes impossible to make such a reductionist analysis; in a world where the gods exist, one cannot be purely 'sentimental' in the modern sense – too much is at stake. What Livy's consul is at pains to establish is not the efficacy or meaning of religion, but that the rites practised by the Bacchists were alien to Rome. But if this is not a case of 'pure sentimentality' then it is worth enquiring what *was* at stake.

Both Numa and the anonymous *prudentissimi uiri* of the consul's speech are known for their expertise and knowledge: Numa was, after all, selected as king for these skills (1.18.1). In Numa's creation of the post of *Pontifex Maximus* the desirability of segregating Roman from foreign rites is implicit (1.20.5-7). Our consul, however, gives his reason as the fear of *dissolutio religionis*, an almost untranslatable phrase which may well owe its formulation partly to the pun of 'dissolving something tied':[166] but even the term *religio* on its own is problematic. It has a host of resonances that cannot be preserved in any translation, referring predominantly not to the practices

---

of Aesculapius in Beard North and Price (1998) I 68–70. Orlin (1997) 106–107, citing Scheid (1985a) 97–98, stresses political aspects in the decision. See further Musial (1990).

[166] The play on *religio* and *religare* is common: see Maltby's *Lexicon of Ancient Latin Etymologies* (Leeds 1991) 523.

of religion but to a religious sense.[167] Put most succinctly, the consul is warning that the practice of foreign rites is destructive of a proper religious sense. Indeed the whole point of the speech, with its manifold reversals of social distinctions and its evocation of appropriate identity[168] and *coniurationes* of 'alternative Romes' is that a Rome without her traditional rites is not Rome.

We cannot say that Livy universally despises foreign rites: at 40.6.1-2 he describes, apparently without distaste, a Macedonian procedure for lustrating the army; but indifference or curiosity would presumably not have been his reaction if a Roman general had attempted to copy it. The gods of foreign cultures are potent, and Livy's narrative is sensitive enough to credit foreigners with religious success at times;[169] but Roman religion is more successful. The assumption that Roman religion is in some way better than its rivals is part of a more general superiority complex: so the inability of the Macedonian seers to provide the naturalistic interpretation of an eclipse which the Romans were privy to is not something we should be surprised at.[170] We know that in a political context, foreigners are also often incapable of learning from *exempla* properly.[171] Nonetheless there is the occasional moment where Livy's indulgence descends to scorn. For instance the bizarre (to him) rites practised by the Samnites against the Romans are described as *superstitiones*: to add insult to injury, they fail to work against the greater piety of the Romans.[172] But the Samnites are condemned chiefly for their incompetence; Papirius' analysis of their rite seems to indicate a number of errors: the mixing of human with animal blood; the use of one oath to enforce the breaking of another (i.e. a treaty); and the compulsion of the Samnite army (10.39.14-17), all demonstrate the basic inability of the Samnites to devise a decent *deuotio*-style rite.

---

[167] For contemporary definitions, Aulus Gellius 4.9; cf. Cicero *On The Nature of the Gods* 2.28. Michels (1976) notes that *religio* is predominantly a word used in prose. There is a brief but useful survey at Beard North and Price (1998) I 216–217, where the point is made that *religio* and *superstitio*, to which we shall turn imminently, should be studied together.

[168] North (1993) 93.

[169] The Aequi seem to be enjoying divine support at 2.62.1-2 and Livy is prepared to credit the Gauls besieging Rome with enough reverence for the gods to explain the success of C. Fabius Dorsuo in passing through their ranks to perform sacrifice (*seu attonitis Gallis miraculo audaciae seu religione etiam motis cuius haudquaquam neglegens gens est*, 5.46.3).

[170] At 26.11.4 Livy tells us that the strange behaviour of the weather was treated as a religious matter by the Carthaginians but it is difficult to know whether he is expecting us 'to know' otherwise or indicating that even the foreigners could see that the gods were intervening. The latter is true when the Bastarnae attribute a fierce storm to the intervention of the gods at 40.58.3.

[171] Chaplin (2000) 71–82 and via index.

[172] Levene (1993) 238–239. The ambivalent traditions about the religious practices of the Sabines and the Samnites are discussed in more detail by Dench (1995) 155–174. Feldherr (1998) 51–64 also has a useful discussion of this episode.

2.4.4 *Superstitio* and captive minds

The description of the Samnite rites as *superstitio*[173] is the only time that the word is not used in connection with Rome or Romans by Livy. The consul is concerned lest it affect the *populus* who see the shrines being dismantled (*ne qua superstitio agitaret animos*, 39.16.10); Tullus, we are told, went from neglecting rites to filling the city with 'superstitious' observances;[174] a similar pairing of excessive religiosity and *superstitio* appears in book 29 in connection with the reporting of prodigies[175] and in book 6 where it is the leading citizens who are afflicted: *in ciuitate plena religionum, tunc etiam ab recenti clade superstitiosis*[176] (*principibus, ut renouarentur auspicia res ad interregnum rediit*, 6.5.6).

But it is unsatisfactory to consider delusion (and therefore scepticism) as the point of Livy's use of *superstitio*. At 39.16.10 *superstitio* seems to refer to an irrational religious fear; the consul continues, explaining that the gods themselves support the actions of the *res publica*: '*omnia diis propitiis uolentibusque [ea] faciemus*' (39.16.11). It is irrational because there is actually nothing to worry about – the gods are at peace with Rome. Such also seems to be the tone of the word as it is used at 6.5.6: Rome needs not worry about the wrath of the gods at this point of victory.

The aside at 29.14.2 (*impleuerat ea res superstitionum animos, pronique et ad nuntianda et ad credenda prodigia erant*) should not lead us to believe that every prodigy in the list that follows is not genuine: it seems most likely that the prodigy list is, as usual, functioning to warn the reader that a recent impiety had aroused the wrath of the gods, despite the optimistic context of the imminent arrival of the Mater Magna.[177] *Superstitio* refers to the excessive reaction of panic and a excessive tendency to see the gods at work: it is in contrast with proper Roman dignity, which drew on the 'knowledge' that Roman religion was sufficient to deal with the situation.

At 4.30.9 the widespread adoption of foreign rites in Rome is described as being due to the citizens being *capti superstitione animi*. Specifically the words *capti animi* are interesting, suggestive as they are of some kind

---

[173] Beard North and Price (1998) I 216–217 make the point that *religio* and *superstitio* should be studied together. On *superstitio*, see also Belardi (1976); Scheid (1985b); Grodzynski (1974). Most recently, and cogently, Beard North and Price (1998) I 214–244. Cicero defines *superstitio* as *timor inanis deorum* at *On The Nature of the Gods* 1.117 and gives an etymology at 2.72.

[174] *repente omnibus magnis paruisque superstitionibus obnoxius degeret religionibusque etiam populum impleret* (1.31.6).

[175] *impleuerat ea res superstitionum animos, pronique et ad nuntianda et ad credenda prodigia erant* (29.14.2).

[176] The only appearance of the adjective in Livy.

[177] 29.14.5-14. Pleminius had just ransacked the temple of Proserpina at Locri, which Livy compares to Pyrrhus' sacrilege in pillaging the same temple. Attention is drawn to the divine punishment that followed (29.8-9). See further Scheid (1985a) 24–26.

of domination of one's sensibilities. This phrase appears elsewhere: when there is a mass poisoning perpetrated by the matrons of Rome, the women are said to be *captisque magis mentibus quam consceleratis* (8.18.11): the only action taken is religious – the revival of the ceremony of the 'nail driven in by the Dictator'. Similar phrasing appears at 7.2.3, when scenic games are introduced to Rome for the first time – which does not meet with Livy's approval: they are introduced at a point when people are not clear in their religious thinking (*uictis superstitione animis*). To underline the point, a prodigial flood occurs almost immediately in the narrative to prevent the Games taking place and Livy emphasises his diagnosis of the cause – *uelut auersis iam dis aspernantibusque placamina irae*.

Both *religio* and *superstitio* indicate not just a type or assessment of a rite, but also the mental propensity associated with correct performance. To be 'overcome' or 'deluded' in some way, and to be less than the master of one's mind, is most undesirable: recourse should always be to traditionally sanctioned responses without panic or impulsive haste. This is surely what underlies the caustic comments about panic in the reporting of prodigies: there really is no need to panic, as the *res publica* has ways and means of dealing with these things.[178] Typically, Livy's criticism is corrective not sceptical: people really should know better.

Thus, with regard to the ritual response, there are aspects of selection beyond the simple one of deciding whether the gods were involved or not. Apart from rare instances where one could approach the wrong sort of gods, the manner and style of approaching the gods needed also to be suitable and this is far more likely to be the point of a judgement or intrusion into the text. It is possible to make a further analysis of the aspects of suitability. Apart from the aspect of identity, there are also signs that inappropriate elements simply fail to work, or backfire; we noted Livy's disapproval of the foreign scenic games at 7.2.3; we have also already discussed the failure (without penalty beyond the failure to secure the *pax deum*) of a rite of which one aspect was dubbed *minime Romano sacro* at 22.57.6. More dramatically there is the farcical death of the king Tullus in book one when he botches an attempt to propitiate Jupiter and is killed by lightning. His incompetence is described as *praua religio* (1.31.8).

The enumeration of examples does not necessarily give us any real sense of the texture or depth of experience inherent in Livy's, and others', reactions to rites that were visibly not Roman. The sense of violation is conveyed in the consuls' speech to a Rome pervaded by the Bacchic rites as a series of ruptures in social as well as religious terms. A rite could not

---

[178] As Champeaux (1996) 70 puts it, 'A Rome, même dans les pires moments, on ne cède pas à la panique; on s'organise, et on fait face.'

necessarily be transplanted to Rome and expected to work; even if it did it might violate other expectations beyond what was tolerable. There was a profoundly complex sense of what was suitable, as was historically the case with the cult of the *Magna Mater*, whose cult was, to use a rather appropriate metaphor, virtually emasculated once it had arrived in Rome.[179] Livy continues this neutering effect in his treatment of the goddess in Rome, though he is perfectly aware of unroman activities of her priests.[180] Opinions on these matters would presumably have varied: some would have had the tolerance to experiment a little; others would have simply dismissed the idea that imported rites could properly obtain the *pax deum*.[181]

Much of the material which has been adduced in relation to the issue of belief or scepticism can thus be more usefully contextualised in terms of the response to, rather than the diagnosis of, divine agency: Livy's use of *superstitio* in particular can now be seen to represent not a state of 'disbelief', occupying and exclusively appropriating the same conceptual space in an individual as 'belief', but a policing of the appropriate boundaries of an entirely different category that *depends on* 'belief'.

The issue of identity has its place but should not be overstated: for the Romans, practical results were a central aspect of religion. The issue of responding to events necessarily depended on the presence and relevance of a question along the lines of 'are the gods involved in this particular event or not?' It is hard not to see this as a consideration when Livy caustically corrects those who saw the divine at work at Cumae. This observation might appear at first sight to authorise the traditional scholarly dichotomy between 'the divine' and 'the non-divine', a fundamental tenet of our current understanding of the ancient world: the distinction between men and gods, represented so vividly in the ancient world both textually and ritually,[182] is not one that should be simply discarded. The similarity between the ancient and modern dilemmas is nonetheless illusory, for the distinction being made in Livy's Rome was not an autonomously objective one, provided by the external world as a factual ontological detail; it was a subjective human designation, made for their particular purposes and *in full awareness* that this was the case, as we shall see.

---

[179] For the regulations placed on participation in the cult see Cicero *On Old Age* 45; Aulus Gellius 2.24.2; Dionysius of Halicarnassus 2.19. There is a discussion by Versnel (1980a) 108–111. For more general discussions, Lambrechts (1951) and (1952); Vermaseren (1977); Thomas (1984) 1525–1528; Turcan (1989) 42–46; Beard (1994); Borgeaud (1996) 89–130; Lane (1996). On the introduction of the cult: Bremmer in Bremmer and Horsfall (1987) 105–111; Gruen (1990) 5–33 and (1993) 1–33; North (1993); Beard (1994); Takacs (1996); Orlin (1997) 109–111.

[180] He refers to *galli* with their *fanaticum carmen* at 38.18.9.

[181] For a reversal of general policy with regard to the openness of the senate regarding foreign elements in general (including religion), see North (1993).

[182] There is extensive discussion of this in relation to Greek material, and the conclusion made there seem transferable to a Roman context: the seminal work is Vernant (1981b).

3

Gods and men in Livy

3.1 Introduction

The discussion thus far has focussed on re-examining Livy's presentation and has argued for a more nuanced approach in reading his religious material. We can now begin analysis of his religious material in earnest. Much of it will lend itself with ease to the kinds of issues raised in the introduction. As a working principle, coherence and intelligibility is maximised, not least as a corrective to previous discussions. This is not to imply that incoherence is absent, or should be explained away; all cultural systems are notoriously contradictory in manifold respects.[1] But the very observation of incoherence relies upon the assumption of a meaningful structure of concepts that have a relationship to one another: much of this system may not be explicit at any given moment. The following account therefore represents what is fundamentally an experimental analysis of the religious system deployed by Livy. No other authors are taken into account – which can be treated as either a strength or a weakness; no essay could attempt to incorporate all sources on these topics in more than a few authors at best, and those that did would run the risk of failing to appreciate the various contexts of the material. This analysis is therefore limited, and thereby all the more precise. It is structured along lines that are familiar to the scholar of Roman literature, though it might be said that the end result is a subversion of that structure. In that it is intended to be a reasonably full answer to many of the criticisms of typically problematic areas, it is more usefully considered a starting point than a final result in itself. Livy is essentially a test case for an argument that might prove useful elsewhere and, in his fullness, seems as good a start as any.

3.2 Explanation

Thus far some simple points have been made about Livy's narrative: the gods do intervene, there are ways of deciding when this happens and, where

---

[1] Though perhaps the term 'contradiction' is itself misleading, especially if one takes no account of the context in which a statement or action is made. See Veyne (1988).

relevant, it is possible to make a practical (i.e. ritual) response. Yet this is too monolithic in its simplicity and is hardly convincing as an end to inquiry. If we posit the answer 'yes' to the question 'did the Romans think that the gods intervened in human affairs?', then we have gained little from the days when we answered 'no'. Identity, for instance, was never treated so simplistically. In fact it is possible to discern no little subtlety and debate in Livy's 'religious' explanations, and in surprisingly familiar territory.

3.2.1 Causal over-determination

It is tempting for the modernist to think that if the Romans believed in their gods, then the only saving grace is that they (or their Greek counterparts) could at least see that some things should *not* be ascribed to the gods. However, this concession to 'the obvious' is completely spoiled by 'causal over-determination', whereby the gods and men are *both* considered responsible for a particular outcome. We thus hear conclusions such as 'the Greeks were just capable of thinking two contradictory things at once' or questions like 'why can't we just say that the Romans were irrational?'[2] Levene sums up the situation thus: 'from Homer on, various ancient writers treat events simultaneously in divine and human terms, with either separately sufficient to explain what happens. To us, it might appear that one or other factor is superfluous; but they seem to have perceived no such contradictions: the divine explanation supplements the human rather than cancelling it out.'[3] 'Causal over-determination' or 'double motivation', as this is normally called, is often cited as an *explanation* of a particular passage, but it fails to do more than *observe* the phenomenon. Either they did not notice the 'contradiction' despite abundant opportunity, or we have failed to understand precisely what is going on.

Causal over-determination is found very frequently in ancient literature, and Livy and his agents are no exception. Consider, as one example amongst many, the vowing of a temple to *Fortuna Equestris*[4] and games to Jupiter Optimus Maximus by Fulvius Flaccus after the victory of the Roman cavalry at 40.40.10 over the Celtiberi. To us, the description of the battle is perfectly sufficient in human terms; yet Flaccus made his vow *after* the rout; it was not a case of *do ut des*, but *do quod dedisti(s)*. We might also note the way that Livy himself assesses responsibility as shared rather than necessarily distinct: for instance, at 5.49.1 he says *sed dique et homines prohibuere redemptos uiuere Romanos*. A variety of approaches has evolved to

---

[2] The two quotes are from a speaker's reply to a question, Loxbridge Post-Graduate Conference, March, London, 1995 and another postgraduate conference in London, February 1997.
[3] Levene (1993) 27.
[4] On which goddess see further Champeaux (1982–7) 131–153.

deal with this supposedly nonsensical situation. Causal over-determination is sometimes considered a 'literary' technique, that is, it does not apply to 'real' life but is merely a 'stylistic' or 'dramatic' strategy. The usefulness of such a distinction is itself questionable[5] and any utility disappears when one is faced with an account of *history* that employs it, or encounters it in connection with the characters in the text. Nor is the decision that the ancients were 'irrational' in some way particularly helpful[6] even if it can be 'proven'. If we are to represent this phenomenon of shared responsibility accessibly to ourselves then our discussion of 'causality' must begin afresh. Ironically it may be that the phenomenon of 'causal over-determination', already perceived to be overly sophisticated, is actually a *simplification* of an even more complex dialogue of which important aspects have been overlooked. Restoring the issue to its greater complexity might actually bring greater clarity in the longer term.

3.2.2 Multiple over-determination
Though the analysis is usually of a diagnosis of divine and human forces at play simultaneously, what we in fact encounter are *multiple* levels of explanation: the human and several distinct categories of the divine. These several categories constitute the divine realm when taken together, and the divide between them is not as sharply defined as that between the human and the divine.

In an example already discussed (above, 71), Livy ruled out the possibility that the consul Gracchus might have been able to avoid his fate after warnings from the *haruspices* (*nulla tamen prouidentia fatum imminens moueri potuit*, 25.16.1-4). These events seem to assume a three-fold categorisation: human; predictable but changeable (assumed by the warnings and attempts at propitiation); and predictable and unchangeable (*fatum*). This is not to say that there was necessarily a highly formalised and schematic categorisation into three rigid categories. For our purposes it is sufficient to say that, in Livy's narrative at least, there was a sense of scale involved within the divine realm. This sense of scale can be further refined: the middle category ('predictable but changeable') can itself be subdivided as we see in the application of solutions to problems. There are a number of occasions when a religious answer to a situation fails to resolve that situation. At 22.57, the prescriptions of the *decemuiri* are deemed to be ineffective but the answer of the Pythia, given at 23.11.1-3, appears to be somehow

---

[5] See Feeney (1998) 1-2.
[6] See Lloyd (1990) for a powerful argument against the idea that different cultures have fundamentally different mentalities; many of the essays in Smith (1978a) also deal with these issues.

more potent. Perhaps the most lavish religious procedures of the entire text are those at 22.9-10 after the defeat at Trasumenae: there are vows of not only a Sacred Spring, but also temples and Great Games. In addition a large-scale supplication and a *lectisternium* are held. If these large-scale rites were successful in propitiating the gods, then, we might ask flippantly, why not perform them each time that a religious problem arises?[7] Presumably the population would refuse to perform a Sacred Spring regularly (the sacrifice of all the offspring of their cattle and flocks) but there are also less expensive rites that seem nonetheless to be more of a concerted effort to restore the *pax deum* than others, such as the complex of rites described at 27.37, which are prescribed by all the major interpretative priesthoods. Yet such large-scale rites are not used every time that there is a breach of the *pax deum*; often the expiations performed seem to be relatively minor. Clearly there is some process of assessment of what is appropriate: expiatory rites are designed to be (merely) *sufficient*. Excess would be wasteful while underestimation would lead to failure.

Assessment of this kind is implied in the notice that Q. Fabius Maximus 'managed' (*peruicit ut*) to persuade the senate to consult the *decemuiri* at 22.9.8, something 'which happened only when the most extreme religious problems were encountered'.[8] The senate was responsible for assessing when experts were required, and which ones were most appropriate. These responses might range from virtual automaticity (as is seen with showers of stones)[9] to the most careful consideration, as when the senate spent an entire day interpreting the prophetic poetry of Marcius (25.12.11) before also consulting the *decemuiri*. Despite the importance laid on such assessment, there is clear evidence that there were times when the experts did not hit the nail on the head at the first attempt, at least in Livy's estimation, which implies that there was a whole range of possible responses. The observation that the Romans were drawing distinctions in the divine realm has repercussions for the distinction between the divine and human levels, especially

---

[7] In fact, the Sacred Spring *is* repeated shortly afterwards (33.44.1), which is astonishing given the lengths to which the Romans had gone to avoid the possibility of error in forming the vow (given in full at 22.10.2-6). On the Sacred Spring, see further Heurgon (1957).

[8] *quod non ferme decernitur nisi cum taetra prodigia nuntiata sunt*. Fabius must have persuaded the senate that the present situation was prodigial or analogous to a portent in some way, possibly along lines of argument noted earlier in connection with prodigies where a situation or event could *haberi prodigii loco*. This would explain why it was an unusual case and therefore why Fabius had to argue for his proposal, whereas usually we are simply informed that the *decemuiri* were consulted in formulaic terms. Fabius must have argued that the recent military failures indicated (or perhaps simply 'were') the *ira deum*.

[9] At 35.9.4-5 and 36.37.3-4 showers of stones are expiated amongst other prodigies on the recommendations of the *decemuiri*: Orlin (1997) 89 suggests that the consultation was linked just to the showers of stones; but the repetition suggests that it was the other prodigies, or possibly the conjunction of the others, that prompted the consultation.

in the light of Horton's suggestion, noted in the introduction, that there are parallels between scientific 'levels' and the way that religious concepts and cosmology are employed as explanatory devices. This is not to say that there are two monolithic thought systems called 'religion' and 'science'. Horton's argument is not hard to apply to other systems of knowledge (or perhaps we could say 'lore'). If we were to experiment with Horton's model of religion, we would note that it is common for religious concepts to be used as part of an explanatory system, an 'abstract' (i.e. intangible, invisible etc.) mode of thought. Essential to this model is the existence of different 'levels' of analysis. This difference in levels appears in conjunction with explanations of different questions which might range from those requiring only fairly 'low-level' answers (why does salt dissolve in water when granite does not?) to those dealing with 'higher' levels of analysis (why does pure water not conduct electricity, while a solution of salt conducts extremely well?). Each level will have appropriate methods: so, to force granite to dissolve, one must theorise and develop solutions on an ionic level. To explain (or affect) conductivity of electricity, however, one must theorise and have an effect at a subatomic level.

The second major point advanced by Horton is that this hierarchy of levels is 'ascended' by trial and error; that is, one starts at the lowest point thought appropriate and proceeds to 'higher' levels until the methods appropriate to the current level solve the problem.[10] Failure is met not with despair and the outright rejection of the interpretative system, but with renewed efforts to discover the appropriate level of response. Though there are obviously enormous difficulties in using such a diffused and large-scale comparison, it does serve to provide a framework of understanding that might allow us to examine the evidence without coming to the conclusion that the Romans were somehow defective or deranged, or possessed of a totally different rationality from our own – the implicit position of many discussions. Horton's cautious comparisons with models of science as familiar thought systems allow us to consider that the different responses to what seem to be different levels of the *ira deum* are not necessarily mutually exclusive, although one may be more appropriate to a particular situation than another. There is a distinction made between what Horton calls 'primary' level analysis, which is based on the senses and everyday experience, and 'secondary' level analysis (which can be subdivided): this is where theoretical, as opposed to tangible, models are used. The further distinctions between secondary models are not so great as this initial difference. But the use of a theoretical model does not preclude the primary, sensory, model:

[10] Horton (1993a) esp. 208–210.

these models are subject to profound overlap yet theoretical integrity. A table can be described in sensory or molecular terms: the possibilities are many. Although these descriptions will each have theoretical integrity, they appear utterly different, indeed incompatible: the practical solutions based on these models will be equally dissimilar. Each is sufficient to explain the relevant properties or phenomena of a substance in its own right, though a 'deeper' analysis might be possible from another vantage point. Thus, one might say, somewhat irresponsibly, that at a certain level of analysis matter does not 'exist', or that the table is made up of more space than substance, which is a superficially reasonable, if ultimately flawed, assessment of the model of a table at a subatomic level. The violent clash between these statements and those based on sensory perception does nothing to undermine the various different levels of theory. While the different levels of analysis remain intact, their very existence is based on a search for greater control over the phenomenon or substance in question. There are points where the primary level, or the 'lower' secondary models, are insufficient. No matter what energy is expended at a level lower than what is required, a solution will not be found: there is greater power perceived only at a higher theoretical model. Sometimes it makes no difference how hard one hits the television; it is time for a technician.

This is what is going on when the Romans invoke the *decemuiri*, or send to Delphi: they are seeking analysis at a 'higher' level than is possible within normal resources. These 'higher' models do not exclude the 'lower' ones but they are likely to be more effective. In a sense none of these levels 'exists' in reality; they are abstractions and so only have any meaning (or even reality) in their application. They are invoked only when necessary and one 'drops back' to a lower level of explanation and response at the first opportunity. This comparison might well be a useful one for indicating the respective scope of the realms of gods and men. Horton suggests that where possible, 'primary' responses will be applied.

Consider three different reports of locust infestation: at Capua in 203 a huge crowd of the insects covered the entire district (*circa Capuam omnem agrum locustarum uis ingens, ita ut unde aduenissent parum constaret, compleuit*, 30.2.10); thirty-one years later there was a similar occurrence at the Pomptine marsh, which was also entirely covered (*Pomptinum omne uelut nubibus lucustarum coopertum*, 42.2.5). These two are both included in a more general list and subsequent expiation. We might venture that it is the scale of the infestation that defines both these as prodigial; the repetition of *omnis* and the mention in the former example that no one could decide where they had come from seem to underline the sense of the violation of the natural order: the senate accordingly accepted that the gods' anger was indicated. But in this case, there is an interesting opportunity for comparison. Shortly after the infestation of the Pomptine marsh, we hear of another cloud (*nubes*) of them appearing in Apulia, blown in from the sea: *lucustarum tantae nubes a mari repente in Apuliam inlatae sunt, ut examinibus suis agros late operirent* (42.10.7).

At first sight we might think that the suddenness (and therefore unpredictability) and scale (we lack the simplicity of *omnis*, but they are still spread *late*) would indicate the hand of the gods but this time there is no mention of any association with the divine; rather we are told of a tedious but very human solution – they were removed by hand (42.10.8). It follows so shortly after the case of the Pomptine marsh that it seems difficult to believe that there had been a general change of interpretation; but there is no indication that anyone thought that the gods were involved.[11] It is tempting to explore the three instances: if there is relatively little difference in reporting, then it may be that in the slight difference is all the interpretation we could ask for. While the prodigial visitations are both 'total', covering the entire district according to the report, Apulia is 'merely' heavily infested. Whereas the earlier invasion at Capua had no clear origin (and its sudden appearance seems to have been a factor in its being considered prodigial), the swarms at Apulia came from the sea. However it seems very difficult to assess with any conviction, since origin is not an issue for the Pomptine marsh.

The division seems clearer in another scenario: at 28.11.6-7, the extinction of the flame of Vesta was more frightening than a long list of prodigies, and the priestess was duly flogged by the *Pontifex Maximus*. But Livy reports in a very matter of fact way that it was not due to the wrath of the gods. Nonetheless, just to be sure, ceremonies to propitiate Vesta were performed.[12] Thus we encountered a human *error*, which seems to have satisfied the search for an explanation. Similarly, in infested Apulia, we have a human *solution* available. The locusts are within physical reach, even though the scale of the attack means that a huge crowd of men is required to deal with it. This seems to be the likeliest factor in deciding the response; the locust swarm is literally within reach in this case whereas before it was not.[13]

---

[11] It is possible that Livy wishes us to *assume* that this is a sign of the *ira deum*, since it is part of a series of domestic notices that follow the cruel punishment exacted on the Ligurians by Popillius: Levene (1993) 110 detects condemnation of Roman actions in the sequences following this episode. But this would be a break from Livy's normal style of reporting; not only is there no mention of any reporting procedure, there is no expiation.

[12] *id quamquam nihil portendentibus dis ceterum neglegentia humana acciderat, tamen et hostiis maioribus procurari et supplicationem ad Vestae haberi placuit.*

[13] At least, as Livy reports: but of course the prodigial swarms landed at some point just as the Apulian insects took to the air.

A second contingency we should expect is some kind of 'trial and error' ascent of the levels, where the initial response was found to be insufficient. When a chasm appeared in the Forum, the initial attempts to sort out the problem were practical and 'primary' (that is, physical). However the effort was unsuccessful. The Romans soon abandoned this and turned to the gods (7.6.1-3). The result is the famous self-sacrifice of Marcius Curtius: the *uates* say that 'the greatest strength of Rome' must be sacrificed (though they do not say say precisely what this is). Curtius declares that it is her youth, before hurling himself into the chasm on horseback.[14] The apparent inability to prescribe correctly on the part of the seers (*uates*) is not necessarily critical: rather, the story is framed in such a way to emphasise the courage and precocious genius (in understanding the riddle) of the young man.[15] The failure of the 'human' solution to a chasm does not preclude a 'natural' cause (*motus terrae*) as a vehicle of the gods' agency. Livy implies that the problem was solved (*post tanti prodigii procurationem...*) although we do not hear that the hole miraculously closed up, as we do in other sources.[16] The level of 'nature' (physical, tangible, human) was 'lower' than that of the divine.[17] The further distinction noted between the inevitable decrees of *fatum* and the negotiable mood of the gods, tentatively suggested above, seems validated by such moments as the aftermath of Decius' and Manlius' night-time apparition. This warned that one of them should perform a *deuotio*: they decided to attempt expiation (*auerruncandae deum irae*) and to follow the dream's instructions if the sacrifice gave confirmation (*si extis eadem quae somnio uisa fuerant portenderentur, alter uter consulum fata impleret*, 8.6.11). Failed propitiation of the gods 'proved' that the situation was indeed one that concerned the inevitable. Presumably faced with *just* these results in a sacrifice the consuls would have persisted in sacrificing to obtain the *pax deum* but in the circumstances this must have seemed rather unrealistic. The apparition was speaking precise Latin when it invoked *fata*.

The positing of differentiated 'levels' of analysis within what we would call 'religious' understanding leads us to expect certain features. Firstly one

---

[14] For a comparative study of this and other acts of self-sacrifice in antiquity, see Versnel (1981b); he points out that the horse is a repeated feature in Roman sources (146-152).

[15] We need not even assume priestly ignorance: the priests' silence might well be linked to embarrassment or tact. After all the declaration that a Roman aristocratic youth must sacrifice himself would create a very awkward scenario. They would have debated the interpretation long and hard if Curtius had not solved the problem.

[16] E.g. Varro L. L. 5.148 = Pocilius fr. 1P; Dionysius of Halicarnassus 14.11.5; Valerius Maximus 5.6.2; Zonaras 7.25. For these authors, the point of the story is precisely that the hole was filled as a result of Curtius' action. See Levene's (1993, 214) comparison of other sources.

[17] A similar 'ascent' of explanatory levels seems evident elsewhere, e.g. at 5.16.8, just before the arrival of the embassy to Delphi: *iamque Romani desperata ope humana fata et deos spectabant*.

would expect a repeated situation to be met with a predictable, almost automatic, response, as was the case with showers of stones for example.[18] Other situations would require a great deal more thought and experimentation before success was achieved. There might even be outright failures, such as seem to be indicated when Livy says of the plague at 7.2.3 that no help was forthcoming from god or man: this led to the institution of the *ludi scaenici* – a mistake, according to Livy. This does not suggest that the gods are insufficient or that their existence is questioned: Livy is not necessarily even implying that the competence of the priests who recommended the games[19] is particularly unreliable, just that the situation was extreme; perhaps extreme measures were called for, even experimental ones. In the broadest possible way we might compare the way that criticism, blame or responsibility is currently assigned (or not) to mechanics, doctors or scientists: it is accepted that there are limits to their expertise, and that at times there is nothing that they can do for a particular situation, however pressing the need or novel the experiment.

Secondly, according to Horton's model, the division between the human and the divine realms should not be a 'hard' distinction but a 'soft' one, of aptness rather than fact. Whatever conceptual framework is being used and however it is expressed, we would expect it to represent the same situation from a different perspective: invoking higher levels of theory with a view to finding a solution would be a question of the type of problem being faced. This can easily be made explicit in the text at times: consider a possible translation of our gold-nibbling rodents at 27.23.2 (*Cumis – adeo minimis etiam rebus praua religio inserit deos – mures in aede Iovis aurum rosisse*); 'At Cumae – to such an extent does incompetent religious interpretation *introduce* the gods even *into* minor matters – there was the report that mice had chewed the gold in the temple of Jupiter.' Livy's incompetents are trying to use a sledgehammer to crack a nut. Only the expert can reliably look beyond the ordinary and mundane to see beyond the ken of ordinary mortals. But it is a question of appropriateness, not of fact. Thus though there was a clear distinction between 'human' resources and 'divine' remedies, at the same time these realms were not utterly separate from one another. As a unified whole they represented a spectrum – a metaphor that can only represent one cross-sectional view of a system that might be more appropriately represented as three dimensional, with specialisation increasing along with scale.

---

[18] Which always prompt a *nouemdiale sacrum* in Livy. Champeaux (1996) 67 notes this and other examples.

[19] We should note that although the episode has the ring of formal procedures, no agent is mentioned, not even the senate. Thus the criticism is somewhat diffused.

In other words, a serious, 'high-level' problem might well have been tackled by any of the relevant priesthoods – the *pontifices*, the *haruspices*, or the *decemuiri*: the deciding factor might have been precedent in one case, or perhaps some more formal jurisdiction; or a more complex (even arbitrary) set of considerations. A premium would therefore have been placed on the ability to operate correctly this whole array of interpretative techniques, appreciating not just scale but also the appropriate areas of expertise. This interpretation was predominantly the responsibility of the senate who would then delegate each situation to the relevant priesthood: we have no idea of how a typical session would have actually gone, since the religious issues are so rarely handled by individuals. The naming of Fabius Maximus as the driving force behind the reference to the *decemuiri* at 22.9.8-9 is a rare case: it was this hero who saw the importance of a situation that, as it turned out, was beyond the resources even of Rome's most technical experts. But we have little sense of how the deeper realities of the Roman religious thought worlds were constructed, or even of the terms used. At best we can hope to identify features that seem to be persistently common and hope that there are not more criteria linking together our examples that a Roman would have thought so obvious that it would not have been worth articulating them.

This elucidation of the interpretative processes forces the reassessment of certain conclusions drawn about Roman religion: in the light of the amount of consideration (whether virtually automatic or protracted and de-tailed) that went on, the conclusion that religion was focussed on 'rite' to the exclusion of 'theory' cannot avoid being a value judgement. It might be that it was possible to have a sophisticated discussion using signifiers drawn from ritual practice, or precedent. 'Is this the sort of situation that calls for a *lectisternium*? Perhaps we should think in terms of a *nouemdiale sacrum*.' Would we call that 'rite' or 'theory'? For all we know, the enumeration of prodigies might well function as a profoundly meaningful theoretical 'code' that is wasted on us: to the educated Roman, Livy's prodigy lists would say something far more specific than some general sense that the gods were *placati* or *irati*. On the other hand they might be as cumulatively meaningful as a list of technical faults on a car: some would be serious enough to merit serious outlay on their own, others would only come to light or matter at all in connection with other faults. Perhaps they paint a coherent picture with consequences characteristic of one particular fault; perhaps they are simply a list of details irrelevant to one another. We have generally assumed that all prodigies were of a similar order: but the little we know of their ritual prescriptions imply strongly that they saw different levels of seriousness.

It therefore seems likely that the *res publica* could tolerate a minor disruption to the *pax deum* as the smooth operation of any machinery or organism can tolerate minor misfunctions, which explains Rome's survival of the occasional moments where prodigies are not noted or expiated.[20] Such suggestions can only be speculative but the experimental effort to gauge the emotional impact of prodigies and other events where the gods were deemed to be relevant is surely valuable, at least to highlight the range of possible options and to disturb the cosy assessments and presumptions that are more usefully associated with than paganism. All models of comparison remain utterly crude in the absence of detailed evidence and personal testimony, neither of which is much available and both of which would probably give us very different results from those we might expect. But in the light of their painstaking effort to assess any number of situations and ascertain the appropriate response, to say that 'all that mattered was the correct performance of rite' is true in one sense: but we might say that this observation is as inadequate as observing that the successful launch of a satellite depends on someone pushing the launch button at the right time. Ritual is, in some senses, the thin end of the wedge. The real work is the interpretative labour.

3.3 The agency of the gods

3.3.1 Introductory comments

A gratifying sense of subtlety is now discernible in Livy's explanatory process: the discussion now has a little colour, or at least some shades of grey. The distinction between 'human' and 'divine' levels is not so rigid as has been thought. It is a designated rather than a fixed category. So, for instance, one category which we are traditionally told by commentators is 'human' and therefore held up for praise or blame is *uirtus*: but at 38.48.7, Cn. Manlius, accused of trying to upset official negotiations with Antiochus by starting a war with the Gallograeci, informs L. Scipio that he prayed successfully that the gods grant him (Scipio) the same *felicitas* as his predecessor received, but also that he would have the same *uirtus*.[21] Apparently we cannot simply assign praise and blame purely to men even for their 'human' qualities. Diagnosing divine agency therefore becomes all the more difficult, since it is clear that we are dealing with a question of different perspectives rather than ontologically different categories. This should warn us that we need to clarify exactly which level we are dealing with at any given point: if there is 'overlap', then the realms are still constructed and

---

[20] As happens at 5.15.1, where of course the situation is ultimately resolved *fato* when the Albine lake is drained.

[21] Cf. Decius' prayer for the same at 10.24.16 on behalf of his colleague and himself.

described along different lines, each with its own theoretical and practical integrity. Some attempt should be made to identify the distinctive way that the gods were deemed to operate in the human world.

There are two principal areas in which the hand of the gods was diagnosed: in nature (that is, prodigies and unexpected events taken as omens); and in human activity (i.e. the explicit help of the gods, and the unfolding of events, especially in battle). Since the latter category is complicated by human action, which is often difficult for us to distinguish from the exertions of the gods, some initial points are best made in connection with the former category of prodigies and the like.

3.3.2 Nature and the gods

As we have seen, prodigies are usually defined as violations of natural law. As such they might appear to offer a useful door into Roman constructions of nature and cosmology. Unfortunately for us, it is a general feature of our various sources that there is little attempt to ascertain *why* a particular prodigy should have appeared: Roman practice, as we hear it in Livy, is corrective of interpretation or action rather than investigatory of causes. We know from Cicero's *On the Haruspical Response* that the priests might well offer causes as part of their diagnoses,[22] but Livy suppresses such details for the most part. With or without causes, perhaps a Roman would have replied to this point to the effect that religious life was full of the consequences of minor errors: prodigies (or more precisely, the *ira deum*) occur in the same way as weeds grow in gardens and it is less important to find out how they occurred than to act before things get any worse.

However useful such investigations would be for us, we do not have the benefit of them, even if they were undertaken, let alone recorded. But we do find reasoning in a number of cases that these events did not appear at random. Although a great number of prodigial events do not seem to us to have an explicable link with what was portended (why, for instance, should the draining of the Albine lake have led to the capture of Veii?) MacBain points out that often the details of the prodigies seem to function as a warning of a particular outcome expressed metaphorically.[23] Where reasonings *are* given they often make the prodigy intelligible to us in this

---

[22] The fragments of the original haruspical response, culled from Cicero's text, are collected in Beard North and Price (1998) II 7.4a.

[23] MacBain 122–124 (the majority of his examples include details taken from authors other than Livy). Cf. Tacitus *Annals* 15.47.1-3 and 15.7.2. Suetonius seems to be explicit on the interpretative process at *Vitellius* 9. We see a similar process much later, with Ammianus (e.g. 28.1.42). With reference to *Annals* 15.47.1-3 see Woodman (1997) 96 and Ash (1997) for discussion of the more general symbolism of 'heads'.

way: we are therefore justified in assuming that a link between the details of a prodigy, or omen, and its predicted outcome was evident to those trained in Roman religion, even if we are not told of these details and are not always in a position to follow their logic. Perhaps some portents were not particularly exposed to scrutiny, but it does not seem beyond the pale to posit that an interpretation was at least considered possible.

This is preferable to the alternative, that some portents 'made sense' to the Romans while others were simply not categorised or analysed. If this line of reasoning holds, then the particulars of disruptions of the *naturalis ordo* are not arbitrary, they reflect a 'deliberate' outcome. Furthermore, we should begin a discussion that will continue in the next section: in dealing with the gods (and therefore nature), there is no 'neutral state'.[24] The evidence that we have might lead one to think that nature is an independent witness to the anger of the gods, but we should note the corollary of the classification of certain phenomena as prodigial, i.e. that an undisturbed nature should not be taken for granted. The gods 'inform' *all* states of nature: the *naturalis ordo* is called the *pax deum* at a higher level of analysis. The alternative to *pax* is *ira*, and vice versa[25] and if one requires a religious interpretation, even *pax* can be emphasised as meaningful and causative. Thus the Romans habitually acknowledged the support of the gods – the *pax deum* – in cult: they were not only interested in problems.

This makes a difference to the way that we receive particular episodes affecting natural forces. For example, it gives a different slant on one notorious episode which is often cited as 'rationalistic': the famous prediction of C. Sulpicius Gallus of an eclipse before the crucial battle of Pydna. The military tribune gave the specific prediction that an eclipse would occur, specifying the time, and saying that it was part of the natural order of events (44.37.6-7).[26]

Gallus, with the consul's permission, addresses the men and predicts an eclipse: he explains that this is a natural occurrence and that they should not take it to be a portent. This does *not* mean that he has dispensed with the category of portents. If he did, then the consul failed to understand the message, as his subsequent sacrifices illustrate. Gallus expanded the

---

[24] *Natura* itself can of course be taken to be a divine force, and not just by 'full-blooded' philosophers: Pliny, for instance, taking a line only partially influenced by Stoicism, treats it as a divine force (Beagon (1992)); the discussion here is inadequate to the complexity of the issues.

[25] For the conclusion that all cosmological paradigms (including science) presuppose 'friendliness' or 'hostility' (but never neutrality) see Midgley (1992), esp. 107–115.

[26] Levene (1993) 119–120 notes a range of alternative versions emphasising Cicero *On The Republic* 1.24 and Valerius Maximus 8.11.1. His others are Quintilian (1.10.47); Pliny (*NH* 2.53); Frontinus (*Strategems* 1.12.8); Polybius (29.16.1-2); Plutarch (*Aemilius* 17.7-10); Justinus (33.1.7) and Zonaras (9.23).

understanding of the workings of the *naturalis ordo*, the reliable state of the cosmos under the benign influence of the gods at peace. By moving the boundary of the 'natural' back to include the eclipse, he has reassured the Romans that they should not take the eclipse to mean that they have lost the support of the gods. What he has *not* done is put forward an interpretation that does away with the gods or their interest in human affairs. He has only reclassified one phenomenon and this process should not surprise us in the least: indeed in a dynamic society such change are to be expected over time.[27] The next logical inference is that all events were 'deliberate' in this sense, including the blessings of *pax*. We should see this principle at work also in the realm of human activity.

3.3.3 The gods and men

The vast majority of notices concerning the gods and men make *both* responsible, which makes it difficult for us to be specific about any differences. We have already seen in discussing 'levels' that the choice between diagnosis of divine or human is more a question of emphasis than strictly demarcated relevance. However much the two are intertwined in practice, it is possible to distinguish different areas of responsibility.

To begin at the most general level of analysis, we can reasonably speculate that the gods were thought to be fundamentally benign: of the two possible states of the natural order, there are good reasons to think that if either state was considered 'normative', it was *pax*. The *benignitas deum* is alluded to frequently;[28] Zeuxis, appealing for generous terms of peace, calls on the Romans to 'lay aside contention with all men and be like the gods, the protectors and fosterers of the whole human race' (37.45.9); and they might indulge in mercy, albeit in a limited way, when their wrath is manifested or a human mistake is made.[29] Indeed, the very existence of the whole apparatus of religion implies that the gods are reasonable beings. When their *ira* has been manifested, there is a 'clean slate': we hear no more of the wrath that cost the consuls their lives at 27.33.11, for instance.

---

[27] Interestingly, Livy keeps religious awe in the frame as Gallus himself becomes the object of such a response, instead of the eclipse (*Romanis militibus Galli sapientia prope diuina uideri*, 44.37.8). The astronomer's knowledge was almost as inaccessible and remote as the event of the eclipse, and presumably only 'almost' because he was visibly mortal. The usual interpretation of an eclipse would be the fall of a king, which can only apply to Perseus. Finally, of course, Perseus' power *is* broken in the battle that ensues as is only 'natural', given the gods' support for Rome. For a more 'godless' interpretation see Lucretius 5.76-81 and 5.751-70.

[28] I note 5.20.3, 7.13.5, 8.4.6, 8.5.3, 8.13.11, 24.38.2, 26.41.6, 26.41.14, 28.11.8, 28.25.7, 29.15.1, 31.31.20, 37.54.10, 39.9.4, 41.24.8 and 45.23.1.

[29] In the episode of the deaths of Marcellus and Crispinus, (27.33.11), Livy ends with the notice that the gods diverted the consequences of their wrath to the consuls personally *miseritos nominis Romani*.

The gods might even be said to promote proper Roman behaviour towards themselves. During the Bacchanalia, the consul assures the assembly that it is the gods who deliberately exposed the cult's actions so that they could be punished and repressed (39.16.11). The consul is not speaking at odds with Livy's account, whereby the cult is brought to the attention of the senate by Aebutia, the aunt of the would-be initiand Aebutius.[30] The particular mechanism of the cult's 'discovery' is relatively unimportant to the diagnosis of divine agency: presumably it would have somehow come to the senate's attention anyway. The gods simply used a convenient vehicle for the inherent tendency to restore *pax*.

The intentionality of the gods is intrinsic to their nature, as they are constructed in Livy's account: for the historian evoking cult practice, they *are* a will that permeates all human existence, and their will has a 'plan' in so far as specific events are willed, often under the explicit aegis of *fatum*. Many other activities are more negotiable and good relations must be maintained at all times. Their 'actions' are not on an equal level to those of humans, who arrange physical resources or manage mental and emotional states; rather the 'actions' of the gods are the fulfilment of their will as the forces that underlie those resources or states. As they were thought to produce results consistent with their will in nature, so too they produce results in the human realm according to their mood. Livy puts it most succinctly at 1.39.4, when he speaks of the adoption of Servius Tullius[31] by Tanaquil and Lucumo: his education was easy because it was what the gods wanted (*euenit facile quod dis cordi esset...*, 1.39.4). The example is useful for us in that it does more than indicate the assumption that the situation had an 'inherent tendency', recognised as the will of the gods: it also serves to represent the human responsibilities of that situation, the provision of the means whereby the will of the gods might be fulfilled. There is another (rather vague) division of duty made at 2.46.6-7: after the fall of Q. Fabius, M. Fabius, the consul, accosts the retreating soldiers and reminds them of their vows, only to be told by Caeso Fabius not to harangue the troops to fight according to their vows, but that the gods will see to it. Their task was to lead by example (2.46.6-7).

Whatever the gods do for men, there is scope and responsibility for those men also: at 3.11.6 we hear of Caeso Quinctius who augmented the gods' gifts and applied them to the state's benefit. Caeso's gifts are explicitly the dispensation of the gods, since he had no part to play in his receiving them:

---

[30] 39.11f.
[31] For analysis of the legends about Tullius see Capdeville (1995) 7–40.

but his development of his potential is ascribed to his credit.[32] What the gods gave was a particular orientation of human resources.[33] Hannibal can similarly speak of the gods endowing Romans and Carthaginians with a particular (warlike) temperament[34] and can himself be told that the gods did not grant him everything: he knew how to win, but not what to do with victory (*'non omnia nimirum eidem di dedere. uincere scis, Hannibal; uictoria uti nescis'*, 22.51.4).

Though knowing how to use victory is designated a gift from the gods, in the criticism is the assumption that Hannibal could act on this deficiency. This argument runs counter to the normal line on the contrasting roles of gods and men: the usual conclusions drawn are that the role of the gods is maximised by writers to mitigate defeat and minimised to allow for the glorification of valorous Romans, as if religious interpretation could be so easily manipulated and still retain credibility. There is always scope for men to excel in the face of scarce gifts from the gods, to maximise already full assets (so Caeso) or squander their gifts (so Hannibal): this is inherent in the representation of responsibility. At times, the gods *are* 'blamed' for a defeat: but this implies a criticism of the human failure to procure the *pax deum* (as much a responsibility of a magistrate as his command of the army). Elsewhere, a bad general is named as such; there is no blanket policy to whitewash what Livy considers to be error.

Religious analysis was not primarily an attempt to produce an academic or abstract analysis: the articulation of any position is stimulated by the desire to provide *exempla*. In his conference with Zeuxis, Scipio asserts the appropriate Roman response to the favour of the gods, saying that of those things that are the gods' domain, they have what the gods have given: but their spirits (*animos*), which pertain to the human mind (*qui nostrae mentis sunt*) they have cultivated and not allowed success or setback to change (37.45.11-12).

Scipio's position marks out both the Romans and himself as prudent operators, and apparently leaves his audience with clearly defined responsibility. It does not, however, claim to be an exhaustive deduction on the respective roles of gods and men, for there are instances where the loss of

---

[32] Cf., amongst many other examples, Perseus' description of Macedonian resources as *omnia quae deorum indulgentia, quae regia cura praeparanda fuerint* at 42.52.13.

[33] This could be added or (presumably) squandered by pious or impious activity: when Q. Marcius Philippus is encouraging his troops before engaging Perseus, he reinforces that appropriate behaviour leads to an accumulation of divine favours (*'ea omnia quam diis quoque inuisa essent sensurum in exitu rerum suarum; fauere enim pietati fideique deos, per quae populus Romanus ad tantum fastigii uenerit'*, 44.1.10-11).

[34] *optimum quidem fuerat eam patribus nostris mentem datam ab dis esse, ut et uos Italiae et nos Africae imperio contenti essemus* (30.30.6).

perspective is itself specifically assigned to the agency of the gods. After the murder of Theoxena and Poris, who cursed Philip and his sons before their death, the king's son Perseus began plotting for the removal of his brother Demetrius: the curses, combined with others, quickly reached the gods, who drove him insane enough to plot fratricide (40.5.1).[35] Perseus suffers similarly later. When he might have crushed the Roman army, the gods robbed him of his wits (44.6.14).

The fact that it was thought possible for the gods to deprive the impious or erroneous of their wits would initially seem to run counter to Scipio's clear demarcation of responsibility, but this is not the case. Though Postumius says at 9.9.10 that the gods robbed the commanders of both sides of their wits, Scipio's advice still might have applied. In this case the time for prudence was not in the midst of battle, when the men and their generals were afflicted with an ominous stupor (9.2.10-15), but on the news of the defeat: the response of the senate is 'slanted as a whole so as to emphasise the Romans' acting freely to resolve their religious difficulties'.[36]

The defeat was the retribution for Roman impiety, as detailed by the Samnite Pontius in 9.1 (which Livy confirms at 9.2.1): but the renewal of the auspices under new consuls and the negotiation of the religious difficulties[37] is exactly the kind of conduct that Scipio was referring to. He is not separating 'attitude' (*animus*) from the influence of the gods, but exalting Roman institutions and *mores* that led them to address incidences of the *ira deum*, and his advice includes the propitiation of the gods in order that the Roman *animus* be free of adverse effects. In a practical sense it both influences and is influenced by the gods' mood, though in different ways. Though the gods affect *animus*, rites, whose instigation and proper performance depend on *animus*, affect gods. The modern desire for a cut-and-dried assignation of roles does not fare well with such subtly exemplificatory material: at every turn, we encounter parallel accounts and diagnoses that offer men opportunities to maximise the possibilities of the situation in which they find themselves rather than an objectifying and inflexible perspective.

In extremely rare circumstances, the gods are deemed to have intervened somewhat more specifically than usual: when Corvus is assisted by a raven in single combat against a formidable Gaul, Livy tells us that the gods interrupted, overshadowing the human aspect (7.26.2), but even then the Roman

---

[35] The plot comes to a head at 40.24 when Demetrius is poisoned. Philip dies 'more sick in mind than body' and haunted by the memory of his murdered son (40.56).

[36] Levene (1993) 228.

[37] 9.9.1-9 and 10.3.

must finish off the job. The gods must have an 'intermediary' to have their effect, whether it be natural forces (e.g. the storm that scuppered the Bastarnae at 40.58.3-7), animal[38] or human.

But such moments are rare and it is an error to rely solely on the gods, even when their favour is evident. In their prosecution of L. Verginius and M. Sergius, the tribunes of the plebs assert that the gods never avenge harms; they simply enable the injured to act on their own behalf (5.11.16). These two had effectively caused an unnecessary defeat at Veii through their rivalry and unwillingness to work together as commanders. When an attempt was made to remove them from their office, they stubbornly vetoed it but they were eventually compelled to resign. The following year, when the burdens of war were pressing hard, the tribunes of the plebs began to stir up sedition, which backfired in that popular ill-feeling began to threaten their own positions. In an attempt to deflect their increasing unpopularity, they launched a prosecution against Verginius and Sergius for their mismanagement of the previous year's campaign. The tribunes, after reminding the people that they had already been calling down the wrath of heaven on these men, called on them to act decisively: 'the gods themselves never lay hands themselves on the guilty – it is enough when they arm the injured with an opportunity for vengeance' (*nunquam deos ipsos admouere nocentibus manus; satis esse, si occasione ulciscendi laesos arment*, 5.11.16). Their audience agreed: the men were duly fined.[39]

Livy's gods are not those of Homer; they do not fight alongside the human combatants. But they do play a most active role, visible in the behaviour of the people concerned. Statements such as those of these prosecuting tribunes did not present a paradox or 'mere rhetoric', as they are sometimes received by modern readers. The vast majority of references to the gods do seem to intertwine the two realms and the ideal formula for success is voiced by King Tullus in his speech after his victory despite the betrayal of his Alban allies. He had reacted swiftly to the news with a vow to found the *Salii* and build temples to *Pallor* and *Pauor* then claimed that their treacherous retreat was part of a planned manoeuvre. His troops, spurred on rather than deterred, went on to defeat the Fidenates and Veientines. The king acknowledges the support of the gods before going on to explain the subterfuge that had just brought victory: his vows clearly assisted in the

---

[38] Corvus' raven is unique as an active assistant but a range of animals, from bees (e.g. 24.10.11) to wolves (e.g. 32.29.2), appear in prodigy lists acting strangely.

[39] Manlius offers a similar line of argument: in his revolutionary rage, he exhorts the plebs to support him, and warns them that he will be killed unless they intervene: they could appeal to the gods, but these would never come down from 'heaven' for his sake: though the plebs are saying that the gods will prevent it, it is *they* who must prevent it (6.18.9).

battle since the enemy fled in fear (1.28.4); he thanks first the gods then the undoubted courage of the Roman army.[40] Even such a dramatic and far-reaching ritual action as the *deuotio* of the elder Decius is not considered to be the single cause of the ensuing victory: Torquatus' generalship was such that victory was virtually guaranteed (8.10.8). Torquatus still had to navigate the various difficulties presented to him after the death of his colleague, and Livy's account does not attempt to distinguish between the authors of the exact details of the various elements of victory; but one wonders whether the army would have performed as it did in the narrative without Decius'*deuotio* of the enemy.

Livy is not preoccupied with demonstrating precisely how the gods intervened: he assumes a familiarity with the conjunction of human efforts towards the fulfilment of the gods' will and only very rarely will he specify where and how they intervened. The distinction was probably one that he would not have understood the need for, since it was 'obvious' both that the gods were in support of Rome, and that Torquatus had performed excellently. To distinguish the two is not an act of empirical investigation but is to look at the same event from a different angle. If we are to find evidence of the distinction between roles we must look elsewhere.

A practical distinction is drawn at 30.31.10, when the conference between Hannibal and Scipio breaks down. To the gods is granted jurisdiction over the outcome rather than the means – the question was to be decided by arms and whatever fortune the gods sent. Aemilius Paullus offers further refinement on the various spheres of responsibility when addressing his unruly troops: while the troops should attend to their fitness, their weapons and sufficient sustenance for unexpected orders. Everything else was the concern of the gods and the general who would orchestrate a good opportunity for battle (44.34.3-5).[41] The area left untouched by Aemilius' definitions of responsibility is the uncertain aspect of the outcome.[42] It was, then, not sufficient to fight, even with courage: one required the blessing of the gods to orchestrate events.

A similar claim is made when Marcus Servilius argues for a triumph on behalf of Aemilius Paullus: he emphasises that it is also a thanksgiving to the gods (45.39.12). That the Romans thanked the gods for the results of battle, while noting the efforts of their men as a means, is well known.

---

[40] Cf. the words of Romulus: '*urbes quoque, ut cetera, ex infimo nasci; dein, quas sua uirtus ac di iuuent, magnas opes sibi magnumque nomen facere; satis scire, origini Romanae et deos adfuisse et non defuturam uirtutem*' (1.9.3-4).

[41] The speech gains a very favourable, and effective, response (44.34.7).

[42] To add to the sustained argument on this point presented throughout these chapters, we might add the notice that *Mars communis et incertus belli euentus esset* (37.45.13).

But if one considers such issues as the courage shown by the troops or an individual as a *result* in itself, then that evokes an analysis that involves the gods: thus L. Scipio's *uirtus* could be sought in prayer as an end in itself, but would be something to praise *him* for when it was exhibited. This is no different from the way that the gods produced specific and meaningful results in nature when they sent prodigies: 'higher-level' explanations can provide very specific results. What is stressed is the joining of resources, the perfect co-operation (for the most part) of the realms of gods and men in fulfilling the destiny of Rome.

3.3.4 *Fors, fortuna* and *fatum*

Though Livy's account has generally been seen as a forum for 'proving' or 'disproving' the value of Roman religion, we can now say that Livy is not even considering such questions. For him, mastery of Roman religion was correct diagnosis of the varying factors in a given situation in order to produce an efficient and effective solution. There is little sign in Livy of any love of study of religious phenomena much beyond this need, little in the way of proactive theoretical debate or anticipation of future difficulties that might require solution: rather there is the reactive process of learning from experience and adding to the store of already existent knowledge.[43] In this interpretative system were a number of categories not yet examined – the interrelated terms *fors, fortuna* and *fatum*.[44] For the most part, scholarly discussion of these has usually assumed a complete dichotomy between *fors* (and often also *fortuna*) and the intervention of the gods, an overlap between *fortuna* (in another of its guises) and divine aid and a superiority of *fatum* over the gods' power to act.[45] Obviously if rigid differentiation of divine and human agency and responsibility is denied, then there are profound consequences for these conclusions. Discussions of these terms, and particularly *fortuna*, typically open with an emphasis on philosophical *tyche* and the 'influence' of Greek philosophy on Roman ideas.

---

[43] Consider the practical lore given concerning *deuotio* at 8.10.11-11.1: see also Linderski (1985); North (1990a) 66. The difference between this type of material and the antiquarian works of the late Republic is discussed by Beard North and Price (1998) I 153. For the records of the *pontifices* see North (1998) and for the introduction of new material during the Republic, North (2000).

[44] A fourth term, *felicitas*, is often considered in connection with these three. The understanding of this term in this chapter is consistent with that of Erkell (1952) 43–128, who establishes that *felicitas* is the continuing favour of the gods towards a particular individual; it is linked to moral rectitude and is used as a good prognosis of success (e.g. Cicero *On the Command of Pompey* 47); also Weinstock (1971) 112–114; Champeaux (1982–7) II 216–218.

[45] See e.g. Kajanto (1957) on 6.41.4f. and 7.6.9: 'It is obvious that Livy... stressed the fact that the consul's destruction was an *accident*, due to chance' (i.e. *forte*): on *fortuna*, see his 84, and on *fatum*, 53–63. Levene (1993) has two sections on 'fate and fortune', 13–15 and 30–33.

The widespread and multi-textual discussion of the impact of Greek ideas on Roman categories can barely be rehearsed here but it is worth considering to what extent the issue has been framed as an 'invasion' of Greek ideas, against which the Romans had little defence, save a resultant incompetence in using clear-cut categories. This analysis forces the scholar to enumerate a variety of categories within each of these terms – usually a mish-mash of 'older Roman ideas' and 'new Greek ideas'. It might be more useful, and almost certainly more historical, to speak of the Roman *appropriation* of these categories and a consequential sophistication of the range of implications.[46] This has the advantage of allowing for the possibility of a synthetic understanding of these concepts – a synthesis that can properly be called 'Roman'. Our task therefore is to consider whether they have any useful continuity of meaning and what place they have in a sophisticated system of analysis. A fresh discussion is also required in the light of the foregoing argument about the contingency of the roles of gods and men. *Fatum* must be located within an interpretative system, and the idea of a contrast between the agency of the gods and *fortuna* and *fors* must be re-examined.

3.3.4.1 Fatum

Fatum has often been central in arguments about Livy's 'Stoicism': for Walsh, there is a number of passages that imply a Stoic position;[47] for Kajanto, Liebeschuetz and Levene, this is overridden by the observation that the majority of the forty uses of the words *fatum*[48] and *fortuna* in Livy's extant text do not indicate peculiarly Stoic ideas and are 'more conventional'.[49] The usual strategy regarding those instances that do imply teleological outcomes is that Livy, by his use of *fatum* and *fortuna*, can steer a path through the twin, but partially contradictory, aims of demonstrating that 'Rome is bound to succeed, and Livy wishes to show this; but he also wishes to show that her success is due to the behaviour of her citizens. Consequently, scope has to be left for individuals to exhibit their virtues, and for the rise of Rome to be presented as the result of those virtues' (Levene (1993) 33). Aspects of this will undoubtedly appear, but in the way that it

---

[46] Feeney (1998) 26–27, 28–31 and 50–52 makes the same point with regard to religious rites and goes on to demonstrate the coherence of Roman practice, with a conspicuous incorporation of Greek-style rites to supplement Roman traditional rites. See also Scheid (1995). We might also note the integration of the Etruscan *haruspices* into Roman public ceremony and diagnosis (Beard North and Price (1998) I 20): Livy occasionally indicates their foreign origins (e.g. at 27.37.6).

[47] Walsh (1958) 53–55.

[48] The figure is that of Kajanto (1957) 63.

[49] The description is Levene's (1993, 31), who has a summary of the important bibliography. See also Liebeschuetz (1967) and Erkell (1952) 162–173.

is presented by Levene, and to a lesser extent Liebeschuetz, Livy appears somewhat cynical about his designations and quite willing to subvert the categories in order to make a political point. However, it is possible to argue the exact opposite: the invocation of *fatum* does not diminish other areas of responsibility for Livy. In fact it is *almost never* exonerative.

The use of *fatum* does not preclude any further analysis of responsibility, as a number of examples indicate: the delegation of the three violent (*praeferoces*) sons of M. Fabius Ambustus, who were instrumental in provoking the Gauls to attack Rome, was described as 'more like Gauls than Romans' (5.36.1).[50] Their bad tempers in the face of Gallic provocation are attributed to the pressing fate of Rome (*ibi iam urgentibus Romanam urbem fatis legati contra ius gentium arma capiunt*, 5.36.6.) Their behaviour remained reprehensible, but for Livy is only one of a complex of causes.[51] Nothing could be worse than the farcical defeat of the Romans at the Allia; it was more like pre-emptive surrender than a battle. It is difficult to see how Livy is avoiding criticism when, for example (and there are plenty from which to choose), he informs us that, amongst other vivid details of the astonishing Roman incompetence, Rome was far from ready for the rapidly approaching Gauls: the consular tribunes ignored all the usual military and religious considerations when they drew up for battle.[52]

The criticism that even the gods were neglected is especially striking when the ensuing narrative demonstrates how it was Roman piety that reversed the run of fortune.[53] There is a similar analysis of Cannae: the allocation of blame is so vivid that Levene finds that 'Varro's factionalism and recklessness lead to defeat, but they do so in a purely human way, and there is little indication of the influence of the divine – Cannae is seen essentially in human terms' (48). However, it would seem that Livy disagrees: at 22.43.9 he speaks of *urgente fato*. In the light of these examples (two crucial moments in Rome's history) the conclusion that the introduction of fate serves to avoid blame cannot be seen as a useful interpretative approach. Rather, it is an important part of the interpretative system as a whole.

The term *fatum* itself, as Kajanto shows, admits of a variety of appropriate translations (he offers 'a prediction', 'a person's lot, his (often predicted) fate' and 'even a synonym for *mors*', 54) but this does not mean that

---

[50] See further on this passage Luce (1971) esp. 269.

[51] Levene (1993) 184, 193–201 explores the various links with Camillus and the progress of the final fulfilment of Roman piety during the war with the Gauls.

[52] *ibi tribuni militum non loco castris ante capto, non praemunito uallo quo receptus esset, non deorum saltem si non hominum memores, nec auspicato nec litato, instruunt aciem, diductam in cornua ne circumueniri multitudine hostium possent* (5.38.1).

[53] Levene (1993) 194f.; Luce (1971) 275 and 277.

the Latin term was necessarily fragmented. These translations share the implication of inevitability, beyond even the reach of the gods.[54] *Fatum* is distinguished from the agency of the gods in a number of instances, as forming a force too potent to counteract. We have already met the example of Gracchus, who died despite his best (religious) efforts to expiate a prodigy: he could never succeed since *nulla tamen prouidentia fatum imminens moueri potuit* (25.16.4: see above, 71 and 88).

Similarly, the veterans of Cannae deploy the category of fate as distinct from that of the gods when pleading for indulgence at 25.6.6: if defeat was not due to the gods or fate, but men, should the soldiers or the generals be blamed? We know that the veterans are wrong (*urgente fato* 22.43.9) but they *are* arguing within the proper boundaries of Roman cosmology. In both examples there is a contrast between destiny and not just the works of men but also, apparently, the reach of the gods: it is in cases like this that scholars invoke Stoic ideas of *heimarmene*. But there is no need to go 'outside' Roman concepts to understand the term here. The mention of 'the gods' in these examples assumes the opportunity of affecting other outcomes, since the gods are approachable.

Fatum is therefore a level of interpretation distinct from the human and the (negotiable) divine: even the gods work within its strictures.[55] But it is important to recognise that it derives its meaning from the context of a fuller interpretative system. *Fatum* acts to preserve the integrity of the entire system: it allows for, and recognises, the occasional failure of the religious system to procure divine support (which can be equated with finding suitable explanations) or, conversely, the continuing success of Rome in the long term despite her occasional neglect of the *cultus deorum*. This latter aspect may well have featured more largely in the lost narrative dealing with the end of the republic, when Rome continued to expand and consolidate her empire, yet fell into chronic civil unrest and, ultimately, a political collapse. Thus, when fate is deemed responsible, it is the religious system of negotiation, if anything, which is off the hook rather than men who have failed to perform their duty.

This is not to say that *fatum* functioned purely as a disorganised residual category for the inexplicable: there is no evidence in the *AVC* that 'God

---

[54] Kajanto (1957) 60 n.1 cites 9.4.16 (*subeatur ergo ista, quantacumque est, indignitas et pareatur necessitati, quam ne di quidem superant*), where *necessitas* equals *fatum*.

[55] Rosenberger (1998) 245 is thus overstating the potency claimed for expiation when he speaks of the lack of 'fate' in the Republic ('das Fehlen eines unverrückbaren Schicksals'). It is however true that fate is invoked far less frequently in Livy than in Tacitus and Ammianus; though we can explore this in each author, whether their depiction reflects the understanding of the society at large is beyond our scope here.

works in mysterious ways'. *Fatum* could have its own intelligible plans, as both Livy's narrative, and his priests, indicate. The Sibylline Books contained predictions based on fate. There would be little point in documenting the inexplicable as predictable. The important point here is that expiation, normally the solution to the *ira deum*, is redundant when one is dealing with *fatum*. Irresistible fate, the most potent force of all, resided at an explanatory level 'above' the level of the gods, a cosmic will: we should therefore expect it to be invoked as an explanation only in specific circumstances. Just as the gods might be invoked when human efforts had been exhausted (cf. the incident of the *lacus Curtius*), so too might *fatum* become a useful candidate when all divine explanations had been attempted, and proved fruitless. This seems to be the case with the unfortunate Gracchus, despite his repeated attempts at sacrifice in keeping with the advice of the *haruspices* at 25.16.4 (above, 71 and 88).

The failure of religious resources might then function as *evidence* that *fatum* was involved, but not necessarily as proof, nor was it the only route to the diagnosis. *Fatum* might be sanctioned by expert interpretation, just as the activity of the gods might be discerned from the pattern of events. Only the highest authorities, such as the *decemuiri* (whose domain was the Sibylline Books of fate) or the Delphic oracle would therefore be in a position to introduce destiny appropriately since it was the most ponderous interpretation available. It remains a *deduction*, as is the gods' intervention, with its own particular criteria.

One of these appears to be repeating significant patterns, on a variety of scales. Scipio Africanus divines the workings of not just the gods but also *fatum*, telling his men that it is Roman destiny to suffer defeat before victory in all great wars[56] – but he is sufficiently cautious to include *quodam* as a qualifier, which mollifies his arrogance into extreme boldness, so to speak. When he confers on Africanus the almost unique title *fatalis dux* at 22.53.6, Livy seems to concur with Scipio's provisional assessment: the only other general to earn this title is another Roman, who also intervened in a 'fateful' war of initial reversal, this time against the Gauls. Camillus is so described at 5.19.2, after the draining of the Albine Lake, and therefore on the eve of the destined defeat of Veii. No other leader earns the title, just as no other campaign linked with *fatum* is effectively ended by one man.

Other long-term patterns attract the designation of *fatum*: P. Decius Mus embraces the *familiare fatum* and follows his father's example, devoting

---

[56] *ea fato quodam data nobis sors est, ut magnis omnibus bellis uicti uicerimus* (26.41.9).

himself in order to gain Roman victory (10.28.12-13).[57] So when Livy refers to *fatum* before the Allia (5.36.6) and Cannae (22.43.9) he is apparently drawing on Scipio's formula:[58] there is no other explanation than that this pattern of failure followed by success seems to be typical of Roman fortunes, despite the efforts of commanders both at the altar and in the field. Religion (and indeed history) offered no other explanatory strategy for this turn of events since mention of the gods always includes the possibility of propitiation. Scipio is perfectly suited to act as a mouthpiece: unafraid of the excess of such a drastic and far-reaching conclusion, he commands respect for his success, whatever hesitations Livy has about his manner.

Generals other than Scipio make particular deductions about fate on a relatively small scale, as Decius did, but the *priests* only invoke fate where there is a positive outcome for Rome. Little wonder, seeing that their credibility and their function depended on their abilities to avert forewarned disaster: they might have the proper authority to speak of Rome's fate, but to do so negatively would not be to their credit. In the face of any difficulties they must always attempt propitiation. If they were to conclude that the hand of fate was present in setbacks it would be tantamount to resignation.[59]

Even more, perhaps, than the diagnosis of divine support or wrath, *fatum* was to be treated with respect, not simply because one could 'get the facts wrong'. It is not that *fatum* is not a *possible* diagnosis in a situation where it is avoided, but that, in a way similar to the tendency to adopt the 'lowest' viable explanation on a scale of interpretations, it does not always *need* to be introduced. If Livy 'believed' that to each was allotted a particular span and type of life, he does not bother to make it especially prominent. Death is the final and most self-evident unchangeable reality of human existence, and thus deserves the designation of *fatum*: but its reliability in some senses liberates Livy from mentioning it at every turn. It follows that, in keeping with the principles adopted for the discussion of the workings of the gods, there will be moments where explicit mention of *fatum* is more appropriate than others.

Consider the abundance of religious errors in connection with the death of the consul Q. Petilius Spurinus. When he dies at Letum, Livy adduces a number of explanations from different sources: firstly we learn that his vow to capture Letum that day provided an ominous pun (*se eo die Letum*

---

[57] Cf. 31.48.12 or Livy's verdict on the Claudii at 9.33.3: *cum ex ea familia,* † *quae uelut fatales cum tribunis ac plebe erat,* † *certamen oritur.*

[58] For the close relationship of Scipio with the narrator at this point, see Feldherr (1998) 71–72.

[59] The appropriate domain of the *decemuiri* is fate, given that they consulted the *libri fatales*: but the old man of Veii, alone of the various *haruspices* through Livy's extant ages, also spoke of the *fata* (5.16.10).

capturum esse, 41.18.11). He was granted his wish, meeting death (*letum*). He had also failed to obtain favourable signs for *Salus* at 41.15.4, and his colleague Gnaeus Cornelius, who also died in office, had reported a strange problem with a disappearing liver after sacrificing the *sescenaris* ox (41.15.1). We can add that Petilius proceeded to battle despite unfavourable omens from the sacred chickens (41.18.14). This was revealed later, as was the mistake in the ritual for drawing lots between himself and his new colleague Valerius (41.18.8). Petilius is also described as careless (*incautius*, 41.18.11), which seems to suggest human error, at the moment of his death. Even if we discount the sign offered by the chickens as simply a warning that all was not well (which we knew anyway), we are left with three religious 'causes': the *ira* of *Salus*, stepping outside the *templum* and the prediction of *letum capiendum*. Yet Livy does not, despite the multitude of errors and the ill-omen of the intransigence of *Salus*, invoke *fatum*.

In contrast the consuls Gracchus and Marcellus, who have each already appeared here more than once, died because of *both* the *ira deum* and *fatum*. It is therefore worthwhile speculating as to whether there are specific features characterising episodes designated to be the outcome of *fatum* rather than any other agency.

One possible reason for the *absence* of *fatum* in the case of Petilius is that specific agency is available. The clear identification of *Salus* as the 'cause' in the matter ends the search for explanation: there is no need to involve any 'higher' explanation. If pressed, perhaps Livy would have offered that it was Petilius' fate to die at this point; certainly, an individual's death elsewhere is linked with *fatum*. Gracchus is the example already introduced, and though he was forewarned, he was unable to avoid his death. In Gracchus' case alone is fate depicted as so potent that there is no contingent explanation. One difference is that the others' errors could be attributed to a specific cause, while Gracchus seems to have committed none: rather he adopted the proper course of action, the repeated effort to propitiate the gods. The statement that no foreknowledge could change *fatum imminens* (25.16.4) is an affirmation by the author that his subject (and his attendant *haruspices*) had done all that he could: since he had performed his rites, the only remaining explanation was that of fate.

Gracchus was warned by the gods of his impending death through ritual (above, 71, 88 and 108): but the case of Marcellus is more complex. Apart from the range of divine and human factors invoked to explain his death, his fall is also linked with *fatum*. When there is the exchange of provinces that sent Marcellus to Sicily to meet Hannibal for the last time, Livy speaks of his *rapiens fatum* that conspired to have him, the first general to defeat Hannibal, to be also the last to die against him (26.29.9-10). Yet when

Marcellus actually dies, this is attributed to the gods, who diverted their prodigial wrath to the consuls and spared the state.[60]

Livy does not use *fatum* elsewhere of the consul's lot, though there are always plenty of causative principles at play. Here then, in particular, is the pathos of such an innocent decision to evoke pity for the brave consul.

There is a further dimension however: Hannibal's fearsome reputation is itself *already* linked with *fatum*. During a dream, the Carthaginian general disobeyed the instruction not to look behind him: he saw an enormous serpent causing devastation and was told that it symbolised the destruction of Italy, and that he was to proceed without further questions to fulfil his destiny (21.22.8-9).[61] The perennial niceties of interpretation will soon engulf the Carthaginian, since the dream says nothing of victory, only of the devastation of Italy. The outcome of the Punic War is, in a broad sense, destined: there is more than the simple motif of piety/success, impiety/failure and Marcellus is caught up in these inexorable events by the exchanging of provinces.

The evocation of *fatum* is not intended to replace the religious explanations for his difficulties, which are sufficient at their own level. *Fatum* rather represents a change of perspective from the particular to the broadest possible viewpoint and it is sanctioned not only by the invocation of destiny in Hannibal's dream but also by Scipio's formula of initial setback/eventual victory. By the repeated use of *fatum*, the historian reveals his knowledge, provided by hindsight, and links the approaching fall of Marcellus to Hannibal's dream. He does this by making explicit what the dream prescribed as secret, that is, the true pattern of Hannibal's fate – to gain a reputation as distinguished as could be hoped for, but short of the status of being the conqueror of Rome. This is made as complete as ever by his victory over all, including the man who first turned the tide by defeating him. Only the *fatalis dux*, Scipio, could stand against him and he was almost superhuman in his own right. Perhaps Marcellus had avoidably blundered into a pattern prescribed by fate; perhaps if Hannibal himself had been less ambitious and remained in Africa, neither would have found their lives entwined by the prescriptions of destiny: but once caught up, they could only play out the almost anonymous roles allotted to them.

We might say that references to fate will tend to accumulate, since once a run of events has been linked with destiny, any aspect of those events is potentially meaningful to that scheme. Thus *fatum* is used repeatedly in con-

---

[60] Above, 44, 46 and 99.

[61] On the differences between Livy's and Coelius' versions (fr. 11 P) of this episode see Pelling (1997) 202–204.

nection with the Punic War, the war with the Gauls and the campaign against Veii, of which the first two are linked to Scipio's scheme of initial defeat and final victory and the last to the fulfilment of an ancient prophecy.[62] Otherwise it is employed rarely, especially in connection with war. Though it might have been possible, if it had been necessary, to incorporate other events into the scheme of destiny, *fatum* is usually too ponderous an explanation to be required. The death of Petilius, compared above (71, 88, 108 and 111) with that of Marcellus and Gracchus, does not belong within such a grand scheme in any meaningful sense, and thus does not merit the *explicit* assignation to fate. It would not necessarily be wrong but neither would it be appropriate or necessary.

One category remains: it is commonly said that *fatum* often 'simply' means 'death'. Though this is true of the fact, it does not reflect the rhetoric involved. A few examples clearly illustrate the variety, and the subtlety, of Livy's usage. At 3.50.8, Verginius, who had just murdered his daughter to prevent her seizure by Appius, contrasts the (presumably natural) death (*fatum*) of his wife with his daughter's death, which was honourable, if unwelcome (*miseram sed honestam mortem*). Verginius is drawing a powerful contrast between the inevitable death (*fatum*) of his wife, which is not described or dated (she is spoken of in the pluperfect at 3.44.3), and the *unnecessary* death of his daughter: he could not save her life, but he did protect her honour. To see *fatum* as a 'simple alternative' to *mors* entirely misses the point of the passage.[63] The death of Philip of Macedon is twice referred to as *fatum* (42.11.5; 41.52.7, and both times with *oppressum*). Each time it is by his son Perseus, and each time it resonates with the reader who remembers Livy's own version at 40.54.1, where he says that Philip was consumed by old age and grief at the death of his son. Demetrius' death was of course engineered by Perseus, driven insane by the gods, whose use of *fatum* in Livy's account underlines his hypocrisy: his brother's (and therefore his father's) death was far from natural.

Such are Livy's strategies in mentioning *fatum*. The rhetorical power of destiny, which stems from its potency and relation to other diagnoses,

[62] According to the Old Man, both the *libri fatales* and the *scientia* of the Etruscans say that victory for the Romans was guaranteed by the draining of the lake, 5.15.11; Delphi concurs. The lack of room for manoeuvre combines with the aspect of prediction to make *fatum* an unavoidable diagnosis.

[63] Decius' death, called *fatum* by the *Pontifex Maximus* Livius, is equally more potent than *mors* would have been at 10.29.3, since it evokes the sense of destiny: just as the consul has 'given away' his life, so too will the Romans conquer the equally doomed Gauls and Samnites. Loesius, last leader of Capua, speaks of *fatum* as death at 26.13.17, but this is because he has asked for those of his colleagues who have chosen to accept death to join him: the word has the chill acquiescence in the inevitable, as it does at 5.40.3.

should not be underestimated, but it should not be concluded, as Kajanto (1957) and Levene so often do, that it 'only' has a 'literary' function, for this depends for its meaning on a sharp division between 'real life' and the realm of 'the aesthetic'. To explain, to give an interpretation, *is* a rhetorical and agonistic venture but it is the evocative process of convincing that is the competitive aspect: any poverty of meaning or superabundance of diagnosis in dealing with words like *fatum* would reveal Livy to be a charlatan. In fact he uses it with great discretion for a number of purposes: as an explanation largely within the bounds of religion (as with Gracchus), for rhetorical effect, but also, and most tellingly, to make sense of grand sweeps of history. In the last case, especially, he acts with great discretion. There is no clumsy statement that fate dictated this or that pattern; rather the human domain remains the arena for action, and the gods and fate as the context in which they operate. Their activities are consistently deduced, and all the dynamics of such interpretation are visibly present. Livy can accordingly operate his narrative at three relatively independent levels, each with their proper mode of action. As a historical explanation for the various tides of history, this makes for an eminently satisfying account, reflecting a much richer fabric of explanation than is possible with simple formulae such as piety/success.

It might be objected that Livy's use of *fatum* undermines his exemplary and religious agenda. After all, if one cannot alter the future, why learn from the great Romans of the past, or propitiate the gods? Livy's text never supports a position remotely like this. Not even his characters adopt this position. In fact, excepting the deaths of individuals, it is very rare that *fatum* is invoked to explain details. More importantly, virtually no character in the *AVC* encounters fate *knowingly*: diagnosing fate is easier with hindsight, easier even than the mood of the gods, since only later can it be known that all attempts to avoid the outcome failed: even then it is rarely necessary or appropriate. The discretion with which *fatum* is deployed is as much a lesson as any other aspect of the text: this is not a category to be invoked too easily. Essentially, therefore, Livy's recommended position can be put without excessive simplification as 'even if it might be *fatum*, try anyway'.

Fatum represents the end of analysis – there is no 'higher' explanation: but it is not simply a term for the inevitable. It is an understatement to say that *fatum* evokes a cosmic will, a grandeur whose dispensation raises Rome above all her rivals. It guarantees the grand sweep of the narrative but does not necessarily determine just how all the details will be played out. Would Rome succeed in harmony, or in crisis? How close to the edge could her fortunes go? That the fates had been safeguarding Rome and planned for her success right from the start was, in a sense, a foregone conclusion, since she had indeed succeeded. But any possibility that Rome owed her position just to a succession of great leaders, or *fortuna*, is forestalled. Paradoxically, it may be that we should invert the traditional formula and claim that Livy worked to find room in Rome's illustrious past for the role of fate, as the capstone of her position in the ancient world.

3.3.4.2 Fors

If *fatum* is at one end of the scale of predetermination, then *fors* is normally taken to be at the opposite end. It is too common to be ignored: though *fors* as a nominative agent appears relatively rarely (Kajanto (1957) offers a count of 16), the ablative *forte* occurs at least 197 times.[64] It requires brief attention here since it is often used as evidence of Livy's scepticism. The usual assumption adopted (excepting Champeaux) is that *fors* indicates a random event *in contrast* to divinely ordered or humanly anticipated events. In modern analysis it corresponds roughly to an intervention that owes nothing to the situation into which it intrudes, yet such a scenario is difficult to reconcile with the image thus far deduced about ancient thinking. For the Romans, a situation was subject to an irresistible propensity towards a particular outcome. As such, we might expect that a 'chance' (i.e. unexpected) event would be drawn ineluctably into that propensity. In a world where results were attributed to the *pax* or the *ira deum*, there seems little scope for utter randomness.

Armed with these considerations, it is possible to examine representative examples. The first of these is the first instance of *forte* in Livy: when Amulius orders the drowning of the infants Romulus and Remus, they are saved by 'some divinely sent chance' (*forte quadam diuinitus*, 1.4.4) when the flooded waters of the Tiber prevent them from being deposited in the river proper. Left in the marshy overflows to drown, they survive. In due course the waters retreat and the boys are left to be found by the she-wolf and Faustulus. The divine intervention is strengthened by Livy's introduction to the story of their conception and birth: he considers (*ut opinor*) that the fates had already decreed the origin and imperial destiny of the city (1.4.1).

The somewhat (deliberately) evasive *forte quadam* reappears, equally unambiguously, at 5.49.1, when the remaining Romans are about to capitulate to the Gauls and ransom the city: the gods did not leave them to live in a state of purchased freedom – the dictator 'happened to arrive', and duly intervened.[65] Thus our tentative assumptions seem confirmed: it is perfectly

---

[64] Kajanto (1957) 76; 197 is Champeaux's (1967) 363 figure.

[65] The importance of the timing, indicated by *forte*, should not be understated: it is the difference between Rome at war and Rome defeated; see Feldherr (1998) 78–81.

possible to have the overlap of divine and 'chance' events. In these two examples both the will of the gods and details ascribed to *forte* coexist.

There is no theoretical reason why a notion of randomness should not co-exist with a complex theory of causation. Indeed the very existence of such a category implies that other aspects were predictable: for instance a broad economic theory might 'explain' why a number of people lost their homes after a rise in the basic rate of interest, but would not define the precise details of each individual case. Or, in a scientific paradigm, the certainty that a particular chemical reaction would take place at a particular rate with a particular result would *not* dictate which particular molecules would react with which and when, even though the time for the whole reaction would be fairly easy to predict. Nonetheless the overall results would be predictable by the theoretical models.

In fact, in these cases, the category of 'chance' is simply a result of forming an interpretative strategy which will represent a particular focus. Anything that falls below that focus is, by definition, a 'chance' event. Thus it is a necessary dismissal of the details: the theory would be unworkable if it attempted to take into consideration all events on a smaller scale. Details might remain perfectly explicable, given a closer focus; but a different set of theories and observations will be part of an answer to these more particular questions.

It actually makes no difference to the category of *fors* whether events are explicitly designated as unfolding according to a divine plan, or are simply those coincidences that occur without any given reason: it always indicates a particular detail, more or less unexpected, that is, a *part* of a chain of events. Ultimately it is a way of drawing the readers' attention to a specific event, of structuring the narrative to indicate an unexpected or new factor. It denotes the human perspective of the unfolding of events and is only relevant to the workings of the divine in so far as the category represents those details that are left to decide themselves, given that greater forces are at play which will decide outcomes in broad terms. In short, there is no polarity between *fors* and the gods, no claim to divine agency (though that might be elsewhere) and certainly no denial of the gods' interest.

3.3.4.3 Fortuna

Fortuna, linguistically an extension of *fors*, is a comparable but distinct entity from its parent. Like its cognate it is linked to events on a human level but, unlike *fors*, is also the name of a prominent deity, or rather a variety of deities.[66] Whereas *fors* designates the unexpected juncture of a specific

---

[66] With the exception of the joint temple *Fors Fortuna*, founded at 10.46.14.

event upon an already existing situation and does not particularly attempt to analyse the causes of that event, *fortuna* is constructed as a more wilful entity 'governing' events in a more general way. *Fors* specifies the coincidence of individual details: *fortuna* is an agent in a more nebulous and circumscribed manner. Nonetheless they share the aspect of a related perspective: both predominantly seek not to explain the workings of heaven but rather *to evoke the human perspective*. Just as *fors* could easily overlap with the workings of fate or the more negotiable will of the gods, so *fortuna* can also represent these workings without claiming a *distinct* jurisdiction. The number of occurrences of *fortuna* (Kajanto (1957) 64 counts 493), excluding mentions of actual recipients of cult) necessitates some general discussion of these frequent examples in Livy's text in some schematised fashion.

Levene offers the conclusion that 'we may accept Kajanto's account: that Livy uses it to mean "luck" or "chance" when he wishes to draw attention to the incalculable, the unpredictable element, especially in battles, over which humans have no control; in this way he can explain mistakes, or else can emphasise Roman *uirtus* by showing that it was superior to *fortuna*... but such an idea ... would have the unwanted effect of diminishing Roman victories. Hence Livy uses it also to mean something like "providence", and here it is used above all to emphasise the divine protection of the city.'[67]

There are problems, both methodologically and textually, with such a position. Firstly, the 'unpredictable element' of battle and other endeavours is precisely that area over which the gods are conceived to have jurisdiction: thus the implications of the modern categories of 'luck' or 'chance' are at best misleading. Secondly, if the intrusion of *fortuna* as a causal agent in the narrative runs the risk of diminishing Roman *uirtus* in success, what are we to make of the dedications of temples to *Fortuna* during or after battle? We have already noted Fulvius Flaccus' vow to build a temple to *Fortuna Equestris* (40.40.10) and Sempronius' vow to *Fortuna Primigeneia* (29.36.8): if we are to follow Levene and Kajanto then the Romans themselves were happy to abandon *any* claim to praise that might have been forthcoming for their victories. Such modesty would be most uncharacteristic and also leaves Kajanto's hypothesis without any support from Livy's agents. Nor does Livy himself shrink from naming *fortuna* as an agent in a Roman victory: to say that it is deployed to maximise credit to Roman virtue simply does not correspond with the text. Thirdly, the conjunction of the ever-successful *fortuna populi Romani*[68] with the suggestion that Roman

[67] Levene (1993) 33, citing Kajanto (1957) 82–84 and 90–91.
[68] Kajanto (1957) 65–67.

uirtus is to be praised over the 'whims of fortune' is also paradoxical, if not downright contradictory. In fact, *fortuna* only makes sense when understood relative to the jurisdiction of the gods.

3.3.4.4 Fortuna and the gods

That *fortuna* is linked with the divine is evident from a number of angles: firstly, because she *is* a goddess and it is far from clear that the Roman reader distinguished what we would call *fortuna* from *Fortuna*.[69] There are reasons to think that she could be construed as a deity in action. In one case, *fortuna* is said have saved the city immediately following the dedication of a temple to her as *Fortuna Muliebris*: when the Volsci and the Aequi join forces and invade Roman territory, they fall out over leadership and end up fighting one another. Livy offers that the *fortuna populi Romani* destroyed both armies (2.40.13).

Furthermore, *Fortuna* receives ritual attention, appropriately enough, after the shrinking of the lots at Caere (21.62.8). We also find that, as is consistent with the juxtaposition of the respective realms of gods and men, human values are placed in apposition to *fortuna*.[70] In the absence of proper human resources, the *fortuna populi Romani* is sometimes sufficient to protect Rome at 2.40.13. At another point any distinction between *fortuna* and the gods is blurred: when a plague leaves Rome undefended, the gods and the *fortuna* of the city conspired to keep her safe (*di praesides ac fortuna urbis tutata est, quae Volscis Aequisque praedonum potius mentem quam hostium dedit*, 3.7.1). It even seems that *fortuna* and the *di praesides* are contingent: the singular verb is not conclusive but the feminine *quae*, if we can make anything of a fairly normal grammatical construction, designates *fortuna* as the dominant grammatical subject.[71]

There are further examples where *fortuna* seems to represent the enactment of the gods' will: the Gauls, having fatefully taken Rome so easily,

---

[69] At 2.40.12 a temple is dedicated to *Fortuna Muliebris*; we also hear of the temple of *Fors Fortuna*, dedicated by Servius Tullius, at 10.46.14; there is a *supplicatio* to *Fortuna* on Algidus at 21.62.8; Sempronius vows a temple to *Fortuna Primigeneia* at 29.36.8; a temple of *Fortuna* without epithet is mentioned at 33.27.4; Fulvius Flaccus offers a temple to *Fortuna Equestris* at 40.40.10. On the broader problems of capitalising abstract deities, see Feeney (1998) 88: 'thinking about the difference between *Pax* and *pax* is not easy, but it would appear to be a good deal easier than thinking about the difference between *PAX* and *PAX*'.

[70] E.g. especially with *uirtus*: *in eo bello et uirtus et fortuna enituit Tulli* (1.42.3); Fabius Maximus is said to have left the Roman army *minus iam tandem aut uirtutis aut fortunae paenitere suae* (22.12.10). Cf. also 7.30.8, 7.34.6, 9.17.3 (where the *ingenium imperatorum* is also mentioned), 23.42.4, 25.24.13, 26.41.9; at 35.42.8 we find *ingenium* in place of *uirtus*.

[71] Cf. the situation in a war against the Gauls where, under the pretext of religious restrictions, the Gauls launch an ambush but *fortuna* defends the Romans from the breach of trust: *successisset fraudi ni pro iure gentium, cuius uiolandi consilium initum erat, stetisset fortuna* (38.25.8).

send troops to Ardea, where, thanks to *fortuna*, they will meet true Roman courage in the form of the exiled Camillus (5.43.6). This would seem to be in keeping with the workings of *fatum*, whereby Rome, in the event of a major war, would reverse initial setbacks.[72] But the gulf between modern and ancient interpretations is obvious in the way that *fortuna* was thought to be at least relatively predictable from its recent record: Philip of Macedon decided to go with Hannibal's cause on these grounds (23.33.4). All the evidence seemed to suggest that the gods were with the Carthaginian; they happened not to be with Philip in the same way.

Fortuna is not, however, always favourable. At 23.24.6 *fortuna* adds to Rome's miseries with the loss of Postumius and his legions: indeed, one of *fortuna*'s traditional characteristics was the unexpected reversal, spectacularly in the cases of Camillus (*uere uir unicus in omni fortuna*, 7.1.9) and Aemilius Paullus, whose success in war was matched by his misfortune at home. He specifically attributes the loss of his two sons to the workings of an envious *fortuna* (45.41.8-12). Aemilius would have us believe (and he was in good company in antiquity) that inherent in *fortuna*'s gifts is the dispensation of failure or loss after a run of success. He was wise enough to foresee this, and hoped that *fortuna* would divert the outcome from the public stage of his successes to his private life.[73] Again, this does not separate the approachable gods from *fortuna*, for when Hannibal shrewdly advises Scipio to beware his good fortune, and not to despise the Carthaginian's offer of peace, he attributes his own reversal at one time to *fortuna* and at another to the jealousy of the gods.[74] In terms of interpretative structure the jealousy of the gods and the mutability of *fortuna* seem to occupy the same category.

What characterises *fortuna* perhaps more than anything else is its unpredictability: the phrase *uaria fortuna*, indicating gains for both sides at different times, occurs at least nine times[75] and often *fortuna* is characterised as capricious or at least unpredictable. However it does not represent

---

[72] 5.37.1-3 – the prelude to the disaster of the Allia – seems to be in the same mould but it is *fortuna* who manifests the gods' will: *cum tanta moles mali instaret – adeo occaecat animos fortuna, ubi uim suam ingruentem refringi non uolt –…nihil extraordinarii imperii aut auxilii quaesiuit.*

[73] Compare the way that the gods diverted the consequences of ritual error to Marcellus and Crispinus, 27.33.11.

[74] 30.30.5, and 4 and 26, respectively. He also attributes the outcome of war to *fatum* (30.30.3). The entire speech is an illustration of the way that *fortuna* will be mentioned to underline the uncertainty of future events (to humans at least), *fatum* to indicate the unchangeable and that it is the gods who dispense the course of events.

[75] I note 2.60.4, 6.25.4, 21.1.2, 22.29.7, 28.12.3, 29.29.5, 29.29.9, 33.37.1 and 40.40.1. There is also the combination of *fortuna* with *uario* at 9.18.11, 10.29.7, 23.5.9 and 23.13.4; the phrase *aduersa fortuna* is used at 3.58.4, 9.18.12 and 33.4.4. Another variation of the wording is found at 2.6.10 (*ibi uaria uictoria et uelut aequo Marte pugnatum est*).

some idea that life is *totally* unpredictable; trends can be discerned, at least broadly. *Fortuna* operates in the same sphere as the gods and in a similar fashion, influencing the various factors that govern the outcome either for or against the protagonists. In a radical sense it indicates 'the situation that occurs' (where *fors* will tend to mean 'the *thing* that occurs'), a particularly colourless phrase in English but one loaded with implications in a Roman setting: there is no modern correlative for *fortuna* in the sense that it is impossible to convey its fuller implications. Like *fors* and *fatum*, it draws attention to events, assigning them to a distinct category: *fors* refers to the particular, *fatum* to the inevitable and *fortuna* to the situation as immediately presented, with all its inherent tendencies. Essentially, *fortuna*'s emphasis is on the human perspective. Thus *fortuna* can refer to the workings of divine favour or displeasure, but what is conveyed by its use would seem to be that a situation 'as is' is represented as 'caused' by *fortuna*.

One extended example will illustrate this: when the Roman army is cut off by the Samnites, P. Decius, a military tribune, offers to take control of an overhang, saying that either the *fortuna* of the Roman people, or their own courage, would grant them success (example (i): *nos deinde aut fortuna populi Romani aut nostra uirtus expediet*, 7.34.6). Having done so he is said to have 'seized the *moment of advantage* for action' ((ii): *fortunam gerendae rei eripuerant*, 7.34.10). When they are surrounded he tells his troops that the Samnites have missed the *opportunity* to destroy the army as a whole ((iii): *delendi omnis exercitus fortuna...usus non sit*, 7.35.5). He plans their escape and exhorts them: '*fortuna* has left us nothing but our swords and courage ((iv): *cum praeter arma et animos armorum memores nihil uobis fortuna reliqui fecerit*, 7.35.8). Shortly afterwards he ends with the appeal, 'You have followed me so far, follow me still, while I follow the same *fortuna* which has brought us here ((v): *me modo sequimini, quem secuti estis; ego eandem quae duxit huc sequar fortunam*, 7.35.12). On his successful return to camp, Decius is praised highly and proceeds to sacrifice an ox to Mars (7.37.3).

Fortuna cannot be represented consistently in English in this episode: we must render it '(tutelary) *fortuna*' (i), 'tide of circumstance' (ii), 'opportunity' (iii), 'circumstances' (iv) and, for the final example, (v), almost any of these translations. What cannot be properly represented is the pregnancy of the usages, except perhaps in Decius' invocation of the *fortuna populi Romani*, which is suggested with caution, as is appropriate for such a junior official.

Decius is treating each new situation as a result or outcome, though as a new one emerges, the previous situation (*fortuna*) becomes part of the means by which he reached that new situation (*fortuna*). All this is characteristic of a 'higher-level' analysis, and reminds the reader of accounts of the gods' agency whose domain *fortuna* structurally represents. Each new situation offers different opportunities and tendencies, and it is these that are most of all alluded to in the use of *fortuna*, not those implications that are foregrounded by our (limited) translations. It is repeated, yet distinct, usages such as these that led Kajanto to schematise his different types of *fortuna*. But there is a greater unity than he allows: at each point that he speaks of *fortuna*, Decius describes the whole of the present situation, and judges its inherent tendencies. When he promises to 'follow the same fortune that brought us here' he is seeing the run of 'luck' that would normally be taken to indicate the support of the gods, which of course he acknowledges in his sacrifice. Yet it is to Mars, god of war, that he sacrifices, not *Fortuna*. That would seem appropriate enough in a military context, but it begs the question, in what capacity was *fortuna* actually functioning as a goddess? The answer would seem to be in the *fulfilment* of divine support: 'the way things turned out/are turning out' is the most emphatic proof of the gods' will towards Rome. In describing *fortuna* as *uaria*, the Romans were therefore acknowledging an observable phenomenon: victory is far from assured – it is in the hands of the gods. The general use of *fortuna* can thus reflect the unexpected loss of the *pax deum* as well as the delivery of favour's outcome. This accounts for the references to *uaria fortuna* at least: a loss of favour, usually due to impiety, is responsible for defeats, as we have repeatedly seen.[76]

Fortuna is unequivocally linked to the dispensations of the gods, which raises the question: if the twists and turns of *fortuna* are so interlinked with the mood of the gods in general, why was it needed as a distinct term? Livy is perfectly happy at other times to say that the gods themselves acted a certain way, or to juxtapose a loss of piety with failure. Why then does he also use *fortuna* so often? The answer would seem to lie in the particular jurisdiction of *fortuna*, the *manifestation* and fulfilment of the gods' will. *Fortuna* represents the experience at human level of the gods' will: this is implicit in the one instance where *Fortuna* is propitiated as a god, after the prodigial shrinking of the *sortes* at Caere where *sors* cannot mean a senseless dispensation of 'chance', or the oracle would be redundant: it must indicate the workings of the gods in human life, one's lot. Such is the jurisdiction of *fortuna*, the way that things will, or have, turn(ed) out for a

---

[76] There may be a similar understanding of the structural contingency between *fortuna* and the gods when Livy reports that, after a shower of stones, a voice was heard on the Alba Mons ordering the Albans to perform their traditional rites, which they had neglected, as if they had abandoned their gods to oblivion with their nation and had adopted Roman rites, or, embittered against fortune, as sometimes happens (*ut fit*), they had abandoned rites altogether (1.31.3).

specified agent. It represents a somewhat different perspective from the invocation of 'the gods', either by name or as a whole, and the wisdom about *fortuna* encapsulated all the knowledge and uncertainties of the complex workings of the gods.

At the same time, the term avoids another set of problems: to speak of *fortuna* did not require the kind of expertise that characterised the negotiation with the gods undertaken by the *res publica* through the senate and priests. The difficulties of exact interpretation are sidestepped by the invocation of *fortuna*, which was not intrinsically interpretative: the gods seem to be in support (or not) and lending support to one or the other side or to be dispensing a particular situation to men, in whatever way. The man who speaks of *fortuna* does not claim to know these details, or does not wish to bother with them. Yet the gods *are* thought, or rather, *known* to be at work, as can be seen by the use of *fortuna* to reflect the appearance of favour. Indeed assessment of the run of *fortuna* is deliberately sought: battle after battle, endeavour after endeavour, has interim reports on the run of fortune. Livy might even evoke fortune when there is no clear advantage. In evenly matched battle against the Hernici, the cavalry rouse themselves to win and Livy reports that it was not easy to see what made the difference, unless it was the ever-present (*perpetua*) *fortuna* of each side that raises or lowers morale (in other words, the Romans won).[77] *Fortuna* is *perpetua*, that is, it always has a hand in events, and each nation (or even an individual) can claim its own, just as each nation calls on its gods for protection. It just happens that those of Rome are greater: of all the uses of *fortuna* in Livy's text, only the *fortuna populi Romani* is constant in its favours.[78] This reliability, of course, can only be spoken of after the event.

Given that *fortuna* is generally unpredictable it comes as no surprise that there is a common preference not to rely on it. One never knows just how far the gods will lend their favour, given the technical difficulties of obtaining it, the ease with which it can be lost, or even the uncertainties of simple jealousy, as encountered so bitterly by Hannibal and Aemilius. There is also the difficulty of knowing exactly how the gods' wishes will be manifested, in detail.

So fortune can take an unexpected turn without indicating a major breach of the *pax deum*, as it does when the patrician consul falls ill and the plebeian Popilius takes full charge at 7.23.2: he promptly defeats the Gauls with his tactics and courage (7.23-4) before his being wounded necessitates

---

[77] *nisi quod perpetua fortuna utriusque populi et extollere animos et minuere potuit* (7.8.4).
[78] Kajanto (1957) 67 interestingly points out that Cicero prefers to refer to the *fortuna rei publicae*: it may be that Livy is polemically emphasising the people as the recipients of the gods' favour.

a Dictatorship.[79] We find that the general who does not entrust outcomes to *fortuna*, such as Marcellus, is praised (23.43.7). In a similar vein, Fabius Maximus chastises his *magister equitum*, M. Minucius Rufus, and asserts his right to authority over his rash colleague, saying that in the hands of a good commander, *fortuna* has but a small role to play (*haud magni fortunam momenti esse*, 22.25.14). Fabius is not speaking theoretically, but practically: it is not that *fortuna* has little impact, it is that the good general does not rely on it in his planning. He should circumscribe the dangers of an uncertain future by making the best use of whatever *fortuna* has offered to date, as Hannibal has learned, and tries to tell Scipio at 30.30.18-23: using *fortuna* four times, he emphasises that the greater the success, the less fortune is to be trusted; that while the choice to make peace is in Scipio's hands, victory is in the gods'. The Roman can make a certain peace or take his chances on the gods' dispensation of fortune: *[tibi] ea habenda fortuna erit quam di dederint.*

It is no disrespect to the gods to say that one should make the most of the *fortuna* that they send: rather it is an acknowledgement of their power over the affairs of men. However much it can be *explained* as being the result of the gods' wishes, to speak of *fortuna* does not seek to explain what is obvious. To deploy *fortuna* is rather to evoke a human reality, a lived experience of the vicissitudes of the best-laid plans. While it relies on the certainty that the gods are active in one way or another it is not particularly an attempt to analyse this. It leaves men to do what they can do, given the opportunities, advantages and setbacks of the way that things turn out. The observation that *fortuna* has favoured a people, as it did the Romans, was (merely) to indicate the self-evident truism that the gods had provided their favour, itself a testament to Roman piety.[80]

3.4 Interpretation and power

3.4.1 Introductory comments

The complexity of deductive principles means that, for the Romans, *any* statement about religion is interpretative rather than empirical. Religious deductions are *practical* in the sense that they are intended to give rise to a particular course of action: they are far from being dry and academic

---

[79] Cf. e.g. 1.23.10: *res Tullo quamquam cum indole animi tum spe uictoriae ferocior erat. quaerentibus utrimque ratio initur cui et fortuna ipsa praebuit materiam.*

[80] Precisely the sentiment of Q. Marcius Philippus, who seems to be claiming at 44.1.10-12 that one route to persistent success is through a nation's conduct (*ea omni [sc. scelera] quam diis quoque invisa essent, sensurum. [Persea] in exitu rerum suarum: fauere enim pietati deos, per quae populus Romanus ad tantum fastigii uenerit*).

conclusions. By being forced by circumstance to formulate a religious (or non-religious) position, Livy and his agents are defining, redefining and possibly reasserting the traditional categories of interpretation. Throughout the text, institutions and individuals make distinctions between 'religious' and 'non-religious' situations, assess the depth of a religious crisis, and suggest solutions. As such, religion forms a system of knowledge, and it stands to reason that religious diagnoses were received in the same competitive atmosphere as 'non-religious' debate in the senate of Rome: to have one's assessment accepted would no doubt have required persuasion of equally opinionated rivals.[81] But the presence of a number of experts in the senate (which of course included the priestly *collegia*) would inevitably entail disagreement, status issues and all the usual paraphernalia of human knowledge: in other words, we should expect religious knowledge to be affected by the factors that always constrain and define social power. Thus, though we should assume their broad familiarity with religious lore, it is doubtful that Roman aristocrats would have freely offered their opinion on religious matters on all occasions: a proper gentleman would, despite his understanding, only under great duress presume to tell the *pontifices* or *augures* their job or to contradict them on their lore. The foregoing sections have elaborated various aspects of the interpretative principles that underlie religious opinion in ancient Rome. This section deals more with the reception of those formulations: the interpretative endeavour did not end with a 'correct' formulation – there were manifold considerations, both social and religious, with regard to the propriety involved in making religious claims.

3.4.2 The authoritative individual

It is evident that, despite the preference for collegiate and senatorial consideration, an individual aristocrat might be required to make a religious assessment: general after general makes some kind of religious statement to his troops;[82] at another juncture, the sworn judgement of a single praetor is taken to be sufficient authority for the 'books of Numa' to be burned (40.29.12) – he had decided that they were dangerous to *religio*.[83] The consul who informed the plebs that the Bacchist cult was a danger to the state was equally sure of his opinion (39.15, 16): these latter two were presumably backed to some extent by precedent, their undoubted acquaintance with

---

[81] As Fabius Maximus found when he persuaded the senate to consult the Sibylline Books at 22.9.8-9.

[82] Kajanto (1957) 37 lists examples where a Roman general explains that the breaking of a treaty by the enemy is said to guarantee Roman victory (3.2.4; 6.29.2; 8.7.5 and 10.39.15).

[83] *animum aduertisset pleraque dissoluendarum religionum esse* (40.29.11). Cf. the phrase *dissoluendae religionis* in connection with the Bacchist cult (39.16.9).

pontifical law and the debates that would have gone on in the high political circles in which they moved. They may even have been priests, but they are not represented as such by Livy. Functionally they are magistrates and for him that is sufficient guarantee.[84]

In noteworthy contrast to their matter-of-fact confidence, two of Livy's most expert religious commentators imply that there is a difficulty inherent in making religious statements – Aemilius Paullus refused to be drawn into certainty at 44.22.3, though he could hope (*spero*), partly on the grounds of omens, that the gods would offer their support.[85] Consider also the combination of caution and confidence in the speech of Papirius before battle against the Samnites: he details his reasons for thinking that the gods will support the Roman cause, though he does note the difficulty of knowing the gods' will for certain. He inserts a caveat when he predicts that the gods will oppose the Samnites, *if* it is permissible to conjecture their mood (*'tum si qua coniectura mentis diuinae sit'*, 10.39.16).

Both men are generally represented as exemplary: Papirius in particular shows his religious acumen when he explains that the *pullarius* who wrongly announced that the omens were favourable has incurred the wrath of the gods through his actions. His analysis is borne out by the death of the keeper of the chickens in the battle (10.40.4-5; 10.40.11-13), though it still requires his somewhat unambitious vow of a cup of sweetened wine to induce the gods to change the signs into favourable ones: Livy tells us that he was successful (*id uotum dis cordi fuit et auspicia in bonum uerterunt*).[86] For a man so evidently skilled in interpretation the caution expressed in his aside that one cannot know the mind of the gods seems noteworthy.[87] Yet it is not that the expression of doubt indicates a level of expertise inferior to more confident diagnoses: his predictions, detailed diagnoses and solutions are shown to be accurate. He is not always cautious: when a raven seems to confirm his diagnosis, he declares that the gods had never before manifested

---

[84] Certainly the historian makes no effort to authenticate their religious authority and does not indicate any surprise that magistrates *qua* magistrates should make such judgements.

[85] '*Deos quoque huic fauisse sorti spero eosdemque in rebus gerendis adfuturos esse. haec partim ominari, partim sperare possum.*'

[86] 10.42.7. Here, presumably, is Livy's answer to the situation of the late Republic where there was exploitation of the need for a formal announcement of omens or the mistaken announcement of favourable omens (Liebeschuetz (1979) 15–17, 20–21 and 24–5). Cf. the comments on 'cheating' oaths by fulfilling the letter rather than the spirit and intended meaning in connection with the Roman hostages sent to Rome by Hannibal at 22.58.8. On this episode see also Linderski (1993) 60–61, and Orlin (1997) 52 who seems to argue that the erroneous announcement was impious in itself and it was this that brought on the death of the *pullarius*. It seems more likely that it was the danger indicated by the sign that cost him his life; his action merely shifted the responsibility to himself, just as the *ira deum* shifted to the consuls at 27.23.4.

[87] He is also cautious about his suggestion that it is the lot of his family to defeat the Samnites at 10.39.14, adding *forsitan* to his deduction.

their presence with such clarity (*adfirmans nunquam humanis rebus magis praesentes interfuisse deos*, 10.40.14). Such a range of responses smacks of an experienced interpreter.

What these two men have in common is that they visibly operate within the deductive principles of traditional practice, as do the generals who assure their troops that the gods are on their side. Working within an interpretative system, they are not only concerned to acknowledge the limits of their knowledge, and the limits of any system of knowledge, but also they respect the fact that they are speaking to an educated audience who would not relish being lectured in the basics of religious understanding. Their modesty is exemplary: they assert their opinions while avoiding the pitfall of charisma and excessive confidence. Instead they negotiate skilfully with the evidence to diagnose divine 'intervention' and to indicate the process of deduction.[88] What they do not do is to doubt the efficacy of the principles by which they are working.[89] If any one man threatened to destroy the integrity of these protocols, it was Scipio Africanus.

> Scipio was almost larger than life (*mirabilis*) not only by virtue of the genuine qualities which he possessed, but also by his cleverness in displaying them, a cleverness which he had developed from early youth. In public, he generally spoke and acted as though he were guided either by dreams or by some divine inspiration, whether because he was really afflicted by *superstitio* or so that his orders and advice would be followed without delay, as if it came from an oracle. He sought to create this impression from the beginning, from the day when he assumed the *toga uirilis*: he never began any public or private business without first going to the Capitol to sit in the temple for some time – and usually on his own and in privacy.

---

[88] Thus when Aemilius says that events *seemed* to indicate the help of the gods, we should not deduce, as some have done, that there is any element of scepticism present: '*rex ipse tradentibus prope ipsis dis in templo Samothracum cum liberis est captus*' (45.41.6). The reticence reflects his desire to avoid boasting that the gods supported him even though he clearly states that he sacrificed to Apollo before engaging Perseus.

[89] This is also true of generals who assert that the gods are in support of their cause: they might omit Papirius' most elegant disclaimers but they do unfailingly rely on general principles such as the general assertion that punishment might come later than expected but come it would in its own time, as is said at 3.56.7: *pro se quisque deos tandem esse et non neglegere humana fremunt et superbiae crudelitatique etsi seras, non leues tamen uenire poenas*. Cf. the statements that the gods will avenge the breaking of treaties by, amongst others, Papirius (10.39.15); for similar statements see also 3.2.4, 6.29.2, 8.7.5. The crucial difference from Scipio in the following examples is that these men are deducing from general principles rather than attempting to make a prediction about a specific instance. It was self-evident that the gods would avenge wrongs committed against them, such as the breaking of a sworn treaty, but that was not the same as an absolute guarantee that they would provide victory at a *particular* juncture.

This habit of his, which he continued all through his life, gave rise to the widespread conviction (whether this was his intention or not) that he was of divine origin. The story was told of him which was frequently told of Alexander – a story equally without foundation as it was fantastic – that he was conceived by a prodigious snake which had been frequently seen in his mother's bedroom. When anyone came near, it would suddenly uncoil itself and slip away. The belief in these supernatural things was never ridiculed by him; rather it grew stronger because he contrived neither to deny nor to confirm them openly. There were many other traits in this youth's character, some genuine, others feigned, which created a greater admiration for him than is usual.[90] (26.19.3-19)

Clearly a number of distinctions are being made here: we must explore this complex in some detail, beginning with his *superstitio* ('In public …oracle'):

pleraque apud multitudinem aut per nocturnas uisa species aut uelut diuinitus mente monita agens, siue et ipse capti quadam superstitione animi, siue ut imperia consiliaque uelut sorte oraculi missa sine cunctatione exsequerentur. (26.19.3-4)

There are two options in each (unequal) half of the sentence (dividing it between *agens* and the first *siue*). In the second half, there are two possible options as to why he should claim unusual knowledge: Scipio is either 'superstitious', i.e. he believes that he has divine inspiration, or he is deliberately pretending to have divine inspiration in order to have his orders taken seriously and obeyed without delay. According to the first half, if Scipio does 'believe' in his mysterious guidance, then it takes one of two forms, either dreams, or some other less specific form. Both of these are

---

[90] *fuit enim Scipio non ueris tantum uirtutibus mirabilis, sed arte quoque quadam ab iuuenta in ostentationem earum compositus, pleraque apud multitudinem aut per nocturnas uisa species aut uelut diuinitus mente monita agens, siue et ipse capti quadam superstitione animi, siue ut imperia consiliaque uelut sorte oraculi missa sine cunctatione exsequerentur. ad hoc iam inde ab initio praeparans animos, ex quo togam uirilem sumpsit nullo die prius ullam publicam priuatamque rem egit quam in Capitolium iret ingressusque aedem consideret et plerumque solus in secreto ibi tempus tereret. hic mos per omnem uitam seruatus seu consulto seu temere uolgatae opinioni fidem apud quosdam fecit stirpis eum diuinae uirum esse, rettulitque famam in Alexandro magno prius uolgatam, et uanitate et fabula parem, anguis immanis concubitu conceptum, et in cubiculo matris eius uisam persaepe prodigii eius speciem interuentuque hominum euolutam repente atque ex oculis elapsam. his miraculis nunquam ab ipso elusa fides est; quin potius aucta arte quadam nec abnuendi tale quicquam nec palam adfirmandi. multa alia eiusdem generis, alia uera, alia adsimulata, admirationis humanae in eo iuuene excesserant modum; quibus freta tunc ciuitas aetati haudquaquam maturae tantam rerum molem tantumque imperium permisit.*

presumably subject to the charge of being either *superstitio* or political manipulation.

The dreams are consistent with the claims made by the general himself in Livy's account[91] and the daytime (if *aut* is taken to be exclusive)[92] inspiration is presumably linked to Scipio's notorious daily consultations with Jupiter Capitolinus. Clearly *superstitio* implies some kind of disapproval. But the details of the criticism are not as obvious as they might appear. To begin with, the criticism is relevant whatever the source or meaning of the inspiration, as both possibilities given with *siue* can apply equally to diurnal or nocturnal activity; for the time being the options governed by *aut...aut* are less important to us. But it cannot be that Livy wishes us to know that he personally is not willing to accept the existence of prophetic dreams, for the text elsewhere acquiesces in their power to predict, in connection with the *deuotio* of Decius Mus. Both consuls dreamed of the same superhuman form that announced that the commander of one army and the entire army of the other side were destined as a sacrifice to the *Dii Manes* and to Mother Earth. Their response was measured when they discovered that the dream was mutual: they immediately proceeded to make sacrifices to propitiate the gods and decided that if the victims portended the same outcome as the dream, that one of them should fulfil this destiny. The *haruspices*, apparently unaware of the dreams,[93] gave a similar prognostication and the consuls duly agreed that whoever found his army retreating would perform the necessary sacrifice.

The text reveals a number of surprises: one might expect the duplication of the dream to convince the consuls yet they make sacrifices to submit the terrifying dream to examination. The consensus of the traditional rites then confirms the veracity of the vision. What is important for Livy is not whether dreams are credible or reliable[94] but how one is to respond to such phenomena. The irruption into the text of the vision is tamed and incorporated as the consuls refuse to be bowed by surprise or haste: they deploy proper Roman traditional procedures, the only appropriate response. Scipio on the other hand promotes dreams to a status equal with auspices and auguries, albeit with an *etiam* to separate them (26.41.18). There is certainly

---

[91] The general mentions his dreams to his assembled soldiers – *idem di auguriis auspiciisque et per nocturnos etiam uisus omnia laeta ac prospera portendunt* (26.41.18).
[92] The force of *aut...aut* here need not be utterly exclusive; it would seem that at any given point one or the other source was effective. Second opinions have been inconclusive on this point.
[93] *ubi responsa haruspicum insidenti iam animo tacitae religioni congruerunt...* (8.6.12).
[94] For the reliability *and* unreliability of dreams as a means of divination see e.g. Suetonius *Augustus* 91. Dreams were, of course, notoriously unreliable in literature, beginning with Homer (*Il.* 2.6: cf. *Aeneid* 6.283-4). See also Pelling (1997).

no indication that he subjected his visions to the sort of stringent checking that Decius and Torquatus observed. This then would be an example of *superstitio*, inappropriate management of possibly genuine religious phenomena.

Livy offers as an alternative the suggestion that Scipio acts as if under the inspiration of a divinity as an alternative *superstitio*: this would not have pleased the educated Roman either. The institutions of Republican Rome were designed specifically to forestall the possibility of one individual appropriating such *auctoritas*. The tradition did, however, tend to cast the great general as 'sincere'[95] in his beliefs, however inappropriate they were, which brings us to wonder why we are uniquely given a 'political' alternative here, namely that Scipio wished to have his orders obeyed and advice heeded. Livy acknowledges the tradition that had Scipio operate in an unorthodox religious fashion but fragments its power by offering a 'political' alternative which, if it characterises the general as a rogue, at least reduces the impact of Scipio as a religious *exemplum*.[96] Any attempt to imitate his charismatic behaviour would now be met with suspicion of political motives for religious claims: better to have a slightly unscrupulous hero than a dangerous religious precedent. In view of the remarkable career that every Roman reader would have been expecting, it is an appropriation of the ultimate authority that allows Livy to cut such a hero down to size at such an early moment.[97] Even Scipio is required to adhere to proper Roman practice: no man is greater than the Republic and that applies to religion as much as other aspects of statehood.

The final clause (*siue ut imperia... exsequerentur*), however, can only be understood in the context of the proprieties of religious announcements. It is assumed that the 'proper' behaviour implied by Livy would be *not* to use religious reasons or authorities. But Scipio's error is not specifically that he made authoritative religious pronouncements, for he was not the first, nor the last, general or senator to invoke religious reasons in his *imperia consiliaque*. Livy's complaint is the way in which he made them: Scipio is excessive in the authority that he arrogates, but not wrong to make any diagnosis at all. The warning seems to allude to two specific instances in the text. The first is Scipio's naming of Neptune as an assisting god in his

---

[95] So Seguin (1974), who contrasts Livy's account with that of Polybius.

[96] Of course 'political manipulation' is not necessarily a criticism: Numa is subjected to a similar treatment in his meeting with Egeria (1.21.4); on both see most recently Feldherr (1998) 69–72. But Livy does imply that Scipio did *not* act on the basis of any genuine charismatic religious *abilities*.

[97] Though he had been (irregularly) elected curule aedile at 25.2.6, Africanus has not yet made much impact on Roman politics.

assault on New Carthage. Scipio ascertains from some fishermen that the harbour can be crossed on foot at low tide. The intrepid general turns this situation to his advantage, but not without first claiming divine assistance:[98] he declares the shallow water to be a prodigy and tells his men to follow Neptune's lead and tread where no mortal foot has gone before.[99]

What is puzzling about this passage is that Scipio's claim of such specific divine help is extremely unusual and, possibly more importantly, *unnecessary*. Thus Livy allows Scipio his charisma but in an example where it is largely superfluous. His men could no doubt have seen the advantages of an unexpected attack on the walls: he would not have had to convince them to act. The incident is normally (of course) taken to indicate Livy's preference for a rational explanation over a divine one, but there is more at stake than rationalism or a rationalising exploitation of religion.[100]

Livy did not 'see through' the deception, rather he decided to curtail the power of the charismatic leader of the historical tradition. He is exploiting the power of suggestion to incorporate Scipio into a more traditional Roman mould: interrogating the locals and discovering a weakness is the sort of thing a Roman general *should* do, although the audience will have heard of the legends of Scipio's exploits and charismatic religious *mores* which are therefore duly acknowledged but rendered tautologous.

A similar reflex seems to be operative in the second instance of Scipio's most charismatic self-presentation when he claims the support of the gods at 26.41.18-20: the general is outrageously emphatic that the gods have supported his election and successes. He proceeds to say that Rome's success is

---

[98] We should remember the comment that some of the supernatural stories about the general are true – *alia uera, alia adsimulata* (26.19.9). The reader is, however, expected to draw his own conclusions as to which are which. For the accretion of these stories see Walbank (1967) and Scullard, (1970) 18–23. For the characterisation of Scipio and the treatment of his death(s) (in perfect accord with the conclusions reached here and below) Kraus (1998) 279: 'over and over the historian shows how hard it is to evaluate Africanus: was he a charismatic manipulator, or the best of all Romans?' Jaeger's (1997) excellent discussion of the trial and death of Scipio (her chapter 5, 132–176) is also relevant.

[99] *adeo nudauerat uada ut alibi umbilico tenus aqua esset, alibi genua uix superaret. hoc cura ac ratione compertum in prodigium ac deos uertens Scipio qui ad transitum Romanis mare uerterent et stagna auferrent uiasque ante nunquam initas humano uestigio aperirent, Neptunum iubebat ducem itineri sequi ac medio stagno euadere ad moenia* (26.45.8-9).

[100] None of this is to say that Livy would like to deny absolutely that the gods had a hand in events. One apparently minor detail, that the wind assisted the retreat of the tide, is not explicitly assigned to the familiarity of the fishermen with the habits of the local area, but appears as an unexpected extra assistance: *medium ferme diei erat, et ad id quod sua sponte cedente in mare aestu trahebatur aqua, acer etiam septentrio ortus inclinatum stagnum eodem quo aestus ferebat* (26.45.8). Such 'minor' details are often assigned to the help of the gods by a significant juxtaposition: the mention of the action of the wind would seem rather superfluous otherwise. To *deny* the involvement of the gods, even without this detail, would be extremely unusual: Scipio did, after all, achieve a notable success here.

assured through augury, auspices and even dreams (*'idem auguriis auspici-isque et per nocturnos etiam uisus omnia laeta ac prospera portendunt'*) and proceeds to say that his *animus* foresees victory in Spain (*'animus quoque meus, maximus mihi ad hoc tempus uates, praesagit nostram Hispaniam esse'*). Scipio is in danger of becoming an oracle in his own right at this point, and Livy, after indulging him this moment, has him immediately add that what his mind divines, reason also supports (*'quod mens sua sponte diuinat idem subicit ratio haud fallax'*).

We should see another adjustment of the historical record here: to be sure, people remembered Scipio saying that he divined this or that; but they may have missed the 'fact' that he confirmed his hunches by solid reasoning, based on facts. Thus the historian undermines the dangerous *exemplum* that would have Scipio rely completely on his charismatic religious attitude, juxtaposing a more traditional, and more suitable, process of deduction. Any Roman who chose to follow Scipio's example could spend as much time as he wished in the temple of Jupiter Capitolinus – just as long as he interrogated locals on campaign and subjected his dreams and inspiration to hard-nosed reasoning.

The particular difficulty that Livy seems to be circumventing is that Scipio's pronouncements claimed to have the authority of an oracle – and it is hard to find a greater authority. To assess this claim from the point of view of rationalism or belief is unproductive: it depends on the predictive power of oracles, not on any question of the existence of the gods. Most importantly, the most contentious issue in the ancient world concerning prediction was not whether or not it could be done, but by whom it was done:[101] prediction was a matter of the appropriation of authority and one's relation to the gods, not the theoretical possibility of telling the future. To operate like an oracle was to move beyond the limitations of mortal knowledge, something which was only appropriate to specific agencies, such as Delphi, or the most skilled of interpreters, such as the *haruspices* – and then, strictly on the basis of their *scientia*.[102] Roman generals, unlike oracles, were expected to

---

[101] For the construction of diviners and prophets in a Roman context see Potter (1994), especially chs. 1 and 2; for an analysis of a more charismatic Greek seer (Teiresias) see Buxton (1980). On Greek poets and prophets see Détienne (1967).

[102] The authority enshrined in oracular utterances is indicated not only by the accuracy of the various predictions made by Delphi, but also where they are used metaphorically, as at 3.34.1. The Old Man of Veii, whose charisma is curtailed to a large extent by his not being a magistrate and his not even having a name, is exceptionally insightful when he anticipates the Delphic response (5.15.1). We should note that his knowledge was *triply* validated: he was inspired (*diuino spiritu instinctus* (5.15.10) and adds that the information is also to be found not only in the books of fate but *also* formed part of the *disciplina Etrusca*. He was hardly acting on his own authority, and once again, Livy's account shows a consistency that few commentators would attribute to him.

use their reason and knowledge rather than their personal, unrepeatable, faculties of divination.

Herein surely lies an essential attribute of Livy's chief objection to Scipio's conduct: the general does not acknowledge the limits of knowledge, still present despite an immensely sophisticated 'technology' to inform decisions. Even the Roman priests might misunderstand those phenomena despite their training and experience: our cautious generals Aemilius and Papirius are therefore, entirely appropriately, mortals exercising skill in a difficult art. Furthermore, they are relying on phenomena, visible indications that require interpretation, whereas Scipio is depending on a non-phenomenological source of knowledge in trusting dreams – an action more inappropriate or dangerous than utterly misled. Indeed, such is their expertise that we might postulate that to realise the limits of prediction from signs is the very height of understanding: human skill is always human, and therefore inherently flawed. Scipio has attempted to circumvent these difficulties by his own charismatic and personal link with the divine. Given that the process of interpretation was one carefully enshrined in appropriate protocol and specialisation, Scipio's pretensions to divine inspiration represent a serious threat to the established structure of the republican response to divine issues. The absence of an appropriate sense of his limitations is a threat to tried and tested Roman practice, and one which Livy at once acknowledges, diffuses and refuses to endorse – whatever its success. After his treatment of Scipio, Livy might reasonably assume that it would be virtually impossible for a leader of a Roman army to be able to arrogate such charisma to himself without his subordinates in some way understanding that individual through Livy's example, thereby cutting their leader down to size, whatever his claims might be.[103] As for the appearance of the snake, this is reminiscent of the way that stories attached themselves to eminent men towards the end of the Republic and under the Empire.[104] This kind of charisma is most

---

The *haruspices* as a body make a prediction at 42.20.4 where they predict a great victory from portents, in contrast to the expiatory responses ordered by the *decemuiri*. It is worth noting that though Livy notes the notorious difficulties of understanding oracular responses at 9.3.8 (*uelut ex ancipiti oraculo responsa*), the Delphic response at 23.11.1 is not only *not* ambiguous, it is actually so similar to Roman practice that it acts more as a corrective to the incorrect prescriptions of the *decemuiri* at 22.57.6 than as a visibly foreign element.

[103] It is quite possible that Livy is casting an eye towards the incipient power of Augustus in composing these books, and the 'special relationship' with Apollo (for which see Gagé (1955) 479–522); but it is equally possible that he is reacting somewhat more generally and espousing what he constructs to be traditional Roman values in response to the possibility of such a leader emerging in the future. That such factors were important to the contemporary audience seems to be indicated by the care that Augustus took in stressing his 'restoration' of the traditional ways.

[104] There is a not dissimilar story about Nero, which Tacitus quashes with equal firmness and rather less tact (11.5.6).

emphatically curtailed: it is the only feature that Livy rejects specifically. To accept it would have placed Scipio beyond reach, both for the historian and for his contemporary society. Roman Republican religion simply could not contain a figure with such associations: thus it cannot even be admitted as a possibility since it is the only aspect of Scipio's religious reputation that simply cannot be recontextualised appropriately.

3.4.3 Naming the gods

There is a further aspect to Scipio's impropriety as a general: in Livy's extant text he is almost unique in assigning the assistance he is claiming to one, and only one, specific god without a simultaneous vow of games or a temple. Scipio's specificity is most uncharacteristic of Roman generals: normally gods are only picked out in connection with ritual but Scipio makes no dedication. Typically it is 'the gods' in a generic and virtually anonymous plural who are thanked and acknowledged for their support.[105] There would appear to be factors inhibiting the naming of a specific deity by non-priests.[106] When Scipio names Neptune, his reasoning seems transparent: it was the sea, the domain of Neptune, that appeared to be offering assistance. This would seem to be a common principle where individual gods are named: the Locrians are quite explicit about the domain of Proserpina in connection with her temple (29.18.1-20) and we find repeatedly that where a particular temple is concerned, the deity is easily specified.[107] But proper understanding is more complex than this. In calling for proper remedies to be applied in response to the complaints of the Locrians, Fabius Maximus refers to the *pontifices* for details of what expiation, to which gods and with which victims Rome should proceed (29.19.8). Livy typically does not give us any details of this province of the experts, and only brings the scruple to our attention as part of his casting Fabius Maximus as an *exemplum*, in some kind of meticulous opposition to the unrestrained Scipio or

---

[105] Livy himself attributes the discovery of a slave plot to capture the Capitol to Jupiter without any qualms, presumably because it would be obvious that it would be Jupiter who protected his domain (4.45.2) but such specificity is extremely rare and this example seems to be a unique venture for the historian.

[106] We are repeatedly told that deities were specified by the various colleges, e.g. at 36.37.5: *consul P. Cornelius, quibus diis quibusque hostiis edidissent decemuiri, sacrificaret*. Ammianus, citing authorities which we cannot date, but which may refer back to this period, tells us that even the *pontifices* were at times extremely cautious about specifying deities (17.7.10). Interestingly, although Scipio was a *Salius*, he was not apparently an interpretative priest according to Szemler's (1972) listing. Even if he had been, it is his functional role that he exceeds. It is as a general that he exceeds normal bounds of public interpretation.

[107] See e.g. the desire of the *pontifices* to know to which deity expiation should be offered in the case of a lightning strike at 27.25.8-9: interestingly they add that it is possible to offer joint sacrifice to certain deities, possibly referring to the temple of Liber, Libera and Ceres.

sacrilegious Pleminius. The care that he urges would seem to indicate that expiation is more complex than simply restoring the property of Proserpina, whose temple it was: there was also the question of addressing the proper jurisdiction of *other* deities.

There is a similar exemplary care in diagnosis when the gods intervene to assist M. Valerius Corvus in single combat with a Gaul. Livy informs us that the gods took an unexpected hand when a raven (*coruus*) appeared unexpectedly and settled on the Roman's helmet, whereupon Corvus delightedly accepted the omen and prayed for the help of whichever god it was that had sent the omen: the raven immediately launched against the Gaul, who, terrified and distracted, was duly slain by Corvus. The raven flew away eastwards (7.26.3-5). The ensuing struggle over the Gaul's armour led to the utter defeat of his countrymen and the victory was the beginning of a distinguished career for the young tribune.[108]

The indefinite formula (*si diuus, si diua esset*) used in Corvus' careful negotiation of the possible specific identity of the god sending him aid is a well-known phenomenon and the formula is often taken to represent hesitancy in the face of possible error.[109] Whether Corvus had some idea of which god helped him or not cannot be securely deduced: he might have known of the raven's association with a particular god but here it might as well be a god of victory as any patron of ravens.[110] However, as we shall see, there may also be other factors at play.

At the other extreme from prudence come a number of agents who are all too ready to name deities: apart from Scipio, the younger T. Manlius, son of the famous Torquatus, is confident that Jupiter will attend the Roman cause (8.7.5-7) but since the incident is symptomatic of his *ferox animus* (8.7.8), it would seem that his outspokenness is misjudged.[111] Manlius follows his father's *exemplum* wrongly here as well as in other respects.[112] His father was also disposed to call on Jupiter by name: when the elder Torquatus sees Annius, the leader of the Latins, lying unconscious after falling on the steps of the temple of Jupiter, he declares without hesitation that the gods have

---

[108] Apart from gaining a *cognomen*, he went on to be consul four times and *dictator*: he also heads the list of great men who would have defeated Alexander the Great, had the latter reached Roman territory, at 9.17.3.

[109] For further examples, see Alvar (1985); also a spectacular and extended example at Livy 22.10.

[110] 'Allegedly gifted with prophetic powers, the raven is described in Latin literature as sacred to Apollo/Helios' (Toynbee (1973) 275). For other remarkable moments with ravens, see also Pliny *NH* 10.60.

[111] We might even go so far as to say that to be so bold as to specify a god's role so precisely is the prerogative of the virtual amateur, or the most enlightened expert, but not a more average serious contender for respectable reputation. Of course Jupiter was in support of Rome, but to *say so* was crass.

[112] Kraus (1998) 270; Feldherr (1998) 105–111.

begun a just war; Jupiter, propitiated by Roman sacrifice, is present and has shown his ill-will (8.6.5-6). This follows his outburst earlier, when he called in indignation on Jupiter, *Ius* and *Fas* to listen to Annius' threats (8.5.8-10). Torquatus' confident diagnosis that Jupiter has taken a hand in events is not simply based on the visible evidence of Annius' incapacitation: he sees the fulfilment of his appeal, an appeal which was based on proper practice – the protection of a treaty by the patron deity of Rome, who is also (probably even more tellingly) the deity at whose temple he is knocked unconscious.

The reader will not be particularly surprised. Before his departure for the city, Annius announced a challenge almost to Jupiter himself: in the god's presence he would demand that Rome agreed to their constitutional demands (8.4.11). Torquatus relies for his diagnosis not just on Jupiter's jurisdiction in respect of treaties but also on his own direct appeal, made just before, and presumably also on the location of Annius' 'accident'. Livy also seems to be adding material in support of the Roman when he mentions Annius' apparently insolent warning to Jupiter in his speech to the Latins. Torquatus was therefore correct in his diagnosis but Livy has hinted that he was far from tactful; even if the historian finds that the consul's outspoken specificity and confidence was acceptable, his manner was not necessarily to be emulated.

It should not be forgotten how unconventional – yet ultimately accept-able – was Torquatus in most of his dealings. He was *par ferociae* to An-nius (8.5.7) and, even as a young man, Torquatus was a fierce opponent and strict disciplinarian. His father had cut him off from public life because his son lacked any eloquence (*lingua impromptus,* 7.4.6) and was dull-witted (*tarditatem ingenii,* 7.4.7). But the tribune who wished to prosecute his fa-ther Lucius for his disgraceful treatment of his son found himself threatened by that very son and forced to break off the prosecution. Thus, in addressing Jupiter so, he was characteristically devoid of tact and propriety in his mode of presentation, yet retained an essential 'rightness'.[113] When Scipio, in a similar manner, assigns his easy access to an undefended New Carthage to Neptune, he may be interpretatively 'accurate', but his boldness is not necessarily appropriate.

This emphasis on caution is not to say that only the priests had any *opinions* as to the identity of a god engaged in active intervention: even if Torquatus' outburst was sanctioned as an exception – or just typical of him – then we should be wary of deciding that a failure to name a deity reflects any general *inability* to discern the respective realms of the gods.

---

[113] The action against the tribune (7.5.1f.), like Torquatus' execution of his son (8.7.20-8 and 8.1), is approved of by Livy despite its extreme nature.

Rather we should be aware of a nexus of considerations that are embedded in an avoidance of competition and a demarcation of proper authority.
Discussion and assignation of roles to gods was the stuff of experts and demanded serious and dignified consideration. To appropriate the authority of
a priest, to represent oneself as distinctive with regard to religion, is a dangerous, unrepublican venture.[114] The vast majority of instances where the
divine is mentioned refer to the gods in the plural. Even when a particular
deity is thought to be relevant, the other gods might be mentioned.[115] This
is not just an avoidance of error but also an act of political tact.

3.4.4 Acknowledgement of the gods

Caution was not, however, an unproblematic solution to the difficulties of
interpretation. Any religious statement was subject to manifold considerations: speaker and audience alike placed religious matters in a complex web;
a veritable array of checks and balances came into play, and the educated
Roman would have been expected to master this. However, men were not
the only audience: the gods were listening too, and far from indifferently.
We know that failure to acknowledge the gods is traditionally a dangerous error: triumphs, for instance, are repeatedly introduced in Livy's text
as both a thanksgiving to the gods *and* a glorification of the commander
concerned.[116]

But acknowledgement was not limited to the context of rite: C. Claudius'
triumph, held for his success over the Ligurians at 41.13.6-14.1, is unusual
for the failure to mention thanksgiving to the gods. This is normally carefully placed, if not emphasised, in the documentation of the requests for,
and granting of, triumphs.[117] It is therefore telling that the Ligurians, not
realising why the Romans have left, immediately organise an uprising. Livy
makes little of this explicitly, but since we have become accustomed to
the significant juxtaposition of events, we can reasonably assume that he
is making a point. The senate orders Claudius to return to the province after

---

[114] Livy claims that such a zeal was the driving force behind Flaccus' despoliation of the temple of
Juno Lacinia: *enixo studio, ne ullum Romae amplius aut magnificentius templum esset* (42.3.1).

[115] Q. Fabius Maximus, in speaking of the breaking of a treaty (i.e. the province of Jupiter), still
takes care to acknowledge the other gods (26.8.5).

[116] Note that Cn. Manlius, under prosecution for attacking the Gallograeci, admits this as a plausible
scenario: '*si graue ac superbum existimarem uirtute gloriari …*' and goes on to emphasise that
the triumph is intended to honour the gods (38.48.14-15). See also the speech of Marcus Servilius which culminates rhetorically (and unfortunately, also fragmentedly) '*quidem† illae epulae
senatus… utrum hominum uoluptatis causa an deorum† honorumque?*' (45.39.13): whatever the
original text, he seems to be placing the gods in the centre. Versnel (1970) is a thorough study of
the practices and probable origins of the triumph.

[117] Phillips (1974) includes useful tables on the reporting of triumphs in Livy, but she is unfortunately
too brief about this particular aspect to go further with this point: she does however demonstrate
that Livy is sufficiently consistent to make any omission look deliberate.

overseeing the elections: Livy pointedly includes in their instructions to return as allies the Histrians whom he had brought from their province for the triumph so that they did not copy the example of the Ligurians (41.14.6). The uprising is swiftly crushed, only for Claudius to repeat the same mistake. He writes in characteristic haste to the senate, not only giving an account of the situation, but also boasting that by his courage and *felicitas* (*gloriaretur sua uirtute ac felicitate*, 41.16.8), there was no enemy on this side of the Alps.

The implication of *gloriaretur* seems to be that the gods were given insufficient mention in the letter. Though *felicitas* is used of a 'run of luck' which implied the special favour of the gods (Erkell (1952) 53f.), it is a word that, even more than others, is subject to political correctness: essentially it is not a word that one uses of oneself, but of others.[118] The next uprising is more damaging to the Romans, and costs Petilius *his* life, after his mistake in ritual rather than the sort of error of judgement that Claudius made. The arrogance, and its consequences, are underlined by the successful subjugation, probably with divine aid (Livy mentions a *miraculum* at 41.11.4), of the Histrians and the *supplicatio* accordingly decreed by the senate (41.12.4): proper religious protocol was applied at that point, and the Histrians, unlike the Ligurians, remained quiet.[119] It is well known that neglect of the gods in ritual leads to the loss of their support, but Claudius' neglect was in speech and interpretation rather than in rite.

---

[118] So, e.g., Hannibal speaks humbly of Scipio's *felicitas* at 30.30.11, though the mention of his adversary's *adulescentia* implies that one day's *felicitas* is the next's *fortuna*; Aemilius Paullus is one of only three Romans (apart from Gaius Claudius above) to speak of his own *felicitas*, but he is contrasting his successful administration of the *res publica* (*qua felicitate rem publicam administrauerim*, 45.41.1) with his private losses. Later in the same speech (45.41.12), he refers to *uestra felicitas* (i.e. of the *populus Romanus*). Manlius is also cautious in assimilating his own *felicitas* with that of the Roman people (*experimini modo et uestram felicitatem et me, ut spero, feliciter expertum*, 6.18.13). The combination with *uirtus* has a particular potency, being highly honorific or critical: thus Sophonisba honours and appeals to Masinissa with such a phrase (30.12.12) and Livy uses it judiciously of Camillus (*consilio et uirtute in Volsco bello, felicitate in Tusculana expeditione*, 6.27.1); L. Aemilius Regillus is thus honoured in a dedication to the *Lares Permarini* (*auspicio imperio felicitate ductuque*, 40.52.5). Decius prays to Jupiter Optimus Maximus for *felicitas* for both himself and his colleague (10.24.16) and Scipio (typically hyperbolically) speaks of his troops' *'uirtus tanta et felicitas perdomita'* (28.32.11). Hannibal is hasty, acting as if the war is over and waits *ut suae in uicem simul felicitati et uirtuti cedatur* (22.58.4). Most emphatically, Hannibal, in wiser mood, speaks to Scipio of the *'pauca felicitatis uirtutisque exempla'* (30.30.23), invoking the *exemplum* of M. Atilius to underline the dangers of arrogance. Claudius would therefore seem to have rather exaggerated his position in the scheme of things.

[119] It seems worthwhile to speculate that in fact the reasoning behind Livy's account is that the Ligurians continued to fight despite the triumph, thus implying some error that squandered divine support; his suggestion that Claudius did not properly recommend the assistance of the gods to the senate might well be his explanation for this. It is worth noting also that the allies were disgruntled at the meagre handout, and showed it by their silence during the triumph, and that the Histrians, who had sued for peace, were mistreated. Elsewhere, Claudius gets a poor press from Livy and is marked out as one who neglects the gods; his own soldiers send him back to Rome to make the vows he has omitted, and get his proper equipment (41.10.5-13).

The care with which the Roman priests propitiated individual deities, and the unusual circumstances that surround most instances where a particular god is named, make it most plausible that, even when there is the clearest of evidence that one particular god is active in a given situation, there may be other gods working for the benefit of the Romans, and that the better men of the senate will be careful to allow for this. The dissatisfaction of just one god would seem to be dangerous: all the gods but *Salus* were in support of Petilius and Cn. Cornelius at 41.15.4.

For the most part 'the gods' are constructed as a unified entity in co-operation with one another, though it stands to reason that there were times when it would be staggeringly obvious to the expert that the aid of a particular god had been crucial. At such a moment, it would be as inappropriate to fail to acknowledge it as it was to fail to acknowledge the gods at all. However, it would be highly inappropriate for a relatively raw aristocrat, even if his knowledge was sufficient, to name a deity publicly as solely responsible for an action. Such a scenario is probably intended to be understood in the case of the inexperienced Corvus, who was a mere military tribune when he received the exceptional assistance from the raven. In the circumstances, his phrasing (*si diuus, si dea,* 7.26.5) was entirely appropriate and successfully negotiated the opposite dangers of neglect and arrogance. In the case of Torquatus' appeal to Jupiter, it may have been inappropriate to be so outspoken as to call on Jupiter alone, but not necessarily incorrect, in the last analysis, for a man of such standing. That is, *if* one was going to be so explicit, then he picked the right deity for the situation.

3.5 Conclusions

Religion has emerged as considerably more complex in Livy than has hitherto been thought, as indeed has Livy. Religious interpretation has gone from being a bipolar argument to a nuanced discussion, which in itself is more historically plausible. It has also become possible to speak of a religious interpretative *system*, though how far we have seen 'through' Livy's account to the 'historically' true version is anyone's guess. Essentially we have an account that must have a claim to verisimilitude but, at the same time, should be treated as visionary in the sense that the selection and presentation of material reflect an exemplary model rather than a 'historical' one. His handling of details is impressive: his presentations of priestly authority in particular are remarkably coherent. There seems little doubt that on religious matters Livy knows his own mind and shaped his material accordingly.

By using traditional elements, Livy has designed a religion for Rome. Perhaps a Roman of the Early and Middle Republic would have nodded his head throughout Livy's account; perhaps he would have been startled at the changes. The dichotomy between 'historical fact' and 'literary representation' cannot be dispensed with, for we have no 'objective' version of events, nor could we ever. *Any* exegesis of religion, at *any* point, would remain representational; the best that we can hope to achieve is a comparison of similarly subjective paradigms at different points in Rome's history.

Far from being a simplistic analysis driven by the issues of scepticism or belief, Livy's treatment of religion is a subtle and complex deductive system that not only enshrines the 'science' of negotiating with the gods, but also accommodates the politics of religious authority: his various characters reflect an array of different takes on the application of religious knowledge, sometimes orthodox masters, sometimes novices. His reporting is varied and nuanced, and reflects the various considerations inherent in prodigy reporting, the mainstay of his Rome's maintenance of relations with the gods; his various agents, including his priests, deduce the workings of the gods in many other contexts and respond accordingly.

Though it was not Livy's deliberate intention to explain to complete newcomers the dynamics of interpretation, we have been able to detect the way that 'levels' of analysis were assumed to operate and, in particular, distinguished the human, divine and destined as specific interdependent categories. But we have seen more than the 'science', the 'hard knowledge' of religious interpretation: inevitably, knowledge carried a social premium and had to be managed. Livy shows us religious experts and novices operating within (or violating) both the science and the politics of Roman religion. He also indicates the degree to which that religion was a deliberate construction, a working set of practices endorsed by tradition (reliability) and innovation, when undertaken with appropriate scrutiny.

For the most part, Livy approves of his reconstructed religious system: his priests, though constrained at times by the difficulties of their task, retain their integrity to the extent that they can act as benchmarks of propriety. His senate can, on the whole, be trusted to resolve the status of potential prodigies. Rome can be relied upon to manage her gods, even if errors are made from time to time.

We should have no illusions about whether Livy has presented us with a historically accurate image of Rome at any particular point: his account is too steeped in contemporary issues for that. As was appropriate for historiography, he has created a model that 'lies (or at least, varies events) to tell the truth'. Its perspective ranges from the vaguely defined onlooker, with specific limits (set most detectably at the point of priestly knowledge), to that of the expert historian deducing and embedding patterns set by the fates in Rome's history. Sometimes Livy deals critically with extremely particular items, one prodigy or one priestly response: or he sets himself parameters which are closely adhered to for the most part – his handling of prodigy reports, for example, is evocative yet varied. Even his manner of listing these reports unfolds as an integral part of the narrative: we can say with certainty that they would have been more significant to his original audiences than they can ever be to us. With varying degrees of awareness of the fact, we have assessed his prodigy lists against *our* understanding of how the world works: we read what we take to be a catalogue of absurdity and assume that this was also their experience, but nothing could be further from the truth. For a Roman, the response would have been generated by their appreciation of the meaning of prodigies for the City. Even the driest prodigy list served an intensely dramatic narratological function as Rome's fortunes unfolded. Thus, chronologically local episodes were dramatically contextualised within a perspective that understood a divine intervention that manifested in the overall tenor of events: individual successes and setbacks were satisfactorily explained, in other words.

His documentation and historical explanations occupy a spectrum of perspectives: by his use of *fatum* in particular, apparently disparate episodes of Roman history could be incorporated into repeating patterns that did more than draw loosely on familiar frames of reference. Both the general propensity of Rome's rise to power and specific movements in history could be attributed to fate, bestowing a grandeur on Rome's empire that would otherwise be lacking. The discrimination between *fatum* and the 'ordinary' (i.e. negotiable) mood of the gods in particular allows Livy to set distinct strands of his narratives at different levels. His readers already knew that Rome would triumph: yet she had neglected the gods in recent times and suffered their wrath. Livy at once documents her decline into neglectfulness (and therefore civil war and all types of social discord) while simultaneously anchoring her success in the decrees of the fates, whose promise of empire comes early in the text (1.4). From that moment, it was not a question of whether she would succeed, rather one of how she did so. Had Rome maintained her relations with the gods, and benefited from the harmony that derived from the *pax deum*? Or were the fates to find Rome hindering the manifestation of their plans, attaining greatness only to turn it upon herself? Apart from providing good entertainment, this allows the historian to demonstrate sophisticated religious reasoning. At least in the surviving narrative, there is often a coincidence of adverse *fatum* and the *ira deum*, as at Cannae.

But his religious structure has more than an explanatory function: subordinating the overall pattern to fate allows Livy to subordinate many of his troublesome characters to Rome's destiny. Scipio Africanus is the prime example: he was characterised in the tradition as perhaps a little too large for his boots. Camillus also threatened the republican paradigm. Yet Livy's precise use of *fatalis dux* in connection with (only) these two casts their achievements as *Roman*, not just individual. One way or another, they enacted a higher will that was not their own. It was *Rome* who defeated the Gauls and the Carthaginians.

By the complex interplay of human, divine and destined, Livy could do more than deploy the formula of success/piety: he could represent the various, often conflicting, sequences of causes and events with more than one explanatory perspective in play. The Rome that lost at Cannae had virtually abandoned her traditional preparations and the neglect of the gods is sufficient to explain her subsequent humiliation, just as the recovery of religious procedure was matched by military success: but Livy does not leave the matter there. The discourse on *why* Rome could have made such an uncharacteristic error in the first place is also approached and its answer set at a different level: it was her *fatum* to suffer initial setbacks in major conflicts. Livy's human agents act within tendencies that shape, influence, hinder or contrast with their own efforts: his achievement in depicting the inter-operation of all these agencies is no minor one. The varied fortunes of his Romans are not a perfunctory exegesis of greater forces: rather they represent the entire range of the human condition. And since it was history, the perspective is that of the *human* unfolding of events: the intervention of the gods is no less documented here than it is in other genres and works, such as Virgil's epic. But it is represented from the point of view of the City's interest rather than any individual's, and by deduction rather than explicit identification. These are matters of literary genre, not personal belief, or philosophical speculation.

One fundamental question remains: what made Livy an expert, such that he could represent Rome's religion with such authority? Two interdependent answers can be offered. The historical one would seem to be that state religion, though its practical maintenance was entrusted to the state authorities, was *everybody's* business: the system of prodigies, in particular, demanded that the populace be steeped in at least the rudiments of analysis, even if only to identify suitable candidates for reporting. It seems a most unlikely scenario that no one dared to venture their own conclusions, or make confident announcements of those deductions in their community. Livy would therefore be fairly typical of a Roman adult male in having sophisticated, possibly even controversial, opinions on the matter.

In considering the source of Livy's expertise, however, another part of the answer is under our noses, so to speak, and is an eminently satisfying one for this study: Livy himself tells us at 43.13.2 (discussed above, 46).

It is the study of history that has provided his knowledge, and therefore authority, in religious matters. He has supplemented what cultural knowledge he had by studying the record of the past. Where better to learn of distinctions made, successes gained, failures suffered? The historians and the annals contained as good a record as any, short of priestly knowledge, which he studiously avoids. Seven centuries of religious material was abundant material for a careful reader to become well versed in prodigies and the functioning of the fates. His mastery of the tradition enabled him to become an expert critic in his own right, or so he thought – and he does not seem to anticipate his claim being a particularly controversial one. Thus, the circle turns completely: he is now in a position to present the material to a new posterity, with adjustments made to their particular needs, *exempla* selected to improve their situation and remedy their deficiencies.

It is therefore his study of history that allows him to set himself up as a critic of contemporary Rome. If the authority of augurs is questioned, the reporting of prodigies neglected, or (worse still) the gods neglected or dismissed, then it is not Livy who inveighs against Rome, but *Rome's history*, the long succession of experts and experience, which issues condemnation and thereby implicitly urges for a return to the superior practices of the past, that is to say *Livy's* historical Rome.

In this, as in so many other aspects of his narrative, Livy appears to defer to an external authority to do his work for him, while in fact retaining full control of those authorities (it is, after all *his* narrative). Like so many contemporary texts, a central concern in the *AVC* is the recent neglect of the gods that almost brought Rome low and led to the principate. Livy writes in the tradition of 'religious decline' 'invented' by Varro and his generation, writers sharply aware of the changes over time to a system that had no mechanism for abandoning previous practices. Though he claimed in his prologue that Rome was beyond repair, Livy set out a template for a religious as much as moral and political restoration.

It could not be any other way: religious issues permeate Roman life in his account and are not easily divorced from moral, political, military and social matters. In a sense, we would expect nothing else from a historian, whose task was to evoke Rome, to recreate the past for the entertainment and edification of the present. In this way, Rome's religious history could continue, both as a literary tradition and as a political reality. Armed with the *AVC*, Rome was equipped to revive and continue her greatness under the watchful eye of benevolent gods. And we, unlike Livy, have the opportunity to see whether his labours bore fruit.

4
Tacitus and the restoration of Rome

Just as the analysis of Livy's religious material required some awareness of his broader aims and methods, so too with Tacitus it is essential to acknowledge the way in which he undertook his project and what that was. Of course society had changed profoundly with the transition to empire and we should not expect that the eminently political act of writing history had not also adapted. Nonetheless we shall see that if circumstances and methods had changed, many similarities remain. Like his predecessor, Tacitus constructed a representation of Roman state religion from the events of the past: he 'made sense' of what had gone before and produced an account that reflect his idealised religious system while organising his coverage of events to argue a case. His was not the only possible version of events, even if we find it plausible historically: the historian/emperor Claudius, for instance, might have left us a very different version, given the chance. We shall therefore not only explore the way that religious institutions are represented, but also explore the agenda that helped to 'inform' the facts at Tacitus' disposal.

What emerges is a coherent programme, shaped by selectivity, powerful timing and presentation, with typically Tacitean vigour. He knew his own mind on religion, though this has not generally been the accepted viewpoint. Though many of the religious notices are apparently neutral, once we appreciate Tacitus' techniques of juxtaposing contradictory information, it will be clear that there is no such thing as 'mere' inclusion: virtually all 'religious' notices are pertinent and combine to create a picture of what is usually best described as incompetence. We shall deal exclusively with Tacitus' *construction* – Tacitus' Rome, Tacitus' Roman religion: the fact that the agents and events are more or less historical does nothing to undermine the rhetorical programme in his historical analysis, though the greater detail means we can track individual characters in far more detail. We find not a grudging and reluctant string of isolated notices, with occasional pithy asides, but a powerful and efficient analysis of Rome's religious conduct, her increasing failures and the inevitable consequences. Tacitus' religious narrative is sophisticated, discriminating and, most of all, *coherent* to a very high degree.

Posterity has perhaps been kinder to Tacitus than to Livy.[1] By the time that Tacitus wrote, the principate, which had barely begun at the time when Livy composed his extant books, had become the established political choice of the city of Rome. It had survived assassinations, the end of two hereditary dynasties and civil war that saw the institution survive intact, despite a rapid turnover of personnel. The solution to these crises saw a new development: for the first time the emperor could be made (*fieri*) outside Rome.[2] Religion has rarely been treated as a significant part of the narrative of events, more as an occasional and erratic ornament that has little or no bearing on any explanation of history. In fact, nothing could be further from the truth.

4.1 Religious categories

As with Livy, we begin by establishing the traditional categories, such as prodigies: a comparable pattern emerges, whereby our historian takes exception to mistaken interpretations on the understanding that the reader will see the refinement of details rather than the dismissal of any category. But we must also take account of the changed circumstances: thus the new dynamics of reporting are also explored. The deployment of *fors*, *fortuna* and *fatum* also bears witness to the dynamics of contemporary interpretation. In addition, Tacitus is as concerned as Livy to demarcate appropriate practices: *superstitio* and other methods of recommendation feature throughout his historical accounts.

Once the religious 'furniture' of the account has been examined, we move on to examine the practice of the *cultus deorum*, beginning with imperial cult, which, rather than being isolated as one particular feature, is located as part of a system of honouring the emperors (including lesser honours and lesser members of the family) within a political arena – the only place where it makes sense, whether that sense is Tacitean or more generally historical. In fact, 'politics' emerges as the appropriate context in which to explain a great deal of the religious narrative: the operation of the *cultus deorum* is fundamentally shaped by the contemporary political and social situation. As the integrity of politics 'declined', so too did religious appointments and the authority of the senate: this process, like most of the others, runs across relatively unbroken from the *Annals* into the *Histories*, or, more correctly, is projected back in time from the start of the *Histories*

---

[1] Woodman (1985) 3 applauds Martin's (1981) 10 description of Tacitus as 'the greatest Roman historian'. Syme's *The Roman Revolution* opens with the same praise.

[2] *H.* 1.4.2.

into the period of the *Annals*. In fact 'religion' and 'politics' make better sense taken as a unity than separately.

As the emperors appropriated authority over religion, so too did interpretation become rather hit and miss: and *all* the emperors fail to provide the kind of expertise that Livy's Republican senate could collectively muster. Tacitus has the intrinsic failure of the aristocracy to address Rome's religious concerns finally culminate in the manifestation of the *ira deum* that dominates the opening of the *Histories,* in the form of civil war and the firing of the Capitoline Temple. Finally, we examine the way that the history of the entire period, especially the success of the Flavians, is contextualised in Tacitus' account by the deployment of *fatum*: there is no surrender to the authority of any individuals, even the 'good' emperors. We are reading of the history of *Rome*, not her rulers, and the religious categories are deployed accordingly.

Throughout both accounts, Tacitus is concerned with finding a formulation of Roman religion that will suit the new Rome with her unpredictable and often damaging emperors. This is not to say that he has an intrinsic problem with the institution of empire itself: Rome had declined morally to the point where imperial rule was a necessity.[3] Where once it was the people, now it was the emperor who had to be understood (*A.* 4.33.1-2). The essentially exemplary nature of historiography therefore adapted to new circumstances while retaining its claims to guidance.[4]

---

[3] There is much bibliography on the issue; the usual interpretation is that Tacitus accepts the empire but is deeply interested in having the political system work, whatever its shortcomings. Scott's (1968) formulation of the issue, which stresses Tacitus' grasp of a variety of different historical constitutions and deeper interest in morality than any political system, is still a good corrective to the usual bipolar approach ('monarchist or republican labels are not particularly relevant to him' (50 n.15)). See also André (1982) 41–43 who argues that, for Tacitus, there is no realistic alternative to monarchy; Shotter (1978) and (1991b) argues that he is more interested in having the co-operation of senate and emperor than any constitutional change as do Wistrand (1979), Percival (1980) and Sage (1991); Classen (1988) allows for a change in behaviour and ideals since the Republic; Havas (1991) argues for a 'conception biologique' of the state in the historian's thinking. If he accepts empire, however, Tacitus does not necessarily spare individual emperors; see e.g. Boesche (1987) for the destruction of the social and political fabric by the hypocrisy and isolation of the emperor. Cogitore (1991) 2 sees the use of different terms for power as an implicit attack on the institution, but the terms could equally be complaints about the use of power in individual cases. Cf. Béranger (1990) and Benario (1992).

[4] Aubrion (1991). Note Sinclair's (1995) expansion of the theme: 'in fact, the most valuable lesson a Roman historian provides when it comes to models of explanation and behaviour for what was felt to be transient in society is furnished by his own example in explicating the causes and motives for events' (38). Plass (1988) 103 also stresses the way that political issues are still treated 'in terms of *moral* incoherence' (my emphasis). For explicit mention of an exemplary programme, see *H.* 1.3.1, 3.51.2 and *A.* 4.33.2; for the use of *exempla* in public life within the account, see (selectively) *A.* 3.31.3-4, 3.50.2, 3.66.1-2, 6.32.4, 11.6.1, 11.23.22-3, 11.24 (esp. 11.24.7), 12.20.2, 13.4.1, 15.20.3, 15.23.2, 15.44.5, *H.* 1.50.2, 2.91.3, 4.8.1 and 4.42.6. For the difficulties of using *exempla* in changed times, see (e.g.) *H.* 4.58.2; Ginsburg (1993); Luce (1986); McCulloch (1984) 189. For further debate see also Luce (1991), esp. 2907-2914 and Woodman (1997) 109 which seem to argue against exemplarity, unconvincingly to my mind.

Tacitus' disposition to provide *exempla* raises a fundamental problem: his supposed 'pessimism'. It is taken for granted that he can be fairly described thus, and there is little incentive for someone to provide correctives if he expects the future to be worse than the present. The impression gains support from the sheer number of times that he castigates the actions of agents in his texts, who seem to many commentators to be involved unknowingly in a retrospective game of 'you can't win' with the historian. This, I shall argue, is a misunderstanding. Tacitus, it is true, acknowledges errors in abundance, but this does not mean that he considers all courses of action to be pointless. For a start, he himself tells us that he will catalogue the worst moments of the period: one should not expect a 'balanced' account.[5]

It will become clear that he had certain expectations, and that when these are met, his agents meet with his satisfaction. His precise sense of what was appropriate may be pedantic, and his verdicts of even minor deviations from the ideal, damning: but just because most of the first century was a catalogue of errors for him does not mean that he is pessimistic. He had lived through the savage reign of Domitian, as commentators rarely fail to point out, and we therefore assume that this experience colours his own account, like an obsession: as we shall, however, see, Tacitus is not only or even primarily interested in emperors – it is with the City of Rome that he deals.

Can we not instead read the account of a man who knows only too well what happens when delicate balances of power are upset, when the worst in human nature runs wild? A man who has known both success and failure in the difficult act of Roman politics, and knows (to his own satisfaction at least) that anything short of the precisely considered response can lead to disaster? The remorseless string of mistakes is balanced by the occasional praise or satisfaction where an agent successfully navigates the nightmare of early imperial politics. All too often we cannot see what a criticised agent 'should' have done but that does not mean that there was not a more expeditious course of action open to them: we will be partly occupied with elucidating the better response, and what Tacitus otherwise expected his reader to know.

This kind of account does not deserve the description of pessimism, however exacting, even exasperating, his high standards might be. The account, with its internal logic intact, shows how misjudgements led to terror, exile and death for many of its (often innocent) participants. Who would *not* wish to highlight the consequences of past political error when dealing with such a period? Failure had a high price in his reconstructed reality. The

---

[5] *A*. 14.64.6. This does not mean his account is not 'truthful' (16.16, 6.38.1).

admittedly depressing series of disasters is perfect material from which to learn: there was no need to repeat past mistakes. What better material for an exemplary historian?

It will, then, be (at times) argued and (elsewhere) assumed that Tacitus saw hope for the future in the bloodbaths and inquisitions of the past. Just occasionally hope could be glimpsed as he himself reports at intervals. This brings us to the second aspect of his 'pessimism', namely the assumption that things had not improved much by the time that he wrote.

Tacitus explicitly tells us that the times in which he lived, under Nerva and Trajan, had improved greatly: it was a 'golden age' when the senate and emperor worked together as colleagues and one could think freely and speak one's thoughts (*principatum diui Neruae et imperium Traiani, uberiorem securioremque materiam, senectuti seposui, rara temporum felicitate, ubi sentire quae uelis et quae sentias dicere licet, H. 1.1.4*). *Textually* then, even despite the loss of large parts of the texts, Rome has improved to an astonishing degree. Unfortunately, the conviction, gained impressionistically from reading his savage indictment of his predecessors' actions, is frequently compounded by the dismissal of favourable comments about the times in which he wrote, with a logic that amounts to 'well, he would say that, wouldn't he?' This textual contentment has therefore met with little acceptance from modern commentators.[6]

Even if we could prove a dissonance between contemporary reality and Tacitus' descriptions of it, there is no reason to proceed to the conclusion of hypocrisy. Consider Thrasea Paetus' praise of Rome and Nero, and severe castigation of Antistius, at 14.48.5. The Stoic inspires the senate and forces Nero to comply with the philosopher's blatantly untrue depiction of a merciful and mature Rome in agreeing to a comparatively lenient sentence of exile. Even if Tacitus' audience were not 'actually' living in an ideal climate, they might take the hint. The facts of the future might be shaped by the lead of those willing to take on the challenge of his recommendations, and any gap between his theory and the practice of real life is thereby politely occluded. At its worst then, the praise of Trajan's reign could be treated as an invitation. More importantly, whatever our speculations, it cannot be denied that Rome is constructed *within the historical narrative* to have emerged from the darkness that dominates the extant accounts. To work with anything else makes us unforgivably selective. We do

---

[6] Cf. *Agr.* 1.2-3. Perhaps most eloquent is Woodman (1997) 92–93 who is rather unwilling to commit himself either way: 'Tacitus' repeated retreat from his own age carries the suggestion (which may of course be as false as it is intentional) that the reigns of Nerva and Trajan did not justify [the claim made] ... for free speech and thought.'

not consider Livy a pessimist, or do not emphasise it as a possibility, even though his preface tells us that Rome's woes are incurable: but we do describe Tacitus in this way, even though he tells us that Rome's problems are firmly in her past. I say this not in order to argue that we should simplistically take the texts at 'face value' but rather that we should not take them automatically at its *opposite*.

It is perhaps not surprising that Tacitus' 'opinions' prove so elusive when we discount the admittedly rare categorical statements that he makes. Tacitus' 'sincerity' is often questioned, particularly in connection with his claim to write *sine ira et studio* (*A.* 1.1.3) or that *neque amore ... et sine odio dicendus est* (*H.* 1.1.4). It would not be a gross exaggeration to say that commentators feel obliged to comment on this theme. Most scholars find his claim unfounded,[7] but assessment by more appropriate criteria tends to exonerate him from hypocrisy.[8] The search for the 'real' Tacitus is misplaced, I think. We are dealing with a pair of texts that constructed a century of Rome in a particular historiographical way: we cannot hope to 'glimpse the real man' or, as Henderson memorably put it: 'we will not catch Tacitus with his rhetorical trousers down'.[9] If we dismiss the notices that times had improved considerably, we fundamentally alter the structure of the texts and the narrative(s): the resultant pessimism, no longer textually checked by the clear statement of an end to terror, can be projected forwards into a future now irrevocably doomed to failure. Whether Tacitus 'believed' that times had improved or not, he undeniably constructed his histories to be capped by a recovery, and we should not emend our texts too hastily to fit our preconceptions. The 'textual' Rome had undeniably improved.

Though Tacitus originally provided a narrative that covered most of the first century, there are two difficulties for us. Firstly, there is the fact that the partial survival of the texts leaves us in the dark about significant periods: we have only parts of the reigns of Tiberius, Claudius, Nero and Vespasian, and nothing of Caligula's, Titus' or Domitian's. Secondly, the *Histories*, covering the years 69–96, were written before the *Annals*, which covered 14–68. Thus, even though the original narrative was unbroken overall, it was not composed as one piece nor in chronological sequence. For instance, the *Annals* and *Histories* would seem to indicate different influences: opinions on the debt to Sallust and Cicero in the *Annals* and the *Histories* respectively have varied. Taken purely as historical sources, these factors are less influential than when they are treated as constructs with their own, possibly

---

[7] E.g. Cizek (1979); Whitehead (1979). Further discussion in Miller (1969); Luce (1986).
[8] See Segal (1973); Woodman (1988).
[9] Henderson (1987) 68 n.4. 'Memorably' perhaps should not apply: this line appears (regrettably) not to have found its way into the revised version (Henderson (1998a)).

distinct, internal logic and agendas. Since we are examining Tacitus' historical account as a progression, we must consider the relationship of the two with some care.

These stylistic differences do not mean that we cannot treat the accounts together. McCulloch (1984) 173–175 suggests simply that 'modern editors ... have divided what Tacitus may very well have intended to be one long work'. On this basis we might speculate that the stylistic differences could be seen as subordinate to the historical agenda; *Annals* 4–16 are more Sallustian[10] because this is intended to highlight the corruption of Rome; the *Histories* would then be more Ciceronian[11] because they deal with the restoration of traditional values. Why Tacitus, rather than fulfilling his declared intention of treating the age of Nerva and Trajan at *Histories* 1.1.5, chose instead to move backwards, can only be a matter of speculation: it may be that he found the period of the *Histories* insufficient to explain just what did happen to Rome under Domitian and that the answers to Rome's sufferings lay further back in the past.

But to make Domitian the focus of Tacitus' interest may be to underestimate the historian: we have a great deal of evidence that he set his sights wider than assuaging a guilty conscience for his supposed compliance with a vicious régime. The contrast between the political failures of the early part of the century and the avowedly improved contemporary situation provides probably the greatest tension with the longest perspective – but *only* if we resist the temptation to dismiss his description of the times of Nerva and Trajan on the grounds that they do not match the rest of his account and are 'inevitably' sycophantic, a position which, as I have said, has a long pedigree but no textual support. From what remains of the text, our best assumption is that he wished to explain how Rome had 're-emerged' from the dark days of the Julio-Claudians into the golden age in which he was writing. Since we lack any remnants of Tacitus' account of Domitian's reign, little can be said for certain: but narratological continuity strongly implies that the *Annals* were intended to support, rather than rival, the analyses presented in the *Histories*. This is generally assumed in the following account: an arbitrary choice, to be sure, but no more arbitrary than assuming otherwise.

While Tacitus did not write annalistic history in the way that Livy did,[12] it will be argued that amongst the differences lies a rich vein of continuity,

---

[10] Woodman (1988) 160–169 and (1992b); Ducroix (1978), with further bibliography.

[11] Woodman (1985) and (1988) 160–196.

[12] On the (mis)use of the annalistic format, see Henderson (1998a) 258, 286–260; also Woodman (1997) 93–94. For discussion of the structure of the *Annals* in hexads (or not) see most recently Martin (1990); Woodman and Martin (1989) 14–19 (who virtually abandon the idea of consensus); McCulloch (1984) 137–176. Goodyear (1970b) 17–18 succinctly disposes of Syme's position on hexads.

especially in terms of religion. In fact, what is remarkable is the lengths to which Tacitus goes to preserve a traditional framework of interpretation.

The continuing interest in Tacitus' works is amply demonstrated by the number of entries in Benario's bibliographies,[13] no few of which centre on 'deciphering' Tacitus. The difficulties of reading this ingenious author are well illustrated by the way that Luce's discussion of 'historical change' finds its summation in the issue of 'the difficulties of discovering the historian's opinions'.[14] The plethora of publications on issues of detail has not always led to any broader consensus, least of all in connection with religion.[15] Though interpretations can vary enormously, there are some relatively consistent themes to be found in scholars' descriptions of our author; pessimism and savagery, bias, reasonable historicity, inappropriate distortion and, rather confusingly, indecisiveness.

The religious material has had a similarly mixed reception. Only one monograph (and that dealing purely with the *Histories*) argues that Tacitus was 'traditional' in his 'beliefs'.[16] It is more common to find that the apparent contradictions hold sway, forcing an interpretation that has Tacitus sceptical about traditional Roman religion but still 'religious' in a broad sense, usually fatalistically.[17] While it is true that fate occupies a more prominent role in the narrative, and is apparently more easily invoked by Tacitus when compared with Livy, this does not simply reflect some 'personal preference', as we shall see. Adoption of the principles applied to

---

[13] The most recent, *CW* 89.2 (1995), contains 672 entries.

[14] Luce (1986) makes useful comments about the difficulties of 'discovering the historian's opinions', discounting as he goes a traditional technique of removing 'troublesome' elements to 'uncover' Tacitus' 'true' ideas.

[15] This chapter claims only to be representative; exhaustive cross-referencing to related topics is no longer a realistic possibility. The most recent and/or significant items on a particular issue are included, not least to provide fuller relevant bibliography.

[16] Scott (1968). A number of briefer articles imply this, but do not deal with the difficulties that have led other authors to conclude that Tacitus is untraditional. Liebeschuetz (1979) 194 is closest to the position argued here when he concludes '[Tacitus' rationalism] is ... that of a man who believes in the science in which he is an expert' but I take issue with his comment that 'the gods did communicate with the Roman state through portents, but the signals should not be taken to be more than vague warnings' (*ibid.* 197) and that 'Tacitus would not have been troubled by problems of free will and predestination if he had not lived in an age dominated by Stoic ideas' (199). The latter statement seems to be putting the cart before the horse. Tacitus has no particular love of philosophers *per se* – see his ridicule of the Stoic Musonius Rufus at *H.* 3.81.1. Though Tacitus does acknowledge the existence of Stoic ideas in Roman society, he cannot be said to privilege them: his categories are traditional.

[17] 'Tacitus' belief in prophecy and portents was never more than hesitant and spasmodic' (Walker (1952) 246); 'it is at least arguable that he never indicates more than the normal human disposition to see, when depressed, omens everywhere' (Miller (1977) 14); Syme (1958a), like many others, seems to consider that religious material features only insofar as the genre 'demanded' it, and then in a rather erratic and spasmodic way. But he does offer a disclaimer – 'Tacitus does not have to worry about consistency' (522). He also refers to 'the scepticism appropriate to that governing order' (523).

Livy's narrative yields a very different picture. In particular we will find that sustained criticism and sarcastic irony are not necessarily tantamount to scepticism, pessimism, bias or indecision.

The first difficulty that the reader of Tacitus encounters is his style. Commentaries include a compulsory notice of the difficulties of his diction,[18] and it is this as much as anything that has made the commentator's task so difficult. Time and again, students with good Latin earnestly ask to know 'what he really meant'. There are, however, reasons to think that 'style' is not just the 'wrapping' of an account that can be usefully removed with perseverance; rather it is integral to the work and its purpose. 'Irrationality ... comes out with special clarity in the *form* of the narrative'.[19] The frequent violation of expectation in Tacitus' historical works evokes the political chaos and *dissimulatio* of the principate. Such considerations begin to address enormous questions such as the difference between the two exemplificatory accounts: Livy, with his 'full-scale working model' of Rome is set against Tacitus, who seems more interested in cataloguing errors than explicitly offering any alternative.

Furthermore, the decipherment of a religious structure in the narrative goes some way towards restoring these markers of improvement by supporting a reading that has a more 'optimistic' Tacitus: in the reading that follows, Rome has good prospects for improvement that will blossom under Nerva and Trajan when our text of the *Histories* breaks off. And rather than seeing Vespasian and Titus as interruptions of an otherwise deepening gloom, we could consider Domitian an aberration in an otherwise steady trend of improvement that ran from Vespasian and Titus through to Nerva and Trajan – just as the author tells us to.[20] A model of recovery under the Flavians, one way or another, fits these textual notices better than our (preferred) image of pessimism.

These trends must be reconstructed from apparently minor notices: our author is not generally given to simplifying the plot. He expects the reader to know what he is talking about and refrains from making bland explicit statements: after all 'Tacitus sets the highest premium on displaying his

---

[18] Irony: Plass (1988); O'Gorman (2000); on syntax see Furneaux (1896) 38–74; for *uariatio* see especially Plass (1992); Woodcock (1959) 11–14; Woodman (1997) 111; Syme (1958a) 342–243.

[19] Plass (1988) 102, original emphasis. See also Plass (1992); Sinclair (1991a) and (1995); Henderson (1987) and (1998) as the foremost proponents of this kind of interpretation. See also Woodman (1985) 18; Williams (1990) 3–10. Further bibliography in Benario (1986), items 126–160 and (1995) items 123–149.

[20] This will be developed further in due course, but even without the argument to follow, we can note from *A.* 3.55 that luxury declined under Vespasian decline because of his example, and under Domitian because of the deterrent of imperial appropriation (on this difficult passage, see Woodman in Woodman and Martin (1996) *ad loc*).

personal mastery over his material. He constantly varies his technique, adjusts his diction, and shifts his points of reference – at all costs he must remain the one person in his narrative who cannot be categorised' (Sinclair (1995) 8).

Sinclair's penetrating analysis of the way that 'narrative in the *Annales* often proceeds through palpable silences' (*ibid.* 164) does not, however, permit us to attempt to fill in the gaps by inference. The silences do more than protect Tacitus' 'real opinions' from possible criticism:

> One aim of irony is precisely to leave uncertain what is ironic …the effect of such writing on a large scale is to create an atmosphere of dry wit and ruthless penetration into a political and moral reality that is often irrational if not idiotic. The tone is at once amusing and dismaying. Both those who make history and those who write it are caught up in pervasive cynicism, though one of quite different sorts – the former an alarming moral cynicism that suggests disorder in high places, the latter an intellectual cynicism gratifying because it exposes the former. (Plass (1988) 4–5)[21]

Under the principate, a carefully placed silence became more than just protective, and traditional motifs, such as juxtaposition within the narrative, were exploited to their fullest potential, as we shall see. They became a tool for political comment. The dangers of speech, probably more than any other factor, led to a sophistication in the use of language.[22] We should be wary of 'deciphering' Tacitus, lest we lose the 'real' message. It is the dissonance in the text that speaks volumes. Traditional materials found in a new guise are the poet's medium for generating experience in the reader, and this is no less true of Tacitus than any other writer.[23] The violation of the traditional

---

[21] See also Baldwin (1977) who amply demonstrates the farcical nature of *Annals* 14, though he does not place the humour in any broader context.

[22] Apart from Henderson (1987), Plass (1988) and Sinclair (1995), Rudich (1985), (1993) and (1997) (esp. his Introduction 'The Rhetoricized Mentality', 1–16), deal with this theme admirably. See also Ahl (1984).

[23] Conté (1994) 111–125, writing chiefly on poetry. For use of poetic motifs and the similarities of historiography and poetry, see Feeney (1991) 42–45, 250–264; Martin (1992); Kenney (1983) 14 calls him 'the arch-poet of ancient historians'; Aubrion (1991) stresses the epic and tragic overtones of the *Histories*; Lossau (1992) finds the 'contamination' of an epic and tragic model; Henry (1991) suggests that a 'sense of tragic doom, together with the assertion of a positive national identity that the sense of doom contradicts, that is the most truly Virgilian element in Tacitus' (2992); for other Virgilian overtones see also Segal (1973); Boyle (1984); Miller (1986); Henry (1991). For historiography as entertainment, Woodman (1979) and (1985).

Roman way of life is reflected in the violation of genre,[24] language[25] and historical record.[26]

This is perhaps most evocatively represented by Henderson's deliberately chaotic 'World in Pieces'.[27] The newer readings of Tacitus have far-reaching consequences for our reception of the religious material that has appeared contradictory and incomplete for so long. Though the categories of interpretation and classification show a large degree of consistency, it is the overall tenor of the religious system that shows change in response to different needs. It is after all *application* that shapes such interpretative systems. The discussion begins by confirming sufficient continuity in the phenomena and categories associated with religion in Livy to allow comparison. By drawing on the religious frames of reference as well as other recent general interpretations, it is possible to question the suggestions that Tacitus is so thoroughly pessimistic and a(nti)traditional, and to assert rather that he is radically conservative in his politics and religion.

4.2 Tacitus: a man of distinctions

4.2.1 Establishing religious categories

Tacitus' *persona* differs markedly, on the surface at least, from Livy's. Whereas Livy established his authority under the aegis of deference, Tacitus, the former proconsul and *quindecemuir*,[28] *appears* at least to be most confident in his scathing remarks (though we shall find no shortage of more subtle rhetorical strategies); unfortunately, taken at 'face' value, these confident remarks appear to *us* to undermine traditional practices. In addition his habitual silence following criticism often leaves us emphatically clear as to where an error was made, but apparently does little to advise on a better course of action.

Thus McCulloch ((1991) 2939) complains that 'what, in fact, makes Tacitus so exasperating for many of his readers is that he himself is not concerned about his failure to account for all historical phenomena in the

---

[24] See e.g. Woodman and Martin (1989) on 4.1.

[25] Plass (1988). Also, amongst others, Cizek (1991).

[26] Where Tacitus can be compared with inscriptions, the results are interesting. While recording a great number of similarities, it is apparent that Tacitus has skilfully placed a different interpretation on the facts: Woodman (1997) 99–100 (on the *Tabula Siarensis* and the decree on the elder Piso); McCulloch (1991) 2941–2944 (on Claudius' speech). Williams (1989a) argues for Tacitus' desire to indicate faithfully the complexities of the historical context. Shotter (1988) argues that Tacitus follows the historical record closely while endeavouring to accommodate the enigma that was the emperor Tiberius. Others are more critical of Tacitus' use of sources, e.g. Develin (1983).

[27] Henderson (1987), rewritten (some would say sanitised) as Henderson (1998a) 257–300.

[28] *A.* 11.11.1.

same way [as those he scorns, such as astrologers]'. The traditional interpretative categories of 'belief' or 'scepticism' lead commentators to conclude that we are usually encountering the latter. More complex are those moments where Tacitus appears to be hesitant or contradictory; the conclusion is usually indecision or, where 'contradiction' is noted, a change of heart. In contrast, the following analysis assumes that Tacitus is the master of his material at all times; as the Foucauldian scholarly analyses accumulate, the coherency of his account and programme is increasingly hard to avoid. The competitive arena is, as with Livy, that of interpretation and propriety rather than scepticism and belief.

We cannot, however, simply transpose the interpretative tools honed on Livy's account. The material, while recognisable in many ways, can also be markedly different. This may represent a deliberate violation of tradition reflected in the text; it might, on the other hand, owe more to the changed political and social context – in other words, to happen to conform to contemporary expectations. To begin with, the traditional categories must be established.

4.2.1.1 Prodigies and omens

As with Livy, it is Tacitus' comments, rather than the prodigies themselves, that require our careful interpretation. Because these comments have been interpreted as cynical or critical, the vast majority of commentators are unwilling to take these phenomena as meaningful 'in reality'. McCulloch, for instance, is sympathetic in general but still prefers to limit himself to textual relevance, in an implied opposition to the constructed reality in which the audience lived. '[T]he issue is not whether Tacitus did or did not believe that such prodigies had an influence on the operation of the natural world. Instead, *within his narrative* they have a portendous significance'.[29] Elsewhere he reasserts Tacitus' scepticism, before speaking of the concepts of *deum ira* and *hominum rabies* as a 'psychological rather than a metaphysical metaphor'.[30] Most of these commentators are highly sensitive to the aestheticised text, but they show a relative lack of sympathy for religious phenomena as events based in reality and depend on a dichotomy between

---

[29] McCulloch (1984) 208 (my emphasis).
[30] McCulloch (1991) 2938, 2941. Plass is extremely sensitive to the function of prodigies in the narrative but draws the line at making a traditionalist of Tacitus: 'portents . . . can be taken seriously as a historiographical category without being taken literally as a religious or historical category' (Plass (1988) 71–78; quote from 76). The list could be extended (e.g. Segal (1973) 110f.) and the trend continues: see Ash (1999) 129–136, especially 130–131; Martin and Woodman (1989) 84 (citing Goodyear's (1972) comments on 1.39). Grimal (1989 and 1989–90) seems more willing to accept a genuine 'belief' in such things, suggesting that Tacitus is rejecting *superstitio* not prodigies and omens *per se*.

literature and 'reality'. Thus, at least judging from discussion in print, it seems that some establishment of the category of prodigies (and by implication, other 'supernatural' events) is necessary before any discussion of details can be pursued.[31]

4.2.1.2 Prodigies as harbingers of doom

If Tacitus were assuming without question that prodigies indicated the wrath of the gods, then he would not need to say so; after all, 'for all Tacitus's domineering, opinionated sententiousness, there are few Latin authors who make greater demands on the reader's ability to understand what is not said'.[32] For instance, when he comments that an ox had spoken in Etruria and that there had been unusual births, and many other things that in more simple times (*rudibus saeculis*) had been noted even in times of peace, but which are now only heeded at times of fear (*H.* 1.86.1), we should not understand him to be dismissing the report by the comparison with earlier, less sophisticated times: Tacitus typically uses *rudis* in two ways. Firstly of specific characters – the naive or the inexperienced; many young adults, with responsibility thrust upon them too young, are called *rudis*.[33] Secondly, he uses it of groups of people who are simple-minded. This might be the gullible (*A.* 6.3.2) country folk who are duly corrupted by the decadent city dwellers (*A.* 1.31.4) or the sort of people who did not require laws – before the gradual encroachment of the need for legislation, in the face of a decadent and immoral society (*A.* 3.26.3).[34] To be *rudi animo* is not a particularly *useful* state in the maelstrom of Roman politics, where shrewdness and wit were required to navigate the complexities of cruelty and obsequiousness; nonetheless it was not necessarily an undesirable faculty in itself.[35] At worst it implies error in interpretation but it seems preferable to understand a lost innocence before the distortions of corruption had taken their toll rather than a naivety that has been 'rightly' outgrown. Very often, therefore, we are left to navigate the assumptions that contextualise these comments by further comparison with his more general position: Tacitus is no more concerned to educate a wholly ignorant readership about religion than Livy was.

---

[31] Much of the following discussion implicitly draws on the framework established in connection with Livy, viz. the assumption that the readership would accept the intervention of the gods and that to explain it would be superfluous and possibly insulting except where details of interpretation (i.e. possible controversy) were concerned.

[32] Sinclair (1995) 164.

[33] Agrippa Postumus is *rudem sane bonarum artium* (*A.* 1.3.4); Drusus is *rudis dicendi* (*A.* 1.29.1).

[34] For the beginning of the decline of Rome with the introduction of laws see Scott (1968) 64.

[35] See McCulloch (1984) 196–199 on the virtues of simplicity and the corruption of laws and *dominatio* ('The administration of justice among the simpler, less civilised Germans (*Germania* 12) stands in contrast to the corruption of the legal system at Rome', 199).

But occasionally Tacitus *is* compelled to spell out the obvious. Consider his comments on the Jews and their folly during the war in Judaea. Among their errors are religious mistakes on a scale that only foreigners could make: the Jews did not think it right (*fas habet*) to resolve prodigies with sacrifices or vows since they were so contrary (*H.* 5.13.1). The implication is that the Jews should have known better and expiated the (very Roman-sounding) prodigies that follow. Where Livy was never put in the position of needing to point out the utility of prodigy expiation, the Jews in their incompetence offer the opportunity for profound scorn from the imperial historian. They can be measured against the fundamental assumptions of 'proper' religious practice. The passage is a series of errors, both institutional and interpretative, that virtually guarantee the failure of their rebellion.

The range of comments that assume the traditional meaning of prodigies as harbingers of doom is further evidence that there has been no major change in the understanding of signs taken to be adverse. One example comes at 12.64.1: *mutationem rerum in deterius portendi cognitum est crebris prodigiis.*[36] The majority of the remaining problematic references are easily susceptible to the kind of analysis pursued in connection with Livy's account: there is a premium on interpretation, of the distinction between genuine prodigies and mistaken ones. In other words our imperial historian is still working with the kind of discrimination (not dismissal) that was seen in Livy.

Deduction from visible signs is still the order of the day: *uelut* is, as was found in Livy, politely indicative of the proprieties of interpretation. This process of 'appearance' or 'initial assessment' being confirmed can be seen when Nero 'seemed' to have polluted a sacred spring by bathing there: the subsequent illness confirmed that he had upset the gods.[37] Tacitus has a preference for a more down-to-earth explanation than divine wrath of the legend dealing with the destruction of what seems to be Sodom and Gomorrah at *H.* 5.7. But this is a genre-specific preference for a discerning interpretation which should always at least *attempt* a 'natural' explanation.[38] That the gods *can* be involved in the destruction of cities, but via human

---

[36] Further examples of traditional interpretation are to be found at *A.* 15.47.1 (*prodigia imminentium malorum*), and in the opening to the *Histories* (*prodigia et fulminum monitus et futurorum praesagia, H.* 1.3.2). Similarly, Paetus suffers when he proceeds into Armenia *spretis ominibus* (*A.* 15.8.1), on which see Meulder (1993).

[37] *A.* 14.22.6: [*Nero*] *uidebaturque potus sacros et caerimoniam loci corpore loto polluisse. secutaque anceps ualetudo iram deum adfirmauit.*

[38] Cf. the disclaimer when he includes the sign connected to Otho's death at *H.* 2.50.2 (*ut conquirere fabulosa et fictis oblectare legentium animos procul grauitate coepti operis crediderim, ita uolgatis traditisque demere fidem non ausim*).

means, is evident from the omen and the interpretation put on it during the siege of Artaxata where *adicitur miraculum uelut numine oblatum*.[39] Twice in the *Histories* we are told of a particular variation of moral panic, whereby inexperienced interpreters took the lack of water to be a prodigy. He adds that things that were taken to be chance or natural occurrences in peace were then called *fatum* and the *ira deum* (*H.* 4.26.2).[40] In the *Annals*, on the other hand, when lightning struck a table at which Nero was dining shortly after the appearance of a comet 'about which the common opinion is that it portends some kind of change of ruler (*rex*)', it strengthened the belief that Nero's days were numbered. But both deductions were errors *pari uanitate ...interpretatio* (*A.* 14.22.2).[41] The priestly interpretation of the birth of a calf by the roadside with its head attached to its leg that another 'head' of state (*rerum humanarum*) was being prepared, but that it would be neither healthy nor secret (*A.* 15.47.3), just underlines the stupidity of those who immediately (in the text) begin plotting to overthrow Nero. Tacitus' superior knowledge textually crushes the conspiracy even before it appears.[42]

Two prodigy notices in particular, one in the *Annals* and another in the *Histories*, do however require more analysis at this point. In the chaotic opening to the *Histories*, Tacitus concludes his account of the dislocation of Roman life with the note that:

> Besides the complex of disasters in human affairs, there were prodigies in the sky and on the earth, both warnings of thunder and signs of the future, auspicious and ill-omened, difficult to interpret and unambiguous; for never was it proven by more terrible nightmares that befell the citizens of Rome or by

---

[39] The passage in full reads: *adicitur miraculum uelut numine oblatum. Nam cuncta [extra tectis] hactenus sole inlustria fuere; repente quod moenibus cingebatur ita atra nube coopertum fulgoribusque discretum est, ut quasi infensantibus deis exitio tradi crederetur* (*A.* 13.41.3).

[40] There is also the note at *H.* 1.86.3 that *a fortuitis uel naturalibus causis in prodigium et omen imminentium cladium uertebatur*.

[41] It is possible that the error with the comet was the equation of a *princeps* with a *rex* rather than the utter vacuity of the interpretation. However, as we shall see (below, 215), there is another possible correction implied here, whereby it is the timing that is at fault (*quasi iam depulso Nerone, A.* 14.22.1).

[42] The conspiracy includes religious error too: Scaevinus' 'lucky dagger', from either the Temple of *Salus* or *Fortuna* in Ferentum (*A.* 15.53.3), is central to the downfall of the plot (15.54 and 55). Neither 'safety' nor 'success' comes their way, though one can understand that they would require the support of at least one of these two. It is possible to speculate on the dynamics of this association: *Salus* and *Fortuna* do abandon Nero in due course (perhaps, we might say, when they get the opportunity). The dagger also gains an association with *Vindex*, since Nero chooses to dedicate it to Jupiter Vindex at *A.* 15.74.2, which is taken to be prophetic after the struggle with Julius Vindex. This may imply that the dagger's divine patronage, unbestowed on the conspirators, did have some potency, if insufficient to their particular task.

more conclusive signs that the gods were not concerned with our well-being, but preferred vengeance.

> *praeter multiplicis rerum humanarum casus caelo terraque prodigia et fulminum monitus et futurorum praesagia, laeta tristia, ambigua manifesta; nec enim umquam atrocioribus populi Romani cladibus magisue iustis indiciis adprobatum est non esse curae deis securitatem nostram, esse ultionem.* (*H.* 1.3.2)

Syme commented on this (amongst others), labelling it 'a striking and ominous phrase, but no confession of a creed';[43] but Tacitus is not so vague. He exploits the ambiguity of the present infinitive *esse* to leave the reader with two possible readings. Firstly that, *at that point*, Rome's gods nursed nothing but malice – such a statement being entirely orthodox (and the one given in the translation above). Thus Rome had failed, apparently spectacularly, to propitiate her gods. Secondly, however, the text also admits of the understanding that this is not a particular, but a general, state of affairs: 'the gods *are* not concerned with our well-being, but prefer vengeance'. This more polemical reading is in stark contrast to the *benignitas deum* that we found in Livy. And Tacitus is hardly immune to the possibilities of language; we should respond to both possible meanings. It is the latter sense that has been exploited by those who would have a disenchanted Tacitus 'losing his faith'; yet a literal reading of one possible interpretation distorts the deliberate violation of expectation that seeks to convey the horror of an imperial civil war. Tacitus is 'exaggerating' (if that simple term can do him justice):[44] to say that the gods were malicious towards Rome is, in Plass' terms, a joke. Only by violating reality (the gods cannot 'really' be so set against Rome) can the violation of social and political norms be represented.[45] Nor is there any room for doubt on this – Tacitus' interpretation of events is beyond negotiation, since he does not equip the reader with sufficient detail to draw a different conclusion: the wrath of the gods is a given fact on a huge scale.

---

[43] Syme (1958a) 521. For all Syme's Tacitean and persuasive prose, exactly what a 'creed' might have looked like to him is not clear.

[44] Compare the way that he generalises from particulars in a way that does not seem to be supportable: Baldwin (1974); Walker (1952) 33–66 and 82–157 is a good survey of the material. There is also a tradition of commenting on his use of innuendo. Most recently and fully, Develin (1983); also Miller (1969); Shatzman (1974); Sullivan (1975); Whitehead (1979).

[45] I am reminded of a comment made by a rescue worker after the attack on the World Trade Centre in New York on September 11th: 'even gravity's got it in for us today'.

At *Annals* 14.12.3, Tacitus offers that 'prodigies also intervened, frequently and without effect . . . they occurred with such a lack of the *cura deum* that Nero continued his reign and crimes for many years' (*prodigia quoque crebra et inrita intercessere . . . quae adeo sine cura deum eueniebant ut multos post annos Nero imperium et scelera continuauerit*). Even for Tacitus, this is a densely packed set of words. The implication in the use of *crebra* that there were many prodigies is characteristically emphatic.[46] This notice in particular has attracted much comment:[47] however the problem is not with the prodigies but with our understanding of the polemical statement. *Cura deum* has consistently been taken to be subjective (i.e. 'the gods did not care about Rome'). However, there is no grammatical reason not to take it to be objective; 'we did not care about the gods'. Comparison in Tacitus' language does not necessarily prove anything, but may advise us. The phrase *sine cura* occurs elsewhere in his works objectively three times.[48] *Cura deum* (or *deorum*), on the other hand, occurs nowhere else in Tacitus' extant texts but does occur elsewhere. External comparisons permit either an objective or a subjective genitive.[49] Since prodigies function in Tacitus' narrative as warnings, 'caring' about the gods must translate into taking action on the warnings. We know that prodigies, as warnings, can be interpreted very specifically. Thus events that were genuinely prodigial presumed intention and meaningfulness, as seems to happen when the *haruspices* interpret the misformed calf that predicts Piso's conspiracy (*A.* 15.47.3).[50] Intelligibility of signs (however obscure many of the prodigies are to us) was tentatively argued for earlier (above, 97)

---

[46] At least it was in Livy: the phrase *multa prodigia* occurs there to indicate the acuteness of a crisis. Whenever he uses it, special expiations are required (5.15.1, where they are not heeded but Rome ends up sending to Delphi), 10.23.1, 21.62.1 (where the numbers lead Livy to question whether the checking procedures had been heeded), 24.10.6, 27.4.11, 28.11.1, and 40.19.1. *Quoque* is also significant since it aligns Paetus' immediately preceding actions with the gods'.

[47] E.g. '[this] suggests that the gods were intervening, as a tribune might, to protest against injustice, but in an ineffective fashion which seems to accord them only limited powers' (Walker (1952) 250); Liebeschuetz suggests that Tacitus is being ironic and contrasts the explicit complaints of Lucan ('frequently') and Silius (6.84) against the gods for not intervening: 'in Tacitus the attack is not explicit but implied' (Liebeschuetz (1979) 194). See however Segal (1973) 112–113 to whom I am closer (although he is nervous of the broader problems, 110).

[48] *A.* 2.14.3 (*sine cura ducum*; objective), *H.* 1.79.1 (without a genitive; but apparently objectively); *sine cura* also used of total indifference at *A.* 11.8.1 (objective).

[49] Objective: Quintilian *Minor Declamations.* 274.12; Martial 1.111; Silius Italicus 7.75; Livy 24.8.10. Subjective: Ovid *Metamorphoses* 8.724; Lucan 5.340; Statius *Siluae* 4.2.15; Ovid *Ars Amatoria* 3.405 and Statius *Thebaid* 5.456. Ovid *Metamorphoses* equates the *cura* of the gods with wrath (4.574).

[50] For the appearance of *haruspices* in the texts, see Briquel (1995), for whom they are uniformly correct and appropriate, with the caution that Briquel is mistaken to connect the description *superstitio* with them at *H.* 2.78.1: [*Vespasianus*] . . . *responsa uatum et siderum motum referre. nec erat intactus tali superstitione* . . .). Tacitus is surely referring to astrology.

and there are good reasons to see continuity into the imperial period.[51] We also know from Cicero's *On the Haruspical Response* that (at that time, at least) prodigies could be interpreted as a warning of strife amongst the nobility: we also hear in Tacitus (and, for the record, Livy) that the *ira deum* can manifest in a cluster of aristocratic deaths.[52] Since Nero is emphatically linked with the slaughter of Rome's more eminent populace as the narrative proceeds, it does not seem overly problematic to conclude that Tacitus understood the prodigies to indicate trouble for the ruling classes. Nero has become such a liability to Rome that his removal would effectively equate with expiation. Put differently, there is no point addressing the warnings without first removing a major cause – the emperor. The hendiadactic link of Nero's *imperium* with his *scelera* seems to mark what was perhaps Rome's last chance to end the decline: later prodigy notices suppress any hint of successful expiation. The gods' intercession was in vain because no one was listening.

For completeness' sake, we should consider here another favourite of the sceptic. A corporate sense of responsibility (rather than cynicism) is behind the polemical assertion at *A.* 16.33.1 of the 'indifference of the gods towards good and bad deeds' (*aequitate deum erga bona malaque documenta*). It is not enough to call on the gods when men are standing by watching.[53] We should probably infer a 'naive' attitude that someone can be responsible for his own behaviour and expect to escape the wider consequences of a more chronic moral and religious failure (many of Tacitus' victims, especially those that curse their enemies, are innocent). Tacitus knows better: in a corrupt Rome, it rained on the just and the unjust alike.

Modern scepticism is not a factor in Tacitus' texts: prodigies retained their traditional meaning. What is more pertinent is Tacitus' handling of them within his narrative.

One fact that has attracted attention is the relative scarcity of prodigies in the *Annals* and *Histories*, when compared with Livy. In addition, Tacitus lists fewer signs than Suetonius. There would seem to be two issues here: not just his selectivity, for which there are reasons, but also an actual decrease in the number of reports that he might have included. If we consider that prodigies, notoriously reported in far greater numbers at times of stress,[54] represented a means for communities to indicate their concerns

---

[51] For instance it seems to be important in the understanding of the omen at *A.* 15.7.2 that *pila militum arsere, magis insigni prodigio quia Parthus hostis missilibus telis decertat.*

[52] *A.* 12.64.1, Livy 40.37.1.

[53] Cf. Manlius' appeal to the plebs at Livy *A.* 6.18.9. See also above, 103.

[54] Livy 29.14.2, 21.62.1, 24.10.6; Tacitus *H.* 1.86.1, 4.26.2.

to Rome,[55] then the historical[56] question of the drop in reports can be answered by reference to the change in the political situation.[57]

Livy's Roman Republic depended on its ability to solve religious crises. It had a range of priesthoods equipped to deal with religious difficulties. At times of the *pax deum* they were therefore relatively redundant. As was outlined above in connection with Livy's prodigy notices, the advent of empire led to an increasing focus on the emperor as eminently and continuously pious, and in permanent favour with the gods. The corollary was a gradual change of emphasis in interpreting any signs that were taken to be adverse. The imperative in the Republic would have been to *regain* lost divine favour, even if repeated sacrifice was required. In contrast, the ideal under the Empire was to *retain* it. The majority of potentially prodigial or ominous material was now interpreted either positively or in connection with a change of ruler, as we see in Suetonius: 'all Suetonius' lists of signs revolve around two issues, and two only. The rise to imperial power and the fall from it.'[58] And there would be no shortage of potential signs, given the obsessive interest documented in Tacitus' Rome. The abundance of (often, but not always, flawed) interpretations is a recurrent theme throughout Tacitus' works.[59] But the divide between public discussion and formal reporting had grown much wider: whereas republican Rome had, according to Livy, been

---

[55] Or for Romans themselves; MacBain (1982) 35–42. Compare the way that Tacitus juxtaposes a prodigy report with other attempts by the plebs to indicate their displeasure to Claudius, *multa eo anno prodigia euenere …frugum quoque egestas et orta ex eo fames …in prodigium accipiebatur. nec occulti tantum questus, sed iura reddentem Claudium circumuasere clamoribus turbidis, pulsumque in extremam fori partem ui urgebant* (A. 12.43.1).

[56] It should be stressed that for the time being, we are dealing with the historical record of prodigies from which Tacitus chose items. His *deployment* of these prodigies is however dealt with below. Obviously, there is a danger of a circular argument here, since Tacitus is a key source for these events. The best control we have on this is the account of Suetonius, who tends to conflate state-related prodigies with signs attached to individuals, often without any clear distinction between what was historically accepted by the state as requiring expiation.

[57] Rosenberger (1998) 244 comes to the same conclusion.

[58] Wallace-Hadrill (1983) 191.

[59] E.g. at Augustus' death, A. 1.9.1; when the Caelian Hill burns down at A. 4.64.1; in connection with Claudius' incest at A. 12.8.2; a private dream becomes common property at A. 11.4.1-5; Nero was supposedly protected by snake(s) in the crib, A. 11.5.6; interpretations at Britannicus' funeral, A. 13.17.2; a comet appears and a bolt of lightning strikes Nero's table at A. 14.22.1-4; the Romans in Britain interpret prodigies fearfully at 14.31-32; the populace disagrees with Nero about the collapse of a theatre at A. 15.34.1-2, probably rightly; a whole spate of prodigies and adverse events (not, apparently, the same thing) receive public attention at H. 1.86 under Otho; we are told that Rome was a city 'where the populace took everything as an adverse sign' (...*apud ciuitatem cuncta interpretantem funesti ominis loco acceptum est*) at H. 2.91.1; public pressure persuades Vitellius to adopt the name Caesar at H. 3.58.3. More specifically linked to the end of a reign (i.e. the death of an emperor): the collapse of the distinction between *fatum* and *ira deum* at H. 4.26.2 seems to allude to the emperor's embodiment of divine favour or disfavour, since *fatum* is more likely to refer to the rise or fall of an emperor. Likewise the dream at A. 11.4.3 is taken adversely for Claudius, as are the signs of 14.22 under Nero.

actively interested in prodigies, no one in their right mind would report one to an imperial senate. Though this factor was never redundant, the extent to which this shaped the perception of events varied according to the emperor of the time. This historical situation is however far from being the only factor in play: though the state of the Tacitean texts makes firm conclusions impossible, comparison with Suetonius suggests that Tacitus is also deliberately omitting signs that were connected with individuals rather than the state.[60] Those remaining are not included at random and their handling in the text is far from a simple reflection of the historical record.

The thorough reshaping of interpretations means that we should be surprised that there were any prodigy reports at all, since one was in danger of implying that the current régime was under threat, a proposition which, one suspects, not many of Tacitus' emperors would have received with equanimity. Those that we do have seem to owe their presence in the historical record to the fact that they were either local and/or unavoidably well known, and Tacitus rarely fails to bring this factor to our attention. Thus the prodigy reports that are available to us are almost exclusively from within Rome itself: they were difficult to ignore. The interpretation of lightning strikes on specific buildings would be too established to redefine (e.g. as expiated by Nero at *A.* 13.24.2) as would the death of men of each magistracy within a few months (*A.* 12.64.1).[61] Reports of events on a large scale, such as lightning striking all fourteen districts of Rome (*A.* 14.12.2), or a comet (*A.* 14.22.1) also appear.[62] Where notices appear from outside Rome, they are highly dramatic and usually what we would call a 'natural' disaster on an extraordinary scale – unmistakable prodigial material in other words.[63]

---

[60] The best example of this is *Otho* 8, in comparison with *H.* 1.86 where Tacitus also discriminates between prodigies and 'natural' adverse conditions. Ash (1999) 131–132 notes the greater number of signs for Vespasian and points out how trenchant his selections can be. As she argues, the choice of the cypress tree as the key omen that promises greatness for Vespasian is deliberately made for its multiple allusions. Apart from the fact that the cypress is associated with death, it is likely that there is a deliberate allusion to the withering of the same tree under Domitian, recorded by Suetonius (*Domitian* 15). Other omissions: the signs listed at *Tiberius* 14; *Nero* 46 has a list that seems to include events historically subsequent to the death of Agrippina (i.e., within the scope of the extant text); *Vespasian* 5 contains a whole array of signs, only a few of which appear in the extant Tacitus.

[61] For this phenomenon as a prodigy, see also Livy 40.37.1.

[62] Note also the wording at *A.* 15.47.2, where Tacitus indicates how public signs were – *bicipites hominum aliorumue animalium partus abiecti <u>in publicum aut in sacrificiis</u> quibus grauidas hostias immolare mos est, reperti.*

[63] A massive earthquake in Campania destroyed a large part of Pompei (*A.* 15.22.2); the same area later suffered a divinely sent hurricane which almost reached Rome. The city did not, however, escape from the mysterious plague that swept through the entire population (*non sexus, non aetas periculo uacua, A.* 16.13.2). Though the events of 16.13 are not technically said to be *prodigia,* Tacitus is in no doubt that the gods were responsible (*foedum annum etiam dii tempestatibus et morbis insigniuere*). In addition, a specific adverse sign is noted when violent storms occur during

Ignoring these events would have been extremely difficult, not least because confirmation would have been abundant. Prodigies are also noted when the soldiers in Britain are sufficiently frightened to note them (*A.* 14.31-2). The *Histories* are not dissimilar. When we get what sound rather more like old-fashioned reports, Tacitus himself notes that the time was one of exceptional worry (*H.* 1.86.1). Whereas many of Livy's notices betray an interest, even diligence, in making reports, it appears that in imperial Rome and its environs signs were noted only when they could not be ignored. Such was the historical position, as far as we can tell. What is more, Tacitus was perfectly aware of it, and even accounts for it: his 'lament' on the decline of prodigies is implied in his narrative by the emphasis he places on the intense publicity that they received when they were noted.

McCulloch suggested that Tacitus, in 'omitting' prodigies from the early books of the *Annals*, reflected 'Tiberius' dislike of superstition' (*sic*).[64] His example, of Tiberius's refusal to consult the Sibylline Books at *A.* 1.76.2, can be complemented. Suetonius notes the emperor's attempts to control means of prediction, including his confiscation of the lots of Praeneste (*Tiberius* 63).[65] But Tacitus did more than restrict his own record, if he did that at all: he was well aware that Tiberius' policies would diminish prodigy reports and, by criticising the emperor's responses, implies that this did nothing to help matters. He pithily informs us that the emperor always gave events a positive interpretation (*nam cuncta, etiam fortuita, ad gloriam uertebat, A.* 2.84.3). But the emperor's strategy was not always limited to propagating positive interpretations where none was warranted: situations that were being interpreted adversely were quickly defused by relief operations. Thus, when the Mons Caelius was ravaged by fire and a religious interpretation was beginning to gain momentum, Tiberius acted on a material level to improve conditions, thereby redirecting attention to his munificence and away from the diagnosis of the *ira deum*.[66]

A similar material response at *A.* 2.47.1-3 after severe earthquakes in Asia may have headed off talk of the *ira deum*: Tacitus, however, presents the episode with the kinds of inversions that were characteristic of prodigies

Britannicus' funeral (*A.* 13.17.2). Obviously Nero was unlikely to treat it as a prodigy, whatever the public said, so this particular event receives no official sanction.

[64] McCulloch (1984) 158 also argues that Nero had an 'interest' in prodigies, and that this is reflected in the later books. It is true that Tacitus structures the Neronian years increasingly by use of prodigies, as his material shows, but it is unproven that this reflects a reflected personal 'interest'. We shall be offering other possible reasons for the increased number of prodigies which are more in keeping with the interpretation that the gods were increasingly 'angry' with Rome.

[65] On Tiberius' reputed aversion to traditional religious diagnoses and his preference for the apparently more 'fatalistic' astrology, see also Syme (1958a) 523 for an older, more cynical reading.

[66] The process is made explicit at *A.* 4.64.1.

and may well thereby be hinting that recourse to the gods would not have been inappropriate. 'Vast mountains, it is said, collapsed; what had been level ground seemed to be raised aloft.'[67] In contrast, though their location obviously made a difference to their relevance to the City, the explicitly prodigial earthquakes at *A*. 12.43.1 in Rome are far less destructive and receive less emphasis in the text. Clearly the potential was there for a religious interpretation, which might well have been made if Rome had itself suffered such a disaster.[68]

Thus imperial generosity was an established response to disaster by the time that Tiberius allays the fears of Rome after the fire at *A*. 4.64.1. If sustained as a practice, inevitably the habits of interpretation would change as victims became accustomed to thinking in terms of imperial largesse rather than the *ira deum* as the appropriate and altogether *practical* response to such a crisis. This seems to be what happens at 6.45 – a fire occurred, which Tacitus implies was exploited by Tiberius to buttress his reputation (*quod damnum Caesar ad gloriam uertit exolutis domuum et insularum pretiis*). This time his (unusual) largesse was appreciated without any hint of ominous interpretation.[69] Thus prodigy reporting in Tacitus' Rome was simultaneously undermined on a variety of fronts: not only was it actively discouraged (more will be said on this later) or radically reinterpreted, but Tiberius' largesse actively undermined the very process of categorising such phenomena as religious *at all*.

Here then is Tacitus on the 'decline of prodigy reports': rather than a general lament of neglect like Livy's, we have an acute depiction of the forces that led to the decline in a given period. It is a testament to his powers of observation and analysis that his account remains highly plausible, though it is not our concern here to test this analysis more widely. We shall see

---

[67] *sedisse inmensos montis, uisa in arduo quae plana fuerint.* Furneaux (1896) *ad loc* notes other sources on this earthquake. Pliny not only testifies to the magnitude of the earthquake but also makes a link to the prodigial: at *NH* 2.86 (200) he calls this 'the greatest (*maximus*) earthquake in human memory' and goes on to add that 'the city of Rome was never shaken without this being a premonition of something about to happen: *nec uero simplex malum aut in ipso tantum motu periculum est, sed par aut maius ostento: numquam urbs Roma tremuit ut non futuri euentus alicuius id praenuntium esset.*

[68] The question of whether the earthquakes were prodigial for Rome, for the cities where they occurred, or both, is complex. Livy's Rome *could* reject their responsibility for a prodigy that did not occur on state land (MacBain (1982) 30): Tacitus assigns the responsibility for local prodigies to the Jews (*H*. 5.13.1-3). On the other hand, Rome had been collecting prodigy accounts from further and further afield for some time (e.g. Syracuse (Livy 41.13.2)). After all, Tiberius took responsibility for the practicalities of recovery but that could be taken to be generous rather than necessary. The politics of taking responsibility for such a foreign portent would obviously have been complex. Earthquakes in Cibyra and Aegium similarly led to a remission of tax at *A*. 4.13.1. Tacitus paints a consistent picture in which the emperor acted to forestall negative religious publicity that, initially at least, was being related to the gods' displeasure.

[69] See also *A*. 12.58.2 and 14.27.1.

later that this is not the only aspect of Tiberius' contribution to the decline of traditional (i.e. functional) religion in Rome. Though we have touched only lightly thus far on the narratological implications of prodigies in the text, we can at least proceed in the knowledge that prodigies are still to be understood as an index of the *ira deum*, and predictions of disaster for the Roman state within Tacitus' text. Other categories seem also to retain their identity and uses within the society and the text.

4.2.2 The boundaries of Roman religion

4.2.2.1 Superstitio at home: credulity, astrology and dreams

A key function of Livy's religious model was propriety. Rome's religion was not just a disparate collection of anything that seemed to work: it was a construction of suitable institutions and desirable relationships. The same is true of Tacitus' account: the mutinous soldiers in Pannonia were, in their ignorance, frightened by an eclipse[70] and lost their nerve: 'once knocked off-balance, men's minds are predisposed to religious error' (*sunt mobiles ad superstitionem perculsae semel mentes*, A. 1.28.2).[71] This made them more malleable to Drusus' shrewd exploitation of their fear *dum superstitio urgeat* (A. 1.29.3).[72] *Superstitio* is an appropriate indictment of the emotional response (panic) as the moon disappears behind the clouds. It was not always commoners whose response was flawed: Vitellius was similarly frightened, and superstitious, enough to think that being called Caesar would make a difference to his situation (*superstitione nominis*, H. 3.58.3).

Superstitio is also used of magical practices (e.g. *magicas superstitiones*, A. 12.59.1). The problem with magic was not that it was ineffective, but that it was unregulated.[73] Tacitus does not explicitly condemn the art, though his

---

[70] A phenomenon that had been incorporated into the *pax deum* for centuries by this time, though we have no way of knowing whether this understanding was generally accepted or not. The notoriety of Gallus' explanation implies the former.

[71] Cf. the stories told by men who had been shipwrecked. They reported many strange things *uisa siue ex metu credita* (A. 2.24.4).

[72] O'Gorman (2000) 31–33 argues that, though Tacitus speaks of *superstitio* and says that *miles rationis ignarus omen praesentium accepit*, the soldier's interpretation has much to commend it: 'it is arguable that Tacitus stacks the cards against his explicit judgement of the soldier as ignorant by the semantic subtlety with which the "ignorant" interpretation is represented'. However, her (rhetorical) question 'Why does Tacitus tell us that the solider is ignorant while demonstrating the range and complexity of his interpretation?' does not do justice to the sophistication of religious interpretation, even by 'commoners'. Compare, for instance, the 'ranking' of anonymous interpretations at A. 6.37.2, the complex correlations made about the circumstances of Augustus' death, or the sophisticated interpretations of the fire. Even in his sophistication the soldier could be wrong, in any number of ways. Gallus' rationalisation of eclipses is as good a reason as any.

[73] Or could not be regulated. See Phillips (1991b) on the difficulties of deciding which was 'good' and which was 'bad', as well as the difficulties of enforcement of this distinction. Of the numerous discussions of the definition of magic see especially J. Z. Smith (1995).

depiction of the death-scene of Germanicus vividly creates an atmosphere of dread (*A*. 2.69.3). It does not seem that the readership particularly needed to be told since 'the use of the term *superstitio* seems to have widened over the first century AD ... the most striking development, however, was that the concept of magic emerged as the ultimate *superstitio*' (Beard North and Price (1998) I 218). Indeed, for Tacitus' period, fear of magical practices seems to have pervaded the nobility and this is documented as part of the climate of fear.[74] Thus magicians were expelled from Italy in 16 (*A*. 2.32.3) and again in 69 (*H*. 2.62.2): astrologers were expelled along with them in 16 and again in 52 by a *senatus consultum atrox et inritum* (*A*. 12.52.3).[75] A major obstacle to ridding Italy of astrologers in particular would have been the fact that it was often the emperor who employed their services, or even, in the case of Tiberius, practised the art.[76]

Tacitus' handling of astrology is highly polemical. Though every single prediction made by an astrologer in his accounts comes true,[77] the art of prediction is skilfully shown to be fraught with difficulties. When Tiberius left Rome (*A*. 4.58.2-3) the popular interpretation of the predictions that he would never return was that his death was imminent but it soon became obvious how the 'truth can be obscured' (*uera ... obscuris tegerentur, A.* 4.58.3), since such a fine line exists between the true art and error. Tiberius was indeed never to return, but of course the assumption that this indicated his imminent death was flawed: no one apparently considered that he might live and not return.[78] Furthermore, if we were working within a framework

---

[74] Note in Tacitus the frequent conjunction of the charges of magic and adultery or even incest, e.g. *A*. 3.22.1 (Aemilia Lepida, wife of Quirinius); 4.52.1 (Claudia Pulchra); 6.29.3-4 (Scaurus) and 16.8.2 (Junia Lepida, wife of Cassius, accused of incest).

[75] For the discrepancies in the sources on the measures at *A*. 2.32.3 see Goodyear (1982) *ad loc*. Barton (1994) documents the rise of astrology towards the end of the Republic and into the imperial period, partly at the expense of haruspicy, though this is probably overstated. Haruspicy was less scandalous and therefore received less exposure in our painfully incomplete records which tend to assume the normal state apparatus rather than foreground it. Nonetheless, the introduction and pervasiveness of astrology from the late Republic onwards does seem to be a historical reality. It is not mentioned in the extant Livy, though this proves nothing historically.

[76] His prediction in Greek at *A*. 6.20.2 that '*et tu, Galba, quandoque degustabis imperium*' owes its presence to a number of factors. It comes amid a series of executions and therefore alludes to Galba's survival. But the irony of a consul being told that he *will later* have *imperium, after* a consultation about state affairs, should not be missed.

[77] Tiberius makes his prediction about Galba's future rule by *scientia Chaldaeorum artis* (*A*. 6.20.2); Thrasyllus convinces Tiberius of his ability by predicting (and thereby averting) his own impending doom (6.21); Thrasyllus' son predicted Nero's reign (*A*. 6.22.6); Agrippina was told by *Chaldaei* that Nero would rule but would slaughter his mother (*A*. 14.9.3) – she (successfully) waited for the *tempus ... prosperum ex monitis Chaldaeorum* before revealing the death of Claudius (*A*. 12.68.3); finally, Ptolemaeus predicted Otho's survival of Nero (*H*. 1.22.2) – in the circumstances (Poppaea being Otho's wife, before she became Nero's consort) this was rather impressive. Libo's trial revealed *questions* that were ridiculous (*A*. 2.30.1-2) but the responses are not recorded.

[78] There are other moments where interpretation is difficult. At 6.28, Tacitus sifts through the legends about the phoenix (*de quibus congruunt et plura ambigua, sed cognitu non absurda promere*

of 'belief/rejection', implicitly based on efficacy, then for Tacitus to accept that astrology could make reliable predictions would be to assume he would advocate its use. Thus it has been common to discuss his 'fatalism', a compound of an apparent respect for astrological predictions and a concurrent disregard for traditional religion.[79] It is sometimes missed that every astrological prediction that Tacitus mentions turns out to be true: but efficacy is not the point.

Apart from the fact that Tacitus prefers not to have a senate more intent on future success than present concerns, it remains that whatever an individual does with astrology, it cannot serve the state. Though the historian never spells out his reasons, this is the most consistent reason for his marginalisation. Study of the stars has no cohesive tendencies, but instead is divisive as rivals attempt to achieve their promised status or thwart each other's ambitions; nor does it have rites to establish proper communication with the gods.

Astrology cannot possibly have a useful role to play for the *res publica*, which has its own expert interpreters of fate, in the form of the *quindecimuiri sacris faciundis*. Thus, astrology is a *superstitio* and there would appear to be censure in the notice that Vespasian kept one 'openly' (*palam*) at court:[80] in short, *mathematici* are a race of men who are 'unreliable to the powerful, and deceptive to the hopeful' (*genus hominum potentibus infidum, sperantibus fallax, H.* 1.22.1). The *fallacitas* is more a question of their use as advisers than their ability to make predictions. Otho was 'betrayed' in the sense that his predicted *imperium* hardly took the form that he expected, and Ptolemaeus seems to have missed, or suppressed, the fact that his client's death would follow on rather more rapidly than one would have liked. The slipperiness of predictions makes astrologers poor guides.[81] More speculatively, astrologers who predicted a mediocre future for their clients might

---

libet); there are competing interpretations at *A.* 6.37.1-2; a possible 'chance' prophecy at 11.31, depending on your interpretation; see also *A.* 15.74.2; and the reply of Basilides to Vespasian at *H.* 2.78.4 is said to be ambiguous. This list is not exhaustive.

[79] It is not uncommon to assert that Tacitus became gradually more depressed and pessimistic as he wrote, changing his opinions as he plumbed the depths of the Julio-Claudians in his writing of the *Annals*. We even have a suggested date for his 'conversion' to 'astral fatalism' in Brakman (1928) 73–74.

[80] *H.* 2.78.1 (both references). For the argument that Vespasian has gone too far in resembling his soldiers, see Ash (1999) 130. However she does not differentiate between the *superstitio* of the common soldiery (displayed for instance at *H.* 1.28.2) and astrology, the imperial *superstitio*, which is mostly practised by (foolish, and usually doomed) aristocrats and emperors in Tacitus' works.

[81] Or they might even find their clients being betrayed by informers who watch their movements, as at 16.14. Barton (1994) 71–94 has case studies that illustrate how complex and improvisory horoscopical interpretation could be.

well have found their services required less often than those who foretold greatness.

Astrology is not the only predictive art that should be avoided by the Roman aristocracy. When detailing the entrapment of Libo, the first to die for charges concerning magic and predictions (*A.* 2.27f.), Tacitus tells us that he was 'prone to dabbling in the ridiculous' (*facilis inanibus*) and it was therefore all the easier to press upon him interpretation of dreams along with astrology and magic. We have already seen that, for Livy, reliance on dreams was as disreputable as any other *superstitio*, not because they were *always* misleading, but because they were unreliable and therefore an inappropriate means of divination. The generally exemplary[82] Germanicus is more proper, keeping his auspicious dream in its place by double-checking with the auspices and preserving a sense of perspective. When he addresses his men he restricts himself to saying only what he understood to be relevant and appropriate (*quae sapientia prouisa aptaque inminenti pugnae disserit*, *A.* 2.14.1). The two knights, both named Petra, found to their cost that ambiguities in dream interpretation could be costly at *A.* 11.4 when a relatively innocuous and impersonal interpretation (famine) was recast as a prediction of Claudius' death by less traditional-sounding interpretations.

Though Tacitus specifically says it was merely a pretext for their destruction, they might have been better off keeping it to themselves.[83] Just to underline their untrustworthy status, the somewhat disturbed (*mente turbida*) Caesellius Bassus was foolish enough to trust a dream about buried treasure (*A.* 16.1.1) and Nero was stupid and greedy enough to believe him.[84]

The only exception to the rule in Tacitus is the sending of dreams by Hercules to his priests in an organised ritual format (*A.* 12.13.3) where the validity of the dreams, guaranteed by the god, is assumed. Tacitus is not concerned here with questions of belief or scepticism, efficacy and prediction: his interest lies in policing the boundaries of *superstitio*.

Superstitio abroad   Livy was not averse to dismissing the rites of Rome's enemies but reserved most of his criticism for Rome and Romans: Tacitus,

---

[82] Formerly considered to be a Tacitean hero, Germanicus' reputation has suffered in recent years: Rutland (1987); McCulloch (1984) 177f.; Pelling (1993).

[83] This is less a problem with dream interpretation than with the political context. The context implies that it is the corrupt imperial court that is 'to blame', since they seize on the dream and change its meaning. Nonetheless, Tacitus' closing comment that it was the consequence of some dream that they were destroyed emphasises how fluid and dangerous dream interpretation could be.

[84] Caecina's terrifying dream, while on campaign in Germany, of the ghost of Varus appears to have no predictive power either, though it was understandable in the circumstances (*A.* 1.65.2). See further on some of these Pelling (1997).

however, is more likely to emphasise the foreign nature of religious practices with reference to *superstitio*,[85] which is liberally applied to a whole range of foreign religions. The Jews are thoroughly dismissed[86] and the Druids reveal their incompetence at every opportunity.[87] The Germans are given to religious error in their considering women divine (*H.* 4.61.2) and the altars on which Roman officers were sacrificed after the defeat of Varus were, rather inevitably, *barbarae* (*A.* 1.61.3).[88] The Egyptians are generally unstable and uncivilised, not least for their *superstitio* (*H.* 1.11.1) and their rites, along with those of the Jews, are again described as *superstitio* when those 'infected' by them are expelled from Rome (*A.* 2.85.4). When Nero instigated a persecution of the Christians with their *superstitio*, it was not their lack of guilt that made people pity them, but his motives (*A.* 15.44.5).

This is not to say that all foreign practices are flawed; Tacitus is ultimately operating within the same framework as Livy, since a number of foreign sites and practices receive a dignified exposition, especially those that advised Vespasian and Titus of their destiny to empire.[89] When the Third Legion salute the rising sun, *ut mos*, they are not castigated for it, though it amusingly leads to a rumour that Mucianus had arrived at the battle-scene and the two armies had greeted one another (*H.* 3.2.4-5).

---

[85] The term is not necessarily dismissive. When a number of cities were questioned by the senate regarding the abuse of sanctuary rights, they relied on *uetustis superstitionibus aut meritis in populum Romanum* to argue their case (*A.* 3.60.2). From this it might seem that Tacitus was dismissive of the various claims that follow which are mostly mythical; but such scorn for apparently well-authenticated claims would be extremely unusual. It may be that the term is not so pejorative in itself, but reflects the assumption that most foreign religions are inferior to the Roman: Tacitus elsewhere has Ptolemy ask Timotheus which god he had dreamed of and what his rites (*superstitio*) were (*H.* 4.83.2). The term cannot represent a paraphrase of the Pharaoh's words if there is a pejorative sense. Finally, the worship of Serapis is described as *superstitiones* but in a context that validates Vespasian's 'miraculous' healings. We should remember that, however valid such rites and cults might be abroad, they do not belong in Rome.

[86] Tacitus speaks of their *peruicaciam superstitionis* at *H.* 2.4.3. *H.* 5.2-13 is an extended condemnation, e.g. *profana illic omnia quae apud nos sacra, rursum concessa apud illos quae nobis incesta*, *H.* 5.2.1; their religion is called *superstitio* again at *H.* 5.8.2 and 3.

[87] Mistaken interpretation of the burning of the Capitol, *H.* 4.54.2; their rites are *saeuae superstitiones* at *A.* 14.30.3 *nam cruore captiuo adolere aras et hominum fibris consulere deos fas habebant*.

[88] Civilis exacts an oath that, although traditional, is also barbarous (*H.* 4.15.1).

[89] *H.* 2.2.2-4 sees Titus visit the shrine of Paphian Venus, and earns the shrine a history with full credentials; he receives a positive prediction from the goddess. Vespasian is also promised success at Carmel, *H.* 2.78.3; when the emperor heals a cripple and a blind man in Alexandria, it is at the instigation of the god Serapis (*H.* 4.81.1). There follows a lengthy excursus on the origin of the god's cult, which legitimises it on several counts. Firstly the dream that bade Ptolemy fetch the god is interpreted not by the (presumably unreliable) Egyptian priests, but by the next best thing to a Roman, the Athenian Timotheus, and his conclusions are based on good investigative work rather than any disreputable charismatic inspiration. The story includes a whole array of proofs, such as the repeated dreams of the god both by Ptolemy and by the king of the territory where Serapis was currently housed, Scydrothemis of Sinope. Serapis himself is then linked with Aesculapius, Osiris, Jupiter and (probably preferably) Pluto (*H.* 4.83-4).

But Tacitus does not only credit foreign cults for which there was a political imperative. A few learned, and uncritical, notices appear elsewhere on foreign customs.[90] For the most part, a grudging respect for venerated traditions is to be found even where the nation is found to be generally wanting. The Jews' heritage is acknowledged, for all the good it did them, and we should note that the Egyptian priests, along with their Greek counterparts, are capable of *some* insight in their documentation of the phoenix at 6.28: Tacitus offers that he is including an edited version of their somewhat, but not entirely, erroneous lore. Similarly, the Egyptians' history of letters is used, apparently unproblematically, as historical evidence at 11.14 when Claudius makes changes to the Latin alphabet. Their reliability is guaranteed by their visibility on stone. Christianity is, on the other hand, a new phenomenon and therefore all the less desirable.[91] The frequency of *superstitio*, allied with his systematic undermining of astrology and dream interpretation, is representative of his deliberate judgement of 'religious' activities: such things might be appropriate to foreigners, or in ritualised contexts, but they are far from being appropriate conduct for a Roman.

Fors Inappropriateness does not exhaust the range of possible errors: a number of interpretations contrast 'chance' or 'nature' with genuine religious phenomena and in this Tacitus is more caustic and explicitly discriminating than Livy: *fors* continues to designate the conjunction of details without intention,[92] often defying expectation.[93] As we found with Livy, the use of *fors* as a category owes nothing to any intent to undermine the category of the gods' intervention, though this has often been assumed.[94] It is a shorthand for refusing to assign that significance to particular items at a specific moment. Thus, just as natural events could be mistaken for prodigies (as, for instance, at *H.* 1.86.1 and *H.* 4.26.2), Tiberius is mistaken in attributing to the benevolence of the gods what the historian says was the *fortuitus* birth of twins to Drusus.[95] Tacitus' mention of the error should be taken as local diagnosis of the specific events rather than exclusive and sweeping dismissals of the categories of 'heaven-sent' phenomena. The in-

---

[90] The origins of the Iberians and Albanians who claim descent from Phrixus includes the note that they do not sacrifice rams, without any caustic asides, *A.* 6.34.2; when Gotarzes offers prayers to Hercules on Mt Sunbulah, there is information, again without disparaging comment, about the way that the god instructs his priests, *A.* 12.13.4.

[91] Certainly Tacitus has nothing positive to say about it whatsoever and its novelty is stressed at *A.* 15.44.3-6.

[92] E.g. *seu dolo seu forte, H.* 2.42.1; *forte an dolo principis incertum, A.* 15.38.1; cf. also *H.* 3.21.2.

[93] E.g. *fors cuncta turbare et ignauorum saepe telis fortissimi cadere* (*H.* 4.29.2).

[94] E.g. Kajanto (1981) 544–546.

[95] *nam cuncta, etiam fortuita, ad gloriam uertebat* (*A.* 2.84.3).

tervention of the gods can come unexpectedly, 'by chance', as it does at *A.* 4.27.1, when *belli semina fors oppressit* ... because *uelut munere deum*, three biremes put in at Brindisi.[96] Conversely, it is possible to assign to chance what pertains to the gods or fate: Galba, typically for him, makes the wrong choice at *H.* 1.18.1 when he decides that well-established signs of the *ira deum* are in fact due to chance.

The distinction *is* more often used than was found in Livy and with a more heightened sense of contrast: but we cannot assume that this reflects a wider change. It is more likely a consequence of their different approaches. Livy represents a Rome that is rarely in error, while Tacitus does virtually the opposite, parading mistake after mistake before the hapless reader. Either way, the *co*-existence of the categories of 'chance' and 'divine' should not surprise us. As before, they do not exclude one another. Drusus' twins were just part of a normal pattern of human existence; as a detail, they did not mark out any special divine favour. One dies soon after (*A.* 4.15.1) and the other, Tiberius Gemellus, died at the hands of his co-heir Caligula (Suetonius *Gaius* 23) as Tiberius had predicted (*A.* 6.46.4). If they had featured more impressively in Roman politics, then perhaps the hand of the gods would have been a more accurate diagnosis.

Fatum   It is striking that while Livy's relatively vast extant text has the word *fatum* only thirty-six times and *fatalis* twenty times (and eight of those are in the phrase *libri fatales*, i.e. the Sibylline Books), it occurs as many as thirty-one times (*fatalis* or *fataliter* nine times) in the significantly shorter combination of the *Annals* and *Histories*. These figures could be explained away by the observation that *fatum* is simply used as a synonym for 'death' – which is a considerably more prominent theme in Tacitus' account.[97] However, this would be simplistic.

As in Livy, *fatum* refers in particular and often rhetorically to *natural* death. A death that was both natural and eminent enough to be worth recording was unusual in those days, as Tacitus pithily remarks at *A.* 6.10.3. When Scipio is asked by Claudius, *adeo ignaro* of Messalina's machinations in forcing the suicide of his wife Poppaea, why he is dining without her, he replies that she had died *fato* (*A.* 11.2.5); the compounding of disingenuous sarcasm and political tact is far from neutral. *Fatum* as a natural death is contrasted with suicide (*finem uitae sponte an fato impleuit*, *A.* 2.42.3) and

---

[96] *Velut* is susceptible to the same analysis as in Livy (above, 59), though it seems likely that he would have reversed the order: the revolt would have been crushed by the help of the gods after the ships arrived 'by chance'. Cf. ... *seu forte lapsa uox in praesagium uertit* (*A.* 11.31.6).

[97] E.g. *A.* 1.3.3, 1.55.3, 6.10.3, 14.12.4, 14.14.4 *et al.*

Cestius Gallus is even said to have died either naturally or of weariness *fato aut taedio* (*H.* 5.10.1) fighting the Jews. Since he was succeeded by Vespasian as a prelude to imperial usurpation, it might well be that he, like Marcellus in Livy, was 'accidentally' caught up in events of a greater destiny that necessitated his removal. It is also still possible for Tacitus to exploit *fatum* to condemn murder as Livy did in highlighting Perseus' hypocrisy: even a simple notice that death occurred *fato* can carry the implication that the person in question escaped Nero's purges.[98]

In dealing with aspects other than the timing and manner of death, there is an irony in Tacitus' dealing with *fatum*. He is never so diffident as when discussing the inevitable.[99] When dealing with individuals, there are aspects within *fatum* relating to careers and social position. One such notice appears in conjunction with an assessment of the exemplary[100] senator Marcus Lepidus, who moderated a great deal of savage political activity without antagonising Tiberius:

> Because of this [Lepidus' success], I doubt whether the liking of emperors for some, and their hostility towards others, is determined by the fate and lot we receive at birth, as are other things, or whether it is, to an extent, a question of our own plans so that it is possible to find a way between defiant obstinacy or degrading slavishness.[101]

There is another excursus at *A.* 6.22.1-3 after the story of the predictions of Thrasyllus, Tiberius' court astrologer:

> When I hear of these and similar events, I suspend my judgement as to whether it is fate and inevitable necessity or chance which determines the outcomes of human affairs. Indeed, among the wisest of the ancients and those who follow their

---

[98] This rather grim idea is grotesquely articulated at *A.* 16.13.2 during a severe plague: *interitus quamuis promisci minus flebiles erant, tamquam communi mortalitate saeuitiam principis praeuenirent.*

[99] Although, according to Hellegouarc'h (1991), Tacitus is normally given to 'dogmatic assertions' in comparison with Caesar, Sallust and Livy.

[100] Sinclair (1995) 163–178 is essential reading on Lepidus and the limits of his exemplary role. Compare the *pontifex* Piso, of whom Tacitus says *nullius seruilis sententiae sponte auctor et quotiens necessitas ingrueret sapienter moderans* (*A.* 6.10.3). For Tacitus' interest in *uirtus*, see von Albrecht (1987). For the use of obituaries in general to frame the account and make historical and political points (in this case, the end of *libertas*), see Gingras (1991–2). *Libertas* is central to his political viewpoint (Shotter (1978); Roberts (1988); Morford (1990) and (1991); Sinclair (1995) esp. 163–169).

[101] *unde dubitare cogor, fato et sorte nascendi, ut cetera, ita principum inclinatio in hos, offensio in illos, an sit aliquid in nostris consiliis liceatque inter abruptam contumaciam et deforme obsequium pergere iter ambitione ac periculis uacuum* (*A.* 4.20.2-4).

teachings you will find conflicting theories, many being convinced that the gods do not concern themselves with the beginning or the end of our life, or with mankind at all in the final analysis. Therefore suffering is repeatedly the lot of the good, and happiness of the evil. There are, on the other hand, others who believe that though there is a correlation between fate and events, it does not depend on the movement of stars, but on primary elements, and on a combination of natural causes. Still, they leave us the choice of what sort of life we will have. Once the choice is made, a sequence of events is fixed. Good and bad are not what people commonly think; many who can be seen to be to be struggling with difficulties are happy but for the most part, there are very many who, although they are endowed with great riches, are completely miserable. This depends on the former tolerating their difficult lot with patience, and the latter make poor use of their wealth. Most men, however, cannot give up the belief that each person's future is fixed right from birth, but that some things happen differently from what has been foretold because of the fake claims of those who speak about things which they do not know about, and that this destroys the credibility of a skill, for which both the past and our own age have provided unambiguous examples of proof.[102]

The passages have often prompted mention of Tacitus' 'indecision' or 'agnosticism' and it has generally been concluded that the concepts are vague or devoid of significance.[103] But there are better reasons for Tacitus' 'hesitation': Martin and Woodman are in no doubt as to the true relevance of 4.20 – it is possible to be a great (states)man even under bad emperors.[104]

---

[102] *Sed mihi haec ac talia audienti in incerto iudicium est, fatone res mortalium et necessitate immutabili an forte uoluantur. quippe sapientissimos ueterum quique sectam eorum aemulantur diuersos reperies, ac multis insitam opinionem non initia nostri, non finem, non denique homines dis curae; ideo creberrime tristia in bonos, laeta apud deteriores esse. contra alii fatum quidem congruere rebus putant, sed non e uagis stellis, uerum apud principia et nexus naturalium causarum; ac multis electionem uitae nobis relinquunt, quam ubi elegeris, certum imminentium ordinem. neque mala uel bona quae uulgus putet. Multos qui conflictari aduersis uideantur, beatos, at plerosque, quamquam magnas per opes, miserrimos, si illi grauem fortunam constanter tolerent, hi prospera inconsulte utantur. ceterum plurimis mortalium non eximitur, quin primo cuiusque ortu uentura destinentur, sed quaedam secus quam dicta sint cadere fallaciis ignara dicentium. Ita corrumpi fidem artis, cuius clara documenta et antiqua aetas et nostra tulerit.*

[103] Probably most succinctly put by Syme (1958a) 527: 'the notions of *"fatum"* and *"fortuna"* continue to be discussed . . . not much emerges. The words belong to literature rather than dogma.'

[104] 'Tacitus is no more seriously concerned with fate and astrological determinism here than at *A.* 6.22.1-3, but uses these concepts as a convenient foil for the characteristic point that *posse etiam sub malis principibus magnos uiros esse*' (*Agr.* 42.2).

We might go further, and reappropriate this material into Tacitus' particular religious stand. One could not discuss fate without raising the question
of *imperial* destiny. Though Tacitus appears to admit the difficulties of interpreting predictions of fate, this is not straightforward 'intellectual doubt'.
To experiment with the dictates of fate in imperial Rome was not only improper but extremely dangerous. By studiously failing to endorse any particular interpretative standpoint Tacitus declares his disinterest in the decrees
of destiny – just about the only sensible position left on the subject for an
aristocrat. Knowledge was power, and absolute knowledge was to be left to
those with absolute power *already*.[105]

Given the fascination for signs that inevitably developed in imperial
Rome, and the speculation that could mark out a man against his will and
best interests,[106] we would expect the expert statesman to be doing more
than just avoiding committing himself. It is in fact Vespasian, the old-
fashioned general who was hardly different from the common soldiery in
terms of appearance and dress (*H.* 1.5.1), and the first emperor to change for
the better (*H.* 1.50.4), who embodies Tacitus' exemplary procedure for dealing with omens.[107] Though he kept an astrologer at court, his attitude to fate
is textually modest. The prophecies made about him as a young man, which
he only remembered when prompted (*recursabant animo uetera omina*), he
had considered fulfilled by his eminence under Nero.[108] He is also suitably
modest when asked to heal the sick: reluctant to act, he takes professional
medical advice first (*H.* 4.81.4). On seeing Basilides in the temple of Serapis in Alexandria, he performs his own extensive inquiries into the location
of the man before accepting his appearance as an omen on the strength of
his friend's name (*H.* 4.81.2). Finally, even with the indications of divine
support, Tacitus emphasises that Vespasian's decision to attempt usurpation
is a choice that the founder of the Flavian dynasty makes after proper consideration (*H.* 2.74.2) and it is *fortuna* that he (appropriately) considers, not
fatum.[109] Rather than placing his hope in predictions, he takes full responsibility for his choice of action, irrespective of omens, unlike Otho, who is
swept along by the assurances of his supporters when they urge astrological

---

[105] Cf. Sinclair (1995), who offers that 'at first sight it may appear that Tacitus generalises on the
human condition, but in both cases his attention is actually very narrowly focussed upon the
question of the political survival of members of the senatorial class' (54–55).

[106] Rubellius Plautus, for instance, was promoted as a rival to Nero after the appearance of a comet
(*A.* 14.22.1). The interpretation was flawed.

[107] *Contra* Ash (1999) 128–136, who sees continuity in the treatments of Vespasian and Otho, and
entrenched criticism of the Flavian in his handling of religious items.

[108] *sed primo triumphalia et consulatus et Iudaicae uictoriae decus implesse fidem ominis uidebatur*
(*H.* 2.78.2).

[109] In Tacitus' text, Vespasian's choice is only sensible: the historian has just informed us that his
card is already marked by Vitellius (*H.* 2.73.2).

predictions on him (*H.* 1.22.1-2). Thus Tacitus, somewhat paradoxically, circumscribes the power of destiny and puts it in its place. Just as Livy's better statesmen thought, whatever one's future, there is also a present (*fortuna*) to attend to.

The only non-imperial destiny treated in the texts is that of Curtius Rufus, whose *fatale* vision at 11.21 and its subsequent fulfilment are recorded with textual and historical impunity. The story is framed within his unexpected rise to prominence, from being the son of a gladiator to the height of senatorial authority. However he can form no precedent for those who sought to know the future, since the man's response to a sign that he did not (textually) seek was to get on with his career in typical contemporary fashion – reprehensibly.[110] He conspicuously let fate take care of itself, as did even the arch-interpreter Tiberius – ultimately.[111]

Thus when he mildly notes in the opening to the *Histories* that 'we only took on board the predictions and signs connected with Vespasian after the event',[112] Tacitus is not exercising a cynicism that these signs were 're-ally' meaningless or fabricated: he is signalling what was probably the only sensible position that could be taken at the time. Even Vespasian did not associate the various signs with empire (*H.* 2.78.2) and, after all, Galba and Otho *also* had imperial destinies to fulfil.[113] When three of four candidates are fated to win the throne, how are we to decide in which order they will do so? Or for how long? Galba, though told by Tiberius that he was destined to rule decades previously, had subsequently lived through the reigns of Caligula, Claudius and Nero. And signs could easily be misunderstood: Vespasian himself thought the signs had already been fulfilled. Why should the senate think otherwise? Galba and Otho are both testaments to the wildly unnavigable outcomes of *fata* when enacted in their human context. Would-be emperors would do well to remember how *uera ... obscuris tegerentur* (*A.* 4.58.3) – not just an intellectual position, but a traditional, and eminently practical one.

The treatment of emperors, the individuals of the time *par excellence*, is very distinctive: it forms a marked contrast with Tacitus' contemporary Suetonius, for whom all signs were linked to the rise and fall of an emperor. As we have seen already, this was part of a more general historical trend.

---

[110] *aduersus superiores tristi adulatione, adrogans minoribus, inter pares difficilis.*

[111] At *A.* 6.46.3 he leaves the succession to fate even though he has foreseen much of the remaining century (*A.* 6.20.2, 6.46) as well as some of what is to come after his death. The irony of his impotence in the face of such knowledge should not be missed.

[112] *occulta fati et ostentis ac responsis destinatum Vespasiano liberisque eius imperium post fortunam credidimus* (*H.* 1.10). *nos* refers to the senatorial order (Sinclair (1995) 50–58).

[113] Vitellius is the only emperor in the *Histories* not to have astrological predictions assigned to him.

In effect, these signs can only be treated as *fatum* rather than the *pax* or the *ira deum*, since there is apparently no room for manoeuvre.[114] Thus, *fatum* would become an overly deployed analysis. Tacitus in fact notes the collapse of the distinction between fate and the *ira deum* at *H.* 4.26.2 (*at quod in pace fors seu natura, tunc fatum et ira dei uocabantur*) but distances himself from the diagnosis of fate by his problematisation of accurate interpretation of destiny (thereby inviting the rehabilitation of the category of the *ira deum*). Though the emperors in the *Annals* receive little in the way of divine validation of their rules, those in the *Histories* are more conspicuously contextualised by fate, as we shall see below. The senatorial and the equestrian historians therefore seem to tend towards different ends of the interpretative spectrum. While Tacitus notes the tendency in a city that 'interpreted almost everything in religious terms' (*H.* 2.91.1), he does not always indulge it. There was an interpretative context even for the *fatum* of an individual, namely the destiny of Rome, and Tacitus does not lose sight of this larger perspective, as we shall see, in discussing his broader deployment of religious items.

4.2.2.2 The cultus deorum

For the basic categories of religious interpretation, we find therefore that from Livy to Tacitus it is a case of '*plus ça change, plus c'est la même chose*'. It is still the historians' business to review interpretation and to establish the Roman way within a welter of practices and styles of worship. What remains to be explored is the institutional operation of the *cultus deorum* and Tacitus' religious narrative, in that order.

Imperial cult   Probably the greatest innovation in Roman state cult since the days of which Livy wrote was the introduction of imperial cult, beginning with the cult of Julius Caesar in the late republic. The format of imperial cult is normally summarised along the lines that in the provinces, the living emperor was worshipped, along with his predecessors, while in Rome and Italy, it was the already deified *diui* who received cult worship rather than the incumbent emperor.[115] Until fairly recently, it was common to interpret imperial cult as an aspect of religious decline. However, Price

---

[114] Suetonius is not the only one. At *A.* 13.47.3, the freedman Graptus attributes Nero's escape from a fictitious plot to *fatum*.

[115] 'Official public cults in the capital were restricted to deceased emperors ... for the living emperor vows were offered on his behalf ... Dio further distinguishes between the cults offered by subjects of Rome ... and those to be performed by Roman citizens resident in the provinces. Whereas the subjects of Rome had cults of the living emperor, Roman citizens had cults of the Roman type' (Beard North and Price (1998) I 349).

(1984), which has dominated discussion since publication, offers a more appropriate approach. For him 'the emperor stood at the focal point between human and divine'.[116] Thus we should expect Tacitus' rendering of imperial cult to reflect this negotiation of power, rather than any broad criticism of whether the cult had any validity.

Tacitus had obviously read his Price.[117] He contextualises religious honours as an important part of the general negotiation of power with the emperor, and those around him. Thus the adoption of an emperor as a *diuus* was a senatorial process. In theory they had a choice, though they might come under pressure to adopt a predecessor in order to validate the present emperor. In other words, when it came to the adoption of a new god, there would not be a marked difference from the introduction of a foreign god; the new deity would have qualities and powers of which Rome wished to avail herself. Since the criterion for selection was the desire to associate the new régime and Rome ongoingly with the deceased *princeps* and all the values and achievements that made up his identity, its opposite would therefore be *damnatio memoriae*, obliteration rather than celebration.

As usual, discrimination has often been taken to be dismissal. Comments about the German prophetess Veleda, for instance, have attracted attention as a backhanded criticism of imperial cult.[118] At *H.* 4.61.3, Tacitus says that 'Veleda, a maiden of the tribe of the Bructeri, possessed extensive authority; for by ancient custom the Germans attributed to many of their women prophetic powers and, as the *superstitio* grew in strength, even actual divinity';[119] and at *H.* 4.65.6 that 'she dwelt in a tower, and one of her relatives was chosen to convey the questions and answer like the messenger of a god'.[120] More specifically, at *Germania* 8, we read that 'in Vespasian's days we saw Veleda, long regarded by many as a divinity. In former times, too, they venerated Aurinia, and many other women, but not like sycophants, nor treating them like gods.'[121] But these passages have no bearing on imperial cult. Tacitus is objecting, not to the notion of deification, but to the excessive reverence for a living woman (*adulatio*, and treating her as a goddess) though he does not seem to consider *ueneratio* for such women inappropriate. These passages are a discussion of criteria, not of the practice

---

[116] Price (1984) 233. See also Price (1987) and Beard North and Price (1998) I 360–361. For documentary studies, see also Fishwick (1978 and 1987).

[117] As well as his Gradel (2002), too late to receive full integration into this discussion.

[118] E.g. Walker (1952) 252. On the following, see Rives (1999a).

[119] *ea uirgo nationis Bructerae late imperitabat, uetere apud Germanos more, quo plerasque feminarum fatidicas et augescente superstitione arbitrantur deas.*

[120] *ipsa edita in turre; delectus e propinquis consulta responsaque ut internuntius numinis portabat.*

[121] *uidimus sub diuo Vespasiano Veledam diu apud plerosque numinis loco habitam; sed et olim Auriniam et complures alias uenerati sunt, non adulatione nec tamquam facerent deas.*

of deification *in toto*. Deifying living prophetesses is an entirely different affair from the deification of departed *principes*.

There are also comments in the aftermath of Augustus' death that have been linked to imperial cult. Various anonymous voices offer their thoughts on the departed emperor and it has been argued that the latter, more acerbic, comments are to be taken as closer to Tacitus' own position (Miller (1969)). Among these are to be found opinions that appear to touch on imperial cult: 'No honour was left for the gods, when Augustus wanted himself to be worshipped with temples and statues with divine attributes, like those of the gods, and with flamens and priests' (*A.* 1.10.6).[122] This has nothing to do with imperial cult in our normal sense, of the emperor receiving direct worship as a deity when living (abroad) or dead (in Rome, and subject to deification). Even if we take the line that this is a reference to imperial cult of a living emperor, there are many hazards. There is no reason to assume that Tacitus is offering these positions for unfiltered digestion by the reader – he is, after all, perfectly capable of stating a position unequivocally without textual intermediaries. Once again, the hope of finding Tacitus' 'true opinions' has misled us: the opinions are not the vehicle of his message, they are the object of his (historical) interest.

McCulloch (1984) documents the way that Tacitus treats rumour as a potent historical force in itself and religious interpretations, a common subject of gossip, are ultimately no different. Like rumours, they can themselves give rise to historical action, but this has no bearing on whether they are true or correct. For Tacitus, as we have noted, Rome is a city peopled by religious interpreters, and this is part of his documentation of life there. The interpretations are typically in error, or exaggerate: Augustus was not voted *flamines et sacerdotes*; he was voted a single priest, and that came after death; and these criticisms are ill-targeted if they are a closet attack on imperial cult – they are aimed at his career while alive, not his cult when dead. Moreover, the critics are inconsistent: Tiberius is criticised in precisely the *opposite* manner – for the refusal of honours at 4.37: some consider his refusal an example of how disregarding one's reputation undermines good practices (*nam contemptu famae contemni uirtutes, A.* 4.38.6).[123] It was not just prodigies that were discussed and debated by the general population of Rome. All plausibly 'religious' matters were fair game and we get the impression that just about every possible position was probably articulated

---

[122] *nihil deorum honoribus relictum cum se templis et effigie numinum per flamines et sacerdotes coli uellet.* See Furneaux (1896) *ad loc* for the translation of *effigie numinum*.

[123] See Martin and Woodman (1989) for the 'wilful distortion of Tiberius's views'. And of course he was also criticised by anonymous speakers when he gave permission for such a request (*arguebatur in ambitionem flexisse, A.* 4.37.2).

by *someone*. Documenting the 'you-can't-win' factor in Roman 'celebrity gossip' is not the same as criticising fundamental aspects of religion.

In fact, imperial cult may well be a mark of *civilisation*. Tacitus says of the Britons that 'a temple also erected to the deified Claudius was ever before their eyes, a citadel, as it seemed, of unending overlordship. Men chosen as priests had to squander their whole fortunes under the pretence of religious practice.'[124] He is not speaking *sua uoce*, but ironically, reporting (supposedly) common perceptions (*aspiciebatur*) among the Britons, or at least the rebels. These semi-barbarians had no idea how to have a proper priesthood, or why.

The *diui*, supposedly such a bone of contention, are actually of less interest to Tacitus than the senate that deified them: the immediate aftermath of both extant imperial deifications re-enacts Rome's relationship with the deceased but not departed *diuus*. When Augustus is deified, the act itself is hardly the centre of attention (*uersae inde ad Tiberium preces*, *A*. 1.11.1) but the senate, along with the heir, is plunged into, not so much the régime of Tiberius, as the overweening and still potent legacy of Augustus. Rome's political masters are a spineless senate and a reluctant emperor who together struggle to pick up where the first *princeps* left off. The senate attempts the recreation of Tiberius in the mould of Augustus, while the new emperor starts as he means to go on: endeavouring to work within Augustan precedents in an attempt to constitutionalise the principate rather than assuming the authority that allowed Augustus to set those precedents. Augustus, uniquely among the *diui* in Tacitus, receives cult honour and the attention befitting a god at various moments in the earlier books of the *Annals*.[125] When Julia Augusta dedicates a statue to *diuus Augustus*, Tiberius is annoyed that his name is placed below hers but there is no perceived problem with the statue itself (*A*. 3.64.3). This emphasis on the first *princeps* is not accidental: it is part of Tacitus' argument that in religious and political terms, Rome struggled and failed to come to terms with the realities of his legacy. In many ways they were still his subjects.[126] Tacitus' unique criticism of the first *princeps* is not a matter of deliberately unorthodox opinion[127] but rather unprecedented textual authority: in these minor notices resides a political assertion. The most persistent focus of attention is

---

[124] *ad hoc templum diuo Claudio constitutum quasi arx aeternae dominationis aspiciebatur, delectique sacerdotes specie religionis omnis fortunas effundebant* (A. 14.31.6).
[125] Germanicus dedicates a mound to Mars, Jupiter and Augustus at *A*. 2.22.1; a *sacrarium* to the Julian family, and statue of Augustus at Bovillae are voted by the senate (A. 2.41.1); *A*. 4.36.2 sees the people of Cyzicus stripped of privileges after neglecting the worship of Augustus.
[126] See e.g. *A*. 4.42.3 for another example.
[127] According to Ceausescu (1974) Tacitus' is the only negative assessment of Augustus in antiquity: for example, he criticises the *princeps'* handling of legislation on adultery at *A*. 3.24.3.

the dynamic between senate and emperor, not the validity of institutions, religious or otherwise.

Thus in the deification of Claudius, the emphasis is on the living and their conduct. Deification re-enacts the relationship of Claudius to his court while alive – theoretically honoured, actually marginalised or even ridiculed. He may have been deified, but mention of his foresight and wisdom provoked laughter (*A.* 13.3.2) and the appointment of his murderer Agrippina as *flaminica* adds insult to injury (*A.* 13.2.6).

Imperial cult is often singled out as if it was problematic for its practitioners. Historically it seems to have been much less of a problem than we often assume.[128] Thus emperors are not the only ones to receive these honours. At *Annals A.* 6.18.2, there is an allegation that Pompeia Macrina's ancestor Theophanes had been a friend of Pompey and after his death had worshipped him as a god with *caelestis honores*, an example of *Graeca adulatio*; this rebounded on her father and brother years later. Doubtless, if Theophanes had rendered cult honours to Caesar instead, there would have been less of a (historical) problem. Nero's short-lived daughter, (Claudia) Augusta, is also deified (*A.* 15.23.4-5). Both the thanksgivings after her birth and the deification are linked explicitly to flattery. Tacitus does nothing to undermine state imperial cult in this: overkill of honours may be part of the terminal decline of the senate but ruler worship receives no special treatment. The posthumous honours are excessive, as usual, but the type of honour is not undermined in itself any more than superfluous thanksgivings and the obsequious voting of temples and statues ever stood for an end to those institutions and practices. There would come a time when all these perfectly appropriate types of honour, including imperial cult, would once again be deployed, with more care, as a useful part of the *cultus deorum*.

More speculatively, there seems little to be gained by the association of Rome with a dead infant. The association would, in effect, be more with her progenitor than herself, since her only achievement was to end the immediate prospects of the dynasty. None of this is to say that the deification was not valid in itself. A poor arrangement is still an arrangement, until it is rescinded or abandoned. A scholar would not argue that a dreadful choice of consul, explicitly criticised in the sources, invalidates the magistracy: there seems no reason to problematise the particular institution in question in the absence of any indications in the text to this effect.

That is not to say that complex situations of assent or denial could not appear in connection with deification and subsequent cult: Poppaea, killed

---

[128] Gradel (2002) appeared too late to receive full attention here but vigorously argues the case that imperial cult was fully integrated into the religious system even at an early stage.

after the proud father kicked her in her pregnant belly, was also deified. Though her rites were foreign, we are told that she received cult honour after her death.[129] Thrasea Paetus acts as a (highly problematic) reference point for propriety in this: he did not attend her funeral, according to his accuser Capito Cossutianus. But as we shall see, Thrasea is not Tacitus' unalloyed mouthpiece and Capito is not a neutral witness. As the narrative has it, Nero observes that Paetus deliberately refused to attend Poppaea's deification (*A.* 16.21.3). However, the Stoic's accuser then adds that his enemy has refused to attend *any* meetings of the senate for three years by this point, nor even those of the *quindecimuiri*; he has not taken part in prayers for the imperial family or other traditional vows for senators and/or priests (16.22).

Despite Capito's and Nero's polemical isolation of Poppaea's case, Paetus has not apparently turned his back on this rite in particular; rather, he has abandoned any attempts at discrimination or ameliorations in the public affairs of Rome as hopeless. He would therefore seem to be refusing to endorse *any* religious or political activity, presumably on the grounds that it was inescapably corrupt. It is not he but his opponents who single out his refusal to accept Poppaea's divinity. But even if we accepted, for the sake of argument, that Poppaea's deification did attract his particular scorn, it does not by any means indicate a rejection of the institution: we do not hear of Paetus' opposition to cult practice concerning Augustus or Claudius, for instance. Nero's musings might as well be an example of his vanity as of any evidence that Paetus particularly scorned the status of the emperor's departed wife: and Tacitus' image shows how trivial and petty is Nero's attitude. The deification of the woman he murdered and her continuing influence shows just how bad things have got.

Apart from these, there are the 'failed' deifications, two in the *Annals*, and the other in the *Histories*.[130] Tacitus notes that Cerialis Anicius, consul-elect, proposed a motion that a temple should as soon as possible be built at the public expense to the Divine Nero and adds that 'some interpreted it as an omen of his death, seeing as such honours were linked to the dead' (*A.* 15.74.3-4). Nothing apparently came of it. Nero had another (posthumous) near-miss: Vitellius sacrificed to him, possibly as a prelude to planned deification, at *H.* 2.95.2. Again, nothing further came of it, except that Vitellius was discredited in discerning circles.

---

[129] Though the notice of her funeral and burial at *A.* 16.6.2-3 does not explicitly indicate her deification, at *A.* 16.21.2 we hear that *deum honores Poppaeae decernuntur* and she is referred to as *Poppaea diua* at *A.* 16.22.5. Furneaux (1896) notes coins and inscriptions of the title *Diua Poppaea Augusta*; see also Dio 63.26.5.

[130] Whose impact we should not exaggerate: they gain a somewhat distorted prominence in the absence of the deifications of Vespasian and Titus especially.

More pertinently, the suggestion that Livia be deified was refused by Tiberius on the grounds that she would not have wanted it.[131] Her case in particular is a useful one in contextualising imperial cult as one part of a spectrum of honours aimed at the imperial family, both living and deceased. For instance, at 1.14 the senate attempted to honour the Augusta but Tiberius vetoed the suggestions, not even permitting them to vote her a lictor or raise an altar commemorating her adoption into the Julian family. His explicit reasons included that women should not be so honoured, which would have been fine except for the fact that her power and influence already pervaded Roman politics. Tiberius' annoyance and jealousy thus set the senate even further back in their attempt to acknowledge, and therefore negotiate, her power.[132]

Tacitus' notices on these serve as more than historical material, and surprisingly credible material given his reputation for 'distorting' the facts: he evokes a system with which he assumes the reader is familiar and selects those aspects that constitute a very narrow set of evidence – the subservience and administrative incompetence of the senate and its emperors. Each religious notice is embedded in the narrative as part of a broader programme to highlight 'moral' decay. Religion is part of the senate's responsibility, and they fail in this as they fail in more overtly 'political' situations. The risk that the Taciteaan senate absolutely refused to take, even in the face of Tiberius' persistent irritation, was under-acknowledgement of the imperial family. Here they fell into precisely the same traps as they did in politics, of allowing sycophancy and fear to govern their decisions. Their willing reduction of their role to one of voting honours at every opportunity was not a solution but a problem in itself. Honours accumulated faster than they were forgotten.[133] The only area in which the senate were willing to exercise any initiative was, apparently, in sycophancy (*adulatio*), which

---

[131] *addito ne caelestis religio decerneretur. sic ipsam maluisse* (A. 5.2.1). But she *was* deified under Claudius (Dio *A.* 60.5.2). Furneaux (1896) 172 notes unofficial use of titles such as *Livia Augusta Dea* outside Rome. Suetonius records that she had specifically requested deification (*Tiberius* 51).

[132] The same pattern is seen repeatedly in politics: cf. the closing event of the succession debate (*Annals* 1.11-1.14): twelve candidates were named for the praetorship (as Augustus had done) and when the senate urged Tiberius to increase the number, he bound himself by an oath not to exceed it. On the debate as a whole (and especially the diagnosis of 'pretence'), see Woodman (1998b).

[133] And some *were* forgotten (*A.* 2.83.4), a rare, possibly unique, acknowledgement of North's suggestion for this method of pruning the *cultus deorum* under the Republic: 'the conservative ethos forbids letting anything drop. But the process of social evolution and the mere passage of time ensure that certain rites will get overlooked, neglected or forgotten' (North (1976) 12). It had not escaped Tacitus' notice, apparently.

meant rivalry and mutual self-destruction[134] and obeisance, and in this they had both the emperor's contempt and enforcement.[135]

Tacitus has little doubt that what motivates the senate is sycophancy:[136] thus they repeatedly vote honours that the emperor disliked and/or opposed. Tiberius' exasperation and repeated attempts to limit these honours seems only to stimulate the religious frenzy, which is not surprising. Tacitus' senate is attempting to locate itself in the face of an increasingly powerful *princeps*, and one medium for this definition of roles is through ritual and honours. The more autocratic (and contrary) Tacitus' emperors become (*refusing* the honours that would fix the relationship between senate and *princeps*), the more the situation demands a clear articulation of the relationship. Thus the senate finds itself in a vicious circle that it fails to escape: though the situation demands, ever more urgently, that it express and codify the power of the emperor, his refusal to allow this leaves it in even greater anxiety as we can see from the persistence of the issue. What we call imperial cult is, in this narrative at least, in fact only the apex of a pyramid of potential honours: the *diui* are not the only eminent dead[137] and their lesser counterparts can be honoured religiously on a lesser scale.[138] Furthermore, the living can be associated with the gods in a way that emphasises their effective power without crossing the line of religious propriety. Thus, when Tiberius and Sejanus (temporarily an honorary member of the

---

[134] A common topic: see e.g. *A.* 14.64.6. Informers, the scourge of Rome, were often linked with *adulatio* (e.g. *A.* 2.32.4), which, though needed in moderation during such times (*A.* 4.17.1), often also undermined the quality of proposals (3.65) and obscured the truth (*A.* 6.38.3). Tiberius gains credit for checking their activities at *A.* 3.56.1 but protects them at *A.* 4.30.5. By *A.* 4.36.5 they are the only inviolable aristocrats.

[135] See *A.* 2.87.2 – 'speech was restricted and perilous under an emperor who feared freedom while he hated sycophancy'; Tiberius hated the senate's compliance ('men fit to be slaves', *A.* 3.65.3); but he protected the informers, a chief cause of the fear which so often transformed into *adulatio* (as at *A.* 4.74.2 and 4.30.5).

[136] For the epidemic of sycophancy and servility see *A.* 1.7.1 (*at Romae ruere in seruitium consules patres eques. quanto quis inlustrior, tanto magis falsi ac festinantes uultuque composito, ne laeti excessu principis neu tristior<es> primordio, lacrimas gaudium, questus adulatione<m> miscebant*), *A.* 2.32.2 (*quorum auctoritates adulationesque rettuli, ut sciretur uetus id in re publica malum*), *A.* 3.65.2 (*ceterum tempora illa adeo infecta et adulatione sordida fuere …*). See also the comments of Segal (1973) 119. Sejanus enjoys the debasement of the aristocracy (*A.* 4.74.4), but Tiberius did not (*A.* 3.65.3); for such epigrammatic contempt, see further Sinclair (1992). *Obsequium* was the appropriate relationship (McCulloch (1984) 181; Morford (1991)).

[137] Germanicus observes what seems to be a useful distinction between Augustus and his father Drusus (*'tua, dive Auguste, caelo recepta mens, tua pater Druse, imago, tui memoria'*, *A.* 1.43.3). He also invokes Drusus alone at *A.* 2.8.1.

[138] When Germanicus dies, *honores ut quis amore in Germanicum aut ingenio ualidus reperti decretique*, *A.* 2.83.1. Nor are such honours voted exclusively in Rome itself (and these are not exaggerated any further by flattery (*A.* 3.2.5)); these are not only matched, but outdone, for Drusus at *A.* 4.9.2; Livia is offered minimal posthumous honours after Tiberius' intervention at *A.* 5.2.1.

imperial family) set up court outside Rome, the frightened senate use religious honours to appeal to them at *A*. 4.74.2, complete with statues of Tiberius and Sejanus, even though they were asked to address entirely different matters.[139] They sycophantically vote an altar to Clemency, an altar to Friendship, and statues round them to Caesar and Sejanus: just in case the message is not obvious, both men are begged to appear in public. Tacitus' material and presentation is a deliberate demonstration of the processes that he saw as characterising the dynamics of the period.

These honours might be granted to the living emperor and his associates[140] and emperors can be compared to gods.[141] We could of course dismiss this type of language as sycophantic (and therefore, by implication, meaningless) but this would be to miss the point that all the textual agents in the *Annals* and the *Histories* are all caught up in the ongoing attempt to find a stable and workable balance between emperor and his subjects. Imperial cult and honours are one way of negotiating the unprecedented *auctoritas* of Rome's greatest family. Tacitus' treatment frames religious matters within the more general political nightmare. His selection and location of material are trenchant but his interest is particular, even narrow: the frequent errors in interpretation, an evocation of the political forces that, for him, shaped first-century politics and the persistent need to recreate patterns of proper, 'truly' *Roman* conduct, whatever the actuality of the period.

There is no shortage of potential alternative responses to the changes of religious practice in this period: one might, for instance, note with interest, rather than contempt, the shift of interest from the state to the individual in the form of omens (as opposed to prodigies) or astrology; a triumphalist account perhaps, that maximised the power of the emperor who sought to preserve the ancient *cultus deorum* despite the traditional decline of morals. Tacitus' agenda, tied very closely to the historical reality, is no less constructed than any other account: he weaves his narrative together so persuasively that if we are to appreciate its nature as a construction, we must make an effort to see that it could have been framed another way. Religion, as an

---

[139] *At pauor internus occupauerat animos cui remedium adulatione quaerebatur. ita quamquam diuersis super rebus consulerentur, aram clementiae, aram amicitiae effigiesque circum Caesaris ac Seiani censuere crebrisque precibus efflagitabant uisendi sui copiam facerent.* For an independent (epigraphic) witness to the senate's desire to have the ruler(s) back in Rome, see Griffin (1997).

[140] Requests to build temples to Tiberius, Livia and the senate: accepted at *A*. 4.15.4; refused at *A*. 4.37.1; honours are suggested for Nero *A*. 13.8.1 and 13.10.1 (refused) where they are also requested for his father and guardian; for him again *A*. 13.41.5, and thanksgivings for his safety at *A*. 14.10.1-4 after his 'lucky escape' from assassination by Agrippina.

[141] E.g. *A*. 3.36.2 and 4.39.2 (by Sejanus).

interpretative system and set of institutions, is something that *did* adapt, for Tacitus, often perfectly reasonably: but for the most part, it was drawn into the maelstrom of indecision and fear that characterises Tacitus' first century, just like other areas that required politically laden judgement. What we do *not* see in Tacitus' version of events is a fundamental disdain for religion: his account is rather a strong corrective, and a documentation of a system which was never given an opportunity to function properly.

The debasement of the cultus deorum Thus far we have outlined synchronically the various categories that were deployed in the understanding of Roman religion in the period covered by Tacitus to establish the basic categories of religious experience. But Tacitus' accounts are also progressive and diachronic: what he made of the first imperial dynasty of Rome, and their immediate successors, can only be explored when we examine the (generally worsening) developments. On all fronts, Tacitus' Annalistic Rome inexorably slides into the disasters of the *Histories*. He documents the march of institutional problems and Rome's collapsing relationship with her gods, caused largely by a political and social (i.e. moral) context that made maintenance of appropriate and workable standards impossible. For Tacitus, the very guardians of Roman religion were, ultimately, either powerless or corrupted during the first century.

Priests functioned as guarantors of the tradition – and trusted experts – in the extant Livy; not so in Tacitus. For the time being we are concerned with subjects of emperors rather than the *Pontifices Maximi* themselves since the continuation of traditions depended as much, if not more, on the senate, who made up the body of priestly members. Though some priests retain the kinds of characters that offset the excesses of the principate, and the grasp of lore that preserved the *cultus deorum*, this is not always the case. Since priests were chosen from the leading men of the senate, we would expect that the weaknesses evident in political life would show up in connection with the religious experts also. In the programmatic opening to the *Histories*, Tacitus says that priesthoods, along with magistracies, were among the spoils of factional war (*et sacerdotia et consulatus ut spolia adepti*, *H.* 1.2.3). No such statement is to be found in the *Annals* but we do find its predecessor, the encroachment of political favour on the appointment of priests. Given that the tendency had become serious enough to warrant mention in the *Histories*, we should expect the reader of the *Annals* to notice the gradual erosion of priestly calibre.

As with so many other aspects, Augustus starts the trend (*A.* 1.3.1) and then a poor (but not yet disastrous) development under Tiberius is the prelude to steady degeneration over the years: even Tiberius sees the need to strengthen the priesthood.[142] The opening books of the *Annals* seem to indicate a mixture of good and bad. The *flamen dialis*, for one, does not acquit himself well when he argues for his right to govern a province (*A.* 4.16.6). He argues that the restrictions were based on rivalry in the republican senate, and that such problems are irrelevant in the principate. The paradox of his breathtaking sycophancy in attributing previous religious decisions to rivalry in a senate that is busy with competitive self-destruction does him little credit. The debate does, however, bring forward the augur Lentulus and unnamed others in opposition. Though we are not given explicit guidance, there are good signs that if any side is to be taken, it is that of the augur; his opponent is discredited by his own statement, and Lentulus' reasoning is not given. Thus his position is effectively irreproachable and his reasoning, unlike that of his opponent, beyond our reach.[143] Some approval of Lentulus' position seems warranted, especially as the precedents – and the decision that emerges – take the same position.[144] Whatever Tacitus' preferred solution was, his senate is capable, at this point, of weighing up such a question and resisting deleterious impulses. There are to be few such occasions as time progresses.

Tacitus makes a point of telling us that Tiberius *lost* good priests such as L. Calpurnius Piso, who refrained from initiating sycophantic measures and intelligently moderated others whenever he could (*A.* 6.10.3) as well as forcing Ateius Capito, a man well versed in both human and divine lore,[145] out of public life (*A.* 3.70.3).[146] Cocceius Nerva, similarly knowledgeable and one of the few trusted by Tiberius (he went to Capri with the emperor at *A.* 4.58.1), starves himself to death at *A.* 6.27.1. As for their replacements, the problem does not always lie with the choice of men but in the way it is done. They are apparently rewarded for political favours, rather than appointed for their experience and expertise. Nero Caesar is similarly made a *pontifex* at the same time as it is requested that he be allowed to stand for the quaestorship five years early. It seems unlikely he had gained the kind

---

[142] Already by *A.* 4.16.4, moves are made to increase the dignity of the priests (*utque glisceret dignatio sacerdotum*).

[143] We can only speculate on what an augur would have said about the jurisdiction of a *flamen*, but there is unlikely to be significance in the unusual note that he was an augur: this was simply a way to distinguish between various homonymous senators of the time which was so common that it found its way into the *Fasti* (Furneaux (1896) *ad loc*). Woodman and Martin (1996) identify him as Cn. Cornelius Lentulus, *cos.* 14 BC, and continue 'he is here deputising for the absent *Pontifex Maximus*' though they do not offer their reasoning.

[144] See however Furneaux *ad loc* who cites Seneca (*de Ben. A.* 2.27.1) to the effect that Lentulus was 'extremely rich, miserly and stupid.' Suetonius (*Tiberius* 49) notes his fearful suicide and that Tiberius was both his heir and the author of his misery.

[145] He is at least credited as such by Macrobius *A.* 7.13.11.

[146] A difficult passage: see Woodman and Martin (1996) *ad loc*.

of experience and knowledge normally desirable for the role. After the trial of Piso, Tacitus makes the point that his chief accusers Publius Vitellius, Quintus Veranius and Quintus Servaeus were rewarded with priesthoods (*A.* 3.19).[147] In fact these men seem to be reasonable choices, as their subsequent activities in the text illustrate.[148] But it is perhaps the precedent that is dangerous. More ominously, Tiberius also blocks the promised priesthood of the disgraced Blaesi for political reasons at *A.* 6.40. All the ingredients for active imperial control of priesthood are therefore present from an early stage: priesthoods are already *spolia* of the 'civil war'[149] under Tiberius, one of many occasions when the *Annals* lay the basis for trends that had gone much further in the *Histories*.

Priests are less conspicuous in subsequent reigns: Claudius notes the decline of haruspicy, and, typically for an emperor, attributes it to lack of use in times of prosperity (*A.* 11.15.1). No priestly activity is recorded for his reign apart from the rites performed by the *pontifices* (and ridiculed by the public) to purify Rome of incest at *A.* 12.8.2-3. Similarly, under Nero, priests rarely figure in the narrative. The emperor expiates lightning strikes under the instruction of the ever-anonymous *haruspices* at *A.* 13.24.2 and they make an accurate prediction at *A.* 15.47.3. No question is made of the priests' performance of their duties, yet it is hard not to come away from the *Annals* with a sense that priests are increasingly *not* in a position to repair the damage that is increasingly caused by the most powerful men in the state.

Moving to the period covered by the *Histories*, Galba is somewhat incompetent himself, as we shall see, and does not always have religious experts to put him straight. His disregard for omens is noted at *H.* 1.18.1-2 and though there is the *haruspex Caesarum* Umbricius[150] on hand to predict

---

[147] See Martin and Woodman (1996) on 3.19:'for other awards to prosecutors see *A.* 2.32.1 and 4.20.2-3'.

[148] Vitellius, a veteran of Germany and therefore associate and friend of Germanicus (*A.* 1.70), commits suicide under accusation of offering the Keys of the Treasury and Military Treasury for 'seditious projects' (*A.* 5.8) – he was therefore not evidently an informer who were normally immune from prosecution; Veranius, another old friend of Germanicus, had been governor of Cappadocia (*A.* 2.56.4) and leaves our narrative at this point without attracting Tacitus' attention for the best and worst of political actions; Servaeus was prosecuted as a friend of Sejanus, though Tacitus notes specifically that he had not abused this position: at *A.* 6.7.2-4, he and his fellow accused, a knight by the name of Minucius Thermus, turned informer and brought down Julius Africanus and Seius Quadratus. Even their betrayal is somewhat mitigated: Tacitus comments on the endemic habit of leading figures becoming informers that it happened 'sometimes in self-defence, often more like a contagion' (*pars ad subsidium sui, plures infecti quasi ualetudine et contactu*).

[149] Keitel (1984).

[150] The deviation in the pattern of naming priests with Umbricius would appear to be explained by his title. His case would therefore seem analogous to that of the *Pontifex Maximus* in that he had an exalted and individual status.

treachery at *H.* 1.27.1, the warning does Galba no good. There may be hints of inauspicious appointments when Otho comes to power: 'Otho continued to discharge his imperial duties ... Sometimes he observed the dignity of the Commonwealth, but often in hasty acts, dictated by the expediency of the moment, he disregarded its honour ... On older citizens, who had already held high office, Otho bestowed, as a crowning dignity, pontificates and augurships, while he consoled the young nobles, who had recently returned from exile, by reviving the sacerdotal offices held by their fathers and ancestors' (*H.* 1.77.5).

When precisely the emperor was acting responsibly and when he was undermining the *res publica* is left to the reader to decide: there are plenty of other candidates for hasty mistakes in the passage other than his priestly appointments.[151] Nonetheless, Tacitus' comments at the opening of the *Histories* (*sacerdotia et consulatus ut spolia adepti*) invite us to feel somewhat uncomfortable about these appointments, given that this is the fullest mention of priestly appointments in the extant text– unless he is referring to later (Flavian) appointments (which of course, included his own). Given the calibre of recently eminent citizens (for an example see Curtius Rufus, condemned as typical of his age, at 11.21), the chances are that those who had held high office were not necessarily the best men for the job: but circumstances would inevitably limit Otho's choice.

Priesthoods, like magistracies, are thus locked into a system where political goodwill rather than expertise has become the criterion for appointment. Given that political favour is preferred over aptitude, the alliance of the aristocracy with the transient political master(s) in preference to the enduring character of the city is one of the chief causes of the profound problems facing Rome. Priestly independence is hardly likely to survive in such a context.

Vitellius was appointed to at least one priesthood, presumably under Nero, but was typically appointed for the wrong reasons: not through any effort on his own part, but because of his father's eminence.[152] His inadequacy in religious terms is, as we shall see, emphatically demonstrated when he becomes *princeps*, but in our texts he appoints no priests, and leaves intact Otho's various appointments, including consulships (*H.* 1.77.4). Under Vespasian the *haruspices* feature once again in the refounding of the Capitoline as expert advisers. In the case of this particular

---

[151] The recall of exiles found guilty of extortion; or the appointment of Verginius and Vopiscus as consuls, for instance.

[152] *consulatum, sacerdotia, nomen locumque inter primores nulla sua industria, sed cuncta patris claritudine adeptus* (*H.* 3.86.1).

priesthood, we might assume that their membership was to some extent protected by their Etruscan origins, even if they are now a *collegium*. As for the other priesthoods, we must assume that the poor appointments of the recent past would persist for some time.[153]

Despite all these hints, priests *qua* priests are not explicitly found wanting in Tacitean Rome; on the rare occasions that they appear, they are entirely proper. Tacitus builds into his account a series of notices that succeed in insinuating that the whole process of appointment had diluted the quality of the priesthoods while strenuously avoiding any statement that brought the institutions *per se* directly into question. When they perform their duties, the priests are still sufficient to their various tasks – a testament to the strength of the institution rather than its current membership. Thus, in Tacitean Rome, the religious personnel are unlikely to be a match for their Republican counterparts. This is true also, even especially, of the senate.

The failure of expertise It is not the priests who were the chief intermediaries in deciding religious matters. Though their expertise might be called upon, it is the senate, including its priests *qua* senators, who are theoretically responsible. In this role, they conspicuously fail to maintain the standards that Tacitus would have liked to see. Though priests inevitably figure in the decline, as members of the senate, they are not, in the following examples, deliberately called upon as religious experts. In addition we encounter the fact that the emperor was himself a priest by virtue of simultaneously being a member of all the major colleges, and *Pontifex Maximus*. Thus, he potentially embodies all the expertise of Rome in religious matters: the senate can be severely circumscribed by his authority. When the emperor speaks on religious matters, does he do so on the basis of his being *princeps*? Purely as a senator or consul with a traditional right to speak on such questions? Or is he assuming the authority of whichever *collegium* would normally have jurisdiction over the item in question? The signs are that it was no more possible for the Tacitean senate to tell the difference than it is for us.

The localisation of religious authority is particularly difficult for the Tiberian senate. Tiberius, who so conspicuously hates the abject servility of the senate (*A*. 3.65.3), acts a number of times as a check on decline. The emperor apparently understands the issue to be one of knowledge, but Tacitus, as we shall see, often places the difficulties in a moral and political context by narrating moments in the senate that tell a consistent story. Though Tiberius, and, to a lesser (explicit) extent, Claudius, see themselves

---

[153] Virtually all the major priesthoods were traditionally held for life. See Beard (1990) 20–21.

as part of the solution, the historian indicates that they are rather part of the problem.

Tiberius makes his displeasure known when Germanicus, inappropriately for an augur, takes part in the building of a burial mound for Varus' troops at *A*. 1.62.2; at *A*. 1.73.5 he forestalls a prosecution for insulting Augustus with the short-lived precept that injuries to the gods are the concern of the gods (*deorum iniurias dis curae*); at *A*. 3.18.2, after the death of Piso, he blocks various measures, including the building of a golden statue to Mars the Avenger and an altar to Vengeance (*Vltio*), on the grounds that celebration is inappropriate. At *A*. 3.64.3-4, under the pernicious influence of *adulatio*,[154] the senate decrees supplications to the gods and the celebration of the Great Games, to be exhibited by the *pontifices*, *augures*, *quindecimuiri* and the Board of Seven, along with the Augustal Brotherhood. Lucius Apronius moves that the *fetiales* should preside also over the Games. Tiberius refuses on the grounds that there was no rule or precedent for this.

When Tiberius refuses to consult the Sibylline Books at *A*. 1.76.3 over a flood, he presumably thinks that he knows better. However the incident is replete with political implications. The suggestion is made by Asinius Gallus, who we know from elsewhere was a *quindecimuir* (*ILS* 5050). Tacitus' silence on this point implies that his request was not made on the authority of his priesthood: it *should* be possible for any senator to make the suggestion. But Gallus is not, in Tiberius' eyes, just 'any' senator. The comments on Gallus in 1.12 and 1.13 imply that Tiberius, nursing a long-standing grudge against the supposedly ambitious senator, would be more open to the suggestion from other members of the senate (and Gallus dies in custody in 33 (*A*. 6.23)). The claim is, after all, based on good precedents: it was done in AD 5 and again in 12 (Dio *A*. 55.22.3, 56.27.4), though we do not know it from the *Annals*. In response to the refusal, Tacitus indicates that his decision obscured divine and human issues (*perinde diuina humanaque obtegens*). *Humana* hints at just how personal a decision this was, far from the kind of professionalism that is normally desired. But the emperor's obfuscation of divine issues presumably means that by refusing to debate the issue, Tiberius does not allow for the rehearsal of the criteria used to make such a

---

[154] As the subsequent narrative indicates (3.65-66). *Obsequium* is the appropriate relationship (McCulloch (1984) 181; Morford (1991)). The senate's 'proper' relationship with the emperor of the day has been much discussed: McCulloch (1984) 179 offers that 'what disgusted Tacitus was not so much the subordination of their role to the dictates of the emperor, but their failure to take an initiative in participating actively in the new order. This psychological enervation (*A*. 1.7.1), representing the failure of the nobility to seek means for expressing their own *aequalitas*, was to Tacitus as much a source of despotism as the bad emperors themselves.'

decision. Persistent similar refusals will inevitably lead to a breakdown in the transmission of such knowledge.[155]

The active, even overweening, intervention of a *princeps* is countered by an explicit comparison, and a reminder that this is not the only possibility: Tacitus celebrates the rare opportunity for the senate to make meaningful decisions on religious matters (*A.* 3.60.6). His lengthy exposition reflects the careful discussion and weighing up of the various claims: thus the senate seems perfectly capable of holding such debates, but, in the circumstances, only at the instigation of the emperor. In practice, it was not possible for the Tacitean senate to act on their own initiative, as a rare attempt (and object lesson in reading Tacitus' coverage of religion and politics) indicates.

Within Tacitus' narrative, when the tribune Quintilianus and the consul Caninius Gallus suggests the introduction of a Sibylline Book into the collection, they are separately rebuked by the emperor for not observing customary procedures: though the tribune is only mildly chastised on the grounds of inexperience, the consul is given more of a dressing down and reminded not just of the Augustan legislation on the topic but also that the college itself should be consulted over the authenticity of the work in question before the senate can legitimately decide to include the 'new' text. But Gallus may be more insightful than Tiberius gives him credit for. Tiberius has already effectively appropriated access to the collection and their interpreters by the abrupt and autocratic refusal of access at *A.* 1.76.3. Traditional protocol, at least in the form that Tiberius frames it, does not take account of this: to submit a new book to the collection, one has to consult the priests themselves. But attempting this would appear to circumvent the emperor – clearly a dangerous venture. However, Tiberius' explicit permission to approach the college cannot be sought directly since the emperor persistently *claims* to endorse republican channels. Asking his permission would be to expose the pervasive game of pretence that characterises Tiberius's dealings with the senate.[156] Gallus is therefore faced with an insoluble dilemma if he wishes the book to be considered, as he must do. Putting the matter to a poorly attended senate, if procedurally inappropriate, at least advertises the issue to all the relevant parties and invites them to act without giving offence by ignoring their spheres of authority. Tiberius' criticism therefore misses the point. As he says himself, though Quintilianus is young and ignorant of precedent, Gallus knows the procedures well. Apparently he

---

[155] It also underlines his monopoly, via the illegal art of astrology, on access to the dictates of fate which, alone of the various *collegia*, the *quindecimuiri* deliberately consider.

[156] Though see Woodman (1998b) on the 'succession debate' for an argument against seeing Tiberius as duplicitous, at least in that episode.

also knows his emperor. Tacitus' agenda is conveyed by apparently simple notices that collectively assemble as a devastating critique of the emperor's supposed safeguarding of religious procedures.

Tiberius' reinstatement of the normal channels of authority cannot but be ironic for the reader, already alerted that Tiberius had appropriated the real power.[157] The religious institutions of Tiberian Rome cannot be safeguarded in these circumstances. But the emperor is struggling with logistical problems which he himself engenders by his autocracy. For instance, Servius Maluginensis, the *flamen dialis* (who could effectively not leave Rome because of religious restrictions) requests the right to govern a province at *A.* 3.58.1, claiming that the religious limitations could easily be circumvented on the analogy of other priesthoods. The senate is willing to take some responsibility – in the form of Lentulus and others, who object (in the absence of the emperor), as we have already seen. Tiberius's intercession ends the debate at *A.* 3.71.2: when a decision is made, it is Tiberius who introduces Augustan and earlier precedents to decide the issue. He has effectively reserved the decision for himself and, at best, the senate needs Tiberius' confirmation.[158] At 4.16, when Tiberius suggests the replacement of the now deceased *flamen*, some of the restrictions on the priest's wife (the *flaminica* who performed ritual actions herself) are lifted through the senate after some debate. The new regulations and appointment seem unproblematic in themselves. But again, it is Tiberius who instigates the debate. The senate is represented as so enervated that they lack the authority or initiative to make such changes themselves. Only at Tiberius' urging do they resolve it and find a modern compromise to some of the archaic regulations that seem to have impeded the *flaminica*, and thereby (presumably) the priesthood. The inexperience and obedience that Tiberius has engendered has now begun to take its toll and the ever less expert senate would henceforth remember to await instructions.[159]

In Tacitus' account, Tiberius discovers that the situation was unworkable. Thus, while his particular religious prescriptions succeed, his attempt to lay down general principles fail because of the climate over which he presides. For instance, he declares at *A.* 1.73.1 that the *maiestas* laws, after beginning under Tiberius, ultimately undermined everything (*cunctaque corripuerit*). At this point, an attempt to prosecute Falanius and Rubrius,

---

[157] *sed Tiberius, uim principatus sibi firmans, imaginem antiquitatis senatui praebebat ...* (*A.* 3.60).
[158] Under the Republic, the senate was not always the final authority for such matters – it might also have involved other authorities, particularly the popular assemblies: see Bleicken (1957b).
[159] In fact, the intercession of Lentulus and the others seems to be the last time in the *Annals* that the senate take any religious action of their own accord, with or without the *princeps* present, apart from the voting of honours, to which we shall return shortly.

the former for selling a statue of Augustus along with a garden and admitting an actor to the group who worshipped Augustus in his home, the latter for violating Augustus' divinity by perjury, led to a stern rebuttal from Tiberius who declared that *deorum iniurias dis curae*. Soon, however, sacrilege against Augustus becomes a well-known charge.[160]

Political insecurity, vividly underlined by the growth of informers and the exercise of absolute authority, guarantees a surfeit of religious honours in Tacitean Rome: this includes the 'defence' of Augustus' position and privilege. This system of acknowledgement begins to collapse as it persistently fails to resolve the tensions in aristocratic society: nor is it the only casualty.

Refusing to locate religious authority in one man was not just a question of power-sharing in Livy's Republic. Given the range of different knowledges inherent within religious understanding, it seems reasonable to assume that it also safeguarded against error. Under Tiberius, the dangers of relying on one man's expertise become a practical concern. Additionally, even religious actions that might have been appropriate in a different context begin to look isolated, even conspicuous, in their context of political machinations. Increasingly, as time passes, the religious system in these accounts begins to falter.

The dislocation of the cultus deorum   The honours and triumph (the latter also implicitly an acknowledgement of the gods) for Germanicus at 2.41 are already undermined in their celebration by the popular remembrance that *breuis et infaustos populi Romani amores*. But it is *Tiberius* who immediately plots for Germanicus' removal from Rome in our text, actively colluding with what had previously been poor luck. Tiberius' programme to renovate and dedicate temples at *A.* 2.49.1 seems entirely proper and might have signalled an improvement in circumstances if we had encountered it in Livy: however, here the subsequent narrative opens with the chilling note that *adolescebat interea lex maiestatis*. The left hand does not seem to know, or care, what the right is doing in Tiberian Rome. We are already close to 'going through the motions'. Averting the *ira deum* does few senators any good as long as they can be terrorised by human means. At *A.* 3.18.2, on the death of Piso, it is suggested that religious honours be voted, but Tiberius interposes with his typically imperial maxim that foreign victories should be celebrated with sacrifices, but domestic woes should be kept quiet (*ob externas ea uictorias sacrari dictitans, domestica mala tristitia operienda*)

---

[160] See *A.* 2.50.2, where Tiberius orders that the charges be investigated and punished, if necessary; cf. 3.66.

which neither he nor the senate are to live up to for long. Tacitus derides the honours offered to Drusus and Tiberius at *A*. 3.57.1-2, or the unimaginative flattery that proposed them. Tiberius' restoration of Pompey's theatre, without erasing the founder's name, seems a worthy venture, but the senate's voting of a statue of the overrated Sejanus to stand within it undermines any credit that might have been achieved at *A*. 3.72.4-5.

These juxtapositions are significant, if difficult to fix in their impact. Even the knowledgeable emperor cannot contain the forces he has unleashed, or live up to the formulations that he himself offers the senate. Whether any of them counts as impiety in the eyes of the gods, we cannot say: but at the very least, some kind of incompetence is indicated. It is not the question of *if* Rome will become misaligned with her gods, but *when*. And Rome will not even be in a position to note the warnings.

Without the independent systems of prodigy reports and consultation of the Sibylline Books, Tiberius' Rome has abandoned its 'early warning system' and opportunity to correct cosmic imbalance. It is therefore no surprise that sooner or later the gods, apparently benign for a while, begin to bear grudges. When it duly comes, the *ira deum* arrives – naturally, in these circumstances – unannounced and unexpectedly. For Tacitus, Sejanus embodies their anger (*A*. 4.1.2).[161] Such is the refusal to see ill that when Sabinus is dragged off on New Year's Day at *A*. 4.70.1-4, bystanders flee, then return, fearful that their flight admitted that something was wrong. The pretence of 'business as usual', applied to the difficult and subjective arena of prodigies for some years, has now reached even the blatantly obvious: it did not require 'expert' interpretation to see that Sejanus' power had encroached on a sacred day. The impropriety is emphasised by the word play on (Se)Janus ('without Janus').[162]

When the cities of Asia offer (or perhaps, request the right) at *A*. 4.15.5 to build a temple to Tiberius, his mother and the senate, the offer is accepted and thanks given by Nero Caesar, who, apart from being hated by Sejanus, reminds his audience of his father Germanicus. We are thereby invited by this allusion to remember *his* fate, and other ill-starred favourites of Rome. Though we have lost the story of the final days of the doomed prince, by

---

[161] The tradition seems to have asserted that Sejanus outwitted Tiberius, and we would probably assume that this occurred on a 'level playing field', but Tacitus offers otherwise in the light of Tiberius' manifest intelligence and unremitting suspicion; the emperor *was* fooled, but because of the *ira deum*. Tacitus is accounting for an historical anomaly – he does not consider Sejanus to be a shrewd enough political operator to undo the wily Tiberius under normal circumstances – by invoking a 'higher level' of analysis. He is similarly impelled to invoke a 'higher' level of explanation to ward off the reaction he expects when recounting a number of deaths in *A*. 16.16.1-2.

[162] Corrigan (1993).

4.60 Sejanus' plots have already begun to tell against him. Tiberius' son Drusus might have received the same honours as Germanicus and more *ut ferme amat posterior adulatio* (*A*. 4.9.2) but only because of his (apparently avoidable) death, which was of course due to the wrath of the gods, as manifested in the rise of Sejanus. If Rome had been more alert to the *ira deum*, then, these two might not have died. Posthumous piety did little for Drusus, especially when the gods continued to be angry. It appears that despite Tiberius' implied claims to adequacy in religion, he cannot compensate for the dysfunction of the institutions which he has so successfully appropriated to his expert guidance.

There is more: Tiberius uses religion as an excuse to leave Rome when he sets off at *A*. 4.57.1 to dedicate temples to Jupiter at Capua and a shrine to Augustus at Nola and he did not return. The discordance between his avowed intentions and his actions relegate a worthwhile religious moment that should have strengthened Rome's solidarity to being a facilitator of its enervation. The artificial preservation of religious practice by the emperor is even more of a sham in such circumstances. In this, as in other matters, he is following the letter of the law while systematically destroying its spirit: Agrippina's death by starvation, which Tacitus implies was engineered by the emperor, is met with a vote of *thanks* for Tiberius (who claims that she starved herself, heartbroken) along with an annual sacrifice to Jupiter to celebrate not just her death but also that of her enemy Sejanus (*A*. 6.25.5). The injustice of the offering to Jupiter on the anniversary of Agrippina's death seems to be underlined by the immediately subsequent decision of Cocceius Nerva, the longtime companion of the emperor, well versed in both human and divine law, to end his life at *A*. 6.26.1 even though his status is intact and his body unharmed. He supposedly foresees danger and chooses to be the master of his own destiny. The mention of his religious knowledge, whose relevance commentators have not been able to explain, may well be present to indicate that Nerva has diagnosed the *ira deum* and can see no solution, just inevitable problems.

Tacitus' Tiberius is paradoxically both a safeguard and the greatest danger to religion: to paraphrase Juvenal, there is no one to guard *this* guardian. His dissimulation creates an atmosphere where the senate can only act with any authority and freedom when under direct instruction.[163] Their normal procedures are paralysed under an emperor who autocratically decides religious matters when republican channels are attempted, and who strenuously

---

[163] Compare Shotter (1989) on *A*. 4.30.5: 'While Tiberius was on hand to check (in many cases) their abuses, the situation probably appeared less dangerous, but the problem raised by his arbitrary interventions was what would happen when he was not on hand to save defendants.'

defends these now worthless channels when his autocracy is openly acknowledged in practice. Such conditions are hardly conducive to the transmission of the inherited wisdom that had been instrumental in governing
the *cultus deorum* for centuries. Even when proper procedures are followed,
they threaten to become increasingly meaningless in context. Though political upheaval does affect religion, the remembrance of proper cult actions
does persist, however isolated it becomes. That isolation is set to grow until
the few aspects of religious practice that have not fallen prey to the corruption of politics become positively conspicuous and virtually futile.

Claudius, like Tiberius, tries to breathe life into a system that is severely
hamstrung by the context in which it is supposed to operate. The creation
of a haruspical college, spurred on by the typically antiquarian[164] diagnosis of declining religion, is set within a respectable context of precedents;
but we note that the senate is by now accustomed to acting on the emperor's instructions. They pass the matter to the *pontifices* after the emperor
has outlined his case. How Tacitus framed his discussion of the Saecular
Games at *A.* 11.11.1 we cannot know, though we should note that this
was the province of the *quindecimuiri* rather than the senate. Nor are the
enlargement of the *pomerium* and the restoration of the *Salutis augurium*
problematised in themselves at *A.* 12.23.3-4; rather they are set within good
precedents. Any hope, however, that the new, antiquarian, emperor might
bring some improvement to the situation is, however, quickly dashed.

The first problem is that the case is made by Claudius and Claudius
alone and the emperor is simply not up to the task, as Tacitus' depiction
makes vividly clear. Any implication that *Salus* will henceforth be an ally
of Rome is textually undermined by the immediately subsequent adoption
at *A.* 12.25.1 of Nero, who will hardly embody the blessings of the god.
At *A.* 12.4.4, Vitellius is allowed to have Silanus struck from the senatorial roll even though the *lustrum* had been closed. Claudius not only fails to
act against this, but colludes with the procedural anomaly by cutting off his
own contact with the disgraced Silanus.[165] Claudius' knowledge of precedent and protocol also seems to fail him when his court persuade him to
marry his niece Agrippina. The incest may have been circumvented legally
by Vitellius (*A.* 12.5.3-5) but there seems little reason to think that this is
sufficient: astonishingly, almost simultaneously in our text, Silanus is prosecuted for supposed incest with his sister and Claudius, endeavouring as ever
to find integrity in law and lore, performs rites to purify Rome, thus confirming a religious dimension to the act. The emperor is, not for the first –

---

[164] North (1976) 12.
[165] Who duly quits office and commits suicide (*A.* 12.8.1).

or last – time, legally correct but out of touch with reality.[166] Shortly afterwards, the *ira deum* begins to irrupt into the text with two sets of prodigies. One, at 12.43, is interestingly coupled with an example of the gods' support for Rome in their relief for famine. A further set follows at 12.64. Amidst the prodigies, it would seem that, while the relationship between Rome and her gods is beginning to suffer more profoundly after years of abuse and neglect, there is still divine 'goodwill' towards the City.[167]

Claudius' antiquarianism may allow for some reasonable reforms but, when combined with his idiocy as emperor, is of little use if he will not attend to those things that were more immediately at hand.[168] The situation has not yet become irrecoverable, but, given the prevailing climate, it is only a matter of time. It would be simplistic to link these prodigies purely to the marriage of Claudius and Agrippina. Yet the acknowledged appearance of prodigies for the first (extant) time means that the goodwill of the gods, while still a potent force, is being lost. The incest at the heart of the *res publica* must be a factor in this, notwithstanding the normal 'wear and tear' on the cosmos.

By this point it is clear that the emperor, partly through his being *Pontifex Maximus*, has assumed a great degree of authority over religious matters. This might seem inevitable but Tacitus does make an effort to prescribe a religious role for the senate under Tiberius, maximising their ever diminishing role until their active intervention has become a distant memory. The benefits of shared expertise and diffused authority threaten to be lost when all religious motions must go through the emperor. This inherent weakness develops over time and is ultimately played out to its logical conclusion under Nero, as a 'religious' narrative of the surviving texts indicates.

Before the reign of Nero (excepting the reign of Caligula, about whom we can only speculate) the senate dealt for the most part with an emperor imbued with procedural tradition. Tiberius may have been instrumental in robbing the senate of its ability to make decisions about religion, and Claudius may have not let the right hand notice what the left was doing, but at least these two were partially equipped to oversee the *cultus deorum*. Under Nero, it is increasingly a question not so much of reliable expertise

---

[166] Tacitus confirms that Claudius has committed incest *sua uoce A.* 13.2.3 (*claudius nuptiis incestis ...peruerterat*). The sham is still visible to the public at 12.5 (*...incestum ac, si sperneretur, ne in malum publicum erumperet metuebatur*). There is also the easily drawn implication that the hypocrisy has become profound, since by the prosecution of Silanus, a purification for incest can be enacted without reference to Claudius. If so, the *ira deum* that follows shortly afterwards may be an indictment of this sleight of hand.

[167] Cf. their assistance at *A.* 4.27.1.

[168] E.g. Claudius is sacrificing in Ostia when Messalina married Silius (*A.* 11.26.1-4). While no censure is attached to the emperor for his observance of ritual, his lack of everyday observation is startling.

but of the extent of incompetence and wilful sabotage. Nero, perhaps not surprisingly given his age, never seems to get much of a grasp of religion in Tacitus' text. Rather, he relates to religion as a way of endorsing his ever more flagrant abuses. The only person who outdoes the now absolutely deplorable senate is the emperor himself. The destruction of Rome becomes a race, where the only merit of the aristocracy is that, after an initial head start, they cannot keep up. As Nero pushes back the boundaries of disgrace, the senate respond by negotiating their moral surrender through religious honours, a tendency hitherto resisted almost solely by the incumbent emperor, yet simultaneously fostered by the various régimes.

Early in the reign, it is true, the senate takes the lead in abolishing any remaining respect for religion, with Nero refusing various honours (*A*. 13.10.1), but this is almost certainly due to the influence of Burrus and Seneca, a moderating influence on the young *princeps* (they had only recently prevented murders by Agrippina and her accomplices, 13.2-3). It does not take long for him to catch up: whereas Claudius overly reinforced his family ties, Nero goes to great lengths to reduce his. After acquiescence in, or ignorance of, the poisoning of his adoptive father by his mother (12.66), Nero poisons his stepbrother Britannicus (*A*. 13.16.2-5), murders his mother (*A*. 14.8.6), executes one wife using the state apparatus (Octavia, 14.64) and murders another on his own (Poppaea, *A*. 16.6.1) along with their unborn child; he also disposes of his mentors Seneca[169] and (in all likelihood) Burrus (*A*. 14.51.1-5) along with anyone else who might set a different example.[170] As these impediments are removed, Tacitus' Nero increasingly shows his 'true colours'.

Very early in the reign, the suborning of religion is virtually complete. Almost the only honours mentioned are those to celebrate fictitious or domestic 'victories'. By *A*. 13.41.5, there have been so many honours, on such a scale, voted for the mediocre reign that Caius Cassius proposes a classification of sacred and business-days to allow for the transaction of normal busines. The thanksgivings, at 14.10-11, after the murder of his mother, show that religious honours, partially resisted by Tiberius, have now become a key feature of the active collusion with the régime. The prospect of Rome maintaining good relations with the gods becomes a distant dream as even the artificially (i.e. imperially) rectified negotiations with the gods slide into the same perverted morass as other senatorial actions, a process vividly enacted as the senate compete to destroy any remaining integrity in thanksgivings. It is a rounding condemnation of the senate, rather than a

---

[169] Hated by Nero, who wanted to be rid of him at *A*. 15.56.2; obliged to commit suicide at 15.60f.
[170] In particular Thrasea Paetus, whose death closes the *Annals* (16.35).

criticism of the man when Thrasea Paetus, one of the last symbols of recti-tude,[171] abandons his accustomed nodded assent or just silence in response to such acts of *adulatio*, walks out of the senate, famously putting himself at risk without inspiring any of his colleagues to *libertas*.[172] He sees no other way to stem the downward spiral (his protest continues if the speeches of his accuser later are anything to go by (*A*. 16.22.2-22.10)). His stand is ap-parently endorsed by the gods, who (textually) immediately send a spate of prodigies (*A*. 14.12.3) *quoque ... inrita*. Nero, freed from the inhibition of his mother's presence, shows what a monster he was to be inhibited by the likes of her.

The way is now clear for the active subversion of religious forms: Nero institutes his Juvenile Games to hide the fact that he wishes to perform on stage (*A*. 14.15.1). Not content with using religion as a pretence, he assaults sanctity by bathing in the source of the Marcian aqueduct at *A*. 14.22.6 and suffers the *ira deum* as a result. With Paetus' divinely endorsed with-drawal from public life, there is nobody to rebuff him except those gods themselves. By the time that Octavia is executed at 14.64 amid massive official celebration, Tacitus virtually abandons documenting the thanksgiv-ings: their bankruptcy is such that the details have become irrelevant:

> How long shall I go on recording the thank-offerings in temples in such circumstances? Whoever learns about what happened then, in my writings or others', can presume that the gods were thanked every time the emperor ordered an exile or murder; and conversely, that events that were once welcomed were now treated as national disasters. Nonetheless I will not pass over in silence, when any senatorial decree reached new depths of sycophancy or humiliation.[173]

After the failed conspiracy of Piso, Rome is a mass of funerals and the Capitol teems with sacrificial victims: one man after another gives thanks for the death of a son, a brother or a friend, 'wearing out Nero's hand with congratulatory kisses' (*A*. 15.71.1). When Nero gives thanks for his

---

[171] As noted above in connection with Nero: earlier, in the trial of Antistius Sosianus, who had satirised the emperor, Paetus earned unstinting praise for breaking senatorial servility: *libertas Thraseae seruitium aliorum rupit* (*A*. 14.49.1). There he did the accused some good by amelio-rating the sentence. But what middle path could there be when celebrating matricide?

[172] *silentio uel breui adsensu priores adulationes transmittere solitus exiit tum senatu ac sibi causam periculi fecit, ceteris libertatis initium non praebuit* (14.12.2).

[173] *dona ob haec templis decreta quem ad finem memorabimus? quicumque casus temporum illorum nobis uel aliis auctoribus noscent, praesumptum habeant, quoties fugas et caedes iussit princeps, toties grates deis actas, quaeque rerum secundarum olim, tum publicae cladis insignia fuisse. neque tamen silebimus si quod senatus consultum adulatione novum aut patientia postremum fuit* (*A*. 14.64.6).

deliverance, his dedication of the dagger to Jupiter Vindex points forward, little though it was realised at the time, to the rebellion by Vindex, or so Tacitus tells us (15.74.2): it seems that Jupiter was less than impressed. Then, after the gods tire of patience, they send unambiguous messages (e.g. the melting of a statue of the emperor by lightning at *A.* 15.22.3) before finally 'planning' to do what Rome should have done for itself, the removal of the emperor, in the form of the rebellion that is the beginning of his end.

The thanksgiving and honours at the birth of little Augusta (*A.* 15.23.4-5) are, as Tacitus acerbically points out, rather fruitless and have to be reworked as tributes when she dies, chronologically four months later, but textually within the same sentence. Nero's ode to the gods when a theatre collapses empty marks out his alienation from the rest of the population who see an adverse sign in the fact of the collapse at 15.34, while the emperor attempts to continue the imperial habit of making positive interpretations. His inability to stop shaking in the temple of Vesta 'either because the goddess inspired terror in him or because of his crimes' (*A.* 15.36.3)[174] meant that he cannot even *consult* the gods about his planned trip to Greece, never mind gain their approval.

Ritual appeasement for the fire at *A.* 15.44.1-2 has no opportunity to unite the city in rite in the *Annals*: it not only fails to secure freedom from anxiety (because of the rumours that Nero had sponsored the fire) but arouses opposition for the cruelty inflicted on the Christians in Nero's games. The subsequent propitiation of the gods smacks of the priests' expertise but the apparently suitable procedures are undermined by the common suspicion that Nero set the fire. The ensuing scramble for resources for the rebuilding programme included the pilfering of many temple funds, a *sacrilegium* that Seneca refuses to endorse (*A.* 15.45.5). Prodigies rapidly follow, and Tacitus vividly condemns Nero: 'Prodigies occurred at the end of the year ... never were lightning flashes more frequent: there was also a comet. Nero expiated each and every one (*semper*) of them with human blood.'[175] As is to be expected, an enormous amount is packed into this memorable image. Given that one function of religion was to stabilise the *urbs*, a more emphatic inversion is hard to imagine. With this vacuation of expiation, which was at least attempted in response to earlier prodigies, Nero puts himself beyond redemption. Nero takes them personally (an interpretation in which he was presumably correct for a change) and acts on them, in

---

[174] *seu numine exterrente, seu facinorum recordatione numquam timore uacuus.* The temple is not, of course, to last much longer. It was one of the casualties of the fire in 64.

[175] *fine anni uulgantur prodigia imminentium malorum nuntia. Vis fulgurum non alias crebrior et sidus cometes, sanguine inlustri semper Neroni expiatum* (*A.* 15.47.2).

contrast to their intended audience, everybody *but* Nero, who continue to tolerate the slaughter. Thus, though the emperor does avail himself of religious experts, their restricted role means they cannot offset the general decline; as fast as the priests attempt to restore the *pax deum*, Nero and his fawning senate restore the damage to the cosmic fabric.

In the meantime, the débâcle continues. The Quinquennial games are textually just a prelude to Nero's killing Poppaea with a kick to her pregnant belly, and more bankrupt rites at *A.* 16.6.2, in a foreign style to boot (*non … ut Romanus mos*); they are even made an opportunity to signal imperial displeasure to Caius Cassius (*A.* 16.7.1). When the senate rename May and June to honour Nero's descent from Claudius and Germanicus, Tacitus continues, 'the gods marked out this crime-stained year with tempest and plague'.[176] While cataloguing crimes Tacitus clarifies at *A.* 16.16.2-3 that the victims are not to blame but that the *ira deum* is the driving force behind the events. At *A.* 16.21.1, 'Nero finally desires to stamp out Virtue herself'[177] when the deaths of Thrasea Paetus and Barea Soranus are planned. The utter alienation of Rome from 'normality' seems complete as the *Annals* close.

The senate, to be fair, do attempt to match his depravity. Any sense of propriety is quickly overcome, and proportion with regard to religious matters is one of the first casualties. The sycophantic impulses that Tiberius had attempted to rein in run riot as the senate elides Tiberius' maxim that foreign victories should be celebrated and domestic sorrows met with silence (*A.* 3.18.2). They willingly collude with the murderous régime, and the honours pile up; and Nero needs their help, especially in conjunction with the destruction of figures who represent a different, more moderate, way.[178]

We do perhaps get the impression that the opposition under Nero is more forthright, but the contrast is all the greater because of the character of the emperor: Tiberius and Claudius at least had more plausible grounds to execute their relatives and did not particularly expect thanksgivings on the same scale (if at all) for their 'deliverance'. The timing of the end of the *Annals*, as the last praiseworthy opponent of Nero slips away, is therefore particularly frustrating for our study. Paetus is the last representative of moral and political opposition to the regime.[179] Given the momentum of the narrative, it seems a safe bet that things got worse after his death.

---

[176] *Tot facinoribus foedum annum etiam dii tempestatibus et morbis insigniuere* (*A.* 16.13.1).

[177] Grant's memorable phrase for *Nero uirtutem ipsam excindere concupiuit.*

[178] Seneca's death is set in motion and justified by the false confession of Natalis at *A.* 15.56.2; Thrasea's enemy Capito Cossutianus presses for his removal at *A.* 16.21.2-22.10.

[179] His 'crimes' are documented at *A.* 16.21.2-22.10; he is particularly effective at *A.* 15.20.2-4 and at *H.* 4.5.4 we are told Helvidius Priscus learned from him a love of *libertas.*

Moving to the aftermath of Nero and into the text of the *Histories*, Galba's reign does not start well in religious terms. His entry into Rome is ill-omened (*infaustus omine*, *H*. 1.6.3); when adopting Piso as his heir, his opening, 'if I were adopting you before the *pontifices*, as is the custom …' at *H*. 1.15.1 underlines the fact that he is *not* doing so, though he is perfectly aware of procedure. When he proceeds to the *contio* to announce Piso's adoption at *H*. 1.18.1, the dreadful weather does not put him off, though such signs were traditionally adverse, whatever the reasons for his proceeding.[180]

Otho, of better character in Tacitus' view than has often been surmised,[181] begins at least by showing some religious acumen. He correctly takes the signs adverse for Galba as favourable to himself (*H*. 1.27.1); he alludes to the *infaustus* adoption of Piso and makes a religious issue of Galba's arrival in Rome at *H*. 1.38.2 (*his auspiciis urbem ingressus*, *H*. 1.37.6), as well as diagnosing, apparently correctly, the conjunction of *ira deum* and the *rabies hominum*. Unfortunately, as Tacitus indicates by his customarily pregnant juxtaposition, his soldiers immediately proceed to mar his own inauguration: 'Neither the sight of the Capitol, nor the sanctity of the overhanging temples, nor consideration of past or future rulers could deter them from committing a crime [i.e. the assassinations of Galba and Piso] which any successor was bound to avenge.'[182] Otho is caught up in events beyond his amateurish control. At *H*. 1.43.2, his murderous envoys ignore the sanctity of the temple of Vesta and at *H*. 1.47.3 the new emperor crosses a forum littered with bodies to the Capitol. The implied comparison with Galba's *infaustus* entry is only partially undermined by his decision to have them buried. By *H*. 1.50.2 we have been told that Otho and Vitellius seemed to be 'appointed by fate for the destruction of the Roman world'.[183] At *H*. 1.89.4, Otho, who had earlier (*H*. 1.77.4-5) appointed magistrates and

---

[180] Galba typically makes his own misfortune whether generous or greedy (Morgan (1992)). For the aspect of *capax imperii*, see Pigón (1990) 370–374; Nawotka (1993) deals more with *nisi imperasset*. For a fuller discussion and further biography see Ash (1999) 95–125 and Murison (1993).

[181] Ash (1999) 83–94.

[182] *nec illos Capitolii aspectus et imminentium templorum religio et priores et futuri principes terruere quo minus facerent scelus cuius ultor est quisquis successit* (1.40). Scott notes that the *lacus Curtius* is the site of Galba's death: 'The vitality of these associations both for Tacitus' readers and for himself may be gauged by the use he makes of the *lacus Curtius*. The death of Galba is presented in terms of a possibly analogous *devotio. Agerent ac ferirent si ita e re publica uidetur* (1.41). But beyond the parallelism of circumstances there exists a fearful contrast in this symbol of sacrifice on which the historian is to insist repeatedly. The self-immolation of Curtius closed the chasm that threatened the destruction of Rome, but the murder of Galba can only symbolise its reopening, pinpointing as it does the beginning of a year of Roman self-destruction' (57–8). See also his 60–64 on the impiety of Galba's murder.

[183] *duos omnium mortalium …deterrimos … and the rivals were indeed uelut ad perdendum imperium fataliter electos.* See further Morgan (1993) 328.

priests as if it were a time of peace, refuses to delay when onlookers point out the need to restore the Salian shields to their proper place. Once again, religious expertise is found wanting at the highest level, and the extent to which the emperor can make mistakes is accentuated by the senate's inability to resist him.

Vitellius, in accordance with the trend for ever-worsening usurpations, gets the worst start yet from Tacitus:

> But Italy was suffering more heavily and terribly than being at war. The soldiers of Vitellius, dispersed through the municipal towns and colonies, were robbing and plundering and polluting every place with violence and lust. In their greed for anything, whether legal or not, they omitted nothing, sacred or not, that they could sell.[184]

Even when he tries to resolve difficulties he plays into the hands of fate in sending away the Batavian legions (*principium interno simul externoque bello parantibus fatis, H.* 2.69.2); his gleeful response to the 'hideous and terrible sight' (*foedum atque atrox spectaculum*) at *H.* 2.70.6 shows him to be a monster. His alienation from rectitude and his isolation from the rest of the population are emphasised in his offering sacrifice personally to the *dis loci*; he is grossly (religiously and otherwise) incompetent at *H.* 2.91, execrable to good men when he sacrifices to Nero at *H.* 2.95.2 (*foedissimo cuique apud bonos*) and, to complete the inversion of the ideal senior statesman, is laughable as a general at *H.* 3.56. At *H.* 3.58.5 he gave in to a superstitious impulse to accept the name Caesar and to cap it all, he could not even abdicate properly (*H.* 3.68).[185]

Vespasian, on the other hand, manages himself with more decorum. His response to omens is more measured than that of his predecessors. He even piously administers vows for Vitellius at *H.* 2.74.1. The silence that he was met with (*per silentium audierint*) indicates just how much the situation is demanding his usurpation: Tacitus engineers a most reluctant assault on the principate by the Flavians. Finally, as we shall see, though he initiates the

---

[184] *ceterum Italia grauius atque atrocius quam bello adflictabatur. dispersi per municipia et colonias Vitelliani spoliare, rapere, ui et stupris polluere. in omne fas nefasque auidi aut uenales non sacro non profano abstinebant (H.* 2.56.1).

[185] For the reception of Vitellius' career and resignation see (somewhat ambiguously) Levene (1997) and Ash (1999) 120–121, who both anticipate pity as the audience's response to Vitellius' situation. Both plot the reactions of the textual audience to gauge the 'appropriate' response, but this seems an unusual and difficult reading of Tacitus' subjects. Despite the sophistication of these arguments, it seems rather out of character for Tacitus to pity one who has so spectacularly failed to live up to the expectation of basic competence; it may be that Vitellius' utter failure even *not* to rule is beyond contempt in the eyes of the historian. Textual audiences are not the most reliable indices of the author's opinions.

reconstruction of the Capitoline temple, he entrusts the task to Lucius Vestinus who immediately consults the proper experts, the *haruspices*. Their stipulations are unproblematically followed. Titus piously emulates his father's example in visiting a shrine at *H*. 2.4. Domitian, not yet identified as a monster,[186] is sheltered by Vesta and the caretaker of her shrine, whom he duly acknowledges and evicts respectively when given the chance (*H*. 3.74.1-2).

The problems that Rome encounters might have been more manageable if the senate had been able to compensate for the weaknesses of its emperor. But their response to the subversion of their religious system is to encourage it, and contribute to the decadence. Under the emperors, Rome abandons its vigilance, and the *ira deum* grows ever more profound. It was suggested earlier that Livy's position on this is that one way or another, the balance of the cosmos tends to become disturbed over time and that, though interpreters might well see a complex and specific significance in this, it is best treated as a simple fact of life. Rome had tolerated many prodigies in its time, thanks to its system of prodigy reports and expert responses. This is, of course, precisely the system that had been allowed, or encouraged, to sink into disrepair. Some prodigies were still noted, as we have seen. But these, by their very nature, tended to be 'major' and we know from Livy that some sense of magnitude could be distinguished in prodigies. Assuming some relationship between the impact of prodigies and the depth of the *ira deum*, the prodigies that are noted are presumably indicative of a cosmic disharmony that is far from being incipient. The wrath of the gods is well under way by the time that Rome begins to listen to the warnings. Tacitus' very silence in the Tiberian books about religious items begins to appear ironic and portentous, as the *ira deum* begins to creep up on a Rome that sees, hears and speaks no evil. Thus, 'wear and tear' on the Roman cosmos would have begun, or increased, under Tiberius, so reluctant to activate Rome's religious systems, and continued apace. Whatever these incremental causes were (and we can only speculate), they were not resolved. The continuing bankruptcy of religious institutions and initiatives means that Rome inevitably sinks into ruin.

Ritual acts as a focus for the decline of Rome and the gradual collapse of political morality, and any expectation that rites have pacified the gods is forestalled: Rome sinks into the chaos that was the *ira deum* and continues on her way into the civil wars of the *Histories*.[187] And civil war was of course traditionally a matter of neglecting the gods. There is no doubt

---

[186] See Ash (1999) 141 on one of the signs, physiognomical in this case.
[187] Though Tacitus implies throughout the *Annals* that Tiberius and Nero are waging civil war against their own people (Keitel (1984)), 'real' civil war was not diminished in its horror by this.

that the gods are angry.[188] In addition, McCulloch understands both the appearance of the phoenix at *A.* 6.28 and the temporary withering of the *ficus Ruminalis* (13.58) to be related to the end of the Julio-Claudian dynasty, even if these harbingers of doom precede the reality by years, or decades.[189] Given the growing intensity of these signs and signifiers, we can proceed on the understanding that Tacitus is constructing an explanatory narrative that includes the gods; far from being 'impotent' or 'psychological', they are a potent force: in fact they are the key to understanding events in their broader context. All the rest is details. But while we are told that they are displeased, there is no explicit documentation in Tacitus of the *causes* of the *ira deum*. Livy used failed rite to explain the *ira deum* (where he did record a cause which is rarely).[190] But Tacitus does not employ the same structure. There are no prodigies under Tiberius, yet we are told that Sejanus' rise to power was the gods' doing. Tacitus' expert diagnosis, based purely on the evidence of events in Rome, thus partially overcomes the lack of prodigies. His diagnosis is not unprecedented: Quintus Fabius Maximus had also discerned the *ira deum* in an adverse course of events at Livy 22.9.8-9 (above, 67).

The formula of *ira deum/pax deum* is still applicable, even if access to traditional wisdom is curtailed. Tacitus' economical use of the terms reflects due caution with precision: it only appears judiciously, when perhaps the reader might require guidance or clarification. It implies that a balance has been lost, and that events will tend towards a downward spiral unless properly checked: and it is the latter aspect, the restoration and maintenance of the *pax deum*, that is the concern of men.

Of course it is tempting to make tentative connections between the *ira deum* and the combination of imperial conduct, the senate and, most of all, the superfluous religious honours that filled the first century; this would account for the acceleration of prodigies and collapse of Rome more vividly than a deduction of incremental decay. And this may be the way in which Tacitus understood things, especially in terms of the inflated honours. But we have no authority for this and it was probably more complex and subtle than any simple equation of conduct with divine will. In a Rome suffering

---

[188] Explicitly at *A.* 4.1.1; there are two prodigies for Claudius in our text (*A.* 12.43.1 and *A.* 12.64.1), and Nero encounters no fewer than seven, if we count *A.* 15.44.1-2 (in response to the fire, which prompts expiation under the supervision of the *quindecimuiri*); see also *A.* 13.24.1-2, 13.58.1, 14.12.3, 15.22.3-4, 15.47.1-3 and 16.13.1 and *H.* 1.86, 2.38.5 and 3.56.1.

[189] McCulloch (1980) and (1984) 206–208; for further discussion of this episode see Dickson and Plympton (1977) and Segal (1973) 114 who demonstrate (*contra* Syme (1958a) 269) that the prodigy is highly significant: 'the order of events which he adopts ... throws into sharp relief the contrast between the corruption and depravity at the centre of the empire and the strenuous exertions and dangers at its western and eastern extremes'.

[190] E.g. 22.57.2-7 and 40.59.6.

the wrath of the gods, *something* will go wrong: in a Rome that cannot restore its balance, things will get worse. A direct 'cause and effect' formula
will not always be appropriate. Thus Drusus died because of the *ira deum*,
but that does not mean that the gods 'intended' for him *in particular* to
perish miserably. A runaway lorry will hit something, sooner or later, and
the faster it travels, the more damage it will probably cause. So precise details are not our concern, even if a contemporary reader might have inferred
more detailed correspondences: what we can reliably say is that long before
Nero was removed from power, he had become so inimical to the restoration
of the *pax deum* that the situation became, in a practical sense, irremedia-
ble: even if the brakes had been working on our metaphorical lorry, it was
too late for them to have much effect, even if they were belatedly applied.
The wealth of prodigies, and the utter failure to address them properly, took
Rome to a point where expiation was no longer a realistic prospect in the
Annals: the city was too fragmented, and incapacitated, to address the *ira
deum* in ritual terms. It might have been theoretically possible to act, but
this did not happen and all the signs are that, in practice, the disintegration
had to run its course.

The burning of the capitol   Over the previous sixty years, practices had
degenerated: Rome had seen imperial incest, every imaginable type of familial murder within a dynasty for whose well-being the entire priesthood
annually prayed, a slaughter of the innocent and the guilty alike; the senate
riven by unnecessary judicial murder, with an increasing tendency to erad-
icate the best characters; the reporting of prodigies threatened to become
bankrupt, and those that were reported failed to convey the intended warning; and astrology had apparently become a permanent and divisive feature
of Roman life. Now came an act that could dwarf these in its magnitude
of disrespect for the gods. The Capitoline temple was burned down in a
siege.[191]

> This was the most deplorable and disgraceful event that had
> happened to Rome since the foundation of the city; for now,
> with no foreign enemy, with the gods ready – if only our be-
> haviour had allowed them – to be favourable, the seat of Jupiter
> Optimus Maximus, founded by our ancestors under solemn
> auspices to be the mainstay of empire, which neither Porsenna

---

[191] In weighing loyalty to an individual friend against loyalty to the state, Cicero deems setting fire
to the Capitol as the ultimate test (*On Friendship* 11.37), quoted by Ash (1999) 70. It seems that
most of Rome fails the test in 69.

(when the city was surrendered), nor the Gauls (when it was captured), had been able to violate, was destroyed by the violent madness of our emperors. Once before indeed during a civil war the Capitol had been destroyed by fire, but then only through the acts of individuals; now it was besieged in plain view, and torched in plain view. And what were the motives of this conflict? What made such a great disaster worth it? Were we fighting for the sake of our homeland?

Id facinus post conditam urbem luctuosissimum foedissi-mumque rei publicae populi Romani accidit, nullo externo hoste, propitiis, si per mores nostros liceret, deis, sedem Iouis Optimi Maximi auspicato a maioribus pignus imperii condi-tam, quam non Porsenna dedita urbe neque Galli capta temer-are potuissent, furore principum excindi arserat et ante Capi-tolium ciuili bello, sed fraude priuata. Nunc palam obsessum, palam incensum, quibus armorum causis? quo tantae cladis pretio stetit? pro patria bellauimus? (*H*. 3.72.1)

In this all the various threads explored above come together. While the destruction of the temple is normally seen as just another sordid act of civil war, in religious terms it is one of the key moments of the entire account and the logical conclusion of the decline of the previous decades. And Tacitus deliberately blurs the locus of responsibility. Obviously the temple could not have burned without the introduction of fire but on this point Tacitus resists closure, aware no doubt that the various versions cannot be taken at face value.

Firstly, and locally, Tacitus refuses to say which of the two sides was to blame for bringing fire to bear. His note that the more popular account blamed the Flavianists (*H*. 3.71.3) is undermined at *H*. 3.75.4: in addition, it is the Vitellianists who had already used fire to storm the gates and arrive with more brands (*H*. 3.73.3). In Tacitus' account, there really is no telling who set the fire. Secondly, he attributes blame more widely in saying that the temple burned *furore principum* (*H*. 3.72.1). Given that neither of the present candidates for the title is present, a great degree of blame is therefore attached to them for the *general* situation reaching the degree of intensity that it did. But though Vitellius and Vespasian are currently at war, we cannot conclude with them. Which *principes* got Rome into this situation, exactly? Vitellius is clearly incompetent and bloodthirsty; and Vespasian, yet to improve for the better in Tacitus' account, has his problems with generals and soldiers alike.[192] But they both rose to prominence in the midst of civil war that was *already* rampant.

In addition, the mention of the Republican burning of the temple and its still-extant dedication by Lutatius Catulus *inter tanta Caesarum opera* shows a long historical perspective that could easily embrace a whole clutch of emperors who contributed to the decline. Nor is that all: Tacitus also pleads that the gods were willing to look kindly on Rome, *si per mores nostros liceret. Nos* usually refers to the senate in Tacitus' accounts (Sinclair (1995) 50–58) but here may be somewhat more diffused.[193] Responsibility for the disaster is thus spread through a much wider section of Roman society than one might initially assume. Though one or the other side had the idea of using fire, the fact that the situation had reached such a crisis point can be attributed to (the) emperors; that this came to pass can, in turn, be attributed to the population of Rome more generally, who resisted the tendency of the gods to assist and preserve Rome, squandered the power of her religious institutions and conspicuously failed to rise to the challenge of imperial rule.

Thus, we are dealing with a hierarchy of causes in the *Histories*. One side or another set the fire, the emperors established a scenario in which some such disaster[194] was unavoidable, but the emperors could only promote this level of chaos in the context of the appalling *mores* of Rome as a whole. '*Mores*' succinctly leaves open the question of specific referents and cannot be restricted to cult practice, though it should include it. Rather, it indicates the culmination of the manifold decline on virtually every front. The gods were not necessarily angry with Rome because Rome was not behaving: but they were angry because they had not been reliably appeased for decades: not, at least, in Tacitus' accounts.[195]

For so much of the texts, the gods have functioned as a barometer of the decline when all human authorities were inadequate to provide a stable reference point against which to measure behaviour. With the burning of the Capitoline temple, even this seems to have been banished from the text. Thus Tacitus articulates, in the vacuum, a human 'plea' to fill the gap, temporarily – if only our behaviour had allowed the gods to lend their support. . .

---

[192] Ash (1999) 55–70 documents the excesses and difficulties of the Flavian campaign.

[193] Tacitus refers to the *populus Romanus* in the following paragraph, and, as we shall see, it will be more then the senate who restore the temple.

[194] The emphasis on *incendi* and the absence of either current emperor imply that *something* drastic was inevitable.

[195] Countless ceremonies must have been performed without Tacitus' recording them, which makes his selection all the more pertinent.

Rome has cut its last connection with 'normality' and is living, as it were, on borrowed time. The city, lacking a 'head', cannot continue long in this state before everything disintegrates completely.[196] We see the beginning of this final stage of disintegration soon after in the text. One of the last customary distinctions, between foreign and civil war, is eroded at *H.* 4.22.2 as each tribe reasserts itself (*mixta belli ciuilis externique facie*); at this point, the sense of identity that made Rome more than just another city is well on the way to oblivion. 'Rome', however, has sufficient momentum for Vespasian's victory, though it is not a clean one (Ash (1999) 55–73). The Druids were mistaken not in diagnosing *fatum*'s hand in events, but in the outcome, because (just) enough of Rome's identity remains to restore what had been forgotten. The refounding of the Capitoline at *H.* 4.53 is the first major religious act that is not juxtaposed with indications of hypocrisy or corruption in either text. It signals a reversal of the trend that had continued almost unabated and with increasing momentum since early in the reign of Tiberius: its significance cannot be overstated. The curiously (and uniquely) full account of the temple foundation[197] in a text that is characterised by its pithiness and economy, the full-scale evocation of the refounding of the temple – this is more than antiquarian interest.

The refounding of the Capitoline is no less than the textual and religious reconstruction of Rome's proper relations with the gods. The passage reflects all of the religious concerns we have traced through the texts; the tone of the passage is dignified, and lacking in rebukes or juxtapositions that undermine its effect. Moreover as a rite it meets the essential criteria: the city acts as a unity, the prescriptions of the priests are followed and, interestingly, the emperor is absent – thus allowing the aristocracy to function properly. Nonetheless his political authority endorses the act, thus stabilising the political situation. It represents a religious and a political model to be imitated for its balance of power and jurisdiction, a balance seen only very rarely in the two texts.[198] Continuity with the past is affirmed by the approximate preservation of the predecessor, though the increased height may reflect the growth of the empire, both geographically and politically, and its self-image.[199] At *H.* 4.78.3 we have seen a Roman victory

---

[196] The symbolism of a 'Rome without a head' is built into the narrative. For the destruction of the Capitol as the 'decapitation of Rome' and the symbolism of decapitation in general, see Woodman (1997) 96.

[197] Compare e.g. those built and/or dedicated under Tiberius. Chilver (1985) *ad loc* offers that this is the only description of its type in extant Latin literature. Even Livy (as we have him) never goes into this kind of detail.

[198] For an analysis of Tacitus' model of a working (i.e. unified) *res publica* see Aubrion (1990).

[199] Cf. the increase of the *pomerium* under Claudius; it was expanded to match the increase in the size of the empire.

that is accomplished *nec sine ope diuina* (presumably panic), the *only* textual occasion on which the gods assist Rome in battle. Though it cannot be ascertained for certain that this occurs after the restoration of the Capitol chronologically, it does occur subsequently in textual terms, and represents the newly refound *pax deum*.

But rite, even on this scale, will not be sufficient to effect a lasting change. If Rome has cleaned her slate, her future progress will depend on checking the trends that had done so much damage for so long. It seems unproblematic to suggest that affairs improved under Vespasian and Titus, and that there was a downturn under Domitian, but Tacitus is unlikely to be so straightforward: in addition, this would be to forget the importance of the senate, enervated and out of practice in real administration. One might reasonably assume that they would gradually come to their traditional senses under the guidance of the first two Flavians, and might well be robust enough to stand up to the last of the dynasty; or, at least, not entirely forget what was right.[200]

This seems to be precisely what is indicated at *A.* 3.55, where Tacitus discusses the improvement of Roman morals, specifically regarding luxury. He asserts that extravagant eating reached astonishing levels between Actium and the accession of Galba, but then began to decline for various reasons, and gradually. Firstly, there was the ruination of old and corrupted aristocratic families by their very expenditure; but the reign of terror under Domitian was also a disincentive to conspicuousness.[201] Improvement was therefore steady overall, though for very different reasons. In line with this trend, provincials brought their own more frugal habits – a tendency shared and supported by Vespasian for a decade, by which time they might well have become sufficiently entrenched to act as a corrective to a decadent emperor.[202] This is our only textual indication of how Rome fared as a moral entity under the Flavians, and may of course be entirely misleading. In the absence of other evidence, its fit with our argument is nonetheless rather encouraging.

---

[200] Suetonius documents Vespasian's resistance to the tendency for spiralling court cases and personal insults at *Vespasian* 10-14.

[201] I rely here on the reading of the passage offered by Woodman in Woodman and Martin (1996) *ad loc.*

[202] Provincials, relatively uncorrupted by all that Rome had to offer (*A.* 3.55), also show their worth when they fail to respond to, or to understand, the politics of attending Nero's games at *A.* 16.5.1. On the theme of corruption and subsequent improvement see the extended comments of Woodman and Martin (1996) on 3.55. On the ameliorative effects of provincial senators, see McCulloch (1984) 189: 'Thrasea, the *nouus homo* of municipal origins, is willing to modify traditional customs for the furtherance of justice ... [whereas] the old Roman *nobiles*, dulled by their servitude, continually looking to the past, a past riddled with their own failures.' See Goodyear (1970a) for the unconventionality of Tacitus' optimism.

Tacitus' senate under Domitian might then have been very different from the one he depicts under Tiberius, irrespective of our traditional guesswork that Tacitus was racked with guilt about his 'collaboration': perhaps instead the later books of the *Histories* showed a senate that heeded the *exempla* of Marcus Lepidus or Thrasea Paetus, quietly mitigating the worst excesses, forever looking for an opportunity to preserve traditional values, biding Rome's time until they, rather than circumstances, could choose their own emperor. No proof exists for this inference, but that is also true of the traditional assumption that Tacitus created his Tiberian senate in the image of Domitian's, or even that he *felt* (let alone was 'racked with') guilt at serving under Domitian.

Rome, as a going concern, has had a narrow escape. At the particular moment when the crisis came, she found the integrity and strength of purpose to establish the foundations for her recovery, not unlike the phoenix who undergoes a crisis when he must find the strength to carry his father to the sun after his birth. In fact, this is precisely what the expert reader has been expecting.

4.2.2.3 The fatum of Rome

Thus far, Tacitus' first century is subjected to the kind of interpretation that Livy used to shape individual years, or series of years: a disruption of the *pax deum* led to problems and ritual correction renewed Rome's relations with the gods. The active, exemplary and moral focus was on Rome's conduct, especially – but not exclusively – in terms of rite. Yet latent within this 'everyday' orientation was the larger category of *fatum*. Since we lack Livy's later narrative, it is hard to say whether *fatum* intruded into the later account any further than it did in our text: in the extant account it is most potent during the Hannibalic War, and then retreats from the active interpretation, though Scipio's formulation that Rome is destined to suffer initial defeats in her greatest wars may well have repeated itself later on. Whether he located the broad decline of Rome within a context of *fatum*, we cannot say, though he is clearly familiar with the category. Though Tacitus' narratives are similarly incomplete, there are signs that he also located the large-scale loss and return of the *pax deum* within a larger context still: that of Rome's fate.

When alluding to the future (and entirely unexpected) reign of Claudius, Tacitus does not mention fate, but *fortuna* (*A.* 3.18.7). In contrast, Vespasian's accession is connected several times with *fatum*. Vespasian receives a whole array of predictions of one sort or another. His fate is already

established in the *Annals*[203] and is elaborated within the *Histories*.[204] Even
the actions of others are attracted into a 'fatal' pattern: not just is Galba's
end 'fatalised', but the fates are also implicated when Vitellius sends away
the Batavian troops *principium interno simul externoque bello parantibus
fatis* (*H.* 2.69). Vespasian begins his campaign *meliore fato* (*H.* 3.1.1) and
the Vitellianists fight his troops *numero fatoque dispares* (*H.* 3.84.3). Thus
a superficial reading of the *Histories* in particular leaves one with the impression that *fatum* 'appointed' Vespasian, a startling contrast with Tacitus'
refusal elsewhere to provide frameworks for individuals to aspire to imperial power. Why should the rise of the Flavians be attributed to fate, when
that of others is not?[205] In this apparently minor difference lies a fundamental point of perspective. We might, no doubt, consider this a result of
Flavian propaganda but Tacitus has shown himself perfectly able to sift such
accounts critically.[206] We saw in Livy how, once *fatum* has begun to take an
active hand, individuals can be attracted into a 'fatal' series of events. This
applies even to the Flavians.

   In the midst of the chaos of the *Histories*, Tacitus informs us that Otho
and Vitellius appeared, not just to the senate and knights but even the people, to be 'appointed for the destruction of Rome' (*duos . . . uelut ad perdendum imperium fataliter electos, H.* 1.50.2). Rome has reached an uneasy
and unpleasant consensus, the first (textual and extant) city-wide agreement
of any kind: *some* sort of deductive unity then. A distasteful *fatum* hov-
ers over the account and is reinforced by other notices: Vitellius and Otho
share omens linked to birds, which Morgan (1993) 328 argues links them to
Rome's destiny – to be torn apart by rivals. 'Tacitus' account of the omen
which opens the Vitellians' campaign . . . reminds the reader of the curse of
fratricidal strife laid on the Romans and the suffering which must flow from
that.'[207] It is therefore more than a passing acerbity: it alludes to a much
greater cycle of events than the *fatum* of any individual in the narrative.

   Since the *fatum* of Rome was probably the greatest interpretative category that any Roman would be likely to refer to in practice, it is of such a
magnitude that it must be treated with enormous respect – the proprieties

---

[203] *A.* 16.5.3: an incident presented to emphasise the workings of destiny (Bartsch (1994) 6–7, 30–
31).
[204] *H.* 1.10.3; 3.1.1 and 5.13.3 all validate the dynasty; thus the oracular predictions made of Vespasian (*H.* 2.78.6-7) and Titus (*H.* 2.4) as well as Basilides' divine apparition to Vespasian at *H.*
4.82 reinforce the *dynastic* rather than the individual destiny.
[205] Nero (*A.* 6.22.6 and 14.9.5), Galba (*A.* 6.20.3) and Otho (*H.* 1.22.1-2) all receive astrological
interpretations but do not explicitly attract the ponderous categorisation of *fatum*.
[206] See Ash (1999) 83–93 on his discerning treatment of the various depictions of Otho.
[207] It may be the same preoccupation that leads people to accept the poisoning of Britannicus
(*A.* 13.17.1) on the grounds that brothers cannot share power easily.

of deduction seem to be observed in the carefully deployed *uelut*. It is not so much that our author is 'unsure' or 'non-committal'. The associations of *fatum* cast an ominous shadow over the narrative, *however* it is introduced, as the reader is invited to contemplate events within this enormous perspective. Tacitus, like Livy, is far too subtle and refined an interpreter simply to throw *fatum* directly into the narrative. Respectful and trenchant allusion is perfectly sufficient. At this point in the story, where more sickening bloodshed is to come and the downward spiral still has no little momentum, Tacitus peers into the abyss of the text's immediate future with just a hint of hindsight from the other side of history. This was no ordinary succession. From Tacitus' perspective, it was the lowest moment in Rome's entire history, when Italy was the site of unremitting civil war that threatened never to end and would finally consume the temple at the heart of the City. The deduction of fate, a massive interpretation for a disastrous situation, is not *difficult* in the circumstances. Technically it is the only viable context if we are right in reasoning that Rome is simply unable to reverse the *ira deum* at this point. However there is more to it than a simple and vague diagnosis that an unexplained fate 'must have' been involved in disasters on this scale. This *fatum* seems to have been contextualised by the system of *saecula* across the two historical narratives.

McCulloch suggests that two signs in the *Annals*, the appearance of the phoenix at 6.28 and the (temporary) withering of the *ficus Ruminalis* at 13.58, allude to the fate of Rome. He notes that the phoenix was associated with the eternity of Rome in oracular literature (*Oracula Sibyllina* 8.136), while the *ficus Ruminalis* was associated with the founding and history of the city, concluding 'the excursus on the phoenix, then, should not be interpreted simply as an omen portending the death of Tiberius and the accession of Caligula; rather, here Tacitus portends the suffering and devastation during the remainder of the Julio-Claudian principate, up to and including the year of the great civil war' (McCulloch (1984) 207–208).

Tacitus alludes to cycles in other ways: in his discussion of the sighting of a phoenix, he says that it traditionally returned *post longum saeculorum ambitum* (*A.* 6.28.1); when he outlines the rise and fall of luxurious banquets in Rome at 3.55, he presents a perfectly coherent 'human' pattern, whereby fashion and experience combine with the appearance of an upright emperor to rectify a long-standing and deleterious habit. He then offers another possible analysis, that human life is governed by cycles (*nisu forte rebus cunctis inest quidam uelut orbis, ut quem ad modum temporum uices ita morum uertantur*). These two levels, the human and the cyclic, are not exclusive: in the latter framework, the details of the previous explanation are just that – details. Somehow or another, this change of morals was bound to happen. The light touch of *nisi forte* ... is rather reminiscent of Tacitus' 'hesitancy' in his dealings with *fatum*, some of which we have already discussed (above, 173). There, his priority was to retain responsibility as the central focus in explaining the past: *fatum*, however potent a force in actuality, was not a recommended concern. A similar pattern is discernible here: Tacitus' readers should not rest on their laurels in the face of difficulties, waiting complacently for the cycle to turn: it was their responsibility to inform and embody these turns of history. It may also be that invoking cycles of ages required some tasteful presentation: as broad deductions, they might well be a ponderous categorisation in the same league as *fatum*.

Secondly, in the opening to the *Histories*, Tacitus refers again to an extended 'cycle of ages' (*longam saeculorum seriem*):

> Now too Italy was prostrated by disasters either entirely novel, or that recurred only after a long succession of ages; cities in Campania's richest plains were swallowed up and overwhelmed; Rome was wasted by conflagrations, its oldest temples consumed, and the Capitol itself fired by the hands of citizens.

> *iam uero Italia nouis cladibus uel post longam saeculorum seriem repetitis adflicta haustae aut obrutae urbes, fecundissima Campaniae ora; et urbs incendiis uastata, consumptis antiquissimis delubris, ipso Capitolio ciuium manibus incenso.* (1.2)

This comment is rarely taken to be part of a significant analysis but it is actually a trenchant contextualisation of recent and imminent events. We are apparently offered two alternatives here. Either Rome's decline was unprecedented (the novel invention of the imperial regime), or (*uel*) it was part of the cycle of ages (*series saeculorum*). The first stresses the novelty and horror of the period, while the latter detects a very broad pattern (which implies predictability). These options are, however not mutually exclusive, as *uel* implies. Rather both explanations have something to contribute to the formulation of an appropriate response to events. After all, there were indeed *nouae clades* in actuality: Roman history did not previously record this kind of internecine strife.

On the other hand, if Tacitus' understanding of the situation is that some kind of 'breakdown' was 'due' because of the circuit of ages, as this and other notices imply, that did not mean that it had to be so *utterly* catastrophic, so callous and cruel. To assign the breakdown simplistically and dogmatically to a cycle of ages is to 'explain' too much, to contextualise these events within a structure of interpretation with too much closure – too much at least for an exemplary history. The 'particular' details can always vary when dealing with broad sweeps of fate: Tacitus' insight combines with his sensitivity to the human situations that he goes on to document. No categorisation, however suitable as an explanation, could do justice to the horror. The reader will therefore consider both aspects as the narrative proceeds, and material is present that feeds into both (non-exclusive) perspectives.

Which events is Tacitus referring to? He might be referring only to those of AD 70. However, is the reader only to think of these particular months? Or, to put it in their terms, did the wrath of the gods descend suddenly, without prior warning? In fact, the string of plurals (*nouis cladibus...haustae aut obrutae urbes ...incendiis*) have plausible immediate referents, but also invite the reader to refer both forwards and back in time. There was an earthquake at Pompeii (noted specifically to be in Campania) at *A.* 15.22 (63 AD) and of course the city was destroyed beyond the limits of the extant text; Tacitus presumably recorded the eruption of Vesuvius. Most of Rome burned down in 64 (*A.* 15.38), before the Capitoline temple was destroyed by fire (*H.* 3.72): this accounts nicely for the plural *incendiis* as well as including sites of the most ancient sanctity (*uetustissima religione*) to make up the plural *delubra*.[208] We might also remember the comet at *A.* 14.22.1, the popular interpretation of which was that a *mutatio regis* was about to occur. Tacitus castigates those who proceeded to act as if Nero were *already* dethroned (*igitur quasi iam depulso Nerone*). With hindsight, of course, the comet was just an early warning and the next appearance at *A.* 15.47.1 presumably acted as a reminder. In religious terms, the *Annals* therefore functions as a prelude to, and basis of, the events of the *Histories*, and we are looking at a long perspective, as befits a *series saeculorum*.

But perhaps the term simply means something like 'our period', without particular definition: for instance, at *H.* 1.86 Tacitus informs us that *rudibus saeculis*, prodigies were better noted. There is no obvious reason from these references to think that a *saeculum* and an even greater context, a *series saeculorum*, are necessarily chronologically or interpretatively precise. However, not only would it be surprising for a *quindecimuir* to be immune to the religious significance of the word, but the cycle mentioned at *A.* 3.55, which lasted from Actium until the civil war of 68–9, was a period that lasted almost exactly 100 years, which, as we shall see, is said

---

[208] Servius' shrine to the moon, the altar at which Evander sacrificed to Hercules, the temple to Jupiter Stator vowed by Romulus, Numa's palace and the temple of Vesta were all destroyed, along with the *penates populi Romani*.

elsewhere to be a Roman *saeculum*. Furthermore, in the *Agricola*, Tacitus twice spoke of the *beatissimum saeculum* under Nerva,[209] while in the *Histories* (2.37), he pointedly refers to the *corruptissimum saeculum*, in which it was, despite some other accounts, rather unlikely that Paullinus, wise as he was, hoped for the choice of a new emperor by the senate and the armies. Unless Tacitus' use of terminology is uncharacteristically slack, we have clear evidence that at some point between the civil wars of 68 and the reign of Nerva, Rome had moved from one *saeculum* to another. There are other reasons beyond these coincidences to think that the term is used with some precision.

Precise long-term dating is clearly an issue in both narratives. The *Histories* opens with the note that it was now 820 years since Rome's foundation. In the *Annals*, the *ficus Ruminalis* is said to have sheltered Romulus and Remus 840 years before (13.58)[210] and the date of the phoenix's appearance at 6.28 explicitly caused some problems: it had not apparently waited long enough (less than half its generally accepted 500 years) and some (*non nulli*) therefore thought that it was a spurious sighting. It therefore seems a very deliberate act to displace it by two years in comparison with other authors.[211] This very precise interest may have something to do with the Saecular Games and the process of the *saecula* and it also hints that the *quindecimuiri* may have found some way to resolve the problems of the dating. Claudius earned ridicule in some quarters for staging these games on the 800th anniversary of Rome's foundation: at 11.11, rather than repeat himself (and unfortunately for us) Tacitus refers to his explanation of the dating issues of the Games of both Augustus and Claudius in the *Histories* (*rationes ... satis narratas*), in connection with Domitian's games in 88, for which he was a member of the quindecimviral college. This account, of course, is now lost to us. What we do know for certain is that he did address the issue of dating and the length of *saecula* in a lost portion of his text.

We tend to think only of the numerical aspects of the dating when we consider the Saecular Games (and the apparent inconsistencies) but for Rome, the *saecula* were far more important indices of Rome's position in the cosmos. Thus 'messier' details like human experience and the overall shape of events would have been involved in the understanding of the cycles of ages. And our historian wrote his accounts *after* he and his colleagues

---

[209] *Nunc demum redit animus; et quamquam primo statim beatissimi saeculi ortu Nerva Caesar res olim dissociabilis miscuerit, Agr. 1.3 and in hanc beatissimi saeculi lucem ac principem Traianum, Agr. 44.*

[210] There may be textual problems here: see Furneaux (1896) *ad loc.*

[211] Dio *A*. 58.27.1 and Pliny *NH* 10.2.5 give 36 rather than Tacitus' 34 AD.

had addressed the issue of these cycles: it would be strange if some of his insights did not appear in his historical accounts.

Thus far the evidence leads to a deliberate and inductive placement of material related to fairly precise *saecula* in the historical record: unfortunately, there are other pieces of evidence that are not so straightforward. In the *Agricola*, Tacitus spoke of the *beginning* (*ortus* and *lux*) of a *beatissimum saeculum* under Nerva, which continued under Trajan – in other words, almost thirty years *later* than the burning of the Temple and the accession of Vespasian (above, 216). To understand what was at stake in diagnosing 'saecular' influences, we must therefore go outside Tacitus' texts to get a sense of the kind of material he would have been working with.

The exact dating of *saecula* was problematic even in antiquity: Censorinus *On The Nativity* records some general information. There are natural and civic *saecula* (17.1). He lists various philosophic systems, which are more than sufficient to prove that measuring a *saeculum* was a highly contentious matter. Each city had decided on its own measurement. The precise length of a Roman *saeculum* is rather problematic: *On The Nativity* 17.9 corrects Livy (book 136) where he mentions the length of a *saeculum* as being 100 years (and this in connection with *Augustus'* games). He does not however quote Tacitus. But he does record the figure of 110 as a decemviral one, though it is not clear if he is referring to their records, the pattern he deduces from the Games or, possibly, Tacitus. More pertinently, he also notes an association of the end of a *saeculum* with prodigies.[212] Tacitus similarly seems to be deliberately linking prodigies with the *series saeculorum* in the opening to the *Histories*.

Dating difficulties are most obvious in examining the history of the Games: the Republican celebrations that seem to provide the ritual background to the Saecular Games occurred in 249 and 146: when the Augustan Games were celebrated in 17 BC, a 'sequence of earlier games was "established" beginning in 456 BC'[213] and these were based on a cycle of 110 years. But this was not the end of the dating issues: even the revised dating should have given games in 16 rather than 17, and Domitian's games occurred in 88 AD, 105 years later and 6 years in advance of the cycle of 110 years.

The discrepancy in dating is notorious but one conclusion that can be drawn is that *saecula* could either be construed as precise and exact, or that,

---

[212] *sed ea quod ignorarent homines, portenta mitti diuinitus, quibus admonerentur unum quodque saeculum esse finitum.*
[213] Beard, North and Price (1998) 205. For a summary of the dating and the problems of the different traditions, see *On The Nativity* 17.3-5; outlined in Hall (1986) 2574–2575.

like the seasons mentioned at 3.55, they merged more gradually. Perhaps as long as the Games occurred in the 'changeover' period of a 'season', they could be considered to be valid. Furthermore, Rome's particular interest in the ages would inevitably manifest in their use for *interpretation* rather than an exercise in numbers. However the notion of the *saecula* arose, we can be sure that the Romans used them to explain the broad sweep of events in the human arena: in other words, they would relate to major political change rather than simple counting, as indeed the Republican games obviously did.[214]

Taken from this perspective, we should think it unlikely that Tacitus the *quindecimuir* did *not* consider the cycles of ages in his explanation of the first century. But on the analogy of *fatum*, we would expect him to treat such a massive and far-reaching category with a great deal of respect, and to go to some lengths to avoid implying that such an interpretation negated in any way the need for an analysis of responsibility. It would not dominate the narrative which is properly (for history) grounded in the human experience. The *saecula* would therefore be gauged with a variety of measurements: chronology obviously featured but there would have been some attempt to map the process of the ages onto the broad trend of human activities, where a whole range of issues would need to be 'understood' with care: history is notoriously messier than numbers.

Tacitus' analogy of seasons may be more pertinent here than it first appeared: any change in human affairs might have occurred gradually and not corresponded exactly with a precise date, just as spring can be said to start at the vernal equinox, or when the daffodils emerge. If we assume that such leeway applied to an individual *saeculum*, then we might assume even greater overlaps with a *series saeculorum*. If the final age of this series ended a century after Actium, then that fits with the destruction of the Capitoline temple and the beginning of the revival. This age is then the one he dubs *corruptissimum* at *H.* 2.37 just before its close. This in turn corresponds with *A.* 3.55, where improvements in banqueting habits gradually followed the year of the four emperors, the lowest point in Roman history. And though the darkest moment, the 'winter solstice', appears with the burning of the Capitoline, the first promise of this 'spring' also appear

---

[214] Beard North and Price (1998) I 71–2 cite Varro for the link between the First Punic War in 249; the games in 146 (or 149) heralded major wars in Africa and Greece. Even the Etruscan *saecula* were reflected in political life: the ninth Etruscan *saeculum*, for instance, began in 44 BC, coinciding with the death of Caesar and the comet that followed: see Barton (1994) and Turcan (1976). I note, but carefully avoid, the kinds of series of 'metal-based' ages mentioned by Ovid *Metamorphoses et al.* We simply do not have enough material to make any useful comparisons, and, knowing Tacitus, the material would need some reworking to be of use in understanding the course of history and particular human behaviour.

in 70 with Vespasian's accession when conditions seem to have begun to improve, spurred on in part by an emperor who brought in an old-fashioned severity even before he changed for the better. The progress to a 'warmer climate' would be gradual: our 'daffodils' therefore only begin to appear in full bloom with the rise of Nerva. In Tacitus' terms, Nerva's age saw the dawn (*lux*) of the *beatissimum saeculum*.

This schema probably resides somewhere between 'speculative' and 'ingenious': its great merit is that it is *completely* consistent with Tacitus' own comments and the general deployment of religious themes within his historical works, not least a whole host of details whose presence has hitherto been met with bemusement or puzzlement. We have the advantage that the issues were definitely addressed by none other than our author and his colleagues. They *did* find some kind of resolution when they held games in 88: it is regrettable that we have lost Tacitus' detailed account of this. At this point he could have drawn together the different threads and linked the various signs that he had embedded without further comment as they occurred – thus reflecting the gradual unfolding of understanding them over time. Tacitus' redating of the phoenix, where he alludes to the *series saeculorum* by his phrasing *post longum saeculorum ambitum* (*A.* 6.28.1), does imply some reasoning process or at least a desire for effect that is not otherwise obviously explicable.

This line of reasoning can, of course, easily be dismissed as random pieces of information that 'happened' to find their way into Tacitus' account, but before dismissing the whole nexus of factors as insoluble, we should consider the 'everyday realities' of interpretation in this situation. The sighting of the phoenix, for instance, did not lead to any contemporary conclusion that several decades later Rome would dissolve into civil war. Rather, it would have 'lurked' in the general memory not yet properly understood, and probably largely forgotten, until a review of fate's signs prompted a connection. In addition, much of the lore was formulated when these regions were distinct entities; with their absorption into Roman *imperium*, it is entirely possible that their relevance would now pertain to Rome, just as the prediction that a ruler would rise from the East was appropriated by a local Roman general (i.e. Vespasian). If the phoenix, noted previously by Greeks and Egyptians and interpreted as relevant to their various dynasties and régimes, now related to Rome, as it seems to in Tacitus' account, that might have explained the interruption of its normal chronology as it remapped its appearance to a different chronological system. Domitian's games do, of course, approximate to the Augustan dating but the lack of precise correlation and the fact of Claudius' dating *must* have invited some review, even just to confirm Augustus' calculations, and that is before they took into account the human arena as an indication of the long-term mood of the gods. If we add the various prodigies and the withering of the *ficus Ruminalis* under Nero to the equation, clearly the *quindecimuiri* had their interpretative work cut out.

Somehow they made sense of these various signs scattered over a period of decades sufficiently to celebrate the Games. Tacitus deliberately brings to our attention his role in the Saecular Games: his scattered allusions to *saecula* in such a generally efficient text cannot but be an allusion to his expertise. His understanding of the cycle of ages as a *quindecimuir* would be *expressed* very differently from his understanding as a historian, but we would expect his priestly knowledge to permeate his historical account. His historical understanding would of course have been different from his understanding in 88 while the tyrant Domitian ruled Rome though it does not seem inconceivable that he and his colleagues hoped that the new *saeculum* would bring better times, in the form of a better emperor for an already improving senate.

While the apparently insoluble problems of the different dates prevent us from reaching any firm conclusions, the contextualisation of the first century of imperial rule, the age of decline, would surely demand some 'higher' explanation, especially from one so learned as our historian. Such immense chronic disasters would not have been explained purely in the human sphere. Thus, the *Histories* see the unfolding of a fate that has overseen the decline of Rome, and will seek also to orchestrate its regeneration.

This is the *fatum* of Rome, not of any individual emperor or dynasty – which makes sense of the way that different emperors are treated regarding *fatum*. The Flavians are 'chosen' as appropriate vehicles of the coming regeneration. Why should this be? The likely answer is that not only that they can provide a candidate *capable* of overseeing Rome's restoration, but also that the first successor, at least, was a worthy one. In many ways, Vespasian is the inverse of the first new emperor, Galba. He has no need to adopt, and neatly inverts the maxim that 'he had a great future as emperor behind him (*capax imperii nisi imperasset*, *H.* 1.49.4) since he was the first to change for the better (*H.* 1.50.4) and accelerated the end of luxury that began after Actium through his attitudes to dress and diet (*A.* 3.55.4). Even Domitian's murderous policies somehow brought forth a 'good' result (the abandoning of consumptive luxury) because of the irresistible trend towards 'rightness' that Rome now found itself in.

What of the 'new age' of Rome? The statement that Tacitus is writing in happier days appears in the *Agricola* (2–3) and is not the only evidence. In discussing historiography, Tacitus tells us that contemporary writing does not suffer the distorting effects of an emperor who could not resist the temptation to interfere with literature, unlike that of the first century of the principate where *ueritas pluribus modis infracta.*[215] Political duress is often suspected in this, and this suspicion leads to interpretations that act as if it has been excised from the text. But, as we have seen, events make good Roman sense viewed from a perspective of decline and recovery. At least in textual terms, we should accept that Rome seems to have found its feet once again by the time Tacitus wrote.

Thus the events of this century become part of the larger fate of Rome. And that goes for all its denizens, even Vespasian. Without the cycle of ages, the narratives are the triumph of a Flavian *fatum*; but if the largest context is the 'life-cycle' of the city itself, then Vespasian, like the others, is put in his proper place as part of Rome's ongoing history, the product of a joint venture of men and greater powers. Thus the Tacitean perspective is longer than most. Dynasties, even political systems, will come; but they will also go, while Rome remains.

4.3 Conclusions

Despite his conservatism, and like his predecessor Livy, Tacitus has dynamically reformulated Roman religion to meet the needs of his day and with a very distinctive perspective: there is no nostalgia, just a representative range of *exempla* or wider lessons from the past. The picture of the religious processes in first-century Rome is highly sophisticated, something that has long been accepted for his political narrative. There is no difficulty now in accepting that his use of language is highly precise and his perspective wide yet possessed of apparently minute details as Woodman (amongst others) has repeatedly shown. There are no longer good reasons to consider the religious narrative with any less sympathy.

Tacitus' reputation for genius has not suffered: his mastery of the genre is complete. Though I have argued that *qua quindecimuir* he would have had a well-articulated perspective on the first century of imperial rule, the *Annals* and *Histories* are fully fledged historical accounts, in the Roman sense. The gods are ever-present but do not dominate the narrative. Their wrath, their exasperation, is never allowed to do more than intervene at a human level: it never becomes the focus of the narrative. We are dealing predominantly with a human world, and a long series of human tragedies, when we read Tacitus: his indication of the role of the gods does nothing to diminish the

---

[215] See also *H.* 1.1.1: *principatum diui Neruae et imperium Traiani, uberiorem securioremque materiam, senectuti seposui, rara temporum felicitate, ubi sentire quae uelis et quae sentias dicere licet* (*H.* 1.1.4).

horror story. The persistent erosion of proper conduct in Rome along with the blatant isolation of the institutions that had, for so long, kept Rome in harmony with her gods – all this must have been extremely powerful reading for the ancient reader. As the religious institutions lose their power to uphold Rome under the weight of political corruption, it is guaranteed that disasters will follow; clearly, the account would be *entertaining*, as befitted history. And political recovery, with Vespasian, is twinned with restoration of proper religious functioning, whatever we think happened under Domitian. At the same time, these events would not make proper sense without their contextualisation, firstly within the realm of the *pax* or *ira deum*, and then also as part of a much larger cycle of events. But we never lose sight of the participants, their decisions, their motives, their suffering.

Religion is central to Tacitus' explanations and characterisation of the century which he narrated, or so it seems from the sections of his texts that we have. Indeed, such are the scattered details that if we had a full text, it might be possible to write a more deliberate 'religious history'. But even that would artificially divorce the *cultus deorum* from its social and political context, an approach which, as he has so clearly demonstrated, would be dangerously misleading. A string of apparently unconnected religious events actually constitutes a careful argument rather than reluctant and irrelevant historical notices for the sake of completion. What emerges is distinctively modified, but far from unrecognisable, from the days of Livy – no mean feat given the pressures to 'adjust' the religious system to the new ideologies. In fact, Tacitus' religion is radically conservative. In the face of profound changes, he preserves the memory of former practices: the decline of prodigy reporting and prodigy interpretation is set carefully in contrast with the way that they *used* to function. Tacitus remembers, by allusion or by 'knowing' comments, the way that prodigies can support Rome in her quest for greatness: an antidote, then, to the various imperial delusions.

Our argument has, somewhat inevitably given the state of the texts, involved various degrees of speculation. I am all too aware of the distance we have travelled from previous discussions that were centred on our author's 'belief', 'scepticism' and 'fatalism' in offering a complex scheme encompassing the whole set of events within *fatum*. The essential building-blocks are, however, unmistakably secure, and anchored in the texts: Tacitus has no doubt that prodigies indicate the wrath of the gods, and that Rome suffered from that wrath increasingly during the first century, and he shows great skill in incorporating them into his narrative. Like his predecessor, he is more concerned with propriety in religion than debating or undermining the efficacy of the religious system. He works *within* the system, noting others' interpretative shortcomings and juxtaposing religious and 'human' material to show their interdependency, highlighting incompetence, hypocrisy and ever-failing standards of conduct.

Yet the door was always open to the better: he does not allow prodigies to fade from the historical record, rather he embeds their proper use into his accounts by alluding to possible interpretations of the *ira deum*. He even accounts for the decline in their proper use – without crediting any excuses. He knows only too well how the system has been distorted, but that does not mean the distortion should not be resisted: the Jews explicitly found out to their cost what happens when prodigies are ignored and there is no reason why Rome's half-baked handling of adverse signs should be any more successful. The reader does not need it spelled out when the City misses the signs of the wrath of the gods. There can be no doubt that the noting of prodigies and their expiation is a viable system: more fool Rome if she declined to use it.

This is no piecemeal and incidental religious interpretation of occasional grudging notices of what could not be ignored in the historical record. Just as we found with Livy, it has different textures and overlapping levels. We deal with angry gods, prodigies and related setbacks, but we can also detect a much broader sweep of events set within orthodox religious categories: fate, and the cycle of ages, which Tacitus, as a *quindecimuir*, was better equipped than any other extant ancient author to comment on. Where he alludes to these, either by analogies or by his deployment of relevant material, his apparently incidental remarks fit very closely with what we might expect from a man of his experience and learning. If the argument about *saecula*, in particular, has something of a 'house of cards' about it, it is built with *Tacitus'* cards in the kind of form that we would have expected. Moreover it reinstates and gives clearer meaning to his comments that Rome's fortunes had improved and places his occasional discussion of decline or recovery in a coherent pattern.

In Tacitus' combined histories, we may well have the most sophisticated and ambitious extant formulation of Roman religion. The reader is steered away from interpretation that will render no practical favours to themselves or the *res publica,* and the state remains the religious focus. Tacitus' persistent interest in the dynamics of power formulates a perspective from which the senate is a crucial player in the maintenance of order on all levels: if they fail, Rome suffers all the more. This is not a simple indictment of the various textual agents: Tacitus is interested in the way that dynamics and relationships affect conduct, and the way that institutions suffer when their integrity is not upheld.

Some of the foregoing argument would no doubt be validated, modified or abolished if the full text of the *Histories* in particular should miraculously appear: the loss of Domitian's reign is not a trivial one. Such is the *fatum* of the ancient historian. In the meantime, we can speak of an account that bears a distinctive and coherent religious structure. The 'pessimism' so notoriously attached to Tacitus may well be misplaced. We have tended to focus on the decline, but not the escape from peril, the criticism rather than the affirmations. As with Livy, the historian's focus is primarily on contextualising events in religious terms and examining the relationship of Rome with her gods through cult – in other words, making sense of the past. If the refounding of the Capitoline is anything to go on, rite remains the principal means of communication from men to gods but Tacitus' politicisation of religion is more insightful than any existing modern account. His ability to contextualise religious actions and weigh up their consequences is remarkable. Not only does he illustrate that the senate required authority to practice religion, he is also skilful in his creation of a working religion for the *res publica*. The *cultus deorum* is reclaimed from both the popular (undiscriminating and pessimistic) *and* the imperial (personalised and overly optimistic) interpretations. Religious events, including those generated by the new fatalistic systems centred on the person of the *princeps*, are firmly reappropriated within a system that puts the city of Rome at its centre.

But religion was not just about the fabric of events: it is not simply a question of finding the right category and embedding each event there. Interpretation and identity remain at the heart of religious discourse. The *Histories* and the *Annals* look to a very different time, but they are sensitive to the potential future deployment of the various categories that inform religious interpretation. The practice of interpretation required not just skill, but discipline: one had to know where to draw the line. Where better to learn this, and much more about religion, than from history, the previous enactment of the art and the documentation of its results?

Tacitus' accounts primarily display *behaviour* and exhibit the best and worst of his predecessors' actions. One of his greatest insights was into the way that religious institutions and methods suffered, not through inadequate rite (which we normally assume is their chief interest), but because of the context in which the personnel were operating. Rite, which is *never* undermined directly, became increasingly isolated as the emperor and senate moved further and further away from the stability that they could have had, if only they had understood the broader picture. Tacitus' combined accounts are therefore reminiscent of Livy's story of Cannae: Rome forgot herself but rallied, put things right with her gods, and became the 'real' Rome once again.

The conservative reader will be suffering by now. Livy, whom we tend to see as triumphing Roman success, displays a far more pessimistic structure than Tacitus: due in part to the accidents of survival, his Rome appears to function well in relation to her gods. Yet he opens with the declaration that his evocation of an exemplary Rome is intended as a remedy for a city that is actually beyond redemption. He represents what might be possible, if the effort is made, though he (textually) offers no hope that the lesson will be heeded. Tacitus, on the other hand, every classicist's favourite pessimist, purports to write of past horrors to an audience who will have to look to their memories to find suffering; it was certainly not to be found in his contemporary Rome. While the *AVC* laid proper conduct before the otherwise forgetful reader, the *Annals* and the *Histories*, then, claim to serve as warnings 'lest we forget'. As he presents it, a future senate under a different emperor might well need his insights and his encouragement to preserve proper *Romanitas*. Even if we accept his claims, one suspects that he saw no room for complacency: relations between senate and emperor were always in a state of constant renegotiation and religious practices could easily be modified when placed in a different political context. Its role was still being passionately negotiated three centuries later.

5

Ammianus and a final settlement

5.1 Introduction

Over 250 years passed between the works of Tacitus and Ammianus Marcellinus. How, exactly, we are to think of the religious aspects of the period in which the latter wrote is a complex question that could easily merit a book in its own right. We can point to the survival of many pagan cults and practices for centuries after Constantine.[1] Or, with our long hindsight, we could point to symbolic moments such as the death of Julian, the last pagan emperor, in 363, as the end of a thousand-year-long era. Perhaps the 'real test' of the slippery process of Christianisation was the position of the aristocracy, which gives us a slightly later and appropriately more nebulous date.[2] We might see the end of state paganism in the refusal of Gratian to be *Pontifex Maximus,* probably in 376,[3] or the failure of the so-called 'pagan revolt' of 394 and the death of the 'pro-pagan' usurper Eugenius in the west.[4] Alternatively, we might adopt a different approach: older models of an all-out contest between paganism and Christianity have been supplanted by models of assimilation, where most aristocrats gradually, and (on the whole) peaceably, became part of the new order.[5] Whatever our criteria, clearly something drastic happened during the fourth and early fifth centuries and any text or other evidence is potentially a part of, and witness to, these processes. Even a single inscription can be a doorway into the politics and religion of the empire on the grandest scale and across generations.[6]

Somewhere towards the end of that century, and in the middle of the often unpredictable but rarely passive processes of Christianisation, Ammianus, a soldier and native Greek speaker, published his *Res Gestae.*

---

[1] E.g. Beard North and Price (1998) II 5.2e (123–4) note that participation in the Lupercalia was still being denounced in Rome around 495, citing Gelasius' *Letter Against the Lupercalia* 16.

[2] '[A]fter about 440 no further pagans are attested among the elite of the city of Rome' (Hedrick (2000) 57).

[3] For bibliography on the dating, see Beard North and Price (1998) I 374, n.29.

[4] On which see most recently Hedrick (2000) 39–50, who stresses the political factors in the usurpation.

[5] Hedrick (2000); Salzman (1992).

[6] Hedrick (2000).

The existing narrative begins with book 14 (353) and closes in 378 with book 31: it is thought that the lost books (traditionally numbered 1–13) dealt with the period from Nerva to the accession of Magnentius.[7] This discussion contextualises the work in two ways; diachronically, as part of the long-standing genre of historiography; and synchronically, within a society undergoing profound political and religious change. As with our previous authors, any conclusions we reach are tentative, however closely they are argued from the text, since, as with Livy and Tacitus, we, unlike the contemporary audience, are dealing with an incomplete work.

5.1.1 Religion in the *Res Gestae*

There is a discernible change in our material as we move across the centuries to Ammianus. Time and again, interpretation and lines of thought that were implicit in the accounts of Livy and Tacitus receive clear attention in Ammianus' altogether more explicit history. As we shall see, this difference is worthy of discussion in itself. As with Livy and Tacitus, the balance of explicit statements and implicit assumptions is a most telling factor in our understanding of the dynamics of religious interpretation in his society and time. Ammianus wrote in a markedly changed political, social and religious climate and quite possibly for a different audience; moreover we should be even more wary of what it means to call him 'Roman' than with his provincial predecessors, as we shall see. Finally, even Ammianus, whose account is so replete with apparently bald statements of religious causality, has been described as 'secular', though he does at least escape the charge of scepticism. The task of establishing that he had a coherent religious position is not initially so demanding as with Livy and Tacitus, since there are fewer reinterpretations required of particular passages and much of the work has been done,[8] but scholarly accounts which marginalise the importance or coherence of religion in the *Res Gestae* still need to be confronted.

Ammianus has undergone some of the most dramatic conversions in religious literary history. Once (rather implausibly) credited with Christianity,[9]

---

[7] Barnes (1998) 20–31 examines the structure of the extant text to suggest that the original work contained 36 books rather than 31, and that we have the latter 18.
[8] I refer principally, but not exclusively, to Rike (1987) and to Harrison (1999).
[9] Not a difficult conclusion to dismiss: Rike (1987) 2 mentions these discussions, which usually depended on his praise of provincial bishops. Henri de Valois disagreed in his 1681 edition of the *Res Gestae*. Rike also refers to J. Gimizaine *Ammien Marcellin, sa vie et son oeuvre* (Toulouse, 1889). The best collection of the early commentators is the *Variorum* edition of Wagner and Erfurdt (Wagner, J.A., and C.G.A. Erfurdt, eds., 1808: *Ammiani Marcellini quae supersunt cum notis integris* Frid. Lindebrogii, Henr. et Hadr. Valesiorum et Iac. Gronovii quibus Thom. Reinesii quasdam et suas adiecit Io. Augustin. Wagner, Leipzig (repr. in 2 vols., Hildesheim/New York 1975)) – a reference I owe to Dr Gavin Kelly.

he turned to Neoplatonism,[10] embraced paganism to the point of evangelis-
ing,[11] only to renounce the divine, at least in public, when he settled in a
neutral stance, that of 'classicising historian in a tradition of secular historiography'.[12] But throughout he is 'confused' – virtually a requirement of
paganism according to some scholars.[13]

It hardly needs stating that this discussion will attempt to secure his further apostasy back to that of pagan apologist, already convincingly argued
for by Rike (1987), to which there will be copious reference throughout
this chapter, and more polemically by Barnes (1998): there is no need to
rehearse the earlier debates in great depth.[14] Though we will expand on
his position, Rike's groundwork enables us to delve deeper into implications of Ammianus' work without the preamble of locating most religious
categories. Ammianus' formulation is traditional in many senses, but the
dynamics of divine interaction with humanity are drastically reformulated.
Ammianus' religion is far from sentimental: it is a profoundly reorientated
system intended for practical deployment.

If we are to have permission to bother at all with the religious material we must first deal with the manifold objections of Matthews (1989)
who sees religion as largely ornamental and secular. He minimises the role
of religion on several fronts:

> Ammianus was not writing a religious history ... [T]he 'high
> places' where true history was accustomed to run (26.1.1) were
> of a secular, not a religious nature ... but it will often be diffi-
> cult to show that a god or a goddess (Mars, say, or Bellona), or
> an allusion to fate or Fortune, is more than a technical device,
> useful, for example, in transition from one subject to another
> or to convey the enormity, or unexpectedness, of the events by
> which the Romans were confronted, but not implying any sig-
> nificant theological or philosophical reflection ... In the great
> majority of cases, fate, Fortune and the gods function in Am-
> mianus as part of the normal equipment of a historian writing in
> the classical manner ... [they] are part of the machinery. What

---

[10] Enßlin *Zur Geschichtsschreibung und Weltanschauung des Ammianus Marcellinus* (Leipzig, 1923).

[11] Rike *passim*; Elliott (1983) 202–220, esp. 210–212.

[12] Irrespective of whether he is a 'vague fatalist' or 'vague monotheist'. These two usually go together, e.g. Momigliano (1977a) 148; Liebeschuetz (1979) 302. See also, Blockley (1975) 168–169; Camus (1967) 133–134, 140, 143–144, 199, 267–268. Herodotus is also thus described – wrongly, according to Harrison (2000) 178–181.

[13] Most writers: many comments are collected by Rike (1987) 3–5 with excellent (and entertaining) criticism.

[14] Rike (1987) 2–7 has an eloquent summary of the previous religious argumentation.

would Classical history and poetry …have done without Fortune and the gods? (Matthews (1989) 425–8)

Though he is aware of Rike's book, he dismisses it in an extended footnote that describes it as 'flawed by an unnecessarily obscure style'[15] and
continues:

> it is essential that a 'theological synthesis' such as that at-
> tempted by Rike should respect the difference between the two
> styles of writing [i.e. narrative as opposed to excurses]. In
> general, I would prefer to look in Ammianus for a range of
> responses to complex and varied situations rather than for a
> single definable 'theology'.

He has not convinced everyone: Barnes, for one, clearly prefers Rike's
position.[16] Matthews has compressed quite a number of issues in his account: we shall examine them in the order that they appear in the citation
above. He first asserts that Ammianus was not writing a religious history
and then proceeds to back this statement up, beginning with reference to
Ammianus' broad comment on historiography. However, there seems no
textual reason at all to conclude that the refusal to include trivia at 26.1.1
has anything to do with religion (which Ammianus nowhere defines as trivial).[17]

On the difficulty of proving that a god or goddess is more than a 'technical device', we might well ask why the burden of proof should be on
proving such an assumption, quite apart from invoking Feeney's (1991, 2)
thoughts on 'literary devices' ('criticising the gods in epic as a literary device is like criticising the carburettors or pistons in a car as an engineering
device'). Matthew's reason for this is that the gods often act to represent
transition or the enormity of events. But it has already been demonstrated
that, in Livy and Tacitus at least, this is precisely the *point* of invoking the
gods, to explain a broader sweep of events. Ammianus gives us no explicit

---

[15] Barnes (1998) 80 n.10 rightly calls this a harsh judgement. The mention of 'an unnecessarily obscure style' seems a particularly unnecessary, or perhaps revealing, assessment. Though Matthews
cannot have had much opportunity to incorporate Rike's work (the two works were published very
close together), the comments he does make show no sign that he would have taken Rike's position
seriously.

[16] 'A recent study ought to put an end to the sterile debate.' I do not fully endorse Barnes' own vision,
of a militant pagan who was a 'prisoner of the past' (Barnes (1990) 83), because Ammianus'
religious formulation is too much of a coherent adaptation from that of his predecessors. However
'pessimistic' or 'nostalgic' he might have been in other areas, Ammianus' religion is a forward-
looking and flexible arrangement.

[17] See further Harrison (1999).

reason to read his text this way, far from it: Matthews is drawing on readings of other authors (which themselves often invoke 'the secular tradition' to bolster *their* readings in a mutually confirming circle). He then sums up by invoking the supposedly familiar tradition of the 'ornamental' role of fate, *fortuna* and the gods in historiography.

This appeal to the secular tradition of historiography seems to be the fulchrum of Matthews' position on Ammianus' religion: earlier historians are sceptical about religion, or deliberately secular, therefore so is Ammianus, who imitates them in many other ways. Unfortunately, even in the days when it was reliably concluded that a historian was secular or sceptical, the reasons for their holding the 'rational' line varied: the tradition invoked by Matthews is not only illusory, and it could only be maintained by special pleading, adapted to each individual author.

Matthews posits an association of the gods with the enormity of events, but Walker (1952) 245 played down the role of divine agency in Tacitus by noting that 'usually the actions attributed to "Fate" are of an *unimportant, even trivial*, kind' (my emphasis): so as Matthews dismisses religious material because it 'only' deals with important events, so Walker does so because it 'only' relates to 'trivia'. The supporters of the 'sceptical' or 'technical device' approach to religion in historians therefore appear to be sharply divided on their criteria for the meaninglessness of religious categorisation: Matthews' position was weaker than it appeared even before a demonstration that Livy and Tacitus took religion far more seriously than had been supposed. The 'tradition' has already lost probably its two staunchest allies and their defection means that we can no longer justifiably talk of a tradition at all. Furthermore, there are good signs that those few other historians cited as loyal to secularity will soon abandon the cause.[18] We can no longer invoke the secular *tradition*, and we should no longer place the burden of proof on defending the importance of religion.

What then if Ammianus was unilaterally adopting a secular manner, irrespective of the tradition? Though this might masquerade as an answer, it raises far more questions. We gain little by effectively dismissing the religious interest of works of the period on the grounds that they are 'secular', even if we can show that they actively avoid religious formulations (which Ammianus certainly does not): we should rather recognise the complexity of the different responses to an unstable situation that were being offered by different authors under different conditions. By Ammianus' time, pagans and Christians were negotiating different strategies to share the cultural

---

[18] For instance, the supposedly 'rational' Caesar. See Marincola (1997) 209 ('what takes the place of the gods in Caesar is *fortuna*') and Feeney (1998) 19–20.

knowledge which often informed their literature. The names of gods are used apparently without concern by Christian authors such as Ausonius and pagan authors with Christian patrons, such as Claudian. A high-ranking pagan with Christian masters would adopt one tactic, a Christian another, and an independent pagan like Ammianus yet another strategy. A great deal was at stake, and even if one finds 'secularity', that should not be treated as an end to exploration, but a beginning. What was there to gain by adopting a secular *persona* in the late fourth century? The possible answers are endless and all of them imply deliberate choice.

In fact, I suspect that the implied contrast of 'secular' with 'religious' is merely an extension of a familiar modern dichotomy, and is not far from 'scepticism' and 'belief' which obscured more than it revealed. The desire to see a disinterest in religion has once again asserted itself and coloured our readings. The conclusion that an author distanced himself from religion is considered to be a way of closing the discussion: the text, we are supposed to believe, now makes good sense.

This supposed closure is, however, no more than an illusion when dealing with antiquity, late or otherwise. If an author avoided religious formulations, should this be taken as a 'sincere' disbelief in religions of any kind? Or, an example to follow, a plea for tolerance by refusing to broach the subject? Or does it perhaps show the desire to command respect and avoid enmity amongst the widest possible audience? A fear that their religious understanding would be found wanting by critical readers? The possibilities mount up.

Clearly a diagnosis of secularity is only a starting point for investigating religion in such texts. Even the threshold of visibility, by which I mean the extent to which religion imposes itself on the reader during the narrative, could easily mislead us. A pagan of the time who had abandoned any hope of the restitution of the *cultus deorum* might rail openly and frequently against Christianity's deficiencies with savage bitterness, lauding at every opportunity the glory of Jupiter and his retinue, and damning the fools who had abandoned their worship, whereas one who still had hope that another, longer-lived, Julian was to come, might quietly put his message across with composure and discretion. Which would be the more religious?

Even if we were to grant, for the sake of argument, that fortune and the gods were somehow empty of meaning and ornamental within the narrative, does this not nonetheless hearken back to the days when a historian would expect his readers to acknowledge Jupiter Optimus Maximus as their 'chief' god in cult? Aligning oneself with a tradition is a multivalent venture: the deduction that by using long-established methods of writing and deliberately aligning oneself with the past, one thereby *excludes* the now (officially) neglected deities of that time is not the most obvious, nor the most telling, conclusion available. We should be on our guard that when we encounter once again the historiographical habit of using meaningful juxtaposition, a preference for 'natural' representations over the fabulous and the delivery of understated criticism of religious conduct, we, rather unimaginatively, see only a bland and modernising secularity.

In conclusion, it seems inescapable that the term 'secular' is somewhat inadequate, given the variety of different political and textual strategies known from the later Empire: while Ammianus is clearly distinct in his approach from the likes of Eunapius or Zosimus, and appears superficially less zealous in his religious outlook, he uses all the erudite tools of his trade to undermine Christianity and enhance traditional rites.

Matthews' criteria for reading Ammianus' religion are not perhaps the most sympathetic, least of all in the light of our foregoing discussion, where 'a range of responses to complex and varied situations' is characteristic, rather than exclusive, of a sophisticated paganism. In practice his reading of Ammianus' religion amounts to a superficially cohesive confusion at best. Consider, for example, his rather negative assessment of Ammianus' excursus on divination at 21.1.7-14, which affirms the power of traditional methods of prediction: it is 'neither more nor less than a learned digression ... the digression itself does not betray a complete mastery of the actual philosophical issues that were involved (430)'. Ammianus' eclectic approach to Cicero, whom he cites here, is said to be 'more literary than philosophical: not that this in any way reduces the warmth of his feeling on the subject'. Matthews closes with the aside that 'if Ammianus had paid equal attention to Cicero's most important work on the subject, the *De Divinatione*, he should have realised that ... it is in the end a devastating attack on the validity of divination' (431), citing Liebeschuetz (1979) 31 to support this view.[19] However, not only is the reference to Liebeschuetz highly misleading (what he says is closer to the opposite), but neither does Matthews refer to the drastically different interpretation of Cicero's work put forward by Beard (1986) and Schofield (1986). Perhaps Ammianus knew his Cicero better than was thought.

Matthews has, despite appearances, taken a strongly polemical line on this material. He is, in effect, arguing that Ammianus is a sub-philosophical pagan who has repeatedly, even reliably, failed to grasp fully

---

[19] A similar attitude to similar material is taken by Amat (1992), who repeatedly, even repetitively, says that Ammianus, depending on Apuleius' work, has muddled originally distinct ideas about justice and Nemesis. The possibility that Ammianus did this deliberately is not really considered. On Ammianus' supposedly 'failed philosophical credentials', see Rike's pertinent discussion on his pp. 3–4.

the significance of those works to which he has undoubtedly been exposed and that he failed to appreciate the keen religious climate. State cult is barely addressed by Matthews as an issue in itself, in sharp contrast to what we find in Rike's study, which retains it as the central focus. Thus Matthews' very approach prejudges the question of religion. At best, with Matthews' rubric, Ammianus could emerge as a well-informed reader of philosophy and the *Res Gestae* as a kind of almanac of partially relevant excursuses strung together by some historical narrative: there is no possibility of a unified or overall coherent position. But this issue is more a question of preference than argument: we can either tend towards the position that Ammianus is not intelligent enough to understand his sources properly, or that he has deliberately recast and subordinated his 'digressions' (particularly the philosophical material) to a supporting role in his history, where they function as a gloss on what religious experts have known for centuries. We can speak of (imperfect) 'influence', 'failure to understand', or otherwise compare Ammianus to a suspiciously modern model of historiography: or, with greater acknowledgement of his rhetorical style and approach, we can explore his deliberate and strategic appropriation of myriad fields of knowledge and their integration into his programme. Detecting philosophical topics and discussions, whether they be Neoplatonic, Ciceronian or Stoic, does not prove that they deserve an exalted status, it merely indicates that they are part of the general discourse of the times. As we shall see, Ammianus wishes to show his knowledge but an important part of his agenda is to put philosophy in its proper place – where it did not threaten traditional religious understanding. It is not a matter of 'fact' but of authority and predominance.

Whichever way we look at it, religion is going to be more significant than Matthews allows. But we not just concerned with an unwieldy 'canon' or 'theology': *whose* Roman religion are we dealing with? A parochial Greek's? A soldier's? An outsider or an orthodox patriot?

5.1.2 The later empire

The Roman world had undergone many changes since the times of Tacitus and Livy. Even listing those features with which this discussion must deal is no mean task, and the criterion of relevance will be strictly enforced.[20] There are few constants and we cannot even number Rome itself amongst them, since the effective capital of the empire was now the

---

[20] I leave broader issues of history and composition to Camus (1967); Sabbah (1978); Elliott (1983) and Matthews (1989).

emperor's court, wherever it might be.[21] The geographical decentralisation and shift of power from the old political centre(s) in the old Roman world was mirrored, of course, in religion. The extant text of the *Res Gestae* covers a period where, with the spectacular and short-lived exception of Julian, Rome had a Christian[22] emperor. Thus, two principal points of reference for the preceding chapters are, if not lost, then drastically modified.

Firstly, the historian has apparently lost his geographical (and therefore religious) fixed centre, since the emperor's presence in Rome was an exception rather than a rule. Whereas earlier writers could draw on Rome's heritage and pantheon, rites and *exempla* in the knowledge that all interpretative roads led to Rome, Ammianus and his empire had no such unified reference point. He could no longer address a society that, if fragmented, plausibly shared enough religious assumptions for him to spell them out briefly (if at all), and then within relatively homogeneous points of reference. Livy and Tacitus wrote for Rome, and (especially in the case of the latter) the senate. Ammianus, in contrast, speculates on whether he will have an audience at all (31.5.10; cf. 14.6.2).[23] Nor can religious authority be so easily located: Livy's republic had the senate and its committees of priests and Tacitus demonstrated the tensions that arose between the emperor and his senate. But religious expertise in Ammianus' empire was a very different matter, with very different issues. Moreover, with regard to religious issues and recommendations Livy and Tacitus wrote *to* the people of Rome *about* the history and conduct of the people of Roman Italy.

However, Ammianus' *persona is* clearly centred in Rome:[24] Ammianus includes the least relevant City prefectures, he includes details on Roman topography to the extent that no other city attracts; and his finest set-pieces

---

[21] More eloquently put by Ammianus himself at 14.6.5.

[22] No claim is made here of continuity between the modern phenomenon and its ancient homonym, nor is any attempt made to explore the enormous, if obscured, differences, some of which are detailed in Smith (1979) and Goodman (1994). See also Markus (1990).

[23] There has been debate about the exact nature of Ammianus' audience and associates (not necessarily the same group); e.g. for Sabbah (1978) 508–510, the *Res Gestae* are aimed at Rome itself but his material could just as easily be taken as acknowledgement of Rome's special status in the Empire, which is undeniably an aspect of his account. See also Cameron (1964) for the argument that we should not conflate Ammianus' position with that of particular senatorial circles; more generally on the construction of an audience, Sabbah (1978) 507–540. The most recent discussion is Frake (2000) who argues that Ammianus wrote with an eye on civil administrators, on the basis that they are the group who feature most in the *Res Gestae*.

[24] The best, and most recent, discussion of this issue is in Kelly (2002), who argues that Ammianus is writing with the 'immediate expectation, nothing more absolute than that, of an audience at Rome'. His second chapter 'Ammianus and the Romans' (13–56) details Ammianus' connection, and relationship, with Rome. Since this work is unpublished, I summarise where relevant the pertinent points and argument that he offers.

are set in Rome.[25] Rome is the storehouse of the past, the great resource of learning through history. So when Ammianus addresses his audience *as if* in Rome[26] and otherwise constructs his perspective as Roman, it might be argued that he was indeed 'writing for Rome'. But the deliberate *restoration* of Rome, despite the historical changes, as the perspective for historiography *par excellence* is a complex and multivalent strategy. If read historically, then it does tend to imply that Ammianus was indeed situated in Rome, and modestly producing a history for local consumption (if Rome can be considered a 'local' area). If read as a literary and didactic strategy, it is rather more: a claim to the entire heritage of Rome history, with all its *exempla*, traditions, successes and failures. None of these claims would have a comparable weight if they were located elsewhere: to write in Rome is to write for the empire. Thus it will be argued here that Ammianus sets his sights wider than his predecessors, and that he intended to have relevance for the wider 'Roman' community: so, for instance, Livy's beloved *fortuna populi Romani* is usurped by the *fortuna orbis Romanae* (25.9.7), an apparently innocuous difference which enshrines a massive change in perspective.[27] If he is going to find a new or redesigned paradigm for religion, it will have to take account of a virtually unprecedented phenomenon: that of choice between religions.[28] It may be that his criteria rather than his results are what enable us to consider him 'pagan', as we shall see.

Nor is this the only major new consideration. The cultural identity of our author is explicitly complex: a self-declared Greek[29] who wrote history (a genre that had its roots in Greek culture) in Latin.[30] Discussion centres, for the most part, on which is predominant. Barnes (1998) argues vigorously that Ammianus 'thought in Greek', against much discussion of the last few decades, while many of his predecessors noted strong identification with the Roman tradition.[31]

---

[25] Cited by Kelly and respectively 14.6.2, 22.15.24 and 28.1.3-4; 14.6, 16.10 and 28.4. Kelly also notes, among other topics, the way that Rome 'defeats' Constantine, who is dumbstruck, and mostly by pagan temples (27–28).

[26] As Kelly reads his use of *peregrini* at 14.6.2.

[27] Noted also by Naudé (1964) 83.

[28] For this issue in the late republic and earlier empire see North (1992); for an overview of the later empire see Beard North and Price (1998) I 278–312.

[29] Ammianus often uses the first person plural (e.g. *dicimus* 22.9.7) to introduce a Greek term: Marincola (1997) 147 cites Ammianus' description of himself as *miles quondam et Graecus* and *ingenuus* (31.16.9, 19.8.6) on which see also Barnes (1998) ch. 7; Sabbah (1978) 510 n.9, 532–535; Matthews (1989) 462–464 and Blockley (1975) 16–17.

[30] There are other Latinising features: he characteristically uses *nos* and its cognates to mean 'the Roman army' (Marincola (1997) 289–90).

[31] Barnes (1998) 65–78 has a summary of the scholarship. The term 'Roman historian', which he opposes, can of course be used to indicate his subject matter rather than his cultural identity, and this may be what was meant.

At one extreme, we have the explicit identification with Greece and Greeks, in tandem with the implicit literary and linguistic associations, and at the other the unassailable fact that he chose to write in Latin. However strongly either side is emphasised, the fact remains that he locates himself in both worlds, as heir to both historiographical traditions. 'Ammianus' history carries a constant claim to emulate all the great historians of Greece and Rome – Herodotus, Thucydides, even Xenophon and Theopompus, Polybius, Sallust, Livy and Tacitus.'[32] This will have repercussions for his interpretations and the boundaries that he sets for religious propriety. In Ammianus, a vast number of historiographical themes are deliberately united: 'He intended his *Res Gestae* to sum up the whole of Greco-Roman historiography'[33] and historiography includes models of religion.

5.2 A religion for Rome

5.2.1 Hallowed practices

Ammianus must, if he is indeed a pagan apologist, construct a religion for Rome within the vastly increased and polarised options realistically available to the denizens of the empire. By now we are accustomed to the recommendatory embodiment of religious habits and protocols; the historian shapes our knowledge both of what works for Rome and what is appropriate. What we will find is that the hallowed pagan practices of Rome are consistently defended – the material is so profuse that only representative or striking examples are cited. If Ammianus is truly heir to the tradition bequeathed by Livy and Tacitus,[34] one of his chief concerns will be the (re)construction of a state cult for Rome and her empire.

Certainly there are signs that paganism is equal to the essential religious task of securing divine support. A pagan response to a crisis is effective when Tertullus appeals to Castor and Pollux to end a storm that is causing

---

[32] Barnes (1990) 72. The appropriation of the Greek heritage stressed: Barnes (1998) 66 and *sub indice*; Marincola (1997) 102 n.199, 255; Matthews (1989) esp. 461–468. Latin: Fornara (1992b); Bowersock's review of Matthews (1989) in *JRS* 80 (1990), 244–50.

[33] Barnes (1990) 72. Sabbah (1978) speaks of Ammianus' 'histoire presque vraiment universelle' (597). For Ammianus' position regarding his contemporaries and predecessors see Sabbah (1978) 31–114, 115–219 (historical), 241–372 (contemporary literature).

[34] On the suggestion that Ammianus deliberately followed and imitated Tacitus as a historian, the consensus is that there is no significant debt. See e.g. Blockley (1973) and (1975) 17, Matthews (1989) 456 and (1994). Most recently, and pertinently, Marincola (1997) 240 and 254–255 (with further bibliography). On the coincidence of Tacitus' ending, and Ammianus' starting, point he says 'this did not mean that his history need be similar to that of his predecessor. It meant that he wished to be seen as the practitioner of a serious history that had been practised long ago, and had . . . fallen into desuetude.'

a grain shortage in Rome – the weather duly abates;[35] a tomb of Mopsus is known for its healing properties;[36] Julian, *incertus de militum fide*, successfully propitiates Bellona (*placata ritu secretiore Bellona*, 21.5.1). Traditional methods of divination still worked: the failure of Julian's campaign against Persia hardly lacks warnings – Ammianus goes to great lengths to establish the misgivings of the *haruspices* and other experts (discounting the philosophers who misled the emperor).[37] Shortly before the 'forced' declaration of Julian as Augustus, at 20.4, a misshapen child with two heads, two sets of teeth and four eyes is born in Antioch and Ammianus offers *his* lament on the decline of prodigies:

> At that same time in Daphne, that lovely and magnificent suburb of Antioch, a portent was born, horrible to see and to report; an infant, with two heads, two sets of teeth, a beard, four eyes and two very small ears; and this misshapen birth foretold that the state was turning into a deformed condition. Portents of this kind are often born as predictions of the outcome of various affairs; but as they are not expiated by public rites, as they were in the time of our forefathers: they pass by unheard of and unknown.[38]

Like his predecessors, Ammianus has anchored a series of trenchant allegations in what initially appears to be a nostalgic, even whimsical, 'aside'. The coincidence that Livy and Tacitus both dealt with the neglect of prodigies, the former explicitly and the latter in a more diffused way, does not mean that this lament lacks meaning or functions as a vacuous mimicking of earlier motifs: the historian's task is precisely to hold the past up to the present as a mirror. The repetition of a complaint should not be mistaken for ornamental and insignificant mimesis. Both Livy and Tacitus could demonstrate to their readers that the neglect of prodigies was a matter of contemporary concern, and this will also turn out to be true in this case: Ammianus may be alluding to an apparently established tradition of Latin

---

[35] *moxque diuini arbitrio numinis, quod auxit ab incunabulis Romam, perpetuamque fore spopondit, dum Tertullus apud Ostia in aede sacrificat Castorum, tranquillitas mare molliuit, mutatoque in austrum placidum uento* (19.10.4).

[36] *manes eius heroici dolorum uarietati medentur plerumque sospitales* (14.8.3): surely a response to the claims made for martyrs' shrines. Note the disclaimer for failures (*plerumque*).

[37] *Haruspices*, to which we shall return, are the object of special focus in Liebeschuetz (1988).

[38] *Tunc apud Dafnen, amoenum illud et ambitiosum Antiochiae suburbanum, uisu relatuque horrendum natum est monstrum, infans ore gemino cum dentibus binis et barba, quattuorque oculis, et breuissimis duabus auriculis, qui partus ita distortus praemonebat rem publicam in statum uerti deformem. nascuntur huius modi saepe portenta, indicantia rerum uariarum euentus, quae quoniam non expiantur, ut apud ueteres publice, inaudita praetereunt et incognita* (19.12.19-20).

historiography but he has emphatically made the motif his own. Whereas his predecessors were concerned with the contemporary lack of respect for prodigies, Ammianus bewails the fulfilment of the earlier decline: prodigies have now been dispensed with altogether by the state. The response of old, public expiation exists now only in memory though the phenomena continue just as they had always done. The notice is more than a historical curiosity: to preserve the memory also preserves the possibility of a restoration.

The short notice embodies almost the whole of his religious programme. The link with the practices of his predecessors is emphatically made, the difference with contemporary habits noted; the divinatory use to which prodigies can be put (by anyone who can interpret them) remains; last, but not least, the possibility of a religious programme that put such useful material at its heart is evoked. To restate a former and abandoned position is not to record mindlessly, but to make possible the restoration of what has been forgotten, and we shall explore a number of moments like this. For now, we can note that what is of immediate narratological and religious interest here is that a prediction is made from the portent, in contrast to Ammianus' predecessors. Livy's extant account hardly concerned itself at all with predictions made from prodigies: rather, a solution was to be sought through ritual. In Tacitus' account, actual expiation was rarer (and often doomed or overshadowed in some way), but the emphasis remained on restoring the *pax deum*; thus both earlier authors steer their narratives towards *expiation*. The purpose of collecting such reports was, after all, to *prevent* those foreshadowed events from occurring in the first place. Livy represents this (rhetorically) as the norm and the proper focus of public interest: Tacitus, while depicting neglect of prodigies and their investigation, generally steers the reader back to tried and tested methods. That is not to say that prediction was impossible: far from it (see, e.g., *Annals* 15.47.3). But it was not the main focus of interest.

Ammianus, though he acknowledges the possibility of expiation, stresses the possibility of (useful and accurate) *prediction* offered by prodigies such as this and promptly avails himself of the opportunity to look ahead to the declaration of Julian as rival Augustus to Constantius: the Roman state will, for a time, have two 'heads'. Nonetheless, the prodigy is 'properly' interpreted, that is, in terms of the state rather than (e.g.) the ruling emperor(s). By limiting his interpretation to the condition of the state, Ammianus 'reminds' us that prodigies are a matter for the *res publica*. Thus, even at this point, signs were not entirely linked to rulers: it would have been so easy to note the connection with the two *Augusti* who are about to launch campaigns for full rule of the Empire, especially when the 'fit' of the portent with impending events is not difficult to see, even down to the detail of two heads and one beard, just like the two *Augusti*.[39] Given that prodigies occur unexpectedly, they can still be used to foresee future events irrespective of the use that the state puts them to.

The conceit that the prodigies are not noted or understood – clearly undercut by his own record – should also not be underestimated. Ammianus has his peers wandering, almost lost, through an abundance of signs, if only they would register them and explore their meaning. His is the voice of memory, arresting the decline by asserting the shadow of past practices, lest they fade entirely from the record. As long as *someone* remembers the (otherwise) *inaudita et incognita*, there is the possibility of what we would call pagan rites being reinstated. That some profit would be derived from so doing is obvious by the link with the imminent civil war.

This notice comes at a significant point in the narrative and it is worth recording the story that the prodigy caps. It involves a section dealing with the intrigues of Paul 'the Chain', whose prosecutions against innocent people begin at 19.12.1.[40] A number of questions submitted to an obscure oracle at Abydum had been forwarded to the emperor 'with malicious intent' (*maligne*, 19.4.5): the implication of Ammianus' account is that some of these requests could be taken as a threat to the emperor, though he is far from unambiguous on the matter. Paul headed a commission to look into the allegations: his 'determination to do harm was unswerving and fixed' (*obstinatum fixumque eius propositum ad laedendum*, 19.12.1) and, though Ammianus recounts a number of failures on his part to secure greater punishment than exile, Paul did cause the deaths or condemnations of many others: many victims were simply wearing amulets, or were accused of necromancy by an enemy because of their passing a grave in the evening (19.12.13).

But not all of the blame is Paul's: responsibility rested firmly with Constantius. The prosecutions were handled, Ammianus tells us, as if Claros, Dodona or Delphi had been consulted about the death of the emperor. He then hastens to point out that protecting the ruling emperor is an entirely legitimate affair, but that pleasure should not be taken from such regrettable necessities, least of all by a ruler, since this (in appearance at least) crosses the line between despotism (*licentia regi subiecti*, 19.12.18) and (legitimate) rule (*potestate*). Cicero is evoked as an *exemplum*: given the choice, a man in power should seek grounds for pardon rather than opportunities for punishment, 'as is appropriate for a mild and considerate official' (*quod lenti et considerati est proprium*, 19.12.18). The account indicates that there was

---

[39] This detail was noted, I am informed, by Theresa Urbainczyk at an Ammianus conference in Durham in 1997.

[40] He first appeared at 14.5.6 and was already up to mischief then.

no need for the trials to be conducted so savagely: the emperor, though he might neglect other important matters, was particularly sensitive to such matters (19.12.5): suspicious and petty, he became enraged and sent Paul to the Orient and gave him *arbitrium* to conduct trials. Another official, Modestus, was also commissioned but Hermogenes of Pontus, the praetorian prefect, was not chosen because, we are told, he was 'too mild' (*ut lenioris ingenii spernebatur*, 19.12.6) for the task at hand. Ammianus also makes a point of telling us that Paul left, 'as instructed, puffing and panting in deadly rage' (*perrexit (ut praeceptum est) Paul, funesti furoris et anhelitus plenus*, 19.12.7) and that free rein was given to every kind of perversion of justice (*dataque calumniae indulgentia plurimis*).

It is not just Constantius' 'enjoyment' of the trials that is brought into question: the entire sorry episode is his responsibility, in his choice of officials and the scope allowed to them. The closure of the episode with a portent that heralds trouble for the state (explicitly) and trouble for Constantius in particular (implicitly) suggests some kind of causal relation between the injustice and improper handling of the matter, and the outcome. Ammianus, it seems, sets out a rather different stall to his predecessors. Justice and divine retribution are a theme to which we shall return more fully, but it is also worth noting that the portent is itself followed (and the book and section closed) by a short account (19.13) of Lauricius' checking of the raids of the Isaurians – a passage which deliberately diminishes the importance of a church council in Cilicia (Barnes (1998) 91–3). The Church is thus set in opposition to traditional, now neglected practices and the Christian emperor found wanting, as both Rike (1987) and Barnes have argued. Though the connection of justice to future events remains as yet to be fully explored, we can say provisionally that his actions may have led in some way to the *ira deum*; they certainly led to the *ira hominum*.

Prodigies and portents, then, still warn of future problems: after a soldier named Jovianus was struck dead by lightning along with two horses, Julian again called in the interpreters, who said that the expedition should not be undertaken, once again using signs for prediction rather than resorting to expiation: they clarified that the thunderbolt was of the advisory kind: 'as are called those which recommend or dissuade' (*fulmen consiliarium esse monstrantes. Ita enim appellantur, quae dissuadent aliquid fieri uel suadent*).[41] The typologising of prodigies is reminiscent of Livy's discrimination between physical and hallucinatory portents, but, as before, we should not

---

[41] 23.5.13. Cf. *portenta ...indicantia rerum uariarum euentus*, 19.12.20; it is unknown even by experts what an unprecedented prodigy (or type of prodigy, *noua portenti species*) heralds at 27.3.1, but it heralds *something* (*nulloque coniectante uentura postea quod portendebatur, euenit*); other examples follow.

assume a dogma, but rather a system of lore, replete with considerations and possible diagnoses. Just how hard and fast Ammianus' subcategories of prodigies are is hard to tell.[42] Other prodigies seem also to function as warnings with a symbolic association (such as brooms which sprout and thereby indicate the political rise of lower ranks at 28.1.42), though at times we are expected to diagnose the details; an ass mounting the tribunal and braying loudly precedes the story of Terentius, a baker who became governor (27.3.1-2). Ammianus explicitly makes the connection between the prodigy and the rise of the low-born *pistor*, who caused a lot of trouble before his execution for fraud. Meanwhile, for those who wish to know the future on demand, there is also the excursus validating augury, haruspicy and divine inspiration (21.1.7-14). The location of this excursus is not haphazard: book 21 is the story of Julian's accession and Constantius' death, and opens with Julian (as Caesar) considering whether he should endeavour to win over the increasingly hostile Augustus Constantius or anticipate the latter's attack.

A crucial influence was the signs he had interpreted as well as dreams that indicated the impending death of the emperor (21.1.6).[43] The historian then breaks off from the historical narrative to survey various divinatory techniques as a response to lingering accusations against Julian: the malicious said that his methods were 'depraved' (*prauas artes*), a term used elsewhere of magical techniques. But Ammianus begs to differ. Divination was rather a branch of learning that a wise man (*sapiens*) could respectably acquire: the omnipresent spirit that directed the elements could thereby communicate with him through the sciences and disciplines of divination. As long as they were properly placated, the ruling powers would supply men with prophetic knowledge based on the dictates of fate (21.1.8). There then follow more specific details: augury and auspices owe nothing to any deliberate or conscious action of birds: their flights are directed by the *deus*, who does so out of kindness or because men deserve it (*benignitas numinis, seu quod merentur homines seu quod tangitur eorum adfectione*, 21.1.9). Haruspicy, another method of telling the future, was, we are told, invented by Tages who rose out of the ground in Etruria (21.1.10). There is also inspired prophecy when the sun, the 'mind of the world', inflames men more than usual, bringing them an awareness of the future: in these cases a variety of (traditional sounding) signs have great significance: voices, thunder,

---

[42] The balls of flame that prevent the rebuilding of the Temple in Jerusalem presumably belong to a different category from that of 'warning', since they are an effective deterrent in themselves (23.1.1f.). For a broader discussion of this prodigy see Phillips (1979).

[43] Julian displays a talent for prophetic dreams elsewhere, e.g. 22.3.3, where he and other dream interpreters detect a problem which turns out to be the burning of the temple of Palatine Apollo back in Rome.

lightning, meteors and the like. Some compression seems to have taken place here: items that sound as if they would previously have been connected to prodigies are now good material for the inspired to see the future. Dreams are a tricky case (and we should remember that this excursus is partly a response to Julian's dreams) but can be validated by observing the sleeper's position, as Aristotle described: 'We are assured by Aristotle that dreams are certain and reliable when the dreamer is in a deep sleep, with the pupil of his eye looking straight before him and not directed to either side' (21.1.12).[44]

Thus far, though Ammianus harks back to the religion of his predecessors, we have already detected some structural differences: though he acknowledges the possibility of expiation, divination, which previously paid second fiddle to placating the gods, has moved to the forefront. We see this not only by virtue of its explicit validation in 21.1, but also in Ammianus' use of the prodigy at Antioch. This latter item also invoked the theme of justice and imperial conduct as a factor in influencing the mood of the gods. Both these aspects will recur at intervals in our discussion.

Divination is certainly then an effective tool for the discerning: but effectiveness was of course not the end of the selection process in constructing a religion. More important is the distinguishing of an *appropriate* constellation of practices within the empire-wide series of possibilities, and its chief rival would of course be Christianity. A survey of material touching on Christianity uniformly indicates that it is unsuitable as a candidate for a state religion.

5.2.2 Christianity

Opinions on the Christian content[45] of the *Res Gestae* have moved from according it priority[46] to surprise that it appears at all. Certainly it has a distinctly marginalised role in the *Res Gestae*.[47] It is not that Ammianus

---

[44] The general scholarly consensus is that Aristotle did not accept that dreams could be reliably used for prediction (Gallop (1988)). This fragment, which cannot be connected with any extant Aristotle, is not normally cited in such discussions.

[45] This section reflects only an overview of the treatment of Christian themes in the *Res Gestae*. The various works cited explore the references in more detail.

[46] See Rike (1987) 2 and Blockley (1975) 123, for further references.

[47] Barnes (1990) 77 takes a strong line which is hard to refute ('Ammianus chose . . . to ignore Christianity wherever he could. It was a conscious choice'); his position is reinforced in Barnes (1998) and see also Hunt (1985); Matthews (1989) 435–451; Rike (1987) 100–111; Neri (1992); de la Beaumelle (1974) and O' Donnell (1979). For Ammianus' tendency to exclude Christian terminology Cameron and Cameron (1964). Blockley (1975) 131–132 shows that Ammianus is, at times, 'non-classical' in his use of Christian terminology. These arguments usually (often tenuously) stress the 'secular' nature of historiography, and (often rightly) the interest in *uirtus* over religious choices and the hazards of imperial prescriptions on religion.

would do away with Christianity altogether; his preference for imperial religious toleration has often been noted,[48] as has his praise for those provincial bishops who live wholly blameless lives.[49] It is tempting to conclude that Ammianus has adopted a 'moderate stance', especially in comparison with his more strident contemporaries[50] but this would be to misunderstand the historiographical habit, where explicit and firm conclusions are 'left to the reader' (that is, the historian embeds signs that require interpretation). In Ammianus' depiction of Rome and her Empire, to marginalise Christianity was tantamount to polemic of an extreme kind. How was Christianity to be remembered? The answer seems to be that it had its place – on the outskirts of society.

Ammianus repeatedly marginalises what were important Christian matters: Barnes (1998) 93–4 detects 'a most remarkable and effective covert insult to Christianity' in the documentation of the Eastern provinces at 14.8. Jerusalem, despite its important ecclesiastical status, is not considered to be a significant city: 'Ammianus deliberately closed his eyes to the importance of contemporary Jerusalem, just as he closed his eyes to the central role that Christianity played in the politics, society and culture of the Roman empire after Constantine'. While demonstrating his familiarity with Christian terminology[51] he repeatedly writes as an outsider to the religion.[52]

Christianity therefore does receive some carefully located praise: but overall it fails to impress in quite a number of ways. Even as it strove to reinvent itself as a state religion, Christianity's claims often rested on the traditional criterion of (military) success.[53] It is, however, conspicuous in Ammianus' account for its failure to provide security within and without the empire. While Christians on the borders of the empire are conciliatory, they are violent and seditious in the cities.[54]

---

[48] See e.g. the praise of Valentinian for his toleration at 30.9.5. Scholars have formulated Ammianus' position with a slightly different emphasis, such as a philosophically based toleration, (Enßlin *Zur Geschichtsschreibung und Weltanschauung des Ammianus Marcellinus* (Leipzig, 1923)), to a more pragmatic patience like that suggested by Rike (1987) 106 n.96 ('toleration, yes, but preparatory to tipping, peaceably, the flow of conversion back ... that is – reconversion').

[49] 27.3.15.

[50] See e.g. Barnes (1998) 80 (on others' views); Paschoud (1988); Matthews (1989) 435 and Harrison (1999) 187 n.43.

[51] For which see e.g. den Boeft *et al.* (1995) 212. I see no reason to conclude, as Barnes (1998) 83 does, that Ammianus, like Julian, is an apostate because of his evident and specific knowledge of many of their terms. Christian language and terminology was hardly a secret.

[52] Barnes (1998) 82 emphasises that Ammianus' glosses on word like *synodos ut appellant* (at 15.7.7 and 21.16.18) persistently undermine the position of Christianity.

[53] Trompf (2000) illustrates just how central this theme was in ancient historiography and continued on into Late Antiquity; he deals almost exclusively with writings in Greek.

[54] Rike (1987) 104–105 for evidence.

When the bishopric of Rome was contested by the equally overzealous Damasus and Ursinus, the violence led to many deaths: Ammianus assures us of 137 dead in the Basilica of Sicininus in just one day. Ammianus concludes that while he can see the attraction of obtaining such ostentatious power that accompanies such posts in Rome, such ambitious characters as Damasus (the eventual victor) and Ursinus might be 'genuinely happy' (*beati re uera*, 27.3.15) if they quit the cities and adopted lifestyles like the provincial priests (*antistites*), who severely limit their diets, dress plainly and keep their eyes downcast, thereby commending themselves *perpetuo numini* as pure and sober men (*puros ... et uerecundos*). But this is not unadulterated praise, far from it: it is an *exemplum* in response to the outrageous schisms that left 137 dead in rioting over rival candidates for the bishopric. The formulation leaves Christians emphatically removed from the halls of power. The contrast between the riotous behaviour in Rome and the (marginalised) provincials could not not be greater: Christianity's place is not in the seats of power. Thus 'no markedly Christian emperor is a hero in the *Res Gestae*'.[55]

Probably the most notorious episode involving an urban bishop is that narrated during the siege of Bezabde at 20.7.7-9, where the bishop went under truce to speak to Sapor: he gently discouraged the Persian leader from continuing his efforts, warning of future losses on both sides. Sapor's 'madness' was such that entreaties could have no effect. Ammianus then reports what was in his view a 'groundless suspicion' (*suspicio uana ... (ut opinor)*) that the bishop had revealed to Sapor the best site for an attack on the wall. The suspicion gained corroboration from the fact that after the embassy, the siege engines were placed with precision at the points in the wall where they would do most damage 'as if those operating them were familiar with which parts would be most easily penetrated'. Whether or not we accept Barnes' argument that Ammianus is here indulging in 'Tacitean innuendo' in order to make a veiled accusation of treachery against the bishop, this Christian action is, at best, rather naive.[56]

There is also the farcical ease with which the Alamanni could enter an unguarded Mainz during a Christian festival (27.10.1-2): it is hard not to see irony in Ammianus' account. The emperor Valentinian had exercised great caution – or so he thought (*ut rebatur ipse*) in going *ad expeditionem*:

---

[55] Rike (1987) 105.
[56] Barnes (1998) 87–88: his analysis relies on the simplistic analysis of similar 'innuendo' in Tacitus but nonetheless has some merit. However, it seems inappropriate (to this reader, at least) in this instance to reduce Ammianus' nuanced picture to a categorical 'statement'. For similar charges elsewhere see de la Beaumelle (1974) 19–23. The story of the fall of Bezabde is often discussed and I make no attempt here to list the many references.

Rando, the prince of the Alamanni, on the other hand, had laid careful plans to capture Mainz. Since he arrived during a Christian ceremony, he was able to carry off a multitude of prisoners and an impressive amount of booty: so much for imperial caution and so much for Christianity's claims to supplant paganism in its role of protecting the empire.

A comparable position is taken on the notorious failure of Constantius abroad coupled with his unreasonable ability to stir up sedition within the empire.[57] The praise of the courage of martyrs at 22.11.10, like the praise of provincials, is not a ringing, or even a grudging endorsement. It appears during the 'martyrdom' of George, bishop of Alexandria. The son of a fuller, who had caused the ruin of many, he had been made bishop against his own, and everyone else's, interest (*contra utilitatem suam reique communis*, 22.11.4) by the city, whose seditious habits were noted even by oracles. George 'forgot his profession' which required him to be just and merciful (*professionisque suae oblitus, quae nihil nisi iustum suadet et lene*) and acted like an informer, bringing many to ruin. He had already alienated the pagan population when he appeared to threaten the temple of the *Genius*.

Before long George had been lynched and torn to pieces, along with some of his retinue. The bodies were taken to the shore, where they were burned and the ashes deposited in the sea. This last tactic was aimed at preventing the appearance of a martyr shrine. Ammianus then offers some recognition of what martyrdom represented: men who kept their faith even at the cost of their lives.[58] But this kind of acknowledgement is far from being exclusive to Christians: philosophers make many similar shows of courage in the face of deadly cruelty.[59] And Ammianus closes the episode of the killing by noting that if George had not alienated both parties, the Christians might have made the effort to save him.

Thus far, Christianity has not proved itself an equal to paganism: Rike (1987) 106–107 also dispenses with the interpretation that the description *religio absoluta et simplex* at 21.16.18 is one of praise: *absoluta* is hardly a commendation in a context of diversity and *simplex* hardly fits with the evidently desirable sophistication praised elsewhere; in addition, as Rike points out, the tendency to describe Christianity as a *lex*[60] contrasts with a

---

[57] See e.g. 20.11.32 for his failures against the Persians and 15.1.2 for his success in killing off internal rivals; 21.16.18 for his excellence in promoting religious schisms. There are other references to this effect (e.g. 14.10.16 and 14.11.8).

[58] He probably distinguishes George and his colleagues from martyrs: the remains were destroyed by the crowd in case they were treated as martyrs (*metuens, (ut clamabat), ne collectis supremis, aedes illis extruerentur, ut reliquis, qui deiuare a religione compulsi, pertulere cruciabiles poenas, ad usque gloriosam mortem intemerata fide progressi, et nunc martyres appellantur*, 22.11.10).

[59] Rike (1987) 106; Blockley (1975) 127; see e.g. 14.9.5-6; 19.12.12 and 29.1.38-9.

[60] Possibly 15.7.7 (an emendation, not adopted in Seyfarth's edition); 15.7.8; 20.7.7 and 25.10.15.

preference elsewhere for less rigid *prudentia* or *mathematica*: Ammianus' religion, like that of Livy and Tacitus, is a sophisticated inductive exercise – evidence is weighed up and a interpretation is necessary to find a nuanced response to a complex situation. A *lex* is simply too inflexible to suit an interpreter's needs. Neri (1992) comes to similar conclusions from a different angle: he sees an acknowledgement in this expression of Christianity's particular claims to a 'simple truth', set in opposition to heresies (*superstitiones*), as distinct from paganism's preference for sophistication and looking beyond the obvious. However, even if Ammianus is acknowledging these claims in a manner that Christians would accept, it is not a ringing endorsement of Christianity: 'There is reason to think that a simple truth is for him a truth for the simple' (Neri (1992) 60). Thus, Ammianus points, once again, at a particular and subordinate role for Christianity as (just) another cult in the varied Roman Empire.[61]

It is true that Ammianus is a long way from liquidating Christianity as a religion, but the role he creates for it is emphatically marginalised. These apparently positive statements that Ammianus makes about Christianity also define a limited context for its utility. It may be a religion that demands its adherents follow blameless lives, but the implications of his formulation are that there is a place for such blameless provincials at the *periphery* of power. Christianity is simply not designed to guide military, civic or imperial administration. Thus there is no reason to disagree with Rike's conclusion that 'Christianity, if to Ammianus a *religio licita* and plainly superior to other barbarian cults, was no serious competitor for virtue with the great civilised religions. Rather these would have to show it how to occupy a socially productive place among the *diuersitates religionum*.'[62]

5.2.3 Foreign religions

One area where Ammianus clearly diverges from his predecessors is on the question of foreign religions.[63] Livy, we should remember, used the term *superstitio* almost exclusively of practices undertaken in Rome but Tacitus was more ready to condemn foreigners even on their home territory, especially the Jews, Egyptians and Druids. With the decentralisation of the Roman empire from Rome comes a difficulty in defining boundaries, especially for Ammianus who had grown up outside the immediate

---

[61] For this vision see also O'Donnell (1979).

[62] Rike (1987) 101.

[63] Once again, this discussion can do little but summarise Rike's excellent findings and argument, though he makes little comparison with earlier sources.

influence of Rome as a fixed point of reference.[64] Though the Jews are still despised,[65] quite possibly for their connection with Christianity, the reputations of Egyptian and Druidic traditions have been strikingly rehabilitated: Egypt is honoured as the ancestral home of religion, and the Druids are famous for their knowledge.[66]

A number of other foreign religious traditions receive a generally favourable reception, most notably that of the Magi, whose traditional practices are treated with great respect: 'the Magi have nothing to do with "magic". They are not performers of suspicious tricks, but serious priests carrying out their duties with a time-hallowed knowledge and expertise.'[67]

Positive treatment is not, however, a rule. The religious traditions of the Huns and the Quadi are not treated so favourably,[68] though there is always the possibility of civilisation. The temples of the Taurians, in some of their cities at least, are free from human victims (22.8.36) although they continue human sacrifice elsewhere (22.8.34). But overall there is a far more open-minded flavour to Ammianus' account: it is at least possible for a foreign nation to teach Rome a thing or two. One might, somewhat simplistically, say that foreign cultures are demonised and stereotyped far less than previously: Ammianus goes further to distinguish foreigners from each other than his predecessor – indeed he includes many more. This gives a fuller range of assessments. The Burgundians for instance are probably the best of a barbarian lot.[69]

The term *superstitio*, formerly used to demarcate foreign religious practices with a touch of disdain, thus gains all the greater impact in its rare usages. Of the five occurrences, it is used once of Christian schism (21.16.18), and also of Manichaeism and its like (15.13.2); conjectural emendations allowing, Sapor may have[70] consulted *superstitiones omnes* before an attack on the Romans (18.4.1), while Julian, like Hadrian, was *superstitiosus magis quam sacrorum legitimus obseruator* (25.4.17) and, at times, a poor

---

[64] I note without comment the disagreements about his precise origins: see Seager (1999), Barnes (1998) 63 and Appendix 6; Matthews (1989) 8–9, (1994) and Fornara (1992a).

[65] They are *fetentes et tumultuantes* at 22.5.5.

[66] Egypt: 22.16.19f; Rike (1987) 96–100. Druids: 15.9.8; Rike (1987) 93.

[67] Den Boeft (1999) 209. Ammianus' deployment of motifs traditionally used to characterise foreigners and barbarians is subtle, according to Wiedemann (1986). On foreign religions, see Rike (1987) 93–95, and especially den Boeft (1999), on the decline of Persian religion. I am grateful to the latter author for providing a draft of his article before publication.

[68] Rike (1987) 87–89.

[69] Not least because of their supposed Roman origins (28.5.11); see further Rike (1987) 92. Wiedemann (1986) finds more generally that Ammianus is likely to assess Roman behaviour in terms traditionally reserved for barbarians, which can further elide the previously rather stereotyped distinctions between Roman and foreign cultures.

[70] Seyfarth adopts *superstitiones*. The manuscripts have a variety of words reliably beginning with *pr(a)est-*, which makes the reading rather weak evidence.

judge of signs (e.g. 24.4.1, where Ammianus distances himself from Julian's assessment). The Huns are at the opposite extreme, being restrained *nullius religionis uel superstitionis reuerentia* (31.2.11).[71]

5.2.4 Undesirable practices

The relative redundancy of the designation *superstitio* does not, however, deprive Ammianus of the means to indicate clearly his preferences for religious conduct. Certain practices are clearly undesirable – Ammianus can scarcely conceal his contempt for Sabinianus' predilection at critical moments for spending time at the shrines of martyrs (18.7.7). Though he was 'chosen in the hurried moment of general danger as the best conductor of an internecine war', he held up the war with his ceremonies.[72] Elsewhere, there are clear signs of continuity, even despite initial appearances.

Dreams receive a treatment comparable with previous discussions: in the earlier period, they required either independent confirmation (Livy 8.6.9) or ritual contextualisation (Tacitus *Annals* 12.13.3). Ammianus draws instead on Aristotle to circumvent their inherent unreliability (above, 242): if the sleeper was observed, their movements would betray whether the dream was genuine or illusory (21.1.12). In practice, of course, this requires an independent (and rather patient) observer and cannot be undertaken alone, thus confirming the difficulties of dream interpretation and a need for expert assistance. Nonetheless, they are treated along with the canon of reputable practices, along with birds, entrails or divine inspiration, all of which are prone to interpretative error (21.1.7-14).

Other detestable rites are still marked out for censure – 'magic' for instance.[73] At 26.10.5, Marcellus' sole praiseworthy deed was that he killed Serenianus, useful to Procopius only because of his *doctrinarum diritas* – these presumably the same *doctrinae* that allowed him to imbue a cap with magical powers (14.7.7); Apronius is praised for hunting down *uenefici*, feared for their *artes nefariae* (26.3.2). At 28.1.14, one Marinus was accused of having tried *artibus prauis* to gain a certain Hispanilla as his

---

[71] Though these rare usages of *superstitio* are entirely traditional, it is worth considering whether the historian avoided the term because of the growing tendency of Christians during the fourth century to refer to paganism as (a) *superstitio*.

[72] I cannot agree with Hunt (1985) 195 that Ammianus is objecting to Sabinianus' succession to the post held by Ursinicus; he may have had a personal axe to grind in this respect, as Hunt argues, but the mockery is specifically religious. It is centred on the rites and their context as much as the delay that they entailed (*ominoso sane et incepto et loco*).

[73] On which term, see Matthews (1989) (indexed frequently); Rike (1987) 37–39 and via index; Blockley 104–123. Ammianus refers to such *artes* variously as *nefandae* (14.1.2), *noxiae* (28.1.26), *prauae* (28.1.14) and *secretae* (unlikely to be a recommendation and in apposition with *uenena*, 23.6.78) but never uses the terms *magus* or *magia* for such things. They are reserved for the respectable Persian Magi (den Boeft (1999) 208–209).

wife; the identity of Valens' successor was sought *detestandis praesagiis* (29.1.6).

Astrology fares slightly better than these purveyors of rather ill-defined and certainly ill-received arts. Though Alexandrian experts in the art seem to be acknowledged warmly at 22.16.17 (*recalet apud quosdam adhuc licet raros consideratio mundani motus et siderum*), most of our references deal with trivialised uses of the art.[74] Thus Ammianus' position is not so far from that of Tacitus. Astrology is efficacious but not necessarily desirable, and prone to every kind of misuse.

Like his predecessors, Ammianus does not apply his discrimination merely to disciplines or practices themselves, but also to the way in which they are used. Even traditional pagan measures can be abused, most spectacularly by Julian, who was 'superstitious' rather than being a proper observer of rites (*superstitiosus magis quam sacrorum legitimus obseruator*).[75]

The only pagan emperor of the extant *Res Gestae* potentially presented Ammianus with serious problems for any rehabilitation of paganism: paradoxically, Ammianus' hero provides the greatest wealth of *exempla quae uites*. Julian's spectacular failure in Persia would appear to play into the hands of polemical Christians. Indeed they openly declared their joy at his death and there were rumours that it was in fact a Roman Christian who had killed the emperor;[76] even without this, the failure of the military campaign against Persia left a lot to be explained, given that such matters were central to the various claims made by both Christianity and paganism.

Ammianus' strategy is to establish that Julian was no ideal adherent of the *cultus deorum*: 'while the *cultus deorum* is made responsible for what was best in Julian's character, his failings are yet portrayed as unrepresentative, personal deviations from what it properly enjoined'.[77] While in Gaul and still a Caesar to Constantius, Julian's rites are eminently successful and proper, though necessarily secret.[78] The secrecy indicates

---

[74] Most amusingly, those who will not appear in public, wash or dine without consulting the stars (28.4.24) but we should also note those who use astrology in legal cases, who are subject to severe censure (28.4.26); Heliodorus is an astrologer and *tartareus ... malorum omnium*, though the two do not necessarily go together (29.2.6).

[75] 25.4.17. For the latest appraisal and bibliography of the charismatic emperor see Smith (1995). The account here is strictly limited and summarised.

[76] 25.6.6-7; Paschoud (1988) 150–153.

[77] Rike (1987) 39, whose two chapters on Julian (2 and 3) are excellent for the documentation of the stages of degeneration in Julian's religious behaviour, especially for the comparison with Libanius' account.

[78] Rike (1987) 40–42 amply demonstrates that though secrecy in religious rites is undesirable throughout antiquity, Julian is compelled by Christianity to hide his worship. In Ammianus (and elsewhere) it is normally associated with black magic (26.3.3; 26.3.4; 29.1.29 and 30.5.11). Theodoret noticed the opportunity, describing how Julian undertook human sacrifice in secret (*Historia Ecclesiastica* 3.26-27). For such charges see also Wiedemann (1986) and (more generally) Rives (1995b) and Beard North and Price (1998) I 233–234.

that Constantius' tyranny rather than an overt religious break was the cause of the civil war that left Julian as sole Augustus. But later he was to exhibit signs of his excessive religiosity (*superstitio*). While his activities in Gaul were characterised by his being occupied with good traditional pagan pursuits,[79] by the time he reached Antioch the strict adherence to tradition had begun to wane. The inappropriate assumption of what should have been priestly regalia was criticised by Ammianus as ostentatious rather than pious (*ostentationis gratia uehens licenter pro sacerdotibus sacra*, 22.14.3). Neither does the entourage of women, also for the sake of appearances, sound traditional. His suppression of his temper allows for an apparently successful propitiation of Jupiter, if the immediately subsequent discovery of the Apis bull is anything to go by (22.14.4, 6). But his *curiosus* search for a *noua consilii uia* (22.12.8) in approaching Apollo, which apparently forms part of a list of criticisms,[80] seems to be connected to the ominous destruction by fire of the temple of Apollo (22.13.1). Julian's failure to note the ample, almost pleonastic, warnings of the various diviners on his Persian campaign clearly put the responsibility for error on the emperor. He had received all manner of propitious omens and signs (or active help, 15.2.8) early in his imperial career: he sets off with favourable auspices (*secundis auspiciis*, 17.8.2); the *Genius Publicus* appears at 20.5.10, promising him support; he reinterprets what seems to others a bad omen (21.2.1-2); he is hailed Augustus by the people of Sirmium (21.10.2) and accepts the sign happily (*euentu laetus et omine*).

Thus far Julian has received only positive predictions, which were certainly to his liking. However, as his fortunes change, we find that he is less willing to accept adverse signs: abundant warnings appear as his death approaches. The rot seems to set in at Antioch, which Julian enters at the same time as the ritual mourning for Adonis, also cut down in his prime (*in adulto flore sectatum est*, 22.9.15); this was taken as a bad sign (*uisum est triste*) and the signs continue apace. The people combine names to read *Felix Iulianus Augustus* at a funeral and about the same time the death of a senior priest indicates the approaching death of Julian, although this is not transparent at the time (23.1.5-6); those skilled in signs diagnosed that an earthquake in Constantinople boded badly for a campaign against another's territory and the Sibylline Books warned in no uncertain terms to postpone the campaign against Persia (23.1.7).

More signs of trouble follow shortly after: a colonnade collapses at Hierapolis, killing fifty soldiers and wounding many more (23.2.6); there is a

---

[79] *haruspicinae auguriisque intentus et ceteris, quae deorum semper fecere cultores* (21.2.4). Note the claim of continuity and, thereby, sanction for the arts mentioned here.

[80] The catalogue is sustained, including excessive (*nimia*) sacrificial victims and ceremonial rites (*immodice*), as well as a superfluity of diviners of all types, some expert and some not (22.12.7).

similar disaster at Batnae (23.2.7). On the night of the fire that destroyed the temple of Apollo in Rome, Julian has troublesome dreams in Carrhae, the site of the slaughter of Crassus' troops (23.3.3) – it was afterwards supposed that he handed an imperial robe to his cousin Procopius there (23.3.2). Julian ignores Sallustius' pleas for delay despite his warning of 'inevitable destruction' (*inreuocabile ... exitium*) without successful propitiation of the gods (23.5.4) and the corpse of an unjustly executed man is an *omen inlaetabile* (23.5.6). As if that was not enough, a captured lion is taken to be an adverse sign by the *Etrusci haruspices* but they are not heeded (23.5.10); their advice on the death by lightning of a soldier, Jovianus, is also ignored (23.5.12-14). A sacrifice to Mars goes wrong, prompting Julian to swear that he would not sacrifice to the war god again (24.6.17): hardly a wise promise for a Roman emperor abroad on campaign. The signs are bad at 24.8.4 and a final cluster of signs at 25.2.3-8 include the departure of the *Genius Publicus*. Julian appears at this point to respond appropriately, commending the future to the will of heaven *uentura decretis caelestibus commendabat* and leaves his modest bed to supplicate the gods, whereupon he sees the star of Mars; horror-struck, the emperor fears that the sign threatens his future (*horroreque perfusus est, ne ita aperte minax Martis apparuerit sidus*). Immediately in time (though not textually; a digression to validate the occurrence of such events intervenes briefly) Julian summons the *haruspices* who cite the ancient *haruspex* Tarquitius to the effect that the emperor should avoid new enterprises. Yet, astonishingly, Julian persisted in ignoring them, despite their pleas that he at least delay his departure. Ammianus attributes this to his opposition to divination (*imperatore omni uaticinandi scientia reluctante*). In practice this translated into a preference for the favourable interpretations of the philosophers.

This all stands in contrast to events before his accession at the beginning of book 21, where he was spurred on by prognostications of Constantius' death. There, Ammianus informs us that Julian took note of various signs, which he interpreted with some skill (or at least familiarity: *uaticinandi praesagia multa (quae callebat)*, 21.1.6) and (most tellingly) dreams of Constantius' death. It would be easy to see contradiction here: Julian begins by noting signs and being acquainted with their interpretation, and at the end is apparently one of those who fail to note such things. The important contrast is between acquaintance with signs (*praesagia ...quae callebat*) and knowledge of the *scientia* of divination.

Julian has consistently shown himself to be a rather haphazard interpreter and a rather poor client: at 22.1.1, he is to be found continuously consulting entrails and auguries in his search for information on Constantius' fate. Aprunculus Gallus, an orator and skilled diviner (*haruspicinae peritus*), was not initially trusted by the suspicious emperor, for fear that he was being told merely what he wished to hear: he then switched his attention away from Gallus to another sign – the fall of a soldier who, like Constantius, had 'helped him up' (in one case onto his horse and in the other to the position of Caesar). He interpreted this sign himself. Only then did he accept the expert's prediction (*iamque uaticiniis credens*, 22.1.2). It emerged that the fall was synchronous with the death of the emperor. He may have been right, but his distrust of the *haruspex* bodes ill. Julian had a strong tendency to reserve too much of the interpretative process to himself, or to trust the wrong experts (usually philosophers) as we shall see in due course. In fact, Julian's problem seems to be that he had an excessive preference for *positive* interpretations, which the philosophers were, at times, more ready to offer than the traditional experts. Early in his reign, the signs were overwhelmingly in his favour, leaving one with the impression that he was happy to abide by them. When his fortunes, and therefore the signs, change, he refuses to be brought into line by the warnings.

In other words, Julian was a *dabbler* in divination: he overrode legitimate authorities and had too much faith in his own judgement and plans; he did not respect the *scientia* involved; though he may have been correct in foreseeing Constantius' death, the fact remained that if he would not submit to the proper authorities on signs, then sooner or later he would come unstuck. His lack of judgement was thus signalled to the discerning reader in this way at the earliest opportunity. It became more obvious as time went by: he is sometimes right, or at least not conspicuously wrong, but the combination of his preference for his own inexpert and noticeably positive interpretations would prove to be his undoing: with his emphasis on the positive, Julian was an old-fashioned emperor in more ways than one. Amid such a profusion of signs that makes even Livy's prodigy lists look sparse, there is no scope for a criticism of paganism since the blame for failure is laid firmly at Julian's feet. Indeed the emperor's failure is a central player in the *validation* of the predictive arts that were so closely associated with paganism. Traditional pagan practices are repeatedly shown to be effective, especially in the hands of experts. Time and time again, even to the point of exasperation, the reader, and the emperor, are reminded of Julian's impending fate: no one could say he was not warned.

5.2.5 The construction of Roman religion
5.2.5.1 Traditional features
The aspects of religious conduct that Ammianus is urging on his audience are as reminiscent of earlier models as his *uitanda*. As if haruspicy is not vindicated by the unheeded warnings of the Persian campaign, then we have

an explicit validation of this ancient craft along with augury and divine inspiration (21.1.7-14) as well as an impressive moment of skill when Marcus, a *haruspex*, divines in Rome that the state has no emperor until the appointment of Valentinian (26.1.5); portents, prodigies and omens are likewise to be ignored at one's peril.[81] Oracles and predictions are generally reliable[82] though there is no guarantee that there will not be idiots interpreting them.[83] Sacrifice, which is discussed in more detail below, is successful if undertaken properly, as for instance at 21.5.1, when Julian gains the support of Bellona. Ironically, for an image of an ideal working religion, it is to the Persian Magi that we should turn (though there is no reason why earlier Romes, lost in the extant account, might not have performed the same function). Den Boeft (1999) 213 suggests that the idealised image of the Persian Magi is set deliberately in contrast with Julian: 'he composed a picture of what religion should be. A cult which is carried out by experts by virtue of their reliable knowledge of the divine world, a knowledge which was not spoiled by superstition.'

5.2.5.2 Knowledge and interpretation

Most emphatically, it is interpretation once again that is the cornerstone of the *cultus deorum*. We have already noted the way that Ammianus implies that Julian's knowledge was not sufficient, if he would not acknowledge the full *scientia* of the arts. Elsewhere in the text we meet both good and bad interpreters, as was true of even potentially undesirable arts like astrology. Of the innumerable examples we might note the appearance of experts

---

[81] Ammianus' terminology is somewhat different from his predecessors. For the most part he reports the sign without saying it was prodigious or portentous. He uses *prodigium* only once (30.5.15) in its strict sense; the word is used in a phrase meaning 'skilled in interpretation of prodigies' several times (18.3.1; 23.5.10; 25.10.1 and 27.3.1 (*prodigialium rerum*)); it is used metaphorically at 31.2.2 (*prodigiose*) and also possibly at 29.1.10 (*prodigiosa feritas*) unless Valens' rage is being designated a religious issue. Livy's Hannibal was already using the word metaphorically (23.45.9) and Tacitus described Vitellius as an *ostentum* (*Histories* 3.56) so there were good precedents for either. *Portentum* appears four times (19.12.20; 23.2.7; 27.3.1 and 31.1.1 (where he seems to be differentiating between *praesagium* and *portentum*)); *praesagium* and its derivatives, most frequently used of actual signs or the act of divination (14.7.7; 21.1.6; 23.3.3; 26.1.7; 25.4.17; 28.1.7 and 31.1.1) is often used with *uelut* to offer conjecture on the source of human reasoning or an assured manner: (e.g. *[ea] ueluti e praesagiis adfirmabant*, 15.3.7; 15.5.34; 20.2.4 and 20.8.20). It generally retains 'religious' overtones, as at 30.1.5 when Papa, king of the Armenians, foresees with 'human' rationality his own death at the hands of Terentius. Characters do not foresee (*praesagire*) less ponderous outcomes.
[82] E.g. 31.1.1-5, 31.14.8-9.
[83] Those men that take THEO to indicate Theodorus instead of Theodosius might so easily have avoided their costly mistake by continuing their investigation (29.1.32). The idiocy of the *uulgus*, previously towards the excessive designation of events as prodigial, is now caricatured at the opposite extreme; Ammianus castigates their *scepticism* about predictions (21.1.13), though this does not justify any hypotheses about a change in popular beliefs. The historians will always find a target to act as a straw man.

in particular disciplines. At 18.3.1 we meet *gnari prodigiorum*; at 22.1.1 Aprunculus Gallus is *inspectu iecoris . . . praedoctus* and *haruspicinae peritus*; after an earthquake at 23.1.7, *horum periti* warn Julian about his Persian campaign and we hear of *gnari rerum prodigialium* at 25.10.1. Not all who claimed such skills are credited; many *ignari* came out of the woodwork under Julian along with genuine experts (*iuxta imperitus et docilis*), arousing the historian's indignation (22.12.7). Divination did not have a captive audience: there is a eloquent refutation of those who reject prophecy at 21.1.13-4, with Cicero invoked as an extra authority:

> It is enough to reply that even a grammarian sometimes speaks inappropriately, that a musician is sometimes out of tune and a medical man ignorant of a remedy, but we have not abandoned grammar, music and medicine because of it. Cicero, among his other notable sayings, tells us: 'The gods give us signs of future events. If we go wrong about them it is not divinity but men's interpretation that is at fault.'[84]

Both Livy and Tacitus, closely focussed on the city of Rome, presented the collegiate priests as religious experts: but with the weakened focus on Rome and more cosmopolitan approach to knowledge adopted by Ammianus, expertise is more diverse. These experts are therefore not generally validated by any institutional connections, yet their status is implied in good historiographical manner: not only are their verdicts reliable, but also, in common with Livy and Tacitus, they are usually in the anonymous plural.[85] Rike's synthesis might equally apply to the priests in Livy's and Tacitus' accounts: 'the faceless preservers of the *doctrinae genus leue* can scarcely be distinguished from their books of ritual. Quietly they wait to be consulted; rooted to their shrines and secretive, they hold unchanged those divine *res gestae* embodied in ceremony that lay at the source of history and religion' (Rike (1987) 71). Their authority is presumed rather than established:[86] when the *haruspices* are forced by Julian's obstinacy to reveal the

---

[84] *On The Nature of the Gods* 2.4.12 (Lucilius speaking): *sufficiet dici, quod et grammaticus locutus interdum est barbare, et absurde cecinit musicus, et ignorauit remedium medicus. Set non ideo nec grammatica nec musica nec medicina subsistit. unde praeclare hoc quoque ut alia Tullius: 'signa ostenduntur' ait 'a dis rerum futurarum. in his siqui errauerit, non deorum natura, sed hominum coniectura peccauit.'*

[85] There are two possible exceptions, but we do not know if the men in question were actually priests: Aprunculus Gallus is named but is apparently an orator first and foremost (*haruspicinae peritus*, *Aprunculus Gallus orator*, 22.1.2) while Marcus, the *haruspex* who divined that there was no emperor before the appointment of Valentinian, is apparently a clear exception (26.1.5).

[86] Though they are criticised (just) once. The priests of republican Rome were irresponsible with the calendar (26.1.12).

contents of their books (23.5.10 and again at 25.2.7) it underlines the emperor's foolishness in the face of such a mighty authority – their honesty and integrity are beyond question. We have seen that Ammianus is dubious about Julian's assumption of the role of the priests in carrying the *sacra* in Antioch (22.14.3). The emperor's religious charisma at the expense of priests is never to Ammianus' liking – the historian's position may be comparable to that adopted towards Scipio by Livy: an agent's activities are constantly measured against what was appropriate for one of his position. Julian took it upon himself to interpret signs all too often, but he was not the only one: the greatest usurpation of authority proper to the priests in Ammianus' account came from the philosophers.

5.2.5.3 Philosophy in the Res Gestae

Broadly speaking, there are three philosophical narrators or agents in Ammianus' text: Ammianus himself ventures to offer us various syntheses;[87] then there are individual men, whether they are agents in the text or men known through their writings; and finally the philosophers who accompanied and advised Julian. The last group were repeatedly and blatantly wrong in their advice on religious matters.[88] As we shall see, priestly knowledge is reliably promoted above that of philosophy.[89] But if he reserves the role of religious interpretation for the priests, Ammianus does not leave philosophers with no role whatsoever. A more suitable model is exemplified by characters such as Demetrius Cythras who had propitiated the god Besa at Abydus without any ulterior motive for many years (19.12.12). Several

---

[87] Which have not been favourably received: see e.g. Matthews (1989) 428–431, who is typical in trying to mix and match Neoplatonic and Stoic ideas before arguing that Ammianus had not understood them perfectly; Camus (1967) 197; even Harrison (1999), who is generally more sympathetic, casts various aspersions (e.g. 'half-digested or inconsistent', 180). Rike (1987) 3–4 has the last word (and fuller references): 'how did Ammianus rank as a Plotinus, Porphyry, or Iamblichus? ... [being] unable to stand such comparison – unless some day the *Enneads* should be tested for its historiographical quality – Ammianus was marked as "no philosopher".' This argument pre-empts many of Matthews' complaints. On Neoplatonic ideas in Ammianus, see Szidat (1982). Barnes (1998) 76–78 charts his reading of and allusions to Plotinus, and suggests an earlier date (340s or 350s) than is usually accepted (380s) for the historian's reading of Plotinus.

[88] Ammianus is notoriously explicit about this, e.g. at 23.5.11, where the advice of the *haruspices* is rejected in favour of the philosophers *quorum reuerenda tunc erat auctoritas, errantium subinde, et in parum cognitis perseuerantium diu.*

[89] Rike (1987) 73, n.20, comments that in the (extant) *Res Gestae*, only one philosopher makes a prediction, when Maximus predicted death for those inquiring into the name of Valens' successor at 29.1.42. But his comment that 'it must be significant that of all the philosophers mentioned by Ammianus, only Maximus gives an oracle' is overstated, despite Ammianus' use of *praedico.* Maximus, a man of undoubted learning (*uir ingenti nomine doctrinarum*, 29.1.42) hardly had his work cut out in making such a prediction, even if it was by divinatory means (something we cannot tell for certain). Either way, he was issuing a warning and a refusal to be involved more than he was delivering an oracle. For a clear example of 'prophecy' (*praesagio*) by 'human' foresight see 30.1.5.

philosophers are exemplary for facing death at the hands of a tyrant[90] but they are not restricted to laughing at torture and burning.[91] Philosophers are experts in their own domains as the numerous citations of Plato indicate.[92] But their knowledge of 'natural science' (for want of a better phrase)[93] is strictly subordinated in authority to the traditional lore of the priests. Though he uses their material, the historian does not enter into any discussion of one type of knowledge over the other, or question the religious in the light of the 'scientific'.

In dealing with earthquakes, Ammianus underscores the difficulties of establishing the identity of the god responsible before embarking on an excursus, predominantly informed by philosophy, about the process by which they occur, and this example can serve as a template for the relative location of different knowledge-systems in the *Res Gestae*. After noting the difficulties of accounting for earthquakes, which had left most philosophers in *aporia* at 17.7.9-10, the priests' evidence is adduced to underline that there are no easy answers – a differentiation of interpretative authority which will become increasingly familiar.[94] The pontifical books do not name a specific deity in connection with earthquakes, in case ritual error should occur in following their stipulations. Thus each case had to be taken on its own merits.[95] Indeed, Ammianus ends his general aetiology with the conclusion, appropriated from Anaximander, that water is a key factor. Thus poets and theologians called Neptune *Ennosigaeos* and *Sisichthon*.[96]

By the enclosure of the philosophical material with different religious interpretations, religious understanding is privileged and unquestioned; even the great Anaximander is, at best, catching up with the religious tradition. In

---

[90] E.g. the young Simonides who kept the secret of the successor of Valens (29.1.37-38).
[91] Rike (1987) 69–86 has an extensive discussion of the appropriate role of the philosopher, drawing more fully on Ammianus and also many other relevant texts that inform the historian's discussion. The discussion here is limited to aspects of knowledge and interpretation. For a broader analysis of the role of philosophers at this period see Brown (1992) esp. 58–70.
[92] 16.5.10, 22.16.22, 25.4.2, 30.4.3 and 30.4.5; cited with the epithet *opinionum insignium amplissimus* at 23.6.32; we also find cited, amongst others, Epicurus (30.4.3); Heraclitus (21.16.14); Anaximander (17.7.12) and Aristotle (17.7.11, 18.3.7, 21.1.12, 27.4.8 *et al.*).
[93] The quotation marks represent my doubts about the habitual tendency of modern scholars to juxtapose 'science' exclusively against 'religion' rather than any superiority complex about the advantages or superiority of modern over ancient science (if there was such a thing) or philosophy.
[94] The chief source for Ammianus' information seems to be Aulus Gellius' *Attic Nights* 2.28 (den Hengst (1992)).
[95] *obseruantibus sacerdotiis caute, ne alio deo pro alio nominato, cum qui eorum terram concutiat, sit in abstruso, piacula committantur*, 17.7.10. Rike (1987) 36, n.114 rightly criticises Wardman (1982) 160 for his assertion that 'the older pagan books were no better than the new; one could not have much confidence in the lore of the pontifical books when they declined to say anything about earthquakes for fear of naming the wrong god'.
[96] 17.7.12. Possibly referring to Juvenal 10.182 and Aulus Gellius 2.28.1.

addition, we should note the easy coexistence of the different levels of explanation. The 'natural science' is effectively a description of 'how' earthquakes happen while the references to the priests and the *poetae ueteres et theologi* underscore the utility of religious responses (dealing with the question 'why?').[97] It might be claimed that Ammianus is claiming, through the authority of Anaximander, to know what the pontifical priests did not, but that is by no means the only interpretation available. *Function* is a crucial consideration here. Without diminishing the importance of a philosopher's reputation, Anaximander's mistakes would not have such a profound impact as any mistake made by the *pontifices*. They too were undeniably privy to the knowledge of the *poetae ueteres et theologi* but respected the dangers of prescribing uniformly for such a vexatious scenario. Decisions were better taken at the time, taking into account other evidence. Their reticence does not indicate ignorance, but laudable caution.[98] In addition, the now-familiar anonymity of priests and the respect for their lore is in marked contrast with the knowledge of specific and named philosophers, who must each prove his worth.[99]

Though he avails himself of every possible source of information, Ammianus consistently prioritises ritual knowledge for practical (including ritual) purposes. One example shows this vividly: when the soldier Jovianus is struck by lightning with his two horses, the *haruspices* summoned by Julian offer that the expedition is emphatically forbidden by the sign because a man of lofty name was struck along with his war-horses. This seems perfectly traditional: indeed they cite the books on lightning to say that the location of such an event should not be looked upon or trodden on, thus anchoring their interpretation in the known, the sanctioned traditions.

The philosophers, on the other hand, maintained that the brilliance of the sacred fire which suddenly appeared was not significant: 'it was merely the course of a stronger mass of air sent downwards from the aether by some force; if it did constitute a sign, it foretold an increase in renown for

---

[97] A similar pattern should be assumed for other such excursuses, even where the divine is not mentioned; e.g. the discussion of plague at Amida at 19.4.1-8; the explanation for shooting stars (unless comets are being described) does not preclude the religious meaning of the sign at 25.2.5. Comets are treated as both religious in significance and susceptible to 'rational' inquiry in natural terms at 25.10.1-3, judging from the fact that the excursus comes at the end of a prodigy list. 'Scientific' explanations never overlap with or exclude divine interpretation; Ammianus is quite capable of criticism, though it is usually of the failure to see divine agency, e.g. at 21.1.13.

[98] Having said that, the usual priests to deal with earthquakes in Livy are the *duumuiri* or *decemuiri* (3.10.6, 4.21.5 and 34.55.1 (after the failure of the expiations presumably prescribed by the *pontifices*, and there we find that a general supplication was ordered)). The instauration of the Roman Games after an earthquake (amongst other prodigies) at 40.59.8 was, however, probably due to the advice of the *pontifices*.

[99] So too Rike (1987) 72–75.

the emperor, as he was beginning a glorious enterprise, since it was common knowledge that flames, by their very nature, travel upwards without
opposition.' To a seasoned interpreter, these reasons might well explain the
physical appearance of the lightning but the signification must have seemed
ludicrous: Rome, as Livy and Tacitus record, had been expiating lightning
strikes on significant places for centuries. To follow such 'clever' and amateurish interpretations in the face of conflicting expert opinion and in such
a situation was even more ridiculous. Julian's preference for the positive
interpretation is a sad indictment of his attitude to divination.

Lest this discussion should appear to create a rigid demarcation between
priestly and philosophical knowledge, we must remember that Cicero was
quoted on interpretation at 21.1.14; no example better underscores the danger of making too firm a distinction between 'philosophers' and others,
since he is also cited as a critic of philosophers (22.7.3-4). In addition, we
should note that Pythagoras gained his insights from the (authoritatively
anonymous) Egyptian priests (22.16.19f.). The philosopher Maximus was
famed for his understanding of religious procedures, though we do not know
it from Ammianus.[100] Ammianus's silence ensures that there is no danger
of a philosopher being mistaken for a *gnarus prodigiorum*.

But if the teachings of philosophers are of value, theirs is a tradition that
will inevitably be erratic. Even if Anaxagoras predicted a rain of stones
and an earthquake (22.16.22) his charismatic abilities could not be reproduced; and a tradition that dies with its founder has no future use for
Rome's religion. The founders of the more durable religious *doctrinae*, like
Tages, founder of the haruspical art (21.1.10), who reportedly rose up out of
the earth in Etruria, contributed far more than any philosopher. 'A threshold exists beyond which even philosophers will become *perseverantes in
parum cognitis*. For Ammianus, it is the function of the priest to conserve
ritual ... while the philosopher is to absorb learning from every source'
(Rike (1987) 75). Whatever their education, philosophers should know their
limits.[101]

5.2.5.4 Poets

The complex of religious knowledge and individuals is not limited to anonymous seers and philosophers. There is a third group, the poets. Ammianus names not only Virgil and Homer, but also, rather surprisingly, the
likes of Menander, and on issues of the most fundamental religious im-

---

[100] Though he is praised for his learning at 29.1.42, it is Eunapius, not Ammianus, who indicates
that he excelled in *religious* interpretation (*Vitae Sophistarum* 477–478, 480, 501).
[101] See Rike (1987) 85–86 for elaboration on this in the political arena.

port. The comic poet is an authority for the existence of the *genius* attached to each individual at birth. Homer is understood to have spoken on the same topic when he portrayed gods fighting alongside men (21.14.5) and we have already noted that the *ueteres poetae* called Neptune *Ennosigaeos et Sisichthon* (17.7.12).[102] In short, the historian recognises that the poets spoke in a particular idiom.[103] The recognition of a different order of knowledge and expression does not permit us to dismiss these moments as meaningless ornament. Like the teachings of philosophy, they have their place in the constellation of religious knowledges.

Distinct in function, if not necessarily in person, from the poets and philosophers are the anonymous *theologi*; the phrase *ueteres poetae et theologi* occurs at 17.7.12, implying a distinction. But it may be hendiadys; poets *are theologi*. On the other hand, much of what the *theologi* have to say sounds equally philosophical.[104] Bearing in mind Ammianus' genre-conscious use of poets elsewhere for information, the answer is likely to be that his information is derived at least in part from philosophical commentaries on poetry (on which see Lamberton (1986)); either way, a functional distinction is the only one available to us. Though the term appears only five times, their evidence is as sure as that of the priests. At 14.11.25, the *theologi ueteres*, critically to the coherence of Ammianus' excursus, regard[105] Adrastia (Nemesis) as the daughter of Justice; at 16.5.5, the *theologicae doctrinae* record[106] that Mercury is the *mundi uelociorem sensum esse motum mentium suscitantem*. At 17.7.12, as we have seen, the *ueteres poetae* and the *theologi* join forces in linking Neptune with earthquakes; at 21.1.8 Themis is said (*dicitur*) to be in charge (*praeesse*) of prophecies;[107] the *theologi ueteres* 'give her a share' (*collocarunt*) in the bed and throne of Jupiter, the *uigor uiuificus*. Finally the *theologi* are in agreement with Menander and Homer at 21.14.3 in saying (*ferunt*) that each man is allotted a *genius* at birth.

---

[102] The poet Philoxenus provides a surprisingly philosophical-style *exemplum* in the face of the threats from Dionysius, upset that the poet alone refused to praise the tyrant's verses (15.5.37).

[103] Of Homer, Ammianus says *fabulatur inflatius* 22.16.10; cf. 23.6.53 *ut Homerus fabulosius canit.* Iris is introduced in connection with the rainbow (20.11.26-30) in a way that suggests the recognition of a different idiom rather than a different 'truth'. Compare the ending of Livy's prologue with his mention of *bonis . . . ominibus uotisque et precationibus deorum dearumque, si, ut poetis, nobis quoque mos esset, libentius inciperemus.*

[104] See Barnes (1998) 167 for good reason to think that Ammianus read Porphyry, and that the philosopher is a source for the crucial passage at 21.1.8; the ideas there are attributed to *theologi ueteres.*

[105] *fingentes*: 'fashion'? 'designate'? 'construct'? 'tell a Platonic mythos'?

[106] *prodidere*: 'transmits'? 'asserts'? 'teaches'? 'informs'?

[107] We should not see here a sceptical distancing, but rather an appeal to unquestioned expertise.

The poets, in common with so many venerated writers of Ammianus' antiquity, are men of profound knowledge, transmitting the heritage and preserving the knowledge of the past. The cultured man of educated knowledge in Ammianus' world would do well to be conversant with their insights. Yet even these great men do not represent the apex of religious knowledge: the key authority on religion in Ammianus is, consistently with our previous subjects, the author himself. Not only is he highly selective in using what must have been a vast amount of potentially relevant literature, he frequently offers his own conclusions without the requirement for any secondary authority; thus he simply informs us that the fates blind those whose death is approaching[108] and in his own person he frequently makes a diagnosis that depends on the divine where it might just as easily have been omitted, as it might indeed have been by our earlier writers.[109] The excursuses typically cite his various authorities to establish Ammianus' position; *they* are subject to *him*.[110] We might recall that, rather like Livy, Ammianus has one single criticism for his otherwise exemplary priests (26.1.12) – the historian's authority is thus established by a method either borrowed or duplicated for the same reasons: tasteful hegemony. It is the same in his approach to knowledge in general.

5.2.5.5 Ammianus peritus omnium

There is one aspect of Ammianus' presentation – and this most emphatically applies to the religious – that we must problematise, somewhat reluctantly after the difficulties encountered with Livy and Tacitus, and that is the apparent *transparency* of much of the religious material. A number of such instances have already been mentioned, such as the explicit isolation of error in interpretation – with even greater serendipity, by reference to Cicero, who predates all three of our historians; the explicit difficulties of the *pontifices* regarding the naming of specific deities for ritual purposes is another example. The list continues: 'higher levels' of reasoning are far more transparent in such excursuses as the one dealing with divination. Nowhere in Livy or Tacitus do we read anything resembling the clear statement that birds do not foretell the future because of any knowledge on their part but because the god (*deus*) directs their flight in such a way as to reveal *futura*; the same logic presumably applies to entrails and other similar disciplines that follow (21.1.8-14). The inference that the divine realm was seen as fundamentally benign, so speculative and

---

[108] *utque solent manum iniectantibus fatis hebetari sensus hominum et obtundi* (14.11.12).

[109] E.g. *uigilauit utrubique superni numinis aequitas* (14.11.24); many of Jovian's troops survive *fauore superi numinis* (25.8.3) *et al.*

[110] As we will find at 14.11.25 in the excursus on justice.

deductive from the religion of Livy, is a bald statement in Ammianus – the fundamental benevolence of the divine is suggested as a foundation for the science of divination, unless it is the divine response to the piety of men (i.e. the opposite end of the same stick) at 21.1.9.[111]

Despite these similarities, we should remember that religious knowledge in its various forms and import was constantly redeployed. To compare achronologically would be to assume a static 'canon'. The abundance, even superfluity, of explicit religious dialectic in our later author should not be thoughtlessly plundered to 'prove' arguments located primarily in earlier periods. Rather the foregrounding of what was previously implicit should be problematised. As a feature, it is central to Ammianus' programme. In Livy and Tacitus, the deployment and exemplification of knowledge and expertise formed part of their broader exemplary programme. Livy's 'there you go' 'milky fullness'[112] was as deliberate as Tacitus' 'you should know better' pithiness. Neither, however, went to the lengths that their successor did to explain religious matters. This merits some comment.

One highly plausible factor in the degree of explicit explanation of religious material is linked to the times in which Ammianus wrote. The literary dialectic of Christianity with paganism was now an established facet of educated writing, though it was not always so restrained. Is Ammianus then taking the opportunity to answer (or even, to educate) Christian critics in such moments as his validation of pagan prophetic practices? While this cannot be ignored, neither can it be the single basis of our answer. It is not just religious interpretation that has moved to the forefront. The previously subtle processes of exemplification have likewise become explicit, to the extent that Blockley (1975), failing perhaps to appreciate the care with which the earlier historians wove their *exempla* into their accounts, can say 'the only surviving historian who makes large-scale use of *exempla* is Ammianus' (163). The difference is not particularly increased *use* of *exempla*; on the readings outlined here it would be impossible to exclude any individual or moment from a list. But in the *Res Gestae*, the appeals to imitate and avoid are repeated and explicit statements, not occasionally generalised comments and ubiquitous assumptions.

From another angle we can see a similar change. In contrast to the rarity of Livy's or Tacitus' naming of another historian (and then usually to criticise or compare) Ammianus will refer, almost needlessly, to a predecessor such as the *auctor amplissimus* Thucydides (23.6.75; he is also mentioned

---

[111] *amat enim benignitas numinis, seu quod merentur homines, seu quod tangitur eorum affectione, his quoque artibus prodere quae impendent.*
[112] Quintilian's phrase: X.i.32 speaks of Livy's *lactea ubertas*.

at 19.4.4).[113] So when religious material is foregrounded, it is not so much that the later age is 'more superstitious', as is often said, since foregrounding of *all kinds* of previously interwoven material and assumptions is now almost a rule; we are dealing with a broader shift in the writer's relationship with traditions of all types. Where his predecessors avoided tastelessly informing the audience of what they surely knew, much of Ammianus' information borders on the superfluous. Though we might reasonably speculate that some of it was less well known,[114] much of the information in the forefront was surely familiar to his audience. It is doubtful whether such asides as *[Apollo] qui sol aestimatur* (19.4.3) were part of a dialectic – it was surely common knowledge, even beyond an educated audience. We should consider that the extensive information is part of Ammianus' proof of his worth. It is doubtful whether, in a society that was far more fragmented geographically and religiously, even a local born-and-bred Roman could have relied on the depth of consensus on religion that our earlier historians assumed without question.

One potential source for this change of style is Ammianus' dual tradition. The presentation of information has much in common with Herodotus,[115] and the structure of his account may owe its basis to Thucydides,[116] though Ammianus has also synthesised two Latin historiographical genres, namely the chronological approach of annalistic history and biographical assessment. But this is not the 'answer': Ammianus is not simply jumping through academic hoops to please the *literati*, although it does demonstrate his worthiness to join the historical tradition. Just as Livy and Tacitus had purpose in their particular version of historiographical traditions, so too did Ammianus. Traditions of the genre were not preserved for empty reasons. The particular pattern of deployment serves a further and altogether deliberate purpose, that of education.

It has often been remarked that Ammianus was a 'snob';[117] that is, he showed a marked preference for those with a traditional education.[118] Though anyone exhibiting such a distinct preference in this day and age

---

[113] It is worth noting that in the extant text, the most recent named author is Virgil: antiquity seems to invite explicit citation.

[114] For instance, the details of Aristotle's safeguards for interpretation of dreams at 21.1.12 or Anaximander's theories about earthquakes and water (17.7.12). Perhaps they *were* well known but it seems reasonable to assume that some of the extensive information, whether philosophical, geographical or historical, was more or less obscure while much of it was part of everyday knowledge. The same dilemma is noted by Blockley (1975) 164 n.50.

[115] E.g. Matthews (1989) 14; Sabbah (1978) 66–67.

[116] Barnes (1990) 68–70, though the broad similarity is not particularly conclusive.

[117] Alfödi (1952) 101–102 and 121f. See now also Henck (2000) 183.

[118] E.g. 21.10.8; 29.1.11; 30.4.2 and 31.14.8: Julian is frequently praised for his education (15.8.10 (by Constantius); 16.5.6-7; 25.2.3 and 29.1.42); Jovian on the other hand and for example is

could rightly be called a snob, we should be more hesitant about judging Ammianus by the same criteria. Education was more than a gloss: it underpinned the fabric of contemporary society:

> Education ... provided the basis for dealing with a grimmer aspect of late Roman politics – with the increased impingement of official violence, directed against members of the upper class. The ideals associated with *paideia* were invoked, with great urgency, to check such violence ... Formalized speech was held to be, in itself, a form of self-control ... It was a fragile speck of order in a violent and discordant world.[119]

Ammianus' criticisms of a lack of education are typically linked to, at best, incompetence and, at worst, cruelty.[120] Valens was ignorant, while Julian was not; the former held numerous iniquitous trials, the latter was merely censured for the occasional lapse – and that in connection with education.[121] Ammianus' lament at 29.2.18 clearly indicates the power of education, where he wishes that Valens might have known better:

> Noble system of knowledge, bestowed on the fortunate by a divine gift, you who have often improved even flawed characters! How much you would have put right in those times, if it had been permitted that Valens should have understood something that the wise say, that power is nothing other than concern for the well-being of others, and that it is the mark of a good ruler to restrict his power and limit the desire for all things, and that (as the dictator Julius Caesar used to say) the memory of cruel deeds makes for a bad store of memories for one's old age ... and not to act with undue haste when an action cannot be undone.[122]

---

mediocriter eruditus (25.10.15) though Ammianus does also acknowledge that he is *magisque beniuolus et perpensius*.

[119] Brown (1992) 48. See his chapter 2 *passim*. Though he draws most heavily on Libanius and sparingly on Ammianus, the overall picture fits very well with our historian. Compare the formulation of Kaster (1988) 27 (in a broader context): '*doctrina* presumed *mores*'.

[120] Blockley 158–159, with the neat quote 'it is quite surprising how many Imperial and other crimes are sins of ignorance' from T. R. Glover, *Life and Letters in the Fourth Century*, Cambridge 1901.

[121] Julian's ban on Christians teaching rhetoric and grammar is something that Ammianus would prefer to be forgotten, though he preserves its memory (22.10.6-7); also noted at 25.5.20.

[122] *O praeclara informatio doctrinarum munere caelesti indulta felicibus, quae uel uitiosas naturas saepe excoluisti! quanta in illa caligine temporum correxisses, si Valenti scire per te licuisset nihil aliud esse imperium, ut sapientes definiunt, nisi curam salutis aliena, bonique esse moderatoris restringere potestatem, resistere cupiditati omnium rerum et, ut Caesar dictator aiebat, miserum esse instrumentum senectuti recordationem crudelitatis ... nec praecipiti studio, ubi inreuocabile factum est, agitari.*

Even a *uitiosa natura* might be improved by the *praeclara informatio doctrinarum*. Constantius, who supposedly failed to grasp his education,[123] was at least *doctrinarum diligens affectator* (21.16.4) and this is linked to a policy of greater clemency.[124] Education was, for Ammianus, a vital part of society and civilisation in a world where court cases could depend on the nod of a single man.[125] If that man was educated by *sapientes*, which now includes Ammianus himself, the court and the empire might be a safer place.

Ammianus' 'snobbery' is therefore part and parcel of an urgent appeal on which lives might well depend; his account exemplifies and contributes to the creation of the ideal Greco-Roman aristocrat, learned, even steeped, in the literary tradition that had worked so hard for so long to define civilisation. Thus while it is true that he is working to gain the acceptance of the learned men of his audience, his method is to *be* one of them and, in this, his credentials are impeccable.[126]

Ammianus' identity is more than a compromise of various factors: he encompasses and synthesises both Greek and Latin traditions. More specifically it is, like his material, his historiography and his empire, cosmopolitan. The 'modest' statement that he might have no audience at all (31.5.10) is tantamount to a refusal to limit his audience; the similar statement directed specifically at his having a foreign (*peregrini*, 14.6.2) audience, while it is a word that typically refers to foreigners in Rome,[127] equally refuses to bar other cultures than Greek and Roman from his audience.

Some cultures have, of course, failed to become civilised (e.g. the Quadi) and it is hard to imagine the Huns reading Ammianus' history and immediately changing their ways. But while the historian cannot guarantee his reception, he considers that his method is the best way forward, to continue the encoding of cultural knowledge in literature. There is always the possibility of civilisation emerging from barbarity and Ammianus' designated medium for this process is education, works such as his own that not only cap the Greco-Roman literary traditions but synthesise and preserve it. We should seriously consider the possibility that the ambition of the *Res*

---

[123] Ammianus is far from fair in this respect according to Henck (2001).
[124] E.g. Valentinian says of Gratian that, once educated, he *librabit suffragiis puris merita recte secusue factorum* (27.6.9). Of course Ammianus interpreted his material in the light of this assumption; it was hardly something that he had 'discovered' from his researches.
[125] As the wise Simonides realised (29.1.37).
[126] Cf. the conclusion of Marincola (1997) 257: 'as a Greek, he is appealing to the tradition of inquiry and learning that distinguishes his work from its competitors, and (more importantly) that places him as a direct line with history's founders and best practitioners, to whom his work, like that of all the great historians, may be seen as both homage and challenge'.
[127] Sabbah (1978) 508 n.6.

Gestae in its civilising mission knew no bounds. The compromise was there for other 'subcultures', less familiar with Rome's grand history and ways, to imitate as a template for a unified and *civilised* Roman empire. The explicit religious dialogue may owe much to this intention.

Nonetheless the *Res Gestae* are not simply an unwieldy collection of literary gems. Even in his learned discourse Ammianus remains true, in his religion, to the tradition whereby the unstated requirements are of interpretation and practical usage. We will find him, like his predecessors, most selectively concerned with responsibility. In addition, the cosmopolitan nature of the *Res Gestae* also helps to make a great deal of sense of the religious material not yet scrutinised. The place in the overall religious scheme of the *numen*; the deployment of *fortuna* and *fatum*; and his particular concern with Justice.

5.3 The fundamentals of Ammianus' Roman religion

5.3.1 *Numen*

Ammianus uses *numen* fifty-six times in the extant *Res Gestae*, thirty-one times in the singular. Though it can mean 'a (particular) god' (e.g. Aesculapius, 22.14.7), or can, in the plural, replace the traditional *di* (e.g. *cultus numinum* 22.5.1 and 25.4.20 or the *pax numinum* at 23.5.4), more often it is used in a sense that has led to discussions of 'neutral monotheism'. The *numen* is *supernum*,[128] *summum*,[129] *sempiternum*,[130] *caeleste*,[131] *superum*,[132] *diuinum*,[133] *perpetuum*[134] and *magnum*.[135] We also meet an anonymous *deus* at 21.1.9 and 24.1.1 and the *caelestis deus* at 24.1.12 and 25.75 (*aeternum dei caelestis numen*). We should, however, consider whether the reports of Ammianus' 'monotheism' have been exaggerated. As Harrison (2000) 181 remarks, 'Ammianus' manner of switching from speaking of a vague, depersonalised divinity or *numen* to a polytheistic world of more clearly individuated deities is something that, far from revealing him as a closet monotheist, he has in common with any number of ancient writers.'[136] For Rike, laudably retaining a focus on cult practice rather than 'theory', 'if someone had asked the historian where specifically he should go to worship

---

[128] 14.11.24, 15.2.8 and 16.12.62.
[129] 15.8.9, 17.7.3, 21.13.14 and 26.6.9.
[130] 17.13.28, 23.5.19 and 31.10.18.
[131] 19.1.14, 26.1.5, 27.6.8 and 31.16.4.
[132] 16.12.18 (in the speech of a standard-bearer) and 25.8.3.
[133] 26.1.14.
[134] 27.3.15 and 29.2.20 (but probably of *Iustitia* in this example).
[135] 29.5.40.
[136] Harrison (1999) 181, citing Feeney (1998) 91.

Numen, Ammianus would most probably have responded by pointing to a temple of Jupiter or Zeus ... his terms *numen* and *deus* will subsequently stand best as innocuous synonyms courteously offered before a mixed audience of pagans and Christians' (Rike (1987) 31–4). This has certainly been the interpretation given in other instances of 'studied neutrality' and has a lot to commend it. The Christian god is, after all, referred to as *numen* (21.2.5). We can take the discussion further, beyond the scope of Rike's formulation, which broadly assimilates Ammianus to a more traditional model.

It has been suggested that the use of *numen* is one way of avoiding conflict with Christianity, an ongoing concern for many writers,[137] but we cannot ignore the fact that the phenomenon appears from the very beginnings of ancient historiography: Herodotus' use of *ho theos* and *to theion* has also led to his being described as a monotheist,[138] long before there were Christians to offend. Ammianus might just as well have been respecting the distinctive local names of gods by his use of a generic term.[139]

Of course, Herodotus' terminology may simply have been adapted gratefully for a contingency he would almost certainly never have envisaged and irrespective of *his* intentions. Yet once again we are in danger of floundering among partial answers: Ammianus is demonstrably so much more than the sum of his numerous parts. He does not avoid offence when he exhibits cutting sarcasm or utter astonishment in connection with the failure of Christian rites to protect the empire.[140] Politeness may not exhaust the deployment of *numen*. A satisfactory answer is within a constellation of considerations, a shrewd deployment of a traditional motif that simultaneously embraces a whole range of factors.

One issue that emerges from the diachronic comparison is that Ammianus lacks a particularly useful method of indicating the mood of the gods towards Rome; where Livy typically deployed prodigies and their expiation (or not), temple dedications and other acts of piety, Ammianus cannot. How many temples were dedicated or supplications held under a Christian emperor? Tacitus also used prodigies and religious signs, but relied for the most part on the reader's interpretation – though he was forced to offer divine explanations for the rise of Sejanus (*Annals* 4.1.2), and reassured the reader of divine aid in the *Histories* (*after* the restoration of the temple: *nec sine ope diuina*, 4.78.2). Both wrote for what was a narrow audience

---

[137] See e.g. Liebeschuetz (1981) 396–398 on panegyric and Symmachus' 'neutral monotheism'.

[138] See Harrison (2000) 179–181 on this, and issues pertinent to the following argument.

[139] So Hunt (1985) 191.

[140] On Sabinianus, and his predilection for martyr shrines see 18.7.7; I cannot agree with Hunt (1985) 195 that Ammianus is objecting to Sabinianus' succession to the post held by Ursinicus; the mockery is specifically religious.

in comparison with that of Ammianus; for the most part they looked in towards Rome (admittedly a Rome set implicitly within its oldest provinces) reinforcing rather than introducing specific modes of religious thought and analysis. Besides, Tacitus wrote chiefly of the wrath of the gods, while Ammianus' Rome knows more successes. Ammianus, with a far wider and decentralised scope, lacks the vehicles of regular expiation to indicate the *pax deum.*

Ammianus had to find alternatives if he was to avoid bald statements: one such vehicle is the use of suitable 'digressions', such as the appearance of a rainbow, to indicate future events (i.e. the mood of the gods)[141] but, even though they amount to a relatively high proportion of his text, to use digressions for every such moment would not be workable. Though he still finds abundant opportunity for warnings of divine wrath, he is also regularly at pains, as we have seen, to give us a fuller explanation than his predecessors would have found tasteful.[142] Thus we are frequently told of divine intervention – where once we would have been expected to understand this from other signifiers – by reference to the *numen: aderatque propitiati numinis arbitrium clemens* (16.12.52); *quibus ita fauore superni numinis terminatis* (16.12.62) (both for Julian); at 19.1.4 the *caeleste numen* misled Sapor, to Rome's advantage; at 19.10.4, the prayers of Tertullus to Castor and Pollux at Ostia are answered *diuini arbitrio numinis* and there are many other examples throughout the text.[143] If such references were absent from the text, would we still talk so easily of Ammianus' monotheism? If *numen*, like *ho theos* in Herodotus, is simply a term for 'the divine', we should be more wary.

Indeed we should not automatically assume that *numen*, even when described as *supernum* or *summum* is any one specific god at all, whether Jupiter or a Neoplatonic One. Often *numen* simply indicates

---

[141] Ammianus deliberately organises his account to accommodate his excursuses (rather than simply going off at a tangent when relevant material cropped up): '[i]n a world that is understood to be full of signs waiting to be interpreted, a deep significance is attributed to these impressive phenomena ... Ammianus, it is true, never spoils the effect of his digressions by telling us in as many words the meaning of these ominous events, but it is the narrative context that puts them in perspective ... apart from their function in structuring the narrative, they serve as signals or echoes on a superhuman level of the actions of his *dramatis personae*' (den Hengst (1992) 46). Thus the historian's deployment is strikingly reminiscent of his (Latin) predecessors.

[142] It is hard to imagine either author recording the *haruspices* pointing to their books in public exasperation as Ammianus' do twice (23.5.10 and 25.2.7) or going to such explicit lengths to validate divination.

[143] Jovian's troops, including Ammianus, are saved by the *aeternum dei caelestis numen* at 25.7.5 and by the *fauor superi numinis* at 25.8.3; Valentinian is elected *numinis adspiratione caelestis* at 26.1.5; 26.1.14 sees the calendar fixed as bisextile *adiumento numinis diuini* and at 29.6.7 the daughter of Constantius was saved by the *fauor propitii numinis* in the form of Messalla's intervention. Gratian conquers the Lentensian Alamanni *sempiterni numinis nutu* (31.10.18).

'the power of the divine realm', as in the phrase *aeternum dei caelestis numen* at 25.7.5. If the appeal of Tertullus to Castor and Pollux invoked the *arbitrium diuini numinis*, should we not consider that *numen*
owes its presence to the desire on Ammianus' part to avoid saying that
these specific gods acted, while still asserting that the abrupt change in
weather was due to divine intervention – a feature typical of historiographical proprieties? In other words, Ammianus is as loath as his predecessors had been to state baldly that a particular god had acted. Where he does,
it is, as before, based on extraordinary evidence and hedged with doubts and
proofs.[144]

Though he has gone further than Livy or Tacitus ever did in explicitly
noting divine orchestration, he has not entirely abandoned their caution
against naming gods, itself as much a 'religious' matter as it is 'literary'.
Even when he adds an epithet, it may be purely descriptive of the divine
realm in its exalted status vis-à-vis the human realm: *caelestis*, *diuinus* (both
of which are somewhat pleonastic and hardly distinctive of any specific
deity), *sempiternus*, *summus* – none of these words need necessarily distinguish one god from any others. Rather they characterise, and diagnose,
the power of the divine realm. To say that the *numen* acted after an appeal
to Castor and Pollux may simply be Ammianus' way of saying what Livy
would have indicated purely by juxtaposition. If Ammianus had specified
the active gods, he would have been writing epic not history.

It may well be that Ammianus' 'monotheism' is purely a manner of
speaking that is more familiar than we thought. The fact that it 'allowed
for' Christianity might be more of a bonus than a formative influence. If so,
it simply prompted pagans to find a slightly modified term where once 'the
gods' sufficed, and even then they were drawing on their own traditions.[145]

5.3.2 *Fortuna*

With over 100 appearances, *fortuna* is as regular a visitor to the pages of
Ammianus as it was in Livy and Tacitus, and for the most part it retains
the privileges and jurisdictions that were found there. It still represents 'the
way things turned out', and outcomes are still the domain of the gods: *fortuna* is still the *executor* of the will of the gods, without any claim implied

---

[144] For instance, when Mars is thought to have fought for the Romans (24.4.24). It has to be admitted
that this is an epiphany on a scale hitherto unprecedented in our historians. Ammianus is careful
to indicate the magnitude of the claim that he makes (he adds *si misceri hominibus numina
maiestatis iura permittunt*).

[145] Matthews (1989) 429 may be making a similar point in his aside that '*deus*' is 'more abstract'
than Cicero's 'gods', but his brevity makes it difficult to be sure.

by her name to the expert knowledge of which god in particular was responsible for a situation.[146] Thus we find, for instance, that the Alamanni
say of the Romans that their ever-present trustworthiness had raised their
fortune to the skies (*quorum fortunam sempiterna fides caelo contiguam
fecit*, 28.2.7); or there is Gallus, who was taken to the heights of fortune
and dropped from there (*assumptus . . . in amplissimum fortunae fastigium,
uersabilis eius motus expertus est*, 14.11.29). He left Antioch *numine laeuo
ductante* (14.11.12); his death was attributed to *fata* (*ibid.*; also 14.11.19),
which in turn were almost certainly linked to his crimes.[147] Gallus suffered a traditional reversal of fortune, which is characterised emphatically
as unpredictable.[148] Livy noted that perhaps the Albans had abandoned their
worship of the gods because of ill-fortune:[149] a similar effect is occasionally found in Ammianus. Procopius, faced with capture, began to complain
bitterly about *fortuna*, 'as happens in extreme situations'.[150]

The reader expected something like this: when he ransacked the house
of Arbitrio, Procopius had got ideas above his station and ignored what no
man should, that *fortuna* could easily reverse his present high status and run
of luck.[151] When the Limigantes are defeated by Constantius, they did not
think they deserved it (*mussantesque audiebantur interdum, fortunae non
meriti fuisse quod euenit*, 17.13.11) – their treacherous negotiations seem
to indicate otherwise (17.13.5 and 7). Ammianus himself indulges in blam-
ing fortune when he complains of the choice of Jovian as successor to Julian
(25.9.7), though his rule had already been indicated by an omen (21.16.21).
As we have seen in the earlier period, *fortuna* is a slippery ally: an unknown text of Cicero is quoted to the effect that *felicitas* is the combination

---

[146] Similarly, Rike (1987) 16, n.25 points out that Sallustius (9) 'particularly favours the worship of
Tyche in cities inasmuch as these required some common focus of ritual for their highly diverse
populations'.

[147] *Eusebius, ita euisceratus ut cruciatibus membra deessent* called on the gods for justice (*inplo-
rans caelo iustitiam*, 14.9.6); given Ammianus' preoccupation with justice (see below) and her
remorseless reprisals against wrongdoers, the connection seems irrefutable. Perhaps Gallus' well-
publicised cruelty made any omens of his death superfluous; none is recorded.

[148] *Fortuna* receives a full retinue of descriptions to this effect. In discussing the number of instances
of its reversals, Ammianus says that it would be mad to attempt to count them (14.11.34); more
specifically, it is *mutabilis et inconstans* (14.11.30); *uersabilis* (23.5.19); *ambigua* (21.5.13); we
hear of *caeco quodam iudicio fortunae* (25.5.8). We should also note: *Romani reflante fortuna
fallaciis lusi* (of Cannae) (31.13.19); *euentus uariante fortuna* (21.16.14); *fortunae struunt uol-
ubiles casus* (22.1.1); *uersa rota Fortunae* (26.8.13); *fortunae uolucris rota* (31.1.1); *fortunarum
uersabiles casus* (31.10.7); *fortuna* can also be also *inclemens* (20.4.13). It is not always adverse.
Note *laetioris fortunae* (17.12.4); *fortuna sequior* (18.6.6) *celsiore fortuna* (20.10.1)). At 15.5.1
fortuna is the saving *fortuna moderatrix humanorum casuum*.

[149] *fortunae, ut fit, obirati cultum reliquerant deum* (26.9.9).

[150] *ut in arduis necessitatibus solet, cum Fortuna expostulabat luctuosa et graui* (26.9.9).

[151] *ultra homines sese . . . efferens, et ignorans quod quiuis beatus, uersa rota Fortunae, ante uespe-
rum potest esse miserrimus* (26.8.13).

of good plans with *fortuna* (*felicitas est fortuna adiutrix consiliorum bonorum*, 21.16.13).[152] For Ammianus, good planning includes all the inherited knowledge about the ease with which the gods can be offended, and that men should know their place.

We can detect, at a superficial level, a greater tendency to attribute reversals to *fortuna*.[153] The number of references to a positive turn of *fortuna* are severely limited, whereas both Livy and Tacitus might well have exploited the effect of an unknowable change of circumstances to convey surprise (or the ignorance of enemies).[154] But we should resist the temptation to consider that there is a greater fixity about the reversals of *fortuna*. Whereas Livy especially would often juxtapose clear favour of the gods (e.g. through successful expiation) with subsequent favourable *fortuna*, Ammianus, lacking many of the traditional techniques of indicating the gods' favour, often abbreviates this structural procedure with a simple statement that a *numen* aided the Romans, as we have seen.[155] This has the effect of displacing many adverse events to *fortuna*, the traditional vehicle for reminding men of their limited knowledge of the gods' will. There is no fundamental 'theological' change: *fortuna* is the will of the gods in action, unpredictable in its course and with a tendency to reversal; thus any success has to be achieved with her aid.[156]

The difficulties of *fortuna* do not, as we found also earlier, prevent people from forming opinions based on a man's past record: Constantius' men are privately relieved when he makes peace with the Alamanni, since he tended to experience good fortune in domestic affairs but the opposite fighting with foreigners.[157] Valentinian's dream of his dishevelled wife represented his *fortuna* (30.5.18). But for the most part, when Ammianus is particularly interested in an individual's relationship with the divine, the term in question is *fatum*.

---

[152] Cf. Valentinian's formulation *ut spero, fortuna consiliorum adiutrix bonorum* (26.2.9).

[153] Naudé (1964) 83.

[154] *Histories* 2, for instance, opens with *struebat iam fortuna* as the focus of the narrative shifts from a divided Rome to Vespasian.

[155] Not that a *numen* is always favourable by any means. At 31.4.9 the Goths are brought into the Empire *quasi laeuo quodam numine*, where *quasi* acts much as *uelut* in the Livian examples of deduction from visible or verifiable evidence.

[156] The traditional assertion or assumption that *fortuna* aided the Romans along with their *uirtus* is found in the form of a 'pact' between *fortuna* and *uirtus* at 14.6.3; which is extremely similar to the formulation of Livy at 8.24.18 when discussing Alexander and is ultimately only a statement of the obvious. The new ways of reporting do, however, tend to focus on its negative aspects; this, like so many other aspects of Ammianus' narrative, may owe as much to his Greek tradition as anything. Herodotus is of course famed for his stories of the reversals of fortune.

[157] *fortunam eius in malis tantum ciuilibus uigilasse; cum autem bella mouerentur externa, accidisse plerumque luctuosa* (14.10.16; see also 14.11.8).

5.3.3 *Fatum*

Fatum continues to represent the inevitable. That is, one *designates* an event as *fatalis* or happening *fato* to conclude that it was unavoidable. Thus we read of the *fixa fatali lege decreta* (21.1.8); or of the *fatalis necessitas* (29.1.32); or that Constantius continued his preparations for war even though the fates were making their own preparations for his death (21.15.2). *Fatum*, or frequently the *sors fatorum*, is greater than any human resource – *nulla uis humana uel uirtus meruisse umquam potuit, ut quod praescripsit fatalis ordo non fiat* (23.5.5). By virtue of this, predictions of fate can be made (e.g. 21.1.8), and errors in this field are, of course, due to human failings; oracles themselves do not help this by their ambiguity (23.5.9). Reputable experts and methods are obviously preferred (22.16.17), though it can equally be done through *detestanda praesagia* (29.1.6). Though it often deals with death[158] and still emphatically *natural* death[159] as well as emperors and the succession,[160] *fatum* can also be linked to lower political office (29.2.22). But its role is not always deadly; Valens, whose death was preordained at his birth (*uitae terminis a primigenio ortu adscriptis*, 17.1.16), is *saved* by *fatum*, determined to grant him his proper lot of life, albeit so that he can suffer later (29.1.16).

Almost anything can conceivably be preordained: Constantius' strange record of success within the empire and failure outside it is linked to *quasi fatali constellatione ita regente diuersos euentus* – presumably a learned circumlocution for a fate that could be predicted from the stars (20.11.32); Gratian's *instabilis uirtus* was undermined by *fata proximique* (27.6.15). Fate continues to indicate the *end* of analysis, at once a recognition that further interpretation is pointless, or not worth the effort. This is probably the case at 19.12.9 when Simplicius escapes prosecution 'by some fate' (*quodam arcente fato*). It simply wasn't his day to die.

Fatum also, under some duress, lends its exalted status to expressing the temporal power of the emperor. After the surrender of the Sarmatians to Constantius, Ammianus comments that they benefited enormously (*incredibile quantum prosperitatis*) from the situation; he then adds that people are right to think that fate can be overcome, or made, by the power of

---

[158] E.g. 17.9.4, 17.11.5.

[159] 27.5.10, 28.4.22.

[160] The deaths of emperors are reliably foreshadowed by omens and mentions of fate. For Valentinian, *diu conpositum ad quietem principis fatum sortem denuntiabat ei supremam prodigiis ingerentibus multis* (30.5.15); Constantius' impending death is linked to an omen at 21.15.2; Julian's lot is part of the *fatalis ordo* (23.5.5) and he knew he was fated to die at Phrygia (25.3.9) by a spear (25.3.6 and 25.3.19); for Jovian's reign, fated to be 'shadowy' (*et cassum et umbratile*, 21.16.21), we see the sad sign of the crying of his own son during his consular inauguration as an omen (*id quod mox accidit portendebat ... praescriptus uitae finiendae dies*, 25.10.11-12).

an emperor (*uerum illud aestimaretur quod opinantur quidam, fatum uinci principis potestate, uel fieri*, 17.12.17).

The idea of an emperor 'changing fate' might appear to make its cosmic significance redundant, but in context it is apparent that there are clear limits to this. The Sarmatians in question had been overcome by their slaves and forced to choose between the protection of Constantius and serving those slaves. The emperor's granting of their freedom and a king restored their dignity and loyalty (17.12.18-21). The statement refers to the great power of a *princeps* over circumstance; that is, he can make or reverse ruin. There is no indication that he can *prevent* it. We might have expected *fortuna* with some qualifying epithet, but that would have done no justice to the extreme reversal of the situation.

But there is another instance where we read *fatum* where *fortuna* or *felicitas* might have been expected: again the context is of hyperbole. Constantius' courtiers praise his *fatum* as *uigens semper et praesens* at 19.12.16. We know that a predilection for flattery was one of his deplorable weaknesses.[161] Perhaps we are to understand from the context that *felicitas* would have been more appropriate but with the profound and longstanding connection of *fatum* with emperors, the courtiers are not being so innovative.[162] The tendency to link an emperor with fate is no more emphasised in comparison with Tacitus' agents.

However traditional the category of fate seems when analysed from these angles, its place in the interpretative structure cannot be said to remain unchanged from the models of Livy and Tacitus. In the former, 'fate' was a diagnosis of the last resort and greatest ponderance, often after the failure of the negotiation of the *pax deum*. Tacitus politely sidestepped issues of the inevitable to urge propriety.[163] In both cases what mattered more was the proper *cultus deorum*: Roman setbacks were reversed after the proper supplication of the gods in Livy, while the refounding of the temple at *Histories* 4.53 under Vespasian seems to have indicated at least temporary relief from the chaos of the *ira deum*.

Yet despite Ammianus' clear paganism and tendency to the explicit, the phrase *pax deum/deorum/numinum* appears (incredibly) only *once* in the entire extant account, where Julian was warned that, since the *pax numinum* had not yet been obtained, he faced inevitable death (23.5.4). Expiation

---

[161] See e.g. 15.5.37. Ammianus' dislike for flattery is clear. For instance, the Persians' flattery of their leader's *felicitas*, overheard by the tunnelling soldiers at 24.4.23, is heavily ironic.

[162] In fact it is not at all unprecedented: at *Annals* 13.47.3, the freedman Graptus attributes Nero's escape from a fictitious plot to *fatum*.

[163] Tacitus' advice was not heeded for long if at all. In Ammianus' text, knowledge of the future is worth dying for (at least some thought so; see 29.1.7).

is not even mentioned as a possibility. In fact, there are *no* expiations of prodigies in the *Res Gestae* nor mention of it when it might be expected.[164] Words linked to *expiare* are used predominantly metaphorically to express enormity or irreversability[165] or of foreign rites.[166] For all the validation of traditional methods of divination, Ammianus has almost nothing to say for expiation.

There are just two moments where it does appear in traditional guise. The first is in his lament at 19.12.20: he tells us that prodigies often appear and warn of future events but that because they are not expiated publicly as they once were, they pass unnoticed and unrecognised (*nascuntur huiusmodi saepe portenta, indicantia rerum uariarum euentus, quae, quoniam non expiantur ut apud ueteres publice, inaudita praetereunt et incognita*).[167] Secondly, in his discussion of divination, Ammianus includes the need to placate deities appropriately if one is to expect signs foretelling the future (*substantiales potestates ritu diuerso placatae*). Expiation is therefore not entirely forgotten, but these subdued moments are the *strongest* statements for expiation in the extant *Res Gestae*.

Thus, though he has preserved the memory of Rome's former expiatory habits, Ammianus neglects almost every opportunity to drive the point home that expiation is a key to one's relations with the gods: Julian's ignoring a massed legion of adverse signs positively cries out for a comment that expiation might have been possible, but none comes. Or (to pick a random example), the efforts to rebuild the Temple in Jerusalem are abandoned without any attempt at expiation because of divine signs and interference.[168] Why were experts not consulted and expiation performed? This was under Julian, after all.

We might easily assume that the banning of sacrifice at various points and the Christian administration of the empire had pushed expiation into the background. But nothing prevented Ammianus from making a stronger

---

[164] Expiation meaning specifically *remedial* action through sacrifice by the state. Sacrifice is still effective in obtaining the *pax deum* (e.g. 19.10.4) but with its removal from the fulchrum of negotiation with the gods, it has to be said that it has been emphatically decentralised.

[165] Domitian *memoriam nominis sui inexpiabili detestatione perfudit* (18.4.5); Nigrinus is presented by the residents of Aquileia as the chief instigator of war so that the city might be 'expiated' from its treachery at 21.12.19; Valens' indiscriminate punishments are *inexpiabile* (29.1.18) – e.g. the *inexpiabile scelus* of 29.6.7.

[166] The death of the son of the Persian ally Grumbates is 'expiated' by the burning of Amida at 19.2.1. It is not clear whether this is considered metaphorical (i.e. avenged) or religious (i.e. the ghost was expected to cause trouble).

[167] The failure to mention expiation at 19.12.20 is noted by Paschoud (1988) 142 and Harrison (1999) 185, but neither contextualises it more broadly.

[168] 23.1.2-3: Ammianus gives no explicit explanation of the strange events, unlike the Christians of the time. For the importance bestowed on this episode by Christians, pagans and Jews see Phillips (1979); for his 'competitive Judaism' see also Goodman (1994), esp. chs. 6–8.

case for its restoration than he does: he has not, after all, been afraid to risk offending Christians. Rather, we should consider the dynamics of pagan practice as a principal cause of the change: the tendency to take adverse signs as indicating fatality for the emperor, only strengthened by the passing years, had served to undermine the role of expiation and negotiation. The warning that the *pax numinum nondum exorata* [*est*] does not function as a prompt for pleading the cause of expiation; in function, it is merely another omen.[169] In a similar vein, the Sibylline Books, once the repository of *solutions* to extreme religious problems, are reduced in effect to a divinatory role.[170] Of course it is quite possible that they might have given such a response in Livy's or Tacitus' day; but as the texts – and therefore the models of religion – stand, this abject failure to respond by addressing the mood of the gods is unprecedented; the single previous instance of their inadequacy was mitigated by the prudence of an embassy to Delphi, which offered a prescription for expiation (Livy 23.1.11).

This change of emphasis is not necessarily that surprising. With the shift of Roman power away from the centre, expiation of the gods would have more readily raised the question 'which gods?' The traditional gods in new locations would probably not have been the answer, since their status had declined over the centuries.[171] With the loss of localised expiation, the relationship of men towards the gods had shifted dramatically.[172] Traditional rites retain their power of prediction but failures no longer act as an initiative to repeated or reformulated sacrifices as once they did. When the army (including Ammianus) consults the *haruspices* as to their best option for escape, both available possibilities are ruled out yet there is no further sacrifice in the hope of obtaining the *pax deum*; they simply set out and manage as best they can (24.8.4-5). In effect, it seems that all prognosticated difficulties are inevitable.

Of course, there are also moments in Livy's text where it is not possible to avoid a prognosticated outcome, as we saw with the doomed Gracchus, for instance (above, 71, 88, 108, 111 and 113). His *fatum* was initially indicated by adverse signs and it was only Livy who had sufficient textual

---

[169] Even more strikingly, it seems that expiation may have been attempted: *nondum* presumably alludes to *perlitatio*, the repeated attempt at obtaining favourable signs. Ammianus refuses to capitalise on this. It should be noted that even Livy's Republic did not always move from failed *perlitatio* to expiation, but the historian only records this when he wishes to offer an explanation for a subsequent failure, and the failure is only with respect to one god (*Salus*, at 41.15.4).

[170] E.g. *Romae super hoc bello libros Sibyllae consultos, ut iusserat, imperatorem eo anno discedere a limitibus suis, aperto prohibuisse responso* (23.1.7).

[171] They had virtually disappeared from the coinage by the time of the Tetrarchy (Liebeschuetz (1981) 395, esp. n.5).

[172] This issue is shamelessly abbreviated here; it merits far greater study, even within Ammianus.

authority and hindsight to diagnose *fatum*. But Livy will document attempts at *perlitatio*, whether they succeeded (23.39.5) or not (41.15.4), because it was the only reasonable cause of action. This is in sharp contrast to his fourth-century counterpart.

But Ammianus is not dooming his empire to fatalistic foreknowledge of the future without any means of negotiation. On a structural level, there are signs that the mood of the gods, and possibly even *fatum*, are to some limited extent negotiable, chiefly through the medium of *iustitia*.

5.3.4 *Fatum* and justice

To the reader of Ammianus' account, the ubiquity of *iustitia* and *aequitas*[173] do not need to be established. They are a central yardstick of his moral assessments of emperors.[174] The *sapientes* offered that there are four principal virtues: *temperantia, prudentia, iustitia, fortitudo* (25.4.1), but the only one which receives a religious excursus in the extant *Res Gestae* is *iustitia* which, according to Julian, is the *excellentissima uirtus omnium* and the only one explicitly linked to the divine.[175] The excursus appears in connection with the death of Gallus and the gruesome fates of Scudilo and Barbatio (who had treacherously promised the Caesar safety when they brought him to Constantius):

> These and countless other things like them are sometimes (if only it was always!) the work of Adrastia, whom we also call by the alternative name of Nemesis: she who punishes evil deeds and rewards good actions. She is, as it were, the sublime jurisdiction of a potent divine power, located, according to human understanding, above the orbit of the moon; or, as others define her, an actual guardian presiding with universal

[173] The two are frequently linked: Julian appeals to Constantius' *iustitia*, which will permit him to act with *aequitas* (20.8.11). Constantius says of Gallus that he *a iustitia ... defecisset* (21.13.11) and then speaks of Julian as operating *aequitate calcata* (21.13.13). A *grauis quidam aequitatis spectator ... iustius incusabit* men who acted as rashly as did those who elected Jovian (25.5.7).

[174] Constantius *iustumque in eiusmodi titulis capitali odio oderat, cum maxime id ageret, ut iustus aestimaretur et clemens* (21.16.11); Julian is praised on this count at 25.4.8; the catalogue of Valentinian's cruelty consists chiefly of the execution of the innocent; though Ammianus does not actually label this as *iniustum*, elsewhere such acts are the height of injustice; Valens was *prouinciarum aequissimus tutor* (31.14.2) and acted *cum magna iustorum iniustorumque distinctione* in matters of lapsed estates (31.14.3) but was *iniuriosus alia et iracundus* (31.14.6). *Iustitia* wept at the death of Ursulus (22.3.7); but for this and similar cases she would have returned to earth during the reign of Julian, which she had long since abandoned because of the *uitia hominum* (22.10.6; virtually repeated at 25.4.19).

[175] It is *iustitia* that will permit Constantius to meet his requests with *aequitas* (20.8.11); he in turn defines equity, supposedly *calcata* in Julian's case as the *parens nutrixque orbis Romani* (21.13.13) before claiming that *iustitia* will aid his cause (21.13.15); link with the *numen*, 29.2.2 (*numen ratione ... iustissima*).

jurisdiction over the destinies of individuals. The ancient theologians treat her as the daughter of justice and record that from an unknown eternity she looks down upon all the creatures of earth. She, as queen of causes and assessor and judge of events, controls the urn with its lots and the twists and turns of human events. Sometimes, changing and altering many things, she gives our plans a different result from that which we intended.[176]

This is the only explicit appearance of Nemesis in Ammianus' text: Adrastia appears once more in the text as the *humanorum spectatrix* who saw to the death of Eusebius, Constantius' chamberlain (22.3.12). Whatever the knowledge status of the statement that *Adrastia/Nemesis* was the daughter of *Iustitia*, the link is undeniable.[177]

For our purposes, there are important ramifications for the total religious system of Ammianus, as it is presented. We should not forget that the key to his selection of material is linked to responsibility rather than 'pure' theology.[178] Justice proves to be a fulcrum between men and gods; it is a prime locus of negotiation, and in Ammianus' paradigm, it partially fulfils the role of the collective gods in the systems of Livy and Tacitus. Justice is expected, for instance, to aid the designs of men. The inhabitants of Nisibis expected *Iustitia* to help them defend their homes as they had found it did in the past (25.9.2); Tripolis was defended by the ever-present eye of Justice,

---

[176] *Haec et huiusmodi quaedam innumerabilia ultrix facinorum impiorum, bonorumque praemiatrix, aliquotiens operatur Adrastia – atque utinam semper! –. Quam uocabulo duplici etiam Nemesim appellamus, ius quoddam sublime numinis efficacis humanarum mentium opinione lunari circulo superpositum, uel, ut definiunt alii, substantialis tutela generali potentia partilibus praesidens fatis, quam theologi ueteres fingentes Iustitiae filiam, ex abdita quadam aeternitate, tradunt omnia despectare terrena. haec ut regina causarum, et arbitra rerum ac disceptatrix urnam sortium temperat accidentium uices alternans uoluntatumque nostrarum exorsa interdum alio quam, quo contendebant, exitu terminans, multiplices actus permutando conuoluit* (14.11.25-6).

[177] Clearly this excursus is extremely rich. The *theologi* are said to *fingere* this idea – a poetic idiom. They were fashioning a way of representing something and though their testimony is here, as elsewhere, given a high status, we should not forget the plethora of knowledges in Ammianus' text. He does not 'agree' with them, but juxtaposes himself close to them. For a historian the appropriate expression is *ius quoddam sublime numinis efficacis* ('some sublime law of the gods that does not hesitate to take action'). We should also note the refusal to make absolute claims: *Adrastia/Nemesis sometimes (aliquotiens)* performs such actions, *sometimes (interdum)* reverses human plans; thus the proprieties of interpretation are observed. The overlap of imagery with the description of *fortuna* is striking (compare the descriptions of *Fortuna* given by Champeaux (1982-7) vol. II 44–47) but that does not mean that *fortuna* 'is' *Adrastia*. Further discussion of the relative status of the construction (*fingere*) is possible but not here.

[178] Amat (1992) 276 detects various philosophical influences here (chiefly Apuleius) but insists to the end on diagnosing 'confusion' rather than radical appropriation and integration for a particular purpose, even though she notes that 'Elle [Justice] n'est donc vraiment ni la Némésis grecque, ni la loi du talion ni la *Fors Fortuna*; elle diffère même de la lointaine Providence des traités philosophiques d'Apulée.'

who noted the last curses of the envoys and governor and brought about the death of Palladius, the imperial envoy. Sent to investigate the *comes per Africam* Romanus, he had instead formed a pact with the count, deepening the province's problems: their ambassadors were now considered guilty of lying to the emperor, to whom they had originally appealed, and a number of their legates were tortured or executed. The episode opens with the promise of Justice's intervention ('let us move on to the sufferings of the African province of Tripolis, over which (I think) even Justice herself shed tears') and is closed with a similar sentiment.[179] Julian also claims that *aequitas* was always normally linked to victory (*aequitati semper solere iungi uictoriam*, 23.5.23). It was Justice who revealed the treacherous plan of the Goths at 31.15.7.

Justice forever watches men,[180] and impious or cruel executions in particular are punished.[181] Most controversially, *fatum* is said to 'depend' somehow on *Adrastia/Nemesis* (*praesidens fatis*, 14.11.24). Yet this does not mean that *Adrastia* can extend or diminish the length of a man's life. Rather it indicates that her intentions, once she is provoked, cannot be thwarted.

The co-ordination of *fatum* with gods is not restricted to *Adrastia*. This religious aspect is not the only one that appears in the text, and once again, we must make the effort to balance the demands of *fatum* and those of the gods. In our earlier accounts, it was concluded that the two interacted: for Tacitus (and rather simplistically, Livy), *fatum* created a broad context and one's relationship with the gods decided on the details. While Nero's horoscope showed his propensity for rule, it was Nero's business that he offended the gods to the extent that he did: no one forced him to bathe in a sacred spring. Ammianus is similarly sophisticated but with a different emphasis. While the date, even the time, of one's death might be

---

[179] *ad Tripoleos Africanae prouinciae ueniamus aerumnas, quas (ut arbitror) Iustitia quoque ipsa defleuit* (28.6.1) ... *non indefensa, quia uigilauit Iustitiae oculus sempiternus, ultimaeque legatorum et praesidis dirae* (28.6.25); the closing statement is attributed to the city officials but Ammianus immediately narrates the downfall of the guilty parties.

[180] To add to the examples already given, there is 29.2.20 *inconiuus Iustitiae oculus, arbiter et uindex perpetuus rerum, uigilauit adtente.*

[181] The philosopher Eusebius did not call on *caelo iustitiam* in vain (14.9.6), since *uigilauit utrubique superni numinis aequitas* (14.11.24). Not only Gallus but the treachery which brought Gallus into Constantius' power are dealt with by *iustitia*. According to Julian, the shade of Gordianus is avenged *ueluti librante iustitia* when his murderers *cruciabilibus interiere suppliciis* (23.5.17); the curses of Maximinus' victims saw fulfilment later (28.1.57); we hear that the *inconiuus Iustitiae oculus, arbiter et uindex perpetuus rerum, uigilauit adtente* at 29.2.20; impending injustice is represented as the advent of the Furies at 29.2.21, as was the case with Gallus; the *manes inultos etiam tum et errantes* are avenged by the *sempiternus ... iustitiae uigor, aliquotiens serus, sed scrupulosus quaesitor gestorum recte uel secus* (30.2.9) and the ghosts of the victims of Valens' cruelty appear to him before his death (31.1.3).

predetermined, the conditions in which one lives and dies are negotiated by one's actions with the gods, and especially with *Iustitia*.

The emperor Valens is a useful demonstration of these interactive elements: his career is a catalogue of cruelty and injustice. Even before his appointment, he is not considered fit for office. When his brother Valentinian consulted his officers about a colleague, Dagalaiphus, the commander of the cavalry, replied that if the emperor loved his family, he had a brother: but if he loved the state, then he should begin his search (*'si tuos amas'* inquit – *'imperator optime – habes fratrem, si rem publicam – quaere quem uestias'*, 26.4.1). Valentinian hid his indignation but hastened to appoint Valens as Augustus. By 26.6.7, Valens, under the vicious influence of his father-in-law Petronius, is already seizing others' property. Petronius, himself cruel and indiscriminate in his punishment of the innocent and guilty alike (26.6.7), fanned the flames of Valens' own natural cruelty and hard heartedness. The emperor was incapable, we are told, of listening to reason or acting justly. By 26.6.9, the population is praying for a change (*permutatio status praesentis, ope numinis summi, concordi gemitu poscebatur*).

During the uprising of Procopius, Valens, after almost disgracefully abandoning his rank (26.7.13), offends *iustitia* when he executes Florentius and Barchalbas who had betrayed the usurper to him. Ammianus clarifies that if they had betrayed a legitimate ruler, their punishment would have been just (*ipsa Iustitia iure caesos pronuntiaret*). Since Procopius was a rebel, however, they should rather have been rewarded (26.9.10). At 26.10.2, Valens' general inclination to cruelty (*ad crudelitatem propensioris*) is identified as a cause of his officials' injustice. At 26.10.9-12 we encounter the spread of Valens' policies of cruelty and injustice and, given his ready ear, a rise in informers. He attracted much hostility: at 29.1.15-16, he was attacked by an officer of the Scutarii named Sallust, and was under threat by others, but was saved by fate, which was preserving him for far worse things in Thrace (*lacrimosis in Thracia discriminibus destinarat*, 29.1.15). His precise moment of death had been decided at his birth (*uitae terminis a primigenio ortu adscriptis*, 29.1.16). In the light of this situation, Ammianus does not begrudge the emperor the right to take precautions but his severity and hastiness in judgement were such that men 'learned they were condemned before they knew they were suspected' (29.1.18). His lack of discrimination in inflicting punishment on the innocent and guilty alike is said to be *inexpiabile*. By 29.1.27 Valens has so far departed from justice and is so accomplished in causing harm that he is compared to a wild beast in the amphitheatre: nor do things improve.

When a plot to discover the name of his successor was revealed, the trials involved many innocent or upstanding men (29.1.28-42) and books were publicly burned on the grounds that they were *inliciti* even though they were actually books of liberal studies or law (*liberalium disciplinarum indices uariarum et iuris*, 29.1.41) – not a situation that would further the much-needed education of the officials.

One of the defendants, Hilarius, admitted that the conspirators had foreseen their own fate (29.1.33), but that the Furies also threatened the emperor himself and his judges, citing a series of verses to that (rather vague) effect:

> Your blood will not fall unavenged
> Wrathful Tisiphone prepares evil destruction for them
> While Mars rages on the plains of Mimas

In due course, Justice became more attentive: the avenging Furies of those put to death 'worked on the everlasting deity with their just complaints, [and] kindled the torches of [the war goddess] Bellona to confirm the truth of the oracle [received by Hilarius] which had given warning that no crime can be perpetrated with impunity'.[182] The rampant cruelty that continued (29.2.4-17) was capped by the emperor's forgiveness of a tribune, Numerius, who excelled in criminality (*malitia quendam exsuperantem*, 29.2.17). He had confessed to performing a caesarean section on a living woman in order to use the foetus to ask the dead about a change of rulers.

Book 31 sees the end of Valens: the book opens with portents of the emperor's death as the narrative prepares for the disastrous battle of Hadrianople. Though one version recorded that his body was never recovered, Ammianus adds a second version, citing the sole survivor as witness, that the injured Valens, along with his remaining retinue, was burned to death in a building. Ammianus' obituary of Valens closes with the note that after his death, a monument was found near the accepted site of his death: it bore an inscription in Greek to the effect that an ancient noble was buried there, by the name of Mimas. By this link to the oracle received by Hilarius that promised him Tisiphone's vengeance for the spilling of his blood on Mimas' plain, Ammianus brings closure to the religious dynamics of Valens' rule. His death, when it comes, is therefore linked not just to Justice but also to Tisiphone and *Bellona*, who are the vehicles and means of his destruction by war by the Goths. His repeated injustices are unambiguously emphasised as a factor in his death. But this is not the whole of the story.

---

[182] *Iustitiae oculus, arbiter et uindex perpetuus rerum, uigilauit adtente. namque caesorum ultimae dirae, perpetuum numen ratione querellarum iustissima commouentes, Bellonae accenderant faces, ut fides oraculi firmaretur, quod nihil inpune praedixerat perpetrari* (29.2.20).

Since Valens' death was preordained at birth, we cannot simply speak of Valens' 'deserving' his fate without taking into account other factors. In some sense we might be able to speak of his cruelty also being 'preordained'. Over-strict interpretations at this point confuse the issue: Ammianus has offered different formulations of how the divine operates from different angles. The exact nature of Valens' death (by fire) was prognosticated by omens of speech (31.1.2-3) and seems particularly apt after his similar execution of the young philosopher Simonides at 29.1.38.[183] Might a just Valens have died heroically in battle? The question is ultimately redundant. It was a *munus caeleste* to have education bestowed (or withheld) (29.2.18). We are not in a position to understand Ammianus' religious stance if we attempt to 'organise' it into a fixed set of designations or see it as a failed attempt to include disparate philosophical elements. Is education a god? It is *bestowed* by the gods, apparently. This is not, however, a 'fact', it is a construction. Education is linked to the divine by the nature of its blessings. Just as the emperor was constructed as a god in an attempt to articulate his power, so too the *praeclara informatio doctrinarum* is associated with the divine because of its power and beneficence. Ammianus *designates* it a prerogative of the divine to convey this. He had no 'personal opinion' on the matter.

So too with *iustitia* and *fatum*; he accounts for a pre-existent reality by linking it to a web of events and working assumptions. Valens' cruelty invoked Justice, who disposed of him suitably. What is interesting is his method of explanation, and the coherence he seeks to bring to what could be taken to be disparate events: the inexorable process of *fatum* is detected in Valens' close shave with death; the forces that shape human existence were not moving in that direction, and events followed their lead. Within his own system of interpretation and with the tools of late antique paganism, Ammianus has made good sense.

Perhaps more conspicuously than with Livy and Tacitus (who were, after all, predominantly attempting to reify a consensus), Ammianus is *creating* religious standpoints, negotiating with traditional claims and contemporary concerns. Christianity was itself particularly concerned with justice as a cosmic reality and practical concern.[184] To abstract his religious excur-

---

[183] See Blockley (1975) 173–174 for the preference for 'suitable' punishments in the fourth century.

[184] Amat (1992) sees the preoccupation with justice as a contemporary (i.e. Christian) concern: Lactantius is especially singled out for comparison, though the few decades between Ammianus and his Christian predecessor might be an enormous gulf given the changes during the fourth century. But the concern is actually more widespread: Trompf (2000) documents the motif of 'justice' (with a fairly loose, but workable, definition) in historical texts from the earliest texts in the West right up to Late Antiquity (dealing predominantly with Christian texts in the later period).

suses and methods from the reality that they explained and exemplified is to cut them off from their lifeblood. In an attempt to interpret the events of the period, Ammianus judiciously uses cultural knowledge about how 'life' works; working at one point from the exemplary question of justice, at another to explain the reasons behind events, he selects, prioritises and emphasises by turns. The description of *Adrastia/Nemesis* might almost have been about *fortuna* (and would not be entirely 'wrong' if it was) but there is one particular aspect of the divine that he wishes to emphasise here. The warning and appeal to his readers is that justice as a cosmic force does not sanction impious acts – even where a wrong might appear justified, as the treachery to bring Gallus to Constantius would have done to many onlookers. *Fatum* is one's lot; the gods are just. The peculiar impact of the two in conjunction is no more awkward than the coincidence of death by simultaneous electric shock and heart attack, the loss of one's home by the synchronous loss of employment and a sharp rise in interest rates. Did Hitler invade the Sudetenland 'because' of a policy of appeasement or because 'he was always going to'?

Valens was 'spared' because the divine self-evidently allocated him a greater span of life. The reason that *fatum* is explicitly invoked is because, like Marcellus and Hannibal in Livy, or the four emperors in Tacitus' *Histories*, *fatum* has already taken a hand in events, in this case because Valens' injustices have set the machinery of fate in motion. Therefore, when he burns to death, it is because of fate: and his death was additionally just, as were the deaths of so many who had perpetrated cruelty. The 'fit' with his burning of Simonides is not made explicit but was perhaps a deduction to be drawn with ease. Ammianus does not speculate about details because there is little need to: *fatum* still represents ('simply') what happened. It is a category of events, not an event – a reliable outcome in the maelstrom of human activity. Outcomes *per se* are still the domain of the gods, whether formulated as unpredictable *fortuna*, anonymous *numen* or decipherable *iustitia/Adrastia/Nemesis*. Valens suffered at the hands of all three.[185]

By his emphasis on *iustitia* and *aequitas*, Ammianus is not expounding a 'personal' ideology. Rather, in historiographical fashion, he is creating a context for political action: those in power are held responsible for their actions. Thus, Ammianus has in common with his predecessors that he offered a paradigm that aimed to shape human action. Tacitus politely (and in vain,

---

[185] 31.1.1 mentions the *Fortunae uolucris rota*, Bellona, the Furies and omens of his fated death, already attributed to *fatum* at 29.1.15-16 and at 29.2.20 we hear that the curses of his victims moved the *perpetuum numen ratione querellarum iustissima*.

as it turned out) warned against cultivating an interest in *fata*; Livy used it sparingly in interpretation, and then with the authority of hindsight. Both were careful to retain the aspect of responsibility. Ammianus has followed in their footsteps in creating a perspective that has contemporary relevance.

Thus when Ammianus informs us that *fata* blind or stupefy the object of their plans,[186] we might note that neither of his predecessors emphasises this; it might have made much sense of the disaster of Cannae in Livy's account (for instance) but to give it such prominence in his account would be to create a dangerous precedent for a Rome that was to attend to its duties, irrespective of any opportunities for excuses.[187] Ammianus, on the other hand, is in a position to do so because he has located the key responsibility earlier in the chain of events, at the point where a man must decide whether he is to be cruel or just. The blinding effect of fate, which would have undermined responsibility in the narratives of Livy or Tacitus, serves here to *reinforce* the need for appropriate action if one wishes to avoid the inevitable consequences. It is emphasised that there is no escape. It was not only Gallus who fell foul of *Adrastia*, but also those who broke their oaths to deliver him to custody. In the absence of expiation, *iustitia* emerges as a key factor in men's dealings with the gods. Every act is a potential negotiation with the divine, the *spectatrix humanorum*.

5.4 Ammianus and the Roman tradition

These conclusions clearly require some location within the traditions that have been outlined in this monograph. It should be stressed that we have been dealing with emphasis not rigorous theology. How possible would it have been to construct Ammianus' particular model in earlier times? Herodotus presents 'a complete moral system [in his religious material]. Unjust actions meet without fail with a just, proportional response'.[188] We may therefore have a deliberate synthesis of Greek and Latin traditions; but this is no slavish imitation, rather it is a typically complex appropriation of traditional material to forge a new and unified religious position. And it may be a question of emphasis: Tacitus recognises the possibility

---

[186] Said of Gallus, going naively to his death at 14.11.12f. One might reasonably posit that Ammianus is also accounting for the Caesar's uncharacteristically meek – even naive – capitulation to Constantius' scheming.

[187] But Livy does assert that *fortuna* can have a similar effect, as the agent of *fatum* at 5.37.1-3 (the prelude to the disaster of the Allia): *cum tanta moles mali instare – adeo occaecat animos fortuna, ubi uim suam ingruentem refringi non uolt – ...nihil extraordinarii imperii aut auxilii quaesiuit.*

[188] Harrison (1997) 107; consider also his comment at 115 ('human justice is not an alternative to divine justice, but works alongside it').

of an interpretation based on the 'just' orchestration of events by the divine, but discards it.[189] Tacitus' agents sometimes offer the kind of curses that, for Ammianus, would make the ears of Justice prick up; in contrast to those in Ammianus' account, no explicit link is offered with the fate of the relevant emperors or other instigators of cruelty. We cannot finally say whether Tacitus intended us to understand that justice would take a hand in events, just that it is not his prime concern. But the issue *was* studiously avoided. For Tacitus, what mattered was the general restoration of proper *mores*. This was approached with a religious focus and achieved by a religious act, the refounding of the Capitoline temple. In other words, he chose not to highlight this line of interpretation. For Livy, who was not averse to linking curses to divine punishment (above, 102) we have a similar pattern in miniature: the perennial likelihood of offending the gods and the consequent need for vigilance in interpretation and expiation. Tacitus' warning to avoid investigation of fate may well have been a dead letter even by the time he wrote it: Ammianus is not at pains to repeat his advice – while the frequent deaths of those who dared to explore such issues are obviously a disincentive, they function chiefly to indicate the injustice of the judges and emperor. Furthermore it should not be forgotten that some of Ammianus' positions are articulated through classical authors. According to Ammianus, it was Cicero who taught that *felicitas* was a combination of *fortuna* with 'good' acts (21.16.13). But it is doubtful nonetheless whether Cicero would have espoused such a model as Ammianus does. The virtual absence of supplication and expiation is startling. This does not mean that he did not 'believe' in it: there is sufficient mention to preserve the memory of former practices, however subdued it is. We are dealing not with a change of belief, but a strategic change of emphasis.

Ammianus' formulation seems acutely pertinent for his times: the halls of power were further removed from him than they had been from his predecessors and had markedly different concerns. His emphasis on justice and her hegemony over the greatest of mortals is an appeal, a threat, a negotiation with the socially and geographically distant powers-that-be, whose whims could send the innocent and guilty alike to their graves. His account is not diminished in any way by this observation, it is merely put in its place, as one of a myriad of possibilities that happened to be articulated – just like Livy's or Tacitus' accounts. The fact that he had a keen eye for the consequences of a Valens led him, one way or another, to address a particular concern. Livy and Tacitus called for a return to the proper judicious handling of prodigies, amongst

---

[189] *aequitate deum erga bona malaque documenta* (*Annals* 16.33), discussed above, 160.

other remedies. Given the abandonment of prodigy expiation by the fourth century, the *ira deum* was virtually guaranteed. How, then, does a pagan address the concerns of his day, when his most obvious remedy is not an option? In this case, he focussed his attention on the relationship between an individual's behaviour, which was presumably corruptible in the chronic divine wrath that the state would attract, and what would happen to them. As a result, his paganism is more 'personal': but only in its particular focus. It is not the only option and the 'fuller' system of paganism, with prodigy expiation, knowledgeable masters of the various *scientiae* and appropriate institutions, waits in the wings for its opportunity.

Ammianus' redeployment of traditional features privileges a pagan system within the range of cosmological options, each of which has its (unequal) place. Though the domination of Christianity is the feature that is perhaps the one that appears most dramatic to us, the contemporary audience would perhaps have also noted the emphatic removal of philosophy from ritual concerns, or the exaltation of the Magi.

To speak of 'compromise' hardly renders a fair account of his project, since Christianity is not received as an equal. Ammianus does cut across supposed 'divides' but this is more a question of reappropriating themes that Christians had recently begun to treat as their own. His toleration, so typical of late paganism, discriminated between permitting a religious system and allowing it to run riot. Christianity's place was *within* a pagan world, not as an equal partner or even alternative to the *cultus deorum*. The many differences are a witness to remarkable flexibility – it can hardly be said that Ammianus wished simply to turn the clock back. The loss of a system that relied on expiation, based on contemporary adaptation to the repeated bans on sacrifices,[190] is not just circumvented: rather it is an opportunity for the historian to lay claim to a central pillar of contemporary interpretation.

Ammianus' back is much closer to the proverbial wall than was the case for his predecessors and if paganism was to survive in any form, it had to find a *modus operandi* that did not *depend* on sacrifice, however effective that was when applied. Another avenue to the gods was required, that did not require even a temple. Here our attempts to understand paganism through rite ironically force us to consider whether we can classify Ammianus with his predecessors. But to refuse him entry into the canon of 'actively' pagan historians would not only be an error but would also be most inappropriate. It was, after all, *his* religious tradition to reformulate.

However striking the cost of Ammianus' strategy, it must be acknowledged that it was potentially very successful. The categories of *fatum* and

[190] On which see Beard, North and Price (1998) 374–5 and 387–8.

fortuna remained intact and events could be assigned to the *numen* and (or) justice, that is, to a *pagan* reference. After Ammianus, to speak of the justice of the divine was not a peculiarly, or even a particularly, Christian act. In this, his model was immune from criticism from what was an increasingly hostile context; indeed it would be hard to avoid using his points of reference in any discussion of politics in the ancient world. Every invocation of justice was, after Ammianus, potentially a pagan act.

Given a free hand to restore paganism, we should not doubt that Ammianus would have opened the temples to appropriate sacrifice, tastefully supplicated the gods, expiated prodigies, consulted the *augures* and other experts – and left the Christians and philosophers to their quiet contemplative lives. But at the end of the fourth century, this would not seem to be a realistic option and, rather than ally himself with what he may have seen was a lost cause,[191] instead the 'lonely' historian spoke with a voice that could grant paganism credibility.

For the last extant time, Rome formulated a pagan religion for itself that might regulate its rulers and subjects and find a route to the gods. The fact that the chosen avenue looks to us in some ways more Christian than pagan reflects not the failure of Ammianus' project but the flexibility of a disappearing religious system. Like Julian's *haruspices*, he could do no more than offer the synthesis of his knowledge to a hostile, ignorant or indifferent world, and hope that it would listen.

---

[191] Exact dates for the composition of the *Res Gestae* vary. It is usually taken to be either around 391, or later in the same decade (most recently: Matthews (1989) 17–27). Sacrifice was banned in 391 but it was prohibited by Constantine much earlier, temporarily in the event or in practice (Beard North and Price (1998) I 374). It may be that Ammianus' strategy deliberately responds to, or anticipates, this extreme blow to the traditional forms of the *cultus deorum*.

6

Conclusions

Religion is a powerful theme in the three authors scrutinised here: indeed it might be said to be the backbone both of the historical record and of the transaction of Roman identity. Virtually every major battle and a great many other events are explained with reference to the gods. Historiography, in its role of explanation and characterisation, appropriated a particular role to itself in its synthesis of the competing religious knowledges: these self-appointed spokesmen for Rome's religious tradition were not directly 'informing the public' of a central canon, thrashed out at some mysterious policy-making thinktank. These accounts are each individual yet deliberately placed at the centre of religious authority: this was, self-evidently to the audience, a construction. The historical accounts created and negotiated a normative position and aimed at procuring enough general assent to facilitate any excursions into expert or controversial areas. Ironically then, the supposedly sceptical historians might be the closest thing we have to the voice of the 'state religion', at least in terms of text; not a specific formulation of a particular detail or set of circumstances (e.g. as Feeney argues for Horace's *Carmen Saeculare*), but a general framework of practice and interpretation.[1]

Religion is central to the texts under scrutiny here: proper methods, pitfalls, the enactment of the gods' will – all represented over and over again for the reader's edification. Noting prodigies, their expiation, propitiating the gods, *not* offending the gods in one's actions (such as stripping a temple) or manner (such as boasting of one's *felicitas*), finetuning one's interpretation – all this is Roman religion in practice. It does not include the *doctrina* of the priests, but they safeguarded their own traditions and were not for the common man to debate. For the general picture of Roman religion, we must look at the historical accounts, or at least the wisdom of the past.

---

[1] Once again these findings are implicitly anticipated by Feeney (1998); his formulation of the rare religious notice in Caesar's historical narrative (*B. Civ.* 3.105.3-6) is that 'the traditional state apparatus of the *res publica* is being superseded by the manifestation of divine favour for the spectacular charismatic individual' (20).

No other genre represents a sustained attempt to produce this kind of formulation: its very persistence over time would seem to bear witness to the way that religious formulation was considered a central aspect of historiography. Indeed it is hard to identify another forum where these kinds of issues were explored in literature: where else is a full working religious system represented? Individual details could be represented in poetry or art but an overview of religion seems to be the peculiar prerogative of historiography. Three important authors are arguably enough for us to speak of a 'tradition', though the likes of Sallust have not entered into our discussion; and we should not think in terms of a linear progression. We have three individuals writing in very different times and we can only begin to speculate about what each would have made of the others' periods or what their contemporaries might have had to say. Scipio's *Res Gestae* (perhaps it would have been called *De Felicitate Mea*) would have made interesting reading: the differences between Tacitus' account and that of his neighbour might have been greater than those between Livy and Ammianus. Nonetheless, if we should be wary of assuming that their contemporaries would have placed emphasis on the same themes, we can reasonably assume that they would have couched their accounts in terms of negotiation with the gods and proper religious conduct.

We have at least made a start on comprehending the place of religion in these historical accounts. Broad outlines have been proposed within which future detailed discussions of individual episodes may flourish: many remain unexplored here. But the questions will have changed: no longer a simple assent to or denial of the elusive 'theologies' of Roman religion, but a textured set of deliberately deployed interpretations and mannered strategies – not unlike the formulations available for poets in fact. What is distinctive about these historians is that they concerned themselves with almost the whole picture of religion: the only area left deliberately obscure was the reasoning of the various priests – a concession to the politics of expertise. Otherwise they were vigorously engaged in an assessment of religious matters, whether they be phenomena, interpretation or the institutions and their changing role. The genre of historiography demanded a predominantly human perspective: one did not expect elaborate descriptions of the gods' debates, wishes or reasoning, as an epic poet would provide. That particular idiom was no less valid, and no more 'true', than the deductive perspective of the historian. The readers were aware that each genre had its own methods of representing reality, and approached their texts accordingly. For this reason alone we should be suspicious of arguments of 'secularity' in historiographical texts, since history aspired to verisimilitude of 'real' life rather than explicit formulation of divine plans and responses. We may not always be sufficiently naturalised to appreciate the difference.

For this reason, I am under no illusions that the sketches presented here are undoubtedly crude: we can trace links between piety and success, the *ira deum* and Roman setbacks, even the connections between particular deities and subsequent events. But we cannot see the 'thickness' of religious causality that most Roman readers would have discerned. The overall structures of our accounts are particularly difficult to discern, not least because of the damage to the narratives. Though I have outlined a possible 'grand' reading of Tacitus' accounts, I have not tackled the 'grand sweep' of Livy's, or Ammianus', histories: we have the barest indications of the completed *AVC* and none of Ammianus' beginnings. Whereas Tacitus' account can be framed by his own statements, granting the possibility of comparing the direction of the narrative with its outcome, all we can say for our other two is that both imply a pessimistic outcome.[2]

But even this is not to be taken at face value: their exemplary accounts are, after all, an attempt at remedy. Even if we ignore 'grand schemes' covering centuries, we have seen too many instances where a historian feels moved to clarify an otherwise implicit religious causality or accounted for this unusual venture, to dismiss a 'religious' narrative. Time and again, events proved to be comprehensible by recourse to the divine disposition at the time. Nor should we overemphasises any canonical aspect to this: each historian has showed traditional colours but *distinctively* so. On the whole, I have declined to compare their accounts with other texts, but occasionally it is worth noting the uniqueness of a religious deduction or formulation.[3] These men have conspicuously worked not just from but *with* the historical record, applying their own hard-won expertise even while the lessons of the past informed their accounts. They had an eye for the minutest detail within broader schemes of religious propriety and offer a discriminating representation of a working religion for Rome.

Religion did not just matter for the sake of explaining Rome's past: the historians had an eye on the present too. They were only too sure of what constituted an appropriate model for religion. Each is committed to

---

[2] Livy opens with his famous statement of hopelessness *nec uitia nostra nec remedia pati possumus* (*pr. 1.9*): Barnes (1998) 184 sides emphatically with those who see in Ammianus no grounds for optimism. Such judgements may well be misplaced; Livy and Ammianus might well both have responded that their interest lay in making recovery possible without indulging in prophecy.

[3] Compare Plutarch's treatment of the miscategorised Cumaean 'prodigy' (Livy 27.23.2) in his *Marcellus* 28.3: it is unproblematic as a prodigy, and is related directly to the general rather than the Roman state. Tacitus' elucidation of the *ira deum* at *Annals* 4.1.2 also seems to be his own work. Ammianus' account of Julian is clearly at odds with his contemporaries.

prodigies in a way that few others match: Suetonius was happy, for instance, to mix omens connected to individuals with items that Tacitus reappropriates as matters of state. Perhaps in this they were more out of step with their contemporaries than we have tended to assume: the elder Pliny, for instance, showed little concern that hermaphrodites were now treated as an entertaining oddity, in contrast to his ancestors, who found them so worrying that they felt compelled to remove the unfortunate children from Roman soil.[4]

They are also wise to the circumstances that led to the decline in the use of prodigies: Tacitus depicts the process of their erosion, while Livy has no truck with the new approaches, and simply calls it 'neglect of the gods'. Ammianus knows that the restoration of prodigies was an even greater challenge than the restoration of a pagan religious system: the challenge he faced was even more daunting than that of his predecessors, however pressing they perceived the need for a restoration of religious *mores*. Each is wise to the way that innovation can undermine a system that worked well for centuries, and, in their own way, refused to endorse most of the changes. This is not just true of prodigies: it applies to a whole range of changes. Foreign and ill-conceived practices had no place in Rome, unless properly sanctioned as a legitimate expansion of the Roman pantheon.

But this has not just been an exploration of historiography: it has as much, if not more, been a study of religion in its own right. The dynamics in interpretation, though discerned in historical accounts, were not unique to that forum: the historians' easy familiarity is a useful witness, but not as an isolated voice. If we can begin to appreciate how the multiple levels of reasoning and accountability functioned (by noting our own use of a very similar set of explanatory levels) then perhaps the 'contradictions' and 'confusions' will become areas in which we can explore the sophistication of an author's formulation rather than a sad indictment of his foolishness.

We should perhaps distinguish our disagreement with those structures of reasoning from our analysis of their workings: we already do this for (e.g.) economic theory (or the lack of it) and a multitude of other areas: why not religion? We might point at the difficulties of reconciling 'fate' with 'freewill' but we have not escaped the dilemma: it is a topical issue in genetics, for instance, and the solutions, which are, like the religious ones found here, overwhelmingly *pragmatic* in nature, have not actually changed a great deal. There is little room for complacency in this respect.

We in the West live in what the *literati* at least consider to be a secular world. But the difficulty of fitting 'gods' into the same sentence as 'rationality' without a negative of some kind has led us astray in our reading of

---

[4] *NH* 7.34.

ancient writers. I do not intend to make a case for ancient religion as an *effective* practice, though I can see the utility of building a temple of Concord at a time of civil instability. Refusing to admit ancient religion as a rational practice is more of a moral judgement than a balanced assessment. While it was constructed as a simple-minded affair for those terminably lacking insight into the self-evident , 'rationality' seemed an overly generous term. Now that it is instead a sophisticated and nuanced set of interpretative strategies, we might need to consider at least dropping our denial, or (if we are more honest) simply noting our disagreement with their inductive principles.

Ancient religion *was* 'rational' in the sense of requiring the cognitive mastery of complex interpenetrating systems of analysis. Being as much a social and political act as a religious one, interpretation had the trappings of power: reasoned analysis with internal coherence was required to gain assent, and one ignored the expertise of the audience at one's peril. It had insightful as well as amateurish practitioners, or so we are told: it is doubtful whether we could ever recover sufficient expertise to step into their shoes and make the kinds of judgement that they made. We may personally consider ancient religion an intellectual folly, but even its sceptics must now at least admit that it is an *elaborate* folly.

Though I have claimed that three authors can represent a tradition, I have declined to discuss many others here: Sallust and Caesar are particularly conspicuous by their absence in the Latin tradition, and so too are Polybius and Thucydides on the Greek side. These latter two especially would require a very sustained analysis if we were to overturn the virtually ubiquitous reading of their texts as secular or religiously untraditional monuments. Given that Greek and Roman historiography were not the same creatures, that would be an entirely separate volume.

Nonetheless, I have perhaps offered starting points: a commitment to using *fortuna* or *tyche* might indicate not a weariness or disenchantment with contemporary analysis of the divine, but rather, in the case of Polybius, the acknowledgement by an outsider that he is not in a position to make specific deductions about the workings of the Roman gods. Similarly, a 'studied avoidance' of the divine by Thucydides (if that is indeed what is going on in his text) might be a refusal to introduce the gods into a situation where it was simply not necessary – and therefore, in a historiographical account, not appropriate. No doubt the methodology employed here would have to change drastically to give a fair hearing: but it represents a more appropriate point of departure than 'belief'.

From this evidence, religion was undeniably a historian's business. Even to avoid mentioning the gods was a historiographical statement. The narration of Rome's past necessarily involved a documentation of how her institutions had fared, and under what conditions. History was the chance to see how one, or one's city, might negotiate with the gods to maintain or restore the *pax deorum*, based on past successes or failures. This would range from the particular to the most diffuse: a reader of Livy might be encouraged to expect, or even call for, a *nouemdiale sacrum* following a rain of stones; Tacitus' reader might be more cautious in responding to a sign, whether acknowledged or ignored; either's peers might compare the handling of prodigies in times past with more recent examples and see room for improvement. It does not seem beyond the pale to say that Ammianus hoped his readers in positions of power would be more circumspect in ordering punishments, if only for their own sakes.

It is hard to know how much of Ammianus' religion was derived from study of the historical record: though he cites non-historiographical authors of the distant past (primarily Cicero) as authorities on religion, he evokes the historiographical tradition by the simple fact that he wrote history: his lament on prodigies, even if an accidental echo of his predecessors, implicitly sends his readers to earlier accounts for the appropriate handling of prodigies. More likely his comments were to be taken as a deliberate allusion to his predecessors. Either way, his religion is anchored in the Roman past. The study of history *explicitly* qualified Livy, at least, to write about religion; conversely Tacitus, *quindecimuir* for the Saecular Games, looked to the past to inform his religion.

If we can adjust our expectations to be closer to theirs, these accounts are a sharp wake-up call on religious matters. Their subtlety, even formality, should not be mistaken for relative indifference. In the cultured climate of the Roman empire, they were clarion calls for change, or at least reflect a caution that standards did not slip again. Given the consequences that they all depict for failing to propitiate the gods, it is hard *not* to see religion as a serious aspect of exemplary history. Indeed, it is tempting to conclude that if one wished to offer a serious revision of current religious practices, historiography was the most obvious method of doing so. The closer we look at religion and historiography, the harder it becomes to tell the difference.

Bibliography

Ahl, F. (1984) 'The Art of Safe Criticism in Greece and Rome', *AJP* 105, 174–208.

Alvar, J. (1985) 'Matériaux pour l'étude de la formule *sive deus, sive dea*', *Numen* 32, 236–73.

Amat, J. (1992) 'Ammien Marcellin et la Justice Immanente (14.11.20–34)', in Holtz and Fredouille (1992), 267–79.

Anderson, G. (1994) *Sage, Saint and Sophist: Holy Men and their Associates in the Early Roman Empire*, London and New York.

André, J.-M. (1982) 'La conception de l'état et de l'empire dans la pensée gréco-romaine des deux premiers siècles de notre ère', *ANRW II* 30.1, 3–73.

Angliviel de la Beaumelle, L. (1974) 'Remarques sur l'attitude d'Ammien Marcellin à l'égard du christianisme', in *Mélanges d'histoire ancienne offerts à William Seston*, Paris, 15–23.

Ash, R. (1997) 'Severed Heads', in J. Mossman (ed.) *Plutarch and his Intellectual World*, London and Swansea, 196–200.

——— (1999) *Ordering Anarchy: Armies and Leaders in Tacitus' Histories*, London.

Athanassiadi, P. and Frede, M. (eds.) (1999) *Pagan Monotheism in Late Antiquity*, Oxford and New York.

Attridge, H. W. (1978) 'The Philosophical Critique of Religion under the Early Empire', *ANRW II* 16.1, 45–78.

Aubrion, E. (1985) *Rhétorique et histoire chex Tacite*, Metz.

——— (1990) 'Tacite et la notion de corps social (*Ann.* 14.27)', *Latomus* 49, 154–60.

——— (1991) 'L'*eloquentia* de Tacite et sa *fides* d'historien', *ANRW II* 33.4, 2597–688.

Auerbach, E. (1973) *Mimesis: The Representation of Reality in Western Literature*, Princeton.

Badian, E. (1993) 'Livy and Augustus', in Schuller (1993), 9–39.

Bakker, J. T. (1994) *Living and Working with the Gods*, Amsterdam.

Baldwin, B. (1974) 'Themes, Personalities and Distortions in Tacitus', *Athenaeum* 52, 70–81.

——— (1977) 'Tacitean Humour', *WS* 90, 128–44.

Banton, M. (ed.) (1966) *Anthropological Approaches to the Study of Religion*, London.

Barnes, T. D. (1990) 'Literary Convention. Nostalgia and Reality in Ammianus Marcellinus', in G. Clarke (ed.) *Reading the Past in Late Antiquity*, Rushcutters Bay, Australia, 59–92.

—— (1998) *Ammianus Marcellinus and the Representation of Historical Reality*, Ithaca, New York and London.

Barton, T. (1994) *Ancient Astrology*, London and New York.

Bartsch, T. (1994) *Actors in the Audience: Theatricality and Doublespeak from Nero to Hadrian*, Cambridge, Mass. and London.

Beagon, M. (1992) *Roman Nature. The Thought of Pliny the Elder*, Oxford.

Beard, M. (1980) 'The Sexual Status of Vestal Virgins', *JRS* 70, 12–27.

—— (1982) 'Decline and Fall? Roman State Religion in the Late Republic', *PCA* 79, 21–2.

—— (1985) 'Writing and Ritual: A Study of Diversity and Expansion in the *Arval Acta*', *PBSR* 53, 114–62.

—— (1986) 'Cicero and Divination: The Formation of a Latin Discourse', *JRS* 76, 33–46.

—— (1987) 'A Complex Of Times: No More Sheep on Romulus' Birthday', *PCPhS* n.s. 33, 213, 1–15.

—— (1990) 'Priesthood in the Roman Republic', in Beard and North (1990), 17–48.

—— (1993) 'Looking (harder) for Roman Myth: Dumézil, Declamation and the Problems of Definition', in Graf (1993), 44–64.

—— (1994) 'The Roman and the Foreign: The Cult of the 'Great Mother' in Imperial Rome', in N. Thomas and C. Humphreys (eds.) *Shamanism, History and the State*, Ann Arbor, 164–9.

—— (1995) 'Re-reading (Vestal) Virginity', in R. Hawley and B. Levick (eds.) *Women in Antiquity*, London and New York, 166–77.

—— (1998) 'Documenting Roman Religion', in Scheid (1998a), 75–101.

Beard, M. and North, J. (eds.) (1990) *Pagan Priests: Religion and Power in the Ancient World*, Ithaca and New York.

Beard, M., North, J. A. and Price, S. (1998) *Religions of Rome*, Cambridge.

Beck, R. (1988) *Planetary Gods and Planetary Orders in the Mysteries of Mithras*, *EPRO* volume 109, Leiden.

Begbie, C. M. (1967) 'The Epitome of Livy', *CQ* 17, 332–8.

Belardi, W. (1976) *Superstitio*, Rome.

Bélier, C. (1991) *Decayed Gods: Origin and Development of Georges Dumézil's 'Idéologie tripartite'*, Leiden.

Bémont, C. (1960) 'Les enterrés vivants du *Forum Boarium*: essai d'interprétation', *MEFRA* 72, 133–46.

Benario, H. W. (1986) 'Recent Work on Tacitus: 1984–1993', *CW* 89.2.

—— (1991) 'Tacitus' View of the Empire and the *Pax Romana*', *ANRW II* 33.5, 3332–53.

—— (1992) '*Principatus* and *imperium*: Tacitus *Historiae* 1.1', in R. M. Wilhelm and H. Jones (eds.) *The Two Worlds of the Poet: New Perspectives on Vergil*, Detroit, 328–34.

—— (1999) *Tacitus' Germany:* Germania, Warminster, England.

Bendlin, A. (1997) 'Peripheral Centres – Central Peripheries: Religious Communication in the Roman Empire', in Cancik and Röpke (1997), 35–68.

—— (2000) 'Looking Beyond the Civic Compromise: Religious Pluralism in Late Republican Rome', in Bispham and Smith (2000), 115–35.

Béranger, J. (1990) 'L'expression du pouvoir sûpreme chez Tacite', in G. Nicolet (ed.) *Du pouvoir dans l'antiquité: mots et réalités*, Geneva, 181–205.

Betensky, A. (1978) 'Neronian Style, Tacitean Content: The Use of Ambiguous Confrontations in the *Annals*', *Latomus* 37, 419–35.

Bispham, E. and Smith, C. (2000) *Religion in Archaic and Republican Rome and Italy: Evidence and Experience*, Edinburgh.

Blänsdorf, J. (1992) 'Tacite, *Annales* IV 32 sq. et la tradition de l'historiographie antique', in R. Chavallier and R. Poignault (eds.) *Présence de Tacite*, Tours, 45–60.

Bleicken, J. (1957a) 'Kollisionem zwischen Sacrum und Publicum', *Hermes* 85, 446–80.

—— (1957b) 'Oberpontifex und Pontifikalkollegium. Eine Studie zur römischen Salkralverfassung', *Hermes* 85, 345–66.

Bloch, M. L. P. (1973) *The Royal Touch*, London.

Bloch, R. (1963) *Les prodiges dans l'antiquité classique: Grèce, Etrurie et Rome*, Paris.

—— (1964) 'Liberté et déterminisme dans la divination romaine', in *Hommages à Jean Bayet*, volume 70 of *Collection Latomus*, Brussels, 89–100.

Blockley, R. C. (1973) 'Tacitean Influence on Ammianus Marcellinus', *Latomus* 32, 63–78.

—— (1975) *Ammianus Marcellinus: A Study of his Historiography and Political Thought*, *Collections Latomus* volume 141, Brussels.

Boesche, R. (1987) 'The Politics of Pretence: Tacitus and the Political Theory of Despotism', *HPTh* 8, 189–210.

Bonfante, L. W. (1964) 'Emperor, God and Man in the Fourth Century: Julian the Apostate and Ammianus Marcellinus', *PdP* 19, 401.

Borgeaud, P. (1996) *La mère des dieux: de Cybèle à la vierge Marie*, Paris.

Bornecque, H. (1933) *Tite-Live*, Paris.

Bourque, N. (2000) 'An Anthropologist's View of Ritual', in Bispham and Smith (2000), 19–33.

Bowersock, G. W. (1990a) *Hellenism in Late Antiquity*, Cambridge.

—— (1990b) 'review of Matthews (1989)', *JRS* 80, 247–8.

—— (1990c) 'The Pontificate of Augustus', in Raaflaub and Toher (1990).

Bowersock, G. W., Brown, P. and Grabar, O. (eds.) (1999) *Late Antiquity. A Guide to the Postclassical World*, Cambridge, Mass.

Boyancé, P. (1972) *Etudes sur la religion romaine*, Collection de l'Ecole française de Rome volume 11, Rome.

Boyce, A. A. (1937) 'The Expiatory Rites of 207 B. C.', *TAPA* 68, 157–71.

Boyer, P. (ed.) (1993a) *Cognitive Aspects of Religious Symbolism*, Cambridge.

Boyer, P. (1993b) 'Cognitive Aspects of Religious Symbolism', in Boyer (1993a), 4–40.

Boyle, A. J. (1984) 'The Broken Reed: Virgil, Petronius, Tacitus', *Classicum* 10, 26–34.

Brakman, C. (1928) 'Tacitus quae de astrologia iudicaverit', *Mnemosyne* 56, 70–8.

Bremmer, J. (1993) 'Three Roman Aetiological Myths', in Graf (1993), 158–74.

Bremmer, J. and Horsfall, N. (1987) *Roman Myth and Mythography, BICS supp.* volume 52, London.

Brenk, F. E. (1975) 'The Dreams of Plutarch's Lives', *Latomus* 34, 336–49.

Brennan, T. C., Dickerson, G. and Lang, M. L. (1991) 'review of Beard and North (1990)', *BMCR* 2.2.1.

Brink, C. O. (1994) 'Can Tacitus' *Diaologus* Be Dated?', *HSCP* 96, 251–80.

Briquel, D. (1995) 'Tacite et l'haruspicine', in *Les écrivains et l'etrusca disciplina de Claude à Trajan*, volume 64 of *Caesarodunum Suppl.*, 27–37.

Briscoe, J. (1973) *A Commentary on Livy Books XXXI–XXXIII*, Oxford.

Brown, P. (1971) *The World of Late Antiquity: from Marcus Aurelius to Muhammed*, London.

——— (1972) *Religion and Society in the Age of Saint Augustine*, London.

——— (1978) *The Making of Late Antiquity*, Cambridge, Mass.

——— (1992) *Power and Persuasion in Late Antiquity: Towards a Christian Empire*, Madison, Wisc.

——— (1995) *Authority and the Sacred: Aspects of the Christianisation of the Roman World*, Cambridge.

Bruhl, A. (1953) *Liber Pater. Origine et expansion du culte dionysiaque à Rome et dans le monde romain, BEFAR* volume 175, Paris.

Brunt, P. A. (1980) 'On Historical Fragments and Epitomes', *CQ* 30, 487–8.

Bucher, G. (1987) 'The *Annales Maximi* in the Light of Roman Methods of Keeping Records', *AJAH* 12, 2–61.

Burkert, W. (1985) *Greek Religion: Archaic and Classical*, Cambridge, Mass. and London.

——— (1987) *Ancient Mystery Cults*, Cambridge, Mass. and London.

——— (1997) *Creation of the Sacred: Tracks of Biology in Early Religions*, Cambridge, Mass.

Burridge, K. O. L. (1969) *New Heaven, New Earth*, Oxford.

Buxton, R. (1980) 'Blindness and Limits: Sophokles and the Logic of Myth', *JHS* 100, 22–37.

Cameron, A. (1964) 'The Roman Friends of Ammianus', *JRS* 54, 15–28.

——— (1989) *History as Text: The Writing of Ancient History*, London.

Cameron, A. D. E. and Cameron, A. M. (1964) 'Christianity and Tradition in the Historiography of the Later Empire', *CQ* n.s. 14, 316–28.

Camus, P.-M. (1967) *Ammien Marcellin: témoin des courants culturels et religieux à la fin du IVième siècle*, Paris.

Cancik, H. (2001) 'Religiongeschichtsschreiung bei Tacitus. Zur Darstellung der germanischen und jedischen Religion im Tacitus' *Germania* und *Historiae*', in Spickerman *et al.* (2001), 49–69.

Cancik, H. and Röpke, J. (eds.) (1997) *Römische Reichsreligion und Provinzial-religion*, Töbingen.

Cannadine, D. and Price, S. (eds.) (1987) *Rituals of Royalty: Power and Cere-monial in Traditional Societies*, Cambridge.

Capdeville, G. (1995) Volcanus: *recherches comparatistes sur les origines du culte de Vulcan*, *BEFAR* volume 288, Rome.

Ceausescu, P. (1974) 'L'image d'Auguste chez Tacite', *Klio* 56, 183–99.

Champeaux, J. (1967) '*Forte* chez Tite-Live', *REL* 45, 363–89.

—— (1982) 'Religion romaine et religion latine', *REL* 60, 71–104.

—— (1982-7) *Recherches sur le culte de la Fortuna à Rome et dans le monde romain: des origines à la mort de César*, Collection de l'Ecole française de Rome volume 44, Paris.

—— (1996) 'Pontifes, haruspices et décemvirs. L'expiation des prodiges de 207', *REL* 74, 67–92.

—— (1998) *La religion romaine*, Paris.

Chaplin, J. D. (2000) *Livy's Exemplary History*, Oxford.

Chilver, G. E. F. (1979) *A Historical Commentary on Tacitus' Histories I and II*, Oxford.

—— (1985) *A Historical Commentary on Tacitus' Histories IV and V*, Oxford.

Chuvin, P. (1990) *A Chronicle of the Last Pagans*, Cambridge, Mass.

Cizek, E. (1979) '*Sine ira et studio* et l'image de l'homme chez Tacite', *StudClas* 18, 103–13.

—— (1991) 'La poétique de l'histoire chez Tacite', *REL* 69, 136–46.

—— (1992) 'A propos de la poétique de l'histoire chez Tite-Live', *Latomus* 51, 355–64.

Classen, C. J. (1988) 'Tacitus – Historian Between Republic and Principate', *Mnemosyne* 41, 93–116.

Cogitore, I. (1991) 'La potentia chez Tacite: accusation indirecte du Principat', *BullBudé* 2, 158–71.

Cohee, P. (1994) '*Instauratio Sacrorum*', *Hermes* 122.4, 451–68.

Cohen, A. (1986) *Symbolising Boundaries: Identity and Diversity in British Cultures*, Manchester.

Cohn, N. (1957) *The Pursuit of the Millennium*, London.

Cole, S. G. (1984) Theoi Megaloi: *The Cult of the Great Gods Of Samothrace*, *EPRO* volume 96, Leiden.

Conduché, D. (1965) 'Ammien Marcellin et la mort de Julien', *Latomus* 24, 359–80.

Conte, G. B. (1986) *The Rhetoric of Imitation: Genre and Poetic Memory in Virgil and Other Latin Poets*, Ithaca and London.

—— (1994a) *Genres and Readers: Lucretius, Love Elegy, Pliny's Ency-clopaedia*, Baltimore.

—— (1994b) *Latin Literature: A History*, Baltimore.

Cook, B. L. (2001) 'Plutach's Use of *legetai*: Narrative Design and Source in *Alexander*', *GRBS* 2.4, 329–60.

Cornell, T. J. (1981) 'Some Observations on the *crimen incesti*', in *Le délit réligieux dans la cité antique*, volume 48 of *Collection de l'Ecole française de Rome*, Rome, 27–37.

—— (1986) 'The Formation of the Historical Tradition of Early Rome', in Moxon *et al.* (1986), 67–86.

—— (1995) *The Beginnings of Rome 753–264 BC*, London.

Corrigan, P. L. (1993) 'A Literary Reading of Tacitus' *Annals* 4.68–70: The Slaying of Titius Sabinus', *RhM* 136, 330–42.

Cousin, J. (1942) 'La crise religieuse de 207 av. J.-C.', *RHR* 26, 15–41.

Cramer, F. H. (1951) 'Expulsion of Astrologers from Ancient Rome', *Class. and Med.* 12, 9–50.

Crawford, M. and Beard, M. (1985) *Rome in the Late Republic*, London.

Croix, G. D. S. (1963) 'Why were the Early Christians Persecuted?', *Past and Present* 26, 6–38.

Croke, B. and Emmett, A. M. (1983a) 'Historiography in Late Antiquity: An Overview', in Croke and Emmett (1983b), 1–12.

—— (1983b) *History and Historians in Late Antiquity*, Rushcutters Bay *et al.*

Cumont, F. (1911) *The Oriental Religions in Roman Paganism*, Chicago.

D'Ambrosio, F. G. (1980) 'End of the Flavians: The Case for Senatorial Treason', *RIL* 114, 232–41.

Davidson, J. (1991) 'The Gaze in Polybius' *Histories*', *JRS* 81, 10–24.

Davies, J. (1999) *Death, Burial and Rebirth in the Religions of Antiquity*, London and New York.

den Boeft, J. (1999) 'Pure Religious Rites: Ammianus Marcellinus on the *Magi* (23.6.33)', in Drijvers and Hunt (1999), 207–16.

den Boeft, J., den Hengst, D. and Teitlerin, H. C. (eds.) (1992) *Cognitio Gestorum. The Historiographical Art of Ammianus Marcellinus*, Amsterdam.

den Boeft, J. *et al.* (eds.) (1995) *Philological and Historical Commentary on Ammianus Marcellinus XXII*, Groningen.

den Hengst, D. (1992) 'The Scientific Digressions in Ammianus' *Res Gestae*', in den Boeft *et al.* (1992), 39–46.

Dench, E. (1995) *From Barbarians to New Men: Greek, Roman and Modern Perceptions of Peoples of the Central Apennines*, Oxford.

Denyer, N. (1985) 'The Case against Divination: An Examination of Cicero's *De Divinatione*', *PCPS* 31, 1–10.

Détienne, M. (1967) *Les maîtres de vérité dans la Grèce archaïque*, Paris.

—— (1979) *Dionysos Slain*, Baltimore.

—— (1981) 'Between Gods and Men', in Gordon (1981), 215–28.

—— (1986) *The Creation of Mythology*, Chicago and London.

—— (1989) *Dionysos at Large*, Cambridge, Mass.

Develin, R. (1983) 'Tacitus and Techniques of Insidious Suggestion', *Antichthon* 17, 64–95.

Dickson, S. K. and Plympton, M. (1977) 'The Prodigy of the Fig-Tree: Tacitus' *Annales* 13.58', *RSC* 25, 183–86.

Donnell, J. (1979) 'The Demise of Paganism', *Traditio* 35, 45–88.

Dorcey, P. F. (1992) *The Cult of Silvanus – a Study in Roman Folk Religion*, Leiden and New York.

Dorey, T. A. (ed.) (1969) *Tacitus*, London.

Dorey, T. A. (1971) *Livy*, London.

Dorey, T. A. and Dudley, D. R. (1971) *Rome Against Carthage*, London.

Douglas, M. (1966) *Purity and Danger: an Analysis of Concepts of Pollution and Taboo*, London.

Dowden, K. (2000) *European Paganism: The Realities of Cult from Antiquity to the Middle Ages*, London.

Drake, H. A. (2000) *Constantine and the Bishop: The Politics of Intolerance*, Baltimore.

Drijvers, J. W. and Hunt, D. (eds.) (1999) *The Late Roman World and its Historian: Interpreting Ammianus Marcellinus*, London.

Drinkwater, J. F. (1974) 'The "Pagan Underground", Constantius II's "Secret Service", and the Survival, and Usurpation of Julian the Apostate', in C. Deroux (ed.) *Studies in Latin Literature III*, 348–88.

Ducroix, S. (1978) 'Histoire d'un portrait, portraits d'historiens: Tacite lecteur de Salluste', *MEFRA* 90, 293–315.

Dudley, D. R. (1968) *The World of Tacitus*, London.

Duff, T. (2000) *Plutarch's Lives: Exploring Virtue and Vice*, Oxford.

Dumézil, G. (1969) *Idées romaines*, Paris.

――― (1970) *Archaic Roman Religion*, Chicago.

Duthoy, R. (1969) *The* Taurobolium: *its Evolution and Terminology*, EPRO volume 10, Leiden.

Eckstein, A. M. (1982) 'Human Sacrifice and the Fear of Military Disaster in Republican Rome', *AJAH* 7, 69–95.

Edwards, C. (1993) *The Politics of Immorality in Ancient Rome*, Cambridge.

――― (1996a) *Writing Rome: Textual Approaches to the City*, Cambridge.

Edwards, D. R. (1996b) *Religion and Power. Pagans, Jews, and Christians in the Greek East*, New York and Oxford.

Eliade, M. (1957) *The Sacred and the Profane*, San Diego, New York and London.

Elliott, T. G. (1983) *Ammianus Marcellinus and Fourth Century History*, Sarasota, Fla.

Elsner, J. (1998) *Imperial Rome and Christian Triumph*, Oxford.

Elsner, J. and Masters, J. (eds.) (1994) *Reflections of Nero: Culture, History, and Representation*, Chapel Hill and London.

Erkell, H. (1952) Augustus, Felicitas, Fortuna: *Lateinische Wortstudien*, Göteburg.

Fabre, P. (1940) '*Minime Romano Sacro*', *REA* 42, 419–24.

Fantham, R. E. (1998) Fasti *Book IV*, New York and Cambridge.

Faraone, C. A. and Obbink, D. (eds.) (1991) Magika Hiera: *Ancient Greek Magic And Religion*, New York and Oxford.

Febvre, L. (1982) *The Problem of Unbelief in the Sixteenth Century France: The Religion of Rabelais*, Cambridge, Mass.

Feeney, D. C. (1991) *The Gods In Epic: Poets and Critics of the Classical Tradition*, Oxford.

—— (1992) '*Si licet et fas est:* Ovid's *Fasti* and the Problem of Free Speech under the Principate', in Powell (1992), 1–25.

—— (1998) *Literature and Religion at Rome: Cultures, Contexts and Beliefs*, Cambridge.

Feldherr, A. M. (1997) 'Livy's Revolution: Civic Identity and the Creation of the *res publica*', in Habinek and Schiesaro (1997), 136–58.

—— (1998) *Spectacle and Society in Livy's History*, Berkeley.

Ferguson, J. (1970) *The Religions of the Roman Empire*, London.

Festinger, L., Riecken, H. W. and Schachter, S. (1956) *When Prophecy Fails*, Minneapolis.

Festugière, A. J. (1954) 'Ce que Tite-Live nous apprend sur les mystères de Dionysos', *MEFRA* 66, 79–99.

Feyerabend, P. K. (1975) *Against Method: Outline of an Anarchistic Theory of Knowledge*, London.

—— (1987) *Farewell to Reason*, London.

—— (1999) *Knowledge, Science and Relativism, Philosophical Papers* volume 3, Cambridge.

Fishwick, D. (1987) *The Imperial Cult in the Latin West: Studies in the Ruler Cult of the Western Province of the Roman Empire*, EPRO volume 108, Leiden.

Fornara, C. W. (1992a) 'Studies in Ammianus Marcellinus. I. The Letter of Libanius and Ammianus' Connection with Antioch', *Historia* 41, 328–44.

—— (1992b) 'Studies in Ammianus Marcellinus. II. Ammianus' Knowledge and Use of Greek and Latin Literature', *Historia* 41, 420–38.

Forsythe, G. (1999) *Livy and Early Rome: A Study in Historical Method and Judgment*, Stuttgart.

Foucault, M. (1978–1986) *A History of Sexuality*, London.

Fowler, W.-F. (1911) *The Religious Experience of the Roman People from the Earliest Times to the Age of Augustus*, London.

Fox, M. (1996) *Roman Historical Myths: The Regal Period in Augustan Literature*, Oxford.

—— (2001) 'Dionysius, Lucian and the Prejudice against Rhetoric in History', *JRS* 91, 76–94.

Frakes, R. M. (2000) 'Ammianus Marcellinus and his Intended Audience', in C. Deroux (ed.) *Studies in Latin Literature and Roman History*, volume X, Brussels, 392–442.

Frank, T. (1927) 'The Bacchanalian Cult of 186 B.C.', *CQ* 21, 128–32.

Frend, W. H. C. (1984) *The Rise of Christianity*, London.

Frier, B. (1979) Libri Annales Pontificis Maximi: *The Origins of the Annalistic Tradition*, Rome.

Fugier, H. (1963) *Recherches sur l'expression du sacré dans la langue latine*, Paris.

Furneaux, H. (1896) *The Annals of Tacitus*, Oxford.

Gabba, E. (1991) *Dionysius and the History of Archaic Rome*, Berkeley and Los Angeles.

Gagé, J. (1955) *Apollo romain*, Paris.

Galinsky, K. (1998) *Augustan Culture. An Interpretative Introduction*, Princeton.

Gallop, D. (1988) 'Aristotle on Sleep, Dreams, and Final Causes', *Proceedings of the Boston Area Colloquium in Ancient Philosophy* vol. 4.

Garnsay, P. (1984) 'Religious Toleration in Classical Antiquity', in Shiels (1984), 1–27.

Geertz, C. (1966) 'Religion as a Cultural System', in Banton (1966), 1–46.

Geffcken, J. (1978) *The Last Days of Greco-Roman Paganism*, Amsterdam and Oxford.

Gell, A. (1992) *The Anthropology of Time*, Oxford.

Gigandet, A. (1998) *Lucrèce et les raisons du mythe*, Paris.

Gill, C. (1983) 'The Question of Character-Development: Plutarch and Tacitus', *CQ* 33, 469–87.

Gill, C. and Wiseman, T. P. (eds.) (1993) *Lies and Fiction in the Ancient World*, Exeter and Austin, Tex.

Gingras, M. T. (1991–2) 'Annalistic Format, Tacitean Themes and the Obituaries', *CJ* 87, 241–56.

Ginsburg, J. (1981) *Tradition and Theme in the Annals of Tacitus*, New York.

——— (1993) '*In maiores certamina*: Past and Present in the *Annals*', in Luce and Woodman (1993), 86–103.

Giovanni, A. (1998) 'Les livres auguraux', in Scheid (1998a), 103–22.

Girard, J.-L. (1980) '*Interpretatio Romana*. Questions historiques et problèmes de méthode', *Rev. Hist. et Phil. Rel.* 60, 21–7.

Glacken, C. J. (1973) *Traces on the Rhodean Shore: Nature and Culture in Western Thought from Ancient Times*, Berkeley.

Goldhill, S. (1994) 'The Failure of Exemplarity', in I. F. J. de Jong and J. P. Sullivan (eds.) *Modern Critical Theory and Classical Literature*, Leiden, 51–73.

Goodman, M. (1994) *Mission and Conversion: Proselytizing in the Religious History of the Roman Empire*, Oxford.

Goodman, M., Price, S. and Edwards, M. (eds.) (1999) *Apologetics in the Roman Empire: Pagans, Jews and Christians*, Oxford.

Goodyear, F. R. D. (1970a) 'Cyclic Development in History: A Note on Tacitus' *Annals* 3.55.5', *BICS* 17, 101–6.

——— (1970b) *Tacitus, Greece And Rome New Surveys in the Classics* volume 4.

——— (1972) *The* Annals *of Tacitus I:* Annals *1.1–54*, Cambridge.

——— (1982) *The* Annals *of Tacitus II:* Annals *1.55–81 and* Annals *2*, Cambridge.

Gordon, R. (1979) 'The Real and the Imaginary: Production and Religion in the Graeco-Roman World', *Art History* 2, 5–34.

——— (1980) 'Reality, Evocation and Boundaries in the Mysteries of Mithras', *Journal of Mithraic Studies* 3.

—— (1981) *Myth, Religion and Society: Structuralist Essays*, Cambridge and New York.

—— (1990a) 'From Republic to Principate: Priesthood, Religion, and Ideology', in Beard and North (1990), 177–98.

—— (1990b) 'Religion in the Roman Empire: The Civic Compromise and its Limits', in Beard and North (1990), 233–56.

—— (1990c) 'The Veil of Power: Emperors, Sacrificers, Benefactors', in Beard and North (1990), 199–231.

Gorman, E. O. (2000) *Irony and Misreading in the* Annals *of Tacitus*, Cambridge.

Gould, J. (1985) 'On Making Sense of Greek Religion', in P. E. Easterling and J. V. Muir (eds.) *Greek Religion and Society*, Cambridge, 1–33.

—— (1994) 'Herodotus and Religion', in Hornblower (1994), 91–106.

—— (2001) *Myth, Ritual Memory, and Exchange: Essays in Greek Literature and Culture*, Oxford.

Gradel, I. (2002) *Emperor Worship and Roman Religion*, Oxford and New York.

Graf, F. (ed.) (1993) *Mythos in mythenloser Gesellschaft: das Paradigma Roms, Colloquium Rauricum* volume 3, Stuttgart and Leipzig.

Graf, F. (1997) *Magic in the Ancient World*, Cambridge, Mass. and London.

Grandazzi, A. (1995) 'Un aspect de la divination chez Tacite, *Annales* XII, 24: quelques remarques sur le *pomerium*', in *Les écrivains et l'etrusca disciplina de Claude à Trajan*, volume 64 of Caesarodunum *Suppl.*, 38–62.

—— (1997) *The Foundation of Rome: Myth and History*, Ithaca and London.

Griffin, M. (1995) 'Tacitus, Tiberius and the Principate', in I. Malkin and Z. W. Rubinsohn (eds.) *Leaders and Masses in the Roman World*, Leiden, 33–45.

—— (1997) 'The Senate's Story', *JRS* 87, 249–63.

Griffin, M. T. (1982) 'The Lyons Tablet and Tacitean Hindsight', *CQ* 32, 404–18.

Grimal, P. (1989) 'Tacite et les présages', *REL* 67, 170–8.

—— (1989–90) 'Religion politique et sens du divin chez Tacite', *BAL* 20, 101–16.

Grodzynski, D. (1974) '*Superstitio*', *REA* 76, 36–60.

Gruen, E. (1990) *Studies in Greek Culture and Roman Policy*, Cincinnati Classical Studies NS volume 7, Leiden and New York.

—— (1993) *Culture and National Identity in Republican Rome*, Ithaca.

Guillaumont, F. (1996) 'La nature et les prodiges dans la religion et la philosophie romaines', in C. Lévy (ed.) *Le concept de nature à Rome: la physique*, Paris.

Habinek, T. (1998) *The Politics of Latin Literature: Writing, Identity, and Empire in Ancient Rome*, Princeton, N.J.

Habinek, T. and Schiesaro, A. (1997) *The Roman Cultural Revolution*, Cambridge.

Hall, J. F. (1986) 'The *Saeculum Novum* of Augustus', *ANRW II* 16.3, 2565–89.

Hallett, J. (1970) ''Over Troubled Waters': The Meaning of the Title *Pontifex*', *TAPA* 101, 219–27.

Hamerton-Kelly, G. (ed.) (1984) *Violent Origins: Ritual Killing and Cultural Formation*, Stanford.

Harmon, D. P. (1978) 'The Public Festivals of Rome', *ANRW II* 16.2, 1440–68.

―――― (1986) 'Religion in the Latin Elegists', *ANRW II* 16.3, 1909–73.

Harries, B. (1989) 'Causation and the Authority of the Poet in Ovid's *Fasti*', *CQ* 38, 164–85.

Harris, B. F. (1962) 'Tacitus on the Death of Otho', *CJ* 58, 73–7.

Harrison, T. E. H. (1997) 'Herodotus and the Certainty of Divine Retribution', in A. B. Lloyd (ed.) *What is a God? Studies in the Nature of Greek Divinity*, London, 101–22.

―――― (2000) *Divinity and History: The Religion of Herodotus*, Oxford.

Havas, L. (1991) 'Eléments du biologisme dans la conception historique de Tacite', *ANRW II* 33.4, 2949–86.

Hedrick, Jnr, C. W. H. (2000) *History and Silence: Purge and Rehabilitation of Memory in Late Antiquity*, Austin, Texas.

Hellegouarc'h, J. (1991) 'Le style de Tacite: bilan et perspectives', *ANRW II* 33.4, 2454–538.

Henck, N. (2001) 'Constantius' *Paideia*, Intellectual Milieu and Promotion of the Liberal Arts', *PCPS* 47, 172–87.

Henderson, J. (1987) 'Tacitus – A World In Pieces', *Ramus* 16, 167–210.

―――― (1998a) *Fighting For Rome: Poets and Caesars, History and Civil War*, Cambridge.

―――― (1998b) 'Livy and the Invention of History', in Cameron (1989), 64–86.

Henry, E. (1991) 'Virgilian Elements in Tacitus' Historical Imagination', *ANRW II* 33.4, 2987–3005.

Herbert-Brown, G. (1994) *Ovid and the* Fasti: *An Historical Study*, Oxford.

Heurgon, J. (1957) *Trois études sur le* 'ver sacrum', *Collection Latomus* volume 26, Brussels.

Hickson, F. V. (1993) *Roman Prayer Language: Livy and the Aeneid of Vergil*, Stuttgart.

Holtz, L. and Fredouille, J.-C. (eds.) (1992) *De Tertullien aux Mozarabes: mélanges offerts à Jacques Fontaine à l'occasion de son 70e anniversaire par ses élèves, amis et collègues*, Paris.

Hornblower, S. (1994) *Greek Historiography*, Oxford.

Horsfall, N. (1990) 'Virgil and the Illusory Footnote', *PapLatLeedsSem* 6, 49–64.

Horton, R. (1993a) 'Lévy-Bruhl, Durkheim and the Scientific Revolution', in Horton (1993b).

―――― (1993b) *Modes of Thought: Essays on Thinking in Western and Non-Western Societies*, London.

Horton, R. and Finnegan, R. (1973) *Modes of Thought: Essays on Thinking in Western and Non-Western Societies*, London.

Hunt, E. D. (1985) 'Christians and Christianity in Ammianus Marcellinus', *CQ* 35, 186–200.

Hunt, L. (ed.) (1989) *The New Cultural History*, Berkeley and London.

Hutton, R. (1991) *The Pagan Religions of the Ancient British Isles*, Oxford.

Izard, M. and Smith, P. (eds.) (1982) *Between Belief and Transgression: Structuralist Essays in Religion, History and Myth*, Chicago.

Jaeger, M. K. (1997) *Livy's Written Rome*, Ann Arbor.

Jameson, F. (1981) *The Political Unconscious: Narrative as a Socially Symbolic Act*, London.

Janssen, L. F. (1979) '*Superstitio* and the Persecution of the Christians', *Vigiliae Christianae* 33, 131–59.

Jocelyn, H. D. (1966) 'The Roman Nobility and the Religion of the Republican State', *JRH* 4, 89–104.

Jones, A. H. M. (1966) *The Decline of the Ancient World*, London and New York.

Kajanto, I. (1957) *God and Fate in Livy*, Turku.

—— (1981) '*Fortuna*', *ANRW II* 17.1, 502–58.

Kapferer, B. (1997) *The Feast of the Sorceror*, Chicago.

Kaster, R. A. (1988) *Guardians of Language: The Grammarian and Society in Late Antiquity*, Berkeley and London.

Kee, H. C. (1983) *Miracle in the Early Christian World: A Study in Socio-Historical Method*, New Haven and London.

Keitel, E. (1984) 'Principate and Civil War in the *Annals* of Tacitus', *AJP* 105, 306–25.

—— (1987) 'Otho's Exhortations in Tacitus' *Histories*', *G & R* 34, 73–82.

—— (1991) 'The Structure and Function of Speeches in Tacitus *Histories* I-III', *ANRW II* 33.4, 2772–94.

—— (1991-2) 'The Function of the Livian Reminiscences at Tacitus *Histories* 4.58.6 and 62', *CJ* 87, 327–37.

—— (1992) '*Foedum Spectaculum* and Related Motifs in Tacitus *Histories* II–III', *RhM* 135, 342–51.

Kelly, G. (2002) Ammianus Marcellinus: Autopsy, Allusion, *Exemplum*, PhD thesis, Oxford.

Kenney, E. J. (1983) 'The Key and the Cabinet: Ends and Means in Classical Literature', *PCA* 80, 7–18.

Knabe, G. S. (1978) 'On the Biography of Tacitus. The Problem of *sine ira et studio*', *VDI* 144, 111–30.

Kolakowski, L. (1982) *Religion*, Oxford.

Kramer, L. S. (1989) 'Literature, Criticism and Historical Imagination: The Literary Challenge of Hayden White and Dominick LaCapra', in Hunt (1989), 97–130.

Kraus, C. S. (1994a) *Livy* Ab Vrbe Condita *Book VI*, Cambridge.

—— (1994b) '"No Second Troy": Topoi and Refoundation in Livy, Book V', *TAPA* 124, 267–89.

—— (1997) 'Livy', in Kraus and Woodman (1997), 51–82.

—— (1998) 'Repetition and Empire in the *Ab Urbe Condita*', in P. Knox and C. Foss (eds.) *Style and Tradition: Studies in Honor of Wendell Clausen*, Stuttgart and Leiden, 264–83.

Kraus, C. S. (ed.) (1999) *The Limits of Historiography: Genre and Narrative in Ancient Historical Texts*, Leiden.

Kraus, C. S. and Woodman, A. J. (1997) *Latin Historians, Greece and Rome New Surveys in the Classics* volume 27, Oxford.

Krauss, F. B. (1930) An Interpretation of the Omens, Portents and Prodigies recorded by Livy, Tacitus and Suetonius, PhD thesis, Philadelphia.

Krill, R. (1978) 'Roman Paganism under the Antonines and Severans', *ANRW II* 16.1, 27–44.

Kuhn, T. (1962) *The Structure of Scientific Revolutions*, Chicago.

Kyle, D. G. (2001) *Spectacles of Death in Ancient Rome*, London and New York.

La Fontaine, J. S. (1998) *Speak of the Devil: Tales of Satanic Abuse in Contemporary England*, Cambridge.

Laird, A. (1999) *Powers of Expression, Expressions of Power: Speech Presentation and Latin Literature*, Oxford.

Lamberton, R. (1986) *Homer the Theologian: Neoplatonic Allegorical Reading and the Growth of the Epic Tradition*, Berkeley, LA and London.

Lambrechts, P. (1951) 'Cybèle; divinité étrangère ou nationale?', *Bull. Soc. belge d'Anthrop. et de Préhist.* 62, 44–60.

Lancel, S. (1998) *Hannibal*, Oxford.

Lane, E. N. (ed.) (1996) *Cybele, Attis and Related Cults: Essays in Memory of M. J. Vermaseren, Religions in the Greco-Roman World* volume 131, Leiden.

Lane-Fox, R. (1986) *Pagans and Christians in the Mediterranean World from the Second Century A.D. to the Conversion of Constantine*, London.

Lawson, E. and McCauley, R. (1990) *Rethinking Religion: Connecting Cognition and Culture*, Cambridge.

Lawson, E. T. (1993) 'Cognitive Categories, Cultural Forms and Ritual Structures', in Boyer (1993a), 188–206.

Lee, A. D. (2000) *Pagans and Christians in Late Antiquity*, London and New York.

Leeman, A. D. (1985) 'Structure and Meaning in the Prologues of Tacitus', in *Form und Sinn. Studien zur römischen Literatur (1954–1984)*, Frankfurt am Main and New York, 317–48.

Levene, D. S. (1993) *Religion in Livy*, Leiden.

—— (1997) 'Pity, Fear and the Historical Audience: Tacitus on the Fall of Vitellius', in S. Braund and C. Gill (eds.) *The Passions in Roman Thought and Literature*, Cambridge, 128–49.

—— (1999) 'Tacitus' *Histories* and the Theory of Deliberative Oratory', in Kraus (1999), 197–216.

Levick, B. (1999) *Vespasian*, London.

Lewis, I. M. (1989) *Ecstatic Religion*, London and New York.

Lewis, S. (1996) *News and Society in the Greek Polis*, Chapel Hill, North Carolina.

Liberman, G. (1998) 'Les documents sacerdotaux du collège *sacris faciundis*', in Scheid (1998a), 65–73.

Liebeschuetz, J. H. W. G. (1967) 'The Religious Position of Livy's History', *JRS* 52, 45–55.

———— (1979) *Continuity and Change in Roman Religion*, Oxford.

———— (1988) 'Ammianus, Julian and Divination', in M. Wisseman (ed.) *Roma renascens: Beiträge zur Spätantike und Rezeptionsgeschichte*, 198–213.

———— (1990a) *From Diocletian to the Arab Conquest*, Great Yarmouth.

———— (1990b) 'Religion in the *Panegyrici Latini*', in Liebeschuetz (1990a), 389–98.

Ligota, C. R. (1982) 'This Story is Not True: Fact and Fiction in Antiquity', *JWI* 45, 1–13.

Lind, I. R. (1992) 'The Ideas of the Republic and Republican Morality', in C. Deroux (ed.) *Studies in Latin Literature and Roman History*, volume VI of *Collection Latomus*, Brussels, 5–41.

Linderski, J. (1985) 'The *Libri Reconditi*', *HSCP* 89, 207–34.

———— (1986) 'The Augural Law', *ANRW II* 16.3, 2146–312.

———— (1993) 'Roman Religion in Livy', in Schuller (1993), 53–70.

Lipovsky, J. (1981) *A Historiographical Study of Livy, Books 6–10*, New York.

Lloyd, G. E. R. (1979) *Magic, Reason and Experience: Studies in the Origin and Development of Greek Science*, Cambridge.

———— (1990) *Demystifying Mentalities*, Cambridge.

———— (1996) *Adversaries and Authorities: Investigations into Ancient Greek and Chinese Science*, Cambridge.

Lossau, M. J. (1992) '*Amartia, anagnorosis, peripateia*: Tacite sur Tibère', *REL* 70, 37–42.

Lowrie, M. (1997) *Horace's Narrative Odes*, Oxford.

Lucas, J. (1974) *Les obsessions de Tacite*, Leiden.

Luce, T. J. (1971) 'Design and Structure in Livy: 5.32–55', *TAPA* 102, 265–302.

———— (1977) *Livy: The Composition of His History*, Princeton.

———— (1982a) *Ancient Writers: Greece and Rome*, New York.

———— (1982b) 'Tacitus', in Luce (1982a), 1003–33.

———— (1986) 'Tacitus' Conception of Historical Change: The Problem of Discovering the Historian's Opinions', in Moxon *et al.* (1986), 143–58.

———— (1989) 'Ancient Views on the Causes of Bias in Historical Writings', *CP* 84, 16–31.

———— (1991) 'Tacitus on "History's Highest Function"', *ANRW II* 33.4, 2904–27.

Luce, T. J. and Woodman, A. J. (eds.) (1993) *Tacitus and the Tacitean Tradition*, Princeton.

Macalindon, D. (1956) 'Senatorial Opposition to Claudius and Nero', *AJPh* 77, 113–32.

MacBain, B. (1982) *Prodigies and Expiation: A Study in Religion and Politics in the Roman Republic*, Collections Latomus volume 167, Brussels.

Macmullen, R. (1967) *Enemies of the Roman Order*, London.

———— (1981) *Paganism in the Roman Empire*, New Haven and London.

Madvig, J. N. (1877) *Emendationes Livianae*, Copenhagen.

Maier, H. O. (1995) 'The Topography of Heresy and Dissent in Late Fourth Century Rome', *Historia* 44, 232–49.

Marincola, J. (1997) *Authority and Tradition in Ancient Historiography*, Cambridge.

——— (1999a) 'Genre, Convention and Innovation in Greco-Roman Historiography', in Kraus (1999), 282–323.

——— (1999b) 'Tacitus' Prefaces and the Decline of Imperial Historiography', volume 58.2, 391–404.

Markus, R. A. (1970) *Saeculum: History and Science in the Theology of St. Augustine*, Cambridge.

——— (1974) 'Paganism, Christianity and the Latin Classics in the Fourth Century', in J. W. Binns (ed.) *Latin Literature of the Fourth Century*, London and Boston.

——— (1990) *The End of Ancient Christianity*, Cambridge.

Martin, R. H. (1981) *Tacitus*, London.

——— (1990) 'Structure and Interpretation in the *Annals* of Tacitus', *ANRW II* 33.2, 1500–81.

——— (1992) 'Tacite, est-il un historien?', in R. Chevallier and R. Poignault (eds.) *Présence de Tacite*, Tours, 189–95.

Martin, R. H. and Woodman, A. J. (1989) *Tacitus* Annals *IV*, Cambridge.

Martindale, C. (1993) *Redeeming the Text: Latin Poetry and the Hermeneutics of Reception*, Cambridge.

Maslakov, G. (1984) 'Valerius Maximus and Roman Historiography: A Study of the *exempla* Tradition', *ANRW II* 32.1, 437–96.

Matthews, J. (1983) 'Ammianus' Historical Evolution', in Croke and Emmett (1983b), 30–39.

Matthews, J. F. (1985) *Political Life and Culture in Late Roman Society*, London.

——— (1986) 'Ammianus and the Eternity of Rome', in C. Holdsworth and T. P. Wiseman (eds.) *The Inheritance of Historiography 350-900*, Exeter, 17–29.

——— (1989) *The Roman Empire of Ammianus*, London.

——— (1994) 'The Origin of Ammianus', *CQ* 45, 252–69.

McCulloch, H. Y. (1980) 'Literary Augury at the End of Annals XIII', *Phoenix* 34, 237–42.

——— (1984) *Narrative Cause in the Annals of Tacitus*, Königstein.

——— (1991) 'The Historical Process and Theories of History in the *Annals* and the *Histories* of Tacitus', *ANRW II* 33.4, 2928–48.

McDonald, M. F. (1960) '*Phoenix Redivivus*', *Phoenix* 14.4, 187–206.

McGinty, P. (1978) *Interpretations and Dionysos: Method in the Study of a God*, New York.

Meulder, M. (1993) 'L. Caesennius Paetus, un avatar du guerrier impie chez Tacite (*Ann.* 15.7–8)', *Latomus* 52, 98–104.

Meyer, B. F. and Sanders, E. P. (eds.) (1980-2) *Jewish and Christian Self-Definition*, London.

Michels, A. K. (1949) 'The "Calendar of Numa" and the Pre-Julian Calendar', *PAPA* 80, 320–46.

────── (1967) *Claudius: The Emperor and His Achievements*, Cambridge.

────── (1976) 'The Versatility of *religio*', in *The Mediterranean World: Papers Presented in Honour of Gilbert Bagnani*, Peterborough, Ont., 36–77.

Midgley, M. (1992) *Science as Salvation: A Modern Myth and its Meaning*, London.

Miles, G. B. (1988) '*Maiores, Conditores*, and Livy's Perspective on the Past', *TAPA* 118, 185–208.

────── (1995) *Livy: Reconstructing Early Rome*, Ithaca and London.

Miles, R. (1999) *Constructing Identities in Late Antiquity*, London.

Miller, N. P. (1969) 'Style and Content in Tacitus', in Dorey (1969), 99–116.

────── (1977) 'Tacitus' Narrative Technique', *G & R* 24, 13–22.

────── (1986) 'Virgil and Tacitus Again', *PVS* 18, 87–106.

Mitchell, S. and Greatrex, G. (eds.) (2000) *Ethnicity and Culture in Late Antiquity*, London.

Moles, J. L. (1988) 'Cry Freedom: Tacitus *Annals* 4.32–35', *Histos* 2.

────── (1993) 'Livy's Preface', *PCPS* 39, 141–68.

Momigliano, A. (1961) *Claudius: The Emperor and His Achievements*, Cambridge.

────── (1966a) 'An Interim Report on the Origins of Rome', *JRS* 53, 95–121.

────── (1977a) *Essays in Ancient and Modern Historiography*, Oxford.

Momigliano, A. D. (1966b) *Studies in Historiography*, London.

────── (1974) 'The Lonely Historian Ammianus Marcellinus', *ASNP* 4, 1393–407.

────── (1977b) 'Popular Religious Beliefs and the Late Roman Historians', in Momigliano (1977a), 141–59.

────── (1984) 'The Theological Efforts of the Roman Upper Classes in the First Century B.C.', *CP* 79, 199–211.

────── (1986a) 'Ancient Biography and the Study of Religion in the Roman Empire', in *On Pagans, Jews and Christians*, Middletown, Conn., 159–77.

────── (1986b) 'Some Preliminary Remarks on the 'Religious Opposition' to the Roman Empire', in Raaflaub *et al.* (1986), 103–29.

────── (1990) *The Classical Foundations of Modern Historiography*, Berkeley, Los Angeles and London.

Moore, T. (1989) *Artistry and Ideology: Livy's Vocabulary of Virtue*, Frankfurt.

Morford, M. (1990) 'Tacitus' Historical Methods in the Neronian Books of the *Annals*', *ANRW II* 33.2, 1582–627.

────── (1991) 'How Tacitus Defined Liberty', *ANRW II* 33.5, 3420–50.

Morgan, M. G. (1992) 'Dispositions for Disaster: Tacitus *Histories* 1.31', *Eranos* 90, 55–62.

────── (1993) 'Two Omens in Tacitus' *Histories* (2.50.2 and 1.62.2–3)', *RhM* 136, 321–9.

────── (1996) 'Vespasian and the Omens in Tacitus' *Histories* 2.78', *Phoenix* 50, 41–55.

—— (2000) 'Omens in Tacitus' *Histories* I–III', in Wildfang and Isager (2000), 25–42.

Morley, N. (1999) *Writing Ancient History*, London.

Moxon, I. S., Smart, J. D. and Woodman, A. J. (eds.) (1986) *Past Perspectives: Studies in Greek and Roman Historical Writing*, Cambridge.

Murison, C. L. (1993) *Galba, Otho and Vitellius: Careers and Controversies*, Hildesheim and New York.

Musial, D. (1990) 'Sur le culte d'Esculape à Rome et en Italie', *DHA* 16, 231–8.

Myers, K. S. (1994) *Ovid's Causes: Cosmogony and Aetiology in the Metamorphoses*, Michigan.

Mylonas, G. E. (1961) *Eleusis and the Eleusinian Mysteries*, Princeton.

Naudé, C. P. T. (1964) '*Fortuna* in Ammianus Marcellinus', *Acta Cl.* 7, 70–88.

Nawotka, K. (1993) 'Imperial Virtues of Galba in the *Histories* of Tacitus', *Philologus* 137, 258–64.

Needham, R. (1972) *Belief, Language and Experience*, Oxford.

Neri, V. (1985) *Ammiano e il cristianesimo, Studi di storia Antica* volume 11, Bologna.

—— (1992) 'Ammianus' Definition of Christianity as *absoluta et simplex religio*', in den Boeft *et al.* (1992), 59–64.

Newlands, C. (1992a) 'Ovid's Narrator in the *Fasti*', *Arethusa* 25, 33–54.

—— (1992b) *Playing with Time: Ovid and the Fasti*, Ithaca and New York.

Nicols, J. (1978) *Vespasian and the* Partes Flavianae, *Historia Einzelschriften* volume 28, Steiner.

Nixon, C. E. V. and Rodgers, B. (1994) *In Praise of Later Roman Emperors: The Panegyrici Latini, Introduction, Translation and Historical Commentary*, Berkeley and Oxford.

Nock, A. D. (1925) 'Studies in the Graeco-Roman Beliefs of the Empire', *JHS* 45, 84–101.

—— (1930) '*A Diis Electa*: A Chapter in the Religious History of the Third Century', *HTR* 23, 264–70.

—— (1933) *Conversion*, Oxford.

—— (1972) *Essays on Religion and the Roman World*, Oxford.

North, J. A. (1968) The Interrelation of State Religion and Politics in Roman Public Life from the End of the Second Punic War to the Time of Sulla, PhD thesis, Oxford.

—— (1975) '*Praesens Divus*', *JRS* 64, 171–7.

—— (1976) 'Conservatism and Religious Change in Roman Religion', *PBSR* 44, 1–12.

—— (1979) 'Religious Toleration in Republican Rome', *PCPS* 25, 85–103.

—— (1980) 'Novelty and Choice in Roman Religion', *JRS* 70, 186–91.

—— (1983) 'review of R. Syme's *Some Arval Brethren* (Oxford, 1980)', *JRS* 73, 216–8.

—— (1986) 'Religion and Politics; from Republic to Principate', *JRS* 76, 251–9.

———— (1990a) 'Diviners and Divination at Rome', in Beard and North (1990), 49–71.

———— (1990b) 'Family Strategy and Priesthood in the Late Republic', in *Parenté et stratégies familiales dans l'antiquité romaine*, volume 129 of *Collection de l'Ecole française de Rome*, Rome, 527–43.

———— (1992) 'The Development of Religious Pluralism', in J. A. North, T. Rajak, and J. Lieu (eds.) *Jews among Pagans and Christians*, London, 174–93.

———— (1993) 'Roman Reactions to Empire', *Scripta Classica Israelica* 12, 127–38.

———— (1995) 'Religion and Rusticity', in T. Cornell and K. Lomas (eds.) *Urban Society in Roman Italy*, London, 135–50.

———— (1997) 'The Religion of Rome from Monarchy to Principate', in M. Bentley (ed.) *A Companion to Historiography*, London, 57–68.

———— (1998) 'The Books of the *Pontifices*', in Scheid (1998a), 45–63.

———— (2000a) 'Prophet and Text in the Third Century BC', in Bispham and Smith (2000), 92–107.

———— (2000b) *Roman Religion, Greece and Rome New Surveys in the Classics* volume 30, Oxford.

Oakley, S. (1997) *A Commentary on Livy, Books VI–X, Volume I: Introduction and Book VI*, Oxford.

Ogilvie, R. M. (1965) *A Commentary on Livy Books I–V*, Oxford.

Orlin, E. (1997) *Temples, Religion and Politics in the Roman Republic*, Leiden and New York.

Orr, D. G. (1978) 'Roman Domestic Religion: The Evidence of the Household Shrines', *ANRW II* 16.2, 1557–91.

Pailler, J.-M. (1986) 'Lieu sacré et lien associatif dans le dionysisme romain de la Republique', in *Collection de l'Ecole française de Rome*, volume 89, Rome.

———— (1988) *Bacchanalia: la répression de 186 av. J.-C. à Rome et en Italie*, *BEFAR* volume 270, Rome.

Palmer, R. E. A. (1974) *Roman Religion and Roman Empire: Five Essays*, Philadelphia.

———— (1997) *Rome and Carthage at Peace*, Stuttgart.

Parke, H. (1988) *Sibyls and Sibylline Prophecy in Classical Antiquity*, London.

Parker, H. C. (1993) '*Romani numen soli*: Faunus in Ovid's *Fasti*', *TAPA* 123, 199–217.

Paschoud, F. (1988) 'Justice et providence chez Ammien Marcellin', in *Studi tardoantichi: Hestìasis: studi di tarda antichità offerti a Salvatore Calderone*, volume 1 of *Studi tardoantichi / Università degli Studi di Messina, Facoltà di lettere e filosofia, Centro di studi umanistici; 1–6*, 139–61.

Pelling, C. (1993) 'Tacitus and Germanicus', in Luce and Woodman (1993), 59–85.

———— (1997) 'Tragical Dreamer: Some Dreams in the Roman Historians', *G & R* 44.2, 197–213.

———— (2000) *Literary Texts and the Greek Historian*, London.
Penner, H. H. (1971-2) 'Poverty of Functionalism', *HR* 11, 91–97.
———— (1989) *Impasse and Resolution: A Critique of the Study of Religion*, New York, Bern, Frankfurt and Paris.
Percival, J. (1980) 'Tacitus and the Principate', *G & R* 27, 119–33.
———— (1992) 'Truth in the Greek and Roman Historians', *JACT Review* 12, 13–16.
Perkins, C. A. (1993) 'Tacitus on Otho', *Latomus* 52, 848–55.
Phillips, J. E. (1974) 'Form and Language in Livy's Triumph Notices', *CP* 69, 265–73.
———— (1982) 'Current Research in Livy's First Decade: 1959–1979', *ANRW II* 30.2, 998–1057.
Phillips III, C. R. (1979) 'Julian's Rebuilding of the Temple: A Sociological Study of Religious Competition', in P. J. Achtemeier (ed.) *Society of Biblical Literature Seminar Papers*, volume II, Missoula, Mont., 167–72.
———— (1986) 'The Sociology of Religious Knowledge in the Roman Empire to A.D. 284', *ANRW II* 16.3, 2677–773.
———— (1991a) 'Misconceptualising Classical Mythology', in M. A. Flower and M. Toher (eds.) *Georgica. Greek Studies in Honour of George Cawkwell*, volume 58 of *BICS supplement*, London, 145–51.
———— (1991b) '*Nullum crimen sine lege*: Socioreligious Sanctions on Magic', in Faraone and Obbink (1991), 260–76.
———— (1992) 'Roman Religion and Literary Studies of Ovid's *Fasti*', *Arethusa* 25, 55–80.
———— (1998) 'Walter Burkert *In Partibus Infidelium:* A Classicist Appraisal of *Creation of the Sacred*', *MTTR* 10, 92–105.
Pigón, J. (1990) 'The Emperor Galba and the Four Virtues: A Note on Tac. *Hist.* 1.49.3–4', *RhM* 133, 370–74.
Plass, P. (1988) *Wit and the Writing of History: The Rhetoric of Historiography in Imperial Rome*, Madison.
———— (1992) '*Variatio* in Tacitus: Form and Thought', volume VI of *Studies in Latin Literature and Roman History*, Brussels, 421–34.
Pohlsander, H. (1986) 'The Religious Policy of Decius', *ANRW II* 16.3, 1826–42.
Porte, D. (1984) 'Les enterrements expiatoires à Rome', *RPh* 58, 233–43.
———— (1989) *Les donneurs de sacré: Le prêtre à Rome*, Paris.
Potter, D. S. (1994) *Prophets and Emperors: Human and Divine Authority from Augustus to Theodosius*, Cambridge, Mass.
Pouillon, J. (1982) 'Remarks on the Verb "To Believe"', in Izard and Smith (1982), 1–8.
Powell, C. A. (1972) '*Deum ira, hominum rabies*', *Latomus* 31, 833–855.
Powell, C. A. (ed.) (1992) *Roman Poetry and Propaganda in the Age of Augustus*, Ann Arbor.
Preston, J. (1997) *Feyerabend: Philosophy, Science and Society*, Oxford.
Price, S. R. F. (1984) *Rituals and Power: The Roman Imperial Cult in Asia Minor*, Cambridge.

―――― (1987) 'From Noble Funerals to Divine Cult: The Consecration of Roman Emperors', in Cannadine and Price (1987), 56–105.

Pulleyn, S. (1998) *Prayer in Greek Religion*, Oxford.

Raaflaub, K. (1986) *Social Struggles in Archaic Rome. New Perspectives on the Conflict of the Orders*, Berkeley.

Raaflaub, K. A. and Toher, M. (eds.) (1990) *Between Republic and Empire: Interpretations of Augustus and his Principate*, Berkeley.

Raaflaub, K. A. *et al.* (eds.) (1986) *Opposition et résistances à l'empire d'Auguste à Trajan: neuf exposés suivis de discusssions, Fondation Hardt Entretiens* volume 33, Geneva.

Rambaux, C. (1992) 'La critique lucrétienne des religions et le christianisme', in Holtz and Fredouille (1992), 361–9.

Rappaport, R. (1999) *Ritual and Religion in the Making of Humanity*, Cambridge.

Rawson, E. (1971) 'Prodigy Lists and the Use of the *Annales Maximi*', *CQ* 21, 158–69.

―――― (1978) 'Caesar, Etruria and the *Disciplina Etrusca*', *JRS* 68, 132–52.

Rich, J. (1996) 'Structuring Roman History: The Consular Year and the Roman Historical Tradition', *Histos* 1.

Rike, R. L. (1987) Apex Omnium: *Religion in the* Res Gestae *of Ammianus*, Berkeley, Los Angeles and London.

Riposati, B. (1974) '*Quid Tacitus de religione senserit quidque inquisierit*', *Aevum* 48, 336–41.

Rives, J. B. (1995a) *Religion and Authority in Roman Carthage from Augustus to Constantine*, Oxford.

―――― (1995b) 'Human Sacrifice among Pagans and Christians', *JRS* 85, 65–85.

―――― (1999a) *Germania*, Oxford.

―――― (1999b) 'The Decree of Decius and the Religion of Empire', *JRS* 89, 135–54.

Roberts, M. (1988) 'The Revolt of Boudicca (Tacitus *Annals* 14.29–39) and the Assertion of *Libertas* in Neronian Rome', *AJP* 109, 118–32.

Rogers, G. (1990) *The Sacred Identity Of Ephesos: Foundation Myths of a Roman City*, London.

Rosenberger, V. (1998) *Gezaehmte Goetter: Das Prodigienwesen in der römischen Republik*, Stuttgart.

Rosenstein, N. S. (1990) Imperatores Victi: *Military Defeat and Aristocratic Competition in the Middle and Late Republic*, Berkeley.

Rossbach, O. (1910) *T. Livi Periochae Omnium Librorum, Fragmenta Oxyrhynci Reperta, Iulii Obsequentis Prodigiorum Liber*, Leipzig.

Rudich, V. (1985) 'Accommodation to Corrupt Reality: Tacitus' *Dialogus de Oratoribus*', *AncW* 11, 95–100.

―――― (1993) *Political Dissidence under Nero: The Price of Dissimulation*, London.

―――― (1997) *Dissidence and Literature under Nero: The Price of Rhetoricization*, New York.

Rutland, L. W. (1987) 'The Tacitean Germanicus. Suggestions for a Re-evaluation', *RhM* 190, 153–64.

Sabbah, G. (1978) *La méthode d'Ammien Marcellin. Recherches sur la construction du discours historique dans les Res Gestae*, Paris.

——— (1997) 'Ammien Marcellin, Libanius, Antioche et la date des derniers livres des *Res Gestae*', *Cassiodorus* 3, 89–116.

Sachot, M. (1991) 'Religion/*superstitio*: Historique d'une subversion et d'un retournement', *RHR* 208, 351–94.

Sage, M. M. (1990) 'Tacitus' Historical Works: A Survey and Appraisal', *ANRW II* 33.2, 851–1030, 1629–47.

——— (1991) 'The Treatment in Tacitus of Roman Republican History and Antiquarian Matters', *ANRW II* 33.5, 3385–419.

Said, E. W. (1978) *Orientalism*, New York.

Salzman, M. R. (1987) '*Superstitio* in the *Codex Theodosianus* and the Persecution of Pagans', *Vigiliae Christianae* 41, 172–88.

——— (1990) *On Roman Time. The Codex Calendar of 354 and the Rhythms of Urban Life in Late Antiquity*, Berkeley.

——— (1992) 'How the West was Won: The Christianisation of the Roman Aristocracy in the West in the Years after Constantine', volume IV of *Studies in Latin Literature and Roman History*, Brussels, 451–79.

Sauvage, S. (1945) '*Remotum A Notitia Vulgari*', *TAPA* 76, 157–65.

Scheid, J. (1978) 'Les prêtres officiels sous les empereurs Julio-Claudiens', *ANRW II* 16.1, 610–54.

——— (1984) 'Le prêtre et le magistrat', in C. Nicolet (ed.) *Des Ordres à Rome*, Paris, 243–80.

——— (1985a) *Religion et piété a Rome*, Paris.

——— (1985b) 'Religion et superstition à l'époque de Tacite. Quelques réflexions', in *Religión, superstición y magia en el mundo romano*, Cadiz, 19–34.

——— (1986) 'La thiase du Metropolitan Museum', in *L'association dionysiaque dans les sociétés anciennes*, volume 89 of *Collection Ecole française de Rome*, Rome, 275–90.

——— (1987a) 'La parole des dieux', *Opus* 6–8, 125–36.

——— (1987b) 'Polytheism Impossible; or, the Empty Gods: Reasons Behind a Void in the History of Roman Religion', *History and Anthropology* 3, 303–25.

——— (1992) 'Myth, Cult And Reality in Ovid's *Fasti*', *PCPS* n.s. 38, 118–31.

——— (1993a) 'Cultes, mythes, et politique au début de l'Empire', in Graf (1993), 108–30.

——— (1993b) 'The Priest', in A. Giardina (ed.) *The Romans*, Chicago, 55–84.

——— (1994) 'Les archives de la piété: réflexions sur les livres sacerdotaux', in S. Demougin (ed.) *La mémoire perdue: à la recherche des archives oubliées, publiques et privées, de la Rome antique*, volume 30 of *Publications de la Sorbonne, série histoire ancienne et médiévale*, Paris, 173–85.

———— (1995) '*Graeco ritu.* A Typically Roman Way Of Honouring the Gods', *HSCP* 97, 15–31.

Scheid, J. (ed.) (1998a) *La mémoire perdue: recherches sur l'administration romaine, Collection de l'Ecole française de Rome* volume 243, Rome.

Scheid, J. (1998b) 'Les livres sibyllins et les archives des quindécimvirs', in Scheid (1998a), 11–26.

Schilling, R. (1962) 'A propos des 'exta': l'extiscipine étrusque et la *litatio romaine*', in *Hommages à A. Grenier,* volume v. 58 of *Collection Latomus,* 1371–8.

———— (1979) *Rites, Cultes, Dieux de Rome,* Paris.

Schochat, Y. (1981) 'Tacitus' Attitude to Otho', *Latomus* 40, 365–77.

Schofield, M. (1986) 'Cicero For and Against Divination', *JRS* 76, 47–65.

Schuller, W. (ed.) (1993) *Livius. Aspekte seines Werkes,* Konstanz.

Scott, R. T. (1968) *Religion and Philosophy in the Histories of Tacitus,* Rome.

Scullard, H. H. (1970) *Scipio Africanus: Soldier and Politician,* London.

———— (1981) *Festivals and Ceremonies of the Roman Republic,* London.

Seager, R. (1986) *Ammianus Marcellinus: Seven Studies in his Language and Thought,* Columbia.

———— (1999) 'review of Barnes (1998)', *BMCR* 1999-04-13.

Segal, C. (1973) 'Tacitus and Poetic History: the End of *Annals* 13', *Ramus* 2, 107–26.

Segal, R. (1993) 'Paralleling Religion and Science: The Project of Robin Horton', *Annals of Scholarship* 10.2, 177–98.

Seguin, R. (1974) 'La religion de Scipion l'Africain', *Latomus* 33, 3–21.

Sfameni, G. G. (1985) *Soteriology and Mystic Aspects in the Cult of Cybele and Attis, EPRO* volume 103, Leiden.

Shatzman, I. (1974) 'Tacitean Rumours', *Latomus* 33, 549–78.

Shiels, W. J. (ed.) (1984) *Persecution and Toleration,* Oxford.

Shorter, B. (1996) *Susceptible to the Sacred: The Psychological Experience of Ritual,* London and New York.

Shotter, D. C. A. (1968) 'Tacitus, Tiberius and Germanicus', *Historia* 17, 194–214.

———— (1978) '*Principatus ac libertas*', *AncSoc* 9, 235–55.

———— (1988) 'Tacitus and Tiberius', *AncSoc* 19, 225–36.

———— (1989) *Tacitus* Annals *4,* Warminster.

———— (1991a) 'Tacitus' View of Emperors and the *Pax Romana*', *ANRW II* 33.5, 3332–53.

———— (1991b) 'Tacitus' View of the Empire and the Principate', *ANRW II* 33.5, 3263–331.

Sinclair, P. (1991a) 'Rhetorical Generalizations in *Annales* 1–6: A Review of the Problem of Innuendo and Tacitus' Integrity', *ANRW II* 33.4, 2795–831.

———— (1991b) ''These are my Temples in your Hearts' (Tac. *Ann.* 4.38.2)', *CP* 86, 333–35.

———— (1992) '*Deorum iniurias dis curae* (Tac. *Ann.* 1.73.4)', *Latomus* 51, 397–403.

—— (1995) *Tacitus the Sententious Historian: A Sociology of Rhetoric in Annals 1–6*, University Park, Penn.

Siniscalco, P. (1989) 'Le sacré et l'expérience de l'histoire. Ammien Marcellin et Paul Orose', *BAGB* pages 355–66.

Smith, J. Z. (1970) 'The Influence of Symbols on Social Change: A Place On Which To Stand', *Worship* 44, 457–74.

—— (1978a) *Map is Not Territory: Studies in the History of Religions: Collected Essays*, Leiden.

—— (1978b) 'Towards Interpreting Demonic Powers in Hellenistic and Roman Antiquity', *ANRW II* 16.1, 425–39.

—— (1982) *Imagining Religion: From Babylon to Jonestown: Collected Essays*, Chicago.

—— (1995a) 'Trading Places', in M. Meyer and P. Mirecki (eds.) *Ancient Magic and Ritual Power*, Leiden, New York and Köln, 13–29.

Smith, M. (1975) '*De Superstitione*', in H. D. Betz (ed.) *Plutarch's Theological Writings and Early Christian Literature*, volume 3 of *Studia ad Corpus Hellenisticum Novi Testamenti*, Leiden, 1–35.

Smith, R. (1995b) *Julian's Gods. Religion and Philosophy in the Thought and Action of Julian the Apostate*, London and New York.

Smith, W. C. (1979) *Faith and Belief*, Princeton, NJ.

Solodow, J. B. (1979) 'Livy and the Story of Horatius', *TAPA* 109, 251–68.

Sperber, D. (1975) *Rethinking Symbolism*, Cambridge.

—— (1985) *On Anthropological Knowledge: Three Essays*, Cambridge.

Speyer, W. (1986) 'Das Verhältnis des Augustus zur Religion', *ANRW II* 16.3, 1777–805.

Spickerman, W. *et al.* (eds.) (2001) *Religion in den germanischen Provinzen Roms*, Tübingen.

Stambaugh, J. E. (1978) 'The Functions of Roman Temples', *ANRW II* 16.1, 554–608.

Starr, J. (1987) 'The Circulation of Literary Texts in the Ancient World', *CQ* n.s. 37, 213–23.

Stewart, C. and Shaw, R. (1994) *Syncretism/Anti-Syncretism: The Politics of Religious Synthesis*, London and New York.

Stewart, D. (1970) 'The Silence of Magna Mater', *HSCP* 74, 74–84.

Storoni, M. L. (1976) *Empire without End*, New York.

Sullivan, D. (1975) 'Innuendo and the 'Weighted Alternative' in Tacitus', *CJ* 71, 312–26.

Syme, R. (1958) 'Obituaries in Tacitus', *AJP* 79, 18–31.

—— (1958a) *Tacitus*, Oxford.

—— (1970) *Ten Studies in Tacitus*, Oxford.

—— (1984) 'How Tacitus Wrote *Annals* I–III', in A. R. Birley (ed.) *Roman Papers III*, Oxford, 1014–42.

Szemler, G. J. (1972) *The Priests of the Roman Republic: A Study of Interactions between Priesthood and Magistrates*, Collection *Latomus* volume 127, Brussels.

———— (1986) 'Priesthood and Priestly Careers in Ancient Rome', *ANRW II* 16.3, 2314–31.

Szidat, J. (1982) 'Die Neuplatonismus und die Gebildeten im Westen des Reiches: Gedanken zu seiner Verbreitung und Kenntnis ausserhalb der Schultradition', *Museum Helveticum* 39, 132–45.

Takacs, S. A. (1996) '*Magna Deum Mater Idaea*, Cybele and Catullus' *Attis*', in Lane (1996), 367–86.

Talbert, C. H. (1978) 'Biographies of Philosophers and Rulers as Instruments of Religious Propaganda in Mediterranean Antiquity', *ANRW II* 16.2, 1619–51.

Tambiah, S. (1990) *Magic, Science, Religion, and the Scope of Rationality*, Cambridge.

Thérasse, J. (1980) 'Croyances et crédulités des Romains d'après Pline l'Ancien et les écrivains latins', in J.-B. Caron, M. Fortin, and G. Maloney (eds.) *Mélanges d'études anciennes offerts à Maurice Lebel*, Quebec, 283–319.

Thomas, G. (1984) 'Magna Mater and Attis', *ANRW II* 17.3, 1500–35.

Tierney, J. J. (1947) 'The *Senatus Consultum de Bacchanalibus*', *PRIA* 51, 95–10.

Tiffou, E. (1977) 'Salluste et la *Fortuna*', *Phoenix* 31, 349–60.

Toher, M. (1990) 'Livy, Augustus and the Evolution of Roman Historiography', in Raaflaub and Toher (1990), 139–54.

Toynbee, A. J. (1966) *Hannibal's Legacy*, London.

Toynbee, J. M. C. (1973) *Animals in Roman Life and Art*, Baltimore and London.

Trompf, G. W. (1979) *The Idea of Historical Recurrence in Western Thought: From Antiquity to the Reformation*, Berkeley.

———— (2000) *Early Christian Historiography: Narratives of Retributive Justice*, London and New York.

Tucker, R. A. (1987) 'Tacitus and the Death of Lucan', *Latomus* 46, 330–7.

Turcan, R. (1976) 'Encore la prophétie de Végoia', in *L'Italie préromaine et la Rome républicaine: Mélanges offerts à Jacques Heurgon*, Paris.

———— (1978) 'Le culte impérial au IIIe siècle', *ANRW II* 16.2, 996–1084.

———— (1989) *Les cultes orientaux dans le monde romain*, Paris.

Turpin, J. (1986) 'Cicéron, *De Legibus* I–II et la religion romaine: une interprétation philosophique à la veille du principat', *ANRW II* 16.3, 1877–908.

Valantasis, R. (ed.) (2000) *Religions of Late Antiquity in Practice*, Princeton and Oxford.

van Seters, J. (1997) *In Search of History: Historiography in the Ancient World and the Origins of Biblical History*, New Haven and London.

Vanggaard, J. H. (1988) *The* Flamen*: A Study in the History and Sociology of Roman Religion*, Copenhagen.

Verbrugghe, G. P. (1989) 'On the Meaning of *Annales*, on the Meaning of Annalist', *Philologus* 133, 192–230.

Vermaseren, M. J. (1977) *Cybele and Attis: The Myth and the Cult*, London.

Vernant, J.-P. (1981a) 'Sacrificial and Alimentary Codes in Hesiod's Myth of Prometheus', in Gordon (1981), 57–79.

———— (1981b) 'The Myth of Prometheus in Hesiod', in Gordon (1981), 43–56.

———— (1983) *Myth and Thought among the Greeks*, London and Boston.

Versnel, H. S. (1970) *Triumphus. An Enquiry into the Origin, Development and Meaning of the Roman Triumph*, Leiden.

———— (1976) 'Two Types of Roman *devotio*', *Mnemosyne* 29, 365–410.

———— (1980a) 'Destruction, *Devotio*, and Despair in a Situation of Anomy: The Mourning for Germanicus in Triple Perspective', in *Perennitas. Studi in onore di Angelo Brelich*, Rome.

———— (1980b) 'Historical Implications', in C. M. Stibbe *et al.* (eds.) Lapis Satricanus, volume 5 of *Nederlands Instituut te Rome, Scripta Minora*, The Hague, 95–150.

———— (1981) 'Self-sacrifice, Compensation and the Anonymous Gods', in *Le sacrifice dans l'antiquité*, volume 27 of *Fondation Hardt Entretiens*, Geneva, 135–94.

Veyne, P. (1984) *Writing History*, Manchester.

———— (1988) *Did the Greeks Believe In Their Myths? An Essay on the Constitutive Imagination*, Chicago.

———— (1989) 'La nouvelle piété sous l'Empire', *RPh* 43, 175–94.

———— (1990) *Circuses and Bread*, London.

Viansino, G. (1985) *Ammiani Marcellini rerum gestarum lexicon I*, Hildesheim.

von Albrecht (1987) 'L'interprétation de l'histoire chez Tacite', *LEC* 55, 369–75.

Walbank, F. W. (1967) 'The Scipionic Legend', *PCPhS* 13, 54–69.

———— (1972) *Polybius*, Berkeley.

———— (1981) *The Hellenistic World*, London.

Walker, B. (1952) *The* Annals *of Tacitus: A Study in the Writing of History*, Manchester.

Wallace-Hadrill, A. (1981) 'The Emperor and his Virtues', *Historia* 30, 298–323.

———— (1982a) '*Civilis Princeps*: Between Citizen and King', *JRS* 72, 32–48.

———— (1982b) 'The Golden Age and Sin in Augustan Ideology', *Past and Present* 95, 19–36.

———— (1983) *Suetonius, The Scholar and his Caesars*, London.

———— (1989) 'Rome's Cultural Revolution', *JRS* 79, 157–64.

———— (1993) *Augustan Rome*, Classical World Series, Bristol.

———— (1997) '*Mutatio morum*: The Idea of a Cultural Revolution', in Habinek and Schiesaro (1997), 3–23.

Walsh, P. G. (1958) 'Livy and Stoicism', *AJP* 79, 355–75.

———— (1961) *Livy: His Historical Aims and Methods*, Cambridge.

———— (1974) *Livy, Greece and Rome New Surveys in the Classics* volume 8, Oxford.

———— (1982) 'Livy and the Aims of "*historia*": An Analysis of the Third Decade', *ANRW II* 30.2, 1058–74.

Wardman, A. (1982) *Religion and Statecraft among the Romans*, London.

Watson, A. (1992) *The State, Law and Religion: Pagan Rome*, Athens, GA.

Weinfeld, M. (1986) *The Organizational Pattern and the Penal Code of the Qumran Sect: A Comparison with Guilds and Religious Associations of the Hellenistic and Roman Age*, Novum Testamentum et Orbis Antiquus volume 2, Fritzburg and Göttingen.

Weinstock, S. (1971) *Divus Julius*, Oxford.

Wellesley, K. (1969) 'Tacitus as a Military Historian', in Dorey (1969), 63–97.

——— (1991) ' Tacitus' *Histories*: A Textual Survey, 1939–1989', *ANRW II* 33.3, 1686–713.

West, D. and Woodman, A. J. (eds.) (1979) *Creative Imitation and Latin Literature*, Cambridge.

Westlake, H. D. (1977) '*Legetai* in Thucydides', *Mnemosyne* 30, 345–62.

Wheeldon, M. J. (1989) '"True Stories": The Reception of Historiography in Antiquity', in Cameron (1989), 33–64.

White, H. (1980) 'The Value of Narrativity', in W. J. T. Mitchell (ed.) *On Narrative*, Chicago, 1–24.

——— (1987) *The Content of the Form*, Baltimore and London.

Whitehead, D. (1979) 'Tacitus and the Loaded Alternative', *Latomus* 38, 474–95.

Wiedemann, T. (1989) *The Julio-Claudian Emperors*, Bristol.

Wiedemann, T. E. J. (1986) 'Between Men and Beasts: Barbarians in Ammianus Marcellinus', in Moxon *et al.* (1986), 189–201.

Wilcox, D. J. (1987) *The Measure of Times Past*, Chicago.

Wildfang, R. L. and Isager, J. (2000) *Divination and Portents in the Roman World*, Odense.

Williams, B. (1989a) 'Reading Tacitus' Tiberian *Annals*', *Ramus* 18, 140–66.

——— (1990) 'Setting out the Rules. Tacitus *Annals* 1 as programme', *Classicum* 16, 3–10.

Williams, M. H. (1989b) 'The Expulsion of the Jews from Rome in AD 19', *Latomus* 48, 765–8.

Wilson, J. P. (1990) 'The Death of Lucan: Suicide and Execution in Tacitus', *Latomus* 49, 458–63.

Winkler, J. J. (1985) *Auctor and Actor: A Narratological Reading of Apuleius'* The Golden Ass, Berkeley and Oxford.

Wiseman, T. P. (1979) *Clio's Cosmetics: Three Studies in Graeco-Roman Literature*, Leicester.

——— (1985) *Roman Political Life*, Exeter.

——— (1987a) 'Practice and Theory in Roman Historiography', in Wiseman (1987b), 244–61.

——— (1987b) *Roman Studies. Literary and Historical*, Liverpool.

——— (1993) 'Lying Historians: Seven Types of Mendacity', in Gill and Wiseman (1993), 122–46.

——— (1994a) *Historiography and Imagination: Eight Essays on Roman Culture*, Studies in History volume 33, Exeter.

—— (1994b) 'Lucretius, Catiline and the Survival of Prophecy', in Wiseman (1994a), 49–68.

—— (1994c) 'The Origins of Roman Historiography', in Wiseman (1994a), 1–21.

—— (1995) *Remus. A Roman Myth*, Cambridge.

—— (1998) *Roman Drama and Roman History*, Exeter.

Wissowa, G. (1912) *Religion und Kultus der Römer*, Munich.

Wistrand, E. (1979) 'The Stoic Opposition to the Principate', *StudClas* 18, 93–101.

Woodcock, E. C. (1939) *Tacitus* Annals *XIV*, London.

—— (1959) *A New Latin Syntax*, Bristol.

Woodman, A. J. (1979) 'Self-Imitation and the Substance of History: Tacitus *Annals* 1.61–5 and *Histories* 2.70, 5.14–15', in West and Woodman (1979), 143–55.

—— (1985) *Tacitus and Tiberius: The Alternative* Annals, Durham.

—— (1988) *Rhetoric in Classical Historiography: Four Studies*, London and Croom Helm Portland, Or.

—— (1989) 'Tacitus' Obituary of Tiberius', *CQ* 39, 197–205.

—— (1992a) 'Nero's Alien Capital. Tacitus as Paradoxographer (*Annals* 15.20.36–7)', in A. J. Woodman and J. Powell (eds.) *Author and Audience in Latin Literature*, Cambridge, 173–88, 251–55.

—— (1992b) 'The Preface to Tacitus' *Annals*: More Sallust?', *CQ* 42, 567–68.

—— (1995) 'A Death in the First Act', *PLLS* 8, 257–73.

—— (1997) 'Tacitus', in Kraus and Woodman (1997), 88–118.

—— (1998a) 'A Death in the First Act: Tacitus, *Annals* 1.6', in Woodman (1998c), 23–39.

—— (1998b) 'Tacitus on Tiberius' Accession', in Woodman (1998c), 40–70.

—— (1998c) *Tacitus Reviewed*, Oxford.

Woodman, A. J. and Martin, R. H. (1996) *The* Annals *of Tacitus Book 3*, Cambridge.

Woodman, A. J. and West, D. A. (eds.) (1984) *Poetry and Politics in the Age of Augustus*, Cambridge and New York.

Woolf, G. (1997) 'Polis-religion and its Alternatives in the Roman Provinces', in Cancik and Röpke (1997), 35–68.

Worsley, P. (1997) *Knowledges: What Different People Make of the World*, London.

Zaidman, L. B. and Pantel, P. S. (1996) *Religion in the Ancient Greek City*, Cambridge.

Zanker, P. (1988) *The Power of Images in the Age of Augustus*, Ann Arbor.

Ziolkowski, A. (1992) *The Temples of Mid-Republican Rome and Their Historical and Topographical Context*, Rome.

Index locorum

Ammianus
Res Gestae
14.1.2, 248
14.5.6, 239
14.6, 235
14.6.2, 234, 235, 264
14.6.3, 270
14.6.5, 234
14.7.7, 248, 253
14.8, 243
14.8.3, 237
14.9.5-6, 245
14.9.6, 269, 277
14.10.16, 245, 270
14.11.8, 245, 270
14.11.12, 260, 269, 282
14.11.19, 269
14.11.24, 260, 265, 277
14.11.25, 259, 260
14.11.25-6, 276
14.11.29, 269
14.11.30, 269
14.11.34, 269
15.1.2, 245
15.2.8, 250, 265
15.3.7, 253
15.5.1, 269
15.5.34, 253
15.5.37, 259, 272
15.7.7, 243, 245
15.7.8, 245
15.8.9, 265
15.8.10, 262
15.9.8, 247
15.13.2, 247
15.47.3, 238
16.5.5, 259
16.5.6-7, 262
16.5.10, 256
16.10, 235
16.12.18, 265
16.12.52, 267
16.12.62, 265, 267
17.1.16, 271

Res Gestae
17.7.3, 265
17.7.9-10, 256
17.7.10, 133, 256
17.7.11, 256
17.7.12, 256, 259, 262
17.8.2, 250
17.9.4, 271
17.11.5, 271
17.12.4, 269
17.12.17, 272
17.12.18-21, 272
17.13.5, 269
17.13.7, 269
17.13.11, 269
17.13.28, 265
18.3.1, 253, 254
18.3.7, 256
18.4.1, 247
18.4.5, 273
18.6.6, 269
18.7.7, 248, 266
19.1.4, 267
19.1.14, 265
19.2.1, 273
19.4.1-8, 257
19.4.3, 262
19.4.4, 262
19.4.5, 239
19.8.6, 235
19.10.4, 237, 267, 273
19.12.1, 239
19.12.5, 240
19.12.6, 240
19.12.7, 240
19.12.9, 271
19.12.12, 245, 255
19.12.13, 239
19.12.16, 272
19.12.18, 239
19.12.19-20, 237
19.12.20, 240, 253, 273
19.13, 240
20.2.4, 253

319

Res Gestae
20.4, 237
20.4.13, 269
20.5.10, 250
20.7.7, 245
20.7.7-9, 244
20.8.11, 275
20.8.20, 253
20.10.1, 269
20.11.26-30, 259
20.11.32, 245, 271
21.1, 242
21.1.6, 241, 251, 253
21.1.7-14, 241, 248, 253
21.1.8, 241, 259, 271
21.1.8-14, 260
21.1.9, 241, 261, 265
21.1.10, 241, 258
21.1.12, 242, 248, 256, 262
21.1.13, 253, 257
21.1.13-4, 254
21.1.14, 258
21.1.7-14, 232
21.2.1-2, 250
21.2.4, 250
21.2.5, 266
21.5.1, 237, 253
21.5.13, 269
21.10.2, 250
21.10.8, 262
21.12.19, 273
21.13.11, 275
21.13.13, 275
21.13.14, 265
21.13.15, 275
21.14.3, 259
21.14.5, 259
21.15.2, 271
21.16.4, 264
21.16.11, 275
21.16.13, 270, 283
21.16.14, 256, 269
21.16.18, 243, 245, 247
21.16.21, 269, 271
22.1.1, 251, 254, 269
22.1.2, 252, 254
22.3.3, 241
22.3.7, 275
22.3.12, 276
22.5.1, 265
22.5.5, 247
22.7.3-4, 258
22.8.34, 247
22.8.36, 247
22.9.7, 235
22.9.15, 250
22.10.6, 275

Res Gestae
22.10.6-7, 263
22.11.4, 245
22.11.10, 245
22.12.7, 250, 254
22.12.8, 250
22.13.1, 250
22.14.3, 250, 255
22.14.4, 250
22.14.7, 265
22.14.6, 250
22.15.24, 235
22.16.10, 259
22.16.17, 249, 271
22.16.19, 247, 258
22.16.22, 256, 258
23.1.1, 241
23.1.2-3, 273
23.1.5-6, 250
23.1.7, 250, 254, 274
23.2.6, 250
23.2.7, 251, 253
23.3.2, 251
23.3.3, 251, 253
23.5.4, 251, 265, 272
23.5.5, 271
23.5.6, 251
23.5.9, 271
23.5.10, 251, 253, 255, 267
23.5.11, 255
23.5.12-14, 251
23.5.13, 240
23.5.17, 277
23.5.19, 265, 269
23.5.23, 277
23.6.32, 256
23.6.53, 259
23.6.75, 261
23.6.78, 248
24.1.1, 265
24.1.12, 265
24.4.1, 248
24.4.23, 272
24.4.24, 268
24.6.17, 251
24.8.4, 251
24.8.4-5, 274
25.2.3, 262
25.2.3-8, 251
25.2.5, 257
25.2.7, 255, 267
25.3.6, 271
25.3.9, 271
25.3.19, 271
25.4.1, 275
25.4.2, 256
25.4.8, 275

Res Gestae
25.4.17, 247, 249, 253
25.4.19, 275
25.4.20, 265
25.5.7, 275
25.5.8, 269
25.5.20, 263
25.6.6-7, 249
25.7.5, 267, 268
25.8.3, 260, 265, 267
25.9.2, 276
25.9.7, 235, 269
25.10.1, 253, 254
25.10.1-3, 257
25.10.11-12, 271
25.10.15, 245, 262
25.75, 265
26.1.1, 228, 229
26.1.5, 253, 254, 265, 267
26.1.7, 253
26.1.12, 254, 260
26.1.14, 265, 267
26.2.9, 270
26.3.2, 248
26.3.3, 249
26.3.4, 249
26.4.1, 278
26.6.7, 278
26.6.9, 265, 278
26.7.13, 278
26.8.13, 269
26.9.9, 269
26.9.10, 278
26.10.2, 278
26.10.5, 248
26.10.9-12, 278
27.3.1, 240, 253
27.3.1-2, 241
27.3.15, 243, 244, 265
27.4.8, 256
27.5.10, 271
27.6.8, 265
27.6.9, 264
27.6.15, 271
27.10.1-2, 244
28.1.3-4, 235
28.1.7, 253
28.1.14, 248
28.1.26, 248
28.1.42, 97, 241
28.1.57, 277
28.2.7, 269
28.4, 235
28.4.22, 271
28.4.24, 249
28.4.26, 249
28.5.11, 247

Res Gestae
28.6.1, 277
28.6.25, 277
29.1.6, 249, 271
29.1.7, 272
29.1.10, 253
29.1.11, 262
29.1.15, 278
29.1.15-16, 278, 281
29.1.16, 271, 278
29.1.18, 273, 278
29.1.27, 278
29.1.28-42, 278
29.1.29, 249
29.1.32, 253, 271
29.1.33, 279
29.1.37, 264
29.1.37-38, 256
29.1.38, 280
29.1.38-9, 245
29.1.41, 279
29.1.42, 255, 258, 262
29.2.2, 275
29.2.4-17, 279
29.2.6, 249
29.2.17, 279
29.2.18, 263, 280
29.2.20, 265, 277, 279, 281
29.2.21, 277
29.2.22, 271
29.5.40, 265
29.6.7, 267, 273
30.1.5, 253, 255
30.2.9, 277
30.4.2, 262
30.4.3, 256
30.4.5, 256
30.5.11, 249
30.5.15, 253, 271
30.5.18, 270
30.9.5, 243
31.1.1, 253, 269, 281
31.1.1-5, 253
31.1.2-3, 280
31.1.3, 277
31.2.2, 253
31.2.11, 248
31.4.9, 270
31.5.10, 234, 264
31.10.7, 269
31.10.18, 265, 267
31.13.19, 269
31.14.2, 275
31.14.3, 275
31.14.6, 275
31.14.8, 262
31.14.8-9, 253

Res Gestae
  31.15.7, 277
  31.16.4, 265
  31.16.9, 235
Augustine
  City of God
    4.31, 4
    6.5, 7
Aulus Gellius
  1.19, 67
  2.24.2, 85
  2.28, 256
  2.28.1, 256
  4.9, 82

Cassius Dio
  10, 58
  53.20.1, 48
  55.22.3, 190
  56.27.4, 190
  58.27.1, 216
  60.5.2, 182
Cato
  On Agriculture 7.4, 5
Censorinus
  On The Nativity
    17.1, 217
    17.3-5, 217
    17.9, 217
Cicero
  Letters to His Friends
    8.4.1, 67
  On Friendship
    11.37, 206
  On Old Age
    45, 85
  On The Nature of the Gods
    1.117, 83
    2.4.12, 254
    2.28, 82
    2.72, 83
    3.46, 80
  On The Republic
    1.24, 98
  On the Command of Pompey, 105
  On the Ends of Good and Evils
    2.61, 58
  Tusculan Disputations 1.89, 58

Dionysius of Halicarnassus
  2.19, 85
  2.19.4, 80
  2.67.4, 66
  4.62, 67
  4.62.5, 65
  14.11.5, 93

Frontinus
  Strategems
    1.12.8, 98

Homer
  Iliad
    2.6, 128

Justinus
  33.1.7, 98
Juvenal
  10.182, 256

Lactantius
  Divine Institutes
    1.6.10-13, 67
Livy
  Ab Vrbe Condita
    Pr. 13, 259
    1.1.6, 54
    1.4.1, 115
    1.4.4, 115
    1.5.1, 57
    1.9.3-4, 104
    1.13.7, 54
    1.16.5, 54
    1.18.1, 81
    1.20.5-6, 71
    1.20.5-7, 81
    1.20.6, 81
    1.20.7, 72
    1.21.4, 129
    1.23.10, 123
    1.28.4, 104
    1.31, 54
    1.31.1, 40, 76
    1.31.3, 121
    1.31.4, 54, 64
    1.31.6, 83
    1.31.8, 45, 54, 84
    1.39.4, 100
    1.42.3, 118
    1.45.3-6, 52
    1.45.4, 77
    1.45.4-5, 53
    1.48.7, 54
    1.54.6-7, 32
    1.55.3, 54
    1.55.6, 31
    1.55.9, 54
    1.56.9, 80
    2.5.10, 57
    2.6.10, 119
    2.8.8, 54
    2.13.10-11, 57
    2.14.3, 54
    2.18.4, 54

Ab Vrbe Condita
2.18.4-5, 54
2.32.2, 56
2.32.3, 54
2.34.5, 77
2.40.10, 54
2.40.12, 118
2.40.13, 118
2.42.10, 39, 70
2.44.12, 61
2.46.6-7, 100
2.58.2, 54
2.60.4, 119
2.62.1-2, 59, 82
3.2.4, 124, 126
3.5.12, 54
3.5.14, 41
3.6.5, 77
3.7.1, 77, 118
3.8.1, 77
3.10.6, 33, 38, 40, 41, 257
3.11.6, 100
3.24.10, 57
3.29.9, 30, 32, 57
3.32.2, 77
3.34.1, 131
3.44.3, 113
3.50.8, 113
3.56.7, 126
3.58.4, 119
3.70.14, 54
4.7.3, 72
4.9.2, 54, 55
4.9.3, 77
4.12.7, 54
4.20.5-11, 48
4.21.5, 257
4.21.10, 54
4.23.1, 54
4.29.6, 54
4.30.9, 83
4.30.9-11, 79
4.37.1, 54
4.41.12, 56
4.44.11, 66
4.45.2, 133
4.56.3, 31, 57
4.60.1, 54
5.11.16, 103
5.14.3, 39
5.15.1, 41, 64, 96, 131, 159
5.15.1-2, 40
5.15.4, 66
5.15.8, 74
5.15.10, 131
5.15.10-11, 80
5.15.11, 113

Ab Vrbe Condita
5.16.8, 69, 93
5.16.9, 80
5.16.10, 110
5.19.2, 109
5.20.3, 99
5.21.16, 54
5.27.12, 54
5.31.3, 54
5.31.5, 77
5.32.6-7, 40
5.32.7, 41, 74
5.33.2, 54
5.36.1, 107
5.36.6, 107, 110
5.37.1-3, 119, 282
5.38.1, 107
5.40.3, 113
5.40.7, 67
5.43.6, 119
5.46.3, 82
5.48.4, 56
5.49.1, 87, 115
5.50.5, 40
5.51.7, 41
6.5.6, 83
6.8.3, 57
6.18.9, 103, 160
6.18.13, 137
6.18.16, 54
6.25.4, 119
6.27.1, 137
6.29.2, 124, 126
6.33.5, 58
6.37.12, 67
6.38.12, 54
6.42.20, 67
7.1.9, 119
7.2.3, 84, 94
7.2.7, 57
7.3.2, 48, 60
7.3.3-4, 77
7.4.6, 135
7.4.7, 135
7.6.1-3, 93
7.6.2, 58
7.6.3, 57, 58
7.6.9, 105
7.8.4, 122
7.13.5, 99
7.23.2, 122
7.26.2, 102
7.26.3-5, 134
7.26.5, 138
7.27.1, 68, 77
7.28.7, 40, 76
7.28.9, 54

Ab Vrbe Condita
7.30.8, 118
7.34.6, 118, 120
7.34.10, 120
7.35.5, 120
7.35.8, 120
7.35.12, 120
7.37.3, 120
8.1, 135
8.4.6, 99
8.4.11, 135
8.5.3, 99
8.5.7, 135
8.5.8-10, 135
8.6.5-6, 135
8.6.9, 58, 248
8.6.11, 93
8.6.12, 70, 128
8.7.5, 124, 126
8.7.5-7, 134
8.7.8, 134
8.7.20-8, 135
8.9.1, 70
8.10.8, 104
8.10.11-11, 105
8.13.11, 99
8.15.6, 59, 72
8.15.7, 66
8.18.11, 77, 84
8.23.14, 59
8.23.14-7, 72
8.23.16, 72
8.24.18, 270
8.26.6, 54
8.30.7, 54
9.1, 102
9.1.5, 41
9.2.1, 102
9.3.8, 132
9.4.16, 108
9.9.1-9, 102
9.9.10, 102
9.17.3, 118, 134
9.18.11, 119
9.18.12, 119
9.2.10-15, 102
9.28.6, 54
9.29.10, 54, 55
9.33.3, 110
9.36.2, 54
9.40.16, 57
9.44.3, 54
9.44.7, 54
9.46.15, 57
10.3, 102
10.9.10, 54
10.9.12, 54

Ab Vrbe Condita
10.11.2, 61
10.11.10, 54
10.17.12, 54
10.19.17-18, 60
10.23.1, 159
10.24.16, 96, 137
10.28.12-13, 110
10.28.12-29, 58
10.28.12-29.7, 58
10.29.3, 113
10.29.7, 119
10.29.1-7, 58
10.36.11-12, 61
10.39.14, 125
10.39.14-17, 82
10.39.15, 124, 126
10.39.16, 125
10.40.4-5, 49, 125
10.40.10, 23
10.40.11-13, 49, 125
10.40.13-14, 23
10.40.14, 126
10.41.5, 54
10.42.6, 54
10.42.7, 125
10.46.14, 116, 118
10.47.7, 80
21.1.2, 119
21.22.8-9, 112
21.28.5, 54
21.46.2, 30, 34, 44
21.46.2-5, 35
21.47.6, 54
21.51.6, 54
21.59.10, 54
21.62.1, 39, 41, 43, 44, 78, 159
21.62.2, 33
21.62.5, 36
21.62.6, 68
21.62.8, 118
21.62.8, 36
21.63.7, 41
22.1.11, 34
22.1.16, 68
22.7.3, 54
22.7.4, 54
22.9.8, 67, 89
22.9.8-9, 65, 95, 124
22.10.2-6, 89
22.12.10, 118
22.25.14, 123
22.29.7, 119
22.31.8, 54
22.34.3, 72
22.36.7, 28
22.40.4, 54

Ab Vrbe Condita
22.43.4, 57
22.43.9, 107, 108, 110
22.51.4, 101
22.53.6, 109
22.53.13, 54
22.57, 88
22.57.2, 66
22.57.2-4, 38
22.57.2-7, 68, 205
22.57.3, 66
22.57.6, 84, 132
22.58.4, 137
22.58.8, 49, 125
22.61.4, 49
22.61.10, 69
23.1.11, 274
23.5.9, 119
23.11.1, 69, 80, 132
23.11.1-3, 88
23.13.4, 119
23.24.6, 119
23.31.13, 59, 72, 73
23.33.4, 119
23.34.4, 54
23.36.10, 71
23.39.5, 71, 275
23.42.4, 118
23.43.7, 123
23.45.9, 253
24.8.10, 159
24.9.6, 48
24.10.6, 39, 40, 43, 44, 75, 159
24.10.7, 34, 39
24.10.10, 37, 38
24.10.11, 34, 44, 103
24.10.11-12, 39
24.17.6, 54
24.31.14-15, 32
24.38.2, 99
24.44.7, 35
24.44.7-8, 41
24.44.8, 41
24.44.8-9, 42
24.44.9, 72
25.1.6, 79
25.2.6, 129
25.6.6, 108
25.11.20, 54
25.12.11, 74, 89
25.16.1-4, 88
25.16.3, 54
25.16.4, 71, 108, 109, 111
25.17.3, 71
25.17.4, 54
25.17.6, 54
25.24.11-2, 56

Ab Vrbe Condita
25.24.13, 118
25.36.13, 54
25.39.14, 53
25.39.16, 54
26.6.8, 54
26.6.14, 70
26.8.5, 136
26.9.9, 269
26.11.4, 82
26.13.17, 113
26.16.1, 54
26.19.3-4, 127
26.19.3-19, 127
26.19.9, 130
26.23.5, 37
26.23.8, 67
26.29.9-10, 111
26.41.6, 99
26.41.9, 109, 118
26.41.14, 99
26.41.18, 128
26.41.18-20, 130
26.45.8, 130
26.45.8-9, 130
26.49.5, 53
26.49.6, 54
27.4.11, 159
27.8.4, 65
27.11.1-6, 37
27.11.2, 37
27.11.2-5, 37
27.11.3, 40
27.16.15, 70, 71
27.23.1-4, 45
27.23.2, 44, 69, 79, 94
27.23.4, 44, 125
27.25.8, 76
27.25.8-9, 133
27.25.9, 46
27.26.13-14, 46, 70
27.33.6, 46
27.33.7, 54
27.33.11, 46, 99, 119
27.37, 65, 72, 89
27.37.1-2, 37
27.37.2, 42
27.37.3, 35
27.37.4, 28, 74
27.37.5-6, 35
27.37.6, 30, 73, 106
27.37.7, 74
27.37.11, 74
27.38.1, 68
27.43.5, 54
28.11.1, 159
28.11.1-4, 38

Ab Vrbe Condita
28.11.2, 35, 37
28.11.4, 39
28.11.5, 73
28.11.6, 66, 76
28.11.6-7, 92
28.11.8, 99
28.12.3, 119
28.25.7, 99
28.32.11, 137
29.1.11, 57
29.10.6, 80
29.11.1, 80
29.14.2, 41, 83, 160
29.14.3, 37
29.14.5-14, 83
29.14.12, 54
29.15.1, 99
29.18.01-20, 133
29.19.8, 133
29.21.2, 54
29.29.5, 119
29.29.9, 119
29.36.8, 117, 118
30.2.10, 41, 75, 91
30.3.6, 54
30.12.12, 137
30.19.11, 54
30.29.7, 53
30.30.3, 119
30.30.4, 22, 39
30.30.5, 119
30.30.6, 101
30.30.11, 137
30.30.18-23, 123
30.30.23, 137
30.30.30, 22
30.31.10, 104
30.38.10, 48, 77
30.43.12, 54
31.5.7, 70
31.31.20, 99
31.34.8, 57
31.48.12, 110
32.1.10, 34
32.1.12, 40
32.1.14, 73
32.6.5, 53
32.6.8, 54
32.6.13, 70
32.9.1-5, 37
32.29.1-2, 36
32.29.02, 36
32.29.2, 38, 103
33.4.4, 119
33.26.6-9, 35
33.26.9, 30

Ab Vrbe Condita
33.27.4, 118
33.30.8, 53
33.30.10, 54
33.36.13, 54
33.37.1, 119
33.44.1, 89
34.15.9, 54
34.22.2, 54
34.45.6, 38
34.45.6-7, 34
34.45.8, 34
34.55.1, 257
34.55.1-4, 73
34.55.4, 35
35.2.8, 54
35.9.3, 37, 48, 77
35.9.3-4, 37
35.9.4-5, 89
35.21.4, 37, 38
35.21.5, 36, 39
35.21.6, 48
35.42.8, 118
36.1.3, 70
36.19.12, 54
36.36.4, 80
36.36.5, 54
36.37.1, 33
36.37.3-4, 89
36.37.4, 68
36.37.5, 133
36.38.6, 54
37.3.2, 37, 38, 72
37.34.6, 54
37.45.9, 99
37.45.11-12, 101
37.45.13, 104
37.48.1, 54
37.54.10, 99
37.60.6, 54
38.18.9, 80, 85
38.23.8, 54
38.24.11, 54, 55
38.25.8, 118
38.28.4, 48
38.41.4, 80
38.48.7, 96
38.48.14-15, 136
38.50.5, 54
38.55.2, 54
38.55.8, 54
38.55.10, 54
38.56.8, 54
39.5.9, 64
39.8.3, 79
39.9.4, 99
39.15.2, 79

Ab Vrbe Condita
39.15.3, 80
39.16.6, 45, 79
39.16.9, 81, 124
39.16.10, 83
39.16.11, 83, 100
39.21.9, 54, 55
39.22.3, 37
39.22.10, 54
39.43.1, 54
39.46.5, 39
39.49.2, 54
39.56.6, 41
39.56.7, 54
40.2.1, 33
40.2.1-3, 38, 76
40.2.3, 77
40.2.4, 33
40.5.1, 102
40.6.1-2, 82
40.19.1, 159
40.19.1-2, 34
40.19.2, 38, 39
40.19.2-3, 34
40.19.3, 77
40.19.4-5, 73
40.24, 102
40.29.8, 54
40.29.11, 124
40.29.12, 124
40.37.1, 77, 160, 162
40.37.2, 73
40.40.1, 119
40.40.10, 87, 117, 118
40.40.11, 54
40.45.1-4, 37
40.45.2, 38
40.45.3, 38
40.52.2-6, 60
40.52.5, 137
40.54.1, 113
40.56, 102
40.58.3, 82
40.58.3-7, 60, 103
40.59.6, 38, 70, 205
40.59.8, 44, 77, 257
41.9.5, 39
41.9.6, 30
41.10.5-13, 137
41.11.4, 137
41.12.4, 137
41.13.2, 164
41.13.6-14, 136
41.14.6, 137
41.15.1, 38, 111
41.15.3, 40
41.15.4, 111, 138, 274, 275

Ab Vrbe Condita
41.16.6, 71
41.16.8, 137
41.18.8, 111
41.18.11, 111
41.18.14, 111
41.21.5, 38
41.21.10, 77
41.24.8, 99
41.27.2, 53
52.7, 113
42.2.5, 91
42.3.1, 136
42.3.3, 80
42.3.9, 80
42.7.9, 54
42.10.7, 92
42.10.8, 92
42.11.1, 54
42.11.2, 54
42.11.5, 113
42.20.1, 77
42.20.2, 72, 74
42.20.4, 70, 132
42.28.12, 80
42.30.9, 70, 74
42.52.13, 101
43.13.1-2, 46, 51
43.13.2, 41, 141
43.13.3, 35
43.13.3-6, 35, 40
43.13.4, 36, 39
43.13.6, 41, 74, 75
43.16.6, 39
44.1.10-11, 101
44.1.10-12, 123
44.6.14, 102
44.13.12, 54
44.14.1, 54, 55
44.15.3, 54
44.22.3, 125
44.29.1, 80
44.34.3-5, 104
44.34.7, 104
44.37.6-7, 98
44.37.8, 99
44.44.4, 80
45.1.6, 54
45.4.3, 56
45.16.5, 34, 36, 40
45.16.5-6, 36
45.23.1, 99
45.28.10, 54
45.39.12, 104
45.39.13, 136
45.40.1, 53
45.40.2, 54

Ab Vrbe Condita
45.41.1, 137
45.41.6, 126
45.41.8-12, 119
45.41.12, 137
45.43.8, 54
Lucan
5.340, 159
Lucretius
5.76-81, 99
5.751-70., 99

Macrobius
Saturnalia
7.13.11, 186
Martial
1.111, 159

Oracula Sibyllina
8.136, 213
Ovid
Ars Amatoria
3.405, 159
Metamorphoses
4.574, 159
8.724, 159

Periochae
41.1, 66
Pliny
Natural Histories
2.53, 98
2.86, 164
7.178, 29
7.34, 76, 289
10.2.5, 216
10.60, 134
Plutarch
Aemilius
17.7.10, 98
Caesar
47, 48
Marcellus
28.3, 44
Numa
10, 66
Roman Questions
96, 66
Polybius
29.16.1-2, 98

Quintilian
Institutes of Oratory
1.10.47, 98
Minor Declamations
274.12, 159

Servius
On the Aeneid
1.235, 13
6.72, 67
Silius Italicus
7.75, 159
Statius *Siluae*
4.2.15, 159
Statius *Thebaid*
5.456, 159
Suetonius
Augustus
91, 128
Caesar
32, 48
77, 48
Caligula
23, 171
Domitian
15, 162
Nero
46, 162
Otho
8, 162
Tiberius
49, 186
51, 182
63, 163
Vespasian
5, 162
10-14, 210
Vitellius
9, 97

Tacitus
Agricola
2-3, 220
3, 216
42.2, 173
44, 216
Annals
1.3.1, 185
1.3.3, 171
1.3.4, 155
1.7.1, 183, 190
1.9.1, 161
1.10.6, 178
1.11-1.14, 182
1.11.1, 179
1.12, 190
1.13, 190
1.14, 182
1.28.2, 165
1.29.1, 155
1.29.3, 165
1.31, 47
1.31.4, 155

Annals

1.39, 154
1.43.3, 183
1.55.3, 171
1.61.3, 169
1.62.2, 190
1.65.2, 168
1.70, 187
1.73.1, 192
1.73.5, 190
1.76.2, 163
1.76.3, 190, 191
2.8.1, 183
2.14.1, 168
2.14.3, 159
2.22.1, 179
2.24.4, 165
2.27, 168
2.27.1, 186
2.30.1-2, 166
2.32.1, 187
2.32.2, 183
2.32.3, 166
2.32.4, 183
2.41, 193
2.41.1, 179
2.42.3, 171
2.47.1-3, 163
2.49.1, 193
2.50.2, 193
2.56.4, 187
2.69.3, 166
2.83.1, 183
2.83.4, 182
2.84.3, 163, 170
2.85.4, 169
2.87.2, 183
3.2.5, 183
3.18.2, 190, 193, 201
3.18.7, 211
3.19, 187
3.22.1, 166
3.24.3, 179
3.26.3, 155
3.31.3-4, 145
3.36.2, 184
3.50.2, 145
3.55, 151, 210, 213, 215, 218
3.55.4, 220
3.56.1, 183
3.57.1-2, 194
3.58.1, 192
3.60, 192
3.60.2, 169
3.60.6, 191
3.64.3, 179
3.64.3-4, 190

Annals

3.65, 183
3.65-66, 190
3.65.2, 183
3.65.3, 183, 189
3.66, 193
3.66.1-2, 145
3.70.3, 186
3.71.2, 192
3.72.4-5, 194
4.1.1, 205
4.1.2, 194, 266, 288
4.9.2, 183, 195
4.13.1, 164
4.15.1, 171
4.15.4, 184
4.15.5, 194
4.16, 192
4.16.4, 186
4.16.6, 186
4.17.1, 183
4.20, 173
4.20.2-4, 172
4.27.1, 171, 197
4.30.5, 183, 195
4.33.1-2, 145
4.33.2, 145
4.36.2, 179
4.36.5, 183
4.37, 178
4.37.1, 184
4.37.2, 178
4.38.6, 178
4.42.3, 179
4.57.1, 195
4.58.1, 186
4.58.2-3, 166
4.58.3, 175
4.60, 195
4.64.1, 161, 163, 164
4.70.1-4, 194
4.74.2, 183, 184
4.74.4, 183
5.2.1, 182, 183
5.8, 187
6.3.2, 155
6.7.2-4, 187
6.10.3, 171, 172, 186
6.18.2, 180
6.20.2, 166, 175
6.20.3, 212
6.21, 166
6.22.1-3, 172, 173
6.22.6, 166, 212
6.23, 190
6.25.5, 195
6.26.1, 195

Annals
6.27.1, 186
6.28, 166, 170, 205, 213, 216
6.28.1, 213, 219
6.32.4, 145
6.34.2, 170
6.37.1-2, 167
6.38.1, 146
6.38.3, 183
6.40, 187
6.45, 164
6.46, 175
6.46.3, 175
6.46.4, 171
11.2.5, 171
11.4, 168
11.4.1-5, 161
11.4.3, 161
11.5.6, 132, 161
11.6.1, 145
11.8.1, 159
11.11, 216
11.11.1, 153, 196
11.14, 170
11.15, 9
11.15.1, 187
11.21, 175, 188
11.23.22-3, 145
11.24, 145
11.24.7, 145
11.26.1-4, 197
11.31, 167
11.31.6, 171
12.4.4, 196
12.5, 197
12.5.3-5, 196
12.8.1, 196
12.8.2, 161
12.8.2-3, 187
12.13.3, 168, 248
12.13.4, 170
12.20.2, 145
12.23.3-4, 196
12.25.1, 196
12.43, 197
12.43.1, 161, 164, 205
12.52.3, 166
12.58.2, 164
12.59.1, 165
12.64.1, 160, 162, 205
12.66, 198
12.68.3, 166
13.2-3, 198
13.2.3, 197
13.2.6, 180
13.3.2, 180
13.4.1, 145

Annals
13.8.1, 184
13.10.1, 198
13.16.2-5, 198
13.17.1, 212
13.17.2, 161, 163
13.24.1-2, 205
13.24.2, 162, 187
13.41.3, 157
13.41.5, 184, 198
13.47.3, 176, 272
13.58, 205, 213, 216
13.58.1, 205
14.8.6, 198
14.9.3, 166
14.10.1-4, 184
14.12.2, 162, 199
14.12.3, 199, 205
14.12.4, 171
14.14.4, 171
14.15.1, 199
14.22, 161
14.22.1, 157, 162, 174, 215
14.22.1-4, 161
14.22.2, 157
14.22.6, 199
14.30.3, 169
14.31-2, 163
14.31.6, 179
14.49.1, 199
14.51.1-5, 198
14.64, 198, 199
14.64.6, 146, 183, 199
15.7.2, 97, 160
15.8.1, 156
15.20.2-4, 201
15.20.3, 145
15.22, 215
15.22.2, 162
15.22.3, 200
15.22.3-4, 205
15.23.2, 145
15.23.4-5, 180, 200
15.34, 200
15.34.1-2, 161
15.36.3, 200
15.38, 215
15.38.1, 170
15.44.1-2, 200, 205
15.44.3-6, 170
15.44.5, 145, 169
15.45.5, 200
15.47.1, 156, 215
15.47.1-3, 97, 205
15.47.2, 162, 200
15.47.3, 157, 159, 187
15.53.3, 157

Annals
15.54, 157
15.56.2, 198, 201
15.71.1, 199
15.74.2, 157, 167, 200
15.74.3-4, 181
16.1.1, 168
16.5.1, 210
16.5.3, 212
16.6.1, 198
16.6.2, 201
16.6.2-3, 181
16.7.1, 201
16.13, 162
16.13.1, 201, 205
16.13.2, 162, 172
16.14, 167
16.16, 146
16.16.1-2, 194
16.16.2-3, 201
16.21.1, 201
16.21.2, 181
16.21.2-22, 201
16.21.3, 181
16.22, 181
16.22.2-22, 199
16.22.5, 181
16.33, 283
16.33.1, 160
16.35, 198
Germania
8, 177
12, 155
Histories
1.1.1, 221
1.1.4, 147, 148, 221
1.2, 214
1.2.3, 185
1.3.1, 145
1.3.2, 156, 158
1.4.2, 144
1.5.1, 174
1.6.3, 202
1.10, 175
1.10.3, 212
1.11.1, 169
1.15.1, 202
1.18.1, 171, 202
1.18.1-2, 187
1.22.1, 167
1.22.1-2, 175, 212
1.22.2, 166
1.27.1, 188, 202
1.28.2, 167
1.37.6, 202
1.38.2, 202
1.40, 202

Histories
1.41, 202
1.43.2, 202
1.47.3, 202
1.49.4, 220
1.50.2, 145, 202, 212
1.50.4, 174, 220
1.77.4, 188
1.77.4-5, 202
1.77.5, 188
1.79.1, 159
1.86, 77, 161, 162, 205, 215
1.86.1, 155, 160, 163, 170
1.86.3, 157
1.89.4, 202
2.2.2-4, 169
2.4, 212
2.4.3, 169
2.37, 216, 218
2.38.5, 205
2.42.1, 170
2.50.2, 156
2.56.1, 203
2.62.2, 166
2.69, 212
2.69.2, 203
2.70.6, 203
2.73.2, 174
2.74.1, 203
2.74.2, 174
2.78.1, 159, 167
2.78.2, 174, 175
2.78.3, 169
2.78.4, 167
2.78.6-7, 212
2.91, 203
2.91.1, 161, 176
2.91.3, 145
2.95.2, 181, 203
3.1.1, 212
3.2.4-5, 169
3.21.2, 170
3.51.2, 145
3.56, 253
3.56.1, 205
3.58.3, 161, 165
3.58.5, 203
3.68, 203
3.71.3, 207
3.72, 215
3.72.1, 207
3.73.3, 207
3.74.1-2, 204
3.75.4, 207
3.81.1, 150
3.84.3, 212
3.86.1, 188

Histories
4.5.4, 201
4.8.1, 145
4.15.1, 169
4.22.2, 209
4.26.2, 157, 160, 161, 170, 176
4.29.2, 170
4.42.6, 145
4.53, 209, 272
4.54.2, 169
4.58.2, 145
4.61.2, 169
4.61.3, 177
4.65.6, 177
4.78.2, 266
4.78.3, 209
4.81.1, 169
4.81.2, 174
4.81.4, 174
4.82, 212
4.83.2, 169
5.2.1, 169
5.7, 156
5.8.2, 169

Histories
5.8.3, 169
5.10.1, 172
5.13.1, 156
5.13.1-3, 164
Tzetzes, *On Lycophron*
1279, 67

Valerius Maximus
5.6.2, 93
8.11.1, 98
Varro
    On the Latin Language
    5.148, 93
Virgil
    Aeneid
    6.283-4, 128
    7.324-7, 80

Zonaras
7.11.1, 67
7.25, 93
8.5, 58
9.23, 98

Subject index

Abydum; oracle, 239
Adrastia, 259, 275; and justice, 275–282; *see also* Nemesis
adulatio, 175, 177, 182–184, 190, 195, 199; *Graeca*, 180
Aeneid, *see* Virgil
aequitas, 160, 260, 275, 277, 281, 283; and justice, 275
Aesculapius, 80, 81, 265; and Serapis, 169
ait, 54
Aius Locutius, 40, 41
Alamanni, 267, 269, 270; capture Mainz, 244
Alexander, 270; and Roman generals, 134; and sign, 127
Alexandria; home of religious experts, 249; Vespasian performs healing, 169, 174
Allecto, 80
Allia, 107, 110, 119, 282
Amicitia; altar established, 184
Ammianus; as Christian, 227; 'confused', 276; Greek, 14, 226, 235, 236; and historical tradition, 261–262, 264; 'nostalgic', 228, 229, 237; as (failed) philosopher, 232; philosophers, 255–258; philosophy, 233, 284; publication, 226; refusal to include trivia, 229; religious toleration, 242, 268; 'secular', 228–233; heir to Tacitus, 236; *see also* authority, *persona*, pessimism
amulets, 239
Anaximander, 256; on earthquakes and water, 262
annalistic history, 262; as interpretation, 25, 74; and prodigies, 30; tradition, 16, 55, 149
Apis bull, 250
Apollo, 35, 250, 262; and Augustus, 132; Julian dreams of, 251; prophecy and ravens, 134; sacrifice to, 126; temple destroyed, 241, 250; Zerynthius, 80
Aprunculus Gallus, 251, 254
Aristotle, 256; and dreams, 242, 248
astrologers; expelled, 166; poor guides, 167–168; successful/inappropriate, 175

astrology, 184, 246; and *fatum*, 167, 172, 173, 212, 271; and imperial destinies, 166, 167, 175, 212; rise of, 166; successful/inappropriate, 166–168, 175, 249; as *superstitio*, 159, 167; in Tacitus, 166; *see also* Thrasyllus, Tiberius
Ateius Capito: as praiseworthy, 186
auctor est, 54
audience, 2, 14, 17, 28; Ammianus', 227, 231, 234–235, 252, 262, 264, 266, 284, 286, 290; Livy's, 24, 25, 29, 32, 45, 46, 58, 62, 126, 132, 136; Tacitus', 147, 154, 225
augurs, 48, 67, 72, 186, 190; appointed, 188; not named, 65; veto elections, 72, 73
augury, 72, 128, 131, 241, 251, 253
Augustus (Octavian), 47–50, 132, 179, 182, 185; criticised, 179; cult honours, 179; imperial cult, 178–179, 181, 183, 190, 193, 195; signs at death, 161, 165
auspices, 72, 83, 102, 125, 128, 131, 137, 168, 202, 206, 241, 250
authority: of Ammianus, 233, 234, 257, 260, 264; deferred, 22, 32; historiographical, 15, 286; of Livy, 48–51, 53, 55, 60, 62–63, 129, 142, 275; and *oratio obliqua*, 30; priestly, 63–73, 136, 138, 190, 255, 256; religious, 139, 141, 142, 189, 193, 234, 286; of Tacitus, 145, 153, 179, 190; *see also* Delphi, Scipio Africanus, senate

Bacchanalia, 26, 45, 79–81, 84, 100, 124
Bacchus, 80
Barea; *see* Soranus, Barea
Bassus, *see* Caesellius Bassus
Bastarnae, 60–61, 82, 103
bees, 30, 39, 44, 103
belief, 2, 5, 8, 17, 21, 23, 27, 78, 131, 139, 154, 167, 168, 222, 231, 283; *see also* scepticism
Bellona, 60, 228, 237, 253, 279, 281
benignitas deum; *see* gods, benevolence of
Bezabde; besieged, 244

Blaesi; priesthood blocked for political
    services, 187
brain-balkanisation, 3
Bruttium; site of prodigy, 40; site of temple,
    80
Burgundians; religion, 247

Caere, 36, 118, 121
Caesar (Julius), 172, 176, 290; and gods, 230;
    on cruelty, 263
Caesar (title of secondary emperor), 241,
    249, 252; Gallus, 275, 282
Caesar (title of sole emperor), 161, 165
Caesellius Bassus: and illusory dreams, 168
Caeso Quinctius, 100
Caligula, 148, 175, 213
Cannae, 72, 107, 108, 110, 140, 141, 224,
    269, 282
Capito, Ateius, *see* Ateius Capito
Capito Cossutianus: accuses Thrasea Paetus,
    181, 201
Capitol, 126, 133, 202; and heads, 31, 209;
    sacrifice at, 199
Capitoline Temple: razed, 145, 169, 206–209,
    214, 215, 218; refounded, 188, 204,
    209–210, 224
Carrhae, 251
Castor, 236, 267, 268
causal over-determination, 19, 87–96
Cerialis Anicius: proposes temple to (living)
    Nero, 181
Cestius Gallus: and *fatum*, 172
Christian(s), 2; approaches to religion, 3, 5, 7,
    11, 96; attacked Julian, 249; and
    education, 263; god as *numen*, 266;
    murdered Julian, 249; patronage, 231;
    persecution, 169, 200; praised, 244;
    terminology, 242, 243; unreliable, 243
Christianisation, 2, 19, 226
Christianity, 170, 242–246; and justice, 280;
    '*lex*', 245–246; marginalised, 240,
    242–246, 284; and paganism, 231, 245,
    248, 249, 261; for simple-minded, 246;
    superstitio, 169; unsuitable for state,
    242–246; *see also* Ammianus
Cicero, 254, 260, 268, 283; cited by
    Ammianus, 232; on divination, 9, 232; as
    exemplum, 239; influence on *Histories*,
    148
Claros, 239
Claudia Augusta (daughter of Nero), 180, 200
Claudius, 148, 175; death predicted, 166;
    appointed by *fortuna*, 211; and
    haruspices, 9; as historian, 143; and
    incest, 187; undermines religion, 196–197
Claudius Gallus (*flamen dialis*): resigns, 67
Gaius Claudius (consul), 136; neglects gods,
    136, 137
Clementia; altar established, 184

Cn. Cornelius Lentulus: responds to *flamen
    dialis*, 205, 211, 212
Cocceius Nerva; as praiseworthy, 186
comet; as sign, 157, 161, 174, 200, 215, 218,
    257
Constantius, 238, 239, 249, 269; death, 241,
    251, 252; and education, 264; and *fatum*,
    271, 272; and Julian, 241, 250, 252, 262;
    and justice, 240, 275; unsuccessful
    abroad, 245, 270
credo; as technical term, 40, 175; Christian
    sense, 41
C. Sulpicius Gallus: reinterprets eclipse, 165,
    198–99
cura deum, 159
Curtius (Marcus); sacrifices self, 58, 93
Curtius Rufus; and *fatum*, 175
Cybele, 80

Dagalaiphus, 278
damnatio memoriae; as opposite of
    deification, 177
decemuiri sacris faciundis, 64, 65, 67–74, 77,
    80, 88, 89, 91, 95, 132, 133, 167, 181,
    190, 191, 196, 205, 216, 220, 257;
    authority, 70; consulted without
    prodigies, 67, 89, 95, 124; and *fatum*,
    110; 'pessimistic', 70, 132; and Sibylline
    Books, 67
decline: of luxury, 151, 210; of morals, 145,
    184; of religion, 4, 142, 144, 161–165,
    176, 182, 185–211; of Rome, 50, 140,
    155, 160, 171, 194, 197–199, 201, 204,
    207, 208, 211, 213, 214, 220, 222, 223;
    and recovery, 151, 210, 220, 221, 223,
    224; of senate, 180, 189–193
deification, 177–181; of Augustus, 179; of
    Claudia Augusta (Nero's daughter), 180;
    of Claudius, 180; failed, 181; of Livia,
    182; of Poppaea, 181; a senatorial
    decision, 177; *see also* imperial cult
Delos, 80
Delphi, 68, 69, 80, 91, 93, 109, 113, 131,
    159, 239, 274; attacked by Gauls, 60;
    oracle unambiguous, 132
deuotio, 58; lore, 105; of P. Decius Mus, 58,
    93, 104, 110, 128; similar Samnite rite, 82
deus, 266
dicitur; validate sign; *see also* reported
    speech
digressions, 1, 233; in Ammianus, 232;
    indicate mood of gods, 267; validate sign,
    251
Dii Manes, 128
divination, 5, 132, 232, 241–242, 251–253,
    260, 261, 267, 273; reliability, 128, 131,
    168, 237; *see also* Julian
Dodona, 239

Domitian, 146, 148, 149, 273; and decline in luxury, 151, 210, 220; as aberration in recovery, 151, 210, 220; and senate, 211; signs recorded by Suetonius, 162; Tacitus' 'guilt', 211; and Vesta, 204
double motivation, *see* causal over-determination
dream(s), 161, 241; credibility, 128, 131, 168, 170, 242, 248, 262; in ritual context, 168; of god, 169, 270; prognosticatory, 128, 251; reinterpreted, 161, 168; of Scipio Africanus, 126–128, 131, 132; shared, 58, 128
Druids, 246, 247; incompetent, 169, 209
Drusus, 195, 206; exploits *superstitio* of soldiers, 165

earthquakes, 164; in philosophy, 258, 262; prodigial, 35, 73, 162–164, 215, 250, 254, 256, 257, 259
eclipse (lunar) as sign, 165; non-prodigial, 82, 98–99, 165
education, 262, 263; bestowed by gods, 280; by literature, 26, 262, 264; and civilisation, 263, 264, 279; and violence, 263, 264; *see also* Christians, Constantius, Gratian, Jovian, Julian
Egeria, 129
Egyptians, 246; note phoenix, 219; priests, 169, 170, 258; and religion, 247; and *superstitio*, 169
Ennosigaeos, 256, 259
Epicureanism, 17, 23
Epicurus, 256
exempla, 14, 261; in Ammianus, 235, 239, 244, 249, 252, 253, 255, 256, 259–261, 281; foregrounded, 261; in Livy, 25–27, 49, 50, 58, 62, 63, 67, 69, 70, 73, 74, 82, 101, 102, 114, 125, 126, 129, 131, 133, 134, 137, 138, 142; and religion, 26–27; in Tacitus, 145, 147, 151, 168, 172, 181, 199, 210, 211, 215, 221, 225; *see also* Piso, Vespasian
expiation, 28, 33, 36, 39, 41, 42, 44, 45, 47, 48, 67, 71, 74, 76, 77, 89, 91–93, 96, 108, 132, 156, 159–162, 187, 200, 205, 206, 223, 238, 242, 257, 258, 266, 270, 283–285; abandoned, 237, 238, 240, 267, 272–275, 282–284; and correct deity, 133; redundant with *fatum*, 109

fatalis dux, 109, 112
'fatalism'; of Tacitus, 167, 222
fatum, 2, 16, 19, 71, 105, 107–110, 115, 118, 140, 150, 173, 174, 228, 230, 241; in Ammianus, 271–282; avoided as diagnosis, 110–113; blinds victims, 282; and death, 107, 111, 113, 171–172; deployment, 211; diagnosis, 114, 142;

171, 213, 219; and emperors, 175, 271, 272, 278, 281; and *exempla*, 114; and flattery, 272; and the gods, 16, 100, 105, 108–109, 140, 157, 161, 277; 'higher' explanation, 19, 106, 108, 109, 111, 112, 114, 117, 120, 176, 223, 271; and individuals, 111, 172, 174, 175, 211, 212, 271, 279; inevitable, 71, 88, 93, 108, 109, 115, 119, 120, 173, 271–282; judicious deployment, 44, 108, 110–114, 140, 176; and justice, 283; in Livy, 105–115; and Nemesis, 277; patterns in, 109–113, 119, 140, 212; and priests, 71, 109–110, 131, 191; response to, 172–175, 215, 260, 282, 283, 289; of Rome, 105, 106, 110, 114, 115, 140, 141, 176, 202, 203, 211–213, 220, 221; and Sibylline Books, 109; and Stoicism, 106; in Tacitus, 171–176, 211–221; 'technical device', 228–230; and *uirtus*, 106–107, 114, 271; *see also* astrology
felicitas; and divine favour, 105, 137, 269, 283; and flattery, 272; prayed for, 96; used of others, 137; used of self, 137
ficus Ruminalis, 205, 213, 216, 220
flamen; of Augustus, 178; *dialis*, 65, 67, 186, 192; disgraced, 66; *flamines*, 64, 66, 67; named, 67; *quirinalis*, 65, 67
flaminica, 192; Agrippina as, 180
flood; non-prodigial, 77; prodigial, 37, 48, 60, 77, 84
foreign; audience, 264; gods, 79–82, 85, 132, 177; *haruspices*, 70, 73, 106; prodigies, 35, 41, 75, 79, 164; religion, 79, 85, 169, 246–248; rites, 79, 81–84, 169, 170, 181, 201, 273; terminology, 40; victories, 193, 201; war, 206, 209, 270; *see also* Burgundians, Druid, Egypt, Germans, Jews
foreigners; in Rome, 235, 264; and religion, 60, 82, 156, 170, 247
fors; as category, 16, 17, 19, 170, 171, 176; as detail, 116, 120, 170; and *fatum*, 115–117, 171, 173; *forte*, 71, 115, 170, 171, 213, 214; *forte quadam*, 115; and *fortuna*, 116–118; and the gods, 105, 106, 115–116, 170, 171; in Livy, 105, 106, 115–116; and randomness, 115, 116, 171; in Tacitus, 170–171
Fors Fortuna, 37, 116, 118, 276
Fortuna, 35, 37, 118, 121, 157, 276; *Equestris*, 87, 117, 118; *Muliebris*, 118; *Primigeneia*, 35, 117, 118
fortuna, 2, 13, 105, 115, 144, 173, 228, 268–270; adverse, 119; avoids exact interpretation, 122; and *fatum*, 19, 106, 174–175, 211; and the gods, 16, 105, 106, 117–123, 269–270; governs outcomes, 117; in literature, 230; in Livy, 106,

116–123; and Nemesis, 276; *orbis Romanae*, 235; as outcome, 175; *perpetua*, 122; *populi Romani*, 117, 118, 120, 122, 235; as providence, 117; *rei publicae*, 122; reversals, 269–270; saves Rome, 118; as situation, 117, 120, 173; survey of uses, 120–121; 'technical device', 228, 229; *uaria*, 121; and *uirtus*, 117, 118, 120, 123, 270; unpredictable, 119–120, 122–123, 269, 281
Furies, 80, 279, 281; and justice, 277, 279

Galba: death, 202; and *fatum*, 166, 175, 212; and rise in luxury, 210, 220; misinterprets signs, 171, 187, 188, 202
Gallus: and *fortuna*, 269; and justice, 275, 277, 282
Gallus, *see* Aprunculus Gallus, C. Sulpicius Gallus
Gauls, 40, 56, 74, 107, 109, 113, 115, 118, 122, 141, 207; buried alive, 68; attack Delphi, 60; and reverence, 82
Genius Publicus, 250, 251
genre, 7, 17, 141, 150, 227, 235, 262, 287; as strategy, 12, 13, 44, 156, 259, 287; violation of, 153
Germanicus, 187, 193, 194, 201; augur, 190; death, 166; and dreams, 168; as *exemplum*, 168; honoured, 183, 193, 195; and imperial cult, 179, 183
Germans: and religious errors, 169, 177; simpler, 155; and *superstitio*, 177
gods, 9, 11, 16, 28, 82, 85, 98; acknowledgement of, 5, 61, 98, 104, 133, 136–138, 190, 193, 199, 270; agency deduced, 10, 16, 18, 22, 44–46, 59–62, 64, 65, 76, 78, 79, 82–85, 87, 91, 92, 94, 96–105, 109, 110, 112, 121–123, 125, 130, 136, 139, 155, 162, 164, 171, 205, 221, 281, 286, 287, 290; appropriateness of, 79, 80, 84, 274; benevolence, 99–100, 142, 170, 173, 208, 261; blamed for defeats, 101; dismissed, 16, 18, 23, 44, 99, 116, 130, 142, 231, 289; domain, 79, 101, 103–106, 108, 118, 120, 123, 140, 160, 171, 229, 259, 268, 281; existence, 2, 17, 81, 94, 131; govern outcomes, 104–105; and impiety, 102, 194, 200; and individuals, 78, 96, 100–105; intervention, 23, 58, 86, 87, 93, 96–105, 114, 115, 117–119, 121, 122, 134, 141, 156, 159, 160, 170, 199, 205, 206, 221, 229, 286; jealousy, 119, 122; in literature, 228–231; mood deduced, 43–45, 69, 83, 91, 95, 114, 125, 126, 130, 134, 160, 161, 200, 206, 208, 266, 267, 270; and naming gods, 133, 135, 136, 138, 231, 266, 268;

neglected, 44, 46, 49, 107, 121, 136, 137, 140, 142, 158, 159, 178, 185, 197, 206, 269, 283, 286, 289; negotiation with, 9, 14, 19, 22, 27, 28, 68, 69, 77, 89, 93, 96, 102, 108–111, 114, 117, 119, 122, 123, 125, 128, 131, 136, 139, 140, 167, 198, 200, 204, 208, 209, 211, 222, 224, 225, 242, 251, 269, 272–278, 282, 284–287, 291; *see also* propitiation; and success/failure, 9, 22, 60, 61, 68, 107, 119, 121, 141, 171, 210; support: *see pax deorum*; and vengeance, 24, 102, 103, 113, 119, 126, 156, 158, 190; give warnings, 46, 47, 49, 111, 150, 200, 201, 254; as a will, 19, 100, 109, 116, 119, 268; *see also* education, *fatum*, foreign, *fors*, *fortuna*, imperial cult, *ira deorum*, justice, multiple over-determination, nature, *pax deorum*
Goths, 270, 277, 279
Gracchus, *see* Tiberius Gracchus
Gratian, 267; and education, 264; and *fatum*, 271; refused post of *Pontifex Maximus*, 226
Greek: buried alive, 68; historians, 3, 17, 235, 264, 270, 282, 290; influence, 106; philosophy; and *fortuna/tyche*, 105–106; phoenix lore, 219; poets, 131; priests, 79, 131, 170; religion, 6, 7, 85, 87, 106

Hadrian: *superstitiosus*, 247
Hannibal, 22, 57, 68, 70, 71, 101, 104, 111, 119, 122, 123, 125, 137; attributes success to gods, 22; and *fatum*, 112
haruspices, 46, 48, 64, 67, 70–72, 74, 95, 97, 109, 131, 159, 187, 188, 204, 237, 250–255, 257, 267, 274, 285; as *collegium*, 64, 196; consulted, 64, 65; not consulted, 40; and *fatum*, 71, 88, 110, 132; and lightning, 72; not named, 65, 66; validate dream, 128; validated, 70, 71, 254
haruspicy, 241, 252, 258; decline, 166, 187; validated, 241
head: Rome 'without' a head, 209
Heraclitus, 256
Hercules, 55, 168, 170, 215
Herodotus, 6, 17, 20, 52, 236, 270; Ammianus' debt, 262; and justice, 282; and 'monotheism', 228, 266, 267
Hilarius, 279
historiography, 2, 12–17, 25, 51, 52, 61, 139, 145, 148, 152, 220, 227, 230, 232, 233, 235, 243, 254, 255, 268, 281, 286, 287, 290; and *exempla*, 25; and justice, 243; and myth, 21; and poetry, 152; and religion, 1–3, 12, 17–20, 236, 287, 289,

291; 'secular', 228–232, 242, 287;
tradition of, 20, 54, 236, 238, 262, 264,
270, 291
Homer, 7, 87, 103, 128, 258, 259
Honos, 46, 76
human error, *see* Druids, Germans, Jews,
priests, ritual, *superstitio*, Vestals
Huns, 247, 248, 264

imperial cult, 144, 176–185; *see also*
deification, Germanicus
impiety; *see* gods, piety
incest, 166, 187, 196–197
informers, 167, 183, 193
interpretatio Romana, 80; *see also* foreign
gods
interpretation, 7, 12, 59, 61; caution in,
125–126, 134, 136, 268; mistaken, 157,
248, 253; as political act, 12, 62,
123–138; positive, 24, 49, 70, 110, 163,
169, 200, 250, 252, 258, 270
ira deorum, 2, 28, 29, 33, 44, 45, 64, 68, 77,
80, 83, 89, 90, 92, 95, 97–99, 102, 109,
111, 115, 125, 140, 155, 157–161,
163–165, 171, 176, 193–195, 197, 199,
201, 202, 204–206, 213, 215, 222, 223,
240, 267, 272, 284, 288; diverted, 23, 45,
46, 99, 112, 119
Iris, 259
irrationality: in narrative, 151–153

Janus, 194
Jews, 170, 172, 246, 247; and religious error,
156, 164, 223; and *superstitio*, 169;
Temple, 273
Jovian, 269, 275; and *fatum*, 271; poorly
educated, 262; troops saved, 260, 267
Julia Augusta, 179
Julian, 226, 234; as apostate, 243; Augustus,
237, 238, 241, 250; Caesar, 241, 249,
252; and divination, 251–252, 258; and
dreams, 241, 242; and education, 262,
263; and *fatum*, 271; and justice, 275;
poor *exemplum*, 249–252, 255;
propitiates gods, 237; *superstitiosus*, 247,
249; *see also* interpretation (positive)
Juno Lacinia; temple despoiled, 80, 136
Juno Lucina, 37
Jupiter, 34, 37, 42, 44, 45, 64, 84, 94,
133–136, 138, 179, 195, 200, 231, 250,
266, 267; Capitolinus, 54, 128, 131;
Optimus Maximus, 87, 137, 206, 231;
and Serapis, 169; Stator, 215; *uigor
uiuificus*, 259; Vindex, 157, 200
justice, 210, 232, 240, 242, 269, 281, 283,
285; avenges Gordianus, 277; and *fatum*,
275–282; and the gods, 240, 276–282,

285; in Herodotus, 282; in Lactantius,
280; mother of Adrastia, 259; in Tacitean
Rome, 155; in Tacitus, 283; as
excellentissima uirtus, 275; weeps, 275,
277; *see also aequitas*, Constantius,
Furies, Herodotus, historiography, Julian,
Valens
Juvenile Games, 199

L. Calpurnius Piso; as praiseworthy priest,
186
Lares Permarini, 60
Lentulus, *see* Cn. Cornelius Lentulus
Marcus Lepidus; as *exemplum*, 172, 211
Liber, Libera and Ceres, 133
lightning; as prodigy, 28–30, 32, 34–39, 42,
45, 60, 65, 72, 76, 77, 133, 157, 162, 187,
200, 240, 242, 257, 258; strikes soldier
(omen), 251, 257; strikes Tullus, 84
Limigantes, 269
Livy, *see* authority, *persona*, pessimism
Locri, 83
Lucretius, 23
Lupercalia; persisted after Christianity, 226
lustrum; abused, 196

Magi, 247, 248, 253, 284; religious
exemplum, 253
magic, 5, 8, 68, 165, 241, 247–249;
prosecutions for, 166, 168; as *superstitio*,
166
magicians; expelled, 166
Magna Mater, 85
maiestas laws, 192, 193
Manichaeism; *superstitio*, 247
Marcus Claudius Marcellus, 44, 46, 56, 70,
76, 99, 111–113, 119, 123, 172; and
fatum, 111–113
Marcius; prophetic poems of, 74, 89
Marcus (*haruspex*), 253, 254
Mars, 120, 179, 228, 251, 279; epiphany,
268; *Vltor*, 190
martyrs, 237, 245, 248, 266
Maximinus; and justice, 277
Menander, 258, 259
Mercury, 259
Mimas; plains of, 279
minime Romano sacro, 68, 84
Mithraism, 7
monotheism, 228, 265–268; *see also*
Herotodus
Mopsus; healing tomb, 237
mules, 30, 32, 33, 76
mystery cults, 5

narrative, 2, 19, 22, 26, 46, 48, 60, 69, 72, 86,
107, 114, 116, 140, 142, 144, 148, 151,

152, 160, 165, 176, 184, 197, 221, 229, 238, 267; and morality, 14
nature, 13, 74, 97, 232, 257; and chance, 13, 170; and the gods, 93, 97–99; and prodigies, 29, 76–79, 82, 91, 98–99, 105, 156, 162, 170, 204, 217; see also pax deorum
necromancy, 239
Nemesis, 232, 259, 275, 276; daughter of justice, 276; and *fatum*, 277; and *fortuna*, 276, 281
Neptune, 129, 130, 133, 135, 256, 259
Nero, 147, 148, 157, 175; adopted, 196; honoured, 184, 198, 201, 203; murders family, 198, 201; offends gods, 156, 157, 159, 160, 200, 201, 206, 277; reign predicted, 166, 277; and signs, 132, 157, 161–163, 168, 174, 176, 199, 200, 205, 215, 220; undermines religion, 197–201
Nero Caesar, 186, 194
Nerva, 151
Nigrinus, 273
nouemdiale sacrum, 95; and showers of stones, 34, 54, 94, 291
Numa, 72, 81; books of, 124; and Egeria, 129; palace, 215
numen, 265–268, 270, 275, 279, 281, 285; indicates mood of gods, 267; of Christian god, 266; polite term, 265–266
nuntiare, see reported speech

Octavian, *see* Augustus
omen, *see* prodigy
omens, 47, 48, 70, 71, 97, 125, 134, 150, 154, 157, 160, 162, 165, 174, 181, 184, 187, 212, 213, 251, 253, 269, 271, 281, 289; favourable, 250; intelligible, 98; misreported, 23, 24, 125; of speech, 280; in Tacitus, 154–165; unfavourable, 111, 250, 271
oracle, *see* Abydum, Caere, Delphi, Sibylline
oracles, 126, 131; ambiguous, 271; reliable, 253; Sibylline, 67, 68
oratio obliqua, see reported speech
Osiris: and Serapis, 169
Otho, 188, 202, 212; and astrologers, 167; and *fatum*, 175, 202, 212; and priests, 188, 202; and religious failure, 202–203; and signs, 156, 161, 174, 212; survives Nero, 166
Ovid, 13; *Fasti*, 9

paganism, 3, 4, 246, 249, 252, 280, 284; approaches to, 96, 226, 228, 232; civic paganism, 3, 4, 233; end of, 226; 'personal', 284; and prediction, 252; restoration, 285; and rite, 96, 284;

survival, 226, 284, 285; *see also* Christianity
Pallor, 103
Paul 'the Chain', 239–240
Pauor, 103
pax deorum, 10, 45, 48, 68, 84, 85, 89, 93, 95, 98, 99, 101, 115, 121, 122, 140, 161, 165, 197, 201, 205, 206, 210, 211, 222, 238, 267, 270, 272–274, 291; as state of nature, 98–99; *pax numinum*, 265, 272, 274; *see also* gods, benevolence of
persona; Ammianus, 231; Livy, 14, 73; poetic, 13; Tacitus, 153
pessimism: in Ammianus, 229, 288; in Livy, 224, 288; in Tacitus, 146–148, 150, 151, 153, 167, 224, 225
pestilence, 118; prodigial, 34, 38, 39, 77, 94
Petilius Spurinus, *see* Q. Petilius Spurinus
philosophers, 6, 7, 150, 237, 245, 251, 252, 255–258, 277, 280, 285; *see also* Ammianus, Greek philosophy
philosophy, 217, 232, 233, 276
phoenix, 205, 211, 213, 216, 219
piety, 4, 22, 60, 82, 83, 102, 107, 112, 114, 121, 123, 141, 261, 266, 288; *see also* gods
plague; *see* pestilence
Pluto; and Serapis, 169
poet; *see* Greek, historiography, Marcius, *persona*
poets, 257–260; as *exemplum*, 259; and *fortuna*, 229; poetic idiom, 12, 14, 103, 256, 258–259, 268, 276; and religion, 7
Pollux, 236, 267, 268
Polybius, 129, 236, 290
Pontifex Maximus; consulted by senate, 73; emperor as, 189, 197; established, 81; and *fatum*, 113; post refused by Gratian, 226; always named, 65, 71; and regulations, 65; and Vestals, 65, 66, 92
pontifices, 64, 67, 72, 124; announce prodigy, 34, 38, 39; appointed, 186, 188; 'bridge-builders', 64; consulted, 65, 71, 72, 74, 95, 133, 196; as *exemplum*, 172; exhibit Games, 190; not named, 65; and naming gods, 256, 257, 260; neglected, 202; and prodigies, 34, 48, 65; and regulations, 64, 76, 81, 105, 133; give remedies, 65, 187, 257
praua religio, 44, 45, 79, 84, 94
priesthood; ennobling, 65
priests, 8, 254; (mis-)appointments, 65, 144, 180, 185–189, 192; of Augustus, 178; in error, 68–70, 73, 254; exemplary, 78; not named, 257; named at death, 66; named when at fault, 67; overlap of jurisdiction, 65, 72; removed from prodigy

assessment, 64; and the senate, 65; in
Tacitus, 185
prodere, 31, 54
prodigies, 21, 24, 160, 162, 184; in
Ammianus, 237–241; first appearance in
Annals, 197; as announcements (*nuntio*),
32–41; assessment, 23, 27–29, 39–45,
47–51, 53, 61, 62, 65, 66, 68–70, 75–78,
83, 84, 156, 157, 159, 161–164, 178, 194;
better noted in earlier times, 215; as
category, 17, 18, 144; classification, 18,
30, 37, 41, 42, 76, 197, 204; under
Claudius, 205; definitions, 29–30; foretell
events, 237–241; as wrath of gods, 28, 29,
42, 44–48, 60, 68, 83, 84, 155, 156,
158–161, 163, 197, 199, 200, 204; in
historiography, 16, 18, 26, 28, 41,
154–155, 160–165; and liminality, 8, 76;
lists, 26, 38, 40, 47, 62, 68, 76, 80, 83,
161; in Livy, 23, 27–58; *loco prodigii*,
76–77; as metaphor, 97; under Nero, 199,
200; noted by *quindecimuiri*, 220;
reporting, 24, 30–44, 46, 47, 74–76, 83,
84, 139, 157, 160–164, 194, 200, 204,
222, 223, 237–239, 289; and *saecula*,
217; symbolic, 159, 205; in Tacitus,
154–165, 223; under Tiberius (lack of),
162–165, 205; *uersa in prodigium*, 77;
uetus prodigium, 40, 76; *see also*
earthquakes, eclipses, expiation, foreign,
flood, lightning, nature, pestilence,
pontifices, showers of stones
Proserpina, 83, 133
pullarius, 23, 24, 49, 125
Pyrrhus; sacrilege, 83
Pythia, 80, 88

Q. Petilius Spurinus: signs at his death,
110–111, 113, 137, 138
Quadi, 247, 264
Quinctius Crispinus, *see* T. Quinctius
Crispinus
quindecimuiri; *see decemuiri sacris faciundis*
Quinquennial games, 201

rainbow, 259
randomness; *see fors*
rationality, 3, 5, 18, 22, 23, 28, 29, 78, 83, 87,
88, 90, 98, 130, 131, 150, 165, 230, 253,
257, 289, 290; *see also* irrationality
raven, 23, 102, 103, 125, 134, 138; *see also*
Apollo, *praua religio*
religio, 41, 45, 47, 59, 79, 81–84, 94, 124,
182, 202, 245, 246; *see also praua religio*
religion; *see* Christian, Christianity, decline,
exempla, foreign, paganism, *praua
religio, religio*, ritual; approaches to,

1–12, 23, 59, 63, 79; 'contradictions', 8,
10, 11, 19, 86, 87, 150, 154; decline of,
198; and emperors, 145, 195–204, 242;
errors, 19; and experience, 5; formulation
of, 3, 27, 51, 69, 70, 81–83, 85, 105, 123,
124, 129, 130, 133, 136, 139, 141, 143,
145, 150, 153, 165, 179, 185, 200,
221–224, 236–242, 246, 253, 258, 261,
265, 286, 287, 289, 290; and
historiography, 17–21, 23, 27, 28, 30, 69,
73, 86, 105, 114, 138, 139, 143, 144, 150,
153, 155, 167, 185, 222, 224, 227–233,
235, 242, 246, 260, 274, 285–288, 290,
291; and science, 6, 10–12, 89–91, 110,
139, 256
reported speech, 30–41, 51–58; and
announcements, 32–41, 51; and *dicitur*,
28, 31, 32, 37, 52, 56–58, 259; and *fama
est*, 28; and *fertur*, 31; and *ferunt*, 31; and
nuntiare, 31–44, 47, 67, 83, 89; *tradere*,
28, 31, 53–58
ritual, 5, 7–10, 12, 19, 58, 71, 72, 84, 87, 104,
111, 118, 183, 192, 197, 200, 204; and
acknowledgement of the gods, 136; error,
66, 67, 82, 111, 119, 137, 205, 256; and
interpretation, 95; knowledge, 257; and
naming gods, 133, 260; prescriptions, 67,
70; and priests, 254, 258, 284; and
propitiation, 206, 210, 211, 238, 269;
social aspects, 209; and theory, 95–96;
untraditional, 69, 84; Vestals, 65; *see also*
dreams, foreign, gods, sacrifice
Rome; and *annales*, 16; and emperors, 207;
and *exempla*, 27, 63, 225, 235; founders,
25, 26, 67, 143, 206, 216, 224; and
historiography, 151, 235; as centre of
narrative, 33–39, 73, 78, 146, 162, 224,
233–235, 247, 254, 267; *see also fatum*,
decline
Romulus, 104, 115, 216; vows temple, 215
rumour; as historical force, 178

Sabinianus, 248, 266
Sacred Spring, 89
sacrifice; banned, 273, 284, 285; human, 68,
169, 247, 249; of self, 93; *see also*
Curtius (Marcius), *deuotio, minime
Romano sacro*, Sacred Spring
saecula, 213, 215, 216, 220, 223; 100 years,
216, 217; 110 years, 217; *beatissimum*,
216, 219; *saeculum corruptissimum*, 216,
218; dating, 216–220; Etruscan, 218; and
prodigies, 217; *series saeculorum*,
213–215, 219
Saecular Games, 196, 216; of Augustus, 216,
217, 219; of Claudius, 216; dating, 216,

217, 220; of Domitian, 216, 217, 219;
political aspects, 218
Salii, 64, 103
Sallust, 172, 236, 287, 290; influence on
Annals, 148–149
Salus, 111, 138, 157, 196
scepticism, 2, 5, 6, 8, 9, 17–19, 22–24,
27–30, 32, 42–46, 52, 56, 58, 59, 61,
83–85, 115, 126, 139, 150, 151, 154, 160,
168, 222, 227, 230, 231, 253, 259, 286
science, *see* religion
Scipio Africanus, 102, 104; as authoritative
interpreter, 101, 109, 110, 112, 113,
126–136, 211; death(s), 130; *fatalis dux*,
109, 112; and *fatum*, 110; and *felicitas*,
137; and *fortuna*, 119, 123; and narrator,
110; and excessive religious authority,
129–135, 141; *see also* dreams,
superstitio
scribit, 54
secular, *see* Ammianus, historiography
secularity, 22, 227, 289, 290
senate: destroy shrines, 80; and emperor, 145,
147, 179, 180, 182–184, 189–191,
194–198, 201, 216, 224, 225; exemplary,
65, 67, 72–74, 78, 95, 102, 138, 139, 147,
167, 211, 220, 224, 225; failure of
authority, 192, 204–206, 224; failure of
expertise, 74, 144, 145, 175, 179, 180,
182–186, 189, 191–192, 194–199, 201,
203, 204, 210, 224; and priests, 64, 65,
68, 72, 73, 185, 189; recipients of prodigy
reports, 32, 34, 39, 42, 64, 73–78, 162;
responsible for *cultus deorum*, 35, 41, 42,
49, 65, 73–75, 78, 81, 85, 89, 91, 95, 100,
124, 137, 169, 186, 189–192, 208, 210,
223, 224; *see also* decline, Domitian,
priests
Serapis, 174; cult legitimised, 169; and
superstitio, 169; *see also* Aesculapius,
Jupiter, Osiris, Pluto
Servius Tullius, 53; favoured by gods, 100;
and *Fortuna*, 118
showers of stones, 35, 37, 38, 40, 54, 76, 89,
94, 121; *see also uetus prodigium*
Sibylline Books, 67, 68, 70; as *libri fatales*,
171; consulted, 40, 65, 73, 77, 124, 194;
proposed for inclusion, 191; Tiberius
vetoes consultation, 163, 190; and
warnings, 250, 274; *see also decemuiri*,
sacris faciundis, *fatum*, oracles
silence; as narrative strategy, 153; in Tacitus,
152
sine cura, 159
sine ira et studio, 148
Sisichthon, 259
Soranus, Barea; death, 201

state cult; *see* paganism
Stoicism; and *heimarmene*, 108; in Livy, 106;
in Tacitus, 150
storm; as prodigy, 37, 38, 59, 60, 76, 236
style; as message, 151, 152
superstitio, 69, 79, 82–85, 126, 128, 144,
154, 159, 165–170, 246–248, 250; as bad
religious practice, 129; depends on
'belief', 85; and Scipio Africanus,
127–129; used of magic, 165; widened
use in 1st century AD, 166; *see also*
astrology, Christianity, Drusus,
Egyptians, foreign religion, Jews, magic,
Serapis, Manicheism
suscipio; as technical term, 41
sycophancy, 182, 183, 201; and religious
honours, 194; of senate, 182, 183, 186,
199

Tacitus, 236; and the *fatum* of Rome,
211–221; his 'opinions', 148, 150, 178,
203; on imperial rule, 145; as
quindecimuir, 153, 215, 218, 220, 221,
223; sincerity, 148; *see also* authority,
persona, pessimism
tact, 93, 135, 136, 171; *see also* interpretation
Tages; founder of haruspicy, 241
Tarquitius (*haruspex*), 251
Taurians: and human sacrifice, 247
Tertullus: prays to Castor and Pollux, 236,
267, 268
Themis, 259
theologi, 257, 259, 276
theology, 2, 228, 229, 233, 276, 282
Theopompus, 236
Thrasea Paetus: death, 201; as *exemplum*,
181, 199, 201, 210, 211; mollifies
sentence, 147; outwits Nero, 147;
protests, 159, 181, 199; rejects religious
practice in Rome, 181; restrains Nero,
198; *see also* Capito Cossutianus
Thrasyllus (astrologer), 166, 172
Thucydides, 236, 290; Ammianus' debt,
262; and reported speech, 52
Tiberius, emperor, 148; astrologer, 166, 175;
and *fatum*, 175; and informers, 183, 187;
limits honours, 178, 182–184; and signs,
166, 213; signs recorded by Suetonius,
162; undermines religion, 185, 187,
189–197, 204, 209; *see also* prodigies,
Sibylline Books
Tiberius Gracchus, 71, 88, 108, 109, 111,
113, 274
T. Quinctius Crispinus, 44, 46, 99, 119
Tisiphone, 279
Titus, 148, 151, 181, 204, 210, 212; and
signs, 169

traditur, see reported speech
Trajan, 151
triumph, 193; as acknowledgement of gods, 104, 136; and neglect of gods, 136, 137

uariatio, 34–36, 39, 42, 54, 64, 74, 151
uelut; and interpretation, 58–60, 84, 110, 119, 127, 156, 157, 171, 202, 212, 213, 253, 270, 277
uideri; and interpretation, 58–59
uirtus, 50, 96, 104, 105, 117, 172, 242, 271; and *felicitas*, 137; and *ingenium*, 118; *see also fatum, fortuna*
Ursinicus, 248

Valens; and cruelty, 273, 277, 278; death, 279–281; and *fatum*, 271, 278; ignorant, 263–264; and justice, 275, 278–281; rage, 253; unfit for office, 278
Valentinian, 244; appointment, 253, 254, 267; and *fatum*, 271; and justice, 275; toleration, 243
Valerius Antias, 31, 53–54
Varro, 4, 7
Veleda; worshipped as deity, 177–178

Vengeance (*Vltio*), 190
Vespasian, 148, 151, 181, 210; and astrology, 167; and *fatum*, 174–175, 211–212, 221; and recovery of Rome, 151, 210, 220, 222; and signs, 162, 167, 169, 174, 175, 203, 212, 219; signs recorded by Suetonius, 162; *see also* Alexandria
Vesta, 200, 202, 215; flame extinguished, 66, 76, 92; propitiated, 92; shelters Domitian, 204
Vestals, 64–66; and human error, 66, 76, 92; inhumation, 68; naming, 65–67; and *stuprum*, 38; *see also* Pontifex Maximus, ritual
Vindex, 200
Virgil, 52, 80, 141, 152, 258, 262
Virtus, 46, 76
Vitellius; and astrology, 175; as Caesar, 161, 165; and *fatum*, 202, 212; poor appointment as priest, 188; and religious failure, 203; sacrifices to Nero, 181

Xenophon, 236

Zerynthius; *see* Apollo
Zeus, 266